A HISTORY OF CHICAGO
1871–1893

By BESSIE LOUISE PIERCE
THE UNIVERSITY OF CHICAGO

A HISTORY

OF

CHICAGO

VOLUME III
THE RISE OF A MODERN CITY
1871–1893

THE UNIVERSITY OF CHICAGO PRESS
Chicago and London

THE UNIVERSITY OF CHICAGO PRESS, CHICAGO 60637
The University of Chicago Press, Ltd., London

© 1957 by The University of Chicago. All rights reserved
Published 1957 by Alfred A. Knopf. Second Impression 1975
Paperback edition 2007
Printed in the United States of America

ISBN-13: 978-0-226-66842-0 (paper)
ISBN-10: 0-226-66842-8 (paper)
Library of Congress Catalog Card Number: 75-24667

♾ The paper used in this publication meets the minimum
requirements of the American National Standard for
Information Sciences—Permanence of Paper for Printed
Library Materials, ANSI Z39.48-1992.

IN MEMORIAM

CHARLES EDWARD MERRIAM
1874–1953

LOUIS WIRTH
1897–1952

. . . gigantic, wilful, young,
Chicago sitteth at the northwest gates,
With restless violent hands and casual tongue
Moulding her mighty fates. . . .

William Vaughn Moody
" An Ode in Time of Hesitation "

PREFACE

THIS, the third volume of *A History of Chicago*, covers the years from the destruction of the city by fire through the World's Columbian Exposition. During this period Chicago achieved maturity and assumed a leadership befitting the second largest city of the country.

Even more than in previous volumes, I have had to exercise arbitrary judgments in the choice of topics and in the selection of persons to exemplify leadership in various endeavors. The years 1871 to 1893 were the most crowded and dynamic the city had known. In describing what took place I have tried to focus attention upon group life rather than upon individuals of the community, in spite of the important part many played. Insofar as possible I have examined all available sources. Many, but by no means all, are cited in the footnotes which document the text. The bibliography is a selective list of some of the most important primary sources used.

During the years in which I have carried on this research I have relied heavily upon libraries in the Chicago area. To the staff of the University of Chicago Library I owe a special word of appreciation, particularly to Miss Winifred Ver Nooy, Mrs. Ruth Foster, and Miss Katherine Hall. I have turned often to the Chicago Historical Society Library, and have enjoyed the co-operation of its director, Mr. Paul Angle, and his staff. I am indebted to Dr. Stanley Pargellis of the Newberry Library for access to various manuscript collections, and to his associates for the courteous attention given my requests. Especially do I wish to mention the helpfulness of Mrs. Gertrude L.

Woodward and Mrs. Amy Nyholm. The resources of the Chicago
Municipal Library, the John Crerar Library, and the Chicago Public
Library were also canvassed. I wish to thank Miss Bernadine Mc-
Laughlin of the Woodlawn Branch of the Public Library who made
available materials from the main and other branch libraries. Besides these, I had access to the Alfred S. Trude private collection, the
archives of Marshall Field & Company over which Mrs. Ina Dorsey
presided, the Marshall Field Estate Office, Swift & Company, Armour and Company, Aldis & Company, the Illinois Bell Telephone
Company, the *Chicago Tribune,* the *Drovers' Journal,* and the
American Elevator and Grain Trade. The Work Projects Administration translations of the foreign-language press provided much
material which otherwise would have been examined with great
difficulty.

Librarians in the Illinois State Historical Library at Springfield,
the University of Illinois Library at Urbana, the Garrett Biblical Institute at Evanston, the New York Public Library, the Detroit Public
Library, the Library of Congress, the University of Michigan, and
the State Historical Society Library of Wisconsin were also accom-
modating. In the case of the last two Miss Agnes Inglis and Miss
Alice Smith were very kind.

I wish to acknowledge the uniform courtesy which I received
when making requests of residents of Chicago. Mr. Harold Swift
was instrumental in opening up hitherto untouched materials on
meat packing. He and members of the Public Relations Department of Swift & Company offered many suggestions which improved the chapter on the livestock trade and meat packing. Messrs.
E. B. Harris, J. A. Schmidt, J. O. McClintock, and John Aitkens of
the Chicago Board of Trade; the officials of R. R. Donnelley and
Sons, especially Mr. Herbert P. Zimmerman; Miss Frieda Foltz of
Mandel Brothers; Mr. Graham Aldis of Aldis & Company; and
Mr. Hermon Dunlap Smith were always helpful when called upon.
Many other Chicagoans have also co-operated in various ways in this
writing of the history of their city. In some cases acknowledgment
has been made at specific points in the volume.

I am especially grateful to Professor Arthur M. Schlesinger, Sr.,
and Professor Merle Curti for invaluable advice on substantially all
chapters. I wish also to express my appreciation to Professors Leon-

ard D. White, Chester Wright, Louis Gottschalk, Philip M. Hauser, and Edward Kirkland, who read portions of the book; and to Professor Gale Johnson who clarified the meaning of economic terms and factors. I am much indebted to my sister Anne E. Pierce who made many constructive comments on the entire manuscript. Professor Alma Hovey read the original draft and offered suggestions on it.

These expressions of appreciation would be incomplete if I did not mention my graduate students and research assistants who have been associated with me in a study of urban problems in late nineteenth-century America. The tasks of those on the staff of the *History of Chicago* project extended from caring for library needs to the preparation of statistical tables and the important verification of facts. Wood Gray, Blake McKelvey, and the late Dorothy Culp initiated the gathering of notes from newspapers. In particular, I wish to thank Alan Bliss, Herbert Wiltsee, Joe L. Norris, Jessie Sue Bynum, Philip W. Young, David M. Behen, Ralph R. Tingley, Margaret Kelliher, Edward O. Elsasser, and Jeanne Humphreys De Novo. Although associated with me for shorter periods than the others, I want also to express my gratitude to Dorothy Einbecker Feltham, Zenos Hawkinson, Phyllis Bate Sparks, Dorothy Forbis Behen, Robert R. Roberts, Marion Bonzi Pratt, Robert W. Twyman, George Hallowell, Martin Lewis, and Eldridge McBride. I am under great obligation to Harold Kolling and Howard Ryan of the present research staff for their competent and unselfish performance of assignments. I am also indebted to Walter M. Hauser and to my friend Miss Jessie Carter, who eased the last steps in the preparation of the manuscript for the press.

Mr. Alfred A. Knopf, the publisher of this and the preceding two volumes, has been an understanding and helpful friend throughout. The Social Science Research Committee of the University of Chicago has made generous grants for research. Besides the financial aid provided I have enjoyed the friendly interest of the Committee's members under the chairmanships of Dean Robert R. Redfield, Dean Ralph W. Tyler, and Dean Chauncy Harris. I wish also to express my thanks to Dr. Stanley Pargellis and the Committee on Awards for a Fellowship in Midwestern Studies of the Newberry Library and to Mr. Oscar Mayer, Jr., for financial assistance to complete this volume.

In dedicating this book to the late Professor Charles E. Merriam and the late Professor Louis Wirth, I am doing so because of their great contributions to an understanding of this city in modern American life. I am deeply indebted to them for wise counsel and their unfailing friendship.

B. L. P.

VOLUME III

CONTENTS

VOLUME III

MAPS AND ILLUSTRATIONS

A HISTORY OF CHICAGO
1871–1893

CHAPTER I

THE GREAT CHICAGO FIRE

> Men said at vespers: " All is well! "
> In one wild night the city fell;
> Fell shrines of prayer and marts of gain
> Before the fiery hurricane.
>
> On three score spires had sunset shone,
> Where ghastly sunrise looked on none.
> Men clasped each other's hands, and said:
> " The City of the West is dead! "
> . . .
>
> . . . Whittier: " Chicago "

THE GREAT CHICAGO FIRE began October 8, 1871. It was Sunday, and the sun shone warmly upon saint and sinner alike. Here in this city of lights and shadows were the prescient signs of urban maturity; the symbols of the faith of her founding fathers that the promise of the future was ever onward and the destiny of the city " among the stars." On this momentous Sabbath, to be reckoned as the end of an era and the beginning of a new, Chicagoans in large numbers devoted themselves to religious services, bravely abstaining from worldly thoughts. Others there were whose minds wandered to secular pleasures: the baseball game between the Chicago White Stockings scheduled with the Rockford Forest Citys the next afternoon, and the opening of the remodeled and redecorated Crosby's Opera House, to be celebrated by the Theodore Thomas orchestra concert on Monday evening.[1] A reading of the Sunday paper also promised devotees of racing a trial of speed between a man on foot and a trotting horse at near-by Riverside on Tuesday. Especially newsworthy was the three-column description in the *Chicago Tribune* of a fire on the West Side the previous evening which had destroyed property worth $1,000,000. The deadly precision with which the flames had spread should have served as a warning to Chicagoans of the dangers in a city made largely of wood. The summer and autumn had been unusually dry; and burning forests and villages in neighboring Michigan and Wisconsin had not been uncommon.[2]

To those who had forebodings of potential danger came actual justification of their fears in the calamity which fell upon the city that October Sunday night. About 9.30 o'clock, as worshippers left evening church services, the Court House bell solemnly announced the beginning of the history-making Chicago Fire, said to have broken out about 8.30 o'clock in a barn behind the Patrick O'Leary house at 137 De Koven Street.[3] Added to the natural dangers of the fire were the factors of mechanical failure and human miscalculation. The telegraph alarms did not register, and the bell tolled by the watchman in the Court House, who saw the flames, directed firemen to a spot about a mile away from the fire.

Even as the flames spread, Northsiders and Southsiders expected the fire would die when it reached the area burned Saturday night, for the wind blew from the southwest. The river, too, gave a sense of security to others. Near midnight, however, flaming brands

[1] *Chicago Tribune,* Oct. 8, 1871; Bessie Louise Pierce, *As Others See Chicago* (Chicago, 1933), p. 151. For a discussion of weather conditions in Chicago on this date see H. A. Musham, "The Great Chicago Fire, October 8–10, 1871," Illinois State Historical Society, *Papers in Illinois History and Transactions for the Year 1940* (Springfield, 1941), pp. 95–96. Crosby's Opera House was located on Washington Street between Dearborn and State.

[2] The area of the fire was bounded roughly by Adams Street on the north, Clinton Street on the west, Van Buren Street on the south, and the south branch of the Chicago River on the east. *Chicago Tribune,* Oct. 8, 1871; Frank J. Loesch, *Personal Experiences during the Chicago Fire, 1871* (Chicago, 1925), p. 7; *New York Tribune,* Oct. 13, 1871; Henry J. Cox and John H. Armington, *The Weather and Climate of Chicago* (Chicago, 1914), p. 197.

[3] The origin of the fire of October 8 is attributed to Mrs. O'Leary's cow's kicking over a lamp which ignited the straw. This has not been established. Bessie Louise Pierce, *A History of Chicago* (New York, 1940), II, 477; Musham, "The Great Chicago Fire, October 8–10, 1871," *loc. cit.,* pp. 99–100; A. T. Andreas, *History of Chicago* (3 v. Chicago, 1884–86), II, 706–16.

jumped from one shore to the other, driven on by their own momentum and a wind with a velocity of about twenty miles. Flames soon licked away the Parmalee stables at Jackson and Franklin streets, set upon the gasworks a block east of the river between Monroe and Adams, and laid in ruins poverty-stricken, crime-ridden "Conley's Patch," east of the gasworks. Terrified and helpless, people from the West Side joined those from "the Patch" in mad flight to the lake shore and the North Side. Soon their numbers were increased by those from the South Side, madly seeking safety from blinding smoke and onrushing flames. Everywhere were misery and terror: streets choked with scantily clothed and panic-filled householders, often searching for lost members of their families and laden with curiously assorted possessions; thieves reveling in the desperation of their fellow men; men, women, and children wretchedly huddled near the shore of Lake Michigan and sometimes standing neck-deep in its cold waters. As the flames darted unchecked into the streets along the river and as bridges caught fire, it was evident that the North Side, too, was doomed. By four o'clock Monday morning the castellated waterworks on Chicago Avenue was gutted. Northsiders who had aided the stricken must now perforce save themselves.

By late Monday night, October 9, 1871, the fire had run its course. On the West Side the use of a steam force pump saved the Oriental Flouring Mills and thus prevented the conflagration from getting a foothold near by. On the South Side Lieutenant General Philip Sheridan's use of explosives slackened the onrushing blaze. By the time the fire had eaten its way to the lake front on the east and to Fullerton Avenue on the north, a beneficent shower tamed its fury, and finally, after raging for hours unchecked, the flames sputtered out for lack of fuel.[4]

On Tuesday the extent of the devastation became apparent. Individual desolation and bewilderment merged into a common realization of the loss to the city as a whole. Approximately two thou-

[4] The area burned Saturday, Oct. 7, lay on the west side of the south branch of the Chicago River and to the northeast of the O'Leary neighborhood. ("Journal Entries Relative to the Chicago Fire, October 8 and 9, 1871," Cox and Armington, *op. cit.,* Appendix III, 367.) The Oriental Flouring Mills were located at the west end of the Madison Street bridge. For a map of the burned area see Chicago Board of Public Works, *Eleventh Annual Report of the Board of Public Works* (Chicago, 1872).

sand acres lay waste; about eighteen thousand buildings were destroyed, and about ninety thousand people left homeless.[5] In the area touched by the fire only a few skeletonized buildings remained in the midst of still smoldering debris.[6] The First National Bank, the supposedly fireproof Tribune Building, the Post Office, and the east wing of the Court House stood gutted, memorials of the aspirations of a busy and confident citizenry.[7] Even iron had melted and the popular "Athens marble," or Joliet limestone, had turned to powder.

But Chicago was no place for weakness. The city's past had not been one of ease but of unceasing toil and daring. In less than forty years nearly three hundred thousand people had entered her gates and transformed a struggling frontier post into the entrepôt of the great Middle Valley.[8] The legacy of their struggle had not perished; nor had the Great Fire wiped out their insatiate desire to conquer physical and economic forces and thus realize eventual empire. Before the fire ended, a youthful resiliency reflected this spirit in the display of signs such as, "All gone but wife and babes and pluck," and

MOOERS AND GOE

HOUSE AND SIGN PAINTERS,

REMOVED TO DES PLAINES CT.,

CAPITAL, $000,000.30.[9]

[5] Chicago Relief and Aid Society, *Report of the Chicago Relief and Aid Society of Disbursements of Contributions for the Sufferers by the Chicago Fire* (Cambridge, 1874), pp. 9–10; *Chicago Tribune*, Oct. 9, 1872. Figures of losses vary in different accounts.

[6] The line of the fire was: to the south, Taylor, Sherman, and Harrison streets; to the north, Clark Street to Belden Avenue, then southwest to Howe Street; and to the west, Howe Street south to the north branch of the river at Canal Street; along the river to Monroe where it crossed the south branch, west to Clinton and south on Jefferson Street to De Koven where the fire started. Chicago Board of Public Works, *Annual Report, 1872*, map. North of Congress Street on the South Side, only Lind's Block at Randolph and Market streets stood. On the North Side the home of Mahlon D. Ogden, later the site of Newberry Library, was not burned. A few buildings at the east end of Kinzie Street and a few directly south of Division Street had been saved. Of the buildings destroyed about 500 were on the West Side, 3,650 (including 1,600 stores) on the South Side, and 13,000 on the North Side. *Chicago Tribune*, Oct. 9, 1872.

[7] The First National Bank was at the corner of State and Washington streets; the Tribune Building was at Dearborn and Madison; the Post Office at Monroe and Dearborn; and the Court House between Randolph and Washington, Clark and LaSalle streets. Portions of the Farwell Block at Wabash and Madison and the Grand Pacific Hotel at Clark, LaSalle, Quincy, and Jackson remained.

[8] When Chicago was incorporated as a town in 1833 the population was 350. In 1870 it was 298,977. Pierce, *A History of Chicago*, I, 44; II, 3, 5.

[9] Mrs. Maria A. Shorey's narrative, Oct., 1871 ("Chicago Fire, 1871" in *Miscellaneous Personal Narratives* [Ms. Chicago Historical Society]); *Chicago Tribune*, Oct. 15, 1871.

In the face of losses, however, there was little time to review the past or to forecast the future. Before the fire had been extinguished, city officials, aldermen, and leading citizens took counsel in the First Congregational Church.[10] A General Relief Committee of seven was named to care for the destitute, but otherwise no definite action was taken at this moment.[11] Other emergency measures followed: the Common Council by ordinance fixed the price of bread at eight cents for a twelve-ounce loaf; the mayor pledged the credit of the city to pay for necessities; by other proclamations he regulated charges for hacks and similar carriers, opened public buildings as places of refuge and as distribution centers,[12] closed saloons for one week at nine in the evening, invited volunteers to serve as an emergency police, and entrusted the preservation of order in large part to Lieutenant General Philip H. Sheridan, United States Army, commanding the Military Division of the Missouri.

While the fire was still raging, Mayor Mason telegraphed to other cities for aid. The response was immediate. Fire engines came from Milwaukee, Detroit, Aurora, Quincy, and Indianapolis. Food and other necessities poured in from cities as far away as Louisville and Pittsburgh. Shortly, delegations from neighboring states and towns arrived to distribute the supplies which had been sent. A Cincinnati committee of citizens and the Common Council reached Chicago on October 10 with eleven carloads of supplies and erected a soup house on North Peoria Street with a capacity of about four thou-

[10] This meeting was on the afternoon of October 9. Mayor Roswell B. Mason presided. The First Congregational Church was located at the corner of Ann and Washington streets. Chicago Relief and Aid Society, op. cit., pp. 15–16; Chicago Tribune, Oct. 11, 1871, Oct. 9, 1872.

[11] Members were the mayor and the following representatives from parts of the city: for the South Division, John H. McAvoy and Nathaniel K. Fairbank; West Division, William B. Bateham and Orrin E. Moore; North Division, Mark A. Devine and John Herting. The activities of groups such as the Christian Union are treated in the chapter dealing with humanitarian trends.

[12] Companies of militia from Illinois towns and the Fifth Infantry from Ft. Leavenworth aided in preserving order until Oct. 13. Governor John M. Palmer held that the state could supply protection. He objected to President Grant's use of federal troops. Chicago Tribune, April 17, 1872; Ernest Ludlow Bogart and Charles Manfred Thompson, The Industrial State, 1870–1893 (Clarence W. Alvord, ed., The Centennial History of Illinois, IV [Springfield, 1920], 67); Chicago, Council Proceedings, 1870–71, p. 325. On Oct. 11 the General Relief Committee was organized with Orrin E. Moore as chairman, Charles T. Hotchkiss, secretary, and Charles C. P. Holden, treasurer. It designated responsible persons to receive, store, and distribute supplies, including water, supervise the issuance of railroad passes, take care of hospital and medical supplies, and the homeless. Chicago Tribune, Oct. 11, 1871, Oct. 9, 1872.

sand gallons a day. The common councils of many cities appropriated sums of money, Brooklyn, New York, for instance, donating $100,000 in cash or its equivalent in needed supplies. Craftsmen rallied to provide the special needs of their fellows, and fraternal groups generously contributed to members of their orders. Among those who gave benefit performances were Edwin Booth, Charlotte Cushman, and Mrs. John Drew and the New York Mutuals and Philadelphia Athletics;[13] and tangible proof of the universal sorrow evoked were the words of sympathy and money and other contributions from Canada, the British Isles, Germany, and even war-weary France.[14]

On October 14 the Chicago Relief and Aid Society, active since 1857, took over the responsibility of municipal relief work by Mayor Mason's order, and on the nineteenth was authorized by the representatives of various cities to care for their supplies and funds. Made up of capable and respected citizens, the Relief and Aid Society had the confidence of those with whom it must deal.[15] About 35,000 people faced starvation when the Society took over. It immediately issued rations, including $1.98 worth of food for a week and one ton of coal costing $4.50 for a month, for a family of two adults and three children. A large number of women, thrown out of work, and women's organizations made clothing.[16] Schools and churches be-

[13] Typical of a widespread humanitarianism was the action of the Boston Post Office clerks who sent funds to brother employees in Chicago. New York booksellers, publishers, and papermakers contributed to the recovery of their Chicago fellows; contributions came from children in the schools of New York and from the hackmen of Washington. A. T. Stewart, New York merchant, gave $50,000 and authorized John V. Farwell, Marshall Field, and Levi Z. Leiter, Chicago merchants, and Mayor Roswell B. Mason to disburse the sum especially to needy women. The *New York Ledger* entrusted John R. Walsh, president of the Western News Company, with $10,000 for the relief of newsmen. The *Cincinnati Commercial* furnished a complete font of type to the *Tribune* and the *St. Louis Democrat* sent sixty-five bundles of paper. *Chicago Tribune,* Oct. 11–31, 1871; Chicago Relief and Aid Society, *op. cit.,* pp. 26, 281–83.

[14] *Chicago Tribune,* Oct. 11, 12, 1871; *The Times* [London], Oct. 10, 17, 1871; *Le Temps,* Oct. 11, 1871. The aid of the English in establishing the Public Library is treated later.

[15] The president of the Chicago Relief and Aid Society was Henry W. King. Wirt Dexter was chairman of the executive board, Oscar C. Gibbs superintendent. Murry Nelson, John B. Drake, George M. Pullman, Thomas M. Avery, Marshall Field, Nathaniel K. Fairbank, Charles G. Hammond, and Dr. H. A. Johnson, among others, were prominently associated in the society's work. Chicago Relief and Aid Society, *op. cit.,* pp. 121, 137; *Chicago Tribune,* Oct. 12, 14, 1871, Oct. 9, 1872.

[16] Food rations for one week were: 3 pounds of pork (5½ cents a pound), 6 pounds of beef (5 cents a pound), 14 pounds of flour (3 cents a pound), 1¼ pecks of potatoes (20 cents a peck), ¼ pound of tea (80 cents a pound), 1½ pounds of sugar (11 cents a pound),

came emergency shelters; and barracks were constructed for some of the shelterless. For those who owned or could lease lots, simple houses with modest furnishings were made available at a cost of $125. By November 18 over five thousand cottages had been erected or were in process of building, housing from twenty-five to thirty thousand people.[17] An unemployment bureau which attempted to aid those looking for work, in some cases furnished transportation to white-collar and skilled workmen to places outside Chicago where work was immediately available.

Individual physicians and those composing a Relief and Aid Society Committee joined the Board of Health in caring for the sick, setting up dispensaries at convenient points, and serving the districts to which they were assigned. A plan to care for patients in hospitals was devised, and so vigilant were the health agencies that the smallpox epidemic which scourged many places in the winter of 1871–72 was kept under control in Chicago, where the rate per 1,000 inhabitants was lower than that of New York. The Medical Committee between October 16, 1871, and September 1, 1872, when it began to restrict its activities, cared for 55,769 sick persons.[18]

A calamity more serious than the Great Fire could scarcely have overtaken any city. But it left unharmed the foundation of Chicago's commercial prowess. Untouched was her strategic location with reference to lake, river, and canal, thus assuring the city a continuing leadership in the waterborne commerce of the Middle West. Great trunk lines still reached possessively into the world's most productive grain and livestock areas. Vast stretches of timber and other raw materials lay within her grasp, and near by were rich deposits of iron ore and coal. By 1871 she had become unquestionably the country's

1½ pounds of rice (8 cents a pound) or 3½ pounds of beans (3¾ cents a pound), 1¼ pounds of soap (7 cents a pound), 1½ pounds of dried apples (8 cents a pound), 3 pounds of fresh beef (5 cents a pound). *Chicago Tribune,* Oct. 9, 1872. For clothing furnished see *ibid.;* also Chicago Relief and Aid Society, *op. cit.,* pp. 152, 157.

17 The barracks were at Washington and Elizabeth streets, Harrison Street and Centre Avenue, Division and Sedgwick streets, and Halsted and North Avenue. Three sizes of houses were constructed: 12 ft. x 16 ft., 16 ft. x 20 ft., 18 ft. x 24 ft. Each house had three windows, a double chimney, two paneled doors, one partition. The walls were lined with thick felt paper. *Ibid.,* pp. 185–88, 192–94, 272–80; *Chicago Tribune,* Oct. 9, 1872.

18 Vaccination was compulsory. Chicago Relief and Aid Society, *op. cit.,* pp. 215–16; Chicago Board of Health, *Report of the Board of Health of the City of Chicago, 1870–73* (Chicago, 1874), p. 79 (hereafter cited as Chicago Board of Health, *Report*); New York Board of Health, *Third Annual Report of the Board of Health of the Health Department of the City of New York, April 11, 1872 to April 30, 1873* (New York, 1873), p. 161.

greatest grain and lumber mart, and held the crown as meat-packing center. Her ascendancy in the production of iron and steel had already begun, following the establishment in the 1850's of foundries and rolling mills. The editorial comment of the *Chicago Tribune,* October 11, was neither bombast nor vain forecast: " In the midst of a calamity without parallel in the world's history, looking upon the ashes of thirty years' accumulations, the people of this once beautiful city have resolved that CHICAGO SHALL RISE AGAIN." [19]

The losses through fire were mainly in buildings, wholesale and retail goods, and personal property, totaling $173,882,000 of the whole material loss estimated at $196,000,000.[20] Only about 24 per cent of the grain in Chicago the day before the Fire and 21 per cent total storage space for grain were destroyed; about 20 per cent of the lumber on hand; and the Union Stock Yard, where the principal packing-houses were, lay outside the badly burned section.[21] Of the manufacturing enterprises through which Chicago was to expand her industrial empire in the years to come, a substantial number were intact. On the West Side alone 600 manufactories and workshops remained, and rolling mills on the North and South sides were saved. The value of manufacturing stock, machinery, and products burned was estimated at only $13,255,000, whereas in 1871 alone Chicago factories produced goods worth $102,350,000.[22]

[19] *Chicago Tribune,* Oct. 11, 1871.

[20] The losses in buildings were estimated as $51,237,000; in wholesale and retail goods as $64,645,000; in personal property as $59,000,000. Chicago Relief and Aid Society, *op. cit.,* pp. 10–12.

[21] Chicago Board of Trade, *Thirteenth Annual Report of the Trade and Commerce of Chicago for the Year Ending December 31, 1870* (Chicago, 1871), p. 44 (hereafter cited as Chicago Board of Trade, *Annual Report), Fourteenth Annual Report, 1871,* pp. 12, 47, 50, 80; Chicago Relief and Aid Society, *op. cit.,* p. 10; The Chicago Times, *New Chicago: A Full Review of the Work of Reconstruction . . . ,* from *The Chicago Times* (Chicago 1872), p. 101. In the North Division a few small packing-houses were burned. Elias Colbert and Everett Chamberlin, *Chicago and the Great Conflagration* (Cincinnati, 1871), p. 332; *Chicago Tribune,* Oct. 11, 1871.

[22] Sixty factories on the South Side and 100 on the North Side were destroyed. The Sixth Ward on the South Side had " innumerable " factories, to quote the *Tribune,* which escaped devastation. The Union Foundry Works at Fifteenth and Dearborn, a leading producer of cast and wrought iron, was not burned. By the time of the Fire Chicago manufacturers produced goods valued at a little less than one-fourth of all the goods sold in the city. (Colbert and Chamberlin, *op. cit.,* p. 173; [The Goodspeed Publishing Company], *Industrial Chicago,* III, *The Manufacturing Interests* [Chicago, 1894], 591; *Chicago Tribune,* Oct. 20, 1871; The Chicago Times, *New Chicago . . . ,* p. 105; James W. Sheahan and George P. Upton, *The Great Conflagration* [Chicago, 1872], pp. 56, 141); Chicago Relief and Aid Society, *op. cit.,* p. 11.

On October 10, the stockholders of the Chamber of Commerce, from whom the Board of Trade held a lease, resolved to rebuild at once. In quick succession leaders of business and industry demonstrated similar confidence that the new Chicago would be better and bigger than the one destroyed. On October 13, Jonathan Young Scammon announced that ground had been broken for a store and office block, renters for which had already been signed. Within the next three weeks many leading citizens took similar steps. M. Laflin and Sons arranged for the erection of twelve four-story structures in the ravaged district; Cyrus H. McCormick ordered the construction of five buildings, and the rebuilding of the Palmer House from the original plans of John M. Van Osdel, well-known architect, was under way. In a little less than four weeks Field and Leiter began business in temporary quarters, in a remodeled car barn at Twentieth and State streets, and other merchants leased for one year land along the lake front upon which temporary wooden structures could be placed. With characteristic foresight leaders of the city pushed out the shoreline by dumping debris from the devastation into the lake, thereby making new and valuable land.[23]

As rebuilding took place, the retail business area shifted further south along Wabash and Michigan avenues and over to State Street, where in the 1860's Potter Palmer and Marshall Field had established themselves. Shortly, from Washington to Monroe, a modernized retail section arose to meet the needs of Chicagoans. Manufacturing enterprises moved from the north bank of the river to the neighborhood of the south branch at Twenty-second Street and Western Avenue, and wholesale houses were located principally along West Monroe, West Madison, and the once vice-ridden section on Wells. Banking interests took over Washington and LaSalle streets.[24]

Some of the newly constructed buildings were made of brick, considered both fire-resistant and relatively inexpensive. Illinois lime-

[23] *Chicago Tribune,* Oct. 11, 14, 16, 18, 20, 21, Nov. 7, 16, 1871; Chicago Board of Trade, *Fourteenth Annual Report, 1871,* p. 17; Andreas, *History of Chicago,* III, 59, 62; Everett Chamberlin, *Chicago and Its Suburbs* (Chicago, 1874), p. 96.
[24] Field had moved into "Palmer's Marble Palace" in 1868. Pierce, *A History of Chicago,* II, 109, 139. The vice area shortly after the Fire lay principally south of Harrison and west of South State Street. Homer Hoyt, *One Hundred Years of Land Values in Chicago* (Chicago, 1933), pp. 103–4. *Industrial Chicago,* II, *The Building Interests,* 132–33; Earl Shepard Johnson, *The Natural History of the Central Business District with Particular Reference to Chicago* (unpublished Ph.D. Thesis, The University of Chicago, 1941), pp. 217–23.

stone brought from Joliet and Lemont by way of the Illinois and Michigan Canal, and sandstone from Marquette and the neighborhood of Cleveland were used by other builders. Notwithstanding lessons which should have been learned, many, in need of immediate housing, put up buildings of wood which the *Tribune* declared were more numerous than before the Fire, and in some cases as dangerous as powder kegs. Even so-called brick structures were often made of wood except the exterior walls, and mansard roofs with outside surfaces of presumably nonignitible material were sometimes only pine covered with tin or slate. A petroleum roof combination was alleged to have induced others to accept its product in spite of the combustibility of the tar roofs on buildings recently destroyed.[25]

Lack of funds complicated the already difficult problem of rebuilding. Of the $196,000,000 loss by fire, only $96,553,720.94 was covered by insurance.[26] Insurance companies, unable to stand the strain, became insolvent. Twenty-six New York companies, seven Connecticut, three Massachusetts, five Ohio, and seventeen Illinois concerns were swept out of business. Especially hard hit were those insurance companies which had invested in Chicago and Cook County securities and in mortgages on Chicago property, and where interest payments on loans were lost or delayed. But men of vision realized that the land upon which burned buildings had stood still remained and that it had appreciated greatly during the city's history. Those of faith and considered judgment also knew that in the end the well-established and large companies would not go to the wall, but that the Fire would prove a purgative of financially unstable companies.[27]

[25] *Chicago Tribune,* Nov. 11, 25, Dec. 2, 1871, Jan. 7, 1872; *The Spectator,* Feb., 1872, p. 193; City of Chicago, *Laws and Ordinances Governing the City of Chicago, Jan. 1, 1866* (Joseph E. Gary, comp., Chicago, 1866), pp. 53, 118, 224–27. Before the Fire, bricks had sold for $6.50 a thousand; two weeks later they sold for $12 to $15 a thousand. *Chicago Tribune,* July 28, Oct. 20, 1872.

[26] Illinois, *Fourth Annual Insurance Report of the Auditor of Public Accounts of the State of Illinois, 1872* (Springfield, 1872), pt. I, 64 (hereafter cited as Illinois, Auditor of Public Accounts, *Annual Insurance Report*). This amount was carried in 201 companies. Of these, 67 were New York companies, 29 Ohio, 23 Massachusetts, 22 Illinois, and 11 Connecticut. Eleven other states had eight or less and Great Britain had six. By 1872 the insurance paid was 39.36 per cent of the amount claimed, with payment of an additional 12.54 per cent expected. *Ibid.,* pp. 63–64.

[27] According to the Illinois auditor of public accounts 68 companies were forced into liquidation. The aggregate capital involved was $24,867,109.32. (*Ibid.,* p. 82.) By 1875 eleven of these companies were again doing business in Illinois. (Illinois, Auditor of Public

The excitement and anxiety of insurance circles in general were matched by the apprehension of most Chicago citizens who feared that insurance organizations might evade commitments. On November 15, 1871 policyholders in nonpaying companies moved to protect their interests by naming a committee of eminent citizens to investigate the financial status of the suspected concerns.[28] When underwriters proposed increasing rates of insurance on grain in storage from 1½ to 5 per cent, grain dealers denounced this as extortionate, and threatened to invest funds formerly devoted to insurance in buying fire-fighting apparatus of their own. This acrimony on the part of policyholders and their impatience at delays in immediate settlement tended to diminish, however, as insurance companies, particularly the British, discharged their contractual obligations. As a result, renewal of insurance policies in the surviving companies, in spite of greatly advanced rates, attested a revival of confidence.[29]

The fear which, for a time, had existed regarding the ability of insurance companies to fulfill their obligations spread, however, to many business enterprises. Money became tight in the New York market, and shortly commissions to the banks of one-fourth to one-half per cent in addition to the usual 7 per cent interest for good risks prevailed. Brokers freely disposed of stocks. Railroad holdings of those lines centering in Chicago were tossed on the market and sold short, precipitating, according to *The New York Times,* a depression the second week of October "without parallel in the violence of panic among the Railways since the first week in October, 1869, succeeding the Gold explosion of the 24th of September." United States government bonds, especially 6's, 5-20's of 1867 and the 10-40's, showed an appreciable decline. The Secretary of the Treasury bought double the regular amount of 5-20's on October 11, giving

Accounts, *Eighth Annual Insurance Report, 1876,* pt. I, 9–14.) *The Spectator,* Oct. 21, 1871, p. 14, Dec. 15, 1871, pp. 574–75; *The Commercial and Financial Chronicle,* XIII (Oct. 14, 1871), 493.

[28] Isaac N. Arnold was chairman. The committee included Charles B. Farwell, Marshall Field, Charles M. Henderson, merchants; Cyrus Bentley, John L. Thompson, Joseph F. Bonfield, Francis B. Peabody, lawyers; John Crerar, railway supplies, and William F. Coolbaugh, president of the Union National Bank and treasurer of the Republic Life Insurance Company of Chicago. *Chicago Tribune,* Nov. 16, 1871; *The Spectator,* Dec. 15, 1871, p. 578.

[29] *Ibid.,* pp. 544, 573; *Chicago Tribune,* Nov. 11, 1871; Illinois, Auditor of Public Accounts, *Fourth Annual Insurance Report, 1872,* pt. I, 38–39, 45; *The Spectator* (Supplement), Oct. 21, 1871, p. 1, Dec. 15, 1871, p. 579, Feb., 1872, p. 95; Harry Chase Brearly, *History of the National Board of Fire Underwriters* (New York, 1916), pp. 30, 35.

New York finance a disbursement of $4,500,000. By doing so he lightened the strain on the money market. Throughout early October, particularly, the ability of New York banks to discount was decreased and the rates of discount outside of banks increased, retarding general trade for the time being and causing anxiety about the money market.

Foreign exchanges were likewise depressed. On October 12 and 13 the rates on London fell two to two and one-half below par of gold or the point at which it could be exported. On October 13 the Bank of Montreal took the larger part of about £750,000, sixty days London, and released $2,500,000 to the use of the market in the Gold Room. By the next day rates on London improved and cash gold was easier. By the third week of October signs of reassurance in the transactions of Wall Street heartened moneylenders and investors in general, and the recognition of the permanence of real estate, upon which much of the wealth of Chicago rested, served to re-establish confidence.[30] The pressing need of capital by a community which hitherto had been considered a place of profitable investment was adroitly set forth by the pioneer banker Henry Greenebaum of Henry Greenebaum and Company in an open letter to European capitalists. First mortgages on real estate, ten-year loans redeemable in currency with interest at the rate of 7 per cent in gold, payable semiannually, and opportunities for various profitable investments were plausibly described in Germany, England, Canada, and other foreign lands.[31]

The tireless perennial booster, William Bross, one of the principal proprietors of the *Tribune* and formerly lieutenant-governor of the state, made equally convincing appeals to Eastern capitalists, upon whom Chicagoans had heavily relied in the past. The faith of William B. Ogden, first mayor of the city and a man versed in financial wizardry who returned after the Fire from his retirement in New York, lent authority to the optimistic forecast of men of the Bross

---

[30] By the third week of October the banks had recovered somewhat but at the cost of a contraction of borrowing of about $15,000,000. *Chicago Tribune*, Oct. 9, 1872, July 23, 1874; *The New York Times*, Oct. 10–25, 1871; *Le Temps*, Oct. 15, 1871. A branch of the Bank of Montreal was opened in Chicago to aid credit operations and to attract English capital desirous of profiting by the unusual opportunity for investment. Colbert and Chamberlin, *op. cit.*, p. 330; *Chicago Tribune*, Oct. 16, 1871.

[31] Henry Greenebaum and Co., to the attention of European Capitalists, Nov. 15, 1871, *Henry Greenebaum Estate Collection* (*Ms.* Chicago Historical Society).

school. This " absorptive market " for surplus capital, which the *Chicago Tribune* loudly trumpeted in convincing words, led New York merchants to extend credits and to conclude that the Fire had no long-time serious influence on merchant paper.

Increased deposits which by November flowed into Chicago banks from the agricultural hinterland further fortified faith in the city as a profitable center of investment. The October grain market had reflected the excitement prevailing elsewhere, and prices had advanced in heavy trading. A meeting of railroad representatives on October 13, however, allayed fears as to the shipment of this commodity, basic in Chicago economy, by taking steps to insure normal movement. On the sixteenth the Illinois Central Railroad, which tapped the rich grain area to the south and west of the city, offered further assurances by contracting to rebuild its station on the old site.[32]

Within two days of the Great Fire Governor John M. Palmer called the legislature to meet in special session the thirteenth of October to consider measures of relief for Chicago. That night both houses adjourned to visit the stricken city and to confer about urgent needs. A committee appointed by the city authorities requested the state: first, to repay approximately three million dollars advanced by Chicago for making the deep-cut improvement of the Illinois and Michigan Canal in anticipation of earnings;[33] second, to relieve Chicago temporarily from paying state and county taxes; and third, to take care of the county poor and criminals. The legislature proceeded to refund $2,955,340 to the city for the amount advanced for the canal.[34] It also passed a bill enabling warehousemen to deliver grain when the receipts had been destroyed by fire, and made

[32] *New York Tribune*, Oct. 17, 1871; *Chicago Tribune*, July 31, Oct. 12–14, 16–18, 22, Nov. 11, 24, 1871, Jan. 15, 1872; I. N. Arnold, *William B. Ogden* . . . (Fergus Historical Series, no. 17 [Chicago, 1882], pp. 32–33); *The Commercial and Financial Chronicle*, XIII (Oct. 14, 1871), 507; *The New York Times*, Oct. 10, 12, 23, 1871. The financial situation in Europe also favored an early recovery.

[33] The deep-cut improvement of the canal was designed to lower the level of the Summit division. This would permit a greater flow of lake water and facilitate the carrying of sewage from the Chicago River into the Des Plaines River. James W. Putnam, *The Illinois and Michigan Canal, A Study in Economic History* (Chicago, 1915), pp. 35–36, 143.

[34] Six per cent bonds payable in ten years were issued. It was provided that between one-third and one-fifth should be used to construct bridges and buildings on their original sites and the remainder should be devoted to the payment of interest on the city's bonded debt, payment of the police, and the meeting of other urgent obligations. Some of the money was available before the end of the year. *Chicago Tribune*, Oct. 9, 1872; Caroline Kirkland, *Chicago Yesterdays* . . . (Chicago, 1919), p. 231.

provision for the restoration of lost or destroyed court records and the purchase of the books of three abstract companies, unharmed by the fire, to aid in the establishment of titles. A reassessment bill for the collection of state and county taxes, another to issue bonds of $1,500,000 to rebuild the Court House and jail, and enactments legalizing the removal of the inmates of the Cook County Reform School to the state institution at Pontiac gave further relief to Chicago.[35]

To facilitate rebuilding, a bill for the relief of Chicago was introduced into Congress which exempted building materials from tariff duties. Stiff opposition immediately arose from lumber interests, which marshaled their forces to exclude their products from the list of exemptions. In the Senate, the fight was led by Senator Thomas W. Ferry and Senator Zachariah Chandler of Michigan, who represented not only their own constituents but prominent Chicagoans with vast lumber holdings in both Michigan and Wisconsin. In a letter read by Senator Ferry to his colleagues, Wirt Dexter, chairman of the executive board of the Relief and Aid Society, made known this opposition, declaring that such a law would result in fraud, and that it would not appreciably aid Chicago where sellers of building materials were prepared to meet ante-Fire prices. Besides, Dexter said, such a move by opening the market to foreign dealers would paralyze one of Chicago's chief economic enterprises. Furthermore, he felt that the 8,000 houses, the largest of which was eighteen by twenty-four feet, built by the Relief and Aid Society as temporary homes for 40,000 Chicagoans, had cared for the most needy.[36]

[35] For the legislative provisions for the relief of Chicago see Illinois, *Journal of the House of Representatives of the Twenty-seventh General Assembly of the State of Illinois, Second Special Session . . . 1871* (Springfield, 1871), pp. 3–7, *Adjourned Regular Session* (Springfield, 1872), pp. 454, 816, 1251 (hereafter cited as Illinois, *House Journal*); *Journal of the Senate of the Twenty-seventh General Assembly of the State of Illinois . . . 1871* (Springfield, 1871), pp. 37, 532, 579, 689 (hereafter cited as Illinois, *Senate Journal*); *Public Laws of Illinois, 1871*, p. 774 (hereafter cited as *Public Laws*); *Statutes of Illinois, an Analytical Digest of All the General Laws in Force at the Present Time (1818–1872)* (Eugene L. Gross and William L. Gross, eds., Springfield, 1872), II, 61, 117–18, 317–24, 327–29 (hereafter cited as *Statutes*); *The Revised Statutes of the State of Illinois A. D. 1874* (Harvey B. Hurd, comp., Springfield, 1874), pp. 314–15 (hereafter cited as *Revised Statutes*). Other acts not noted in the text can be found in Illinois, *Statutes*, II, 211, 251–52, 316; *Revised Statutes*, pp. 438–39.
[36] *Chicago Tribune*, March 20, 1872; *Congressional Globe*, 42 Cong., 2 sess., pt. I, 4, 57–58, pt. III, 1801–2. Dexter was a member of the law firm Walker, Dexter and Smith. Like many prominent Chicagoans he had investments in lumber. The number of houses built by the Relief and Aid Society as of May 1, 1873, was 7,983. Chicago Relief and Aid Society, *op. cit.*, p. 188.

Dexter's participation in the controversy ran head on into criticism from those opposed to the protective tariff. "The protective tariff," the *Tribune* irately declared, " is the foul fiend of American politics today, as much as slavery was ten years ago." Nor was it, some held, a proper activity for Dexter, in view of his official connection with the Chicago Relief and Aid Society, to express an opinion for or against the pending Relief Bill. More to the liking of proponents of the bill was the resolution of both houses of the state legislature urging Illinois representatives to use their influence to reduce the tariff on lumber and other building material to be used in rebuilding Chicago.[37] In the end, lumber was not included. Cumbersome regulations by the Treasury Department and the limited scope of the bill as passed gave far less relief to Chicago than had been anticipated.[38]

By October, 1872, only a year after the Great Fire, a new city had risen. An unofficial estimate showed new buildings valued at $34,-292,100 on the South Side, at $3,848,500 on the North Side, and at $1,893,000 on the West Side. Along once naked streets healthy young saplings stretched upward, and the increased use of stone in buildings promised an architecturally more beautiful city. Trade was satisfyingly greater than in the year of destruction, real estate sold at advanced prices, and bank clearings attested the confidence generally held. Pessimistic forecasts and the hopes of rival cities that Chicago would never rise from the ashes had proved unfounded. The currents of trade of the Great Middle Valley still flowed through Chicago, the unsurpassed gateway of the middle empire of America.[39]

[37] *Chicago Tribune*, Feb. 14, 16, 1872. Some Chicago lumbermen, chiefly manufacturers, were reported as not opposed to the bill. Among the firms said to oppose the bill were E. W. Blatchford and Company, dealers in lead pipes, linseed oil; Daniel B. Shipman, lead; Culter Savidge and Company, lumber; T. K. Holding of the Phoenix Iron Works. (*Ibid.*, Feb. 16, 1872.) Dexter, in a communication to the *Tribune*, Feb. 17, 1872, declared his letter to Senator Ferry had been written at the suggestion of Turlington W. Harvey, well-known lumberman, and under the impression that all lumber coming to the Port of Chicago would be admitted free. Harvey and others raised no objections to a rebate of duty as long as it was on lumber for the burned part of the city only, Dexter further stated in his letter of defense to the *Tribune*. (See *Chicago Tribune*, Feb. 18, 1872.) Illinois, *Public Laws, 1871*, pp. 786, 793.

[38] U. S., *Statutes at Large*, XVII, 51. The bill became law April 5, 1872. Other acts of relief included the restoration of United States court records, the construction of the Post Office and Customs House, and the repayment of taxes on distilled liquors in bond. *Ibid.*, XVII, 24, 40, 162, 610–11.

[39] *Chicago Tribune*, Oct. 9, 1872; *The Times* [London], Aug. 15, Oct. 25, 1872; *Industrial Chicago*, II, *The Building Interests*, 146; *The Chicago Times*, Feb. 2, 3, 1872; Mabel McIlvaine, ed., *Reminiscences of Chicago during the Great Fire* (Chicago, 1915), pp. 10–11.

On October 30, 1872, Chicagoans, mindful of the destruction of their physical past and envisioning an enticing and glorious future, assembled to lay the cornerstone of a monument in Central Park as an everlasting reminder of the dreadful calamity and " the glorious resurrection which so quickly followed." The monument was designed further to perpetuate " the triumph of energy and enterprise, an example worthy of emulation to the end of time," and to honor those who so generously sent aid from various parts of the world.[40]

Other manifestations of pride in the rebuilt city followed, to the amazement of the world at large. The London *Times* thought such exercises fraught with indelicacy, but generously suggested to its readers that the gratifying signs of a new city might warrant a disposition to boast. *The New York Herald* considered Chicago indeed " a singular city," remarkable for " its marriages and its divorces, for its sensation stories, its house-raising and its rats," and for planning, within two years, celebrations of the anniversary of its own destruction. Observance of such an anniversary by flag-flying, parades, and music reminded *The Herald* of the Westerner who had settled down in a neighboring village for six or seven years and was noted for his quiet, sober manners. But on one particular day of each year he shed his customary sedateness, put on his best clothes, took a holiday, gave himself up to fun and frolic, and generally ended in retiring to bed in his boots. An inquiry disclosed the fact that the day thus set apart for a private celebration was the anniversary of his wife's death. " That man," commented *The Herald,* " must have hailed from Chicago." [41]

In Chicago, however, where a thing was no sooner said than done, it seemed not only proper but natural to give external expression to the exultations of the spirit. In June of 'seventy-three a jubilee week again celebrated the progress in rebuilding made since the Fire, and at the same time advertised to an estimated sixty thousand visitors the Grand Pacific Hotel, the Lake Shore and Michigan Southern, and the Chicago, Rock Island and Pacific railroads, which sponsored the undertaking.[42]

40 *Chicago Tribune,* Oct. 28, 31, 1872. The monument was not completed. Central Park in 1881 was renamed Garfield Park. Andreas, *op. cit.,* III, 179.
41 *The Times* [London], Oct. 25, 1872. See also *ibid.,* Oct. 18, 1873; *The New York Herald,* Oct. 10, 1873.
42 *Chicago Tribune,* June 5–8, 1873. The celebration was held June 5–7, 1873.

Of greater pretentiousness was the Inter-State Industrial Exposition held from September 25 to November 12, 1873, to exhibit the material and cultural progress of Chicago and the Northwest. Planned in the spring of 'seventy-two, the exhibition building of glass and iron stretched from Adams to Jackson and was visited by about sixty thousand people.[43] Within and without they beheld a city reconstructed, risen Phoenix-like from its ashes. Chicago, that " concentrated essence of Americanism," [44] had conquered disaster and was on the march toward the enviable rank of second city of the United States.[45]

[43] William W. Boyington was the architect. Stockholders of the enterprise chose a board of directors of twenty-five leading citizens including Thomas M. Avery, William F. Coolbaugh, William E. Doggett, John B. Drake, Marshall Field, Charles B. Farwell, Nathaniel K. Fairbank, David Gage, Turlington W. Harvey, Wirt Dexter, Thomas B. Bryan, Joseph Medill, Anton C. Hesing, and Potter Palmer. *Chicago Tribune,* April 11, 25, 27, May 19, June 29, Aug. 31, Sept. 26, Oct. 5, 10, Nov. 9, 1873; [Van Arsdale & Massie], *The Inter-State Exposition Souvenir; Containing a Historical Sketch of Chicago; and a Record of the Great Inter-State Exposition of 1873* (Chicago, 1873).

[44] *The Saturday Review* [London], quoted by *Chicago Tribune,* Jan. 18, 1874.

[45] In addition to the sources cited in footnotes of this chapter, many firsthand accounts of the Chicago Fire are available. They include the following: Mrs. Charles True Adams, " The Chicago Fire " (n.d.); Joel O. W. Bigelow to Messrs. S. and O. Bigelow, October 10, 1871; Ada Rumsey Campbell, " The Chicago Fire " (n.d.); William H. Carter to his brother, Oct. 15, 1871; H. W. S. Cleveland's narrative, Nov. 10, 1871; Jennie E. Counselman, " Reminiscences of the Chicago Fire and Some of My Girlhood Days," March, 1928; W. J. Davis's narrative (n.d.); Daniel Goodwin to George M. Higginson, Feb., 1895; Mrs. Alfred Hebard's narrative (n.d.); George M. Higginson, " Account of the Great Chicago Fire of Oct. 9, 1871 "; Mrs. G. Higginson to Mrs. Mark Skinner, Nov. 10, 1871; George Howland to S. H. Peabody, Oct. 14, 1871; Kiler R. Jones, " Recollections of the Great Chicago Fire," Nov., 1879; Mrs. N. B. Judd to Mrs. Mark Skinner, Nov. 23, 1871; Mrs. Henry W. King to friends in the East, Oct. 21, 1871; Arthur M. Kinzie's narrative (n.d.); Mrs. Julia Lemos, " My Experiences of the Fire of 1871 in Chicago " (n.d.); Gilbert Merrill to " Mother," Oct. 27, 1871; Bernard Moos to his mother and sisters in Germany, Oct. 24, 1871; George Payson's narrative, Sept. 28, 1880; Mrs. Maria A. Shorey's narrative, Oct., 1871; John G. Shortall's narrative (n.d.); Lambert Tree, " The Experiences of Lambert Tree and the Several Members of his Family during the Great Chicago Fire of Sunday and Monday, October 8th and 9th, 1871 " (n.d.); John Witbeck to Frederick Carney, Oct. 12, 1871; " Chicago Fire, 1871," *Miscellaneous Narratives* (Mss. Chicago Historical Society); Paul M. Angle, ed., *The Great Chicago Fire, Described in Seven Letters by Men and Women Who Experienced Its Horrors, and now Published in Commemoration of the Seventy-Fifth Anniversary of the Catastrophe* (Chicago, 1946); Mary Emily and Eliphalet Wickes Blatchford, *Memories of the Chicago Fire* (Chicago, 1921); W. A. Croffut, " Reconstruction," in *The Lakeside Memorial of the Burning of Chicago, A. D. 1871* (Chicago, 1872); Alexander Frear, " Chicago: The Full Story of the Great Fire: Narrative of an Eye Witness," in Pierce, *As Others See Chicago,* pp. 191–204; Frank J. Loesch, *Personal Experiences during the Chicago Fire, 1871* (Chicago, 1925); James W. Sheahan and George P. Upton, *The Great Conflagration; Chicago: Its Past, Present and Future . . .* (Chicago, 1871); Joseph Kirkland, " Notes on the Chicago Fire," *Joseph Kirkland Papers* (Mss. Newberry Library).

CHAPTER II

THE FABRIC OF SOCIETY

CHICAGO'S METEORIC RISE to an enviable position among the great cities of the United States in the last half of the nineteenth century was but the fulfillment of the dreams and boasts of her citizens. Louder than the voices of those who, viewing the devastation of the Great Fire of 1871, expressed the fear that Chicago would never rise again, were the voices of others, optimistic and daring, who prophesied that their city would outstrip her rivals and even challenge the great port of New York.

In the years that followed, there poured into a new city streams of newcomers to add to the approximately 298,000 residents already there, to invigorate and inspire an already aggressive and tireless people on the quick-stepping march toward economic hegemony. Within only ten years after the Fire the population rose to 503,185, and by 1890 it had passed the million mark to make Chicago second city of the continent.[1] Even in an era characterized by rapid urban expansion, a growth of nearly 268 per cent in the twenty years following 1870 was breath-taking.

This expansion reflected not only a change in numbers but the coming of a mature society. Chicago had now cast aside the simple ways of pioneering days and had acquired the externals of a more settled social order. This approaching ripeness appeared in the com-

[1] U. S., *Ninth Census, 1870*, I, "Population," 380–91, *Tenth Census, 1880*, [I], "Population," 536–41, *Eleventh Census, 1890*, [I], "Population," pt. I, lxvii, 580–83, 670–73. In 1890 Chicago was a city of 1,099,850. Unless otherwise indicated, the United States census is the source for population figures in this chapter.

position of the population. In the various age levels women had almost attained numerical equality with men, although they still did not predominate in the productive age group, fifteen to forty-five, as they did in the older cities of New York and Philadelphia.[2]

As in the days before the Fire, Chicago was as yet a cosmopolitan city, but a growing number of her inhabitants claimed the United States as birthplace.[3] So many were the nationalities which had so quickly come that the distinction between native and foreign born was not always clearly and appropriately made, and observers remarked that perhaps here on the shores of Lake Michigan might eventually be found the composite photograph of mankind.[4] As in the twenty years before the Fire, Chicago increasingly drew upon the Old Northwest, and at the same time attracted fewer people from New England and the Middle Atlantic states. Still, this northern region continued to provide so large a part of the native population that its regional social patterns remained those of the dominant group of the city. Only briefly after the Civil War did Southerners, enticed by an enlarged economic opportunity, swell the tide of this extraordinary ethnic sea. Then they came chiefly from the border states. From 1870 to 1880 the proportion of Southern-born residents of Chicago to the city's total population had declined to the prewar level. At the same time from beyond the Mississippi River there trickled into the city only a small proportion of Chicago's native inhabitants.[5]

[2] In 1870, the sex ratio, males per 100 females, was 104.6; in 1880 it was 104.3; in 1890 it was 107.0. In 1850, it was 119.3.

[3] In 1870, the foreign-born population of the city constituted 48.35 per cent of the total; in 1880, 40.7 per cent; and in 1890, 40.98 per cent. For further details see Appendix tables.

[4] See, for example, F. Herbert Stead, "The Civic Life of Chicago," Review of Reviews, VIII (July, 1893), 94.

[5] Place of birth of native Chicago residents:

Year	Persons living in Chicago born in Illinois		Persons living in Chicago born outside Illinois (Per cent of total population)				
	Per cent of native population	Per cent of total population	Born in the Old Northwest	Born in New England	Born in Middle Atlantic	Born in the South	Born in the Trans-Mississippi West
1870	56.98	29.43	33.88	4.60	10.17	2.43	.55
1880	66.28	39.30	44.67	3.18	8.24	2.36	.83
1890	67.23	39.68	46.11	1.84	5.88	2.36	1.28

Although readily absorbed into the life of the new city, the native born continued their ties with the state of birth through the organization of societies. The Sons of Vermont, the Sons of New Hampshire, the Sons of New York, the Sons of Massachusetts, and the Virginia Society, among others, reflected the lasting affection of migrants and their children for their earlier homes. Social engagements served to strengthen these bonds and afforded opportunities to extol the past while looking toward the future.[6]

Generally speaking, native residents continued to hold their position of influence, but more than in earlier years their numbers were augmented by the sons of those who, in 1850, had been counted as aliens. By 1890, 77.9 per cent of the city's population was of foreign parentage derived from almost every civilized quarter of the globe. To these were added immigrants coming yearly from abroad who saw the city in a wondrous light, nestled in the midst of the land of plenty, richly endowed with economic and political well-being. The eager of Europe and even from the Far East drifted to Chicago, with the Germans and Irish leading in numbers.

Of all immigrant groups, the Germans added the most to the city's population from 1870 to 1890, just as they had in the twenty years before.[7] Like less numerous foreign units they tended to cling to one another, especially at first, flocking to the near North Side, where they glorified, in street names and businesses, German poets and artists and other Teutons of renown. By the mid-'eighties their growing numbers forced expansion, and the Fourteenth, Fifteenth, and Sixteenth wards on the North and Northwest sides cared for concentrated settlements with smaller communities on the Southwest Side in the Fifth, Sixth, and Seventh wards. Teutonic names also were heard in the other twelve wards by 1880, evidencing a coalescence of Germans with the American born and their rather widespread participation in many activities of the city.[8]

[6] *Chicago Tribune*, Jan. 12, 18, Feb. 23, 1883, Jan. 17, 25, Feb. 8, 1890.

[7] The term "Germans" includes all coming from the states composing the German Empire of 1871 and Austria proper. The method of listing the Germanic States differs with the various censuses. In the 1850 census Germany and Austria were listed separately; in the 1860 census Austria was included under "German States"; in the 1870 and 1880 censuses Austria and Germany were listed separately; in the 1890 census, "The Germanic Nations" included Germany and Austria. For population and employment figures see Appendix. For location of foreign born see map.

[8] Andrew Jacke Townsend, *The Germans of Chicago* (unpublished Ph.D. Thesis, The University of Chicago, 1927), pp. 14, 27, 34; *Illinois Staats-Zeitung*, Jan. 25, 1892; Chicago

Although they were not possessors of the greatest wealth in the community, the Germans were by no means the poorest. Fortunes amassed in brewing and distilling, in various factories, and in other business undertakings, placed them among the captains of industry.[9] German workers in large numbers found employment in the semi-skilled trades from which they frequently moved up rather than down. Their participation in government and politics was aggressive and important, and their hold on political emoluments tenacious and jealous.

Their gregariousness found an outlet in a wide variety of societies dedicated to mutual aid and to social and cultural aspirations. The Order of Harugari, founded to preserve German culture and spread the German language, continued the activities to which it had been dedicated as early as 1863 in Chicago. The Chicago Turn Gemeinde, dating from 1853, Die Deutsche Gesellschaft from 1854, and the Germania Männerchor of 1869 were typical of the long-range interest of these people. Stock companies and groups of amateurs presented plays about Germans in German, and underscored German contributions and customs through the vehicle of the theater. Turn-vereine, primarily reflecting the enthusiasms of the athletically minded, sometimes became involved in the pressing economic and political controversies of the day, as did numerous other organizations. The German Mutual Benefit Society and the German Society for the Protection of Immigrants and the Friendless, designed to shield unsuspecting newcomers from Chicago sharpers, embodied the humanitarian instincts man has for humankind. Women's sections were occasionally affiliated with the organizations of men, furthering the aims of the older society and encouraging social activities.[10]

Department of Health, *Report of the Department of Health, City of Chicago, For the Year 1885* (Chicago, 1886), p. 18 (hereafter cited as Chicago Department of Health, *Report*). For location of wards see map.

[9] Among the wealthy Chicagoans of German extraction may be listed Jacob and William Beidler (lumber interests), Jacob Rehm (brewing and distilling), Bernard Roesing (brewing), Hermann Schaffner (banking), Peter Schuttler with Christopher Hotz (wagon factory), Conrad Seipp (brewing and distilling), Henry Shufeldt (distilling).

[10] *Chicagoer Arbeiter-Zeitung*, Feb. 28, 1881, Jan. 4, March 10, 1884; *Der Deutsche Pionier*, VI (1874), 137–39; Pierce, *A History of Chicago*, II, 471–72; *Illinois Staats-Zeitung*, Jan. 28, 1876; Eliza Roth, *Die Stadt Chicago . . .* (Chicago, 1894), pp. 143–48; *The Workingman's Advocate*, Jan. 8, 1876; *The Knights of Labor*, IV (Aug. 11, 1888), 1; *Abendpost*, July 28, 1890, March 3, Oct. 26, 1891; *Chicago Tribune*, Aug. 22, 1890, Feb. 28, 1892;

A German press offered news of the new home along with that of the Fatherland, and provided German readers pabulum ranging from the conservatism of the *Illinois Staats-Zeitung* to the radicalism of the *Chicagoer Arbeiter-Zeitung*.[11] The obeisance paid by authorities to this great segment of the population was exemplified in the issuance of public notices in German as well as in English, and the teaching of German in the public schools, in which the number of teachers increased from eight in 1870 with 2,597 pupils to 242 teachers in 1892 and '93 with 34,547 studying the language.[12] By 1885 the grammar schools held classes in German, and within five years the subject was introduced in the third and fourth grades. The requirement by law in 1889 that the medium of instruction in all schools be English evoked a demonstration of solidarity against the statute which led some to speculate whether the German element was German or American in its first allegiance.[13]

Into the mixed population of Chicago were also drawn many Irish, who continued to be an important factor in various aspects of city life. The numerical significance of these newcomers diminished as the years advanced, but their influence, particularly in the realm of politics, increased. Here, generally affiliated with the conservative branch of the Democratic party, they enjoyed political advantage in which Daniel O'Hara, their countryman, became an important force. Their cohesiveness was pronounced, and, despite the absence of a language barrier, they remained a strongly unified part of Chicago's

[Albert Nelson Marquis], *Marquis' Hand-Book of Chicago* (Chicago, 1885), John J. Flinn, *Chicago . . . A Guide, 1891* (Chicago, [1891]), and other directories list such organizations. See *Chicago Tribune*, May 16, 1886, for a list of some German societies of that year. Newspapers carry frequent announcements of meetings and of new organizations.

[11] Leading German newspapers in Chicago during the years covered by this volume were *Illinois Staats-Zeitung*, founded in 1848; the *Chicagoer Arbeiter-Zeitung* or *Arbeiter-Zeitung* begun as a weekly in 1872 and as a daily in 1876; the *Chicagoer Freie Presse* founded in 1874; and the *Abendpost*, which issued its first number as a daily in 1889. William F. Scott, *Newspapers and Periodicals of Illinois, 1814–1879* (Illinois State Historical Library, *Collections*, VI. Bibliographical Series, I. rev. ed. Springfield, 1910), pp. 107, 125, 129; Work Projects Administration, *Bibliography of Foreign Language Newspapers and Periodicals Published in Chicago* (Chicago: Chicago Public Library Omnibus Project, 1942), pp. 25, 41–42, 88 (author hereafter cited as W.P.A.).

[12] Chicago Board of Education, *Thirty-ninth Annual Report . . . , 1893* (Chicago, 1894), p. 126, *Thirty-first Annual Report, 1885*, p. 138.

[13] Act of May 18, 1889, Illinois, *All the Laws of the State of Illinois . . . , 1889* ([Chicago], 1889), pp. 237–38 (hereafter cited as *Laws*); *Chicago Tribune*, Oct. 18, 24, 1890; *Chicago Daily News*, Oct. 14, 16, 21, 28, 1890; *Abendpost*, April 21, Oct. 24, 30, 1890; *Illinois Staats-Zeitung*, April 22, May 9, Nov. 1, 1890.

cosmopolitanism. Attacked by old-line Americans not only for their religious unity but because they openly attempted to take over the political patronage, the Irish kept their eyes unwaveringly on the goal they had in mind. Although living in every ward in the city, they were thickest in the Fifth, Seventh, and Eighth wards on the Southwest Side, close to the lumberyards and stockyards where many found employment. Some furnished to the community the brawn so important in establishing the comforts as well as the necessities of living. The public works profited greatly from the picks and shovels which they wielded, often under the direction of an Irish boss. Evidences of such contributions to the physical well-being of the city multiplied so noticeably in the months immediately following the Fire that it gave rise to the boast that it was the Irish who had rebuilt the city.[14]

Recurrent religious festivals and nationalistic celebrations kept the Irish conscious of the Old Country. Numerous Irish societies such as the Ancient Order of Hibernians, the Clan-na-Gael, and the Fenian Brotherhood fed abundantly a congenital attachment to the national cause. The 'eighties saw more than half a hundred separate organizations accenting such fidelities, and these attained united action at times through delegates to the Irish-American Council, organized in 1869. A chauvinistic response to the names of all Irish heroes was as ardent as it would have been in Dublin and was matched, in turn, by an equally passionate Anglophobia.[15] The annual celebration of St. Patrick's Day gave free rein to Irish loyalties, at times so pervasive that the wheels of government were stopped by order of the city council.[16]

[14] Chicago Department of Health, *Report, 1885*, p. 18; *The Chicago Times*, March 7, Aug. 6, 1875, Dec. 1, 1881, March 2 1882; *The Western Catholic*, Dec. 9, 1871.

[15] *Chicago Tribune*, Nov. 23, Dec. 23, 1873, Feb. 9, 1880, Jan. 15, March 4, June 17, 18, July 3, Oct. 16, 1883, March 18, 1885, Feb. 9, May 10, Oct. 29, 1887, Nov. 30, 1890, March 18, 1891; *The Western Catholic*, Jan. 25, 1873, Jan. 10, 1874, March 27, May 1, 22, 1874, Aug. 2, 31, 1878, Feb. 5, 1881, Feb. 2, 1884, Jan. 22, March 26, May 14, 1887; *The Irish World and American Industrial Liberator*, Aug. 30, Sept. 27, 1884; *The Catholic Home*, V (June 23, 1888), 2. For notices of meetings of Irish societies see the various Chicago newspapers. *The Irish World and American Industrial Liberator* and *The Western Catholic* also are good sources. For beginnings of some of these organizations see Pierce, *A History of Chicago*, II, 14–16. See also city directories and handbooks for organization data. The anti-British attitude of Chicago Irish at times kept Irish saloonkeepers from patronizing English syndicate breweries.

[16] For example, the city council ordered the offices of the City Hall closed on March 17, 1883, 1891, and 1892. Chicago, *Council Proceedings, 1882–83*, p. 258, *1890–91*, p. 1742, *1891–92*, p. 2021.

The work of Michael Davitt and the Irish Land League received
hearty support, and by 1880 Chicago proudly pointed to its own
branch of the League. In 1881 and in 1886 the national convention
of the League was held in Chicago, and along with the Irish of
thirty-seven other places Chicagoans supported the program of the
Irish nationalists. Whenever Michael Davitt and other leaders visited
the city in the 1880's their messages were enthusiastically heard.[17]
And when Alexander Sullivan, formerly president of the United
Irish Societies of Chicago and prominent in the Clan-na-Gael, was
named president of the Irish National League of America, in 1883,
the Irish of the city acclaimed it an appropriate recognition of the
contributions, financial and spiritual, which they had given.[18]

These signs of solidarity were, however, not indicative of harmony
within organizations or between societies. The conservative and
clerical Irish openly and ardently opposed secret societies and all
that this secrecy entailed. Within the spirited United Brotherhood,
commonly called the Clan-na-Gael, two factions warred for control,
" The Triangle," led by Alexander Sullivan, and the faction guided
by Dr. Patrick Henry Cronin. The murder of the latter under mys-
terious circumstances for years agitated and horrified the public. The
story of Dr. Cronin's answer to a professional summons on May 4,
1889, when he was picked up by a man driving a buggy drawn by a
white horse; the discovery on May 22 of his nude and beaten body
stuffed into a catch basin in sparsely settled Lake View; and the indictment for murder of seven men, with their trial marked by charges
of jury bribery and a feverish public concern as to the real meaning
of such nativistic manifestation, filled the columns of the daily
press for weeks.[19]

[17] Michael Davitt, *The Fall of Feudalism in Ireland or the Story of the Land League
Revolution* (New York, 1904), *passim; Chicago Tribune,* Dec. 1–3, 1881, June 29, 1882,
Aug. 19, 1886.

[18] The Irish Land League was renamed the Irish National League of America in 1883.
Chicago Tribune, April 28, 29, 1883; Davitt, *op. cit.,* p. 390; *The Chicago Times,* April 28,
1883; William Clarke to H. D. Lloyd, May 23, 1883, Henry Demarest Lloyd, *Papers (Mss.*
Wisconsin Historical Society).

[19] The men indicted were Patrick O'Sullivan of the O'Sullivan Ice Company for whose
injured employee Dr. Cronin was called; Daniel Coughlin, a detective, charged with renting the horse and buggy; Frank J. Woodruff, alias Black, called " the champion story-teller "
of Cronin's flight; Martin Burke, aliases Delaney and Williams, laborer; Patrick Cooney,
" the Fox," the purchaser of furniture found in the " murder cottage "; John Kunze, laborer,
alleged to be the driver of the horse; and John F. Beggs, lawyer and active in the Clan-na-
Gael, as Senior Guardian of Camp 20. (*Chicago Tribune,* May 11, June 17, 18, 19, 20, 30,

So strong was the suggestion that the murder had been engineered to prevent revelations of the allegedly dishonest activities of Alexander Sullivan in the Clan-na-Gael that he too was arrested, but evidence of direct complicity in the murder was insufficient to warrant his trial.[20] On December 16, the jury rendered its verdict on those tried. One was acquitted, one received three years for manslaughter, and three were sentenced to life imprisonment for murder.[21] On appeal, the state Supreme Court reversed the Cook County Court decision and ordered a new trial for one of those sentenced to life imprisonment, on the ground that two jurors in the trial court had been prejudiced.[22] Thus ended what had seemed to Chicagoans not only an evidence of deplorable morals but of shadowy connivances between ethnic factions. For later-day residents of the city the significance of the case lay chiefly in the realization that, in spite of such nationalistic feuds and apparently alien loyalties, the city was weaving an American fabric tough and enduring, with its dominant pattern shaped in the American manner and form.

Less numerous in 1870 and '80 than the Germans and Irish were the Scandinavians, who increased from 9.53 per cent of the city's foreign born in 1870, 12.34 per cent in 1880, to 15.9 per cent in 1890, when they took second place from the Irish. The Danes represented the smallest number; Swedish immigrants in 1880 and 1890 exceeded those from Norway. Like the Germans and Irish, the Scandinavians concentrated at first in certain sections, especially in the Fourteenth and Seventeenth wards. As they gained economic sta-

---

July 2, 1889.) Six men, including two court bailiffs, were indicted for attempts to bribe the jury. In all, ten were said to have made such attempts. *Ibid.,* Oct. 13–16, 23, 1889, Feb. 11, 19, 21–23, April 1, 1890.

20 *Ibid.,* June 15, 1889.

21 Beggs's connections with the murder were unproved and he was acquitted; Kunze was sentenced to three years for manslaughter; and Coughlin, Burke, and O'Sullivan were given life imprisonment for murder. Woodruff was granted a separate trial. The case against him was deemed insufficient and he was taken to Kansas for punishment as a horse thief. Patrick Cooney escaped from the city. *Ibid.,* Dec. 17, 1889; *L'Italia,* Dec. 21, 1889; Lloyd Lewis and Henry Justin Smith, *Chicago: The History of Its Reputation* (New York, 1929), 259–60; *The Times* [London], Dec. 17, 1889; Eugen Seeger, *Chicago the Wonder City* (Chicago, 1893), pp. 272–99. This book is inaccurate in some details but gives an extended and colorful account of Coughlin *v.* The People, 144 Ill. 140 (1893). For a contemporaneous and journalistic account see Henry M. Hunt, *The Crime of the Century or the Assassination of Dr. Patrick Henry Cronin* . . . (Chicago, 1889).

22 O'Sullivan and Burke died before the Supreme Court rendered its decision. Seeger, *op. cit.,* p. 298; *Chicago Tribune,* Jan. 21, 1893.

bility, dispersion was not uncommon. By the early 'nineties they were moving westward into the neighborhood of Indiana Street and Milwaukee Avenue. The Fifth, Sixth, Fourteenth, and Seventeenth wards became the homes of Swedes in particular. The Danes were attracted to the Ninth and western portion of the Eleventh and Twelfth wards and near Humboldt and Wicker parks, while the Norwegians, although more migratory than other Scandinavians, tended to settle on the West Side.[23]

A measure of Scandinavian coalescence in the American society of the time was manifested by their membership in American fraternal organizations and their celebration of American holidays.[24] Their confidence in American secular education and an avowal of faith in the process of Americanization, to which all aliens were subjected, facilitated participation in indigenously American concerns. " What is then that Americanization process that we hear so much about? " rhetorically inquired the Swedish *Svenska Tribunen,* as it denied that becoming an American destroyed a person's old identity. Indeed, in America, said the editor, " one becomes more elastic and pliable and learns to view a matter from several angles " through the development of a man's " inherent characteristics." [25] Unlike nearly all other alien groups the Scandinavians did not urge the teaching of their native languages in the schools, where, said the editor of *Skandinaven,* they wanted their children to learn English and not foreign languages, " not even the speech of the Norsemen." [26]

All this should not imply, however, that their affection for the homeland was in any sense slight or wavering, for the preservation of native traditions was openly and assiduously encouraged. Like others, each of the Scandinavian groups had its publications and organizations designed to keep alive national traditions. The Swedish press with its *Svenska Tribunen, Hemlandet,* and *Svenska Amerikanaren,* the Norwegian *Skandinaven,* and the Danish *Norden* and

[23] *Ibid.,* Oct. 2, 1882, March 21, 1886, March 23, 1890; *Svenska Tribunen,* June 23, 1888; *Skandinaven,* Dec. 31, 1891, Feb. 2, 1892.
[24] See, for example, *Svenska Tribunen,* Sept. 25, 1886, Aug. 18, 1888; *Skandinaven,* March 27, 1872, July 9, 1878. *Skandinaven,* Aug. 10, 1891, describes a joint picnic of the Norwegian Turners and German Turners of Pullman. The Scandinavian Free Thinkers' Society celebrated Thomas Paine's anniversary. *Illinois Staats-Zeitung,* Jan. 30, 1877.
[25] *Svenska Tribunen,* July 2, 1891.
[26] *Skandinaven,* March 5, 1893. See also *ibid.,* June 11, 1893; *Chicago Tribune,* March 21, 1886.

Hejmdal, with other publications both secular and religious, acquainted their nationals with the new country and served as a strong link with the old.[27]

By the close of the 'eighties the Swedes could boast of at least eighteen societies which invaded the sphere of influence long enjoyed by the Svea Society. Singing clubs like Svenska Sångföreningen; the Svithiod Sångkör, formed of members of the Independent Order of Svithiod, a benefit organization, and the Svenska Glee-Klubben betokened the deep-seated love of music these people had. The Swedish Vasa Society and the Svithiod Society provided sick aid and burial expenses for needy members, and organizations such as the Swedish Brotherhood of Painters and Decorators served the craft-conscious. Like the Germans, who honored their heroes by the raising of statues, so the Swedes erected to Carl von Linné a statue in Lincoln Park.[28]

Norwegians and Danes followed the same pattern to preserve their national integrity, carrying on an active community life within the larger fellowship of Chicago. The Norwegian Turner Lodge, founded in 1867, the Norwegian Dramatic Club, organized in 1868, the Norwegian Singing Society of Chicago, active since 1870, the Norwegian Relief Association, and the Viking Cycle Club of 1893 all served to implement the purposes their names denoted. The Norwegian Society, with a continuing devotion, celebrated Norwegian Constitutional Day and other Norse holidays, and the Norwegian Old Settlers' Society each year made merry in dancing and feasting.[29]

Although an old segment of the Scandinavian population, the

[27] See *Svenska Tribunen,* Nov. 30, 1892, for specific expression of these purposes.

[28] Pierce, *A History of Chicago,* II, 20; Ernest W. Olson, *History of the Swedes in Illinois* (Chicago, 1908), I, 706–17, 738, 895; *Svenska Tribunen,* Jan. 29, 1879, Aug. 13, 1887, Feb. 4, 1888, Feb. 2, 1889, May 8, Aug. 7, 1890, June 28, 1891, Feb. 17, May 14, 1892, March 15, 1893; *Chicago Tribune,* Aug. 20, 1888, May 5, 1889, May 23, 24, 1891; *Illinois Staats-Zeitung,* May 8, Aug. 7, 1890, May 23, 1891. The Germans erected statues to Alexander von Humboldt in Humboldt Park and to Johann Christopher Friedrich von Schiller in Lincoln Park. *Illinois Staats-Zeitung,* Oct. 17, 18, 1892.

[29] *Chicago Tribune,* May 17, 1881, Jan. 19, Oct. 30, 31, 1890, Feb. 11, 1892; *Illinois Staats-Zeitung,* March 17, 1877; Theodore C. Blegen, *Norwegian Migration to America, The American Transition* (Northfield, Minn., 1940), pp. 484–85, 572; Birger Osland, "Norwegian Clubs in Chicago," *Norwegian-American Studies and Records,* XII (Northfield, Minn., 1941), 111; *Skandinaven,* Jan. 3, July 24, 1872, May 17, 1883, Jan. 16, 1884, Jan. 22, Oct. 18, 1893, Nov. 18, 1900; *Chicago Daily News,* May 18, 1887. Leif Erickson was honored in festival, painting, and sculpture.

Danes were relatively few in number. In their homes on the West Side they kept alive their folkways and mores and in many cases clung tenaciously to their native language. Their largest society was the male Dania Club, incorporated in 1865, to which Swedes and Norwegians were admitted as nonvoting members. Social engagements and sick and death benefits made the organization a vital concern to the Danes. In 1887, to give force to the old dictum that " as the twig is bent so is the tree inclined," the Danish People's Society organized a Danish Youth Society to perpetuate the culture of their land. Through the Hans Christian Andersen Monument Association, incorporated in 1891, the Danes paid homage to their great literary compatriot.[30]

Although Americans often failed to consider the Scandinavians in their different national entities, each was self-conscious and frequently jealous of the accomplishments of the others.[31] Still, the bond of being Scandinavian was sufficiently strong to encourage the formation of the United Scandinavian Singers and the Scandinavian Convention, made up of the leading societies to provide charity to the needy. A Scandinavian Engineering Society held meetings devoted to matters of professional interest, and the Scandinavian Press Club, organized in 1891, aimed at harmony in its constituency. The Scandinavian Workingmen's Society by 1874 held meetings to canvass subjects of immediate concern, but unlike some of the German workers' associations it steered a course away from economic and political radicalism. The Swedes and Norwegians were generally Republican in politics, but the Danes often belonged to the Democratic party.[32] To those unable to speak English, national-language hotels and banks rendered needed service.[33]

[30] Illinois, *Private Laws of the State of Illinois . . . , 1865*, I, 67 (hereafter cited as *Private Laws*); *Chicago Tribune*, March 21, 1886; *Hejmdal*, Oct. 13, 1874; *Skandinaven*, Jan. 12, Feb. 2, 1892; *Danish Times*, Nov. 13, 1936; *Revyen*, May 20, 1911; *Illinois Staats-Zeitung*, Oct. 26, 1891; *Skandia*, Dec. 6, 1913; *Chicago Tribune*, Jan. 30, 1892.

[31] For illustrations of internal dissension in the Scandinavian groups and for objections raised to the appellation " Scandinavian " see *Svenska Tribunen*, May 21, 29, June 5, 19, 1886, Jan. 16, June 3, 1892; H. H. Boyesen, " The Scandinavian in the United States," *The North American Review*, CLV (Nov., 1892), 531; Kendric C. Babcock, " The Scandinavians in the Northwest," *The Forum*, XIV (Sept., 1892), 103–9.

[32] *Skandinaven*, Jan. 13, 1883, Nov. 26, 1890, Nov. 15, 1891; *Hejmdal*, Oct. 31, 1874, Jan. 16, 27, 1875, March 10, 1876; *Svenska Tribunen*, May 11, 22, June 12, 1886, Aug. 18, 1888, June 18, 1891; *Chicago Tribune*, March 21, 1886; Gustav Elwood Johnson, *The Swedes of Chicago* (unpublished Ph.D. Thesis, The University of Chicago, 1940), pp. 36–39.

[33] Dannevirke provided hotel accommodations for all Scandinavians. There were, of

To an unusual degree the Scandinavians possessed the virtues of frugality and steadiness. A desire to own their own homes rather than to rent was frequently a realization of a much cherished dream, and their places of business were among the most neatly kept in the city. Their well-known love of the sea was manifest in the number who were lake captains and seamen, and they often found employment in shipbuilding. Domestic service and unskilled labor claimed a good number, although there were, in 1880, in the latter work only about half as many Scandinavians as Irish. At that time they outranked both Britishers and Germans in manufacturing and mechanical pursuits and were most numerous of all as tailors, dressmakers, and milliners.[34] The deference of all three groups to law and order is well reflected in the less than 3 per cent of arrests recorded from 1880 to 1890, an enviable record in contrast with the number of Irish and Germans who were apprehended.[35]

Besides the Irish, the British Isles contributed English, Welsh, and Scotch who made up the group next to the Scandinavians in size, and who maintained an almost constant proportion of the whole from 1870 to 1890, furnishing about 10 per cent of the foreign born of the city. Of this number England sent more than two-thirds, with Scotland coming next, and Wales providing a negligible number. The British-Americans also maintained a fairly steady proportion of Chicago's foreign born. In about equal numbers Canadians came, hopefully looking to Chicago " as the Mecca of their ambition." [36]

---

course, hostelries for each nationality. (*Skandinaven*, March 11, 1879, March 29, 1881.) The Scandinavian Bank, for example, in 1875 offered 6 per cent interest on savings. *Hejmdal*, June 11, 1875.

[34] *Skandinaven*, May 4, 1880, April 29, 1889. The Norwegian Sivert Amundsen, who came to Chicago in 1844, was a large shipbuilder. He died in 1880. *Ibid.*, May 4, 1880. See Appendix table.

[35] The following is the percentage of arrests as given in the reports of the Department of Police:

Year	Danes	Germans	Irish	Norwegians	Swedes
1880	.26	11.84	17.62	1.09	1.75
1890	.38	11.07	10.33	1.26	2.53

Chicago Superintendent of Police, *Report of the General Superintendent of Police of the City of Chicago Made to the City Commissioner for the Fiscal Year Ending December 31, 1880* (Chicago, 1881), p. 30, *1890*, p. 52 (hereafter cited as Chicago Superintendent of Police, *Report*).

[36] In 1870, the English made up 6.9 per cent of the foreign born; in 1880, 6.37 per cent; in 1890, 6.29 per cent. The Scotch composed 2.9 per cent in 1870; 2.0 per cent in 1880; and 2.0 per cent in 1890. The Welsh in the same years had .39, .35, .36 per cent

Because of likeness in speech, in institutional background, and in appearance, the immigrant from the British Isles was welded quickly and inconspicuously into the American structure. His was the same pride of heritage as that of old-line Americans who had come in the early days and still retained leadership in economic and cultural life. Special organizations like St. George's Benevolent Association combined English social and humanitarian aspirations. Its Scotch counterpart, the Illinois St. Andrew's Society, recalled memories of the native land. In 1883 the Caledonian Society was formally constituted for the avowed purpose of encouraging Scottish national games and the wearing of traditional costumes, of cultivating a taste for Scotch poetry and music, and cementing friendship among those of Scotch descent. For Welshmen the Cambrian Benevolent Society fostered the same sentiments. In picnics, athletic events, balls, and festivals the British-American Association, as well as the others, renewed friendships and indulged in praise of the home of their birth.[37]

The German states, Ireland and the rest of the British Isles, and the Scandinavian countries had constituted the main source of the foreign born in the 'fifties and 'sixties. They continued to predominate, but in the course of the 'seventies and 'eighties others came in increasing numbers to add to the complexity of the urban pattern. Many of these newcomers, moved by economic or other necessity to better their lot, were from central, southern, and eastern Europe. Within the 'nineties they were to make Chicago, of all American cities, the home of the largest number of Poles, Bohemians, Croatians, Slovakians, Lithuanians, and Greeks. This new immigration, which also included southern Italians, posed many and complex problems, but it did not change the basic pattern of nine-

respectively. The British-Americans had 6.67 per cent in 1870; 6.79 per cent in 1880; and 5.39 per cent in 1890. Canadians made up 6.18 per cent in 1870; 6.48 in 1880 of the foreign born. No figures are furnished for Canadians in 1890. See Appendix table. See Marcus Lee Hansen, *The Mingling of the Canadian and American Peoples* (New Haven, 1940), I, 206.

[37] *Chicago Tribune*, Dec. 2, 1871, Aug. 7, 10, 11, 23, 1873, June 2, Aug. 30, Nov. 30, Dec. 1, 1883, April 27, 1885, Dec. 1, 1886, Feb. 27, 1889. Other organizations, such as the Scotch Thistle Club, the Highland Association and the Heather Club were also active. See *ibid.*, Aug. 15, 23, 1873, Oct. 2, 1882, Aug. 10, 1883, Aug. 24, 1884, Jan. 16, Oct. 30, 1886, Jan. 22, 1893; Pierce, *op. cit.*, II, 16, 17.

teenth-century society in either an alarming or an appreciable degree.[38]

From central Europe came the Czechs of the ancient Kingdom of Bohemia, in the nineteenth century part of the Austro-Hungarian Empire. Constituting about 5 per cent of the foreign-born population of Chicago in the 'seventies and 'eighties, the Czechs (Bohemians) were a closely knit people, clinging to their own cultural, social, and linguistic heritage with a tenacity that resisted easy Americanization. They probably had first come to Chicago in the 'fifties, men of education and culture, exiles from a political despotism. As time passed, peasants, artisans, and skilled laborers arrived, motivated by the desire to be economically secure.[39]

Within the city there developed several Czech or Bohemian settlements, small cities within the larger city. The largest was on the Southwest Side in the Fifth and Sixth wards, with smaller numbers living in the Seventh and Eighth wards. Stretching from Halsted Street to Ashland Avenue and south of Sixteenth, the most highly congested Bohemian colony came to be called Pilsen from the native city of that name. Here, the streets, lined with Bohemian provision stores, clothing shops, restaurants, and other businesses, appeared transplanted from the home across the sea, reminders of a place and day now gone.[40]

Situated as the Bohemians were along the south branch of the river, they often had employment in the lumberyards and furniture factories. Others, fewer in number, could be found in the Fourteenth Ward along the north branch where employment in woodworking could be had. Bricklaying, painting, and the work generally associated with the building trades at first claimed many of their num-

[38] On the changing character of immigration see U. S. Senate, *Report of the Committee on Immigration,* 52 Cong., 2 sess., S. Rept. 1333, II (3 v. Washington, 1893), ii.

[39] See Appendix table. The census reports of 1850 and 1860 do not list the Czechs (Bohemians). They were probably included in Austrian immigration. *Svornost,* June 6, 1890; Emily Greene Balch, *Our Slavic Fellow Citizens* (New York, 1910), pp. 210, 217; Residents of Hull House, *Hull-House Maps and Papers* . . . (New York, 1895), p. 116; John J. Reichman, *Czechoslovaks of Chicago* . . . (Chicago, 1937), p. 6.

[40] *Ibid.,* p. 115; *Svornost,* May 27, Aug. 23, 1884; *Illinois Staats-Zeitung,* Jan. 25, 1892; Jacob Horak, *Assimilation of Czechs in Chicago* (unpublished Ph.D. Thesis, The University of Chicago, 1920), p. 24; Paul Frederick Cressey, *The Succession of Cultural Groups in the City of Chicago* (unpublished Ph.D. Thesis, The University of Chicago, 1930), p. 187. Ward boundaries and street names are often different from those of a later time.

bers. By the 1880's, however, some had entered various business enterprises as clerks and eventually as owners, and another ten years saw them well represented in the professions. By thrift and perseverance they came to have property and through building and loan associations even the lowliest was enabled to own his home.[41]

In these well-run communities the Czech language was heard until the children of the first immigrants abandoned it for English, learned both in their own Bohemian schools and the American public school. In religion, Free Thinkers had invaded the onetime solid phalanx of Catholicism, and the followers of John Hus were numerous enough to propose a memorial to him in Douglas Park. Clubs devoted to music and dramatics and athletic associations of Sokols linked their membership through common pleasures and ties of blood. By 1892 three newspapers, *Svornost, Chicagské Listy,* and *Denní Hlasatel,* enjoyed gratifying circulations.[42]

Like the Czechs, the Poles formed a group whose nationalistic aspirations were not satisfied in Europe. Fleeing from unhappy economic conditions imposed by a restrictive German land policy, by Russian famine, and by the decline of Galician economy, they came in increasing numbers after the Fire. Bismarck's policy of repression directed against the Poles in Prussia, and the ukases of the Russian czar also planted seeds of discontent, so that the less than 1 per cent of the Polish among Chicago's foreign born in 1870 grew to 2.7 per cent within the decade, and by 1890 this percentage had about doubled.[43]

Their several colonies, clustered about the Roman Catholic Church and parochial school, formed a unitary cultural segment of Chicago's cosmopolitanism. The oldest of the Polish settlements was on the Northwest Side; to it was attached the Roman Catholic Church of St. Stanislaus Kostka, at Noble and Bradley streets.[44] By 1886 at least

[41] *Illinois Staats-Zeitung,* Jan. 25, 1892; *Svornost,* May 27, Aug. 23, 1884; *Chicago Tribune,* March 7, 1886; *Bohemian Building and Loan Associations and their Influence on Home Building* (Ms.) quoted in Horak, *op. cit.,* p. 75.

[42] *Chicago Tribune,* Feb. 9, 1890; Robert E. Park, *The Immigrant Press and Its Control* (New York, 1922), p. 264.

[43] See Appendix table.

[44] In 1877 the district embraced by Milwaukee Avenue, the Chicago and North Western railroad tracks, Augusta Street, and Noble Street was inhabited by Poles. *Narod Polski,* May 2, 1917; *Chicago Tribune,* Feb. 3, 23, 1877.

25,000 Poles were reported living in this district; in 1892 the number reached the 30,000 mark. Others dwelt at Seventeenth and Paulina streets in the Sixth Ward, in the vicinity of the Church of St. Adalbert, and between Laurel Street and Ashland Avenue in the Fifth Ward. Smaller groups established homes along Ward Street, with St. Josaphat's Church as the center of community life, and in the neighborhood of Thirty-ninth and Ashland Avenue. Bridgeport had its settlement on the outskirts of the city and South Chicago claimed those who were attracted by the rolling mills. Even so far out as Pullman and the Lemont stone quarry others could be found.[45]

Most of these men of Polish birth were peasants, who now in their new home had to seek work in occupations common to a growing city. Many became laborers, as did a majority of their fellows from other lands. Like the Bohemians they worked in the sawmills, lumberyards, and woodworking establishments. They became blacksmiths, bricklayers, carpenters, mechanics, and shoemakers. When drawn into business they engaged in the clothing industry, cigar and cigarette manufacturing, baking, and meat marketing. By the mid-'eighties they had entered the political arena, voting both as Republicans and Democrats, and had some appointive offices in the city government as well as membership on the police force and in the fire department.[46]

Because many were poor upon arrival, overcrowding and bad housing complicated their way of living, until frugality lifted them to better conditions. They invested their savings in real estate, and building and loan associations assisted those desiring to possess their homes.[47] To supplement the meager wages of the men, women and children sought employment, especially in cigar factories, and, like

[45] *Chicago Tribune*, March 14, 1886, June 12, 1892; *Illinois Staats-Zeitung*, Feb. 22, 1892; *Dziennik Chicagoski*, Oct. 19, 1892; Miecislaus Haiman, "The Poles in Chicago," [Polish Pageant, Inc.], *Poles of Chicago, 1837–1937* . . . (Chicago, [1937]), pp. 3–4. See also *ibid.*, pp. 56, 95–114.

[46] *Chicago Tribune*, March 14, 1886; Robert F. Lessel, "The Rise of Poles in American Politics," *Poles of Chicago, 1837–1937*, pp. 21, 23; Thaddeus Lubera, "Poles on the School Board," *ibid.*, p. 13; *Illinois Staats-Zeitung*, Feb. 22, 1892; *Zgoda*, July 25, 1888, March 3, 13, 20, 27, June 5, 1889; April 9, Sept. 10, 12, 24, Oct. 22, 1890, March 9, 16, May 25, Nov. 23, 1892; X. Waclaw Kruszka, *Historja Polska w Ameryce* (13 v. Milwaukee, 1904–8), III, 130.

[47] By the mid-'eighties 40 per cent were said to own their homes. The *Tribune* reported in March, 1886, in the Fourteenth Ward there were six Polish building and loan associations, two in the Fifth Ward, and one on the North Side. *Chicago Tribune*, March 14, 1886.

the Bohemians and Italians, they moved into the sweated industries.[48]

Social life among the Poles centered about societies, the two most important being the Polish Roman Catholic Union and the Polish National Alliance of North America. The former, stemming from a conference in Detroit in 1873, held its first annual convention in Chicago in 1874. Its primary purpose was to preserve the Catholic faith and its secondary to perpetuate the national spirit. In 1880 the Polish National Alliance was born, in the shadow of the birthplace of American freedom, in Philadelphia. Its avowed objectives were to glorify Polish national aspirations, to guide the immigrant in his entrance to the new land, and eventually to lead him into American citizenship. An intense rivalry between the two societies tended at times to obscure the national heritage upon which both rested, and the anti-Catholic stand taken after 1881 by *Zgoda,* organ of the Alliance, alienated conservative and strongly religious Poles.[49] Both organizations afforded benefits of various kinds to a people greatly in need of direction and aid, but the animus which developed between them profaned the higher achievements for which they had been constituted.[50]

Several organizations provided insurance and sick benefits and the Poles proudly asserted that they did not place on others the care of their dependents. A variety of associations furnished cultural and other diversions. The Polish-American Falcons, similar to the Bohemian Sokols, directed interest into cultural and physical training. In 1893 the Union of Polish Sokols was established. Military societies, such as the Cadets of St. Michael and Kosynieri, and the St. Stanislaus Kostka's cadets, appealed especially to youth, just as in the case of other national groups. Gmina Polska, an organization of nationalistic bent, put on Polish plays, sponsored choral groups, and promoted nature-study classes and lectures on popular subjects. In

[48] Joseph Kirkland, "Among the Poor of Chicago," *Scribner's Magazine,* XII (July, 1892), 23–25; *Chicago Tribune,* March 14, 1886.

[49] *Zgoda* was established in Milwaukee in 1881 and transferred to Chicago in 1888.

[50] *The Catholic Encyclopedia,* XII (15 v. New York, [1907–12]), 208; Kruszka, *op. cit.,* III, 142–46, IV, 75, V, 3–6; Stanislaw Osada, *Historya Związku Narodowego Polskiego* (Chicago: [Polish National Union], 1905), pp. 97, 151, 639–744; *Dziennik Chicagoski,* March 21, 1891, Feb. 29, Sept. 2, 5, 13, Oct. 13, 1892; *Zgoda,* July 16, Aug. 28, 1890; Paul Fox, *The Poles in America* (New York, 1922), p. 90; Karol Wachtel, Z. P. R. K. (Chicago, 1913), pp. 397–565 (Dzieje Zjednoczenia Polskiego Rzym.-Kat. w Ameryce [Polish Roman Catholic Union]).

1893 women were given a part in the activities of Organizacya Patryotyczna (Patriotic Organization), and thereupon entered a sphere which had been largely restricted to men.[51]

Festivals and commemorative exercises followed the nationalistic patterns set by other groups. For the heroes of other lands the Poles substituted Pulaski and Kosciusko, naming a hall for the former and erecting a statue of the latter.[52] Newspapers and other publications promoted by Gmina Polska kept alive an awareness of Polish needs and aspirations. Of these, the *Gazeta Polska* began as a weekly in 1873. During the 'seventies several publications primarily religious in tone were started. *Dziennik Chicagoski,* issued first in 1890, a daily, and *Wiara i Ojczyzna,* founded in 1887, a weekly, served a considerable public, although the number of illiterates among the newcomers even as late as 1892 was high.[53]

Despite the appearance of unity which these various organs presented and the still more effective controls and direction given by the Church and the parochial schools, divided loyalties developed. Native backgrounds accounted for some of this division. To Chicago came Poles from Posen and Silesia, said to be about 75 per cent of all in the 'eighties, and from Warsaw, Lithuania, and Austria. This was not a homogeneous group. In it were the Jews whom Christian Poles disdained, often shunning their business establishments and treating them as social outcasts. "The Poles," said M. Osuch, president of the Polish National Alliance in 1888, "are one thing and the Polish Jews are another." [54]

Such animosities, however, extended beyond the Jews. The Poles, in spite of their Catholicism, were unfriendly to the Irish, and regretted that they had to use Irish priests, a situation which they tried to change by opening their own seminaries. But this attempt to iso-

[51] *Chicago Tribune,* Sept. 27, 1880, March 14, 1886; *Zgoda,* March 13, 1889, Aug. 14, 1892; *Dziennik Chicagoski,* Feb. 1, 4, 5, Aug. 5, 19, Nov. 12, 1892, May 23, July 10, 17, 1893; *Poles of Chicago, 1837–1937,* pp. 159–61; Kruszka, *op. cit.,* IV, 53.

[52] *Chicago Tribune,* Nov. 30, 1880; *Dziennik Chicagoski,* May 4, 5, 1891, May 19, Sept. 18, 1892, Jan. 1, 1893; *Zgoda,* July 13, 27, 1892; *Poles of Chicago, 1837–1937,* p. 137. The statue of Kosciusko was unveiled in Humboldt Park in 1904. (*Chicago Record-Herald,* Sept. 11, 12, 1904.) The cornerstone of Pulaski Hall was laid July 10, 1892. *Zgoda,* July 13, 1892.

[53] Kruszka, *op. cit.,* IV, 113, 115; Osada, *op. cit.,* pp. 17–46; U. S. Senate, *Report of the Committee on Immigration,* 52 Cong., 2 sess., S. Rept. 1333, II, ii.

[54] *Chicago Tribune,* Sept. 5, 1888. See also *ibid.,* March 14, 1886; *Zgoda,* Oct. 31, 1888; *Dziennik Chicagoski,* June 11, 1891.

late the members of their faith by erecting barriers of nationality failed, and the insistence of the papacy that all Catholics in America be one people operated in favor of eventual Americanization. Upon the Germans, the Czechs, and the Slovaks the Poles likewise cast an unfriendly eye, especially when they worked in the same plant and had day-by-day contacts with those whose language they could not always understand. Criticized as being ignorant and vicious and for toiling for lower wages than many others, Poles succumbed less readily than they might otherwise have done to the processes of assimilation and naturalization, although urged by their leaders to become American citizens and to participate in politics.[55]

The Jews of these early contingents were separated from their countrymen by religion but endowed with national characteristics just as other immigrants were. Those who came from Germany dominated early settlement, but in the 'fifties and 'sixties Polish Hebrews were represented among those who sought the beneficences so freely advertised throughout Europe. During the last twenty years of the nineteenth century the Jews of Russia, hoping to escape pogroms and to better their economic lot, joined the trek westward. Of all Russians leaving their country during this time, three out of every four were said to be Hebrew. Many were reported departing from the neighborhood of Odessa. The less than 2 per cent of the foreign born of Chicago in 1890 credited to Russia may very well have been composed chiefly of Jewish emigrants. By the early 'nineties thirteen nationalities were found among the Chicago Jews, and, as in other cases, this difference in birthplace often led to disunity rather than unity, to the inhumanity of Jew toward Jew such as he suffered in social and economic contacts at the hands of gentiles.[56]

[55] Zgoda, Feb. 5, 1890; Dziennik Chicagoski, Feb. 13, 14, 1891, Jan. 4, April 8, July 22, Oct. 6, 1892, Feb. 18, 1893.

[56] Philip P. Bregstone, Chicago and Its Jews . . . (privately printed, 1933), p. 8; Edmund J. James, ed., The Immigrant Jew in America (New York, 1906), pp. 14, 57; U. S. House of Representatives, Reports of Diplomatic and Consular Officers Concerning Emigration from Europe to the United States . . . by the Select Committee . . . to Inquire into the Immigration of Paupers, Convicts, Contract Laborers, and Other Classes, 50 Cong., 2 sess., H. Rept. 3792 (Washington, 1889), pp. 144–45; Hyman L. Meites, ed., History of the Jews of Chicago (Chicago, [1924]), pp. 142–43; Thomas Randolph Hall, "The Russian Community of Chicago," Papers in Illinois History and Transactions for the Year 1937 (Springfield: Illinois State Historical Society, 1938), p. 103; The Occident, Oct. 4, 1889; Charles Zeublin, "The Chicago Ghetto," Hull-House Maps and Papers, pp. 98, 99. See Louis Wirth, The Ghetto (Chicago, 1926), pp. 153 et seq. for a discussion of Chicago Jewry. Because

Congregated in communities on the West Side, the Jews could be found principally in the Seventh, Eighth and Nineteenth wards where, in 1880, an estimated 10,000 lived. By the early 'nineties this number had doubled, but even the highest conjecture does not make them a large part of Chicago's 450,666 foreign born.[57] As their condition improved, they moved from the first site and gave way to the next wave of newcomers. The German Jews advancing southward abandoned their original settlement to their co-religionists from Russian Poland. By 1892 what was known as the " Poor Jews Quarter " lay along the western end of the Twelfth Street bridge and southward to the Italian quarter on the West Side. Neither trees nor grass added comfort and beauty to the poorly ventilated and insanitary shanties, the one- and two-story tumble-down wood cottages, and the three- or four-story brick tenements which fringed the narrow, uneven streets and alleys. Here were often the workshops of sweated workers, within range of noisome garbage-containers overflowing on narrow streets which swarmed, day and night, with children and adults.[58]

Some engaged in cigarmaking, shoemaking, bookbinding, and similar pursuits; others entered the sweated trade of tailoring. Junk shops were numerous, with their heaps of rags and scrap iron or piles of disorderly and mixed pickings. Here could be found street merchants hawking their wares, the Jewish rag and junk peddlers and the " glass puddin' men." A variety of goods was advertised in the Hebrew language on store signs and windows, and " kosher " restaurants and meat markets catered to the purely Jewish trade. When capital was very limited, the Jews took up fruit and vegetable selling. Licensed peddlers, chiefly Russian, dispensed old and second-

the census listed Jews according to national origin, an accurate enumeration cannot be reached.

[57] Board of Delegates of American Israelites, and the Union of American Hebrew Congregations, *Statistics of the Jews of the United States* ([Philadelphia]: Union of American Hebrew Congregations, 1880), p. 35. The greater Ghetto, according to Zeublin, in the early 1890's was located in the area of Polk Street on the north, Blue Island Avenue on the west, Fifteenth Street on the south, and Stewart Avenue on the east. The lesser Ghetto was in the Seventh Ward between Twelfth, Halsted, and Fifteenth streets, and Stewart Avenue. In this latter section about nine-tenths of the population were Jews. The Seventh Ward was the largest Jewish ward. In the Sixteenth Ward lived Polish and German Jews as well as in the Seventh. In the Nineteenth Ward, bordering the Seventh at the north, Jews dwelt alongside Germans, Italians, Irish, and others. *Hull-House Maps and Papers*, pp. 92, 93, 95.

[58] *Ibid.*, pp. 94–95; *Chicago Tribune*, July 19, 1891; Meites, *op. cit.*, pp. 33–34; *The Reform Advocate*, July 2, 1892; Wirth, *op. cit.*, pp. 174, 180–81; *The Occident*, Oct. 4, 1889.

hand goods throughout Chicago to the displeasure of "old-timers," who protested that this cast "odium upon Judaism," and was "a disgrace" brought about by the coming of the Russians.[59]

As soon as they could speak English the Jews engaged in business of their own. By the 'eighties their energy and acumen had made them entrepreneurs, manufacturers of ready-to-wear garments, particularly cloaks, who indulged in the sweatshop practices of their gentile contemporaries. At the top of the economic ladder were merchants of the older stock such as Leon, Simon, and Emanuel Mandel, and the members of the firm of Schlesinger and Mayer. Notable in the annals of banking and other Chicago enterprises was Henry Greenebaum, then at the height of his success, who, along with other older residents, had now attained a leadership in the economic life of the city comparable to that of the original American stock.[60]

The Standard Club, organized by well-to-do German Jews in 1869, the Zion Literary Society, formed in 1877, and the Hebrew Literary Association, started in 1885, among other organizations, reflected the economic and social well-being these Jews had attained.[61] Social and cultural aspirations found expression also in various Jewish lodges of which the branches of the Independent Order B'nai B'rith, already a national organization of power, were most prominent. In 1872 Chicago had five chapters. In 1876 the Independent Order of the Free Sons of Israel in an imposing ceremony established in Chicago its first District Grand Lodge of the West to carry out purposes similar to those of B'nai B'rith. Sick and death benefits and other humanitarian aims implemented its motto of "Friendship, Love, and Truth."[62]

[59] *The Jewish Era*, I (April, 1892), 63; *Chicago Tribune*, July 19, 1891; *The Occident*, Dec. 16, 1881, April 14, 1882. Armour and Company was reported by 1892 as having a special department for slaughtering cattle for orthodox Jews. (*Chicago Tribune*, Sept. 25, 1892.) Four kosher meat markets were on South Clark Street south of Polk, and five along the southern part of Canal Street in 1883. *Ibid.*, July 8, 1883.
[60] *The Universal Jewish Encyclopedia;* J. Seymour Currey, *Chicago: Its History and Its Builders* (Chicago, 1912), V, 357.
[61] *The Occident*, Feb. 22, 1889; *Chicago Tribune*, Feb. 27, 1880, Oct. 14, 1890; James, *op. cit.*, p. 177; *Illinois Staats-Zeitung*, April 15, 1872; Herman Eliassof, "The Jews of Illinois," *The Reform Advocate*, XXI (May 4, 1901), 273–399; Herman Eliassof, "German-American Jews," *Deutsch-Amerikanische Geschichtsblätter, Jahrbuch der Deutsch-Amerikanischen Historischen Gesellschaft von Illinois* (Chicago, 1915), XIV, 369. The Zion Literary Society sometimes appears as the Zion Literary Association.
[62] *Chicago Tribune*, May 26, 1879, Oct. 14, 1890; Pierce, *A History of Chicago*, II, 24; [Independent Order of B'nai B'rith], *Constitution of the Independent Order B'nai B'rith,*

The interest members took in the functions of these organizations was so great at times that criticism arose that these activities alienated members from religious orthodoxy, a situation that proselyting Christians individually and in societies like the Western Hebrew Christian Brotherhood zealously encouraged.[63] The majority of Jews, however, living more humbly than did their rich brethren, clung to the old-time faith and avoided the Reformed Group, which tended to be German rather than Russian or Polish. Around the rabbi, generally an immigrant national of the group to which he ministered, and the synagogue, much of the religious and educational life of the people revolved. Deficient public school instruction, found here as in other foreign quarters, the Jewish Training School supplemented. There, after September, 1890, the generosity of wealthy Jews provided industrial instruction. An evening school, sponsored by the Order of B'nai B'rith, operated successfully after May 28, 1888 in the Russian colony, advancing the use of English and knowledge of this country by a study of United States history and government. The Talmud schools, however, using Jüdisch instead of English, perpetuated the past and postponed the day of induction into American society.[64]

Although the newspapers most often at hand were printed in Jüdisch, other periodicals, some of which were short-lived and unprofitable economic ventures, were available in English. The weekly *Jewish Advance* in 1878, the daily and weekly *Jewish Courier* from 1887, *The Occident* from 1872, and the quarterly *Jewish Era* after 1892 were supplemented by New York publications and the *B'nai*

Revised and Amended in the General Convention of the Order Held in . . . Richmond, Va. June 1st to 5th, 1890 (New York, 1890), p. 3; *The Jewish Advance*, June 21, 1878, June 21, 1881; *Illinois Staats-Zeitung*, April 15, 1872; *Chicago Tribune*, Oct. 9, 1876. The Independent Order of the Free Sons of Israel was founded in 1849 in New York City. *The Universal Jewish Encyclopedia*.

[63] *The Jewish Advance*, Sept. 6, 1878. The Western Hebrew Christian Brotherhood was organized in 1868. *The Advance*, May 21, 1868, Feb. 24, 1870; *Chicago Tribune*, Feb. 15, 16, 1870.

[64] *Hull-House Maps and Papers*, pp. 105–7; Moshe Davis, "Jewish Religious Life and Institutions in America," in Louis Finkelstein, ed., *The Jews: Their History, Culture, and Religion* (Philadelphia, 1949), I, 380; *The Occident*, Oct. 4, 1889; *Illinois Staats-Zeitung*, April 15, 1872; *The Jewish Advance*, Aug. 12, 1881; *Chicago Tribune*, April 2, 1893; [Independent Order B'nai B'rith], *Report of the Secretary to the Twenty-first Annual Convention of District Grand Lodge No. 6 . . .* (Chicago, [1889]), pp. 30–31; *ibid.*, 1892, pp. 26–28.

B'rith Magazine and *The American Israelite,* published in Cincinnati.[65]

Like other children of the Old World the Jews endeavored to care for their own afflicted. The Jews of German forebears, usually of happier economic estate, were the largest contributors, sometimes acting with a condescension inconsistent with a common faith. The United Hebrew Relief Association of Chicago among its various humanitarian endeavors sponsored Michael Reese Hospital, established in 1881, found work for the unemployed, and provided a "Shelter House" to aid Russian Jews in particular. A Home for Aged Jews and one for Jewish Orphans cared for these two dependent groups, and the Young American Hebrew Association, after 1885, took steps to promote the well-being of both Jews and gentiles. The Jews bestowed charity not only through local, but also through national organizations, Chicago Israelites, for example, co-operating with the Jewish Alliance of America in assistance to Russian newcomers to this country.[66]

The Italians, constituting little more than 1 per cent of the foreign born as late as 1890, desired, even more than many others, to establish themselves in their own communities — in the vicinity of Grand Avenue west of the river in the Seventeenth Ward, in the Twenty-second Ward east of the Chicago River in "Little Sicily," in the First Ward, located at the edge of the Loop and extending westward across the river, and north of Twelfth Street in the Nineteenth Ward, known as "the bloody nineteenth." Successors to the now more prosperous Germans, Irish, and Scandinavians, the Italians

---

[65] *The American Jewish Year Book 5694 September 3, 1933 to September 9, 1934,* XXXV (Philadelphia, 1933), 224–25; *The Occident,* Nov. 25, 1887; *Hull-House Maps and Papers,* p. 107; *The Reform Advocate,* June 17, 1893. The *Israelitische Presse* was a short-lived weekly Yiddish paper in 1879 published in the Russo-Polish idiom. In 1883 it was moved to New York because of better prospects. (*The Occident,* May 25, 1883; Wirth, *op. cit.,* p. 179.) The dates of publication vary in different sources. When the publication itself was not available, newspaper guides are the source.

[66] *The Jewish Advance,* Jan. 21, 1881; *The Occident,* May 23, 1884; James, *op. cit.,* p. 57; Eliassof, "German-American Jews," *loc. cit.* p. 369; Pierce, *A History of Chicago,* II, 23; Wirth, *op. cit.,* p. 173; Meites, *op. cit.,* pp. 159–60; [United Hebrew Charities], *First Annual Report of the United Hebrew Charities of Chicago . . . 1888–89* (Chicago, 1889), p. 8. The United Hebrew Relief Association was incorporated Feb. 25, 1867. (Illinois, *Private Laws, 1867,* I, 130–32.) United Hebrew Relief Association, *Twenty-fourth Annual Report of the Executive Board . . .* (Chicago, 1884), p. 6. See also reports of other years. Anita L. Lebeson, "The American Jewish Chronicle," in Finkelstein, *The Jews: Their History, Culture, and Religion,* p. 335; *Chicago Tribune,* June 7, 1891.

dwelt in run-down shacks and tenements, the former homes of these earlier immigrants. Many lived in the neighborhood of Halsted and Taylor streets and along South Clark around Harrison, in a " Little Italy." Near the Twelfth Street viaduct lay " The Dive," with its gaunt and grimy houses, where often an entire family existed in a single room, witnessing birth and death within the narrow and choking confines of four dingy walls.[67] Of all the foreign born in Chicago by the early 'nineties, they made up the largest proportion of the slum population. They became a conspicuous segment of the population because of the physical similarity of the majority — the short stature, the dark skin and eyes of the southern Italians.[68]

Born to rural ways they took awkwardly to urban living. Their purpose in coming to the New World was economic betterment sufficient to lift them from the poverty of their native land, where many hoped eventually to return. Sometimes induced to emigrate by the alluring promises of general emigration agents and sub-agents, or their runners, these immigrants became the victims also of so-called Italian bankers who advanced the money for prepaid tickets and who profited from carrying on a business in contract labor.[69]

When at first the Italians reached their new home, they often toiled as unskilled laborers — street sweepers and pavers, railroad workers — or went into personal service as bootblacks, barbers, and scissors-grinders. Later they might attain the envied status of small merchants and fruit peddlers or seek jobs in the factories. A few became keepers of saloons and restaurants serving, in particular, their own nationals. But those who occasioned the most comment were

[67] In 1880 the Italians numbered 1,357. In 1890 they were 5,685 (1.26 per cent of the foreign born) although unofficially said to be more numerous. Virgil Peter Puzzo, *The Italians in Chicago, 1890–1930* (unpublished M.A. Thesis, The University of Chicago, 1937), p. 23; *Chicago Tribune*, Feb. 23, 1890, Feb. 6, 1891; Alessandro Mastro-Valerio, " Remarks upon the Italian Colony in Chicago," *Hull-House Maps and Papers*, p. 136; *Illinois Staats-Zeitung*, March 7, 1890; Grace Peloubet Norton, " Chicago Housing Conditions, VII: Two Italian Districts," *The American Journal of Sociology*, XVIII (Jan., 1913), 509–42; U. S., *Eleventh Census, 1890*, [IV], " Vital and Social Statistics," pt. II, " Vital Statistics," 161–62.

[68] In the slum district 57.51 per cent were foreign born. The Italians made up 16.73 per cent. U. S. Commissioner of Labor, " The Slums of Baltimore, Chicago, New York, and Philadelphia," *Seventh Special Report* . . . (Washington, 1894), p. 41.

[69] Giovanni E. Schiavo, *The Italians in Chicago* (Chicago, 1928), p. 22; Joseph Kirkland, *loc. cit.*, pp. 6–8; *Hull-House Maps and Papers*, pp. 131, 133; *Chicago Tribune*, March 4, 1886, March 2, 1890; Herman J. Schulteis, *Report on European Immigration to the United States* . . . (Washington, 1893), pp. 28–41; U. S. House of Representatives, *Reports of Diplomatic and Consular Officers concerning Emigration* . . . , 50 Cong., 2 sess., H. Rept. 3792, pt. II, 110–23.

the rag pickers, searching industriously in gutters and refuse heaps for filth-encrusted bones, cigar stumps, and bits of cloth. Forlorn and despised by even their fellow countrymen, they were the flotsam of the Italian colony. Their state of wretchedness was paralleled by that of the ragged and distressingly dirty little girls, who also wandered about collecting cigar and cigarette butts.[70] Through the city's streets roamed also the picturesque organ-grinder, despite an ordinance prohibiting his playing. Juvenile musicians, victims of a traffic in kidnapping carried on by the notorious *padrones,* played and sang as they strolled down the thoroughfares, hopeful that their day's earnings would be enough to forestall a beating by the Italian masters who had bought them. Little boys hawked newspapers from dawn to dark, and child bootblacks assiduously combined shoe shining with begging and at times the picking of pockets, avocations for which their elders had trained them.[71]

These conditions and habits inevitably evoked disparaging remarks directed especially toward the arrivals from southern Italy, despite the low percentage of Italians according to official statistics apprehended for crimes.[72] Led by Oscar Durante, aggressive editor of *L'Italia,* a campaign to Americanize these people was actively carried on. While not ignoring the faults of their compatriots, Durante and other leaders, however, appealed for fairness of judgment and denied the alleged presence in Chicago of an organized Mafia. At the same time all Italians were counseled to abandon their much publicized knives as weapons and to forsake intemperance of all kinds; they were urged to join political clubs and to participate in elections, not only for the purpose of guarding their own interests

[70] U. S. Commissioner of Labor, "The Italians in Chicago," *Ninth Special Report . . .* (Washington, 1897), pp. 23, 44; Schiavo, *op. cit.,* pp. 154–55; *Hull-House Maps and Papers,* pp. 132–34, 138–39; *Chicago Tribune,* Aug. 11, Sept. 3, 1873, March 4, April 11, Dec. 19, 1886; *L'Italia,* Oct. 11, 1890, Sept. 19, 1891, Jan. 23, 1892. The picking up of garbage of all kinds except by employees of the Health Department was forbidden by city ordinance Sept. 24, 1888, but the ordinance was not enforced. Chicago, *Council Proceedings, 1888–89,* p. 381.

[71] A city ordinance in 1874 prohibited those under eighteen years of age from playing instruments upon the public streets or in any saloon (unless employed in the saloon) to earn money. (Chicago, *Council Proceedings, 1873–74,* p. 148.) *Chicago Tribune,* Aug. 11, Sept. 3, 1873, Jan. 19, 1874, July 27, 1879; *L'Italia,* Sept. 3, 1887, May 26, 31, Aug. 1, 11, 18, 1888, July 25, 28, 1891, March 5, Jan. 23, Dec. 17, 1892.

[72] *Ibid.,* Feb. 6, 1892; Chicago Superintendent of Police, *Report, 1883,* p. 30, *1886,* p. 26, *1890,* p. 52. The percentage was less than one until 1890 when it was 1.2.

through government, but to dispel the general attitude of " contempt " in which they were held by Americans.[73]

But the process of assimilation proved slow. An inbred love of the homeland and the centering of much of their interest in the Catholic Church, presided over by a priest of Italian stock, retarded their participation, for the most part, in the pulsating life of the city. Of the 31.27 per cent of all foreign-born males twenty-one years of age or over still not naturalized, the Italians in 1890 made up 46.19 per cent.[74] Like other nationals they wanted their own language taught in the schools attended by their children. Their societies and their observance days bespoke loving remembrance of things Italian.[75] Newspapers, notably *L'Italia* and *La Colonia,* printed in the mother tongue, perpetuated an attachment to their native land while striving earnestly to foster love of the new country to which they had come. Hotels and restaurants, among them the Colombo Hotel on Wells Street, Hotel Venezia at Indiana and Franklin, Club Italiano (of Persichetti), and Rome Restaurant (of Alpini), featured Italian food.[76]

As Chicago became rich and the Italian community grew older, some who at first had been poverty-stricken became men of substantial means. In the professions Italians held an enviable leader-

[73] *L'Italia,* Nov. 8, 15, 22, Dec. 6, 13, 20, 1886, April 2, 9, 16, 1887, June 16, July 21, Aug. 4, 11, Sept. 22, 29, 1888, March 2, Oct. 6, 1889, Nov. 1, 8, 1890, April 4, 1891, Jan. 1, Sept. 17, Oct. 8, Dec. 17, 1892, Sept. 16, 1893; *Chicago Tribune,* Dec. 19, 1886; *Hull-House Maps and Papers,* p. 138. *L'Italia* furnished an escort and interpreter to the naturalization office and paid the fifty cents registration fee if desired. *Ibid.,* Nov. 29, 1886, Sept. 17, 1892.

[74] U. S. Commissioner of Labor, *Ninth Special Report,* pp. 22–23; *L'Italia,* Aug. 1, 25, 1888. The first Italian church, the Church of the Assumption of the Blessed Virgin Mary, was located at West Illinois and Orleans streets in 1881. Marvin Reuel Schafer, *The Catholic Church in Chicago, Its Growth and Administration* (unpublished Ph.D. Thesis, The University of Chicago, 1929), p. 30.

[75] *L'Italia,* April 4, 1891. The fraternal Societa di Unione e Fratellanza Italiana was twenty-five years old in 1892. (*Ibid.,* July 16, 1892.) Benefit organizations also included Bersaglieri di Savoia and Societa Cristoforo Colombo. (Schiavo, *op. cit.,* pp. 53, 56–57.) These societies not only held natal festivities, but celebrated the holidays of their adopted land. *Chicago Tribune,* Sept. 21, Dec. 6, 1891; *L'Italia,* April 17, 1892, June 3, 1893; *The Chicago Times,* July 29, 1888. These are typical organizations.

[76] *L'Italia,* daily, was established in 1886 by Oscar Durante (Schiavo, *op. cit.,* p. 107.) Durante generally was Republican in politics, but urged the formation of Democratic clubs in his paper, *L'Italia.* He died in 1945. *La Colonia,* a weekly newspaper, ran from 1888 to 1892. *Ficcanaso* (The Curious One, literally " The Nosey One "), a monthly periodical, had an existence of only one year after its establishment in 1891. W.P.A., *Bibliography of Foreign Language Newspapers . . . ,* pp. 70–74. A list of hotels and restaurants to which Italians could go appeared in *L'Italia,* July 8, 1893.

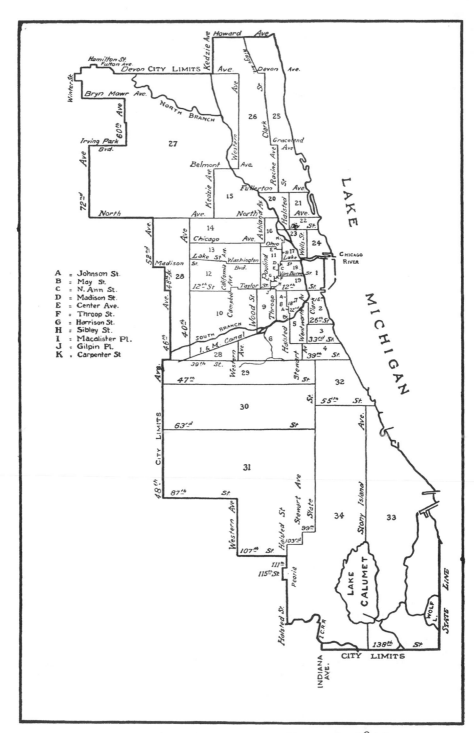

WARD BOUNDARIES IN CHICAGO, 1893

(From Chicago Association of Commerce, *Smoke Abatement and Electrification of Railway Terminals in Chicago.* Chicago, 1915. By permission of Chicago Association of Commerce.)

ship. Dr. Antonio Lagorio, founder and director of the Chicago Pasteur Institute of Rush Medical College, was the Chicago-born son of a Genoese immigrant; Vittorio Carpi, native of Bologna, and Eliodoro de Campi, born of Italian parents in Egypt, were musicians of repute. John Ginocchio, a lawyer prominent in Republican political circles, and Oscar Durante, editor of *L'Italia,* who was born in Naples in 1869 and who, when sixteen years old, had come to Chicago, assumed active roles in city development, lending their energy and prestige to shaping their fellow nationals in the American pattern.[77]

The only other European group which constituted at least 1 per cent of the foreign-born population was the Dutch. Even less numerous were the Asiatics, who had, by 1890, merely a few hundred. They engaged chiefly in the laundry business in the vicinity of Clark and Harrison streets. Their festive celebrations of the Chinese New Year fascinated Chicagoans, as did their stores and restaurants. Toward them, on the one hand, some directed a Christianizing zeal which far outweighed the results attained, while others manifested the kind of hostility reserved for those not of the white race. A semimonthly periodical, *The Chinese American,* established in 1893, occasional intermarriage with the whites, and the adoption of Anglicized names reflected their desire to embrace the American way of life.[78]

To these rudiments of society were added the native white of foreign parents — a group not quite twice as numerous as the native white with native parents in 1890. Children under fifteen years of age made up over half this number.[79] Often they heard one language at home, another at school and play, and the process of Americanization, intended to join and solidify, sometimes served to set them apart from the elder generation.[80] Nor did the tie of homeland exclude jealousies and internal antagonisms. The "older immigration"

[77] Schiavo, *op. cit.,* pp. 107, 155, 156, 181; *Chicago Tribune,* May 3, 1891, May 9, 1948.

[78] Joseph Kirkland, *loc. cit.,* p. 8; *Chicago Tribune,* Aug. 14, Nov. 23, 1873, June 17, Aug. 5, 1878, Feb. 9, 1883, July 8, 1884, April 11, 1886, May 14, 1889, Jan. 24, 1890, Jan. 24, Feb. 6, 1891, June 26, 1892; *Skandinaven,* Sept. 4, 1889; *Chicago Daily News,* Sept. 17, 1884; W.P.A., *Bibliography of Foreign Language Newspapers,* p. 2.

[79] Population of Chicago, 1890: native white, native parents, 223,206; native white, foreign parents, 412,164; foreign whites, 449,628.

[80] The editor of *Skandinaven,* for example, was urged to print his paper in both English and the Scandinavian tongues so that the younger and older generations could enjoy it equally. *Skandinaven,* Dec. 1, 1893.

tended to disdain " the new," for they looked upon it as alien. Now feeling themselves part of the elder citizenry, those who had come from the north of Europe joined those of native stock in urging federal laws to slow up the coming of men whose standard of living encouraged low wages, and whose education and habits of living made them disparate groups of humanity.

Although Negroes were not numerous among the migrants, they formed a cohesive community in the South Division along Clark and Dearborn streets. Fewer than 3,600 in 1870, they increased to 6,480 during the decade following, and reached 14,271 by 1890. Chiefly employed as unskilled laborers, waiters, and domestic servants, they had, by 1885, attained a status sufficient to warrant the publication of a professional and business directory, replete with biographies of leading Negroes and sketches of business and social organizations. Among colored workers unionization had begun; a Negro fire company of ten men, known as Engine Company No. 21, was organized in 1872; and four policemen and five post-office clerks were to be found by 1885.[81]

Of the Negroes who attained political success and standing the most notable was John Jones, who, in 1871, was elected member of the Board of County Commissioners for the short term and in 1872 re-elected for three years, the first of his race to receive such recognition. In 1875 he celebrated the thirtieth anniversary of his arrival in Chicago, where he had attained a reported $100,000 estate before the Fire. As a member of the Colored Masons he exercised a considerable influence over his Masonic friends as well as the Negro community in general.[82]

In 1878 the *Chicago Conservator* and the *Chicago Observer* appeared as Negro newspapers, the latter having a short existence. Beginning in 1887 the Colored Men's Library Association, promoted by Herman H. Kohlsaat, provided a place where men could spend

[81] I. C. Harris, *The Colored Men's Professional and Business Directory of Chicago* . . . (Chicago, 1885–86), pp. 13–62; Estelle Hill Scott, *Occupational Changes among Negroes in Chicago* (Chicago: W.P.A., 1939, mimeographed), pp. 20–23; St. Clair Drake, *Churches and Voluntary Associations in the Chicago Negro Community* (Chicago: W.P.A., 1940, mimeographed), p. 60; *The Knights of Labor,* I (Nov. 27, 1886), 1; *Abendpost,* Jan. 22, 1891.

[82] *Chicago Tribune,* March 12, 1875; Harris, *op. cit.,* p. 36. Jones died May 21, 1879, leaving an estate of $60,000. His mother was mulatto, his father German. He was a tailor. (*Chicago Tribune,* May 22, 1879.) For an example of one of Jones's speeches see *Chicago Tribune,* Jan. 2, 1874.

their leisure time, read, and hear lectures on such topics as "Modern Man and His Reading," by the Reverend Frank W. Gunsaulus, and "Money, Its Use and Abuse," by the Reverend Poindexter S. Henson. Dramatic and musical inclinations led to the presentation of plays and the formation of the Ivy Singing Club. Educational improvement and benevolence were the aims of the Knights of Tabor, the reorganized pre-Civil War society established in 1855 to broadcast news of the emancipation activities of Northerners among southern Negroes. The tabernacles of the Daughters of Tabor paralleled the temples of the Knights, and gave free rein to social aspirations and a love for fanciful display and pageantry. Even more important than the aims of education and benevolence of these lodges was the social prestige the members enjoyed.[83]

Political cohesiveness found expression in an organization such as the Fourteenth Ward Republican Club. For their recently won freedom Chicago Negroes had a jealous concern, and at times instituted suits to prevent or punish discrimination against the members of their race. When the United States Supreme Court in 1883 invalidated the first and second sections of the Civil Rights Law of 1875, they earnestly protested the decision. But in spite of the fixing of penalties by the courts where cases of discrimination were tried, Negroes did not enjoy the privileges of the whites.[84] Business considerations frequently determined treatment, although, regardless of the attitude of the whites, some Chicago theaters sold seats to any

[83] *Chicago Tribune*, Jan. 6, 1878, April 6, 1880, May 2, June 14, Dec. 4, 11, 1887; Ralph Nelson Davis, *The Negro Newspaper in Chicago* (unpublished M.A. Thesis, The University of Chicago, 1939), pp. 8–10, 22–23; St. Clair Drake and Horace R. Cayton, *Black Metropolis* (New York, 1945), pp. 47–51; St. Clair Drake, *Churches and Voluntary Associations in the Chicago Negro Community*, p. 65. The presentation of *Othello* in 1889 is amusingly described in the *Tribune*, Jan. 19, 1889.

[84] *Chicago Post and Mail*, Jan. 26, 1876; *Chicago Tribune*, Oct. 25, 26, 1883. A Negro charged $3.55 for a 35 cent order of roast beef and a 5 cent cup of coffee at the Brevoort House sued and was awarded $25. (*Chicago Tribune*, April 24, 1888.) In the civil rights case of Josephine M. Curry against the People's Theatre the judge declared that the placing of colored people in a part of the theater by themselves was as much color discrimination as excluding them from the theater. The proprietor was fined $100. (*Chicago Tribune*, March 16, 17, 1888; *Chicago Daily News*, March 17, 1888.) A bartender at Chapin and Gore's refused to serve drinks to a colored man at the bar. The Negro was told to go to a side room to drink. Judge Jonas Hutchinson of the Superior Court of Cook County held this a clear violation of the Illinois statute prohibiting discrimination because of color. He imposed the minimum fine of $25. *Chicago Tribune*, Feb. 1, 1893; *Mixed Drinks*, Feb. 8, 1893. The preceding are typical cases and decisions of the court. The Illinois law was approved June 10, 1885. *Laws, 1885*, p. 64.

purchaser irrespective of color.[85] Although theoretically the color line might not be drawn by businessmen, a quiet evasion of the law was general. Nor were Negroes welcomed as neighbors in white residential areas. That Chicago recognized a race problem was evident in private and public discussion, and in meetings such as that at the Central Music Hall February 9, 1890, attended by both whites and colored. These reflected a growing consciousness of a problem which was to assume major proportions in the years to come.[86]

An expansion in territory accompanied the city's amazing growth in population; between 1871 and 1893 the area included within the corporate limits increased from a little more than thirty-five square miles to slightly more than 185 miles. The density of the annexed area was below that of the city proper, which in 1870 was 8,505.2 per square mile and by 1880 was 14,314.5. By 1890, as a result of the annexation, density had fallen to 6,343.4, the lowest of the great cities of the country.[87] This extension of territory, however, had not come without controversy. Along with better government, lower taxes, and more protection of public health and safety, the proponents of annexing outlying towns saw improved housing for a constantly growing number of people. Those who objected to becoming a part of the city feared not only the opposite of these benefits,

[85] The Grand Opera House, Adelphi, and McVicker's without protest sold seats at regular rates to Negroes, a *Times* reporter declared. The Sherman House and the Palmer House would give a Negro a room if he insisted. (*The Chicago Times*, March 16, 1875.) Theoretically there was no color line drawn in the sale of tickets in Pullman cars, but few Negroes could afford to travel so luxuriously. *Ibid.*, April 8, 1875.

[86] *Abendpost*, Aug. 12, 1890; *Chicago Tribune*, Feb. 10, 1890.

[87] The relative standing of the large cities was as follows:

City	Population density per square mile		No. persons per dwelling	
	1880	1890	1880	1890
New York	29,932	37,563	16.37	18.52
Philadelphia	6,567	8,092	5.79	5.6
Chicago	14,314.5	6,343.4	8.24	8.6
Boston	9,806	12,358	8.26	8.52

U. S., *Eleventh Census, 1890*, "Population," pt. I, cxci; Chicago Department of Public Works, Bureau of Maps and Plats, *Map of Chicago Showing Growth of the City by Annexations and Accretions* (Chicago, 1933). To arrive at density, population figures were divided by area. Chicago area figures for 1890 were taken from the map cited. Computation is as of June 1, since 1890 census figures are of that date. The total Chicago annexation of June 29, 1889, alone was 125.363 square miles.

but also the coming of the saloon, a rise in real estate prices, and generally less responsible government.[88]

But the 150 square miles added to the city by 1893 did not solve the housing problem, which was already assuming formidable proportions. Despite the large decrease in the number of people per square mile, the number of persons per dwelling remained substantially the same in 1890 as ten years before. Nearly twice as many lived in the slums as in the city at large. Around the central business district stretched an arc of homes belonging to those on the lowest rung of the economic ladder, the latest arrivals. With enhanced economic status, they too moved farther away from the business section into modest abodes of wood and, occasionally, of brick, devoid of distinctive architectural beauty but less crowded and more comfortable. Still farther out, businessmen, among others, sought the Elysian remoteness of the outskirts of the city where they could, if desired, have horses, a cow, and chickens, and where spaciousness and light contrasted refreshingly with the circumscribed and grimy surroundings of the downtown district. As early as 1874 a contemporary observer declared that " ninety-nine Chicago families in every hundred will go an hour's ride into the country, or toward the country, rather than live under or over another family, as the average New Yorker or Parisian does." [89]

Railroads in alliance with real estate promoters encouraged and facilitated the migration to the suburbs by offering service to would-be commuters. As time passed, Southsiders in increasing numbers were furnished accommodations by the Illinois Central, the Chicago, Rock Island and Pacific, the Michigan Central, the Baltimore & Ohio, the Pittsburgh and Fort Wayne, the Michigan Southern, the Chicago & Eastern Illinois, the Grand Trunk, and the Chicago and Western Indiana. By 1874 the Illinois Central, for example, had twelve trains daily at ten cents a trip for the residents of Hyde Park. The Rock Island attracted others to Washington Heights and Mor-

[88] The most spirited opposition to expansion arose in the town of Hyde Park. The number of wards, eighteen in 1875, became thirty-four in 1889. Chicago, *Council Proceedings, 1889–90*, pp. 336–37. See map.

[89] In the slums the population in 1890 averaged 15.5 persons per dwelling. (U. S. Commissioner of Labor, *Seventh Special Report*, p. 19.) Chamberlin, *Chicago and Its Suburbs*, p. 188.

gan Park. To the north and northwest the Chicago and North Western, the Chicago, Milwaukee and St. Paul, and the Chicago and Evanston served in similar manner. The Chicago, Burlington & Quincy, the Wisconsin Central, and the Chicago, Alton and St. Louis carried residents of the West Side to and from their work. By 1887 combined suburban trains transported about 27,000 persons daily. At their insistence the legal rate of speed within the city limits was increased in 1890 from ten to twenty miles per hour and to thirty in the outlying areas.[90]

But those who toiled long hours in the factories and served in unskilled occupations could neither spend time in commuting nor afford the luxury of suburban living. Their homes, perforce, must be near the place of work and remote from quiet and space. Within two years after the Fire, humble, wooden cottages reflecting in design and color the national idiosyncrasies of Germans, Swedes, and other laborers, rose outside the fire limits.

From the North Side at Fullerton Avenue west of Lincoln and southward to North Avenue and westward to the north branch of the river, workmen, particularly skilled mechanics, profiting by the prosperity induced by rebuilding the city, put up their own unpretentious homes. Investors followed this example. Similar construction proceeded to the west of Milwaukee Avenue and south to Kinzie Street, and from Madison Avenue to Ogden Avenue east of Western to Twelfth Street. South of the Chicago, Burlington & Quincy tracks at Sixteenth Street still more workmen's houses dotted the level stretches of land, until they embraced territory near Blue Island, Brighton, Thirty-third and Western Avenue, the stockyards section, and the Rock Island carshops at Fifty-first and Wentworth Avenue.

Fringing these streets were the dwellings of others who, also affected by the necessity of an inexorable economy, had built small, inartistic cottages with little regard to sanitation. At Canalport, about six miles southwest of the downtown district, the reaper manufacturers, C. H. McCormick and Brother, constructed near their factory one-story cottages for their workmen and two-story houses for

---

[90] *Ibid.,* pp. 353, 410, 420, 445; *Chicago Tribune,* Jan. 4, 1883, June 12, 1887, March 11, 14, 1890; Citizens' Association of Chicago, *Annual Report . . . , 1886* (Chicago, 1886), p. 9; Chicago, *Council Proceedings, 1889–90,* pp. 1448–51.

their mechanics, who, because of poor transportation facilities, could not reach their place of work by seven o'clock in the morning.[91]

Still farther away from the central business district was the company town of Pullman, after 1881 the much publicized social and industrial experiment of George M. Pullman and the Pullman's Palace Car Company. Here, by 1884, lived 8,203 people — clergymen, company officers, and operatives — in red-brick and terra-cotta cottages, usually of two stories, predominant among buildings of "advanced secular Gothic" and Queen Anne design. Monotonous in appearance, even the smallest of the houses nonetheless afforded physical comfort to the occupants, providing them with water, gas, and closets, and in the largest with the luxury of a bathroom.[92]

Different indeed were the ramshackle dwellings of the poor on the periphery of the business section. Workingmen whose daily pay made possible only the bare necessities of life dwelt in nearness to one another in one- and two-story houses. Rear-lot shacks without foundations or plumbing stood close by the house at the front of a lot 25 by 125 feet. One-family houses pocketed several swarming hives of children and adults. Within one room, entire families had a noisome abode, a place of women's work by day and sleep by night. Co-operative households, usually made up of men, divided the expenses of shelter and food in cramped, insanitary quarters. Dank, darkly shadowed cellars, pantries and clothes-closets converted into sleeping-rooms, housed the habitual lodger, who, at times, also shared the bed of a member of the family. In the slums, privacy was a luxury seldom enjoyed.

Because they could find no other place to live, newcomers of the lowest income bracket flocked into these run-down houses, shacks, and even barn lofts, places "unfit for habitation by a civilized people."[93] Overcrowding and filthiness were their lot and custom. Un-

[91] Hoyt, One Hundred Years of Land Values in Chicago, pp. 104–7; Chicago Tribune, May 18, 1873; Industrial Chicago, I, The Building Interests, 66; William T. Hutchinson, Cyrus Hall McCormick, II, Harvest 1876–1884 (New York, 1935), 513.

[92] Pierce, As Others See Chicago, pp. 245–49; Bogart and Thompson, The Industrial State 1870–1893, pp. 208–9; Charles Dudley Warner, "Studies of the Great West, IV Chicago," Harper's New Monthly Magazine, LXXVII (June, 1888), 126; Richard T. Ely, "Pullman: A Social Study," ibid., LXX (Feb., 1885), 452–66. The paternalistic philosophy back of the Pullman experiment and the effect of such a plan on workers met occasional criticism. Ely, in his article, pointed out the meritorious features, but drew attention to what he considered defects.

[93] The words of William H. Genung of the Bureau of Tenement and Factory Inspection.

der such conditions only the neighborhood saloon offered the comforts and congeniality coveted after a day's hard work; consequently expenditures for beer were disproportionate to those for nourishing food. The prevalence of rickets in children was sad and convincing evidence of the lack of a proper diet.[94]

Within three years after the Fire so unkempt and dirty had these houses become that the Board of Health urged municipal regulations to deal with the most odious and dangerous practices. But a lethargic city council and a passive public opinion proved unresponsive. Not until 1880 did a municipal ordinance give the Department of Health the right to inspect and regulate sanitary conditions even in places of employment. Only by permission of an owner could a domicile be entered, except in cases of smallpox and cholera. An active campaign of education by health officials and the press to overcome the opposition of those who insisted that a man should have complete jurisdiction of his home resulted in a statute enacted by the state legislature in 1881.[95] This law required plumbers and architects to submit building plans to the health commissioner before beginning construction. Thus strengthened, the Department of Health proceeded to establish rules as to lights, drainage, plumbing, air shafts, and the ventilation of rooms and water closets.[96]

Upon the passage of the law, inspectors from the Health Department surveyed plans for new tenements and examined previously erected dwellings, directing many improvements and correcting some unsatisfactory conditions.[97] But the canons of decent living and

Chicago Department of Health, *Report 1881 and 1882*, pp. 5, 30, 48; *The Sanitary News*, I (Nov. 1, 1882), 16; *Hull-House Maps and Papers*, pp. 3–6; Edith Abbott and Associates, *The Tenements of Chicago, 1908–1935* (Chicago, 1936), pp. 17–18. The reports of the Department of Health are an excellent source on housing conditions.

[94] Chicago Department of Health, *Report 1881 and 1882*, p. 31; U. S. Commissioner of Labor, *Ninth Special Report*, pp. 44, 45; Joseph Kirkland, *loc. cit.*, p. 26.

[95] The ordinance of 1880 was for "the regulation and inspection of factories, workshops, stores, warehouses, yards, and all other places of employment." (Chicago, *Council Proceedings, 1880–81*, p. 157; Chicago Department of Health, *Report 1879 and 1880*, p. 14.) A similar ordinance passed in 1879 was defective and no appropriation was made for its operation. *Ibid., 1881 and 1882*, p. 25, *1879 and 1880*, p. 14; Chicago, *Council Proceedings, 1880–81*, p. 157; Chicago Department of Health, *Report 1886*, pp. 48–54. Tenement houses were defined as "houses sheltering three or more families keeping house independently." (*Ibid., 1881 and 1882*, p. 30.) Act of May 30, 1881. Illinois, *Laws, 1881*, p. 66.

[96] Chicago Department of Health, *Report 1883 and 1884*, pp. 46–47, *1881 and 1882*, p. 25. The Department of Health drew plans for a model tenement to guide future builders. *Ibid.*, pp. 28–29; Citizens' Association of Chicago, *Annual Report, 1880*, pp. 11–12.

[97] Chicago Department of Health, *Report 1886*, p. 54, *1883 and 1884*, pp. 14–16,

the admonitions of the Department of Health continued to be disregarded. Privy vaults, even in sections where there was a public sewer, remained in common use. As late as 1886 it was estimated that more than one-third of the population had no other toilet accommodations, a situation which prompted the Department of Health to urge legislation " to stamp out this disgusting and unnecessary practice among a civilized community of this enlightened age, and to prevent a further pollution, of not alone the soil upon which we dwell, but also the very air we breathe." [98]

Pollution of water used in both cooking and drinking which came from " filthy tanks in water closet rooms," unhealthful arrangements of piping waste matter, and other revolting conditions also alarmed vigilant health officials, powerless to effect improvements as rapidly as cleanliness and the public health required. Reports on mortality in the various wards of the city showed a close correlation between sanitation and health. In 1882 fully half the children of Chicago died before reaching five years of age, and the next year the Department of Health pointed out the distressing fact that deaths in the tenement wards outnumbered those in the residence wards almost three to one. In the Fourteenth Ward, the most thickly settled of the city, with a large foreign population, the highest rate of child and zymotic mortality occurred.[99]

All these conditions of living existed in the several divisions of the city where dwelt the poor. But as the years advanced they were especially prevalent in the West, as factories multiplied in this section and the supply of housing proved unequal to the demand. Near Hull House, in a third of a square mile containing large undigested groups of foreigners, all the sorry and sinister aspects of such an ex-

---

1881 and 1882, p. 61, *1885*, pp. 65–66. *The Municipal Code* of 1881 listed in considerable detail rules of health and sanitation for the " owner, lessee or keeper of any tenement-house, lodging-house, boarding-house or manufactory . . ." City of Chicago, *The Municipal Code of Chicago* (Chicago, 1881), pp. 330–35.

[98] Chicago Department of Health, *Report 1886*, pp. 60–61. See also *ibid., 1892*, pp. 64–65. It was not until 1894 that the Council outlawed the privy vault on premises " abutting upon or adjoining any street, alley, court or public place," in which was located a public sewer. Chicago, *Council Proceedings, 1894–95*, p. 809.

[99] Chicago Department of Health, *Report 1881 and 1882*, pp. 52, 84, *1883 and 1884*, p. 16, *1885*, pp. 19, 43. The Fifth, Sixth, Seventh, Eighth, Fifteenth, Sixteenth, and Seventeenth wards had high mortality. It should be noted that the birth rate of native whites of foreign-born parents was higher than that of native whites of white parents. See Appendix table.

istence could be found. From this section, as from all others of like character, the better-to-do inhabitants moved away at the first opportunity, leaving to newly arrived immigrants a legacy of dilapidation and filth.[100]

Before the 'nineties the slum and its accompanying sorrows reflected the transition of Chicago from village to city — in far less time than the transition had taken elsewhere. As early as 1881 in the Fourteenth Ward alone 1,107 buildings housed 18,976 persons, of whom 10,113 were adults and 8,863 less than fifteen years of age.[101] In this predominantly German section, Poles and Scandinavians pressed hard upon the earlier German arrivals and upon each other, until over 55,000 of its 65,000 people dwelt in houses caring for three or more families. At the same time in the southwest wards where the Bohemians resided, more than one thousand families averaged but two rooms to a family.[102] By the 'nineties, over 49 per cent of the people lived in dwellings housing more than ten occupants. By 1893, the slum population was estimated as 162,000, second largest in the country. Although not so tightly packed as those of New York, Chicago slums possessed all the planlessness of the urban development which typified late nineteenth-century America.[103]

Anxiety as to how people were to be sheltered extended beyond the

---

[100] The section was bounded by Halsted Street on the west, State Street on the east, Polk Street on the north, Twelfth Street on the south. *Hull-House Maps and Papers*, pp. 3–14; Jane Addams, *Forty Years at Hull-House* (New York, 1935), pp. 97–101; Abbott, *op. cit.*, p. 30.

[101] The Fourteenth Ward was in the West Division. It was bounded on the east by the north branch of the Chicago River. Its boundary ran south along Ashland to North Avenue, west on North Avenue to Crawford (city limits until 1889), south on Crawford to Chicago Avenue, east on Chicago to Ashland Avenue, south on Ashland to Ohio and east on Ohio to the river. Chicago, *Council Proceedings, 1874–76*, p. 578, *Municipal Code, 1881*, p. 129.

[102] Chicago Department of Health, *Report 1881 and 1882*, pp. 30–31, *1885*, p. 18. In 1882, W. H. Genung pointed out in his report of Tenement and Factory Inspection that "the whole number of occupants of tenement houses is about equal to the foreign population, not because of their nationality, but because it is the wage-workers of *all* [*sic*] nationalities who are compelled to occupy tenement houses . . . The tenement houses occupied by native Americans are well furnished in flats and otherwise arranged for separate families, containing a small proportion of children. The tenements of Germans are usually comfortably built but having less of the so-called modern conveniences; but the other nationalities, as a rule, live in close quarters . . ." *Ibid., 1881 and 1882*, p. 47.

[103] U. S. Commissioner of Labor, *Seventh Special Report*, p. 19; Marcus T. Reynolds, "The Housing of the Poor in American Cities," American Economic Association, *Publications*, VIII (1893), 18–19.

lowest income group to employees further up the economic ladder — bookkeepers, clerks, and mechanics, who, too, were plagued by the housing shortage. " The renting public," Chief Inspector Genung of the Bureau of Tenement and Factory Inspection chose to call them, as he urged the construction of fireproof buildings, part to be devoted to stores and shops and part to two- to four-room apartments having outside light for each room.[104]

The building of suites of rooms for small families who did not find it economically satisfactory to move to the suburbs had, as early as 1868, received attention in the press. Here in " family hotels," as one advocate dubbed them, Chicagoans could " keep up appearances " by not living in a small cottage, at times rumored to be the sign of " falling fortunes " and of a " departure from the ranks of ' gentility.' " During the last quarter of the century such accommodations increased, affording the residents more sanitary conveniences and permitting a greater concentration of people than single dwellings of the moderate income group allowed.[105]

As land rose in value during the 'seventies, the economy of high buildings close to the business district made apartment construction practicable. The " flat " craze spread rapidly among people of moderate means. By 1883 a real estate reporter noted that apartments had sprung up " almost as if by magic on every main and cross street of the city." At first from three to five stories high, these buildings had, by the 'nineties, eight and more stories, as the use of the elevator spread from business structures to other buildings. Like other domestic and business places they were constructed of pressed brick in the Romanesque, Gothic, Renaissance, and Moorish styles. Among the earliest of these " fashionable " structures were the Mentone on Dearborn Avenue, the Beaurivage on the northwest corner of Michigan and Van Buren, and the Cambridge on Thirty-ninth Street. Because of the wood interiors and the general lack of fire escapes, agitators for better housing soon were alarmed by the dangers apparent even in the buildings where the outside was of brick. But the craze for this kind of housing spread until, in 1891, it could be said

104 Chicago Department of Health, *Report 1883 and 1884*, pp. 48–51.

105 *The Illustrated Chicago News*, June 13, 1868, p. 114; Hoyt, *op. cit.*, p. 189; *The Sanitary News*, III (Dec. 15, 1883), 43; Chicago Department of Health, *Report 1881 and 1882*, pp. 46–47.

that the French flat or apartment had come not only to stay, " but to increase in number, size and elegance." [106]

Parallel to and not far from the abodes of other Chicagoans were the mansions of the rich, the homes of the aristocracy of the thriving city on the shores of Lake Michigan. The " libels on art which the people tolerated " before the Fire were, according to a contemporary writer, replaced during the next two decades by a cosmopolitan style, especially in the buildings of the late 'seventies and early 'eighties. In the latter decade and in the early 'nineties Chicago architects were particularly concerned with adapting old forms to new conceptions, in which they modified the Elizabethan, the Jacobean, the Queen Anne, and the Greek, Italian, and French, achieving, according to a local enthusiast, a design freed from " rubbish " and one which embodied " an alloy of the little worth that was in them." In general the exteriors tended to reflect the eclecticism existing throughout the country at large, although the greater popularity was given the English Gothic and French Renaissance.[107]

Thus houses dissimilar in color, material, and design gave to Chicago an individuality not possessed by many other places. Unlike the well-to-do in other cities, who occupied a semicircle running out from the central business district, Chicago's rich erected homes in lines lying parallel to the lake with their residences detached and different from the block-like, compactly built homes of the older cities of the East. Nor did the wealthy concentrate in any one part of the city. Of the approximately six thousand socially elect which the 1885 *Elite Directory and Club List* named, an estimated 2,613 resided on the South Side, 1,934 on the West Side, and 1,424 on the North Side. On the South Side, Michigan Avenue led with roughly 556 living there, followed by Indiana and Wabash, with the most exclusive street, Prairie Avenue, ranking fourth with 300 names.[108]

[106] *Chicago Tribune*, March 16, 25, 1883. [The Chicago Times], *Chicago and Its Resources Twenty Years After, 1871–1891* (Chicago, 1892), p. 7; Hoyt, *op. cit.*, p. 127; Chicago Department of Health, *Report 1881 and 1882*, p. 52; *Industrial Chicago*, I, *The Building Interests*, 240–54; *The Drovers' Journal*, Jan. 27, 1883.

[107] *Industrial Chicago*, I, *The Building Interests*, 56–57, 259; Thomas E. Tallmadge, *Architecture in Old Chicago* (Chicago, 1941), pp. 184–85; Addie Hibbard Gregory, *A Great-Grandmother Remembers* (Chicago, 1940), p. 225.

[108] Julian Ralph, *Our Great West*, p. 19 as quoted in Pierce, *As Others See Chicago*, p. 302; *Industrial Chicago*, I, *The Building Interests*, 259; Charles Dudley Warner, " Studies in the Great West. III Chicago," *Harper's New Monthly Magazine*, LXXVI (May, 1888), 874; Abbott, *op. cit.*, p. 24; *Elite Directory and Club List of Chicago 1885–6* (Chicago,

As the South Side gained in popularity, land values appreciated correspondingly. Along Indiana and Prairie avenues, from Eighteenth to Twenty-second Street, $700 a front foot was paid in 1882, and $1,000 a front foot was bid in 1889 for the corner of Prairie Avenue and Twentieth Street. Indiana, Prairie, Calumet, and South Park from Eighteenth to Thirtieth streets had high favor until the late 'eighties and early 'nineties, when Drexel and Grand boulevards from Thirty-ninth to Fifty-first, Kenwood, and Hyde Park provided competition as areas to the south of the city for the well-to-do.[109]

In the construction of their houses they spared neither effort nor expense in order to equal in size and elaborateness the homes of the rich elsewhere. By summer, 1873, Marshall Field had moved into a new mansion at 1905 Prairie Avenue, which the renowned New York architect Richard M. Hunt had designed, and which had been begun in 1871.[110] Of red brick edged with stone, the house rose three and one-half stories above street level. The third floor was under a mansard roof, a feature which betrayed the architect's predilection for French styles. Elaborate stone-carving and grillwork added to the majestic appearance of the Field structure. Here the Fields entertained not only the " Prairie Avenue set " — the Philip D. Armours, the George M. Pullmans, the William G. Hibbards, and others — but also people of renown from all parts of the world.[111] Not far from the Field home on Prairie Avenue lived the John J. Glessner

1885); *Chicago Tribune,* Jan. 2, 1885; Herma Clark, *The Elegant Eighties* (Chicago, 1941), p. 153; Caroline Kirkland, *Chicago Yesterdays,* p. 271.

109 Hoyt, *op. cit.,* pp. 93–94, 189, 190; *Chicago Tribune,* Jan. 5, 1873; Pierce, *As Others See Chicago,* pp. 302, 354.

110 The Field lot, house, furniture, stables, horses, and carriages cost about $175,000. (Marshall Field, " Statement of My Affairs, January 1, 1874," Memorandum, *Marshall Field Papers* [Ms. Marshall Field and Company Archives]). At first the number of the house was 723 Prairie Avenue, renumbered by city ordinance in 1879. (Chicago, *Council Proceedings, 1879–80,* p. 292.) Field bought two lots in 1870 and a third in 1878 on Prairie Avenue. The cost of the first two was $57,632, of the third, $14,000. (Chicago Title and Trust, *Book 564 of Deeds,* p. 199, *Book 615 of Deeds,* p. 69; Cook County Office of Recorder, *Record Book, 688,* p. 478; *Chicago Tribune,* Aug. 27, 1870.) Mr. Richard E. Schmidt, of Schmidt, Garden and Erikson, Architect-Engineers, graciously provided information on the Field house and other architectural matters.

111 The houses of the wealthy on Prairie Avenue represented various architectural styles. The Robert B. Gregory home was Hudson River Gothic, the William W. Kimball house, elaborate French château style. For illustrations of Chicago houses see John Drury, *Old Chicago Houses* (Chicago, [1941]). Arthur Meeker's *Prairie Avenue* (New York, 1949) is a novel which gives a vivid picture of Prairie Avenue society. Book I deals with the years 1885–86.

family in a solidly constructed house of rough-hewn stone with most large windows facing an inner court. Built in 1886 of Romanesque style upon the specifications of Henry Hobson Richardson, the Glessner residence was recognized internationally as one of the best examples of Richardson's work.[112]

Despite the growing favor in which the South Side was held, prominent Chicagoans had not entirely deserted the North Side. Joseph Medill, editor of the *Chicago Tribune*, lived in a Marquette brownstone at 101 Cass Street; Joseph T. Ryerson, a leader in the iron and steel business, had his home at 615 North Wabash, and Cyrus H. McCormick, of reaper fame, resided at 675 Rush Street in a brownstone house designed in late-Renaissance style. Within four years after the Fire, Julian Rumsey, Republican mayor in the trying days of 1861, had rebuilt on the site where his burned-out home had stood at Cass and Ontario streets. By 1887 William Borden, prominent lawyer, moved into his newly completed French château at 89 Bellevue Place, later to be numbered 1020 Lake Shore Drive.

In 1882 Potter Palmer erected his famous residence on a filled-in frog pond on the North Side. Overlooking the lake, this magnificent structure, designed in English-Gothic style by Henry Ives Cobb and Charles Sumner Frost, became the scene of brilliant entertainment over which presided the regal Mrs. Potter Palmer, the former Bertha Honoré. The Palmer " castle " with its embattled tower and turrets, deep-set square windows, and pretentious porte-cochere, gave prestige to the new Lake Shore Drive, which soon blossomed with other mansions. Land values in this neighborhood rose from $160 a front foot in 1882 to $800 in 1892. Here, not long before, cattle, not satisfied with the pastures north of Diversey Avenue, browsed, when homeward bound at night, on the Drive's green grass, until the desperate owners of property impounded the unruly animals.[113]

On the West Side, Samuel J. Walker, before the crash of 1873

---

[112] Henry-Russell Hitchcock, *The Architecture of H. H. Richardson and His Times* (New York, 1936), pp. 277–78, 280. John J. Glessner was a member of the firm of Warder, Bushnell and Glessner, with its harvester factory at Springfield, Ohio. In 1870 he came to Chicago and managed the business from this place. In 1902 he joined with others of like interest in forming the International Harvester Company.

[113] *Industrial Chicago*, I, *The Building Interests*, 260; Caroline Kirkland, *op. cit.*, pp. 131, 265, 288–92; Hoyt, *op. cit.*, pp. 189–90. The construction of Lake Shore Drive was ordered by the park commissioners May 18, 1870. Chicago Lincoln Park Commissioners, *Report of the Commissioners and a History of Lincoln Park* (Chicago, 1899), p. 40.

known as the "Napoleon" of Chicago real estate dealers, promoted the development of the vicinity near Ashland Avenue, once named Reuben Street. Washington and Jackson boulevards also vied for the residences of social leaders. In this part of the city, for some time not far from the sparsely settled prairie, members of a Kentucky colony, including the Carter H. Harrisons, lived in sociability and in comfort.[114]

Appropriately, the interior furnishings, as elaborate and expensive as the mansions themselves, represented not only the taste of the owners but that common to the wealthy of the day. The interior of the Charles B. Farwell Queen Anne-style house was characteristic of the decorative work of the 'eighties, with the entrance hall of paneled wainscot of golden oak.[115] Especially luxurious was the home of the merchant prince Emanuel Mandel at Thirty-fourth and Michigan, where taste ranged widely in spacious rooms furnished in different styles, Moorish and Renaissance dominating the entertainment rooms. On the first floor were reception-hall, reception-room, library, music-room, conservatory, dining-room, and ballroom. From the elegantly appointed music-room opened the conservatory with its rare plants. Satin damask, worked in gilt, adorned the walls of the reception-room, and canvas covered the walls of others. The house was lighted by electricity which, in the course of the 'eighties, had supplanted oil and gas in many homes of the rich.

In the white marble mansion of the railroad capitalist and lawyer Perry H. Smith on the northwest corner of Huron and Pine streets (later North Michigan Avenue), stately suites of drawing-rooms, finished in black walnut, and a little theater, with a rising semicircle of seats, were the scenes of elaborate entertainment. Large mirrors could be pulled across the long windows at night, and a butler's pantry contained a sink with three faucets; from two could be drawn hot and cold water, and from the third, upon special occasions, champagne. Especially pretentious also were the furnishings of the Cyrus McCormick house, its main hall frescoed in the pattern of a

114 Caroline Kirkland, *op. cit.*, pp. 167, 169; Carter H. Harrison, *Stormy Years . . .* (Indianapolis, 1935), pp. 18, 19, 27; Chamberlin, *op. cit.*, p. 257.

115 The Charles B. Farwell house was at 120 East Pearson Street. It stood next to his brother John V. Farwell's house, which was of Romanesque architecture. Tallmadge, *op. cit.*, pp. 180–81; *Industrial Chicago*, I, *The Building Interests*, 260–61; *Northwestern Lumberman*, XXIX (April 2, 1887), 2.

castle of King Henry IV of France. Tapestries of Henry's day decorated the walls of the dining-room, and the ceiling was painted in the design of the Cross of the Legion of Honor, a reaper and sheaves of grain, and the names of Pomona, Flora, Ceres, and Diana. Equally elaborate was the ceiling of the drawing-room upon which the sky, flowers, and birds were done in oil.[116]

Within these palatial edifices could be found murals by Gabriel Ferrier and paintings by famous artists, the acquisitions of men who, upon the attainment of wealth, became art collectors and patrons. Samuel M. Nickerson, president of the First National Bank, had in his private gallery the works of Doré, Inness, Corot, Schaefels, Klombeck, Hübner, and Mücke. The traction magnate Charles T. Yerkes possessed the Dutch masters, as did Charles L. Hutchinson, banker, and president of the Board of Trade in 1888.[117] Statues of bronze, scimitars, antlers, Oriental lamps, and sculptured busts, some of members of the family, made by famous foreign artists, all vied for attention.[118] Eastlake furniture claimed the approval of some. By the 'eighties a revival of the English, French, and Italian Renaissance gained various devotees, the last appealing to the greatest number of Chicagoans. The rococo of late eighteenth- and early nineteenth-century France had a ready market, and carved work on bedsteads, bureaus, sideboards, and other pieces of furniture demonstrated a love for the ornate so typical of these years. The brass bedstead had already made its appearance, and by the 'nineties richly upholstered chairs, sofas, and lounges of all designs could be had. Throughout the city, except in the closely settled areas of the workers' tenements, people in the warm summer evenings sat on rugs thrown on doorsteps sometimes a half story above street level, or enjoyed the relaxation of the popular rocking chair on the veranda — or piazza as it was more often called.[119]

[116] *Chicago Tribune*, Feb. 2, 18, 1892; Caroline Kirkland, *op. cit.*, p. 265; Hutchinson, *op. cit.*, II, 743–44. The preceding list of the homes of prominent Chicagoans is by no means complete.

[117] *Chicago Tribune*, July 8, 1883, Feb. 15, 1885, Nov. 8, 1890, Nov. 30, 1941; *The Knights of Labor*, IV (Aug. 11, 1888), 3; Flinn, *Chicago . . . A Guide, 1891*, p. 133. Art interests are discussed in Chapter XIII, "Patterns of Urban Living."

[118] Salvatore Albano, of Florence, Italy, for example, made a bust of the Marshall Field child in 1875. Marshall Field to Preston Powers, July 2, 1875 (*Ms. Marshall Field, Letter Books*, Field Estate Office, Chicago).

[119] *The Inland Architect and Builder*, III (Feb., 1884), 4; *Northwestern Lumberman,*

Thus, as the number of people in Chicago nearly quadrupled in the fast-moving years from the Fire to the Columbian Exposition, the frontiers of living moved north, south, and west from three miles from the center of the business district to about five miles. To the less fortunate fell the necessity of a life in the deteriorated sections upon which factory and business establishments pressed hard.[120] By 1893 the Chicago of pre-Fire days was gone. " It is a common remark," commented the *Tribune* as early as 1873, " that Chicago was set forward ten years by the fire. The mingled town and village aspects are gone, with the buildings of the early day that held the latter character in the centre of the city. The tendency is to the metropolitan in everything — buildings and their uses, stores and their occupants. And village notions are passing away with them. Even advertisers cease to insist on locations at easy distance from the Post Office, and a mile of our present area seems less than four or five blocks a few seasons ago. We are getting to be a community of strangers. No one expects to know . . . half the audience at the church or theatre, and, as to knowing one's neighbors, that has become a lost art." [121]

XXIX (April 2, 1887), 2; *Chicago Tribune*, July 8, 1891; *The Western Catholic*, May 22, 1875.

[120] Within three miles of the center of the business district 81.9 per cent of the population lived in 1870. Within five miles, 82.3 per cent lived by 1890. Hoyt, *op. cit.*, p. 484; Johnson, *The Natural History of the Central Business District with Particular Reference to Chicago*, p. 484; U. S. Federal Housing Administration, *The Structure and Growth of Residential Neighborhoods in American Cities* (Washington, 1939), p. 82.

[121] *Chicago Tribune*, March 30, 1873.

CHAPTER III

THE ECONOMIC EMPIRE
OF CHICAGO

BEFORE 1871, Chicago had become unquestioned mistress of western commerce, holding in her hand primacy through trade in grains and lumber, and outranking her rivals in livestock and its ally, meat packing. These economic enterprises formed the foundations of the structure upon which Chicago early rested a widening economic leadership. In the future, as in the past, her unrivaled position as terminal point on lake, canal, and railroad certified a continuation of these achievements. And, carried onward by the impulse of the economic revolution in the years following the Civil War, she was thus able to forge ahead of her hopeful rivals, outstripping them through robust daring and deft planning.

The fecund years of late nineteenth century saw also the development of varied and great manufacturing industries, so assiduously promoted as to guarantee a persistent well-being and to make Chicago by 1890 second manufacturing point of the country, judged in gross value of products.[1] These engagements and those allied to them, along with the basic economic resources of grains, lumber, livestock, and meat packing, assured to Chicago an impregnable position as core city of the Mississippi Valley, and contributed to the far-flung and diversified hegemony which she came to enjoy.

---

[1] In value added by manufacture, New York and Philadelphia outranked Chicago. "Value added by manufacture," used in the 1910 U. S. Census as a better measure of an industry's contribution to income than the gross value, is defined in Chapter V, note 2.

THE GRAIN TRADE

THE GRAIN TRADE, the most important economic undertaking in the early history of Chicago, first established the city's leadership by making her the exchange point of the fruitful Middle Valley. In 1851 Chicago became the greatest corn market in the United States, and in 1854 the greatest wheat center, acclaimed by her boosters the greatest grain market in the world. Throughout the history of the city the power of grains has persevered and has given her an unequaled influence and authority in the grain exchanges of the world. Proximity to the source of supplies combined with peerless transportation facilities assured her continuing dominance.

As the mileage of railroads was extended, the supply area widened and moved in the same direction. For the eastern roads the city became the western terminus, and for the roads tapping the West it became the eastern end. Next to Chicago's matchless geographic position, the network of rails which extended fan-shape from the city's center was the most significant of all the factors in her leadership. Four major railroads dominated the grain-carrying trade and marked off the supply area: the Chicago and North Western; the Chicago, Burlington & Quincy; the Chicago, Rock Island and Pacific; and the Chicago, Milwaukee and St. Paul. After 1872, for over twenty years, these four roads and the Illinois Central maintained, with few exceptions, positions among the five leading carriers of wheat. At the same time they, among the leading midwest railroads, most frequently serviced the states producing the corn, oats, rye, and barley marketed in Chicago.[2]

As the center of wheat-growing moved westward, the pre-eminence of Chicago was threatened by aggressive aspirants nearer the

[2] During the 1870's the Chicago and North Western Railway carried the most wheat into Chicago, to be passed in the early 1880's by the Chicago, Burlington & Quincy. In 1886, 1887, and 1889, the Chicago, Milwaukee and St. Paul had heavier receipts than other roads. On the whole, however, the Chicago, Burlington & Quincy during the 1880's and early 1890's ranked as first carrier. The Chicago and North Western and the Chicago, Burlington & Quincy led most consistently in the carriage of grains. For receipts and shipments of grains by principal carriers in the decades 1872–81 and 1882–91, see Appendix tables. The routes of the major railroads serving Chicago are shown on the map of transportation routes.

place of production. Cities having good transportation facilities and close to the source of supply laid claim to the primacy Chicago had enjoyed. This challenge to the city's distinctive position an omniscient Board of Trade explained as an inevitable consequence of the transit of peoples to a more recently developed part of the country, the wheat belt traveling " westward on an even pace with civilization."[3] As early as 1862 Milwaukee had become temporarily the largest primary wheat market in the world, and in 1881 Minneapolis passed Chicago, to establish herself two years later as the top receiving point in the country.[4]

Yet in the marketing of corn Chicago continued to be the leading center, tapping the lush lands of the North Central States which, by 1890, were producing over 62 per cent of all the corn grown in the country. In the race for priority Chicago had outdistanced all other competitors.[5] The 38,157,232 bushels received in 1873 considerably more than doubled in the next twenty years.[6] Except in 1871 and 1888 the Burlington poured into Chicago more of this cereal than did other railroads. During the 1870's the Illinois Central, the Chicago & Alton, and the Rock Island were among the four top carriers, the Central to be outdistanced in 1880 by the North Western, which maintained this lead to the end of the decade. In the 'eighties the Wabash, St. Louis and Pacific and the Chicago, Milwaukee and

[3] Chicago Board of Trade, *Fifteenth Annual Report, 1872*, p. 11. See also editorial expressing the same opinion in *The American Elevator and Grain Trade*, V (Oct. 15, 1886), 85.

[4] Bayrd Still, *Milwaukee: The History of a City* (Madison, 1948), pp. 181, 184–85, 326. Minneapolis's wheat receipts in 1881 were 16,316,950 bushels. Chicago's were 14,824,990 bushels. From 1886 to 1890 Minneapolis's annual receipts were more than twice those of Chicago. For the same period Chicago continued a leadership in wheat shipments, sending out 82,724,249 bushels to the 54,891,085 bushels dispatched by Minneapolis. Minneapolis led in shipments of flour by 1890. Chicago Board of Trade, *Twenty-fourth Annual Report, 1881*, p. xvii, *Thirty-fourth Annual Report, 1891*, pp. 18, 19, *Thirty-sixth Annual Report, 1893*, p. 20; Minneapolis Chamber of Commerce, *Fifth Annual Report, 1887*, p. 75, *Eighth Annual Report, 1890*, p. 73, *Ninth Annual Report, 1891*, p. 77, *Eleventh Annual Report, 1893*, p. 77.

[5] U. S., *Eleventh Census, 1890*, " Agriculture," pp. 12, 76–77. See the optimistic forecast of Chicago's continued dominance by the editor of *The American Elevator and Grain Trade*, VII (Sept. 15, 1888), 64.

[6] Chicago Board of Trade, *Sixteenth Annual Report, 1873*, p. 12, *Thirty-fifth Annual Report, 1892*, p. xxxiv. In 1870 United States corn production was 760,944,549 bushels, of which 439,244,945 bushels (57.7 per cent) came from the North Central Division. Illinois held first place, Iowa second, Ohio third, Missouri fourth, and Indiana fifth. In 1890, United States production was 2,122,327,547 bushels. The North Central Division produced 1,598,870,008 bushels. U. S., *Twelfth Census, 1900*, VI, " Agriculture," pt. II, 80, 81. See Appendix table.

St. Paul, strongly competing with the Alton and Rock Island, were counted among the important roads delivering to the city the corn of the states through which they passed. On the whole, these railroads also brought to the Chicago market the oats, rye, and barley, the four roads having priority in corn maintaining a similar leadership in small grains. At the same time, the Illinois and Michigan Canal, the transport hope of the 1840's, lost noticeably to its speedier competitors as their lines penetrated the ever widening and lengthening stretches of fertile farm land.[7]

As a primary transfer market no city was the peer of Chicago. In 1880 she received more than two and a half times as much grain and flour as did her closest competitor, St. Louis. In 1890 about 41 per cent of all taken in by the ten chief markets came to Chicago, and two years later the city touched the highest point up to that time, aggregating 255,832,556 bushels.[8]

The pattern of shipments of grain from the city to the markets of the East and South for domestic use and for export abroad bears a striking resemblance to the one established by receipts, a few carriers consistently maintaining a leading position. From 1871 to 1893 the Lake Shore and Michigan, the Michigan Central, the Pittsburgh, Fort Wayne and Chicago, the Chicago and Grand Trunk (beginning 1880), the Pittsburgh, Cincinnati and St. Louis, and the Baltimore & Ohio (after 1874) were the leading rail carriers. They, too, were the lines over which most of the rail-borne flour moved. Throughout the twenty years following the Great Fire, however, the lake transported nearly twice as much grain, other than flour, as was shipped over the six leading railroads combined, and in the carriage of flour it surpassed the amount of any one of these roads.[9]

In comparison with the millions of bushels of grain and flour sent eastward, shipments south seemed small indeed. Although improve-

---

[7] Putnam, *The Illinois and Michigan Canal*, pp. 115–18; *The Railroad Gazette*, XI (Jan. 17, 1879), 33; Chicago Board of Trade, *Fifteenth Annual Report, 1872*, pp. 90, 94.

[8] In 1880 Chicago received 165,855,370 bushels of grains, including flour, and St. Louis 59,625,610. In 1890 Chicago received 223,320,031 bushels to 77,795,232 taken in by St. Louis, the closest competitor. For the above information the statistical sources used vary slightly. See Chicago Board of Trade annual reports; Louis Bernard Schmidt, " The Internal Grain Trade of the United States, 1860–1890," II, *Iowa Journal of History and Politics*, XIX (1921), 414–55; U. S. Federal Trade Commission, *Report . . . on the Grain Trade* (Washington, 1920), V, 27–43, (hereafter cited as FTC).

[9] Within a ten-year period, say 1872–82 or 1882–92, the order of primacy of railroads sometimes shifted slightly.

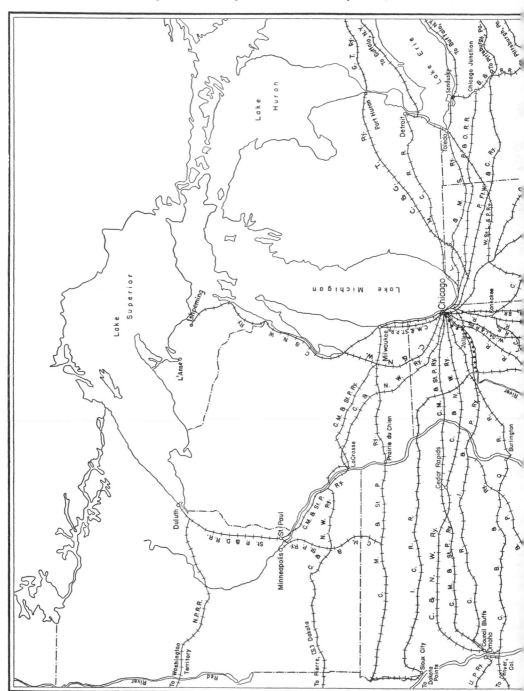

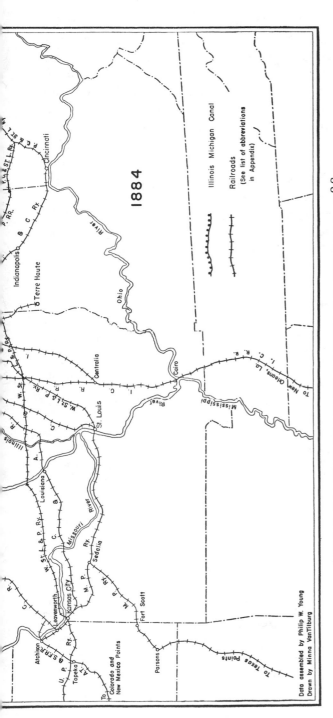

1884

Illinois Michigan Canal

Railroads
(See list of abbreviations
in Appendix)

Data assembled by Philip W. Young
Drawn by Minna VanTilburg

CHIEF TRANSPORTATION ROUTES OF CHICAGO, 1884

Abbreviations Used on Railroad Map

A T & S F R R   Atchison, Topeka and Santa Fe Railroad
B & O R R   Baltimore & Ohio Railroad
C & A R R   Chicago & Alton Railroad
C & E I R R   Chicago and Eastern Illinois Railroad
C & G T Ry   Chicago and Grand Trunk Railway
C & N W Ry   Chicago and North Western Railway
C B & Q R R   Chicago, Burlington & Quincy Railroad
C M & St P Ry   Chicago, Milwaukee and St. Paul Railway
C R I & P Ry   Chicago, Rock Island and Pacific Railway
C St L & P R R   Chicago, St. Louis and Pittsburgh Railroad
C I St L & C Ry   Cincinnati, Indianapolis, St. Louis and Chicago Railway

G T Ry   Grand Trunk Railway
I C R R   Illinois Central Railroad
L S & M S Ry   Lake Shore and Michigan Southern Railway
M C R R   Michigan Central Railroad
M P Ry   Missouri Pacific Railway
N P R R   Northern Pacific Railroad
P C & St L Ry   Pittsburgh, Cincinnati and St. Louis Railway
P Ft W & C Ry   Pittsburgh, Fort Wayne and Chicago Railway
St P & D R R   St. Paul and Duluth Railroad
U P Ry   Union Pacific Railway
W St L & P Ry   Wabash, St. Louis and Pacific Railway

ments in the navigation of the Mississippi River at one time offered hope to those who thought of New Orleans as a cheaper point of export than eastern ports, expectations of a greatly expanded business in the South were not realized. In the 1880's, however, orders for the domestic consumption of corn increased, and at the same time the use of oats as a food for horses gained in popularity.[10] But the advantages of the northern route to the eastern seaboard, fed by both railroad and lake, and the shorter distances of St. Louis from New Orleans encouraged practical Chicago shippers to market their grain by the west-to-east highways.[11] Europe, too, provided a much-needed market in times of surplus production. A satisfying increase, particularly in wheat, corn, rye, and flour exports, not only to Great Britain and Ireland but to Continental Europe, developed in the twenty-year period following the Great Fire. Wheat took the lead and corn came next, going in heaviest amounts to Great Britain and Ireland.[12]

To overcome a prejudice against corn as a food for man, an active publicity campaign was undertaken from 1890 to 1893 by a commission of the United States Department of Agriculture under the leadership of Colonel Charles J. Murphy. This the enterprising Board of Trade of Chicago commended highly. It viewed with great

[10] No exact figures are available for the part of Chicago in such movements. Chicago Board of Trade, *Thirtieth Annual Report, 1887*, p. xiv, *Thirty-first Annual Report, 1888*, p. xxxviii.

[11] Chicago Board of Trade annual reports; *The American Elevator and Grain Trade*, X (Jan. 15, 1892), 227; U. S. Bureau of Statistics, "The Grain Trade of the United States," *Monthly Summary of Commerce and Finance of the United States, 1899–1900*, no. 7 (Washington, 1900), pp. 1979–80; U. S., *Tenth Census, 1880*, III, "Agriculture," 155, 156; Louis Bernard Schmidt, "The Internal Grain Trade of the United States, 1860–1890," III, *Iowa Journal of History and Politics*, XX (1922), 118–31.

[12] U. S. exports of breadstuffs (flour, wheat, corn, rye) to Great Britain and Ireland (column I), and to Continental Europe (column II):

	Flour, barrels		Wheat		Corn		Rye	
	I	II	I	II	I	II	I	II
1871	1,227,624	136,638	22,488,021	2,430,762	5,905,445	191,399		
1872	328,544	15,315	19,017,411	3,667,327	25,779,331	973,679		756,842
1881	4,610,415	530,476	82,550,921	59,007,799	53,014,142	28,882,344	163,589	1,754,027
1882	3,289,909	187,601	65,600,582	25,452,924	28,664,924	9,009,774	63,961	907,686
1891	7,037,420	530,516	29,820,650	21,771,681	14,131,181	9,538,602		308,607
1892	9,603,910	1,285,747	67,293,960	84,416,357	36,503,653	33,087,524	438,069	9,111,242

Chicago Board of Trade, *Thirty-fifth Annual Report, 1892*, p. 160.

satisfaction the publication of recipes in Danish which would appeal to the people of Denmark, the adoption by the German army of a flour of equal parts of corn meal and rye, a publicity campaign in Sweden, and the endorsement of corn as a food by teachers of local cooking schools and charitable societies and boards of public institutions in Great Britain. All this seemed to promise for the great American market a less uncertain sale, and the Board of Trade confidently looked forward to bigger exports than ever before. This would, to quote in part its secretary George F. Stone, thus incalculably benefit this country's great agricultural regions and confer " a valuable boon upon the peoples of the old world, in giving them a highly nutritious food at economical prices." [13]

The inexorable laws of supply and demand both plagued and blessed the promotion of the grain trade. Because of its significance in the economy of the city this trade became an important barometer of the general well-being of Chicago. Although commercial recessions, both national and international, laid their mark on the city's grain exchange as on other economic endeavors, their effects seemed less hurtful and of shorter duration than eastern centers experienced. When financial panics struck, the sale of grain provided Chicago a ready currency. " Chicago," commented the secretary of the Board of Trade in 1890, " is not exposed to the monetary fury which occasionally rages in Wall Street; her loans are made on tangible securities, and the basis of our financial system is in the great crops of the country for which there is always a market close at hand." [14]

But the road to uninterrupted good fortune had pitfalls for both producer and seller. Chicago traders were undersold by eastern dealers who practiced the mixing of different grades of wheat; [15]

[13] *Ibid.*, p. xxxv, *Thirty-sixth Annual Report, 1893*, pp. xxiv–xxv; U. S. Department of Agriculture, *Report of the Secretary of Agriculture, 1893*, pp. 22–23, 48. Further information on Murphy's promotion can be found in Merle Curti and Kendall Birr, *Prelude To Point Four American Technical Missions Overseas 1838–1938* (Madison, Wisconsin, 1954), pp. 25–27.

[14] Chicago Board of Trade, *Thirty-third Annual Report, 1890*, p. xxiii.

[15] The suggestion of establishing uniform grades of grain by the federal government to avoid the difficulties caused by mixing different grades was disapproved by most Americans at this time. See for this attitude *The American Elevator and Grain Trade*, VIII (Nov. 15, 1889), 116, XI (Dec. 15, 1892), 196. In 1916 the United States Grain Standards Act provided for the federal establishment and control of uniform grades of grain. The administration of the act and the promulgation of standards were left to the Secretary of Agriculture, under whose auspices tentative grades were established by 1917. In states where grain inspection systems already existed or might be set up, the Secretary of Agriculture was

they suffered the bane of high transportation costs when rates from western to eastern points were lower than to Chicago and thence east; and the far-flung market Chicagoans so ardently coveted was at times threatened by competition from foreign wheat growers, particularly in Russia, Australia, India, and South America.[16]

The resolution of some of these predicaments, observed the Commissioner of Agriculture as early as 1877, could be accomplished if only " the valleys and plains of the great West be divided between the herder and the shepherd," and the farmer " market his grain in his stable," and send his product abroad in the form of meat.[17] Others saw the solution of these problems in improved transportation and new routes of transit. And those who wished to escape heavy transfer charges at Buffalo, and be " set free from the clutch of the New York railroad grain elevator combine and from the high rates of the rail carriers " looked favorably toward proposals of a direct route to Europe by way of the Welland and St. Lawrence canals.[18]

Tied in with the Canadian canals discussion was the question of reciprocity agreements which would serve East as well as Middle West and be acceptable to the Canadian government. Such an arrangement the *Tribune* strongly endorsed as a means of getting rid of the customhouses and as a measure to strengthen the friendship of the two countries. The Board of Trade also actively supported the suggestion, but efforts to this end in the 'seventies and 'eighties were fruitless. A revival of the agitation through the reciprocal trade provisions of the McKinley Tariff Act of 1890 led to a conference in 1892 by federal government officials and agents of the Canadian government, but again a basis of concurrence was not found and the

authorized to license state inspectors. U. S., *Statutes at Large, XXXIX*, pt. I, 482–85; U. S. Department of Agriculture, *Annual Report, 1917*, p. 467. For opinions of representatives of grain-growing states see *Cong. Record*, 63 Cong., 3 sess., LII, pt. VI, 269–70, 553–58, 949–60.

[16] Chicago Board of Trade, *Twenty-seventh Annual Report, 1884*, pp. xvii-xviii, and *Reports, 1885*, p. xxiv, *1886*, pp. xvi-xvii, *1893*, p. xxii; *The American Elevator and Grain Trade*, I (March 15, 1883), 144; U. S. Department of Agriculture, *Report of the Commissioner of Agriculture, 1886*, p. 411.

[17] U. S. Department of Agriculture, *Report of the Commissioner of Agriculture, 1877*, p. 382.

[18] *The American Elevator and Grain Trade*, I (Sept. 15, 1882), 29, 44, (May 15, 1883), 173, IX (Oct. 15, 1890), 99, X (Feb. 15, 1892), 265, (Aug. 15, 1892), 57, XII (Aug. 15, 1893), 52–53; *Chicago Tribune*, Jan. 1, Feb. 3, 1877, Jan. 1, 1878; Chicago Board of Trade, *Fifteenth Annual Report, 1872*, pp. 17–18, and reports *1874*, pp. 13–20, *1891*, pp. lxii-lxiv.

reciprocal settlement so earnestly desired by Chicagoans was not achieved.[19]

The imagination of the Board of Trade and other aggressive promoters of commerce who wished freedom from tolls and a share in the favors granted Canadian nationals over the Welland Canal by their government was also fired by the proposal of a Lakes-to-Gulf waterway. Urged on the ground that by such an improvement Chicago would become the port of the Middle West and that military security would be strengthened, the project, like plans for reciprocity, failed of realization.[20]

Without an expanding storage space the grain trade of Chicago could not have flourished as it did. The Fire destroyed six of the seventeen elevators standing in 1871. By 1872, however, room for 12,800,000 bushels was available. This space was outdistanced in 1893 by a capacity of 32,800,000 bushels in elevators classified as regular and 10,000 more in private warehouses, by far the largest grain depository in all the country. Yet this amazing enlargement did not always keep ahead of the rich offerings which poured into the city. The greatest elevators in the world were in Chicago, huge five- to ten-story structures, capped by tower-like attics of thirty or more feet, most of them, in the 'seventies and 'eighties, lying in the neighborhood of Nineteenth and Twentieth streets near the south branch of the Chicago River and adjacent to the railroad tracks. Those of first class cost about $500,000 and were elaborately equipped with chutes to receive grain from the cars, with elevator buckets to deposit it, with bins to hold 1,700 to 6,500 bushels, and hoppers to move it to the shipping elevators.

The handling of the grain was efficient and speedy, and upon the elevators depended producers, carriers, and commission men. By

19 J. Lawrence Laughlin and H. Parker Willis, *Reciprocity* (New York, 1903), pp. 65–69; National Board of Trade, *Proceedings of the Fourth Annual Meeting . . . 1871* (Boston, 1872), pp. 21, 141, *Proceedings, 1872*, pp. 39, 120, *Proceedings, 1873*, p. 158; Dominion Board of Trade, *Proceedings at the Annual Meeting . . . 1871* (Montreal, 1872), p. 39, *Proceedings, 1878*, pp. 59–60; Chicago Board of Trade, *Seventeenth Annual Report, 1874*, pp. 12–13. The Board of Trade and other promoters also recommended reciprocal trade relations with South America. *Thirty-fifth Annual Report, 1892*, p. xiii.

20 Chicago Board of Trade, *Fifteenth Annual Report, 1877*, pp. 17–19, *Thirtieth Annual Report, 1887*, pp. xxvi–xxvii, *Thirty-fifth Annual Report, 1892*, p. xxv; U. S. Senate, *Report of the Select Committee on Transportation to the Seaboard*, 43 Cong., 1 sess., S. Rept. 307, pt. I, 236–37. The Chicago Board of Trade also recommended a strong merchant marine. *Twenty-eighth Annual Report, 1885*, pp. xix–xx, *Thirty-second Annual Report, 1889*, pp. xiv–xv.

1891 one elevator could unload 1,500 cars in a day, and in an hour could put in vessels or cars as much as 300,000 bushels.[21] By the early 'nineties the migration of those engaged in the elevating business to the Calumet River area, where approaches were less crowded than along the Chicago River, was well under way.[22]

As the years advanced, concentration of ownership within a few hands mounted. In 1872, for example, out of a total of fifteen elevators, Munger, Wheeler & Company possessed only two, the Air Line and the Galena, with a capacity of 750,000 bushels each. By 1880, out of a total of twenty-three warehouses, this organization had eight, with space for 6,400,000 bushels. This expansion in holdings came about chiefly by buying out competitors, toward which a start was made with the acquisition of two elevators in 1874, upon the breakup of George Armour and Company.[23] In 1889 the Munger-Wheeler property was purchased by an English syndicate, the City of Chicago Grain Elevators Company, Limited, in the hope, it was said, that this investment, along with other warehouses in the North-west, would free the British from the grip Americans had over the grain trade. During that year another syndicate of English origin took over the properties of the Star Elevator Company of Minne-apolis and of the G. W. Van Dusen Company of Rochester, Minne-sota. This new combination, known as the Chicago & Northwest Granaries Company, Limited, had a London board of directors but its board of management resided in Chicago.[24]

[21] Chicago Board of Trade, *Thirteenth Annual Report, 1870*, p. 44, *Fourteenth Annual Report, 1871*, pp. 47, 50; *The American Elevator and Grain Trade*, III (Oct. 15, 1884), 76, IV (Dec. 15, 1885), 134–35; U. S. Treasury Department, *Report on the Internal Commerce of the United States, 1891*, pp. xx–xxi, *ibid., 1881*, pp. 108–10; Ernst von Hesse-Wartegg, *Nord Amerika, Seine Städte und Naturwunder, Sein Land und Seine Leute* (3 v. in one, Leipzig, 1880), II, 35–48. For elevators and their capacities see annual reports of the Board of Trade.

[22] *The American Elevator and Grain Trade*, III (April 15, 1885), 230, (June 15, 1885), 276, IX (Jan. 15, 1891), 183, X (March 15, 1892), 300, 301, XI (Sept. 15, 1892), 97. The construction of an elevator by Charles Counselman in 1892 was considered a forecast of what other important warehousemen would do.

[23] In 1880, Munger, Wheeler & Company managed, in addition to the Air Line and the Galena, the North-Western, the City, the Fulton, the Union, the Iowa, and the St. Paul. The last two were constructed in 1880. The total number of Chicago elevators then was twenty-three. In 1889 and 1892 it was twenty-seven. Chicago Board of Trade, *Fifteenth Annual Report, 1872*, p. 44, and reports for *1874*, p. 56, *1876*, p. 61, *1880*, p. 72, *1889*, p. 122, *1892*, p. 36.

[24] In 1889 elevators of the Minnesota and Northwestern Co., the Atlantic Elevator Co., with elevators in the Northwest, the Pillsbury and Washburn Mills, and two water-power companies in Minneapolis fell into the hands of British syndicates. *The American Elevator*

Between elevator men and the railroads existed well-knit arrangements which strengthened the power of the marketing center over the farmers' grain.[25] Railroads having terminal facilities in Chicago sometimes built their own granaries or leased their land and trackage to others, who put up the warehouses and operated them to the advantage of both parties.[26] Such a contractual relationship, for example, existed between the great grain railroad, the Chicago, Burlington & Quincy and Armour, Dole & Co., from 1860 to 1886, the latter providing more storage space as the road needed it and giving priority to the railroad's grain over that of any others. Following the withdrawal of George Armour from the elevator company and the sale of the elevators to the CB & Q, Dole & Co. took over, on August 1, 1886, purchasing the elevators and entering into a lease similar to that of its predecessor. In 1891 the Armour Elevator Company,[27] under the presidency of the prominent meat packer, Philip D. Armour, followed Dole & Co. as proprietor under a new arrangement, which provided for the lease of lands, buildings, and equipment for five years at an annual rental of $40,000.[28]

---

and Grain Trade, VIII (Nov. 15, 1889), 113, (April 15, 1890), 252, 259, IX (April 15, 1891), 268, X (Oct. 15, 1891), 114, (Dec. 15, 1891), 184; *The Economist*, II (Nov. 9, 1889), 998–99, 1027, VIII (Oct. 22, 1892), 579, Investor's Supplement, 1897, p. 34; *Chicago Tribune*, Jan. 1, 1890.

[25] For carriers serving elevators in 1893, the capacity of warehouses, and their proprietors see Appendix table.

[26] Guy A. Lee, "The Historical Significance of the Chicago Grain Elevator System," *Agricultural History*, XI (Jan., 1937), 21–22; *The Railroad Gazette*, V (Dec. 13, 1873), 495, XIV (March 31, 1882), 201; *The American Elevator and Grain Trade*, III (April 15, 1885), 218.

[27] The principal officers of Armour, Dole & Co. were Allison A. Munger (who succeeded his father Wesley Munger, who died in 1868), George Armour, and Charles S. Dole; the principal officers and partners of Dole & Co. were Charles S. Dole, Henry E. Southwell, Franklin H. Head, and James Darrell. During the 1880's the elevators were known as A, B, C, D, and Annex to D (after September 1, 1884) or the CB&Q elevators. (Chicago Board of Trade, *Twenty-sixth Annual Report, 1883*, p. 88, and reports for *1887*, p. 113, *1889*, p. 122.) The Armour Elevator Company, under the presidency of Philip D. Armour, should not be confused with Armour, Dole & Co., which was active prior to the incorporation of Armour Elevator Company under Illinois law in 1888, but presumably organized the year before. The capitalization of the latter was $100,000. (U. S. Bureau of Corporations, *Report . . . on the Beef Industry, 1905* [Washington, 1905], p. 293.) Chicago, Burlington & Quincy Archives, *Contracts, 1852–1900, Contract File, 1866–82, Elevator Papers, 1879–1887, Elevator Statements, 1886–1902, Miscellaneous Papers, 1878–1879*. (Mss. Newberry Library. Used by permission of Dr. Stanley Pargellis); city directories; *The American Elevator and Grain Trade*, X (Aug. 15, 1891), 51, 53.

[28] The agreement was renewed in 1896 for five years. The elevators under Armour became known as Armour Elevators C, D, Annex to D, E, formerly A, and F, formerly B. (Chicago, Burlington & Quincy Archives, *Contracts, 1852–1900*.) The Armour Elevator

These relationships appeared in most instances to have worked to the advantage of all participants. Independent elevator proprietors, however, complained of discriminatory rates and rebates of which they were not the beneficiaries. Farmers inveighed against what they considered the twin abuses of manipulating the market and the practices of the warehouses. To the grain producer both were as offensive as the discrimination in rates of which the railroads were roundly accused.

For some time protests were heard. Out of this discontent came Article XIII of the Illinois Constitution of 1870, which empowered the state to enact laws relative to railroad controls and warehouse regulation in cities of not less than 100,000 inhabitants. In the exercise of this grant, the legislature in 1871 passed a series of measures which are commonly called the Granger Laws. The constitutionality of the enactment affecting warehouses was tested before the United States Supreme Court in the well-known case of Munn *v.* Illinois. The Court upheld the validity of the Illinois statute, ruling that private business " in which the public has an interest " must submit to control by the public for the common good. The decision dismayed not only warehousemen but other businessmen unwilling to abandon the treasured conviction that government should exercise no such control over economic enterprises of this nature. Recalcitrant warehousemen, however, capitulated. The *Tribune* summed up their change of heart when it said: " The proprietors of the grain elevators in this city consider themselves thoroughly reconstructed. They bow to the inevitable, and regard the decision of the Supreme Court of the United States as final." [29]

The Warehouse Act of 1871 deprived the Chicago Board of Trade of power, but despite this the Board set forth in 1877 and in succeeding years some general rules affecting elevators and related matters.[30] The inspection of grain, however, fell, under the new statute, into

Company was also lessee of the Armour Elevator in 1890 and others in 1891 which were serviced by the CM&St.P Railway. Chicago Board of Trade, *Thirty-third Annual Report, 1890,* p. 34, *Thirty-fourth Annual Report, 1891,* p. 34.

[29] Illinois, *Debates and Proceedings of the Constitutional Convention . . . 1869,* II, 1878; Munn *v.* Illinois, 94 U. S. 113 (1876); *Chicago Tribune,* March 8, 1877.

[30] Illinois, *Public Laws, 1871–72,* pp. 618–25; Chicago Board of Trade, *Act of Incorporation, Rules, By-Laws and Inspection Regulations . . . in Force January 1, 1878, 1882, 1893* (published at intervals until 1886 and annually thereafter. The *Act of Incorporation, Rules . . .* is usually found bound with the *Annual Report* for the preceding year).

the hands of a state inspector appointed by the governor and confirmed by the Senate.[31] Opposition to the provisions of the new statute united frequently incompatible groups. Warehousemen and Board of Trade members joined hands in endorsing bills in the legislature to restore inspection to the Board. Beaten by the downstate vote, the opponents of state inspection finally accepted the outcome.[32] State inspection certificates became a medium of trade the world over, and owners of grain shipping through Chicago to the eastern market eventually requested inspection, although it was compulsory only for the grain stored in Class A warehouses.[33]

The body of law that set up the Illinois Commission with mandatory regulative powers over both railroads and warehouses was unique among state enactments. That such a statute was desirable did not assure obedience. The prescription relating to warehouse receipts proved particularly difficult to enforce. The burning on August 5, 1872, of the Iowa Elevator, a remnant of pre-Fire days, revealed the issuance of receipts for nearly four times as much corn as was actually stored. It was common talk that other elevators engaged in similar practices, and confidence in the validity of receipts in circulation declined.[34] Allegations of short-weighing, failure to return and cancel warehouse receipts, the exchange of receipts among warehousemen to cover up emergency deficits, prohibitive

[31] The first commission was made up of Gustave Koerner, prominent Belleville lawyer and Republican, chairman; Richard P. Morgan, Jr., civil engineer and onetime employee of the Chicago & Alton Railroad; and David S. Hammond, farmer with political connections in Cook County. Gustave Koerner, *Memoirs of Gustave Koerner, 1809–1896* . . . (2 v. Cedar Rapids, Iowa, 1909), II, 525–26; Illinois, *First Annual Report of the Railroad and Warehouse Commission, 1871*, pp. 3, 27; *The American Elevator and Grain Trade*, XI (Jan. 15, 1893), 234.

[32] *Chicago Tribune*, May 2, 1877; *The American Elevator and Grain Trade*, I (Oct. 15, 1882), 60, (March 15, 1883), 139–40, XI (Dec. 15, 1892), 198–99, (Jan. 15, 1893), 234; Chicago Board of Trade, *Sixteenth Annual Report, 1873*, pp. 22–23, *Nineteenth Annual Report, 1876*, pp. 25–26, *Act of Incorporation, Rules* . . . , *1882*, pp. 99–100. The newly organized state Railroad and Warehouse Commission adopted almost unchanged the rules already established by the Board of Trade. The chief grain inspector was to be "a suitable person" and not a member of the Board of Trade, and one not interested in any warehouse in Illinois. *Public Laws, 1871–72*, p. 767; *Statutes, 1871–72*, II, 442.

[33] Illinois, *First Annual Report of the Railroad and Warehouse Commission* . . . *1871*, p. 15, *Twenty-second Annual Report, 1892*, pp. 18–19, 159–60, *Twentieth Annual Report, 1890*, pp. 32–33.

[34] Both Ira Y. Munn and George L. Scott were expelled from the Board of Trade because of irregularities in the Munn and Scott elevators. *Chicago Tribune*, Aug. 6, 7, 14, Sept. 25, Nov. 26, 28, Dec. 4, 1872; Chicago Board of Trade, *Fifteenth Annual Report, 1872*, pp. 138, 141; Illinois, *Second Annual Report of the Railroad and Warehouse Commission, 1872*, pp. 16–17.

and unfair storage and handling charges, the cutting of rates by giving rebates, the false declaration of " hot " corn to force down the market for the advantage of short sellers, also cast some warehouse- men in the role of despoilers and lawbreakers.[35] By the close of the 'seventies, however, abuses appeared to decrease in frequency and severity. With the 'eighties the rise of competing grain centers, in- creasing shipments directly through the city in rail cars, and the establishment of through freight rates tended to lessen the power over shippers which the owners of elevators had enjoyed.[36]

Out of this changing pattern of the grain trade emerged a weak- ened influence of both warehousemen and commission men. The former, in order to keep their elevators filled, went directly to the country and purchased grain on the plea that increasing competi- tion from other grain centers close to the source of supply would divert traffic from Chicago. That such direct purchase could be called " illegitimate," as the commission men declared, was stoutly denied by the owners of the elevators, who insisted that an elimina- tion of the service fees of middlemen would result in higher prices for the producer.[37] In turn, the Board of Trade, in whose member- ship commission men were very influential and numerically im- pressive, engaged in controversies with the elevator men on the

[35] *Chicago Tribune*, June 21, 27, 28, 30, July 3, Oct. 9, Nov. 7, 11–14, Dec. 13, 1873; Illinois, *Second Annual Report of the Railroad and Warehouse Commission, 1872*, pp. 16–17; Chicago Board of Trade, *Sixteenth Annual Report, 1873*, pp. 11–12; *The American Elevator and Grain Trade*, VIII (Jan. 15, 1890), 180.

[36] In 1876 13 per cent of the grain arriving in Chicago was not stored; in 1880, 20 per cent; and in 1885 nearly 57 per cent. (Chicago Board of Trade, *Twenty-eighth Annual Report, 1885*, p. xliv.) In 1892 of about 247,000,000 bushels of grain inspected and graded by the Chicago department of the Railroad and Warehouse Commission, about 110,000,000 bushels went into storage in class A warehouses. Class A warehouses were in places of 100,000 inhabitants and over. Chicago was, therefore, the only city to which this part of the law was applicable. U. S., *Reports of the Industrial Commission*, IV, *Transportation*, "Testimony" (Washington, 1900), 354, 370–71, 405; Interstate Commerce Commission, *Third Annual Report, 1889* (Washington, 1889), p. 77 (hereafter cited as ICC); U. S., *Statutes at Large*, December, 1885, to March, 1887, XXIV, 379–87; Illinois, *Nineteenth Annual Report of the Railroad and Warehouse Commission, 1889*, pp. 119–20; Benjamin F. Goldstein, *Marketing, A Farmer's Problem* (New York, 1928), p. 122.

[37] U. S., *Reports of the Industrial Commission, 1900*, IV, *Transportation*, "Testimony," 371, 393, 396, 406–7; *The American Elevator and Grain Trade*, VI (March 15, 1888), 205, VIII (July 15, 1889), 13, (Oct. 15, 1889), 80, (Feb. 15, 1890), 206, (May 15, 1890), 292, IX (July 15, 1890), 12–13, XI (May 15, 1893), 376, XII (March 15, 1894), 305, XIII (July 15, 1894), 13–14, 17; *The Economist*, III (Jan. 18, 1890), 53–54, IV (July 5, 1890), 6. The example of exporters of Baltimore, Philadelphia, New York, and other eastern cities buying directly from the country dealers was cited as a good example.

mixing of grains, storage charges, and similar matters.[38] With the coming of the 'nineties, along with many others in the evolving business structure, the owners of elevators were charged with attempting to establish a trust, which, in the case of grain, contemporary writers declared, meant the strangulation of both dealers and the Board of Trade.[39]

In the Board of Trade centered the chief activities of grain traders, just as they had since its organization in 1848. Its growth in membership from the original 82 to 1,903 in 1892 and its numerous committees, ranging from flaxseed inspection to transportation and meteorology, attested to its extensive influence and usefulness, and in a very real sense measured the economic horizon of this miraculously growing city. Upon its broad floor assembled those who carried on business through the Board, and whose frantic and delirious shouts and gestures heralded transactions which fed the springs of the economic destiny of the city. Within their respective " pits " men dealt in grains and provisions, and what they did was flashed by busy, tireless telegraph operators to a waiting world.

Rules governing trading were set up by the Board subject to state law, and the Board was the judge of the qualifications of its members. In 1875 membership was made transferable and acquired a market value that reflected the general condition of the trade. In 1856, to induce members to assemble, the Board had served a free lunch; by October, 1881, men were paying an initiation fee of $5,000, and this fee was to be doubled within a year's time.[40] By

[38] *Chicago Tribune,* Dec. 24–29, 1889, Jan. 4, 24, June 25, 29, July 1, 2, 8, Aug. 5, 6, 1890; *The American Elevator and Grain Trade,* III (Oct. 15, 1884), 81, V (July 15, 1886), 18, (Sept. 15, 1886), 60, VII (Sept. 15, 1888), 160, (Oct. 15, 1889), 89, VIII (June 15, 1890), 319, IX (July 15, 1890), 12–13, 14, (Aug. 15, 1890), 36, XII (June 15, 1894), 416, 423, XIII (July 15, 1894), 17; U. S., *Reports of the Industrial Commission, 1900,* IV, *loc. cit.,* 403, 411; *The Economist,* IV (July 5, 1890), 6. In 1890, for example, President William T. Baker and eleven of fifteen directors of the Board of Trade were commission men. For a biography of Baker see Charles H. Baker, *Life and Character of William Taylor Baker* (New York, 1908).

[39] *The American Elevator and Grain Trade,* XIII (July 15, 1894), 13–14; *The Economist,* III (Jan. 18, 1890), 53–54. The farmers for some time had charged the elevators with monopoly practices. See, for example, *The American Elevator and Grain Trade,* III (Dec. 15, 1884), 132.

[40] In 1892 the initiation fee was still $10,000. Changes in fees and the market value of memberships are detailed in the Board of Trade annual reports. See also *The American Elevator and Grain Trade,* III (May 15, 1885), 244, X (April 15, 1892), 341; *The Economist,* Annual Number (Jan. 1, 1890), 5; *Chicago Tribune,* Dec. 31, 1882, Jan. 1, 1884.

1880 the organization had become so large and so prosperous that it sought quarters elsewhere than in the Chamber of Commerce Building, into which it had moved on October 9, 1872. Over the opposition of property owners, banded together under the name of the Union Building Association,[41] the Board put up a building of Fox Island granite at Jackson and South LaSalle streets.

On April 30, 1885, it took over the occupancy of its " new temple of commerce," which with the site was said to have cost about $1,800,000.[42] The occasion was celebrated with appropriate ceremonies attended by representatives of trade associations from Liverpool, New York, Montreal, St. Louis, Philadelphia, Baltimore, and other important cities. But the *camaraderie* of economic brotherhood thus inspired was shadowed by the noisy and unwelcome tones of the leaders of the International Working Peoples' Association and by the manifestations of ill will on the part of laborers who, according to the *Tribune,* had been given " full employment " during the period of construction and were now bent on destroying " the sources of their support." Two thousand marched in the parade to protest against the erection of a building they described as " a grand temple of Usury, Gambling, and Cut-Throatism." Nevertheless, members of the Board rejoiced in having a trading hall 152 by 160 feet which would permit them to escape the smothering attic where, in the past, their transactions had been carried on.[43]

To facilitate operations and to decrease the possibility of large failures, a clearinghouse, with functions similar to those of banks,

---

Rules of the Board of Trade appear frequently in the annual reports. Insofar as possible, trading terms which have a special meaning in " the pit " are not used in this study. For terms " put " and " call," see footnote 78.

[41] The opposition claimed that removal of the Board of Trade would affect rentals near the Chamber of Commerce Building and alleged that $25,000 had bought Council votes. An injunction to prevent the vacating of LaSalle Street was obtained from Judge Murray Tuley of the Superior Court. A decision of the Illinois Supreme Court in March, 1882, however, removed judicial obstacles. (City of Chicago *et al. v.* The Union Building Association, 102 Ill. 379 [1882].) For the story of the struggle see *Chicago Tribune,* June 27, 28, July 17, 21, 29, 31, Aug. 1, 1881; *The Chicago Times,* Dec. 25, 1880, June 26, July 31, 1881.

[42] *Chicago Tribune,* April 30, 1885; Chicago Board of Trade, *Twenty-second Annual Report, 1879,* p. 24, *Twenty-eighth Annual Report, 1885,* p. xlii; Chicago, *Council Proceedings, 1881–82,* pp. 43–44; Charles H. Taylor, ed., *History of the Board of Trade of the City of Chicago* (3 v. Chicago, 1917), I, 428–29, 431.

[43] *Chicago Tribune,* April 30, 1885; *The American Elevator and Grain Trade,* II (Feb. 15, 1884), 144, III (May 15, 1885), 254; Taylor, *op. cit.,* II, 711–15; John Moses and Joseph Kirkland, *The History of Chicago, Illinois* (2 v. Chicago, 1895), I, 352.

opened September 24, 1883. From that date until January 1, 1884, total clearings amounted to $35,341,936.50, a significant showing for the few weeks during which the new organization had functioned. In essence, the clearinghouse was a department of the Board of Trade, used to settle closed trades in the greatest futures market of the world.[44]

In addition to the Board of Trade, the most important agency in transactions in produce, the Open Board of Trade and the Chicago Provision, Grain and Stock Board, better known as the Call Board, served similarly but on a smaller scale. The beginning of the Open Board in 1877 was informal, arising from the desire for an organization which could deal in smaller amounts than were permitted on the large Board. Incorporated in 1880, the Open Board at times ran afoul the more powerful body, as did the bucket shops with which it was at times said to be in collusion. Although in some cases the membership of the Open Board and the larger and more powerful Board was the same, the less pretentious undertakings of the former were reflected in the much smaller fee for the privileges of the organization.[45]

Older than the Open Board was the Call Board, founded to provide an organized market for provisions. It grew out of a lengthy controversy between grain and provision dealers on the Board of Trade as to hours of trading and the desirability of adding a call on grains to the call on provisions. A definite split came in 1876 under the leadership of Benjamin P. Hutchinson, when the Provision, Grain, and Stock Exchange was organized. Less than a year later differences developed within the new organization regarding the question of continuing the call on grain, probably because many members were also members of the Board of Trade. When the call was abolished in April, 1877, by what was described as "a most arbitrary use of power" on the part of directors, those favoring the

[44] *Chicago Tribune*, Sept. 25, 1883, Jan. 1, 1884, Jan. 1, 1886; James E. Boyle, *Speculation and the Chicago Board of Trade* (New York, 1920), pp. 78–79; *The American Elevator and Grain Trade*, III (Oct. 15, 1884), 81. See Board of Trade annual reports from 1884. In the establishment of the Board of Trade Clearing House Cyrus Hall Adams played an important part.

[45] FTC, *op. cit.*, II, 128; *Chicago Tribune*, Jan. 1, 1883, Jan. 1, 1884, May 1, 1885, July 1, 1887; *The Drovers' Journal*, April 21, 1890. See *The American Elevator and Grain Trade*, I (1883) — IX (1891) for interesting items on the Open Board. The floor of the Open Board was available to the public. This Board first started in 1868 but was discontinued in 1870. Taylor, *op. cit.*, I, 373, 414–15.

continuance of the call withdrew to form a new Call Board made up of practically the same men who had organized the late Provision, Grain, and Stock Exchange. It became known as the Provision, Grain and Stock Board to avoid confusing it with its predecessor.

To the meetings of the new group, members of the Board of Trade were invited, leading the *Tribune* to remark that " a treaty of eternal peace having now been concluded, it will be preserved forever — unless somebody gets mad again." In 1884 the Call Board dissolved upon the fulfillment of the Board of Trade's promise to maintain an afternoon session from two to two-thirty o'clock to meet the needs of those who had late orders to fill.[46] In 1887 the Chicago Board of Trade Stock Exchange was established, with membership limited to members of the Board of Trade, but in the year following its inauguration was dissolved.[47]

As in the years before the Fire the urge to speculate continued to exercise its spell over many. The greatest speculative market in the world grew up in Chicago. Prices were at times determined by it, and it became the source of power far beyond the confines of grains and provisions. Looked upon as a legitimate form of business risk by some who indulged in it, speculation was criticized roundly by those who, seeing no honesty and benefit in it, considered it no less than the practice of gambling. Even transactions for future delivery were confused by many with dealings of chance, although for the former the Board prescribed contracts specifying date of delivery, quantity, quality, and price of the commodity traded.

To some, whose holdings the Great Fire had seriously reduced or destroyed, speculative trading seemed a speedy and easy means of recouping lost fortunes. By it men of small estate were magically and quickly transported to the fullness of affluence, and just as magically

[46] The secretary of the Chicago Provision, Grain and Stock Board was James E. Henneberry, also secretary of the Chicago Provision, Grain, and Stock Exchange. B. P. Hutchinson was a director of the new Call Board. Nathaniel K. Fairbank was president of the first Call Board (1876–77), an indication of the importance of the provision men in that association. William N. Brainerd was made president of the new board. *Chicago Tribune*, April 14, May 2, 1877, Jan. 1, 1883, May 14, 1884; Taylor, *op. cit.*, II, 691; Chicago Board of Trade, *Twenty-seventh Annual Report, 1884*, p. xxxiv; *The American Elevator and Grain Trade*, I (April 15, 1883), 158, 196, II (June 15, 1884), 248, (May 14, 1885), 219.

[47] *Chicago Tribune*, April 14, June 2, 1887; Chicago Board of Trade, *Thirty-first Annual Report, 1888*, p. lvii; *The American Elevator and Grain Trade*, V (April 15, 1887), 222, (May 15, 1887), 249. See Chapter VI, " Banking, Investments and Finance," for a discussion of the Chicago Stock Exchange.

and quickly plunged into the emptiness of poverty. This aspect of the get-rich-quick ardor of the times held not only the grain dealers of Chicago captive, but the traders of all the grain marts of the country, Canada, and Europe, many of whom played the game in Chicago according to Chicago rules and Chicago conditions. Although details of the pattern sometimes differed, the main design was much the same, ever dependent upon the skill of the manipulator, the size of the crop, the state of the domestic and foreign markets, and the conduct of the producer.

The culmination of the speculative frenzy of the year after the Fire came in the celebrated Lyon wheat deal of August 21.[48] This involved John B. Lyon, of the commission firm John B. Lyon and Company, the elevator men Ira Y. Munn, George L. Scott, and Hugh Maher, all of Chicago, associated in widespread reports with Thomas Chisholm of Toronto. In July wheat went to $1.25. To corner August wheat and force the price up, settling at $1.40, appeared to these bold manipulators the golden key to success. But the price rose to $1.60 a bushel, bringing to market the farmers' reserve. Next, the request of the cornerers for a million-dollar fund was refused by William F. Coolbaugh, president of the Union National Bank, unless security in the form of grain certificates was deposited. Thereupon the price fell to $1.45. Unparalleled excitement gripped the grain dealers, wild tumult reigned on the Board of Trade floor. "Men grew frantic, yelled, foamed at the mouth, knocked one another down, tore off coats, hats and shirts; broke up tables, smashed out windows and converted the hall into a pandemonium until they were turned into the street," reported *The American Elevator and Grain Trade*. The price of No. 2 wheat fell to $1.20 that day and sank to $1.11 the next. The operators controlled 6,000,000 bushels but their loss was said to be $750,000; and other failures were numerous and far-reaching.[49]

Similar corners followed, mounting in volume and in the finesse

[48] *The American Elevator and Grain Trade*, VI (July 15, 1887), 15; Chicago Board of Trade, *Fifteenth Annual Report, 1872*, p. 11; *Chicago Tribune*, June 19, 1872.

[49] It was claimed that a large amount of wheat had been graded as No. 2 when it was of lower grade. Lyon was reported to have used $200,000 of his fortune to help in the settlement. *The American Elevator and Grain Trade*, I (Jan. 15, 1883), 100; Chicago Board of Trade, *Fifteenth Annual Report, 1872*, pp. 59, 137; *Chicago Tribune*, Aug. 21, 1872; *The Chicago Times*, Aug. 27, 1881; Henry D. Lloyd, "Making Bread Dear," *The North American Review*, CXXXVII (Aug., 1883), 124, 127.

with which they were conducted. Before the 'seventies closed, not only was the ability to read the crystal ball of future market conditions important, but large accumulations of capital were required to play the market successfully. To speculative undertakings were attracted men of the financial stature of Philip D. Armour, who, with the Milwaukee financiers Peter McGeoch, John Plankinton, and Alexander Mitchell, carried on successful operations in wheat during July and August, 1878, making gains reported from $100,000 to $500,000.[50]

The big flurry of the late 'seventies came in the famous James R. Keene corner of 1879. English by birth, but a resident of California, Keene was a successful speculator in railroad and Western Union Telegraph Company stocks who operated generally out of New York. One million dollars were said to have been deposited in the First National Bank through the agents of the combination, and "untold millions" of bushels of wheat, variously estimated from twenty to seventy, were bought up.[51] For almost a year and a half Keene and his associates ran the corner. The cash price of No. 2 spring wheat ranged from 81⅞ cents in the first week of January, 1879, to $1.33½ a bushel in December. An immense incoming crop flooded the market by the last week of August, 1880, lowering the price to 86½ cents. Again nature had done what man was unable or unwilling to do. So much grain poured into Chicago that all storage space, even in abandoned houses, was used. Elevators were so crowded that one finally burst, spilling over the street a reported 15,000 bushels. Avid men, women, and children, entranced by the power of grain to build fortunes, eagerly gathered the treasured foodstuff in bags, baskets, and even in pillowcases, sheets, and bedspreads. The estimated losses in the corner ran from a million and a half to three million dollars.[52]

[50] *The American Elevator and Grain Trade*, VII (Nov. 15, 1888), 98; Taylor, *op. cit.*, I, 562–64; *Chicago Tribune*, July 31, Aug. 1, 1878, Jan. 1, 1879. In the Aug. 1, 1878, issue of the *Tribune* a satirical drama, lamely imitating Shakespeare's *Hamlet* and entitled *King Philip the First, Another Drama in Several Corners*, sets the scene in a house on Meadow Avenue in "King Philip's dressing room, then in a room in Swillporkee at the Plankwankston House," and last in "a sleeping chamber in a house by the lake shore of Swillporkee." The main characters are King Philip, MacGrath, and John.

[51] *The American Elevator and Grain Trade*, I (Jan. 15, 1883), 100.

[52] Chicago Board of Trade, *Twenty-second Annual Report, 1879*, pp. 12–13, 24, 95, *Twenty-third Annual Report, 1880*, pp. 78–79; *Chicago Tribune*, July 7, 1879, Jan. 1, 1881; *Rand, McNally & Co.'s Bankers' Monthly*, I (May 14, 1884), 42; Henry D. Lloyd

The Keene corner was but the prelude to equally important and extensive battles in the years which followed, nonresident promoters, especially from Cincinnati, taxing Chicago facilities to such an extent that orders had to be declined.[53] The climax of these spectacular engagements originated by other than Chicago promoters came in 1887, in general a year of unusual dullness in speculation. Led by Edward L. Harper, an official of the Fidelity National Bank of Cincinnati and an investor in iron and railroad undertakings, his syndicate on May 1 controlled, according to contemporary accounts, about forty million bushels of wheat in Chicago and the supply in St. Louis, Toledo, New York, and San Francisco.[54] Already known to Chicagoans through earlier attempts to corner the market, Harper and his associates monopolized the space for storage and at the same time blocked railroad shipments. Drastic maneuvers failed to halt the retaliation of the " shorts " who, by June 14, had become very active. Then came the action of the Board of Trade to break the storage blockade by declaring more houses regular. From June 14, " Black Tuesday," to the next day, prices fell from 92 to 69 cents. Commission houses went down in failure and the principal plunger defaulted an estimated $3,500,000, wrecking the Fidelity National Bank of Cincinnati.[55] " The fate of the Keenes, the Handys, and the Harpers should henceforth be suggestive to the gentlemen of the commercial and financial ' highway,' that this Board does not present an inviting field for their favorite operations," commented President Abner M. Wright of the Chicago Board of Trade in his annual report of 1887.[56]

to Charles L. Hutchinson, May 2, 1888, Charles L. Hutchinson, Papers, 1866–1922 (Mss. Newberry Library); Van Buren Denslow, " Board of Trade Morality," The North American Review, CXXXVII (Oct., 1883), 382.

[53] Chicago Board of Trade, Twenty-fourth Annual Report, 1881, p. xvii. In July and August Truman B. Handy and other Cincinnatians, including Edward L. Harper, ran the No. 2 wheat price up to $1.36 and then sold. They were said to have made a profit of $3,000,000. Some, however, stayed in too long and lost on September sales. Taylor, op. cit., II, 621–25; The American Elevator and Grain Trade, I (Jan. 15, 1883), 100; Chicago Tribune, Sept. 1, 1881; The New World, XI (Sept. 20, 1902), 8.

[54] Control of Liverpool wheat by the syndicate was alleged. The American Elevator and Grain Trade described Harper " as a blind " for a " Standard Oil and California crowd." Ibid., V (June 15, 1887), 272.

[55] Ibid., V (May 15, 1887), 254, (June 15, 1887), 272–73, 276, VI (July 15, 1887), 13, XI (May 15 , 1893), 378–79; Taylor, op. cit., II, 752; Cincinnati Chamber of Commerce and Merchants' Exchange, Thirty-ninth Annual Report, 1887 (Cincinnati, 1888), p. 84; Chicago Board of Trade, Thirtieth Annual Report, 1887, p. lx.

[56] Ibid., pp. xxxii–xxxiii, lviii–lvix. The President's comment is on p. lix.

Of the colorful and bold adventurers who through the 1880's became important figures in the market, none was more astute than Benjamin P. Hutchinson, familiarly known as " Old Hutch." In 1888 he ran his first actual corner. Before this he had played a significant role in various crises on the Board and had helped sustain the market when it was about to collapse.[57] Believing that the crop would be poor in the summer of 1888, he quietly cornered September wheat. Contrary to the practices of some of his contemporaries, he operated openly and freely, warning those attempting to sell grain they did not possess that disaster awaited them. Prices shot up five to ten and twenty-five cents a bushel " at command," to quote the secretary of the Board of Trade, and went to close contracts at $1.25 to $1.60 a bushel. A few sales of car lots were made at two dollars. It was common talk that Hutchinson held more than half the wheat in Chicago elevators and that he had bought millions of bushels in addition. Under the hammering he skillfully administered, those who had acted as " bears " were forced to retreat. On this September wheat corner it was estimated that he cleared a million or more dollars.[58]

The editor of *The American Elevator and Grain Trade*, not given to praising this form of undertaking, concluded his discussion of the September corner by saying: " A good deal of rot is indulged in by the daily press about making bread dear, as if there were no such thing as a producer. The corner which Mr. Hutchinson constructed did the country at large no harm." Indeed, he continued, only two grain corners had ever been really successful, one by Joseph in the ancient days and that by " Old Hutch " in 1888. " Both Joseph and Mr. Hutchinson," he pointed out, " bought the actual grain, and stored it, in anticipation of contingencies which turned out correctly, and the results to each were the same — enormous profits." [59]

[57] Hutchinson was said to have sustained the market in the McGeoch lard corner and the Harper wheat corner in 1887. *The American Elevator and Grain Trade*, VII (Oct. 15, 1888), 85. Corners in other products than grain are discussed in sections dealing with the special product.

[58] Among others said to have benefited from the corner were William T. Baker, commission merchant and Board of Trade president in 1890 and 1891, and Nathaniel K. Fairbank, lard refiner, president of the Board of Trade in 1878. Both are reported to have made $500,000. *The American Elevator and Grain Trade*, VII (Oct. 15, 1888), 83, 85, 87. See also Chicago Board of Trade, *Thirty-first Annual Report, 1888*, pp. xxxii–xxxiii. How much men made in these undertakings is usually conjecture or rumor.

[59] *The American Elevator and Grain Trade*, VII (Oct. 15, 1888), 85, XIII (Feb. 15,

"Old Hutch's" amulet, however, although compounded of fore-sight, boldness, practicality, and capital, did not always forestall adversity. His wheat corner of September, 1888, which the *Tribune* described as "the most successful deal in grain ever conducted to a close," was followed by reverses in the corn market. In the next three years he had a mixture of good and poor fortune. During the period of his greatest activity he was probably the most talked of man on the 'Change. He persistently denied that he ever engaged in running a corner, and asserted that not two out of ten succeeded in doing so. His appearance in the pit was invariably a signal for wild buying. Years after he had ceased to be an important operator, his name still had the ring of magic — "Old Hutch," with his black slouch hat, the first on the floor and the last to leave it.[60]

> In dealing on 'Change whether little or much,
> All wholesomely fear the insatiate Hutch;
> O'er eyes of the sharpest he "pulleth the wool,"
> 'Mid "bulls" as a "bear," and 'mid "bears" as a "bull."
> How plaintive the tone as crieth each mourner,
> He'll find — thank the Lord — in heaven no corner.[61]

Like Hutchinson, Edward W. Pardridge dwarfed, outthought, and outmaneuvered most of his contemporaries in speculative under-takings.[62] Starting in the 'eighties, he operated through various brokers chiefly as a "bear," upon occasion selling "privileges" or buying "puts" to the amazement of his opponents. By such a shift in January, 1892, he was able to purchase a million bushels of wheat in an hour's time, profiting $10,000 on this deal alone. Before March ended, his gains were approximated at a million and a half dollars. But, like others, he could not resist the call of the 'Change. In a wheat manipulation in April, 1893, he lost heavily, between five and

1895), 285. For a flattering account of Hutchinson see Edward J. Dies, *The Plunger* (New York, 1929).

[60] Chicago Board of Trade, *Thirty-second Annual Report, 1889,* pp. xxxiii–xxxiv; Taylor, *op. cit.,* II, 792, 809, 817, 819, 821, 823, 835, 842, 862, 867; *Chicago Tribune,* Sept. 25, 28, 29, 1888, Jan. 1, 1889; *Chicago Record-Herald,* March 19, 1904; *Mixed Drinks,* I (Sept. 2, 1889), 6; *The American Elevator and Grain Trade,* VII (Oct. 15, 1888), 85, 87; Henry D. Lloyd to Charles L. Hutchinson, May 2, 1888, *Hutchinson Papers.* B. P. Hutchinson's point of view on the legitimacy of corners can be found in his article "Speculation in Wheat," *The North American Review,* CLIII (Oct., 1891), 414–19.

[61] *The American Elevator and Grain Trade,* VII (Oct. 15, 1888), 83.

[62] Edward W. Pardridge was a dry goods merchant besides engaging in grain specula-tion.

six hundred thousand dollars, as the shadow of the nation-wide depression fell across the Chicago grain pits.[63]

Such traders and even those men not engaged in speculative undertakings on the floor of the Board of Trade spoke in large figures, and for them its services were reserved. But men of few goods were no less agitated by the prevailing eagerness for wealth and the prestige it promised. If they could and would, these men of small estate might take their chance in the bucket shop, "the poor man's Board of Trade." Here, on small sums, wagers could be placed on price fluctuations; men could trade on slender margins and could deal in far smaller amounts in grains and other goods with which the Board was concerned. Neither the actual commodity nor warehouse receipts, for example, were necessary as in the pit of the regular Board. [64]

When Chicago's first bucket shop opened is not known, but about 1877 the Public Produce Exchange was started to deal in grain, pork, lard, and other commodities. By 1882 eight or more such establishments flourished not far from the Board of Trade, along notorious "Gamblers' Row," and provided as well facilities to those who wished to play faro and other games of chance. Two of the bucket shops were operated for women only, and to their floors were attracted women from various walks of life, from schoolteachers to practitioners of spiritualism.[65]

[63] *Ibid.*, VIII (March 15, 1890), 225, X (Jan. 15, 1892), 232, (June 15, 1892), 406; *Chicago Tribune*, Jan. 5, 7, 11, 13, 15, 16, 17, 20, 21, 22, 23, 27, 1892, Jan. 1, 1893; Taylor, *op. cit.*, II, 829, 840, 859. Two important speculative undertakings in corn in the early 1890's should be mentioned: that of S. V. White and Company in 1891 and of Coster and Martin in 1892. Both ended disastrously. The latter carried with it important commission firms including Schwartz, Dupee & McCormick. This firm was composed of Gustavus Schwartz, John Dupee, Jr., and William G. McCormick. (Chicago Board of Trade, *Thirty-fourth Annual Report, 1891*, pp. xli, 274, *Thirty-fifth Annual Report, 1892*, pp. 264, 280, 292; *The American Elevator and Grain Trade*, X [Oct. 15, 1891], 118.) Space considerations prevent the inclusion of other speculative undertakings of this nature. *The American Elevator and Grain Trade* and the daily press give rich descriptions. The Board of Trade reports seldom name the participants, although generally treating the episodes.

[64] In 1885 the Board permitted trading in smaller lots than previously, that is, in 1,000-bushel lots. This may be surmised as an attempt to strike at the bucket shops. Chicago Board of Trade, *Twenty-eighth Annual Report, 1885*, p. xliii.

[65] Gamblers' Row or Alley was in the neighborhood of Randolph, Monroe, and Clark streets. Before 1885 the Board of Trade was located at LaSalle and Washington. On January 1, 1883, the *Chicago Tribune* declared there were about 270 bucket shops in Chicago and elsewhere in the country. In Chicago some were soon located in the stockyards section and around Forty-second and Halsted. (*The Drovers' Journal*, March 31, April 4, 1890.) Many were reported as having failed in 1890. (*The American Elevator and Grain Trade*, VIII

Beginning with the 'eighties the Board of Trade waged a relentless but seldom successful war on the shops in an effort to put them out of business. It refused its price quotations in December, 1882, and induced the Western Union Telegraph Company to discontinue its services to the shops in January, 1883. By various devices such as wire tapping, encouraging the co-operation of Board members to reveal the state of the market, and delaying tactics in seeking injunctions against the Board and the telegraph companies furnishing quotations, the shops managed at times to bypass this inconvenience.[66] In 1883 and 1884, however, several court decisions were adverse to the claims of the shops in declaring that the telegraph companies did not have the right to furnish market quotations without the Board's consent.[67]

Unsuccessful in the courts and still further hindered in their activities by the Board of Trade's regulation of 1885 forbidding its members to patronize them, the bucket shops sought relief from the state legislature. Here, too, they were doomed to failure. In 1887 anti-bucket shop legislation known as the Riddle Bill was passed. An Illinois Supreme Court decision in 1890, which ruled that brokers' agencies not providing for deliveries of all sales were illegal, further sealed the fate of the bucket shops as legal organizations.[68]

This ruling had been preceded by a decision of the same court on January 25, 1889, that the Board of Trade, although a private corporation and its market quotations private property, must hereafter furnish these quotations to all persons willing to pay for them and to conform to all reasonable regulations. This finding rested

[June 15, 1890], 319.) *Ibid.*, I (Feb. 15, 1883), 120, 123, III (March 15, 1885), 194, IV (July 15, 1885), 9, V (Nov. 15, 1886), 113, VI (July 15, 1887), 8; *The Chicago Times,* Dec. 3, 1880, Dec. 16, 1882, May 25, 1883; *Chicago Daily News,* June 9, 1892.

66 *The Chicago Times,* Dec. 16, 1882, Jan. 3, Feb. 3, March 13, 1883; *Chicago Tribune,* Jan. 1, 1883; Chicago Board of Trade, *Twenty-fifth Annual Report, 1882,* p. xxiii, *Twenty-ninth Annual Report, 1886,* p. xl, *Thirtieth Annual Report, 1887,* p. lix. *The American Elevator and Grain Trade,* II (1883) — X (1892), gives interesting details.

67 The cases are discussed in the daily newspapers and in *The American Elevator and Grain Trade,* I (March 15, 1883), 138, II (July 15, 1883), 3, III (Nov. 15, 1884), 10, (Dec. 15, 1884), 131; Chicago Board of Trade, *Twenty-fifth Annual Report, 1882,* p. xxiii, *Twenty-sixth Annual Report, 1883,* p. 22; Lewis H. Bisbee and John C. Simonds, *The Board of Trade and the Produce Exchange, Their History, Methods and Law* (Chicago, 1884), p. 97.

68 Chicago Board of Trade, *Act of Incorporation, Rules . . . 1886,* p. 17; *The American Elevator and Grain Trade,* I (April 15, 1883), 158, (May 15, 1883), 178, V (June 15, 1887), 276, IX (Aug. 15, 1890), 41; Illinois, *Laws, 1887,* pp. 96–97; William Soby *v.* The People of the State of Illinois, 134 Ill. 66 (1890); *The Drovers' Journal,* June 13, 1890.

on the ground that through its conduct the Board, with the co-operation of the telegraph companies, had created a standard for agricultural products to which the public conformed.[69] As a result, the
Board decided to limit the supply of its quotations to its members,
for whom special wire service was to be provided.[70] A series of injunctions instigated by bucket-shop owners and the decisions of the
lower courts, however, led the Board, on April 1, 1890, to discontinue its quotation department altogether.[71]

No one of these measures restrained for long the hardy owners and
zealous patrons of the shops, although the worst were plagued by
police raids on the ground that they were common gambling places.
On July 18, 1892, the Board, realizing that its struggle was actually
ended, restored telegraph wires to its floor and started to furnish quotations to all.[72]

The uncertainties of these speculative engagements, the machine-
like precision with which they were carried on, and the mounting
volume of grain and money involved, especially on the floor of the
Board of Trade, roused in the cautious fears as to what the fever of
speculation might do if allowed to run unchecked. In 1874 an apprehensive public opinion led the Illinois legislature to pass an " anti-
corner " law which, however, proved ineffective in even slowing up
the climbing number of speculative undertakings, more and more
furthered by men of wealth and political influence. Nor did regulations, designed by the Board of Trade to prevent corners and to promote adjustments on defaulted contracts, stem the increasingly
stormy and uncertain adventures of the daring.[73] A rising agrarian

[69] The New York and Chicago Grain and Stock Exchange *v.* The Board of Trade of
the City of Chicago, *et al.* 127 Ill. 153 (1889). The principles announced in Munn *v.* Illinois, 94 U. S. 113 (1876) were applied here. *Chicago Legal News,* XXI (July 13, 1889), 777.

[70] The Board of Trade had disseminated its market quotations to correspondents, regardless of membership, who paid for the information. Chicago Board of Trade, *Twenty-
eighth Annual Report, 1885,* p. xliii.

[71] *The Drovers' Journal,* July 2, 1885; *The American Elevator and Grain Trade,* VII
(Sept. 15, 1888), 63, VIII (April 15, 1890), 266; *The Economist,* III (March 29, 1890),
361, (April 5, 1890), 392, (April 19, 1890), 459; Chicago Board of Trade, *Thirty-third
Annual Report, 1890,* pp. lxv–lxvii.

[72] Chicago Board of Trade, *Thirty-fifth Annual Report, 1892,* pp. xlviii–xlix; *Chicago
Tribune,* Jan. 1, 1893; *The American Elevator and Grain Trade,* IX (Nov. 15, 1890), 121,
X (Oct. 15, 1891), 119, 155, 161, (May 15, 1892), 371. The bucket shops claimed to serve
country dealers who did not operate on the floor of the Board of Trade.

[73] Illinois, *Revised Statutes, 1874,* p. 38; Chicago Board of Trade, *Eighteenth Annual
Report, 1875,* p. 23, *Act of Incorporation, Rules* . . . , *1886,* p. 18. Various state courts declared option trading to be mere gambling. The editor of *The American Elevator and Grain*

distrust of what was believed urban chicanery placed these manipulations alongside monopolies of other kinds. When the farmer beheld the evidences of comfortable, even costly, living of those to whom he sent his produce and compared them with the rewards of his own labor, distrust and bitterness deepened the gulf separating the producer of grain from the dealer.[74]

All this the Board of Trade recognized as dangerous to its prestige and its announced purposes. Its punishment of some of the most prominent habitués on its floor for infractions of rules included violators of regulations governing future transactions.[75] But the abstract principle of speculation it openly and stoutly defended.

Speculation [it said] stimulates enterprise; it creates and maintains proper values; it gives impulse and ambition to all forms of industry — commercial, literary, artistic; it arouses individual capacities; it is aggressive, intelligent, and belongs to the strongest and ablest of the race; it grapples undismayed with possibilities; it founded Chicago, and developed the great West, which is the basis of the Nation's prosperity and the impelling commercial power of the continent.[76]

Trade remarked that " legal decisions and even legislation cannot prevent people from speculating, or ' gambling,' if you like, on the strength of their judgment or foresight." (*The American Elevator and Grain Trade,* I [Dec. 15, 1882], 92.) The *Tribune* held dealing in regular future contracts " strictly legitimate," but disapproved of " privileges " transactions, pointing out that they erroneously were synonymous in the public mind with options. *Chicago Tribune,* Jan. 1, 1878.

[74] See Edward Winslow Martin, *History of the Grange Movement: or, The Farmer's War Against Monopolies* (Chicago, 1874), pp. 306–7.

[75] For example, Jack (William N.) Sturges was disciplined in 1874. He conducted a corn corner with disastrous results. He was suspended from Board membership, but was reinstated later upon bringing suit for restoration. The principals in the John B. Lyon and elevator group wheat corner in 1872 were also disciplined. The Board punished members, of course, for other offenses. Cross-trading, dealing in privileges, trading after hours were among the offenses which brought about punishment. See Chicago Board of Trade reports; also William N. Sturges *v.* Board of Trade of the City of Chicago, 86 Ill. 441 (1877), James Baxter *v.* Board of Trade of the City of Chicago, 83 Ill. 146 (1876); *The Advance,* VIII (Nov. 12, 1874), 187. In September, 1875, the Board was upheld by the Illinois Supreme Court in disciplining members for trading in privileges. Aquilla H. Pickering *et al. v.* Henry Cease, 79 Ill. 328 (1875).

[76] Chicago Board of Trade, *Thirty-fourth Annual Report, 1891,* pp. xviii, xix, xxii. The right to trade in futures was considered inalienable because it involved a contract, and laws, it was contended, could not nullify the effect of supply on prices. For the Board's attitude see also John Hill, Jr., *Gold Bricks of Speculation* (Chicago, 1904). The advantages of stock and produce exchanges are noted in Henry Crosby Emery, *Speculation on the Stock and Produce Exchanges of the United States* (Columbia University, *Studies in History, Economics, and Public Law,* VII, no. 2, New York, 1896), and Albert C. Stevens, " Futures in the Wheat Market," *Quarterly Journal of Economics,* II (Oct., 1887), 63.

Public resentment, part of which was miller- and farmer-inspired, culminated in the Hatch-Washburn Antioption Bill in Congress in 1892–93.[77] It was widely proclaimed by the grain interests as socialistic and as harmful to the trading guild, inasmuch as every man was believed in essence to be " the best custodian of himself and his own affairs." With other leading exchanges the Chicago Board of Trade vigorously campaigned against the measure. When the House of Representatives failed on March 1, 1893, to accept by the necessary two-thirds vote the Senate amendments, the Board indulged in open and sincere rejoicing.[78]

The Board could now look optimistically to the future. Its actual cash business had assumed flattering proportions and its scheme of trading for future delivery had, in its opinion, yielded satisfaction. And Chicago, the city which it called home, was circled by the lush lands of the great grain-producing states of the Middle West, whose rich bounties appeared in truth to be everlasting.[79]

THE TRADE IN LUMBER

VYING IN SIZE with the tower-like granaries that stored the abundant supply of grain were the huge stacks of lumber, board piled on board, fringing the banks of the Chicago River. West and south they

[77] The bill prescribed an annual license fee of $1,000, a tax on lard, bacon, raw cotton, hops, most grains, grass seed, flaxseed, and similar products bought or sold on options. A person applying to the collector of internal revenue for a license would be required to file a $40,000 bond and keep a record of all options or future contracts. Penalties for evasions were a fine of from $1,000 to $10,000 and six months' to ten years' imprisonment. *Cong. Record,* 52 Cong., 1 sess., XXIII, pt. VI, 5071–73, *ibid.,* 52 Cong., 2 sess., XXIV, pt. III, 2357–58.

[78] A result of the anti-option bill was an attempt of the Board of Trade in 1892 to stop trading in privileges. The Board had made other attempts. (*Chicago Tribune,* Jan. 1, 1893.) Two kinds of privileges, the " put " and " call," were practiced, at times openly and, if forbidden, sometimes covertly. A " put " is a privilege or option purchased from another to " put " (deliver) a specified amount, at a specified price, and within a stated time. A " call " is the right to demand a certain amount of stock, grain or other commodity at a fixed price, at or within a certain time agreed upon. In both transactions the general intention was not to deliver the articles. The state law, 1874, and Board of Trade rules prohibited option sales under this condition. Both regulations were ineffective.

[79] Even in the panic year 1893, the Board could report a good cash business. For export and for domestic use more than 180,000,000 bushels of grain alone had been shipped. Its grain and provision business aggregated not less than $250,000,000. Chicago Board of Trade, *Thirty-sixth Annual Report, 1893,* p. xlix.

rose twenty to thirty feet above the ground, affirmations of Chicago leadership since 1856 as the world's greatest lumber mart. Located chiefly in the Twenty-second Street district, the yards stretched along the south branch of the river southward, often with planing mill and sawmill near by.[80] Here in the late 'sixties facilities for docking had been greatly expanded. Up canals one hundred feet wide and from twelve to fourteen feet deep steamers and other watercraft carried their immense cargoes to waiting facilities which, by the 'eighties, lined about twenty miles of water front.[81]

Shortly, the excellence of these accommodations and a growing trade produced such high dockage rates that new quarters were sought in the vicinity of Thirty-fifth Street and near the stockyards, a move followed in the mid-'eighties by a migration to the Calumet area. By 1891 lumber docks lay along the north bank of the Calumet River from Ontario Avenue to The Strand, from Ninety-first to Ninety-fifth Street.[82] Other yards were situated on either side of the main branch of the Chicago River at its mouth and on or near Goose Island on the river's north branch. In time, the concentration near waterways was less conspicuous as rail service was provided, especially to the South Side yards in locations not so likely to be flooded in wet weather.[83] As business grew, officials of the yards moved into the downtown district. Executives, manufacturers, wholesalers and retailers, jobbers operating on margin, and straight commission men mingled with aggressive promoters of other thriving business enterprises. The Chamber of Commerce Building alone by 1893 housed twenty-two leaders in the lumber trade.[84]

Until the late 'eighties white pine was king of the softwoods and

[80] By 1890 the yards south and west lay principally along Robey, Lincoln, Wood, Ashland, Loomis, Archer, and Lumber streets.

[81] Andreas, *History of Chicago*, III, 368; [The Chicago Herald], *Illustrated History of Chicago* . . . (Chicago, 1887), p. 81; *Lumberman's Gazette*, XX (Jan. 4, 1882), 1.

[82] Ontario Avenue was renamed Brandon in 1913. *The Chicago Times*, Feb. 7, 1884; *Chicago Tribune*, Jan. 1, 1885, Jan. 1, 1887; *Northwestern Lumberman*, XVII (Feb. 12, 1881), 8, XXIII (Feb. 9, 1884), 10; *Lumberman's Gazette*, XX (Feb. 1, 1882), 5; *The Economist*, V (March 7, 1891), 375, VI (July 25, 1891), 164. The R. L. Henry & Co. was among the important firms which moved to the Calumet area. It and C. B. Flinn & Co. had yards at Riverdale. *The Economist*, VII (Feb. 13, 1892), 241.

[83] *Industrial Chicago*, III, *The Manufacturing Interests*, 528–29; *The Lumber Trade Journal*, XXII (July 1, 1892), 1. Goose Island was on the north branch of the Chicago River where the river divides into the north branch canal and the north branch, between West Chicago Avenue and West North Avenue.

[84] *Ibid.*, XXIV (Oct. 15, 1893), 5. The Chamber of Commerce Building was at Washington and LaSalle streets.

ranked high in construction tastes. At Chicago's very door lay the richly forested states of Michigan, Wisconsin, and Minnesota whose loggers industriously and unstintingly supplied her market. Close by, too, stretched the open prairie and the land beyond, rapidly settled by people craving means of shelter; and to the east were growing cities demanding wood for the construction needs of their physical expansion. Thus fabulous supply and ravenous demand met at Chicago and thrust the city upward in her mercurial rise to economic dominance.

The lumber business, from the first notch of the logger's ax to the manufacturer's finished product, was one for men of daring and imagination. Thousands of acres of wooded land, millions of dollars invested in the exploitation and distribution of billions of board feet, these were the units of measurement. Throughout, from 1871 to 1893, receipts at Chicago were over those of pre-Fire days. In 1872 more than a billion feet of lumber came into the city. This was in addition to shingles, lath, pickets, and cedar posts; enough, declared one observer, if " piled twenty feet high to cover about 3,000 acres of ground." [85]

As early as 1874 local lumber merchants were handling more than double the amount of any other receiving point, and the 153 firms had an invested capital estimated at $10,000,000. More than 300 boats manned by 2,500 sailors were employed to transport the year's cargo, and 7,000 men were needed to transfer, pile, and sort it. Another 2,000 worked in the mills of the city manufacturing the raw materials into doors, sash, and dressed lumber. All in all Chicago promoters looked with satisfaction upon each year's figures, translating those of 1881 into the boast that during the year the city had actually received the whole product of 300 square miles, and by 1893 that local consumption alone amounted to the entire trade of New York, the second largest market of the country.[86]

Chicago enjoyed her peak receipts in 1882, 1888, 1891, and 1892, and during these years, just as in the years before, she tapped the timberlands of the Lake States which lay close at hand. By the mid-'eighties, however, loggers had chopped out much of the stumpage

[85] Chicago Board of Trade, *Fifteenth Annual Report, 1872*, p. 84; *Lumberman's Gazette*, III (Aug., 1873), 39.

[86] *The Chicago Times*, Jan. 1, 1874; *Lumberman's Gazette*, XX (Jan. 4, 1882), 1; *The Lumber Trade Journal*, XXIV (Jan. 1, 1894), 2.

from the sections where access to lake shipping was easy. Then they sought the wooded parts of the interior from whence the raw or milled product had to be railroaded to the lake shore, there to be transshipped as water cargo. More and more the rail lines shuttled into the forested sections and made possible a continued high level of delivery to Chicago even though the Lake States were losing out as the nation's lumber-producing section.[87]

The lake was the greatest of all the highways to Chicago. From 1872 to 1882 it carried twelve times as much as the six leading railroads combined. Its leadership, however, was cut nearly in half from 1882 to 1892, although, even so, more lumber passed over it than by rail. From 1871 to 1893 boats brought to Chicago docks nearly eight times as much as came in through the six leading rail carriers combined.[88]

Of the railroads which penetrated the forested areas, the North Western from 1871 to 1893 stood highest in the amount hauled, conveying into the city over a billion feet of lumber and dislodging the Michigan Central as the main rail feeder of the Chicago market from 1872 to 1882. The Chicago & Eastern Illinois came next with approximately 72 per cent as much as the North Western load, followed by the Illinois Central, the Chicago, Milwaukee and St. Paul, the Michigan Central, and the Pittsburgh, Cincinnati and St. Louis.

In the shipment of lumber from Chicago water transport played only a small part. From 1871 to 1893 the Chicago, Burlington & Quincy Railroad took over five billion feet, nearly two and a half times the load of its closest rival, the Chicago & Alton. To the total carriage of 12,812,381,111 feet the Illinois Central, the North Western, the Rock Island, and the Wabash contributed, ranging from approximately two billion feet to about one-half that number. The

[87] Chicago receipts were 2,117,545,000 feet in 1882; 2,066,927,000 in 1888; 2,045,418,000 in 1891; and 2,203,874,000 in 1892. See Chicago Board of Trade annual reports. U. S., *Sixteenth Census, 1940*, "Manufactures," II, pt. I, 518–19; U. S. Bureau of Census, *Bulletin 77*, "Census of Manufactures: 1905, Lumber and Timber Products," p. 42.

[88] The total by lake, 1871–1893, inclusive, was 30,337,540,150 feet of lumber. The total for the six leading railroads was 3,894,747,390 feet. Only 1,634,817 feet were received over the Illinois and Michigan Canal. The total by all these routes was 34,233,922,357 feet. For detailed figures see Appendix tables showing receipts and shipments of lumber. The total number of shingles received in Chicago 1871 to 1893 by lake, the six leading railroads, and canal was 14,965,293,373; of lath, the stock on hand in Chicago rose from 27,751,520, Jan. 1, 1872, to 62,608,845, Jan. 1, 1893. Of the total received only about one-fourth was shipped out.

lines which brought the livestock, corn, and small grains to the city were, in general, those whose freight cars bore lumber on the return, the Burlington holding leadership in all.

All this redounded frequently to the advantage of Chicago over competing centers in freight rates, for large and sure return shipments promised lower rates and hence better prices.[89] A continuous struggle, however, went on between shipping interests and the railroads. The latter, in order to get business, at times undercut each other until agreements put a stop at least temporarily to such practices. Competition among lumber carriers from Chicago, Burlington (Iowa), Quincy (Illinois), Hannibal (Missouri), St. Louis, and points in Louisiana had, as early as 1871, become so keen that various railroads agreed to abandon rebates. To insure obedience to the compact, provision was made for an inspector of one line to examine the shipments of another, and, in case of disputes or violations, for a board to resolve the difficulty. Among the railroads participating in the arrangement which were large carriers of Chicago lumber were the North Western, the Illinois Central, the Rock Island, and the Chicago & Alton.[90] These mutually protective covenants among carriers, although not always binding if it seemed advantageous to any one to ignore the arrangement, nevertheless cut down what was alleged to be unfair and unprofitable competition.[91]

To Chicago distributors any attempt to bypass the city in the con-

[89] *Railroad Gazette*, VII (Feb. 20, 1875), 75. A suit by the Railroad and Warehouse Commission in McLean County against the Chicago & Alton to the effect that the road had unlawfully charged more for 110 miles from Chicago to Lexington than for 126 miles from Chicago to Bloomington resulted in a decision by the State Supreme Court adverse to the Commission. This case and the reaction of the Illinois farmers toward conditions of transportation are discussed in Bogart and Thompson, *The Industrial State, 1870–1893*, pp. 82–106; Illinois Railroad and Warehouse Commission, *Second Annual Report, 1872*, pp. 8–9; 67 Ill. 11 (1873).

[90] Other signers to the agreement, dated Oct. 14, 1871, were the Burlington and Missouri River Railroad, the Toledo, Wabash and Western Railway, the Missouri Pacific, the North Missouri Railroad, the Hannibal and St. Joseph Railroad, and the Chicago and South-Western Railway. Chicago, Burlington & Quincy Archives, *Miscellaneous Papers* (Mss. Newberry Library). The Burlington and Missouri River Railroad (Iowa Branch) running between Burlington and East Plattsmouth, Iowa, passed under the control of the Chicago, Burlington & Quincy on Jan. 1, 1873. A controlling interest in the Hannibal and St. Joseph Railroad running between Hannibal and St. Joseph, Missouri, was purchased by the Chicago, Burlington & Quincy in 1882. Henry V. Poor, *Manual of the Railroads of the United States, 1888* (New York, 1888), pp. 381, 766.

[91] The advantage of these pools was affirmed, for example, by the traffic manager of the important Chicago, Burlington & Quincy Railroad. Chicago, Burlington & Quincy Archives, *Traffic Manager's Report, 1876–78*.

signment of lumber, shingles, and such wood products by direct shipment from mill to buyer was a particularly sore point. Even after the establishment of the Interstate Commerce Commission, dealers individually and collectively tried, at times with success, to force an abrogation of tariffs not in their favor.[92] By the late 'eighties, however, rulings of the Commission against discriminatory practices began to lessen the effectiveness of the jockeying for advantage which had been conspicuous earlier.[93] A process of decentralization of wholesale distributing points was now under way in lumber and allied commodities, just as in the sale of grains and meat products. The expansion of the transportation net bringing producer and buyer closer to one another and the growing integration of the processes of lumbering were, as early as the 1880's, about to break the virtual monopoly Chicago had possessed, in spite of her stubborn resistance to these economic compulsions.[94]

Still, Chicago remained the greatest single lumber center of the United States. For loss of her onetime uncontested primacy in the sale of lumber throughout the country, the city enjoyed the rich compensation of a large local consumption. With population nearly quadrupling from 1870 to 1890, demands for timber mounted. Between 1871 and 1893 the city put up 98,838 buildings of all types, covering a frontage aggregating 2,268,303 feet at an estimated value

[92] *The Lumber Trade Journal*, XIV (Aug. 15, 1888), 8, XIX (May 15, 1891), 6, XXIV (Nov. 15, 1893), 16; *The St. Louis Lumberman*, VI (Dec., 1890), 19, 24; Agnes M. Larson, *The White Pine Industry in Minnesota* (Minneapolis, 1949), pp. 396–97.

[93] C. [Charles] E. Perkins memorandum Sept. 20, 1887, dealing with lumber rates between Chicago and the Missouri River and Nebraska points. Perkins noted the adjustment of rates to Omaha and western Iowa on an equitable basis. (Chicago, Burlington & Quincy Archives, *Pools, 1880–89*.) Various cases against the railroads dealt with discriminatory practices between large and small places. The Commission ruled that the base for determining rates should be distance, not size of shipping point. See, for example, the following cases against railroads: Euclid Martin and others constituting the freight bureau of the Omaha Board of Trade *v.* the Chicago, Burlington & Quincy Railroad Company, the Chicago & Northwestern [*sic*] Railway Company, the Union Pacific Railway Company, the Chicago, Rock Island and Pacific Railway Company, and the Burlington and Missouri River Railroad Company in Nebraska. (ICC, *Second Annual Report, 1888*, p. 115); B. S. Crews *et al.*, Committee, etc., *v.* the Richmond and Danville Railroad Company (*ibid.*, p. 107); The Manufacturers' and Jobbers' Union of Mankato, Minn. (ICC, *Fourth Annual Report, 1890*, pp. 97–98); Eau Claire Board of Trade (ICC, *Sixth Annual Report, 1892*, pp. 16–17, 99–100).

[94] *Lumberman's Gazette*, XVI (April 28, 1880), 4, XVIII (June 8, 1881), 2, XX (Jan. 4, 1882), 1, XXII (Jan. 10, 1883), 1, 2, (June 6, 1883), 2; *Chicago Tribune*, Jan. 1, 1885; *Northwestern Lumberman*, V (Feb., 1875), 40, XXII (July 7, 1883), 5; Ralph Clement Bryant, *Lumber Its Manufacture and Distribution* (New York, 1938), p. 382.

of $449,227,126.[95] The long-term growth of the city dwarfed the large construction program necessitated by the Fire, although great quantities of materials were required for rebuilding the devastated areas. Fortunately for this aspect of recovery, supplies were in part immediately available. Only 13 of the 121 lumberyards had been burned, and not over 20 per cent of the 300,000,000 feet of lumber on hand and less than 6 per cent of the 1,039,328,375 feet received in 1871 had been destroyed.[96]

Between 1870 and 1890 the city grew in each of its " mile-zones," that is, measured by the mile radially from State and Madison streets. In the latter year twice as many people lived in the eleven-to-twelve mile-zone as had been in the five-to-six mile-zone in 1870, although both represented the outer limits of metropolitan population in those years. Population of the five-to-six mile-zone leaped from 1,000 in 1870 to 70,000 twenty years later, while that in the one-to-two mile-zone increased from 115,000 to 250,000. All this growth and territorial extension of living-quarters meant more buildings, and the expansion of manufactories of wood products also added to the other demands.[97]

Ever-mounting local consumption was by the late 'eighties and early 'nineties the most important stimulus to the lumber sales of the city. In 1892 the largest receipts in Chicago's history had come in answer to the incentive of a building boom attributed to the World's Columbian Exposition, which opened to visitors from all over the world on May 1, 1893.[98] In addition to the Fair building, Chicagoans, moved by a personal and civic pride, repaired old houses and business establishments, and put up new ones even to the outskirts of the city.[99]

The lumbering business of Chicago was vivified and given direc-

[95] Hoyt, One Hundred Years of Land Values in Chicago, pp. 473–75, 483.

[96] Chicago Board of Trade, Fourteenth Annual Report, 1871, p. 80; George W. Hotchkiss, History of the Lumber and Forest Industry of the Northwest (Chicago, 1898), p. 679; Moses and Kirkland, op. cit., I, 382.

[97] Hoyt, op. cit., p. 484. Wood used in manufactured products is treated later in this volume.

[98] Receipts in 1892 were 2,203,874,000 feet. (Chicago Board of Trade, Thirty-fifth Annual Report, 1892, p. 98.) The World's Fair buildings, including the State Building and those on the Midway Plaisance, were reported as using nearly 125,000,000 feet of lumber. The St. Louis Lumberman, XI (April, 1893), 36.

[99] The Lumber Trade Journal, XIX (March 15, 1891), 12, XXI (Feb. 15, 1892), 5, (June 1, 1892), 17, XXIII (April 1, 1893), 16.

tion by the same invincible triad which energized its companion economic endeavors: the geographic location of the city, transportation by both water and rail, and the presence of intrepid and adventurous promoters. Turlington W. Harvey, Jesse Spalding, Jacob and Henry Beidler, Charles and Nathan Mears, Anthony G. Van Schaick, Thaddeus Dean, and Martin Ryerson, men of long-time leadership, continued to build up their separate undertakings alongside more recent arrivals.[100]

Their rewards were rich; they, too, belonged to the ranks of those who could count their wealth in the millions. Their interests and influence reached far beyond mere lumbering into real estate, banking, railroads and other vehicles of transportation, as well as the increasingly important mining of iron and the production of steel.[101] Their far-flung investments touched the forests of the country's northern boundary and even beyond into Canada;[102] they dipped into the deepest timberland of the South and the Far West. An omnivorous appetite for a continuing enlargement of business took them into richly wooded Mexico and the hardwood land of Hon-

[100] Pierce, A History of Chicago, II, 103–4; Victor F. Lawson to Henry Hall, Business Manager of The [New York] Tribune, May 8, 1891, Victor F. Lawson, Papers (Mss. Newberry Library); Chicago Tribune, April 6, 1890.

[101] Typical were Harvey and Spalding. Harvey, among his many investments, held shares of stock and was a onetime director of the Metropolitan National Bank and the American Trust and Savings Bank. He built lines of rail into his timberlands. He was president of the Harvey Steel Car Company and the town of Harvey, Illinois, was named for him. By 1890 he was reported worth $2,000,000. Jesse Spalding, born in 1837, onetime "raftsman" on the Susquehanna, incorporated his firm in 1871. The name of the firm became in 1882 the Spalding Lumber Company. He was a heavy investor in the Chicago and North Western Railway and in Chicago street railways and director of various banks. When he died in 1904 his wealth was reported to be $10,000,000. Chicago Record-Herald, March 18, 1904; Moses and Kirkland, op. cit., II, 697–99, I, 778–80; Industrial Chicago, III, The Manufacturing Interests, pp. 388, 390, 391–93; Currey, Chicago: Its History and Its Builders, IV, 295; Chicago Tribune, April 6, 1890.

[102] The question of free trade agitated Chicagoans interested particularly in Canadian and Mexican lumber. When agitation in favor of reciprocal arrangements between the United States and Canada came up, Chicago sentiment was divided; but wholesalers tended to favor no tax. Lumberman's Gazette, IX (March 15, 1877), 183, XXII (Feb. 28, 1883), 2, 3; The St. Louis Lumberman, IX (Feb., 1892), 35, X (Dec., 1892), 31; The Lumber Trade Journal, XXIV (Dec. 1, 1893), 4. For Chicago as a market for Canadian raw wood materials see A. R. M. Lower, The North American Assault on the Canadian Forest (Toronto, 1938), pp. 160, 177, 178. A convention of commercial reciprocity with Mexico proclaimed June 2, 1884, was endorsed by important Chicago businessmen. Among the products to be admitted from Mexico were wood and timber of all kinds, unmanufactured. Cong. Rec., 48 Cong., 2 sess., XVI, pt. I, 503; U. S., Treaties and Conventions Concluded between the United States of America and Other Powers since July 4, 1776 (Washington, 1889), pp. 714–20.

duras.[103] First, they embraced the heavily timbered lands of Michigan and Wisconsin, particularly those close to the lake with rivers near by. Then they moved farther inland, taking over thousands of acres which supplied the Chicago market with its white pine.[104]

Ownership was extended from spurs of rails to boats to docks to yards. Various companies passed through a similar evolution and shared with others the satisfactions of prosperity. Among the older concerns was the Peshtigo Company, organized by William B. Ogden in 1856, whose 160,000 acres of Wisconsin pine land yielded a cut of forty-eight to fifty million feet a year. By 1867 the company instituted carriage by barges, a type of transport which was to become increasingly popular, only to be superseded in favor in the 1880's by steam-propelled vessels.[105]

Associated with Ogden was the influential and nationally known Isaac Stephenson, onetime member of the House of Representatives and the United States Senate and holder of Wisconsin government offices. Through investments in lumber this important political figure was able to buy sizable amounts of railroad, mining, and bank stocks. Like other Wisconsin lumbermen, he and his brother Samuel M. became important figures in the economic development of Chicago. From Wisconsin to California and Louisiana, Stephen-

[103] The Honduras Lumber Company hoped to turn out 100,000 feet of lumber daily. Its possessions were valued at $7,773,000. The president was C. Sherman Wynn. (*The Lumber Trade Journal*, XIX [April 1, 1891], 7.) Advertisements of the various kinds of wood appear in the newspapers, lumber journals, and directories. See, for example, that of Hayden Brothers in 1884, "Importers in Foreign and Domestic Hardwood Lumber, Mahogany, Cherry, Walnut, Quarter Sawed Oak, Quarter Sawed Sycamore, Quarter Sawed Gum, Red Oak, White Oak, Ash, Bird's-Eye Maple, Red Birch, Etc. Etc." The advertisement included a picture of a Central American logging scene. Rand, McNally & Co., *Directory and Shipping Guide of Lumber Mills and Lumber Dealers in the United States and Canada* . . . (Chicago, 1884), facing p. 25.

[104] Harvey by the early 'eighties held some 40,000 acres in Michigan and Wisconsin. Spalding owned 120,000 acres in Wisconsin which supplied his Menekaunee mill and about 140,000 acres for his Cedar River mill. The Kirby Carpenter Company, of which Augustus A. Carpenter was president, owned 123,000 acres of pine land by the early 'eighties near the company's mill at Menominee, Michigan. [Reed & Company] *The Lumber Industry of Chicago* . . . (Chicago, [1882]), pp. 60, 69; *Industrial Chicago*, III, *The Manufacturing Interests*, 388, 389, 390–91. Many others were similarly interested.

[105] General William E. Strong, Ogden's nephew by marriage, was president of the Peshtigo Company 1873–1891. *The Lumber Industry of Chicago*, pp. 33–34; *Northwestern Lumberman*, XXI (April 21, 1883), 5–6; Isaac Stephenson, *Recollections of a Long Life, 1829–1915* (Chicago, 1915), pp. 166–70; *Industrial Chicago*, III, *The Manufacturing Interests*, 465.

son purchased wooded territory. In California, alone, he, his brother, and Henry Swartz owned 800,000,000 feet of redwood.[106]

In the 1880's acquisitive Chicagoans turned their attention to the increasingly important forests and sawmills of Minnesota. Here investments were made in 1881 and '82 by Samuel K. Martin, familiarly known as " Skinny Martin," a leading wholesaler, with whom Edward Hines was associated from 1884 until 1892 when he formed his own concern. Robert L. Henry, who had impressive holdings in Michigan and in the city of Chicago, too, became a big purchaser of Minnesota lands. During that decade the names of Morton B. Hull, Samuel B. Barker of S. B. Barker & Co., William I. Reed, and Edward H. Reed were also added to the roster of prospectors.[107] As the benefactions of the near-by white-pine states lessened, prophecies of their complete depletion assumed enough significance to influence enterprising investors to move to the South, which would become the nation's leading lumber-producing region after the turn of the century.[108]

As early as 1881 whitewood and walnut were imported from Tennessee, and a lively demand for ash on the part of Chicagoans was widely publicized among southern producers. In 1885 Chicago received her first stock of southern cypress, later to rank in favor with the previously popular white pine as finished wood. The ten-story

[106] Isaac Stephenson was not only connected with Ogden in the Peshtigo Company, but was interested as early as 1858 in the N. Ludington Company, of which he eventually held controlling interest. He became president in 1883. He became president of the I. Stephenson Company in 1888. His brother Samuel was associated with Abner Kirby. In 1861 Samuel Stephenson and Kirby, with A. A. and William O. Carpenter, established the firm of Kirby Carpenter Company. " Sam " Stephenson was with the Chicago concern until 1887. [The American Lumberman], *American Lumbermen* . . . ([3 v.] Chicago, 1905-6), I, 247, 252–54; Allen Johnson, Dumas Malone, Harris E. Starr, eds., *Dictionary of American Biography* (21 v. New York, 1928–44), XVII, 582–83; Hotchkiss, *op. cit.*, pp. 301–3; Henry Hall, ed., *America's Successful Men of Affairs* . . . (2 v. New York, 1896), II, 759.

[107] Larson, *op. cit.*, pp. 250, 274, 280; *American Lumbermen*, II, 133; Hotchkiss, *op. cit.*, pp. 542, 545, 575, 576. In the Duluth district 2,000,000 acres of pine-timber lands were offered from the public lands and 1,000,000 acres in the St. Cloud district in 1883. About 268,000 acres were sold in both districts at an average price of $1.90 an acre. U. S. Commissioner of the General Land Office, *Annual Report . . . for the Year 1883* (Washington, 1883), p. 5.

[108] *Lumberman's Gazette*, XXII (Jan. 3, 1883), 1. In 1909 the timber industry in Michigan, Wisconsin, and Minnesota dropped to 12.3 per cent of the nation's total output. In 1899 the South cut 24 per cent, nearly equaling the 24.9 per cent of the Lake States. *Ibid.*; U. S., *Sixteenth Census, 1940, loc. cit.*; U. S. National Conservation Commission, *Report*, 60 Cong., 2 sess., S. Doc. 676 (3 v. Washington, 1909), I, 56.

Montauk Block at 111 to 117 Monroe Street, designed by the architectural firm of Burnham & Root, was the first large structure to have southern pine throughout, which forecast increasing approval of this wood in building. By 1892 Chicago imports of southern pine and cypress approximated 100,000,000 feet.[109]

With the repeal of the Southern Homestead Act in 1876 and the announcement by the press in the early 'eighties that the South had over 236,000,000,000 feet of standing pine, Chicagoans, anticipating direct shipments from the South to the consumer, had turned with accelerated eagerness to that section. By 1890 the *Chicago Tribune* reported that 800,000 acres of timber in Louisiana alone were in the hands of the city's investors. Plots of wooded areas of Arkansas, Tennessee, Mississippi, and Florida had also been purchased for $1.25 an acre or less,[110] later to be sold for forty to fifty times the original price.[111]

Thither were attracted not only those directly concerned with merchandising lumber but men interested primarily in other economic enterprises who, along with many leading lumbermen, were convinced that the highest returns came not so much from logging as from the rise in the value of the stumpage. Among others, Henry W. King, wholesale clothing merchant, Franklin H. Head, railroad patron and an early promoter of iron, and Nathaniel K. Fairbank, lard and lard oil manufacturer, saw in the southern woods opportunities to enhance their even then considerable fortunes. Head purchased 109,645 acres in Louisiana, and Fairbank, in conjunction

---

[109] *Chicago Tribune*, Jan. 1, 1883, Jan. 1, 1890; *The Lumber Trade Journal*, VI (June, 1885), 19, XXXII (Aug. 15, 1897), 38; *Lumberman's Gazette*, XX (Jan. 25, 1882), 5, XXII (Jan. 3, 1883), 1; *The St. Louis Lumberman*, X (Sept., 1892), 27, XI (Jan., 1893), 29; *The Architectural Record*, XXVIII (July, 1915), 3, 7; *Industrial Chicago*, III, *The Manufacturing Interests*, 111; U. S., *Tenth Census, 1880*, IX, "Report on the Forests of North America," pt. III, 489.

[110] U. S. Bureau of Corporations, *The Lumber Industry*, pt. I, "Standing Timber," (Washington, 1913), 195–97; *Chicago Tribune*, Jan. 1, 1883, Jan. 1, 1890; *Northwestern Lumberman*, XIX (June 14, 1882), 4, XXIII (May 31, 1884), 7; *The St. Louis Lumberman*, VI (Aug., 1890), 28, X (Oct., 1892), 26, 47; *The Lumber Trade Journal*, XIX (Jan. 15, 1891), 6, XXIV (Oct. 15, 1893), 5; *Lumberman's Gazette*, XVIII (Jan. 26, 1881), 5; *The Rand-McNally Bankers' Monthly*, VI (Jan., 1889), 10.

[111] U. S. Bureau of Corporations, *The Lumber Industry*, pt. I, "Standing Timber," 256–58, pt. III, "Land Holdings of Large Timber Owners," 236. The Commissioner of the General Land Office throughout the 'eighties complained of the low price paid by lumber speculators in various sections and of the way in which they got the land. See, for example, U. S. Commissioner of the General Land Office, *Annual Report, 1883*, p. 5, *1886*, p. 80, *1887*, p. 87; *Northwestern Lumberman*, XXI (April 28, 1883), 41.

with the resourceful Harvey, said to be the largest lumber operator in the country in the 1880's, bought 86,159 acres at $1.25 an acre. This they shortly sold to the Long-Bell Company, a Missouri corporation, at a good profit.[112] Before the 'eighties closed, Van Schaick and A. A. Carpenter had also added 70,274 acres to their already large holdings, and Samuel B. Barker, through a purchase of 28,380 acres, touched the perimeter of the rich Middle Country with timberland in both Minnesota and Louisiana.[113]

Florida land, too, was cheap and available. R. L. Henry in 1888 got 122,000 acres, for a part of which he was said to have paid as little as twenty-five cents an acre. The Florida Land Syndicate composed of Chicagoans took up 120,000 acres in that state at a reported $125,000. Later it was rumored that by sale a profit of 450 per cent was realized on the investment. Still another group pooling their resources in a common undertaking was directed to Georgia by the Illinois and Georgia Improvement Company. Capitalized at $1,000,000 and organized in 1890 not only to complete a Georgia railroad but to obtain timbered land, the company included among other Chicagoans Alexander C. Soper, an important dealer in the city since the mid-'sixties.[114]

At the end of 1888 the investment in the city in stocks, carrying vessels, and other aspects of the business was estimated at about $35,000,000, and in lumber plants, standing timber, and subsidiaries of the business tributary to the Chicago market totaled more than $80,000,000. By 1892 wholesalers alone were reported doing a business of $43,000,000.[115] With more capital available, large lumber dealers opened line lumberyards in towns in the consuming area, even as

[112] Paul Wallace Gates, "Federal Land Policy in the South, 1866–1888," *The Journal of Southern History*, VI (Aug., 1940), 313–26; U. S. Bureau of Corporations, *The Lumber Industry*, pt. II, "Concentration of Ownership in Important Selected Regions," (Washington, 1914), facing p. 148; *Moody's Manual of Railroads and Corporation Securities, 1913* (New York, 1913), II, 4915.

[113] Anthony G. Van Schaick, a member of Ludington, Wells & Van Schaick Co., held large tracts of land in Michigan and Wisconsin besides establishments at Menominee and Escanaba, Michigan. His firm owned docks along a half-mile waterfront in Chicago. Hotchkiss, *op. cit.*, p. 308; *The Lumber Industry of Chicago*, p. 87; *Lumberman's Gazette*, XIV (April 23, 1879), 7.

[114] *The St. Louis Lumberman*, VI (Aug., 1890), 28; *The Economist*, IV (Aug. 16, 1890), 254; Gates, "Federal Land Policy in the South, 1866–1888," *loc. cit.*, pp. 323, 325, 326. Advertisements of available land appeared in newspapers and lumber periodicals purchasable through Chicago and southern realtors. The Illinois Central conducted excursions of lumbermen. *Lumberman's Gazette*, XXIII (Dec. 26, 1883), 3.

[115] *Chicago Tribune*, Jan. 1, 1889; *The St. Louis Lumberman*, XI (Jan., 1893), 35.

far west as Colorado and Wyoming. The Chicago Lumber Company, with a cash capital of about three million dollars by 1884, had 102 yards chiefly in towns of Kansas, Iowa, Nebraska, and Missouri. The Harvey interests owned over ninety yards in the same states. With competition at times keen, these outlying yards and the traveling salesmen, dispatched throughout the consuming areas, often served effectively in the sale of the central management's goods and aided in retarding the inroads of aspiring competitors.[116]

At the same time the number of small operators, both wholesale and retail, grew less. Combinations multiplied, able to adjust the supply to the demand and to enjoy, until the late 'eighties at least, frequent favors in rates for transportation. As ownership of timberland, mill, and lumberyard came to reside more and more in the hands of men of capital, companies selling shares of stock also became more numerous.[117] Throughout, commission men were significant figures in the commercial hierarchy, although the heyday of their importance passed as manufacturers acquired more capital with which to carry on their activities.[118]

At hand, too, was the day of the specialized dealer when one type of product was carried exclusively. An important lumberman and investor in Mexican and Arizona timberlands, Edward E. Ayer, sold railroad materials; Edgar E. Washburne and Son handled only one kind of wood, black walnut; Norwood & Butterfield Co. emphasized the sale of yellow pine; and Everett W. Hotchkiss advertised California redwood lumber and shingles.[119]

[116] The Harvey yards were under the National Lumber Company, the White Pine Lumber Company, the Jones & Magee Company of which Harvey was president. *Industrial Chicago,* III, *The Manufacturing Interests,* 387–90; Currey, *op. cit.,* V, 251; *The Lumber Trade Journal,* VII (March, 1885), 10, VIII (Jan. 1, 1886), 5; Andreas, *History of Chicago,* III, 374, 379; *Northwestern Lumberman,* XXI (Jan. 27, 1883), 9, 12; Bryant, *op. cit.,* pp. 382, 388.

[117] Paul W. Gates, *The Wisconsin Pine Lands of Cornell University* (Ithaca, New York, 1943), p. 123; *Northwestern Lumberman,* VII (July 22, 1876), 236, XXI (April 21, 1883), 10, (April 28, 1883), 4; *Lumberman's Gazette,* XVI (April 14, 1880), 4, XX (Jan. 4, 1882), 1, XXIII (Aug. 8, 1883), 3; *The St. Louis Lumberman,* VI (Aug., 1890), 28. The H. Witbeck Company and the Oconto Company were typical of stock-sharing firms. Nathan and Charles H. Mears were connected with the latter. *Northwestern Lumberman,* XXXVII (April 18, 1891), 5; Hotchkiss, *op. cit.,* pp. 434–35; *The Lumber Industry in Chicago,* pp. 15, 28–29.

[118] Among the important commission men were Robert H. McElwee, H. G. Billings, and William J. Carney of McElwee, Billings and Carney with offices at 244 South Water Street. In 1890 the firm was McElwee and Carney.

[119] Ayer was president of the Mexican Lumber Company, incorporated in 1884 with

The propensity to organize, which Alexis de Tocqueville in the 1830's observed as a striking characteristic of Americans, was abundantly illustrated in Chicago in a variety of associations which sprang up. The Lumberman's Exchange, chartered in 1869 and lasting longer than some of its contemporaries, provided its members much needed statistical material on the state of the market and other information helpful to an understanding of an increasingly complex mechanism. Smaller than the Board of Trade, it nonetheless exercised a considerable influence in lumber transactions. It served as the spokesman of those who, despite pronouncements favoring unrestricted competition, objected to its literal application, particularly as it affected prices. The Exchange became the focal point of the feud which developed between jobbers and manufacturers, each sparring for control of the offices. On February 28, 1891 the Exchange was reorganized as the Lumbermen's Association of Chicago, and was joined by the Chicago Lumber Yard Dealers' Association and the Chicago Hardwood Dealers' Association. Much of its attention was to be pointed toward the ubiquitous problem of freight rates in the hope of obtaining favorable tariffs for Chicago, a matter upon which all segments of the trade could agree.[120]

As early as 1874 a Retail Dealers' Association primarily to encourage the proper inspection of lumber was formed. In 1877 the National Retail Lumber Dealers' Association, with headquarters in Chicago, took over the functions of the earlier local group. Composed largely of men in Kansas, Missouri, Iowa, and Illinois, it endeavored through a united front to provide protection for its members from what was held the encroachment of manufacturers and wholesalers in retailing supplies. In 1890 the Association broke up

a capital of $150,000. He had a sawmill at Flagstaff, Arizona. Frederick W. Norwood and John S. Butterfield of Norwood & Butterfield Co. in 1890 established the town of Norfield, Mississippi, where they erected a mill and bought 50,000 acres of timberland. They had other land in Mississippi. *The Lumber Industry of Chicago*, pp. 26, 62; Hotchkiss, *op. cit.*, pp. 708–9; *Northwestern Lumberman*, XXIII (March 29, 1884), 3.

120 Pierce, *A History of Chicago*, II, 104–5; Hotchkiss, *op. cit.*, pp. 683–84; Moses and Kirkland, *op. cit.*, I, 387; Chicago Lumber Institute, *Charter and By-Laws* (Lumber Trade Association of Cook County), p. 4; *Northwestern Lumberman*, XXI (March 10, 1883), 2, (March 31, 1883), 4; *The Lumber Trade Journal*, XIX (March 1, 1891), 6; *The Timberman*, XXIII (Aug. 21, 1897), 118. The highest membership the Lumberman's Exchange had was 156. *The American Lumberman*, April 8, 1905, p. 23. George W. Hotchkiss was secretary of the Lumberman's Exchange from 1881 to 1887. He wrote extensively on the subject of lumber including the *History of the Lumber and Forest Industry of the Northwest* (Chicago, 1898), and was president and editor of *The Lumber Trade Journal*, 1887–1905.

and was replaced generally by state organizations, an Illinois Retail Lumber Dealers' Association taking care of Chicago men.[121] For those of specialized retailing the Chicago Hardwood Dealers' Association was typical. Organized in 1888 on leaving the Lumberman's Exchange, it continued its interest in rules for the inspection of lumber products. Upon the withdrawal of commission men and inspectors from the Exchange, it joined in the reorganization of the latter in 1891 and became a member of the newly formed Lumbermen's Association of Chicago.[122]

For wholesalers the Chicago Lumber Yard Dealers' Association beginning 1888 waged a tireless battle to get the railroad tariffs it desired.[123] It had been preceded as an agency of special purpose by the Lumber Manufacturers' Association of the Northwest, which had, by the mid-'eighties, enlisted as members the producers of about one-half the output of the mills of the Wisconsin, Michigan, and Minnesota region to promote fair trade and stability in business.[124] The far-flung and varied investments of Chicago lumbermen cultivated an attachment to regional and national as well as local organizations. Although not always as effective as the pressure blocs of a later day, activities were well enough directed to cause the *Northwestern Lumberman* to observe in 1876 that " trade organizations, local and general, have come to be regarded as essential aids to commerce." [125]

The spokesman of the Chicago lumber interests was the *North-*

---

[121] Chicago Board of Trade, *Seventeenth Annual Report, 1874*, p. 12; *The St. Louis Lumberman*, IX (Feb., 1892), 40; *Lumberman's Gazette*, XI (Aug. 30, 1877), 2, XIV (Jan. 8, 1879), 1, XXII (May 16, 1883), 6, 16, (May 23, 1883), 4, XXIII (Sept. 19, 1883), 1; Bryant, *op. cit.*, p. 315. The United States Lumberman's Association, established in Chicago in 1890, became the agency of retail secretaries. In 1896 it became the Lumber Secretaries' Association and included the secretaries of all branches of lumbering. *Ibid.*, p. 317.

[122] *Northwestern Lumberman*, XXIX (March 19, 1887), 3; Hotchkiss, *op. cit.*, p. 684.

[123] For a meeting of Chicago dealers with representatives of the Chicago and North Western Railway to prevent Menominee, Michigan, yard men and manufacturers from shipping directly to consumers see *Northwestern Lumberman*, XXII (July 7, 1883), 5. See also, for complaints of yard dealers, *The Lumber Trade Journal*, XIV (Aug. 15, 1888), 8.

[124] The Chicago Herald, *Illustrated History of Chicago*, p. 83; *Northwestern Lumberman*, XXI (March 17, 1883), 6, (March 24, 1883), 4, XXV (Jan. 3, 1885), 7; *The Timberman*, I (Sept. 25, 1886), 6; Bryant, *op. cit.*, pp. 303, 319; *The Lumber Trade Journal*, XIV (Aug. 15, 1888), 8; *Industrial Chicago*, II, *The Building Interests*, 352. The Chicago Sash, Door and Blind Manufacturers' and Dealers' Protective Association in 1885 lobbied against the state lien law. *Northwestern Lumberman*, XXV (March 7, 1885), 16. Organizations of wood manufacturers are discussed later in this volume.

[125] *Northwestern Lumberman*, VII (March 18, 1876), 34. Chicago was an important place for conventions of regional and national associations.

western Lumberman, styled by its contemporary, the Bay City, Michigan, *Lumberman's Gazette,* the epitome of "brass" and "egotistic vanity," and that "North Windy Lunkhead of Chicago." [126] It was, despite this uncomplimentary description, a journal of great influence, with its statistical reports of market conditions and other important aspects of the lumber trade, and its pronouncements on the gold standard for the currency, so-called "patent monopolies," and "working-class agitation." [127] *The Lumber Trade Journal* began publication in 1882 primarily as an organ of retailers, and *Hardwood* sought to serve the needs of a specialty dealer. With the *Lumberman's Gazette* of Bay City, Michigan, *The St. Louis Lumberman,* and other trade periodicals, Chicago publications provided the lumber interests up-to-date information of local, national, and even international significance.[128] In their pages were reflected the hopes and fears of the special group they represented.

On her journals as upon other parts of the lumber trade Chicago looked with pride, satisfied that not even the great market of New York excelled her. Despite this enviable standing, however, trade in lumber failed to attain the position held by the thriving traffic in grain. Nor did it, during the years between the Great Fire and the Columbian Exposition, match the huge dollar volume of the vastly expanding industry of meat packing.

126 *Lumberman's Gazette,* XXII (May 16, 1883), 6. The *Northwestern Lumberman* was established in 1873 and ran until it combined with *The Timberman* January 1, 1899, to form the *American Lumberman.* It changed from a monthly to a weekly in 1876. *The Timberman* was started July, 1886, with James Elliot Defebaugh and A. [Albert] H. Hitchcock editors.

127 *Northwestern Lumberman,* V (Feb., 1875), 44, VI (Nov., 1875), 161, VII (Feb. 26, 1876), 60, XXI (May 12, 1883), 3; *Chicago Herald,* May 11, 1886; Gates, *The Wisconsin Pine Lands of Cornell University,* p. 227.

128 *The Lumber Trade Journal* was published first in 1882. In 1931 it was merged with the *Southern Timberman.* In 1895 it was moved from Chicago to New Orleans. *Hardwood* began publication in 1892 and in 1897 merged with *Hardwood Record.* The *Lumberman's Gazette* (Bay City, Michigan) was published 1872 to 1886, and then taken over by *The Timberman.* *The St. Louis Lumberman* was published 1888 to 1918 when it became *Lumber* with separate editions for dealers and manufacturers, and then the *National Lumberman.* The last was merged in 1932 with the *American Lumberman.*

CHAPTER IV

THE ECONOMIC EMPIRE
OF CHICAGO: LIVESTOCK
AND MEAT PACKING

FASCINATING AND AMAZING as the chronicle of the trade in grains and lumber may be, it is no more so than that of the traffic in livestock and the growth of the city's meat-packing industry. When the Union Stock Yard opened for business on Christmas Day, 1865, the supremacy of Chicago in this domain was already acknowledged — a leadership which would be fortified in the decades succeeding the Fire by astronomical records in both receipts and shipments.

The 'seventies and 'eighties were marked by a notable shift from the marketing of live cattle and swine to their conversion into meat by the packing industry. Controlled by men of indomitable courage and bold vision, the industry was destined to become the greatest of its kind in the world, its products widely accepted as a part of the diet of civilized man. This phenomenal expansion was reflected in the years from 1872 to 1892 by hog receipts jumping about 137 per cent, cattle 422 per cent, and sheep 591 per cent.[1] More important than the increased numbers of live animals received was the growing

---

[1] Receipts of live hogs reached 3,252,623 in 1872; 5,817,504 in 1882; and 7,714,435 in 1892; of cattle, 684,075; 1,582,530; 3,571,796; of sheep, 310,211; 620,887; 2,145,079; of horses, 12,145; 13,856; 86,998. Chicago Board of Trade, *Thirty-sixth Annual Report, 1893*, pp. 42, xxxiii. See also The Drovers' Journal, *Drovers' Journal Yearbook of Figures of the Livestock Trade, 1934* (Chicago, 1935). The Chicago Board of Trade reports and the United States decennial census provide statistical information. These sources at times are inconsistent for the same items over a series of years. For example, calves are sometimes enumerated separately and sometimes with cattle. Figures for Cook County are substantially those for Chicago. For receipts and shipments of livestock and meats by principal carriers in the decades 1872–81 and 1882–91, see Appendix tables.

proportion slaughtered and packed in the city.[2] The measure of growth evidenced in the dollar value of the packers' products was equally impressive and prophetic. The $19,153,851 of 1870 appeared insignificant indeed in the light of the $85,324,371 of 1880 and the $194,337,838 of 1890 — an expansion of over 900 per cent in twenty years! At the same time capital mounted 511 per cent. From 1870 to 1890, also, the proportion of the city's workers employed in meat packing approximately doubled, their absolute number increasing by 719 per cent and their earnings by more than 2400 per cent.[3]

This well-being clearly mirrored the changes which had taken place since the days when Archibald Clybourne, George W. Dole, and Gurdon S. Hubbard drove cattle, hogs, and sheep from the Wabash, at first to supply a pressing local need, and then to send the surplus either as live or packed beef and pork to outlying districts served by lake and canal. As the agricultural frontier extended westward, the area of greatest livestock production moved with it. By the 1880's primacy in the yield of cattle and swine slipped from the East North Central States to the West North Central, and with this change Chicago profited greatly. Located in the heart of the Corn Belt where hog production was highest and where cattle and sheep from Texas and the western range states were sent for fattening, the city enjoyed a natural superiority over other marketing centers.[4]

[2] The beef pack (March 1 to March 1) multiplied almost 157 times in twenty years, increasing from 15,755 cattle in 1872–73 to 697,033 in 1882–83, and 2,469,373 in 1892–93. The pork pack approximately tripled, growing from 1,456,650 hogs in 1872–73 to 4,222,780 in 1882–83, and 4,352,095 in 1892–93. If one assumes that the difference between total receipts of live cattle and hogs and total shipments of the same represents the number slaughtered in the city during the year, slaughtered cattle increased over fourteen times in this period, from 174,050 in 1872 to 661,521 in 1882, and 2,450,121 in 1892. The number of hogs slaughtered increased over three times, from 1,417,029 in 1872 to 4,069,782 in 1882, and 4,778,290 in 1892. Conversely, receipts of dressed hogs declined from 235,905 in 1872 to 5,272 in 1892. Slaughtered sheep increased over ten times, from 165,195 in 1872 to 314,687 in 1882, and 1,661,711 in 1892.

[3] The 1870 value-of-product figure is that given in the census for Cook County, meat, packed, pork. Capital increased from $6,361,000 in 1870 to $38,878,995 in 1890. The increase was 511.2 per cent. In 1870, 2,129 employees were paid $425,560 in wages; 7,478 received $3,392,748 in 1880; 17,439 in 1890 got $10,691,692.

[4] Percentage of the nation's total:

	Swine			Cattle		
	1870	1880	1890	1870	1880	1890
East North Central	28.79	27.31	26.11	22.75	19.23	15.67
West North Central	16.22	29.19	39.11	12.33	20.68	27.01

Further advantages arose from the increasing lines of rail that stretched, like the spokes of a wheel, into the surplus-production areas which poured their bounties into the self-proclaimed " Garden City of the West." Those roads which fetched to the city the grains of the surplus-supply states carried also the livestock to be converted into meat products or to be sent on to other slaughtering points. The Chicago, Burlington & Quincy was most often in first place, with the Chicago & Alton, the Chicago, Rock Island and Pacific, the Chicago and North Western, and, after 1883, the Chicago, Milwaukee and St. Paul holding positions among the five leaders. The same roads, with the exception of the Illinois Central rather than the Chicago & Alton, were consistently among the upper five in the transport of hogs and sheep.[5]

In the shipment of cattle, hogs, and sheep from Chicago concentration of traffic within a few leading roads is also found, lessening, as time went on, because of a greater number of available carriers. As with receipts, however, the highest ranking railroads continued substantially in the lead, the Pittsburgh, Fort Wayne and Chicago and the Lake Shore and Michigan Southern being the recipients of the greatest patronage and indicating that at this time movement was chiefly eastward.[6] For barreled pork and beef in the 'seventies, the same roads, joined by the Michigan Central, were most often the leading carriers, but lake transport cut into and sometimes usurped their leadership. In the 'eighties and early 'nineties the Chicago and Grand Trunk and the Wabash at times disputed the primacy of the principals of the 'seventies, while the lake continued to threaten rail dominance. By the early 'eighties dressed beef was conveyed in largest amount by the Grand Trunk, superseded in the 'nineties by the

East North Central States include Ohio, Indiana, Illinois, Michigan, Wisconsin. West North Central include Minnesota, Iowa, Missouri, North Dakota, South Dakota, Nebraska, Kansas. In 1890 the Mountain States assumed leadership in the production of sheep and lambs. U. S., *Fourteenth Census, 1920,* V, " Agriculture," 572, 586, 598, 740.

[5] In 1875 the Illinois Central was third but dropped behind other roads until after 1893. The Wabash Railway ranked fifth in carrying sheep in 1893, pushing out the Rock Island.

[6] Young calves from states east of Chicago, especially Michigan, Ohio, and New York, found their way through Chicago to Iowa, Missouri, and Illinois in the early 1880's, particularly when eastern pasturage was poor. In comparison with the movement of cattle to the East, the westward movement was a mere trickle. The greatest number came west by the Lake Shore and Michigan Southern, the Michigan Central, and the Baltimore & Ohio, 1881–84. U. S. Department of Agriculture, Bureau of Animal Industry, *First Annual Report, 1884* (Washington, 1885), pp. 250–53; Chicago Board of Trade reports, 1881–89.

Michigan Central. Occasionally other lines, such as the Illinois Central in the carriage of barreled pork, gained enough to offer a challenge to earlier leaders.[7]

As the proportion of live animals shipped out of the city decreased, the mounting demand for processed meats was in every way a rich compensation. This trade, wavering with the mood of the market, enhanced the significance of Chicago as meat provisioner of the world.[8] To this vast enterprise, which tapped deeply the fount of Chicago's expanding empire as probably no other single business venture did, was brought, after the mid-'seventies and throughout the 'eighties, the economic imagination and commercial acumen of " the Big Three " — Philip D. Armour, Gustavus Swift, and Nelson Morris. The emergence of these men marked the passing of an old order in supplying meats to consumers, at first in this country and then other parts of the civilized world. Each had risen when still young from the lowly estate of measuring the return of his labor by a day's pay to the heights of counting his wealth in millions.

The first of this triumvirate to reach Chicago was Nelson Morris, familiarly known as " Nels," born of Jewish parents in Hechingen, Germany, in the shadow of the Black Forest. He came to America following the Revolution of 1848, and for three months after his arrival in 1851 earned a scanty living as an apprentice peddler in Massachusetts and New Hampshire, then for a year as charcoal burner in Connecticut, to engage next in hard manual labor in the coal fields of Pennsylvania. In 1854 he made his way west, working for his passage on an Erie Canal boat to Buffalo and then on a freighter to Michigan City, journeying from there on foot to Chicago and fortune. Here he found employment with John B. Sherman, operating stockyards on the old Myrick property north of Thirty-first Street at Cottage Grove Avenue, at five dollars a month in addition to room and board. Offered $100 a month at the end of his second year, Morris, endowed with imagination and resolution, went into business for himself. With money he had saved he bought disabled stock, speculating at first in dead hogs and those which

---

[7] Dressed beef is listed in Board of Trade reports beginning 1883. For details of transportation see Appendix tables.

[8] Within only three years, 1881–1884, for instance, nearly 89 per cent of the dressed beef received in Boston, New York, and Philadelphia bore the mark of Chicago. U. S. Bureau of Animal Industry, *First Annual Report, 1884*, p. 267.

others considered unsalable. His shrewdness was next directed into the packing of meats, begun in 1859. The Civil War gave him, as it did Armour, an opportunity to acquire army contracts which, with a trade developed in Europe, lifted him to the millionaire class.[9]

Morris was thus well established in Chicago when Armour and Swift arrived. The rise of Philip D. Armour, from ditch-digger in California in the 'fifties to the greatest pork packer of his day, is as extraordinary as was that of Morris. He came to Chicago in 1875, bringing with him Michael Cudahy, superintendent of the Plankinton and Armour packing plant of Milwaukee in which he had been a partner.[10] Within the next decade Armour's insatiable ambition and uncanny insight into the economic processes of the day made him master of packing, elevator, and storage interests not only in the Middle West but in the East as well. By 'ninety-three net profits of his business were said to be $2,000,000, the rate of profit on net worth reaching 16.7 per cent. In 1890 Armour's wealth was estimated at $25,000,000.[11]

Gustavus F. Swift, like Armour, was born in the East, and also like the famous pork baron reached Chicago in 1875. Here, in the already

[9] The estimated wealth of Morris in 1890 was $8,000,000. (Paul Gilbert and Charles Lee Bryson, *Chicago and Its Makers* [Chicago, 1929], p. 706.) Ira Nelson Morris, *Heritage from My Father* (New York, 1947), pp. 2–10; Nelson Morris, "Personal Reminiscences of the Chicago Market," *Breeders' Gazette*, XLVI (Dec. 2, 1904), 1156; *The Universal Jewish Encyclopedia*, VII, 656; U. S. Federal Trade Commission, *Food Investigation. Report . . . on Private Car Lines, 1919* (Washington, 1920), p. 28 (hereafter cited as FTC, *Report on Private Car Lines, 1919*); *Chicago Record-Herald*, Aug. 28, 1907; *The Drovers' Journal*, July 12, 1887; Rudolf A. Clemen, "Nelson Morris," *Dictionary of American Biography*, XIII, 217–18. California Cooperative Canneries, Appellant *vs.* United States of America, Swift & Company, Armour & Company *et al.*, appellees. Court of Appeals of the District of Columbia, Jan. term, 1924, no. 4071. "Answer of Morris and Company," pp. 77–78, Packer Consent Decree, 1920, I.

[10] The Rev. Dr. Frank W. Gunsaulus, "Philip D. Armour: A Character Sketch," *American Monthly Review of Reviews*, XXIII (Feb., 1901), 167–76; Harper Leech and John Charles Carroll, *Armour and His Times* (New York, 1938), pp. 1–35; Cora Lillian Davenport, *The Rise of the Armours An American Industrial Family* (unpublished M. A. Thesis, The University of Chicago, 1930), p. 54; *Mixed Drinks*, III (Nov. 1, 1890), 5; Still, *Milwaukee*, p. 187; Pierce, *A History of Chicago*, II, 96. A useful chronology of packing firms can be found in FTC, *Report on the Meat-Packing Industry, 1919*, Summary and pt. I (Washington, 1919), 237–40.

[11] Armour profits, according to company figures, mounted from $199,000 in 1873 to $1,705,000 in 1882, while the estimated net worth rose from $258,000 to $5,500,000. The net worth in 1893 was put at $12,000,000. FTC, *Report on the Meat-Packing Industry, 1919*, pt. V, "Profits of the Packers," 21; Gilbert and Bryson, *op. cit.*, p. 705; *The Rand-McNally Bankers' Monthly*, V (Feb., 1888), 45. J. Ogden Armour joined his father's business in 1883. In a year he became a partner. Edward N. Wentworth, *A Biographical Catalog of the Portrait Gallery of the Saddle and Sirloin Club* (Chicago, 1920), p. 176.

great transshipment point of the country, he beheld the rising star of
his empire. In 1853 at the age of fourteen his education in meats began under the tutelage of his brother in a Massachusetts butcher
shop. As independent slaughterer and meat dealer, and as wholesaler
of cattle, he singly and with others developed a widespread trade in
meats before coming to Chicago. His early experience thus gave him
an advantage which proved invaluable in establishing him later as
the leader of the beef-packing industry.[12]

Like his contemporaries, Swift tolerated neither sloth nor timidity,
and, undaunted by the start of other pioneers, this cattle buyer soon
turned his talents to dressed beef, which, in the winter of 1877, he
began shipping to Boston. Although other cattle dealers may have
appreciated what the shifting supply areas signified for the hungry
of the East, Swift, probably more than most of his contemporaries,
realized that prosperity eventually would pass to shippers supplying
meat in other than the form of the live animal.[13]

Each of these men, Morris, Swift, and Armour, kept the control of
his enterprise in the hands of the immediate family.[14] Fairly early,
however, Swift turned to selling shares of stock to obtain capital for
permanent improvements, disposing of his first issue largely to
Easterners, men interested in the sale of meat, both wholesale and
retail. New issues of stock paralleled a gratifying expansion in business. Incorporated in 1885 with a capitalization of $300,000 and 6
shareholders, expanding in 1886 to $3,000,000 and 109 stockholders,
Swift's concern had, by 1893, a capital of $15,000,000 and 1,604 stock-
holders.

Both audacity and wizardry motivated him in the consistent extension of his undertakings regardless of the condition of the money
market. Turning back into the business a substantial share of the
profits, Swift, from the time of the incorporation of his company,
April 1, 1885, however, distributed satisfying dividends, paying as
much as 27 per cent in 1892. In order to indulge his yearning for expansion, he borrowed heavily. In 1893 his company owed about

[12] Louis F. Swift in collaboration with Arthur Van Vlessingen, *The Yankee of the Yards* (Chicago, 1927), pp. 13, 16–18, 26–28, 49, 52, 91; Helen Swift, *My Father and My Mother* (Chicago, 1937), pp. 3–4, 6, 29; Thomas W. Goodspeed, "Gustavus Franklin Swift," *The University* [of Chicago] *Record*, VII (April, 1921), 90–98.
[13] See, for example, U. S. Department of Agriculture, *Annual Report, 1870*, pp. 250–54.
[14] FTC, *Report on the Meat-Packing Industry, 1919*, Summary and pt. I, 87–89.

$10,000,000. When the Panic of 1893 came, Swift & Company, with this considerable indebtedness to banks, particularly in the East, was seriously threatened when loans were called in. So confident, however, were friends and employees of Swift's ability to put through any program he had initiated, that they poured into his keeping enough to tide him over his difficulties. When September came, his $10,000,000 indebtedness to banks was reduced to $1,000,000.[15]

Armour, like Swift, not only borrowed whenever he felt it desirable, but he turned back into his undertaking a substantial portion of his profits. From 1868 to 1880, alone, he reinvested over 80 per cent in order to keep abreast of the rapid development of his meat business. Through speculation he further enlarged his financial resources, playing the market heavily in both pork and grain, extending his holdings over the warehousing of grain, buying salt mills in New York, as well as financing fruit acreage in the South and transporting its harvests.[16]

Like grain, pork was a commodity which aroused the instinct for speculation in men like Armour, men willing to take long-range hazards. In July, 1879, Armour and Company began to purchase pork at $8.00 a barrel. When it rose to $14 Armour sold, making, according to reports, a neat $2,000,000. He, however, continued to buy and the price receded to $9.25 a barrel, snapping up gains and an additional million. Not deterred by this loss, the company, in April, 1880, started purchases at an average of $10 a barrel, until it had acquired an estimated 250,000 to 350,000 barrels of spot pork and 1,250,000 of options by draining supplies in both Europe and the

[15] Louis F. Swift entered business with his father in 1875, Edwin C. Swift, Gustavus's brother, in 1878, a second son, Edward F., in 1880, and another son, Charles H., in 1893. (Swift & Company, *Yearbook, 1925,* p. 50.) L. F. Swift, *op. cit.,* pp. 27–44, 203; U. S. Commissioner of Corporations, *Report on the Beef Industry, 1905,* pp. 30–31, 286; Swift & Company, *Yearbook, 1900,* p. 21; *The Economist,* Investor's Supplement, May 8, 1897, p. 39, IX (May 6, 1893), 631; Swift & Company, *Yearbook, 1938,* p. 30; *The Dovers' Journal,* Sept. 15, 1883, July 24, 1884; Swift *Ms.* (Swift Library). When Swift in the summer of 1893 asked for a loan of $1,000,000 of the First National Bank he received it, although he then owed the bank $2,500,000. Helen Swift, *My Father and My Mother,* p. 98.

[16] J. Ogden Armour, *In the Matter of the Investigation of the Packing Industry,* testimony before the U. S. House of Representatives Committee on Interstate and Foreign Commerce, Jan., 1919, p. 12; *The Drovers' Journal,* March 2, Aug. 10, 1887; *Chicago Tribune,* Aug. 3, 1891, Jan. 7, 1901; J. Ogden Armour, *The Packers and the Private Car Lines and the People* (Philadelphia, 1906), pp. 26–28; L. D. H. Weld, *Private Freight Cars and American Railways* (Columbia University, *Studies in History, Economics and Public Law,* XXXI, New York, 1908), pp. 19–20; *The Knights of Labor,* III (June 6, 1888), 1; U. S. Commissioner of Corporations, *Report on the Beef Industry, 1905,* p. 33.

United States. In October these purchases were sold for as high as $18.50 a barrel and Armour profited to the tune of from six to seven millions. Between April and October, because of his activities, the price of pork more than doubled, and provision prices mounted throughout the world in what the London *Times* described as " one of the largest and most successful speculations that ever excited the brain of Chicago." [17]

In 1884 Armour engineered another successful corner. With a large amount of pork on hand following the collapse of Grant & Ward, New York brokers and bankers, he was forced either to move boldly and quickly or to lose heavily, because a pool headed by New York speculators began selling to break the market. To protect his own holdings Armour gave orders to buy all that was offered, with the result that brokers soon found that they had sold him more pork than all the packing houses in the country could produce in six months. To fill their contracts, they then had to buy from him. Again he profited richly, this time about four million dollars.[18]

Although the so-called " Big Three " undoubtedly set the pace, others of impressive stature also played their parts in making Chicago the greatest meat-packing center of the world. Sometimes George H. Hammond of the George H. Hammond & Company packing house at Hammond, Indiana, made up a fourth in the commonly designated " Big Four." [19] Incorporated as beef packers in 1881 with a capital of $1,500,000, the firm reached a capitalization of $2,500,000 in 1888, although after Hammond's death in 1886 the importance of the company waned. In 1890, following the organization of the G. H. Hammond Company, Limited, under the English

[17] *The Chicago Times,* Oct. 2, Nov. 5, 1880, Aug. 27, 1881; Chicago Board of Trade, *Twenty-third Annual Report, 1880,* p. xix; *The Times* [London], Nov. 19, 1880; *The Knights of Labor,* I (Jan. 29, 1887), 9.

[18] *Chicago Tribune,* Jan. 7, 1901; *New York Tribune,* May 7, 8, 1884. Ex-President U. S. Grant was a member of the Grant & Ward firm. For the William A. Young pork corners of 1874 in which Young was said to have lost a half million, most of which went into the pockets of Plankinton and Armour, see *Chicago Tribune,* Jan. 1, 1875. For Armour's speculative activity of the 1860's see Pierce, *A History of Chicago,* II, 99.

[19] Hammond moved to Detroit in 1854. He had, however, large interests in the Chicago stockyards. Hammond, Indiana, was named for him. *Chicago Tribune,* Dec. 31, 1886; *The Drovers' Journal,* Sept. 8, 1883, Dec. 30, 1886, Aug. 10, 1889; U. S. Senate Select Committee, *Report of the Select Committee on the Transportation and Sale of Meat Products,* 1890, 51 Cong., 1 sess., S. Rept. 829 (Washington, 1890), p. 4; Howard C. Hill, " The Development of Chicago as a Center of the Meat Packing Industry," *Mississippi Valley Historical Review,* X (Dec., 1923), 269.

Companies Act, the Chicago-Hammond enterprise passed into the hands of an English concern with plants and agencies at Chicago, Hammond, Omaha, Detroit, Boston, New York, Liverpool, and London.[20]

Destined later to assume a position of prominence in meat-packing history, the Cudahy organization had its beginning in 1890. Michael Cudahy was an Armour associate until 1887, at which time he joined his brother Edward and Armour in purchasing a plant in South Omaha. In 1890 Michael bought out the Armour holding in the Armour-Cudahy establishment and sold his interest in Armour and Company. The new venture, the Cudahy Packing Company, with $750,000 capitalization, had as its president Michael Cudahy and as its vice-president Edward A. Cudahy, who was in charge of operations in South Omaha. The firm had its headquarters in Chicago and began its climb to a place of importance among Chicago packing interests.[21]

The members of the "Big Four" had been preceded by Libby, McNeill & Libby, who continued their operations in the canning of beef started in 1868. Incorporated in May, 1888, the firm had the blessing of Gustavus and Louis Swift although it was distinct from the Swift organization. In 1875 Libby, McNeill & Libby arranged with the Wilson Packing Company for joint rights and privileges under the patents held by the latter for a compressed product. From 1875 to 1885 the market expanded greatly, Libby slaughtering more than 1,200,000 cattle and packing more than forty million cans of beef to delight the palates of Englishmen, Germans, Canadians, and Americans.[22]

[20] The firm was at times hard pressed financially. In 1903 it fell into the hands of the National Packing Company, a holding company, upon whose board of directors sat members of the Armour, Morris, and Swift families. U. S. Commissioner of Corporations, *Report on the Beef Industry, 1905*, pp. 26–27, 35; *The Economist*, V (May 23, 1891), 895–96, VIII (July 16, 1892), 85, Investors' Supplement, May 8, 1897, p. 35, Investors' Manuals, May 6, 1899, p. 42, May 7, 1898, p. 37, May, 1901, p. 68, May, 1902, p. 71, May, 1903, p. 73; Leech and Carroll, *op. cit.*, pp. 205–6.

[21] U. S. Commissioner of Corporations, *Report on the Beef Industry, 1905*, p. 37; W.[William Terence] Kane, *The Education of Edward Cudahy* (Chicago, 1941), pp. 125–30; John M. O'Rourke, *The Cudahy Packing Company: A History, 1890–1924* (published by the Cudahy Packing Company, U.S.A., 1925), pp. 3–6, 54–55; *The Drovers' Journal*, March 24, 1890.

[22] U. S. Commissioner of Corporations, *Report on the Beef Industry, 1905*, p. 289; U. S. Bureau of Animal Industry, *First Annual Report, 1884*, p. 262; *The Drovers' Journal*, Nov. 28, 1885, April 10, 1886. The Wilson Packing Company is not the same as a later Wilson & Co. established in 1916.

For the greater savoriness of the product of the 'seventies over that of earlier days, William J. Wilson of the Wilson Packing Company was responsible. Packing the preserved beef in a pyramidal can in 1874, Wilson at first met rebuff as he carried his samples by basket in an attempt to interest the New York trade. By 1878, however, the Wilson concern and Libby's were flourishing, not only sending out their compressed cooked product, but selling choice cuts of fresh beef to hotels, restaurants, and retail shops which could not use to advantage all parts of the animal. Within a short time competition developed with the St. Louis Beef-Canning Company and other firms, which took over the processes they used despite the patent rights. Suits carried through the United States Supreme Court, however, offered the Chicago group no protection because, the Court held, the processes patented were not novel. By 1884, after the canning of compressed beef revolutionized the preservation of this meat, the output surpassed by several millions that prepared by all other methods during the first seventy-five years of the nineteenth century. For Libby alone the amount was said to be 35,775,663 cans or an estimated 214,654,000 pounds.[23]

To the meat-packing capital of the world were attracted also the savings of British investors. The Anglo-American Packing and Provision Company, an offshoot of Fowler Brothers, was organized in 1874 and, in 1890, as the Anglo-American Provision Company, was absorbed by Fowler Brothers, Limited. The Chicago Packing and Provision Co., Limited, acquired most of the capital stock of the Chicago Packing and Provision Co. and of H. Botsford & Co. in 1890, and in 1892 the International Packing and Provision Co., Limited, took over several concerns. Even with such amalgamations, the newly formed companies failed to measure up to the already established leaders in the field in working capital, in numbers they could employ, and in what they could produce and market.[24]

[23] U. S. Bureau of Animal Industry, *First Annual Report, 1884,* pp. 262–63; Packing Company Cases, 105 U. S. 566 (1881). Armour began the canning of meat in 1878. *Armour,* I (June, 1935), 10.

[24] The following meat-packing concerns were acquired by the International Packing and Provision Co., Limited: International Packing Co., T. E. Wells Company, Allerton Packing Co., John Cudahy, John C. Hately, Hately Brothers Company, Jones & Stiles Packing Co. A partial consolidation of H. Botsford & Co. and the Chicago Packing and Provision Co. had been effected before the Chicago Packing and Provision Co., Limited, took over. *The Drovers' Journal,* Nov. 20, 1885, July 9, 14, 1890; *The Economist,* III (June 28, 1890), 843–44, IX (Oct. 22, 1892), 579–80, (May 6, 1893), 631, Investors' Supplement, May 8, 1897,

As the animal-raising areas moved westward in conjunction with the production of cereals, slaughtering and packing establishments arose to care for the northward and eastward movement of cattle and swine. By the late 'eighties, Omaha, Nebraska City, and Lincoln, Nebraska, Atlantic and Sioux City, Iowa, Kansas City and St. Joseph, Missouri, had plants, satellites of the Chicago packers.[25] Looked upon as the touchstone of economic advancement by the promoters of the new centers, the building of slaughtering and packing plants was warmly welcome. To the Chicago slaughterers and packers were offered, at times, not only free land for sites but bonuses, which, in anticipation of the future, acted reflexively to raise the price of the town's real estate.[26] Subsidies in stock from stockyards companies, freely given to important packers, certified an overwhelming desire that their city participate in the entrancing growth of the Chicago concerns. Unsuccessful local owners found the sagacious Swift and far-sighted Armour quick to sense the advantages of nearness to the source of supplies, and, therefore, willing to provide relief to those finding themselves encumbered with an unprofitable investment.[27]

Thus before 1890 the selling of beef came to be concentrated in Chicago, Kansas City, Omaha, St. Louis, Cincinnati, and Pittsburgh. Aside from Pittsburgh, these cities were also the pork-packing centers of the country to which were added Milwaukee, Louisville, and Indianapolis. In the 'eighties mutton had a place in the output, but

pp. 33–34, Investors' Manual, May 7, 1898, p. 49; The Times [London], July 10, Oct. 29, 30, 1890, May 23, Oct. 24, 1892, Oct. 24, 1893; Illinois, Second Annual Report of the Factory Inspectors, 1894, pp. 106–7.

[25] The Drovers' Journal, May 24, 1890, reported that Armour with other packers had purchased a tract of land at Hunter's Point at the southern tip of San Francisco to set up a beef-canning and pork-packing plant. The Armour offices, Chicago, have no record of such a plant. Cudahy was reported to have purchased a plant in Los Angeles in 1892. (Kane, op. cit., p. 147.) Meat packing on the West Coast as late as 1900 was not extensive. U. S., Twelfth Census, 1900, IX, "Manufacturing," pt. III, 408–10.

[26] Chicago Board of Trade, Thirty-second Annual Report, 1889, p. xxvi; The Drovers' Journal, Jan. 12, 30, 1885, July 13, 1886, Feb. 24, Mar. 26, July 8, 9, Aug. 12, Oct. 2, 1887, Feb. 23, 1888, March 26, July 16, 1890, Dec. 2, 1891; FTC, Report on the Meat-Packing Industry, 1919, pt. III, "Methods of the Five Packers in Controlling the Meat-Packing Industry," 32, 36–37; L. D. H. Weld, A. T. Kearney, and F. H. Sidney, Economics of the Packing Industry (Chicago, 1925), p. 43; Kane, op. cit., pp. 147–48; L. F. Swift, op. cit., pp. 15, 132–34.

[27] U. S. Commissioner of Corporations, Report on the Beef Industry, 1905, p. 288; The Drovers' Journal, May 28, July 13, 1886; FTC, Report on the Meat-Packing Industry, 1919, pt. III, 32, 36–38; L. F. Swift, op. cit., pp. 132–34.

it did not approximate the other two meats. Over all ruled Chicago, her leadership assured by a vast supply of capital and the organizational skill of her packers.[28]

The standing of Chicago as meat center was enhanced appreciably by the development of the refrigerator car which, along with, but even more than, the expansion of railroad service in large part revolutionized the eating habits of civilized men. It sketched a new pattern in production and distribution and, in the case of meats, it extended the packing year from the winter months to a year-round business, and made possible long-distance shipping without spoilage. In 1874 Nelson Morris is credited with sending frozen beef to Boston in a boxcar. But it was Gustavus F. Swift, "the Yankee of the Yards," who first made the shipment of dressed beef a commercial success. Having experimented in refrigeration at his packing plant, he then turned his attention to cars in which to ship his beef.[29]

In what later appeared only crude iceboxes on wheels, Swift, between 1877 and 1879, inaugurated a business which mounted in volume with the passage of years.[30] With his usual good judgment, he turned from the railroads carrying the largest shipments of livestock to the East and, therefore, having a vested interest in such shipments, to the Chicago and Grand Trunk Railway. When this railroad refused to build refrigerator cars for him, Swift furnished his own and routed them over the Grand Trunk until the Interstate Commerce Commission after 1887 eased his way with the leading

[28] The U. S. Senate investigation, 1888–90, dealing with the influence of Chicago, is discussed later in this chapter.

[29] Morris was not the first to experiment in this way. George H. Hammond in 1871 is said to have attempted to ship by way of a crude refrigerated boxcar patented by William Davis. Nofsinger and Company shipped dressed beef from Kansas City in 1875 to Boston and Philadelphia. The Zimmerman car with a V-shaped tank along its top was used for two or three years. *The Buzzer*, V (Dec., 1917), 23–32; *The Drovers' Journal*, Jan. 5, 1887; L. F. Swift, *op. cit.*, pp. 198–200; U. S. Bureau of Animal Industry, *First Annual Report, 1884*, pp. 265–66; *Dictionary of American Biography*, XIII, 217–18; *The Armour Magazine*, XI (Oct., 1922), 24; FTC, *Report on Private Car Lines, 1919*, pp. 25–29. For earlier attempts to ship refrigerated meat see Pierce, *A History of Chicago*, II, 98–99.

[30] U. S., *Twelfth Census, 1900*, IX, "Manufactures," pt. III, 416; L. D. H. Weld, *Private Freight Cars and American Railways*, pp. 16–17; FTC, *Report on Private Car Lines, 1919*, pp. 28–30; U. S. Senate Select Committee, *Testimony . . . on the Transportation and Sale of Meat Products*, 1889, p. 219; FTC, *Report on the Meat-Packing Industry, 1919*, Summary and pt. I, 239. *The Buzzer*, a Swift journal, declares that "the first cars of perfectly refrigerated western beef arrived sweet and wholesome in New England on Thanksgiving morning, 1878." (*Ibid.*, V [Dec., 1917], 26.) According to G. C. Reitinger, Swift & Company's Public Relations Department, Swift's first refrigerated cars were built in 1877.

eastern lines which composed the Trunk Line Association. By 1880 "Stave's Wild West scheme" had become a success. His first markets were in New England where he was well known, and where he entered into partnership with butchers and dealers, shortly to invade New York in the same way.[31] He extended his initial advantage by setting up icing stations along the route of shipment and providing ice for them. At strategic locations he established branch houses to assist in the promotion of his business, or opened new markets by sending out so-called peddler cars from which to distribute his products.[32]

In 1882 Armour started shipping refrigerated dressed beef to consumers east of Chicago, his first consignment going to East Saginaw, Michigan, in May, 1882.[33] Like Swift he set up a branch-house system to distribute his products, the first opening in New York in 1884 and the second in Albany in 1885. By 1890 he had forty in operation. A car-route system was inaugurated about 1892 to supply communities along the way, and just as for Swift these cars served, in a real sense, as moving branch houses. By 1886 the four concerns, Swift, Armour, Hammond, and Morris, the chief shippers of dressed beef, used about 1,500 refrigerator cars.[34]

[31] The story of Swift's perseverance in the face of obstacles is told in his son Louis's *The Yankee of the Yards*, pp. 182–202. At Buffalo and other junction points the Grand Trunk turned over to American roads shipments to New York City and to New England. Swift & Company, *Yearbook, 1926*, pp. 18–19; L. F. Swift, *op. cit.*, pp. 208–9; *Railroad Gazette*, XIX (April 29, 1887), 290; Wentworth, *op. cit.*, pp. 162–63.

[32] FTC, *Report on Private Car Lines, 1919*, pp. 37–38. Swift had his own wholesale organization at Clinton and Fall River, Massachusetts, for his earliest shipments. (L. F. Swift, *op. cit.*, pp. 188, 191–92.) In the spring of 1888 he opened a branch house at Ishpeming, Michigan, to be followed that autumn by one at Milwaukee. (*The Buzzer*, VI [July, 1919], 23.) Swift & Company of New York was incorporated Feb. 8, 1893, to control some of the branch houses handling Swift products in the state of New York. (U. S. Commissioner of Corporations, *Report on the Beef Industry, 1905*, p. 287.) By 1890 eastern packing plants were also controlled by Swift. The Boston plant of Charles H. North & Company became the North Packing and Provision Company in 1890 with Swift as president. *The Drovers' Journal*, Jan. 6, 1890; Rudolf Alexander Clemen, *The American Livestock and Meat Industry* (New York, 1923), p. 388.

[33] The Armour refrigerator car at first had such wide eaves that the first one attempting to go through the Hoosac Tunnel got stuck. The car had to be backed out and the eaves sawed off. *Excerpts from "Armour and Company — Pages from the History of the Nation's Meat Business,"* Typescript, Armour and Company Library; *The Armour Magazine*, IX (March, 1920), 9; *Armour Magazine and Morris Standard*, XV (Sept., 1926), 7.

[34] *Excerpts from "Armour and Company . . . ,"* Typescript; Rudolf A. Clemen, *The American Livestock and Meat Industry* (New York, 1923), p. 389; *Armour Magazine and Morris Standard*, XVI (April, 1927), 4, 7, 26; *Daily Commercial Bulletin*, Dec. 31, 1885; *The Drovers' Journal*, May 8, 1886. For the volume of dressed-beef traffic 1881–1884 see U. S. Bureau of Animal Industry, *First Annual Report, 1884*, p. 266.

It was not without misgivings that local butchers witnessed this invasion of what they considered their special province. As they saw their old-time business opportunities disappearing, they organized for action. Protest meetings stressed "the dangers" of eating meat shipped for long distances, and drew up resolutions against the sale of dressed meat at a lower price than the local butchers asked. The organization of the Butchers' National Protective Association of the United States of America coalesced individual dissatisfactions and centralized opposition. The Association exerted influence upon union labor to boycott Chicago beef. It not only urged that union slaughter-houses be built so that Association butchers would not be forced to purchase meat from the dressed-beef producers, but it attempted to enlist the help of the range-cattle men. In their obstructionist tactics the butchers had the open approval and sometimes active support of livestock shippers and carriers, who, too, feared their star of empire fading.[35] By the mid-'eighties their fears were definitely realized. Capitulation of the opposing forces was inevitable in the light of cheaper costs for Chicago dressed beef, toward which generally favorable freight charges, sometimes the result of freight wars among the carriers, contributed.[36]

The advent of the refrigerator car, however, posed problems for those railroads which carried not only animals but other foods susceptible to spoilage. Since the carriers had at first refused to construct the new type of car, the packers found it necessary to supply them at their own expense. Although the former eventually began to furnish some refrigerator cars, and others were put in service by

[35] *Chicago Tribune*, Aug. 24, 25, Sept. 2, 1882, May 25, 1887; U. S. Senate Select Committee, *Testimony . . . on the Transportation and Sale of Meat Products*, 1889, pp. 150–51; *The Drovers' Journal*, Feb. 6, 1884, April 15, 1887; Swift & Company, *Yearbook*, 1926, p. 20; FTC, *Report on Private Car Lines, 1919*, p. 34; C. E. Griffin, *Railway History of Illinois* (unpublished M. A. Thesis, University of Illinois, 1918), pp. 115–16; *Railroad Gazette*, XIX (April 29, 1887), 290. Restrictive state legislation directed against dressed-beef packers, to the effect that all beef should have been inspected within twenty-four hours of slaughter, was passed, for example, in Minnesota. It was finally declared unconstitutional by the U. S. Supreme Court. *In re* Barber, 39 Federal Reporter 641 (1889); Minnesota *v.* Barber, 136 U. S. 313 (1890). Because of a similarity in laws, Indiana took part in this case with Minnesota. *The Drovers' Journal*, Dec. 24, 1890. See also Swift *v.* Sutphin, 39 Federal Reporter, 630 (1889).

[36] *The Chicago Times*, Oct. 13, 1882; *Lumberman's Gazette*, XXII (May 9, 1883), 1; *Chicago Daily News*, Sept. 22, 1884; *Railroad Gazette*, XVIII (Oct. 5, 1886), 709; *Daily Trade Bulletin*, Dec. 31, 1888, Dec. 30, 1892; *The Thirtieth Annual of the Chicago Daily Commercial Report, 1889*.

private car companies and fast freight lines, the large packing firms, as their business increased, found it advantageous to own a sufficient number to cover their needs. By the early 'eighties railroad competition for tonnage enabled the packing companies to obtain from the railroads the payment of mileage on both loaded and empty movements of their cars. This arrangement apparently was derived from a similar agreement between the fast freight lines and the carriers after the Civil War. It did not extend to the small packers lacking financial resources to build their own cars, who, if not content to do merely a local business, must get transportation for their products at the convenience of those who maintained such cars.[37] Through the dual role of owner and shipper the large packers, furthermore, enjoyed a more favored position than the private stock car companies of the mid-'eighties, for although these companies received corresponding mileage rates from the railroads on their " palace " or Pullman stock cars, they originated no traffic.[38]

To determine the extent and character of such payments, the Interstate Commerce Commission investigated the situation in 1889. It discovered through statements and testimony by the railroad companies that, although no set rule prevailed, the usual rate, since May 1, 1889, on refrigerator cars carrying dressed beef east and southeast of Chicago was three-fourths of a cent per mile. One road to the east and nearly all the roads operating west paid one cent a mile. The origin of the one-cent rate on the western lines was a five-year contract between Armour and Company and the Chicago, Milwaukee and St. Paul Railway, in which Armour held stock, that had gone into effect on December 17, 1887. Under the terms of the contract, Armour and Company agreed to supply the railroad with refrig-

[37] Interstate Commerce Commission, " In the Matter of Private Cars," 50 ICC *Reports*, pp. 656–57 (hereafter cited as ICC); FTC, *Report on Private Car Lines, 1919*, pp. 43, 62–64; ICC, *Seventh Annual Report, 1893*, pp. 60–62; Charles Edward Russell, " The Greatest Trust in the World," *Everybody's Magazine*, XII (Feb., 1905), 154. Swift & Company was reported in 1886 as having 900 refrigerator cars. (*The Drovers' Journal*, May 5, 1886.) Armour and Company, the *Tribune* declared, owned and operated 1,500 in 1889. *Chicago Tribune*, Jan. 1, 1890.

[38] In 1884–85 an active campaign for traffic was carried on by these stock car companies. They demanded high mileage rates from railroads and shippers for the superior shipping equipment in their cars. In 1887 a test case came up before the Interstate Commerce Commssion. See the complaint of the Burton Stock Car Company of Chicago against the CB&Q and ten other railroads. ICC, I ICC *Reports and Decisions . . . April 5th 1887 to April 5th 1888* (New York, 1888), 132–44; ICC, *First Annual Report, 1887*, p. 88; *The Drovers' Journal*, Sept. 11, 1885.

erator cars for their own business and all other business requiring such cars on the one cent per mile basis.[39]

With these mileage rates, refrigerator and other private cars sometimes were found to pay for themselves in two or three years. Refrigerator cars, costing from $900 to $1,000 and with an average life of eight years, brought in 25 to 50 per cent or more annually. On the basis of the evidence, the Commission concluded that three-fourths of a cent per mile was ample allowance for the use of freight cars of any kind; that special cars should be the property of the carriers, not of the shipper or private company, for in the latter case too great an advantage gravitated to certain shippers with large holdings and "probably" encouraged the granting of rebates. Despite this and other pronouncements, the jurisdiction of the Commission was disputed, though the subject of private cars and rates continued to be a matter of frequent consideration by governmental agencies.[40]

The adoption of mechanical advances was paralleled by an expansion in the utilization of waste products by the big packers who, after the 'seventies, more and more took over what had been at one time chiefly a manufacture independent of them. As early leaders in the field both Armour and Swift engaged in the by-products industry on a big scale.[41] So satisfying was this adjunct that it became, in general, a part of the engagements of all important packers. Indeed, so complete was the utilization of waste from slaughtered animals that it gave rise to the remark that "everything of the pig was used except the squeal." [42] Before the mid-'eighties dried blood and tankage were used in making fertilizer. Skin and thigh bones sent

[39] *Chicago Tribune*, May 9, 11, 1889; *The Railroad Gazette*, XXI (April 19, 1889), 264; *Railway Age*, XXXIV (Nov. 7, 1902), 497; ICC, *Third Annual Report, 1889*, pp. 15–16. The ICC report does not identify the eastern road. The twenty-six railroads asked to submit evidence are named on pp. 177–78 of this report.

[40] *Ibid.*, pp. 16–18; FTC, *Report on Private Car Lines, 1919*, pp. 12–15, 65–72; I. L. Sharfman, *The Interstate Commerce Commission: A Study in Administrative Law and Procedure*, pt. II (New York, 1931), 120–41. The ICC investigation, 1890, revealed the 70,000 private cars in use earned, at the rate of three-fourths of a cent a mile, more than $30,666,000 as against a total cost of the cars of $91,000,000, thus paying for themselves in about three years. ICC, *Seventh Annual Report, 1893*, p. 63.

[41] Pierce, *A History of Chicago*, II, 100–1; Swift & Company, *Yearbook, 1912*, pp. 5–6; *The Armour Magazine*, XI (Nov., 1922), 27; *Armco*, IV (Jan., 1915), 6; Armour, *In the Matter of the Investigation of the Packing Industry, 1919*, p. 11; Leech and Carroll, *op. cit.*, pp. 47–48.

[42] This remark is generally attributed to P. D. Armour, but Louis F. Swift ascribes it to his father, who said: "Now we use all of the hog except his grunt." L. F. Swift, *op. cit.*, p. 12.

to the East and England, principally for manufacture, went into knives, brush handles, and buttons, $80 per ton being paid for cattle thigh bones in 1886.

In 1884 Armour took over the Wahl Brothers glue factory located about a mile northwest of the stockyards, thereby starting his Thirty-first Street auxiliaries which, within the next four decades, were to have products running into " many millions of dollars annually." [43] Isinglass, gelatine, and bone meal also contributed to extending the packers' horizon from butcher to manufacturer of diversified products. In 1885 Armour organized his pharmaceutical laboratories for the purpose of making pepsin and pancreatin. In that year also, he introduced a new method of reclaiming useful materials from the water of the rendering tanks, reported as netting the company over $100 a day profit. By 1890 more than forty otherwise wasted parts were utilized for an ever increasing number of products. Even the hair of the lowly pig, sold to furniture-makers at four and five cents a pound, enriched the packers by about $197,149 in the year ending March, 1886.[44] As the Chicago humorist Finley Peter Dunne ("Mr. Dooley") put it: "A cow goes lowin' softly in to Armours' an' comes out glue, gelatine, fertylizer, celooloid, joolry, sofy cushions, hair restorer, washin' sody, littrachoor an' bed springs so quick that while aft she's still cow, for'ard she may be anything fr'm buttons to pannyma hats."

Before 1880 sausage, bologna, and frankfurters, canned meats including corned beef, roast beef, ox tongue, lunch tongue, brawn, and potted ham could be had, as Armour joined the firms in canning meat. Of the many products put out, oleomargarine, variously called oleo, suine, and butterine, had the stormiest history. By 1880 three Chicago establishments were manufacturing it, with a total amount worth $437,800. Because of its cheapness and similarity to

[43] *The Armour Magazine,* XI (Nov., 1922), 27; *The Armour Magazine and Morris Standard,* XVI (April, 1927), 24–25, 30, 32; *Armco,* IV (Jan., 1915), 6; Armour, *The Packers, the Private Car Lines and the People,* pp. 190–209; *The Drovers' Journal,* Feb. 6, 1883, Aug. 5, Nov. 30, 1885, May 28, 1886. See *The Drovers' Journal,* March 22, 1889, for Swift's interest in glue manufacturing.

[44] *Chicago Tribune,* Jan. 1, 1887; *The Drovers' Journal,* Nov. 30, 1885; Armour, *In the Matter of the Investigation of the Packing Industry, 1919,* p. 11; Chicago Board of Trade, *Thirty-third Annual Report, 1890,* pp. xxviii–xxix; Swift & Company, *Yearbook, 1912,* p. 5; *The Drovers' Journal,* June 18, 1886. The figure on pigs' hair is reached by using the reported number of 4,928,730 hogs packed in Chicago March 1, 1885, to March 1, 1886. Chicago Board of Trade, *Twenty-eighth Annual Report, 1885,* p. 58.

butter, the new product quickly captured public favor, and, because it returned higher profits to the retailer, he promptly offered it for sale. Shortly unscrupulous producers appeared whose inferior output was often sold for the best.[45]

Restrictive legislation, therefore, was demanded. An act of May 31, 1879, passed by the Illinois legislature to prevent frauds in the manufacture of butter and cheese, compelled the manufacturer and seller to label the product " with its true and appropriate name." This was followed in 1881 by further legislation to protect the consumer by prohibiting food adulteration in general, and specifically prescribing labels for oleo and similar products with real names and the proportion of ingredients used. Only active lobbying on the part of producers in later years prevented more state limitations.[46]

Dairy interests, however, not satisfied merely with state regulation, turned to the federal government and were successful in getting a law defining butter and taxing and regulating the manufacture, importation, and exportation of oleomargarine. Chicago packers, joined by the Live Stock Exchange, had fought the law on the ground that chemists had declared oleo a good food, and that the price of butter was high for the moderate income group.[47] Its passage focused the eye of the public upon the advertised merits and alleged defects of the product. The larger manufacturers recognized the advantage of co-operation with the government inspectors. Butter manufacturers and other opponents of oleomargarine, including livestock men, continued their attacks, however. Yet despite the per-

[45] In 1890 four Chicago establishments had an output worth $1,864,800. U. S., *Tenth Census, 1880*, " Manufactures," p. 393; *Eleventh Census, 1890*, " Manufacturing Industries," pt. I, " Totals for States and Industries," 392–93, pt. II, " Statistics of Cities," 140–41. Creamery butter in 1883, for example, sold at 28 cents a pound and butterine at 18 to 20 cents. Dealers sometimes made as much as 15 cents per pound profit. *The Drovers' Journal*, Oct. 19, 1883, March 23, 1886.

[46] Illinois, *Laws, 1879*, pp. 116–17. The penalty in the 1879 law for disobedience was a fine, prison sentence, or both. Act of June 1, 1881, *Laws, 1881*, pp. 74, 75. Lobbying was especially active in 1885. *The Drovers' Journal*, Jan. 4, 1887; Illinois, *Journal of the Senate of the . . . General Assembly of the State of Illinois, 1885*, pp. 16, 27, *Journal of the House of Representatives of the . . . General Assembly . . . 1885*, pp. 110, 212, 288, 332, 410, 338.

[47] The law defined oleo as well as butter and prescribed the filing with the Collector of Internal Revenue of a $5,000 bond by manufacturers who should also pay a tax of $6,000. Retailers who sold in quantities of less than 10 pounds were taxed $48; wholesalers were taxed $480. Detailed instructions as to packaging and labeling were a part of the law. The manufacturer must pay a tax of 2 cents a pound on all sales. U. S., *Statutes at Large*, XXIV, 209–13; *The Drovers' Journal*, May 11, 1886.

sisting antagonism of this politically influential bloc, the production of oleo continued, Armour alone producing one and a quarter million pounds in 1892.[48]

Toward lard, as well as oleo, was directed the opposition of those demanding a "pure" product, or, if adulterated by chemicals and cottonseed oil, that it be so labeled. In 1883 McGeoch, Everingham & Company charged before the directors of the Board of Trade that Fowler Brothers had put tallow and cottonseed oil into their prime steam lard. This, the *Drovers' Journal* pointed out, was a question of the gravest importance to the American people, because of the "startling proportions" in which adulteration frauds were being carried on. Although the defendants stoutly denied the allegation, the Board of Trade, having reviewed the case from June 6 to August 21, criticized their business procedures without imposing other penalty. All of this, thought the *Drovers' Journal,* was enough to induce the Fowlers to resort to prayer, appropriately phrased "Good Lard, deliver us!"

Throughout the 'eighties agitation against the use of chemicals and other ingredients, alleged to be "more or less deleterious to health," in the manufacture of lard, continued not only locally but nationally. Promoted in large part by the Butchers' National Protective Association, the movement against "imitations of pure hog's lard" resulted in the Lard Anti-Adulteration Bill passed in 1889 by the Illinois legislature, which required that any lard product not "pure" lard should be labeled "lard compound."[49]

The use of cottonseed oil in making lard had, however, attained an importance sufficient for P. D. Armour to tour the South in 1887 with the avowed purpose of erecting mills there, to break the monopoly then held by the American Cotton Oil Trust. This ambitious project of mills in Alabama, Arkansas, Mississippi, Texas, and elsewhere included as stockholders soapmakers and lard renderers with a rumored capital of $10,000,000, Armour having a controlling interest. During Armour's trip cottonseed-oil certificates under the

[48] *The Drovers' Journal,* March 8, July 18, 1887; Chicago Board of Trade, *Twenty-ninth Annual Report, 1886,* pp. xxxiii–xxxiv; *Armco Advertising News* [Armour], II (Oct., 1913), 13–14. The repeal of the national oleomargarine tax became effective July 1, 1950.

[49] *The Drovers' Journal,* June 11, 20, Aug. 17, 22, 1883, Dec. 19, 1887, March 31, 1888, Feb. 22, 1889; *The Knights of Labor,* III (Feb. 22, 1888). Act of June 3, 1889, Illinois, *Laws, 1889,* p. 111. In 1888 the manufacture of "adulterated foods" was prohibited in the District of Columbia by federal law. U. S., *Statutes at Large,* XXV (1888), 549–51.

pressure of "a raid," carried on in alliance with Nelson Morris, N. K. Fairbank, and others, declined thirty-one points, netting them over one million dollars. Eventually Armour withdrew from the group in opposition to the American Cotton Oil Trust, having frightened the latter to his satisfaction and reaching a compromise with it.[50]

Lard, like grain and pork, figured prominently and sometimes disastrously as a speculative commodity on the floor of the Chicago Board of Trade. Attempts to decrease prices and market supplies by declaring prime steam lard adulterated allegedly motivated the McGeoch attack against Fowler Brothers in 1883, resulting in a loss of about $3,400,000 to the speculators and carrying several other concerns with them. Besides, according to the *American Elevator and Grain Trade,* it placed a " stigma of impurity " upon the product which lasted for years and hurt the export trade.[51] But one disaster seldom prevented others. On August 1, 1893 John Cudahy, considered " a phenomenally successful speculator," with A. W. Wright and others, saw the market sag rapidly after an attempted corner on pork and lard, pork prices falling from $19.25 to $10.50 and lard tobogganing from $9.75 to $5.90 a tierce overnight. Four or five million dollars were reported lost besides the securities sacrificed.[52]

Receptive to the same propulsive forces as other meat products, lard production mounted from 50,277,600 pounds in the winter packing season 1871–72 to 173,670,933 pounds in the year ending March 1, 1892. Along with an increasing number of other derivative products, the produce trade, and subsidiary undertakings, it added substan-

<hr />

[50] The American Cotton Oil Trust had purchased N. K. Fairbank & Co., large lard producer. It tried to buy the Armour refinery, but the Armour firm would not sell. A rival company to the American Cotton Oil Trust, the Southern Cotton Oil Company, was, however, chartered in New Jersey, March, 1887. Henry C. Butcher of Washington Butchers' Sons, Philadelphia, became president. Frederick and John Oliver of South Carolina, prominent in cottonseed oil in the South, also held offices. It was this group with which the Armour firm intended to associate itself, but did not. *The Drovers' Journal,* March 1, 2, 12, Oct. 31, 1887; *The Knights of Labor,* II (March 19, 1887), 1; *New York Tribune,* March 4, 8, 1887.

[51] *The American Elevator and Grain Trade,* II (July 15, 1883), 12, VII (Nov. 15, 1888), 98; *The Drovers' Journal,* June 18, 1883. Daniel Wells, Jr., of Milwaukee was reported to have shared the loss with McGeoch, who had interests also in that city. Still, *op. cit.,* pp. 327, 368, 371.

[52] *The American Elevator and Grain Trade,* XII (Aug. 15, 1893), 52; *Chicago Tribune,* Jan. 1, 1894. When the demand for lard was high and the market for pork poor, Armour, upon occasion, converted pork into lard. *Armco,* IV (Jan., 1915), 5.

tially to the rich offerings of packers not only to the American public but to Europe as well.[53]

By the 'nineties, the combined shipments of beef and pork attained undreamed-of heights as the total value of the industry's products in 1890 reached $194,337,838. Declining proportions in the shipment of live animals to meat reflected accurately the changing character of the market, although live animals nevertheless represented a considerable business. The large dealers in livestock of other cities still turned to Chicago for their supplies, and even farmers in the corn-belt states, especially Illinois and Iowa, bought here the animals they wished to fatten.[54] By 1874 the Board of Trade was proudly pointing also to the expanding sale of pork products and provisions which Chicago had with the South, and by 1879 the *Tribune* happily characterized the demand for Chicago meat and provisions as "vigorous." Before the 'eighties closed, Armour and Company had branch houses in Atlanta, Savannah, Charleston, Memphis, Charlotte, and other southern points, the outposts chiefly of their Kansas City house, while Swift was located in Birmingham, Alabama.[55]

Not content with developing new markets for their products in the United States, Chicago packers and livestock dealers envisaged a lucrative market across the Atlantic, especially in England, where Chicago salt beef had long been popular. The late 'seventies and the decade of the 'eighties witnessed the steady rise of an export trade in live cattle and dressed and canned beef, and the decline of the ex-

[53] Chicago Board of Trade, *Fifteenth Annual Report, 1872*, p. 168, *Thirty-fifth Annual Report, 1892*, p. 49. Swift & Company entered the produce business in 1890. (Swift *Ms.* [Swift Library].) Through an arithmetical computation by which $7.21 per hundred pounds is reached and allowing for some unknown factors, it seems possible to set Chicago's lard output for 1892 at more than $12,000,000. Figures for computation are taken from U. S., *Twelfth Census, 1900*, IX, "Manufactures," 412, and Chicago Board of Trade, *Thirty-fifth Annual Report, 1892*, p. 46.

[54] The Monroes of Boston, Schweistahl and Son of Philadelphia, Eastman and Company and Schwarzschild and Sulzberger of New York, besides dealers in Detroit, Cleveland, and Pittsburgh, were among the purchasers. *The Drovers' Journal*, Jan. 5, 1885; U. S. Senate Select Committee, *Testimony . . . on the Transportation and Sale of Meat Products*, 1889, pp. 48, 212, 218, 231, 234, 498–99. See Norman J. Colman, "Dressed Meat Traffic," U. S. Bureau of Animal Industry, *Third Annual Report, 1886*, p. 278, for a table showing comparative shipments of cattle and dressed beef from Chicago, 1880–85.

[55] Chicago Board of Trade, *Seventeenth Annual Report, 1874*, p. 12; *Chicago Tribune*, Jan. 1, 1879. The yellow-fever outbreak virtually stopped this trade in the summer and fall of 1878. *Ibid.*; U. S. Senate Select Committee, *Testimony . . . on the Transportation and Sale of Meat Products*, 1889, pp. 366–67.

port of salt beef. With livestock in England lagging behind the needs of a rapidly growing urban population, cattle exports from the United States mounted to 104,444 head by 1883, to jump to 394,836 in 1890.[56] The center of this trade was Chicago. Not only did local firms capitalize on the new opportunity, but many leading eastern and Canadian shippers bought here where they could obtain the best selection of cattle. To Nelson Morris fell the distinction of inaugurating the export of both live cattle and dressed beef to the British Isles. In 1868 he shipped a few cattle to London and Glasgow, and by 1887 he had contracted with the Belgian government to deliver fresh meat at Antwerp.[57]

In 1890 France and, in 1891 Germany permitted American cattle to invade their markets, despite the lack of an adequate exports-inspection law. For this entrance Morris, Secretary of Agriculture J. M. Rusk, and the Chicago Live Stock Exchange were largely responsible. Now, at last, commented the *Drovers' Journal,* was the American steer " allowed to sniff the classic air of the continent." [58] But British regulations after 1878 on imported cattle, combined with high shipping rates, improved refrigeration, and the damage suffered by cattle in shipment shifted the emphasis by 1890 to the export of dressed beef, or " dead beef," as trade journals persisted in calling it.[59]

[56] *The Drovers' Journal,* Oct. 3, 1887; U. S. Senate Select Committee, *Report . . . on the Transportation and Sale of Meat Products,* 1890, p. 27, quoting *The Scotsman* [Edinburgh], Jan. 29, 1890; U. S. Bureau of Animal Industry, *Sixth and Seventh Annual Reports, 1889 and 1890,* pp. 23, 71. Figures are for fiscal year ending June 30 in each case.

[57] Nelson Morris, George H. Hammond, and William H. Monroe were probably the largest Chicago dealers in this field. *The Drovers' Journal,* March 3, 1886, Oct. 28, 1887; U. S. Senate Select Committee, *Testimony . . . on the Transportation and Sale of Meat Products,* 1889, pp. 513–14; U. S. Bureau of Animal Industry, *First Annual Report, 1884,* p. 261; Joseph Nimmo, Jr., U. S. Bureau of Statistics (Treasury Department), *Report in Regard to the Range and Ranch Cattle Business of the United States* (Washington, 1885), p. 198.

[58] *The Drovers' Journal,* Aug. 30, 1890, March 19, 24, 1891.

[59] U. S. Senate Select Committee, *Report . . . on the Transportation and Sale of Meat Products,* 1890, p. 30, quoting the *Breeders' Gazette,* April 2, 1890; *The Railway Age,* I (Aug. 3, 1876), 155; *The Chicago Times,* Feb. 18, March 12, 1877; *The Drovers' Journal,* July 14, Oct. 3, 1883, July 5, 1890, Jan. 16, 1892; *Chicago Tribune,* Jan. 1, 1880, Jan. 1, 1881; [U. S. Department of State], *Papers relating to the Foreign Relations of the United States . . . 1890* (Washington, 1891), p. 281 (hereafter cited as U. S. Foreign Relations). An act of Congress of March, 1891, providing for proper ventilation, sound construction, and good attendance on livestock boats reduced loss of cattle in transit overseas, for example, from 1.60 per cent in 1891 to 0.47 in 1893. (Act of March 3, 1891, U. S., *Statutes at Large,* XXVI, 1089–91; D. E. Salmon, " Report of the Chief of the Bureau of Animal Industry,

Difficulties, however, attended the new venture, for at first the expense of putting dressed beef in the British markets was almost prohibitive, and British prejudice against American beef, fanned by reports that diseased animals were used, alarmed exporters. Gustavus Swift made more than one goodwill mission to disabuse the minds of the coveted customers. From the modest but first sizable shipment to England of 36,000 pounds of refrigerated beef by Timothy C. Eastman of New York in October, 1875, exports from the United States rose satisfyingly, so that the United Kingdom for the year ending June 30, 1893, was receiving 197,065,493 pounds.[60] Morris, Hammond, and Swift at first took the lead, with Armour entering into competition on a large scale with them in the early 'nineties. Long-term contracts to hold available ship space and even all the ships of a line by the big exporters eventually squeezed out small shippers, and the financial ability of the big shippers to install, at their own expense, necessary refrigeration equipment before steamship lines were prepared to furnish it, also operated to the disadvantage of the less powerful and venturesome.[61]

Despite protests by English agricultural interests, especially vehement in the late 'seventies and early 'eighties, that the new business was ruining the country's farmers by bringing the American prairies

1893," U. S. Department of Agriculture, *Annual Report, 1893*, pp. 134–35.) For the British restrictions see Great Britain, *Law Reports, The Public General Statutes . . . 1878* (London, 1879), XIII, 581–619; Great Britain, Royal Commission on the Importation of Store Cattle, *Report of His Majesty's Commissioners Appointed to Inquire into the Admission into the United Kingdom of Live Stock for Purposes other than Immediate Slaughter at the Ports* (London, 1921), Appendix, pp. lx–lxiv.

[60] *Chicago Tribune*, Feb. 12, 1877, Jan. 1, 1881; L. F. Swift, *op. cit.*, p. 91; *The Drovers' Journal*, Oct. 5, 1883, March 23, 1886, Sept. 28, 1892; James Trowbridge Critchell and Joseph Raymond, *A History of the Frozen Meat Trade* (London, 1912), p. 26; *The Chicago Times*, Feb. 18, 1877; Joseph Nimmo, Jr., U. S. Bureau of Statistics (Treasury Department), *Report on the Internal Commerce of the United States, 1884* (Washington, 1885), p. 162; Nimmo, *Report in Regard to the Range and Ranch Cattle Business of the United States*, pp. 66, 172; U. S. Department of Agriculture, *Annual Report, 1877*, pp. 374–75; Chicago Board of Trade, *Nineteenth Annual Report, 1876*, pp. 17–18, *Thirty-sixth Annual Report, 1893*, p. 167.

[61] *The Drovers' Journal*, Dec. 20, 1884, July 17, 1889, June 3, 1890; U. S. Senate Select Committee, *Report . . . on the Transportation and Sale of Meat Products*, 1890, pp. 31–32, *Testimony*, 1889, pp. 555–57; U. S. Bureau of Animal Industry, *Sixth and Seventh Annual Reports, 1889 and 1890*, pp. 25–26. In 1879 Armour's first shipment to England was in the steamship *Circassian*. (Letter to author from E. L. Heckler, Department of Public Relations, Armour and Company, Chicago, May 23, 1950.) In 1891 Swift Beef Company, Limited, London, was incorporated. As early as 1889 Swift was shipping refrigerated meats to England. (Letter to author from Swift & Company, Sept. 29, 1944.)

to Britain's very door, the chief market for dressed beef was England. With improvements in refrigeration the prosperous markets Americans had acquired were endangered by shipments of frozen beef and mutton to England from Australia, New Zealand, and Argentina.[62]

By 1890 the Chicago export market expanded appreciably through the shipping of large quantities of compressed beef. As canning methods were perfected, canned beef increased in popularity, especially in England. As early as 1877 the Wilson Packing Company slaughtered between 15,000 and 16,000 cattle yearly for canning, and one-half of their product found its way to Britain; while three-fourths of the canned beef prepared by Libby, McNeill & Libby was shipped to destinations in the same country.[63] By the mid-'eighties European governments with armies and navies in tropical climates had become heavy buyers, although Chicago producers had to meet the competition of Australian beef, which sold generally at slightly less a pound. In 1884 the British government ordered 740,000 pounds of compressed beef for the Nile expedition. In the spring of the next year Armour and Company alone exported 2,500,000 pounds for this campaign, the abundance of the Armour label in the Sudan evoking a punning doggerel on "Gladstone and Armour; or Khans and Cans."

> The roast beef of old England
> Is famed in song and story
> Without it where was English brawn
> That won old England glory?
> But in these days of England's gloom,
> When war's dread notes alarm her,
> What does she send to save Khartoum?
> Corned beef canned by Phil Armour.

[62] *The Economist* [London], XXXIV (Feb. 3, 1877), 125–26; *The Drovers' Journal*, Feb. 23, March 3, 5, 1885; Critchell and Raymond, *op. cit.*, pp. 76–85; testimony of Philip D. Armour in U. S. Senate Select Committee, *Testimony . . . on the Transportation and Sale of Meat Products,* 1889, pp. 416–17.

[63] James Macdonald, *Food from the Far West* (London and Edinburgh, 1878), p. 187; Chicago Board of Trade, *Nineteenth Annual Report, 1876,* p. 18. Export of canned beef was first shown in 1884 as a separate item. Before then it was generally included under "Meats, preserved," but, according to Nimmo, consisted chiefly of corned beef. Nimmo, *Internal Commerce of the United States, 1884,* p. 166. In 1873 these preserved meats were valued at $575,407 and at $3,939,977 in 1877. (*Ibid.*) In 1884 canned-beef exports from the United States were valued at $3,173,767. Chicago Board of Trade, *Twenty-seventh Annual Report, 1884,* p. 13.

When Gladstone first resolved on war,
  No lack of ammunition
Delayed the movement up the Nile,
  The problem was nutrition.
" Our cannonade," the Premier said,
  " Must needs be sharp and brief,
Our cannonade therefore shall be
  Phil Armour's canned corned beef."

" To P. D. A.: Send p. d. quick,
  Care John Bull, London docks,
Two million pounds of canned corned beef,
  Ox tongues, pigs' feet and hocks."
" To W. E. G.: (Send C. O. D.) "
  Swift flashed the ready answer,
Wired per Mackay-Bennett line,
  " I will, because I can, sir."

At every mile along the line
  Fanatics like El Mahdi
Will soon be skirmishing to find
  A soul to fit a body.
The prophet had a host of Khans,
  And some were brave and able;
But then, you see, they couldn't win —
  They lacked the Armour label.

In 1885 the French government gave to Morris the first order for 2,200,000 pounds of canned beef for its army and navy. Prior to this, French officials had been unable to get Chicago firms not only to place their product in a can different in shape from the usual container and holding one kilogram, they had failed to induce the packers to undergo inspection of the shipment upon arrival in France.[64]

Pork, more than other meat products, was subjected to condemnation by foreign dealers and government officials who feared consumers might become ill from eating the American importation. A report of the English consul in Philadelphia to his foreign office on hog mortality in Illinois and other hog states because of a cholera epidemic,

---

[64] *The Drovers' Journal,* June 1, 1883, Sept. 15, 1884, Dec. 10, March 23, 24, April 17, 1885; Critchell and Raymond, *op. cit.,* p. 11; U. S. Bureau of Animal Industry, *First Annual Report, 1884,* pp. 264–65.

confused with trichinosis, created panic in Europe, especially in Great Britain, and caused a decline in the demand. The British government warned the public of the situation in February, but, as in Belgium, the lower cost of the American product seemed to outweigh alarm.[65] A presidential decree on February 18 debarred American salted pork during an investigation by a French parliamentary committee. Austria and other countries likewise took action. In 1883 Germany prohibited the import of all American hog products except lard, completing a policy of exclusion begun in 1880. Under such restrictions exports from the United States fell off greatly.[66]

Retaliatory action was demanded by the Chicago Board of Trade and the packers, who held the foreign press responsible for the circulation of " senseless and wicked reports " and European governments for their " insane desire to protect the home market." [67] In 1880 Armour and Company complained to the American legation in Germany that a decree of that country had cut off their sale of canned brawn there. The next year through Armour's influence the State Department inquired into the effect of the condemnation of pork products by the American press. The situation had reached a point by 1883 that the company was vigorously advocating retaliation against France and Germany.[68]

The phalanx of American protestants against the action of the

[65] Between 1880 and 1881 the export of United States hog products declined 23½ per cent. Chicago Board of Trade, *Twenty-fourth Annual Report, 1881*, pp. xii–xiii, xxi; Alice Felt Tyler, *The Foreign Policy of James G. Blaine* (Minneapolis, 1927), pp. 293, 301; *U. S. Foreign Relations, 1881*, p. 403; *Chicago Tribune*, Jan. 1, 1880, Jan. 1, Dec. 31, 1881.

[66] *U. S. Foreign Relations, 1881*, pp. 399, 403, *1882*, p. 150, *1883*, p. 293, *1884*, pp. 129, 360, *1890*, p. 281; *The Times* [London], Feb. 19, 1881; Tyler, *op. cit.*, pp. 293–95; U. S. Senate, *Report of the Committee on Foreign Relations on Swine Products of the United States*, 48 Cong., 1 sess., S. Rept. 345 (Washington, 1884), pp. 349–50, 360–61, 376; Edgar E. Bramlette, " Prohibition of American Pork in Germany," U. S. Department of State, *Reports from the Consuls of the United States*, XXX, no. 107 (Washington, 1889), 458; Chicago Board of Trade, *Twenty-sixth Annual Report, 1883*, pp. 11–12, *Thirty-sixth Annual Report, 1893*, p. 169.

[67] Chicago Board of Trade, *Twenty-fourth Annual Report, 1881*, p. xiii. See later reports for the Board's increasing resentment. For a petition for retaliatory legislation to the Senate see *Cong. Record*, 47 Cong., 1 sess., pt. I, 257 (Jan. 5, 1882); *ibid.*, 48 Cong., 1 sess., pt. I, 403–4 (Jan. 15, 1884). For press reaction at this time see *Chicago Tribune*, Jan. 9, Feb. 11, 16, 17, 1884; *The Drovers' Journal*, Feb. 20, 1883, Jan. 18, 1884; *Illinois Staats-Zeitung*, June 11, 1881; *Bradstreet's*, X (Aug. 23, 1884), 114. Retaliatory action was urged against the importation of wines which were described as more injurious to health than American pork. *U. S. Foreign Relations, 1883*, p. 284; Chicago Board of Trade, *Twenty-seventh Annual Report, 1884*, p. xviii, *Thirtieth Annual Report, 1887*, p. xxix.

[68] *U. S. Foreign Relations, 1882*, pp. 148, 408–10, *1883*, pp. 355–56; *The Drovers' Journal*, Jan. 24, Feb. 4, 1884.

French and German governments was further solidified by a report of a commission named by President Chester A. Arthur in 1883 to investigate conditions in hog raising and in the packing industry. The report now gave comfort to the pork interests in its official endorsement of their stand that they had been subjected to " so gross a slander." [69] But it did not solve the disturbing problem of making pork products a part of the exports to Germany and France. In the circumstances the Board of Trade, although carrying on a local inspection of provisions, requested the government in 1889 to take action to remove " the stigma of false and injurious accusations " against this " source of great national revenue." The next year Congress passed a meat inspection and retaliation act. It made the importation into the United States of adulterated or unwholesome food, drugs, or liquors unlawful, and provided for the inspection of salted pork and bacon intended for export. In March, 1891 inspection was extended to cover cattle for export or for slaughter and export and all animals slaughtered for interstate trade, as well as the condemnation of any found diseased. In June, 1891 inspection began in Chicago plants, and shortly beneficial results were seen in an increase of exports.[70]

With all these manifestations of power through prosperity and at a time when combinations of those of like economic interest were becoming more and more numerous throughout the country, it is not strange that alliances and amalgamations took shape among live-stock men and among dressed-meat producers. One of the most publicized among the former originated between 1873 and 1875, when a dozen or more Chicago livestock shippers, including Samuel Allerton, Nelson Morris, and Isaac Waixel, joined the great trunk rail-

[69] An extensive statement from Armour and Company as to their methods of packing was given. Eliphalet W. Blatchford was suggested by the Board of Trade to serve on the Commission and became a member. He was president of the Chicago White Lead and Oil Company and was nominated because he was said not to be personally interested in the investigation, and had the personal qualities needed in such an investigation. Chicago Board of Trade, *Twenty-sixth Annual Report, 1883*, pp. 12–13; *U. S. Foreign Relations, 1883*, pp. 103–6, 282–83.

[70] *Ibid., 1889*, p. 165. For the Board's provisions inspection of 1878 see its report of that year, pp. 20–21. U. S. Bureau of Animal Industry, *Eighth and Ninth Annual Reports, 1891 and 1892*, pp. 36, 39; U. S., *Statutes at Large*, XXVI, 414–17, 1089–91. Hog products were readmitted in countries from which they had been excluded as follows: Germany, Sept. 3, 1891; Denmark, Sept. 8, 1891; Italy, Oct. 17, 1891; Austria-Hungary, Dec. 4, 1891; France, Jan. 1, 1892; Spain, May 21, 1892. Chicago Board of Trade, *Thirty-fifth Annual Report, 1892*, p. xxxiii; *Chicago Tribune*, April 15, Sept. 4, 1891.

roads, the Pennsylvania, the New York Central, and the Erie, in an agreement to regulate the shipping of livestock from Chicago to New York and, beginning in 1877, to New England. For each carload the carriers charged $115, awarding $15 to the livestock men participating in the agreement, who for this payment pledged themselves to ship as many cattle by any designated route as would be necessary to equalize or even up shipments. Each railroad company transported whatever it was offered, but if the returns of any month indicated that any one carrier had received more than its proportion of all shipments, the so-called " Cattle Pool," or " Eveners," effected an equalization the next month. " The practical result of this arrangement, of course," commented the railroad journal *The Railway Age,* " is to give the ' Eveners ' a control of the business. They alone can command the capital, appliances, and information necessary for conducting it this way. So far as shippers generally are concerned they can neither afford to ship in competition with the pool without the rebate, nor can they afford to accept the rebate with the condition that they are to ship when and how they may be called upon." [71]

Under fire from small shippers and St. Louis livestock interests, who saw the combination bringing unparalleled advantage to Chicago, the railroads apparently made at least one effort in 1877 to rid themselves of an arrangement which had incurred the animus of those not included. But the attempt was unsuccessful, for the Eveners, alarmed, as the *Tribune* put it, that they might be " legislated out of existence," threatened counter measures. Within the next two years, however, the combination became inoperative, as the dressed-beef trade grew more and more vigorous, and by this time the St. Louis cattle market no longer threatened Chicago.[72]

The Eveners' controversy of the 1870's was but the prelude to a much more bitterly waged struggle during the 'eighties between the livestock and dressed-meat shippers. In it trunk-line railroads con-

[71] *The Railway Age,* III (Jan. 31, 1878), 67; U. S. Senate Select Committee, *Report . . . on the Transportation and Sale of Meat Products,* 1890, pp. 2–3, *Testimony,* 1889, pp. 57–59, 181, 219, 232–33; J. F. Rusling, *The Railroads! The Stock-Yards! The Eveners! Expose of the Great Railroad Ring that Robs the Laborer of the West of $5,000,000 a Year* (Washington, 1878), p. 4; *Chicago Tribune,* Sept. 28, Oct. 3, 9, Dec. 11, 12, 1877.

[72] *Ibid.,* Dec. 17, 23, 1877; U. S. Senate Select Committee, *Report . . . on the Transportation and Sale of Meat Products,* 1890, pp. 2–3; *The Railway Age, loc. cit.,* p. 67. The Eveners' arrangement was reported as extended in late 1877 to St. Louis to pacify influential livestock shippers there.

tinued to play a major role, because upon their co-operation depended the retention of a leading position by those shipping livestock to be slaughtered in the East, as against the rising powers of western packers who were concerned primarily with getting their dressed meats to eastern markets. The resolution of the conflict was hindered by short-lived railroad pools, agreements, and rate wars, and was complicated by privately owned stock cars for shipping live animals and refrigerator cars for transporting dressed meat.

As dressed-meat shipments to the East became a major enterprise by the early 'eighties, the question of the relationship between freight rates on live animals and packing-house products took on considerable significance. Livestock shipments yielded a greater gross tonnage and required less specialized and less expensive equipment. The special incentive of fees to railroads having stockyards along their lines, such as the Vanderbilt roads and the Pennsylvania, swung them to the side of livestock shippers, while the B&O and Grand Trunk were at first used by the packers.

The railroads held that higher rates should be paid on dressed beef because valuable shipments could be made in smaller space. By June, 1879 the dressed-beef rate, after a number of downward changes, was 67½ cents per hundred pounds, with live cattle shipping at 35 cents from Chicago to New York. Western packers complained bitterly of discrimination. The formation of a company by William H. Vanderbilt, T. C. Eastman of New York, and other livestock shippers, rumored in 1882, was interpreted as a direct move to eliminate Hammond & Company and Swift & Company.[73]

In the spring of 1883 a meeting of railroad officials, livestock men, and dressed-beef shippers, with P. D. Armour, Gustavus Swift, and G. H. Hammond representing the dressed-beef shippers and T. C. Eastman and Samuel Allerton the livestock men, reflected the strained relations then existing. Data gathered at the conference provided the basis for the judgment of Albert Fink, commissioner for the trunk lines, of a proposed rate of 77 cents per hundred pounds on dressed beef and 40 cents on livestock. This the packers rejected on

[73] J. W. Midgeley, "Private Cars," *The Railway Age,* XXXIV (Nov. 7, 1902), 494; *The Drovers' Journal,* April 21, 1883; Armour's Livestock Bureau, *Monthly Letter to Animal Husbandmen,* VII (Nov., 1926), 2–3; Paul I. Aldrich, ed., *The Packers' Encyclopedia: Blue Book of the American Meat Packing and Allied Industries* (Chicago, 1922), pp. 257–59; *Chicago Tribune,* Nov. 11, 1882.

the ground that the actual cost of transportation should determine charges, and that the dressed-beef rate should not be more than 75 per cent above the cattle rate.[74]

Failure to reach agreement brought about the appointment by the railroads in September, 1884 of a three-man committee to arbitrate the matter — Gustavus Swift and Samuel Allerton, with Judge Thomas M. Cooley as chairman. The immediate effect of naming the committee was to cause a decline on the rates of both live cattle and dressed beef, but the final result was the decision of Judge Cooley which established rates on livestock and dressed beef from Chicago to New York in the ratio of 40 to 70.[75] The cessation of hostilities was, however, short-lived, for a rate change in February, 1886 by the Trunk Line Executive Committee boosted dressed-beef shipping costs from 43½ to 65 cents per hundred pounds, while the live-cattle rate was only increased from 25 to 35 cents per hundred pounds.[76]

The air was now filled with bitter exchanges, each side accusing the other of disregarding the welfare of the consuming public. The assurances of Commissioner Fink that his committee had striven for neutrality did not stem the tide of name-calling. There seemed little left to do to check all this maneuvering for advantage except to turn to the government, declared the exasperated *Drovers' Journal*, if pro-

[74] Midgeley, *loc. cit.*, p. 494; *The Drovers' Journal*, April 21, July 11, Aug. 21, 1883, Feb. 19, 1886.

[75] *Ibid.*, Oct. 14, 1884; *The Railway Gazette*, XVI (Nov. 14, 1884), 826, XXXIV (Nov. 7, 1902), 494; Armour's Livestock Bureau, *Monthly Letter to Animal Husbandmen*, VII (Nov., 1926), 3; ICC, *Fourth Annual Report, 1890*, p. 216. The position of arbitrator was originally held by Charles Francis Adams, Jr., who resigned.

[76] ICC, *Fourth Annual Report, 1890*, p. 216; *The Railway Age*, XXXIV (Nov. 7, 1902), 494–95; Aldrich, *The Packers' Encyclopedia*, p. 257; *Chicago Tribune*, Feb. 3, 19, 20, 1886; *The Drovers' Journal*, Feb. 19, 20, 1886. Complaint of discrimination against Chicago packing-house interests, carried on by nine railroads running west of Chicago, was lodged by the Chicago Board of Trade with the Interstate Commerce Commission on Feb. 27, 1889. The railroads involved were C B & Q, Chicago & Alton, C M and St. P, C R I and P, Chicago, St. Paul and Kansas City, Chicago, Santa Fe and California, Illinois Central, the Wabash, and the Chicago and North Western. The roads were accused of charging higher rates on hogs to Chicago than upon the manufactured product, thereby giving an advantage to western packers. The ICC ordered an equalization which lowered hog rates, later modifying this ruling, because of the railroads' objection, so that the rate on live hogs was not to be higher than on packing-house products. Chicago Board of Trade, *Thirty-first Annual Report, 1888*, p. xlvi; Chicago, Burlington & Quincy Archives, *Pools, 1880–89*, pp. 10–12 (Courtesy of Newberry Library); *The Railway Age*, XV (Sept. 6, 1890), 655, (Oct. 25, 1890), 746, (Nov. 15, 1890), 801, XXXIV (Nov. 21, 1902), 550; *The Drovers' Journal*, Nov. 8, 1890; ICC, *Third Annual Report, 1889*, pp. 166–68, *Fourth Annual Report, 1890*, pp. 100–3, 192.

tection were to be given " an already badly choked public." Many, therefore, welcomed the setting up of the Interstate Commerce Commission in 1887. Following its establishment Swift, Armour, Hammond, and Morris filed complaints against a number of their railroad antagonists, to be withdrawn at the time that allegations of a packers' combination, or beef pool, filled the public press, of which more and more had been heard as the 'eighties advanced.[77] With a growing consciousness of a preponderant power in the buying, processing, and selling of meats, located in a few cities of the Midwest, with Chicago as leader, an increasing number feared the effect of a centralization so astutely and presciently conceived, one which operated in alliance with the carriers and which, in the end, determined the price the consuming public paid for meat.

Prodded by public opinion, the Senate, on May 16, 1888, resolved to set up a five-man committee to investigate the transportation and sale of meat products.[78] Meeting in Chicago September 2 to 4, 1889, the committee encountered what it considered both evasiveness and concealment in the testimony of commission men doing business at the Union Stock Yard, and of employees of the packing and dressed-beef interests. Process servers failed, in some cases, to achieve success, Philip D. Armour, Nelson Morris, and Louis F. Swift, among others, declining to obey the subpoena. Refusal to appear before the committee at this time, Armour declared, was based on the prejudice Chairman Vest as live-beef man was alleged to have against the Chicago packers.

In November, however, Armour attended the committee session in Washington and answered the questions put to him. He denied that there was agreement among the packers which would result in diminishing prices paid the producer and yet keep up costs to the

[77] The Drovers' Journal, Feb. 19, 20, 26, 27, 1886; New York Journal and Price Current quoted in The Knights of Labor, I (April 10, 1886), 10; Chicago Tribune, Feb. 24, 1886; Midgeley, loc. cit., pp. 494–96. Samuel Allerton, for example, charged that large rebates and secret rates were given beef shippers by the railroads. For Fink's specially prepared statistics see Bradstreet's, XIII (March 6, 1886), 155. The Chicago Tribune sided with the dressed-beef shippers in the controversy. For the specific complaints of the packers against the railroads see the Interstate Commerce Commission reports for 1887 and 1888.

[78] Members of the Committee were George G. Vest, Missouri, chairman; Preston B. Plumb, Kansas; Shelby M. Cullom, Illinois; Charles F. Manderson, Nebraska; Richard Coke, Texas. At the end of the Fiftieth Congress Charles B. Farwell replaced Senator Cullom. Hearings were held in St. Louis, Washington, Chicago, Des Moines, Kansas City, and New York between Nov. 20 and Jan. 28, 1890.

consumer. Although the committee did not contradict these statements, it concluded that the effects of such co-operation were apparent, if not by direct packer agreement, then through that of the packers' agents. Nor did the committee agree with Armour that the low prices paid for beef cattle were due to overproduction and overmarketing at a time when demand was stimulated by an increasing population and an expanding export market. Inasmuch as an agreement among the Chicago packers as to the slaughtering of hogs was admitted to have existed since 1886, the committee further concluded that it was not unlikely that there was such an arrangement among those dealing with beef cattle.[79]

This investigation, with its suppositions and revelations, did not long stay the formation of new combinations. Nor did the passage of the Sherman Anti-Trust Act in 1890 prove an effective deterrent. By March, 1892, Armour, Swift, and Morris were reported as again refusing to bid against each other in the livestock market, from which numerous old-time butchers, unable longer to compete successfully, had largely disappeared. Indeed, commented the muckraking Charles Edward Russell a little while later, such activities had become " a power greater than the government, greater than the courts or judges, greater than legislatures, superior to and independent of all authority of state or nation." Upon the carriers and those who thus controlled the markets of meat and other food, Henry Demarest Lloyd, like Russell censorious and combative, envisaged an American people dependent, held in bondage for their daily necessities throughout life.[80]

Alongside hidden agencies of buying and selling as vested in the big packers and dealers in livestock, there grew up associations openly designed to effect unity and promote business. As in the Board of Trade rested transactions in grain, so there also was the center of speculative trade in provisions. On March 13, 1884, the Chi-

[79] U. S. Senate Select Committee, *Report . . . on the Transportation and Sale of Meat Products*, 1890, pp. 1, 4–5, 7–8, 10–16, *Testimony*, 1889, pp. 81, 93, 131–34, 182–83, 208, 213, 218, 226, 242, 251–52, 327–28, 364, 367, 384, 387–91, 433–34, 440, 468, 481, 613–15; FTC, *Report on the Meat-Packing Industry, 1919*, Summary and pt. I, 46, pt. II, 13. For Armour's testimony as to agreements among packers see *Testimony* before the Committee, especially pp. 364–65. In this it inferentially may be assumed he acknowledges such arrangements.

[80] *Chicago Tribune*, March 20, 1892; Russell, *loc. cit.*, p. 147; Henry Demarest Lloyd, *Wealth Against Commonwealth* (New York, 1894), p. 37.

cago Live Stock Exchange, made up of men interested in breeding, feeding, shipping, selling, slaughtering, and packing livestock, was chartered. Organized to define standards, to prevent the cutting of commissions, to protect the trade from scalpers receiving and disposing of crippled and diseased animals, the Exchange fought against legislation it held undesirable, improved the dockage system and gained concessions on rail rates favorable to shippers of mixed meats. With an early membership of 200 in 1885 organized to fight the establishment of a Bureau of Animal Industry in the Department of Agriculture, the Exchange succeeded, after an ardent wooing of Congressmen, in having the original bill modified.[81] Its initial gratification in this was shortly dimmed by reverses precipitated by the hostility of farmers, through whose influence the Illinois legislature in 1891 appointed a committee to investigate the Exchange to determine the extent, if any, of a combination of commission men and buyers working against feeders and sellers. The committee found buying and selling practices and prices in the hands of the Exchange, but its critics were not able to pass the bill drawn up to prevent such combinations.[82]

In the Union Stock Yard, with its pens of wood and ugly, somber buildings of board and brick, resided the authority and action of the greatest enterprise of its kind in the world; a place of mud and smells, of overhead runways, and of shabbily clothed men seated on horses, cracking their whips over the incoming herds to hurry them on their way. Here in the Union Stock Yard was not only the seat of the packing industry but the headquarters for the forwarding of livestock. This little town, skirting the outlying part of the city along Fortieth and Forty-fourth streets and west of Halsted to Centre Avenue, with its own hotel, post office, town hall, and fire department, was the embodiment of an ingenuity which had solved the problems of concentrating diverse and complicated operations in the preparation of meat for the many. " Hard work " was its watchword and mass skilled production its satisfaction.[83]

[81] Elmer Washburn, president of the Union Stock Yards National Bank, was president; Peter H. Beveridge, vice-president; Charles W. Baker, secretary, *Chicago Tribune*, Jan. 1, 1885; *The Drovers' Journal*, March 18, 21, 1884, Jan. 9, 1885; *Chicago Commerce, Manufactures, Banking, and Transportation Facilities, 1884* (Chicago, 1884), p. 83.

[82] Illinois, *House Journal, 1891*, pp. 245–46, 771, 840–46, *Senate Journal, 1891*, pp. 278–79, 770–76, 846, *Laws, 1891*, pp. 222–23.

[83] FTC, *Report on the Meat-Packing Industry, 1919*, pt. III, 12, 194–95; U. S. Senate

A PHOTOGRAPH OF PART OF THE UNION STOCK YARDS
MADE IN THE EARLY 'NINETIES

From Frank T. Neely, *Neely's Photographs* . . . (Chicago: F. T. Neely, 18—).

A LUMBERYARD PHOTOGRAPHED FROM THE NORTH PIER LIGHTHOUSE
IN THE EARLY 'NINETIES

From Frank T. Neely, *Neely's Photographs* . . . (Chicago: F. T. Neely, 18—).

By 1891, the capital stock of the Union Stock Yard and Transit Company had reached $13,200,000 and of its 400 acres about 200 were used for the yards, the remainder intersected by the trains of twenty-one railroads, delivering and receiving huge numbers of cattle, calves, hogs, sheep, and horses. Upon the management of this vast enterprise, " the eighth wonder of the world " according to the *Tribune,* was heaped the denunciation of western shippers for high charges on yardage and feed, and controls exercised over weighing and dockage. Upon it fell also the accusation by the Humane Society of cruelty to animals. Advocates of sanitation were horrified by the " filth " especially of the hogpens, and by the army of bluebottle flies which infested not only the stockyard itself but near-by homes and stores.[84]

In 1890, weeks of financial maneuvering went on among eastern capitalists, including the Vanderbilt interests and officials of the Pennsylvania Railroad, and English investors represented by the City of London Contract Corporation, Limited. From these negotiations the Chicago Junction Railways and Union Stock Yards Company, a New Jersey corporation, acquired 98 per cent of the stock of the old company. A minority had strongly opposed the disposal of stocks to the English group or any " alien corporation," going so far as to apply for an injunction against such a sale. The constituency of the new company reflected the far-flung interest of investors in Chicago enterprises, inasmuch as four of the ten directors were residents of London, five were financial promoters of eastern United States, and only one was a Chicagoan.[85]

Select Committee, *Testimony . . . on the Transportation and Sale of Meat Products,* 1889, p. 245; *Chicago Commerce, Manufactures, Banking, and Transportation Facilities, 1884,* p. 81; MacDonald, *op. cit.,* p. 181. Nearly all foreign visitors to Chicago reported on the stockyards. See, for example, the accounts in Pierce, *As Others See Chicago,* pp. 223-24, 233-35, 257-61. Centre Avenue later became Racine Avenue.

[84] *The Drovers' Journal,* June 1, 1883, March 18, April 17, July 31, Aug. 14, 15, 1884, Jan. 13, 1885, April 3, July 6, 1886; *Chicago Tribune,* Jan. 1, 1878, Jan. 1, 1879, Jan. 1, 1884; U. S. Senate Select Committee, *Testimony . . . on the Transportation and Sale of Meat Products,* 1889, pp. 183, 191, 244; *Illinois Reports, 1873,* IV, 239-41. The ownership of the stock was widely dispersed among people in Massachusetts, New York, and elsewhere as well as in Chicago. Railroads were heavy investors. See, for example, *Illinois Reports, 1873,* IV, 237-38.

[85] Nathaniel Thayer of Boston was president of the Chicago Junction Railways and Union Stock Yards Company. *The Drovers' Journal,* June 13, 14, 17, 28, July 1, 2, 3, 1890; *Chicago Tribune,* June 15, 1890; *The Economist,* III (May 24, 1890), 647, (June 21, 1890), 800, IV (July 5, 1890), 12, Investors' Manual, 1898, p. 45; FTC, *Report on the Meat-Packing Industry, 1919,* pt. III, 202.

At the same time, the big packers, Armour, Swift, and Morris, led negotiations to buy over 3,950 acres of land about twenty-five miles southeast of Chicago in Lake County, Indiana, to establish a stockyard of their own, and build new packing-houses provided with an adequate supply of water which was unavailable in the rapidly growing stockyards section. It was a matter of controversy whether the reason for the acquisition of the so-called " Tolleston land purchase," to be known as the Chicago and Calumet Stockyards, was primarily for room to expand, as the packers declared, or whether it was a real estate speculation and a way to force concessions from the Stockyards. Those who looked upon the new location as advantageous pointed out that through the Chicago and Calumet River Terminal Railway eastern lines would be more accessible, and that taxes and other expenses of manufacturing would be lower. Others saw inconvenience because of the greater distance from the western railroads which brought to Chicago the cattle of the western ranges for conversion into meat products.[86]

Meanwhile, fourteen smaller packers, called " the little men," finding their position untenable, started negotiations for yards at Stickney, in Lyons Township.[87] Alarmed by the prospect of a double desertion, the new Union Stock Yards Company looked about for ways to appease the packing interests. Not until January 15, 1892 were the differences between " Big Packers " and the Company resolved, and then only after court battles. For 1,000 acres of Tolleston lands and a promise to remain in Chicago and not establish a competing yard in this area for fifteen years, the packers in July received $3,000,000 of 5 per cent noncumulative income bonds and representation on the board of directors of both the New Jersey and the Yards company.[88]

[86] *The Drovers' Journal*, Jan. 11, Nov. 17, 1890; *The Economist*, IV (Aug. 2, 1890), 178–79, (Nov. 1, 1890), 698, 701–4, (Nov. 8, 1890), 744, (Nov. 15, 1890), 791, V (Jan. 1, 1891), 12; *Chicago Tribune*, Nov. 2, 15, 1890; *Railroad Gazette*, XXIII (July 31, 1891), 526–27; FTC, *Report on the Meat-Packing Industry, 1919*, pt. III, 200–1.

[87] *The Economist*, IV (Dec. 6, 1890), 915. The fourteen concerns and individuals known as the Chicago National Stockyards Company were, according to *The Economist*, VI (Aug. 22, 1891), 330: Chicago Packing and Provision Company, Anglo-American Provision Company, Libby, McNeill & Libby, Allerton Packing Company, Underwood & Co., John Cudahy, International Packing Company, T. E. Wells Company, Wm. H. Silberhorn Co., Jones & Stiles Packing Co., John C. Hately, Moran & Healey, Samuel W. Allerton, and G. W. Simpson. Allerton was represented as a packer and also as an individual shipper. Simpson represented an eastern beef company expecting to be established in Chicago.

[88] *The Economist*, VI (Dec. 19, 1891), 1001; FTC, *Report*, pt. III, 203–4; *The Drovers'*

With the small packers, too, the Chicago Junction Railways and Union Stock Yards Company effected a reconciliation on June 11, 1892. The small packers agreed to remain at the yards for at least five years, and, in return, they received a reported $300,000 in 15-year income bonds and $100,000 in cash.[89] With peace established, local capitalists now foresaw a lucrative return on investments, and by autumn, 1892 were reported as holding an estimated $2,000,000 of the capital stock of the New Jersey company.[90]

Along with this satisfying expansion of business organization went the development of better breeds of animals. The American Fat Stock shows, held annually in Chicago from 1878 through 1893 with the exception of 1892, attracted exhibitions not only from this country but from the British Isles, France, and Canada. Buyers from various places flocked to the city to purchase the meats demanded by a critical public.[91] At the same time the importance of Chicago as a horse market attested her growing dominance in the traffic of all livestock. The chief center of trade was at the Union Stock Yard where 82,492 horses were received in 1893. At the Horse Exchange, first established in 1866, transactions between sellers and buyers took place, as stablemen in " hickory shirts and faded trousers " led the horses from a row of red brick stables, their tails wrapped in red flannel and tags marked " sold " flying from their halters.[92]

By the early 'nineties the effects of the dynamic forces which had been at play in the marketing of livestock and the vast enterprise of

---

Journal, Nov. 5, Dec. 19, 1891, June 13, Aug. 13, 1892; U. S. Commissioner of Corporations, *Report on the Beef Industry, 1905*, App. I, p. 293.

[89] The struggle between the packing interests was marked by action in the courts. A " combine " of small packers made up the Consolidated Packing Company, which, with the International Packing and Provision Company, Limited, and the Chicago Packing and Provision Company, planned to work with the Anglo-American Provision Company against the " Big Three " in bargaining sessions. In 1891 the " Big Three," known as the Associated Packers, were said to have slaughtered 84 per cent of all Chicago slaughtered cattle. The small packers, or the " Non-Associated Packers," chiefly packed hogs. *The Economist*, VI (Dec. 26, 1891), 1035; *The Drovers' Journal*, Jan. 16, March 10, 1892.

[90] *The Economist*, VII (May 28, 1892), 805–6, VIII (Aug. 13, 1892), 234, (Sept. 3, 1892), 334; *The Drovers' Journal*, May 10, 18, 25, 26, Aug. 13, 1892.

[91] Illinois Department of Agriculture, *Transactions*, from 1881 to 1893, *passim; Chicago Tribune*, Dec. 4, 7, 1878, Nov. 12, 15, 1879, Nov. 16, 17, 1880, Nov. 11, 16, 1882, Nov. 15, 19, 1883, Nov. 12, 15, 21, 1884, Nov. 11, 1885, Nov. 9, 10, 16, 1886, Nov. 18, 1887, Nov. 14–18, 1888, Nov. 13, 14, 1889; *The Armour Magazine*, VI (Dec., 1940), 20, 88; Chicago Board of Trade, *Thirtieth Annual Report, 1887*, p. xlix.

[92] Chicago Board of Trade, *Thirty-sixth Annual Report, 1893*, p. xxxiii; Flinn, *Chicago . . . A Guide, 1891*, p. 356.

slaughtering and meat packing were clearly seen. And responsive to these forces, able and aggressive men, looking upon the competitive system as a failure, had turned boldly to combination and large-scale organization. If, in doing so, they participated at times in monopolistic practices, they but conformed to the pattern of their contemporaries in other major endeavors, who, in the words of *The Railway Age,* held that "the experiment of competition" should be abandoned for "combination." [93]

[93] *The Railway Age,* II (June 14, 1877), 1042; *Industrial Chicago,* III, *The Manufacturing Interests,* 626; Chicago Board of Trade, *Thirty-third Annual Report, 1890,* p. 1.

CHAPTER V

THE ECONOMIC EMPIRE OF
CHICAGO: MANUFACTURING
AND MERCHANDISING

ON NEW YEAR'S DAY, 1884 the *Tribune* significantly commented on the changes which were coming to Chicago in the course of her metamorphosis from city of commerce to city of manufacturing. "The tendency is to make here the goods sold here," said the writer, observing also that other signs of urban maturity were likewise at hand. The jobbing business formerly carried on in Chicago, he noted, was moving toward the wholesale supply of western jobbers who now were often taking over in their own communities. As further evidence of the city's economic ripening he pointed to the significance of a lessened dependence on New York for currency to move the western crops. Indeed, ever since the day of physical restoration following the Fire, the city had been deliberately and energetically encouraging those forces apparent before 1871 which foretold the overshadowing of commission merchant and middleman by the manufacturer and his agents.

In the realization of this aspiration, the economic potential was aided substantially by the increased numbers of people settling not only in the city but particularly within a range about a thousand miles square. Between 1870 and 1880 the center of population moved westward fifty-eight miles, the second greatest advance in the country's history, to be followed by a westward move of forty-eight more miles in the next ten years. To these old and new inhabitants, Chicago became the largest easily accessible city which could translate raw supplies into finished products and transfer them to consumers at smaller cost than could eastern cities, chiefly because of lower freight charges. By 1880 only New York and Philadelphia surpassed Chicago as a manufacturing point.[1] The decade which followed witnessed mounting figures for all, with Chicago advancing to second place in the gross value of products. More important as a measure of growth was the western city's gain in the increment created by the processes of manufacturing,[2] and, although still behind New York and Philadelphia, she pressed hard upon the latter, outdistancing her before the 'nineties closed.

These products, diverse and varying in their contribution to the economic sustenance of the city, embraced, however, many of the wants of man, from bread to soda water, from the prosaic iron nail to the elaborately ornamented iron hitching post. Versatile producers converted corn into glucose, made cream of tartar, flavoring extracts, yeast, and baking powders. As early as 1873 the manufacture of confections was said to have assumed " immense proportions," a situation, declared one observer, which showed the demands of the rising generation for candies " was as imperative as those of older people for, perhaps, more pernicious indulgences." [3]

Despite Chicago's undisputed position as the greatest grain mart in the world, the city's flour mills did not keep pace with the advance of the industry in other places, particularly Minneapolis and St. Louis. By the early 'seventies Chicago had to import flour to meet the needs of the growing population, which more and more demanded food baked outside the home.[4] More important was the use

[1] See Appendix table.

[2] The relative rank in importance of the various industries to the economy is based on " value added by manufacture." " Value added " is determined by deducting the cost of materials used, including fuel, from the value of the products. (See U. S., *Thirteenth Census, 1910*, VIII, " Manufactures, 1909," 23.) The value of the gross product is significant, however, for the part played in the city's commerce. For Chicago's fifteen most important industries, a statistical presentation appears in the Appendix in order to supply exact figures which are not always given in the text.

[3] U. S., *Eleventh Census, 1890*, " Manufacturing Industries," pt. II, 130–33; *Industrial Chicago*, III, *The Manufacturing Interests*, 615, 629, 632, 795–97; *Lumberman's Gazette*, III (Nov., 1873), 145, 147, XXII (May 30, 1883), 13; *The Drovers' Journal*, April 30, 1886; *The Rights of Labor*, VIII (April 1, 1893), 5, (June 17, 1893), 5. Among the concerns later well known were the Dr. Price Baking Powder Company and the Calumet Baking Powder Company.

[4] U. S., *Tenth Census, 1880*, " Manufactures," pp. 392, 411, 412, 417, 432, 440, *Eleventh Census, 1890*, " Manufacturing Industries," pt. II, 134–37, 334–37, 342–45, 398–401, 510–13,

of grain in the making of alcohol. From 1870 to 1890 the combined capital invested in distilled and malt liquors and malt establishments mounted from $7,131,000 to $22,772,763 and the value of the product from $6,018,567 to $22,583,681, while a correspondingly satisfying increase in number of employees was paralleled by higher wage totals.[5]

Subscribing to the practice of some promoters of other economic endeavors, distillers entered into pools and other arrangements to control prices. In November, 1881 the Western Export Association was organized and within a few months raised prices, only to break up in May, 1882, because of the refusal of some of its members to pay assessments. This was shortly followed by other pooling agreements, continuously affected by the exigencies of the moment and generally accompanied by the dissatisfaction and wrangling of some of the members.[6]

The inability of the pool to keep members within the restraints imposed led to the organization of the Distillers' and Cattle Feeders' Trust on May 10, 1887, patterned on the Standard Oil Trust and having headquarters at first in Chicago and then in Peoria. The alliance between the two groups, now openly confessed, had operated effectively for some time, and was illustrated in the naming of Peter J. Hennessey of the Chicago Distilling Company as trustee and the important livestock dealer Nelson Morris as director.[7] Like others, Morris fattened his cattle on the slops from distilleries with which he had connections, a practice until the late 'eighties countenanced by

---

578–81; *Illustrated History of Chicago . . .* , p. 49; *Industrial Chicago*, III, *The Manufacturing Interests*, 610–11. In 1872 Chicago received 1,532,014 barrels of flour and shipped out 1,361,328. In 1892 only 542,000 barrels were manufactured in the city. Chicago Board of Trade, *Fifteenth Annual Report, 1872*, p. 10, *Thirty-fifth Annual Report, 1892*, pp. 2–3, 4.

[5] Chicago Board of Trade, *Twenty-fourth Annual Report, 1881*, pp. xvii–xix; the U. S. Census for appropriate years.

[6] Jeremiah W. Jenks, "The Development of the Whiskey Trust," *Political Science Quarterly*, IV (June, 1889), 301–5; U. S. House of Representatives, *Reports of Committees . . .* , III, 50 Cong., 2 sess., H. Rept. 4165, "Trusts" [Whisky] (4 v. Washington, 1889), 15; U. S. Industrial Commission, *Preliminary Report on Trusts and Industrial Combinations . . . , 1900* (Washington, 1900), I, pt. I, "Report," 5, pt. II, "Testimony," 200 (hereafter cited as U. S. Industrial Commission, *Report, 1900*); *The Drovers' Journal*, Jan. 21, April 21, 22, June 18, Aug. 16, Sept. 18, 1886.

[7] Of eighty-one members in 1888 six were in Chicago. U. S. Industrial Commission, *Report, 1900*, I, pt. I, 47, 76–77, pt. II, 169–71; U. S. House of Representatives, *Reports of Committees*, III, 50 Cong., 2 sess., H. Rept. 4165, 57–58, 64, 70, 91; Jenks, *loc. cit.*, p. 306; *The Distilling and Cattle Feeding Company v. The People ex rel.* 156 Ill. 448 (1895).

the law, but then prohibited under an increasingly articulate popular disapproval.[8]

Not long after this, a growing antagonism toward the trusts and the action of the New York Court of Appeals against the Sugar Trust in 1890 aroused the apprehension of the trustees of the Whisky Trust that a similar step might be taken against them by the Illinois court. They, therefore, during that year sought safety in the incorporation of a new organization, the Distilling and Cattle Feeding Company, capitalized at $35,000,000. The separate companies of the old trust surrendered their charters and became branches of the one large corporation, but continued the management and conduct of the business as under the trust. By November, 1892, the company practically monopolized the making of distillery products and held virtually all distillery property north of the Ohio River. When reluctance to participate was expressed, as in the case of the Henry H. Shufeldt and Company and Calumet distilleries of Chicago, strong-arm methods eventually brought recalcitrants into line. In 1895 the Illinois Supreme Court dissolved the Distilling and Cattle Feeding Company as a trust in disguise. Certain properties went at public auction for $9,800,000 to the American Spirits Manufacturing Company, organized under New York laws by a committee and capitalized at $35,000,000.[9]

As time passed, Peoria came more and more to be the chief distillery point of Illinois, and Chicago a center of the brewing industry. By 1890, the latter stood sixth in the nation as producer of malt liquors measured by gross value of the product. But even so, Chicago breweries could not satisfy demand, and thirsty Chicagoans had to import supplies, especially from Milwaukee.[10] Indeed, so popular

[8] *The Drovers' Journal*, Sept. 15, Oct. 14, Nov. 9, 1887; Chicago, *Council Proceedings, 1888–89*, pp. 302, 341; Citizens' Association of Chicago, *Annual Report, 1888*, pp. 24–25. For the affiliation of brewers and packing house owners see *Mixed Drinks*, VIII (Jan. 18, 1893), 1. See also U. S. Industrial Commission, *Report, 1900*, I, pt. II, 168.

[9] 156 Ill. 448–92 (1895); U. S. Industrial Commission, *Report, 1900*, I, pt. II, 167, 171, 172, 176–81, 195, 198, 204, 234–35; U. S. House of Representatives, *Reports of Committees . . .* , III, 52 Cong., 2 sess., H. Rept. 2601, "Whisky Trust Investigation" (3 v. Washington, 1893), 16–30; *Chicago Tribune*, Dec. 11, 12, 1888, Feb. 12, 13, 14, June 5, 9, 1891, June 25, 1892; *Chicago Daily News*, Feb. 12, 14, June 5, 1891; The *Drovers' Journal*, May 26, 1890.

[10] John E. George, "The Saloon Question in Chicago," American Economic Association, *Economic Studies*, II (April, 1897), 71; *Mixed Drinks*, II (June 16, 1890), 1, VI (Feb. 24, 1892), 1; *The Western Brewer*, I (Oct. 15, 1876), 67, III (July 15, 1878), 423, VII (July

had malt liquors become that *Mixed Drinks, The Saloon Keeper's Journal* proudly declared in January, 1890, that for every man, woman, and child in Chicago forty-nine gallons were consumed, more than twice as much as the per capita for Germany. At any rate, in 1890 Chicago was credited with drinking up 1,673,685 barrels and in the World's Fair year something over a million more.[11]

Most Chicago brewers were of German birth and generally spoke and read their native tongue with greater ease than they did English. By 1882, however, the German supplement to *The Western Brewer* was abandoned when a questionnaire revealed that the journal's readers preferred that it be printed in English. Even so, German continued for some time to be used in newspapers and other printed matter, in local and national conventions, indeed wherever Germans assembled.[12] Of the leading brewing firms all but two were headed by German immigrants, of which Conrad Seipp's company was the largest. Upon the death in 1872 of Frederick Lehmann, his partner, Seipp, organized a stock company, the Conrad Seipp Brewing Company. Its 95,167 gallons in 1877 put the brewery fifth in the list of such establishments in the country, and second in the Middle West, with Philip Best of Milwaukee ahead.

Peter Schoenhofen, Michael Brand of M. Brand and Company, Kasper G. Schmidt and Herman O. Glade of Schmidt and Glade, and Matheui Gottfried were, like Seipp, of German background and well versed in their craft. With the English Corydon E. Downer and Henry V. Bemis of Downer & Bemis Brewing Company and the Irish John and Peter Fortune Brothers, they brought to Chicago the skills of their industry. Associated with Downer and Bemis was John H. McAvoy, after 1865, when the concern changed from brewing ale to making the increasingly popular lager beer.[13] Although

---

15, 1882), 1061; Thomas C. Cochran, *The Pabst Brewing Company: The History of an American Business* (New York, 1948), p. 80.

[11] The statement of *Mixed Drinks* was an exaggeration of less than two gallons. *Mixed Drinks*, II (Jan. 15, 1890), 1; George, *loc. cit.*, pp. 83–84; U. S. Commissioner of Internal Revenue, *Report . . . , 1890* (Washington, 1890), p. 204, *Report, 1893*, p. 211. As late as 1900 the annual per capita consumption in the United States had reached only 16.01 gallons. Herman Schlüter, *The Brewing Industry and the Brewery Workers' Movement in America* (Cincinnati, 1910), p. 83.

[12] *The Western Brewer*, II (June 15, 1877), 201, III (June 15, 1878), 343, 348, VII (March 15, 1882), 371; *Constitution and By-Laws of the Alumni of the American Brewing Academy* (Chicago, 1901), pp. 1, 4.

[13] *Illinois Staats-Zeitung*, June 2, 1880; [The Western Brewer], *One Hundred Years*

many brewers relied upon plants devoted primarily to malting, others, like the company headed by Frederick Wacker and in 1884 by his son Charles H., manufactured at least part of the malt needed.[14]

As in other profitable undertakings, foreign capital sought out liquor-making establishments. In 1889 the McAvoy Brewing Company, successor of the Bemis & McAvoy Brewing Company (formerly Downer & Bemis Brewing Company), and the Wacker & Birk Brewing and Malting Company fell into the hands of an English-owned syndicate, the Chicago Breweries, Limited. Shortly other investments were made, although local men in general were in charge of the Chicago plants.[15] In 1890 the City of Chicago Brewing and Malting Company, Limited, captured about one-third of the shares of five leading brewing and malting concerns, later affiliated as the Chicago Consolidated Brewing and Malting Company, incorporated under Illinois laws, with the Northern Trust Company of Chicago serving as trustee of the bondholders.[16] In 1891 the Milwaukee and Chicago Breweries, Limited, absorbed the United States Brewing Company made up of five leading Chicago breweries. The important Milwaukee concern of V. Blatz was also taken over, and Blatz was made president.[17]

of Brewing (Chicago, 1903), pp. 321, 322, 612; *Mixed Drinks,* I (Nov. 15, 1889), 1, II (Feb. 1, 1890), 1; *Chicago Tribune,* Jan. 1, 1880; *The Western Brewer,* III (Dec. 15, 1878), 829, IV (April 15, 1879), 297, V (July 15, 1880), 702, VII (Jan. 15, 1882), 56; John P. Arnold and Frank Penman, *History of the Brewing Industry and Brewing Science in America* (Chicago, 1933), p. 94.

[14] One of the firms devoted primarily to malting was the L. [Louis] C. Huck Malting Company, incorporated in 1878 but operating from 1871. Louis was the son of the well-known brewer John A. Huck. F. Wacker & Company was sold in 1875 to the Northwestern Malting Company. In 1880 Frederick Wacker and his son started F. Wacker & Son. In 1882 the Wacker & Birk Brewing and Malting Company was incorporated with Frederick Wacker as president.

[15] Stock in the Peter Schoenhofen Brewery was also taken by the City Contract Company of London, which had been the purchaser of the McAvoy and Wacker firms. (*The Economist,* II [Oct. 5, 1889], 890.) *Mixed Drinks,* I (Dec. 1, 1889), 1; *The Economist,* III (May 17, 1890), 608–9.

[16] Included in the transaction were the Conrad Seipp Brewery and its subsidiary, the West Side Brewery, the F. J. Dewes Brewing Company, the L. C. Huck Malting Company, and the George Bullen Malting Company. The purchase price was said to be $9,500,000. *Ibid.,* III (May 17, 1890), 609, (June 6, 1890), 730.

[17] The Chicago breweries were those of M. Brand Brewing Company, Ernst Brothers Brewing Company, Bartholomae and Leicht Brewing Company, Bartholomae and Roesing Brewing Company, and K. G. Schmidt Brewing Company. *Ibid.,* I (June 8, 1889), 471, V (March 7, 1891), 380–81, VI (Nov. 28, 1891), 809; *One Hundred Years of Brewing,* p. 498; *Chicago Tribune,* March 4, 1891; Cochran, *op. cit.,* pp. 158, 406. The capitalization of the new group was reported as $11,000,000.

Alongside what appeared well-placed investments, overexpansion occurred; overproduction resulted, accompanied by price-cutting. Old-timers to protect themselves joined hands in the Chicago and Milwaukee Brewers' Association and in 1890 fixed the price at $6.00 a barrel, which, the *Economist* declared, meant a 15 per cent profit on common stock. Still, "beer wars" cut deeply into profits, but, even so, public confidence in brewery shares seemed in general unshaken. Chicago stocks declined neither on the English nor the American market. Even the depression in the early 'nineties did not seem to affect the national and local thirst; Chicago brewers continued to make money.[18]

By adopting the London device of "tied houses" manufacturers and wholesalers forced retailers into a position of dependence. The latter in many cases became merely the managers of saloons owned by producers. Both the Chicago Brewing and Malting Company, Limited, and the Milwaukee and Chicago Breweries, Limited, sold beer wholesale and retail through their representatives, the City of Chicago Investment Company and the United States Security Company. In their hands lay $6,000,000 for the purchase of property for beer saloons largely in the manufacturing and residential areas. Frequently, too, brewers paid the saloonkeeper's license fees or bonds, besides at times setting up their own agents as retailers. Thus the producers of beer attempted to keep in existence the retailers of their product, having, for example, in 1893 financial interests in no less than half of the approximately seven thousand saloons in the city.[19]

By no means were saloons the only place dealing in intoxicants, for groceries, meat markets, and even some dry goods stores sold their customers' favorite brands. Saloonkeepers bitterly but incorrectly complained that these merchants were not legally obliged to

[18] The president of the Chicago and Milwaukee Brewers' Association in 1890 was Rudolph Brand; the vice-president was Charles H. Wacker. (*Mixed Drinks*, III [Aug. 1, 1890], 1); Cochran, *op. cit.*, pp. 148–49; *One Hundred Years of Brewing*, p. 572; *The Economist*, VIII (Sept. 10, 1892), 369, (Oct. 22, 1892), 579, X (July 15, 1893), 45, (July 22, 1893), 76, 79; *American Brewers' Review*, VI (Aug. 18, 1892), 118, 120, (Sept. 15, 1892), 179, (Oct. 13, 1892), 236, VII (July 27, 1893), 57; U. S. Commissioner of Internal Revenue, *Report, 1893*, p. 371.

[19] George, *loc. cit.*, pp. 73–76; *Mixed Drinks*, VIII (Aug. 2, 1893), 1, (Sept. 27, 1893), 1; *The Economist*, VIII (Sept. 10, 1892), 369–70, X (July 22, 1893), 79; *American Brewers' Review*, VI (Dec. 15, 1892), 177, 385; *The Western Brewer*, V (Jan. 15, 1880), 58; Chicago, *Council Proceedings, 1885–86*, pp. 133, 134, *Annual Reports of the Various Departments . . . 1893*, p. 7.

take out a retail license, and broke the law which forbade them to dispense liquor in amounts less than a gallon. And when so-called " high-toned " clubs of some of the richest and most prominent men of the city allegedly paid only the $25.00 federal fee, despite the council ordinance, saloonkeepers held it the rankest kind of discrimination. Nor were they happy when they thought of hotels, Turkish-bath parlors, and amusement places also permitted, again it was said, to sell, without tax, even hard liquor. Forced after 1884 to pay $500 for licenses, saloonkeepers were convinced that no other class of merchants received such unfair treatment.[20] And where else could the lover of beer get a glass of the amber fluid for five cents, with a free lunch of sausages, roast meat, sauerkraut, baked beans, boiled potatoes, bread, and pickled pigs' feet? [21]

A solidarity of craft-consciousness bred associations to counteract the influence of the forces of Prohibition and to lobby for favorable legislation in the various lawmaking bodies which controlled the trade. Chicagoans played a part in national and state as well as local organizations which pointed up the interests of manufacturers, wholesalers, and retailers.[22] All groups rebelled against laws which imposed restraints upon the traffic in which they were engaged. New names took over the policies of old. The retailers' Liberty League of 1873, for example, transmitted its philosophy to the Chicago Wirts-Verein in 1877, which directed its ire against " The Citizens' League and unprincipled cranks" generally in their endorsement of the statute forbidding the sale of liquor to minors.[23]

[20] *Mixed Drinks*, II (May 15, 1890), V (Oct. 15, 1891), 1, (June 15, 1891), 1, VI (Jan. 27, 1892), 1; *Chicago Tribune*, June 16, 1892; *The Western Brewer*, I (Aug. 15, 1876), 9, 16; Chicago, *Council Proceedings, 1882–83*, p. 304, *1883–84*, pp. 414–15, *1885–86*, pp. 130–31, *Laws and Ordinances . . .* , *1890*, pp. 700–1; U. S., *Statutes at Large, 1877–79*, XX, 333. Clubs mainly served wine. Beer was the chief drink in amusement parlors and similar places. Druggists, prior to 1883, were exempted from the license fee if intoxicating liquor was dispensed for medical, chemical, or sacramental use. In 1883 a fee of $25 was charged; in 1885 one dollar.

[21] *Mixed Drinks*, VIII (Jan. 11, 1893), 3; George, *loc. cit.*, pp. 93–94; *The Drovers' Journal*, May 21, 1886.

[22] Among the local groups was the Distillers', Brewers', Bottlers', Maltsters', and Wholesale Dealers' Association organized in 1880, a rare case of several interests merging. (*The Western Brewer*, VI [Jan. 15, 1881], 47.) The Chicago and Milwaukee Brewers' Association was organized in 1881. (*One Hundred Years of Brewing*, p. 572.) A Brewmasters' Association of Chicago and vicinity was organized in 1886. *Ibid.*, p. 578.

[23] *Mixed Drinks*, II (Jan. 1, 1890), 1, VII (Dec. 21, 1892), 1; Illinois, *Laws, 1891*, p. 105. The Chicago Liquor Dealers' Association organized in Jan., 1893, urged Congress to permit the opening of the World's Fair on Sunday. *Mixed Drinks*, VIII (Jan. 11, 1893), 3.

Despite this common program, dissension and jealousy often separated the various branches of the trade. Brewers openly advertised their product as safer than other drink, asserting that whisky makes "a man ugly and corrodes his stomach," while "wine dozes him. Water thins him, lowers the physical tone and makes him frigid, besides filling him full of all manner of strange animals." Saloonkeepers, unable to mount the ladder leading to social éclat, looked with bitterness upon the growing economic and social importance of producers, who often had risen from the ranks of poor employees to rich employers. Palatial residences, membership in exclusive clubs, penetration into other economic undertakings, conspicuously symbolized the advantages acquired through wealth.[24]

As in other industries, producers and sellers had their organs of publicity and education. *The Western Brewer* preached "the gospel of BEER, a gospel good and wholesome and healthful and invigorating, as against the Gospel of Puritanism, of Prohibition, of Personal Thralldom." The journal sponsored experimentation for improved methods of brewing, endorsing, in particular, mechanical refrigeration, in 1876.[25] *Der Braumeister* was the official spokesman for the Master Brewers' Association, which was organized in 1887, as well as serving other groups of brewmasters. About 1891 it was taken over by the Danish immigrant Dr. Max Henius and Dr. Robert Wake of the Scientific Station for Brewing of Chicago, and changed from a German publication to a bilingual organ, the *American Brewers' Review*.[26]

Mixed Drinks, The Saloon Keeper's Journal, under the editorship of Robert J. Halle, prominent member of the Liquor Dealers' and

---

[24] *The Western Brewer,* V (March 15, 1880), 266, XI (Jan. 15, 1886), 90, (Oct. 15, 1886), 2165–66, (Nov. 15, 1886), 2402; Schlüter, *op. cit.,* pp. 67–68; *Mixed Drinks,* I (Nov. 1, 1889), 4. Mildred Walker's *The Brewers' Big Horses* (New York, 1940) fictionalizes the life and social status of a brewer's family. The marriage of Marshall Field, Jr., to Albertine Huck, daughter of Louis C. Huck, was an event of social significance.

[25] *The Western Brewer,* I (Aug. 15, 1876), 13. *The Western Brewer* was published under this title until 1920; June, 1920 to December, 1932 as the *Beverage Journal;* January, 1933, to May, 1934, as *The Western Brewer;* from May, 1934, as *The Brewers' Journal.* One Hundred Years of Brewing, a bulky and extensive study of brewing, appeared as a supplement to *The Western Brewer* in 1903.

[26] *Der Braumeister* ran from 1887 to 1891; *American Brewers' Review,* 1887 to 1939, took over *Der Braumeister* with its July 8, 1892 issue. *Brauer und Mälzer,* published in German and English for a time, served brewers and maltsters 1882 to 1889. It merged with the *Brewers' Journal* and was known as the *Brewer and Maltster and Beverageur* until 1937, when it ceased publication.

Manufacturers' State Protective Association, caustically voiced the opinion of saloonkeepers against Sunday closing, high licenses, woman suffrage, and Prohibition as opposed to " the course of equal rights and liberty." In its columns appeared, as well, news of the trade, personal ephemera, and recipes for new cocktails such as " Two Nips " and " The Glacier," so perfected, the paper declared, that they made the drinker " feel OK " with himself and " the world in general." [27]

Learned chemists and other scholars, sometimes derisively called " beer doctors " by the less scientifically trained brewers, set up schools, carried on experiments, and evolved new techniques in the making of various kinds of liquor. The Zymotechnic Institute, established in 1868 by the German Dr. John Ewald Siebel, and schools run for brewmasters by individual companies insured a more scientifically prepared product. The Takamine Ferment Company, exploiting the process of fermentation which substituted corn for the usual malt in the production of alcohol, profited greatly from the experiments carried on by the Japanese Jokichi Takamine. Indeed, so popular was the method that in March, 1891, the stockholders increased the capital stock from $1,000,000 to $10,000,000.[28]

The capacity for growth shown by Chicago in other fields of economic enterprise, like the city's pivotal position on the important east-to-west passage of men and goods, stimulated the production of iron and steel. This initial and inherent thrust was nurtured by the great consuming market provided not only by an insistent local demand but by the needs of an increasingly populous region near at hand. By 1890 the consumption of pig iron, aside from what was made into steel, reached approximately four hundred thousand tons a year. In 1870 Illinois attained first rank in railroad mileage, and along with her sister states of the North Central Division maintained this enviable priority until 1903. As a result, at an early time Chicago began the production of rails and Bessemer steel; her im-

[27] *Mixed Drinks,* I (Aug. 15, 1889), 2, (Oct. 1, 1889), 1, (Nov. 15, 1889), 1. *Mixed Drinks. The Saloon Keeper's Journal* was the title 1878 to 1894. It was followed by *Fair Play* 1894 to 1897, *Champion of Fair Play,* 1898 to 1929.

[28] Arnold and Penman, *op. cit.,* pp. 15, 122, 124, 129, 130; *Chicago and Its Resources Twenty Years After, 1871–1891,* p. 93; *Chicago Tribune,* Jan. 1, March 6, 1891. See also, for other technical and scientific advances, American Brewing Academy of Chicago, *Tenth Anniversary Reunion Alumni and Former Students* (Chicago, 1901), pp. 19–20, 25, 144–45; *American Brewers' Review,* VII (Nov. 10, 1892), 299–300.

portance as rail-producing center was inescapable. The city's expanding manufacture of steam cars, of the varied products of foundries and machine shops, and of agricultural implements presaged the day in the late 'eighties when Chicago would attain the enviable position of second iron and steel center of the country.[29]

Between 1872 and 1882 ore receipts jumped threefold, to be followed in the next ten years by a fivefold increase, most of it brought in by the lake.[30] This period of expansion saw the movement of the industry from its early location near the Chicago River southward as far as the Calumet district along the lake shore; and from here large-scale production, begotten of multiplying blast furnaces, improved mechanization, skilled management and craftsmanship, was rapidly achieved. In the Calumet district artificial harbors could be constructed without difficulty because of the flatness of terrain and the easily dredged lake bottom; here the district was skirted by an abundance of level, vacant, low-cost land, unexploited for residential purposes and accessible to the large volume of clean water required by the industry.[31]

Scarcely less important as a factor in encouraging the growth of the industry than accessibility to raw materials was the availability

[29] The Lake Superior mines of Michigan, Wisconsin, and Minnesota were the chief sources of supply. The Marquette and Menominee ranges were the two closest to Chicago. George W. Cope, *The Iron and Steel Interests of Chicago* (Chicago, 1890), pp. 7–9, 12–13; *Chicago Tribune*, Oct. 9, 1872, also Jan. 1 annually 1872–1893; U. S. War Department Corps of Engineers, U. S. Army and Shipping Board, *Transportation on the Great Lakes* (Washington, 1926), pp. 243–48, 286; *The Iron Age*, LVIII (Sept. 10, 1896), 459; U. S., *Eleventh Census, 1890*, pt. II, 138–39, 160–61, 454–55, 544–45; American Iron and Steel Association, *Annual Statistical Report, 1890*, p. 53, *1893*, pp. 48–49. Joseph T. Ryerson and Son (after 1888, Joseph T. Ryerson and Son, Inc.) was one of the important links between iron and steel producers and manufacturers. Beginning in 1842, their large iron and steel warehouse became one of the important factors in the western trade. *The Iron Age*, LXVII (April 4, 1901), 31.

[30] From 1872 to 1882 the lake brought in 94 per cent. In 1880 the Chicago and North Western reached the Menominee Range, the closest to Chicago by an all-rail route. In 1886 the Chicago, Milwaukee and St. Paul entered the range. The estimates of receipts are based on a tabulation of receipts of ore from the annual reports of the Board of Trade, 1872–1882. After 1882 statistics of rail receipts and shipments are not available. Mounting tonnages in lake receipts, however, make plausible the inference that the transport of ore to Chicago was chiefly a lake-carried problem. See Appendix tables.

[31] Richard Hartshorne, *The Lake Traffic of Chicago* (unpublished Ph.D. Thesis, The University of Chicago, 1924), pp. 17–18; Hoyt, *One Hundred Years of Land Values in Chicago*, pp. 134–35; John B. Appleton, *The Iron and Steel Industry of the Calumet District* (Urbana, *University of Illinois Studies in the Social Sciences*, XIII, no. 2, 1925), p. 122; U. S. Senate, *Economics of Iron and Steel Transportation*, 79 Cong., 1 sess., Sen. Doc. no. 80 (Washington, 1945), p. 20.

of coal, coke, and limestone. Before 1890 Chicago drew most of the soft coal needed from Illinois, Indiana, Pennsylvania, and Ohio. Illinois sources were but fifty to seventy-five miles away, and the block coal of western Indiana only approximately 175 miles by rail from Chicago. Especially adapted to Bessemer steel production, the Indiana beds supplied the first Bessemer steel mill in Chicago and the first steel works in near-by Joliet. Besides, a considerable amount was imported from southeastern Ohio and western Pennsylvania. The main source of coke was the Connellsville ovens of Pennsylvania.[32] From quarries, especially those at Hawthorne, about seven miles away, Chicago mills got much of their limestone for fluxing, while the Joliet mills found theirs on the spot.[33]

By the late 'eighties the march was well under way, for, in little more than a decade, Chicago and her satellites cut sharply into the heavy leads in production traditionally maintained by Pennsylvania and Ohio.[34] The years following were to see the beginnings of vertical combinations, large-scale production of both iron and steel, and an increasing diversification of products, incontestable signs of the industry coming of age.

On May 1, 1889 the Illinois Steel Company was formed, a combination of three large concerns: the North Chicago Rolling Mill Company; the Joliet Steel Company, with its plant at Joliet and blast furnaces along the south branch of the Chicago River; and the Union Iron and Steel Company.[35] Shortly Illinois Steel became a se-

[32] American Iron and Steel Association, *Annual Report, 1872–73* (Philadelphia, 1873), II, 64, *Annual Report, 1874*, III, 28; American Iron and Steel Association, *Bulletin*, XVI (March 1 and 8, 1882), 660, XXVIII (March 21, 1894), 59; George E. Plumbe, *Chicago, The Great Industrial Center of the Mississippi Valley* (Chicago, 1912), p. 28; *The Railroad Gazette*, XVII (Oct. 16, 1885), 665; Cope, *op. cit.*, pp. 12–15; U. S. Senate, *Economics of Iron and Steel Transportation*, p. 157. See Appendix table.

[33] National Association of Iron Manufacturers, *Statistical Report . . . for 1872* (Philadelphia, 1873), p. 22; Cope, *op. cit.*, p. 14; John B. Appleton, *The Iron and Steel Industry of the Calumet District*, although primarily devoted to a later period than this volume, has some pertinent information for the years to 1893.

[34] Early statistical material often appears for counties and states rather than for separate cities. For the place of Illinois and Chicago in various lines of iron and steel production see American Iron and Steel Association, *Annual Report, 1871*, I (Philadelphia, 1872), 13, *Annual Report, 1879*, VIII, 29, *Annual Statistical Report, 1889*, XVIII, 36, 41, 44; U. S., *Tenth Census, 1880*, "Manufactures," pp. 106–7, 740, 742, 761, 762, *Eleventh Census, 1890*, "Manufacturing Industries," pt. II, 138, pt. III, 393; *Industrial Chicago*, III, *The Manufacturing Interests*, 615; *Iron Age*, LVII (Jan. 2, 1896), 21–24.

[35] The Chicago Rolling Mill, established in 1857 and in 1864 known as the Chicago Rolling Mill Company, was first located on the north branch of the Chicago River. It was said to have rolled the first Bessemer steel rail in the country in 1865. (American Iron and

rious competitor not only for the American but for the world market. Organized to effect economies in the assembly of raw materials, cost of management, and the distribution of its products, the new company had possession of ore lands, coal deposits, timber lands, stone quarries, and means of transportation.[36] Expansion of business was rapid. In 1890 the company through its five plants produced 680,274 tons, and the following year doubled its seventeen coke blast furnaces and other parts of its productive machinery directed principally into the manufacture of rails. Its report for 1892 showed net earnings of $2,019,268 as compared with $1,038,777 for 1891. A dividend of 13.51 per cent payable in company scrip was declared that year besides a cash dividend of 5 per cent. Upon its board of directors were found such important figures as Marshall Field, the merchant prince, Henry H. Porter, former chairman of the Union Steel Company and a heavy investor in railroads and timber lands, and leaders of the iron and steel industry, John Crerar of the Joliet company, and Orrin W. Potter and his son Edward of the North Chicago Rolling Mill Company.[37] Expanding its facilities on the lake front, the Illinois Steel Company brought production in the Chicago area to a peak, and rivalry between Chicago and Pittsburgh was noted with apprehension by the eastern city.[38]

Steel Association, *Annual Report, 1872–73*, II, 43–44.) In 1869 it became a part of an enlarged organization, the North Chicago Rolling Mill Company. In 1878 the company took over the Milwaukee Iron Company of Bay View, Wisconsin. In 1880 the South Works were constructed with lake frontage and an exposure on the north side of the Calumet River's mouth. The Union Iron and Steel Company was in South Chicago near the river. *Chicago Tribune*, May 5, 1889; *The Economist*, II (May 4, 1889), 356; *The Rand-McNally Bankers' Monthly*, VI (April, 1889), 73.

[36] The extension of the Illinois Steel Company to these different enterprises important to it was not unique. For example, a syndicate of Chicago and New York capitalists in spring, 1887 took over the Duluth and Iron Range Railroad and the Vermilion mines of the Minnesota Iron Company, at a reported price of $6,000,000. Among those said to have participated were Henry H. Porter of Pullman's Palace Car Company and the Union Steel Company; Marshall Field; Jay C. Morse of the Union Steel Company; Darius O. Mills of New York; and John D. Rockefeller, of the Standard Oil Company. The American Iron and Steel Association, *Bulletin*, XXI (May 11, 1887), 125, XXIII (May 15, 1889), 132; H. H. Porter, *A Short Autobiography* (Chicago, 1915), p. 35.

[37] *Chicago Tribune*, May 5, 1889; *The Railway Age*, XV (Jan. 4, 1890), 3; *The Economist*, V (Feb. 21, 1891), 289; *The Railway Age and Northwestern Railroader*, XVIII (Feb. 10, 1893), 120.

[38] Smaller iron and steel companies included the Calumet Iron and Steel Company at Cummings, near South Chicago. Inland Steel Company was incorporated October, 1893, and soon became very important. *Chicago Daily News*, March 1, 1888; Cope, *op. cit.*, p. 38; Wayde Grinstead, *50 Years of Inland Steel* (Chicago, 1943), pp. 5–7. See American Iron and Steel Association, *Directory to the Iron and Steel Works of the United States . . . cor-*

Flourishing factories rapidly turned out railroad cars, wheels, and other equipment, as well as the rails over which they passed, individually and collectively testifying to the annually growing importance of the city as a manufacturing point. Of the companies making railway equipment the most famous was Pullman's Palace Car Company, founded in 1867 as a stock company and capitalized at $100,-000.[39] As in other important enterprises, the 'eighties especially witnessed amazing growth. The healthy state of business, for which the master hand of George M. Pullman was mainly responsible, was evidenced in assets and capital stock mounting over two and a half times from 1883 to 1893. Equally impressive was the gain in earnings and the annual surplus, and the consistently satisfying dividends on stock paid quarterly, which ranged from 6 to 8 per cent. Although not without competitors, Pullman and the associations controlled and operated by his company invariably carried the greatest number of travelers in his *"wagons de luxe,"* as the French economist Paul de Rousiers so appropriately called them.

By autumn, 1890 the company reported an 18 per cent gain over the 4,242,542 passengers of the year before, matched by a corresponding increase in miles traveled. At the same time conditions of travel improved. By 1889 steam heat and electric lights, and separate toilet facilities for men and women were installed in cars running from Chicago to San Francisco, San Diego, or Los Angeles, for which a charge of fifty cents a night, or four dollars the entire way, was made. Between Chicago and the East equally attractive features were found, the Pintsch gas system lighting a car of twelve sections, the smoking-room, drawing-room, and buffet.[40]

Imbued, as were other economic leaders of the day, with the prevailing zeal for expansion, Pullman reached out eagerly for new

rected to *July 25, 1882* (Philadelphia, 1882), pp. 144–47 for Chicago mills of that date. Directories of later years supply similar information.

[39] Incorporated in 1867 as Pullman's Palace Car Company, it was commonly called the Pullman Palace Car Company. It was the predecessor of the Pullman Company (1899), in 1927 Pullman, Incorporated.

[40] *The Railway Age and Northwestern Railroader,* XVIII (Oct. 27, 1893), 787; *The Economist,* VI (Oct. 24, 1891), 690–91; Pullman's Palace Car Company, *Annual Statement, 1889, 1890, 1891* (courtesy of The Pullman Company, Chicago); *Railroad Gazette,* XXI (Feb. 15, 1889), 115, (Aug. 16, 1889), 544, XXII (Aug. 15, 1890), 575, (Oct. 24, 1890), 746. The capital stock in 1883 was $13,269,000, and in 1893 it was $36,000,000; assets in the same years were $23,095,369 and $61,791,643; earnings $4,093,245 and $9,200,685; annual surplus in 1893 was $4,006,448; in 1889 it had been $2,251,530.19.

fields he might conquer. In 1873 he shipped palace cars to England where they were introduced alongside the American system of checking baggage. Two years later he opened a shop at Turin, Italy. Before the 'seventies closed, drawing-room and sleeping cars rode the rails of six of England's and Scotland's main lines.

The success which the Pullman Company enjoyed was illustrated by an increasing number of shops, including those at Elmira, Detroit, and St. Louis, which turned out not only the so-called palace and dining cars and the chair car, but all kinds of passenger coaches and freight cars. The town of Pullman, located in the vicinity of 111th Street, provided permanent workshops after 1881 — the physical embodiment of the idea of its founder, George M. Pullman, just as was the sleeping car which bore his name.[41]

Besides Pullman's Palace Car Company other manufacturers undertook to satisfy the mounting demand for railroad and other transportation equipment.[42] In 1890 the Grant Locomotive Works erected a plant in Cicero, proposing to bring out 250 locomotives a year. With the use of steel gaining popularity throughout the country, men interested in industrial expansion entered this field, devoting themselves solely, as did the Harvey Steel Car Co. of Harvey, Illinois, to steel car construction.[43] And, as the city extended its territorial limits and streetcar lines were built to meet the requirements

[41] Pierce, As Others See Chicago, pp. 241–49, 264–66; Joseph Husband, The Story of the Pullman Car (Chicago, 1917), pp. 28–54, 61, 63, 83–84; The Chicago Times, April 1, 1873, June 26, 1874, April 25, 1880, April 3, 1881; Chicago Tribune, April 1, 1873, Oct. 18, 1889, Oct. 17, 1890; The Economist, VI (Oct. 24, 1891), 690; Thomas A. Dunlap, comp. and ed., Wiley's American Iron Trade Manual of the Leading Iron Industries of the United States (New York, 1874), p. 256; Steel Facts, April, 1947, p. 7; Illinois Bureau of Labor Statistics, Third Biennial Report, 1884, pp. 638–54; Corrall R. Harding, George M. Pullman (1831–1897) and the Pullman Company (The Newcomen Society, New York, 1951. Courtesy of Pullman, Incorporated), pp. 16, 20–24, 30.

[42] As early as 1873 the Joliet Steel Company had made a steel rail. In ten years the North Chicago Rolling Mill Company and the Joliet Steel Works were two of four plants producing a considerable number of steel rails. (American Iron and Steel Association, Directory to the Iron and Steel Works of the United States, 1882, pp. 145–47.) During the 1880's the Sargent Co. manufactured railroad brake shoes. The Union Foundry and Pullman Car Wheel Works and the Wells and French Co., the latter making both railway cars and bridges, were among those supplying railroad equipment.

[43] Chicago Tribune, Dec. 22, 1889, Jan. 30, 1890; The Economist, IV (July 19, 1890), 118, V (Feb. 14, 1891), 250, (May 2, 1891), 748; The Railway Age, XV (Jan. 4, 1890), 15, (Jan. 11, 1890), 19, 23, (March 22, 1890), 197, (April 26, 1890), 300; American Iron and Steel Association, The Bulletin, XXVI (March 25, 1892), 149. Among the incorporators of the Grant Locomotive Works was Edward T. Jeffery, also connected with the Harvey Steel Car Co. The Grant Locomotive Works moved to Chicago from Paterson, New Jersey.

of the residents of the new sections, the manufacture of this kind of transportation sprang up by the late 'eighties. Here again was a demonstration of the practicality and timeliness motivating Chicago investors, of that spirit which the Frenchman Paul Blouët called Chicago " go-aheadism," of which the city was the most typical example in the United States. In this new undertaking could be counted the Calumet Car Company of Placerdale and the Day Railway Car Company, the latter producing, among other things, both surface and elevated railroads and rolling stock. Both had been preceded, however, by F. E. Canda & Co., with works at Blue Island, who, as early as 1874, put out streetcars along with those for railroad passengers and freight. In addition, Canda built water stations, turntables, and iron bridges.[44] The construction of " floating monsters of iron," and then of steel, to replace the onetime ships of wood, and orders for iron and steel viaducts bore further testimony to the growing importance of Chicago as a manufacturing point.[45]

In iron and steel lay the roots of many other thriving enterprises. So lusty was this growth that establishments like the Washburn & Moen Manufacturing Company of Worcester, Massachusetts, put up works in near-by Waukegan to make barbed wire, with its offices of management located in Chicago.[46] Foundry and machine shops flourished abundantly both in quantity and variety of output. By 1890 the capital poured into them placed them fourth in amount invested in manufactures — over twenty-five and a half million dollars, more than five times that recorded in the previous decennial census. Relatively, they rated third among the major manufactures, both in

[44] Max O'Rell (Paul Blouët) and Jack Allyn, *Jonathan and His Continent* (Madame Paul Blouët, trans., New York, 1889), p. 43; *Wiley's American Iron Trade Manual*, p. 255; *The Economist*, I (April 6, 1889), 272; *The Railway Age*, XVI (Feb. 28, 1891), 179. Placerdale was about one and a fourth miles west of Pullman and Kensington and on the road to Morgan Park, between 115th and 119th streets. Jesse S. Hildrup was a large owner in the Calumet Car Company and the Morgan Park Street Railway Company. St. John V. Day was one of the leading incorporators of the Day Railway Construction Company.

[45] Important bridge builders were the Lassig Bridge and Iron Works, the Chicago Bridge and Iron Company, the American Bridge Works and the Kenwood Bridge Co. (Moses and Kirkland, *History of Chicago*, II, 426–27.) The steel steamer *Maritana*, reported the largest in fresh water, was launched in 1892 from the yards of the Chicago Shipbuilding Company, of which Emmons Blaine was president. The vessel was to be used in the iron ore trade. (American Iron and Steel Association, *The Bulletin*, XXVI [June 22, 1892], 181.) *The Railway Age*, XV (Jan. 4, 1890), 15, (Jan. 11, 1890), 34, XVI (Feb. 21, 1891), 159; Chicago Board of Trade annual reports; *Chicago Tribune*, Jan. 1, 1890, Nov. 20, 1892.

[46] *The Economist*, V (March 28, 1891), 514–15, (April 11, 1891), 600.

number employed and in the value thus created. Typical of the broadening and deepening of the opportunities afforded those so engaged was the enlargement of Crane Bros. Manufacturing Co. from the modest copper and brass foundry of Richard T. Crane of the 1860's to the manufacture of not only valves and lead and iron pipes, but pumps and hydraulic elevators. In 1886 the company further extended its business to include the jobbing of plumbing fixtures, more and more in demand as the urbanization of Chicago and her satellites progressed.[47]

Although pipes and other essentials for the installation of water closets, washbowls, bathtubs, and sinks could generally be purchased locally and were frequently made in Chicago, the conveniences themselves were most often obtained from eastern factories and then distributed through the usual merchandising channels, such as Crane's, to local and hinterland customers. Chicago manufacture of these appliances lagged appreciably behind trade. As early as 1866, however, the L. Wolff Manufacturing Company added to its manufacture of copper vessels, used in distilling and brewing, the making of plumbers' supplies. About 1873 Wolff bought the right to produce the Fuller patent cocks, advertised as preventing leakage. He is also credited with putting out the first copper bathtub in Chicago, which, by the late 'seventies, was preferred, as a rule, over the crudely built zinc- and lead-lined tubs of Chicago plumbers. These, a few years later, were superseded in the best homes and hotels by the more attractive porcelain and painted cast-iron tubs.[48] By the 'nineties the "Flume and Crystal Closet," in which Henry Huber & Co. specialized, offered stiff competition to other makes, and was considered good enough to be installed in the mansions of Emanuel Mandel, Max M. Rothschild, and Chauncey Keep.[49]

[47] Anon., *History of Crane Co.* (Typescript. Courtesy of Crane Co.), *passim;* Pierce, *A History of Chicago,* II, 112.

[48] *Industrial Chicago,* II, *The Building Interests,* 50–56, 622; Moses and Kirkland, *op. cit.,* II, 423; [Manhattan Publishing Company], *A Biographical History with Portraits of Prominent Men of the Great West,* p. 447. By the mid-'eighties porcelain and painted cast-iron tubs could be purchased in Chicago from the agency of the J. L. Motts Iron Works, a New York concern.

[49] *Chicago and Its Resources Twenty Years After, 1871–1891,* p. 94. Mandel, prominent retail dry goods merchant, lived at 3400 Michigan Avenue; Rothschild, a member of the clothing firm of E. Rothschild & Bros., lived at 2112 Prairie Avenue; and Chauncey Keep, lumber dealer 1879–82 and vice-president of Raymond Lead Co. 1888–93, had his home at 2825 Prairie Avenue.

Alongside advances in the construction of the bathtub were improvements in other equipment. In 1873 the Palmer House installed the first so-called sanitary water closet in the city, imported from the British Isles. In the 'eighties keen competition developed among an increasing number of makes, Chicagoans in particular looking favorably upon a new invention, an automatic flush toilet designed by their fellow townsman Benezette Williams, and described as disposing effectively of the sewage from any building. James B. Clow & Son, founded as jobbers in 1878, acted as agents in the 'eighties for the Alexander closet, made in Detroit and advertised as " the best in the world, free from sewer gas, smell from traps, no overflowing and no getting out of order." [50]

Besides the modest attempts to manufacture sanitary fixtures, fledgling stove works and small factories for making steam-heating apparatus sprang up to satisfy some of the needs of the local market. As early as 1875 the production of iron bedsteads was undertaken, and a cutlery establishment joined in the varied procession on its way, Chicagoans declared, toward a millennium of prosperity. To the dream of emancipation from the East with an accompanying leadership of the Middle West, even the reduction of metals was considered a possible contributor. As early as 1874 the reduction of ore and crude bullion reached 20,000 tons, with gold and silver leading and valued at $2,500,000, while twelve million pounds of lead smelted carried an estimated value of $780,000.[51] Establishments fabricating tin cans for storage and shipping boasted a good business as early as the 'seventies.[52] At the same time nonferrous metal pro-

[50] U. S. Commissioner of Patents, *Annual Report, 1882*, pp. 3, 570, *1883*, pp. 664–65, *1884*, pp. 604–5; *The Sanitary News*, I (Nov. 15, 1882), 2, (April 15, 1883), iii. Clow dealt in boiler tubes and iron pipes. The firm began the manufacture of cast-iron pipes in 1892. The corporation of James B. Clow & Sons was formed in 1894. William E. Clow, *My 60 Years in the Cast Iron Pipe Business* (Chicago, privately printed, 1938. Courtesy of Miss Katherine Hieber, of the James B. Clow & Sons staff).

[51] Two of the best-known stove products of Chicago make were the Gold Coin stoves and ranges put out by the Chicago Stove Works and the Jewel Vapor stoves and ranges made by George M. Clarke & Co. Cribben, Sexton & Company were stove manufacturers of importance. Andreas, *History of Chicago*, III, 472–77, 483; *Chicago and Its Resources Twenty Years After, 1871–1891*, p. 111; [International Publishing Company], *1837–1887. Half-Century's Progress of the City of Chicago . . .* , pt. I, " History of Illinois " (Chicago, 1887), 355; *The Economist*, II (Nov. 16, 1889), 1057, III (June 14, 1890), 769; Chicago Board of Trade, *Eighteenth Annual Report, 1875*, p. 226; W. L. Fawcette, " Currency and Banking in Chicago," *The Lakeside Monthly*, IX (Feb., 1873), 134.

[52] To Edwin Norton, of Norton Brothers, Maywood, is ascribed credit for rolling the first solder from molten metal for tin cans. This firm had factories also in New York and

duction increased, and by 1880 the *Tribune* pointed to no fewer than 177 firms with a combined capital of $3,573,000 and products valued at $6,435,000.[53]

Probably no product of Chicago factories was more widely known than agricultural implements, which already enjoyed international acclaim. By 1890 the city's six factories produced about one-seventh of all machines made in this country. Their estimated value added through manufacture had soared about six times within ten years, putting the industry among Chicago's top eight, an impressive advance from the position of fourteenth ten years earlier. During that period those who earned their living in the various factories multiplied nearly four times, while the capital invested mounted about nine times, enough to make it by 1890 the third highest capitalized of Chicago's major industries. Of the important makers of agricultural implements the best known was the firm of C. H. & L. J. McCormick. In 1879 it became a joint stock company, the McCormick Harvesting Machine Company, in which Cyrus H. McCormick held controlling interest.[54] Expansion of the business both at home and abroad was gratifying, net profits swelling from $325,000 in 1877 to $1,232,781 in 1881. But dollar gains did not certify happy personal relations, and in 1890 Leander and Hall McCormick withdrew, selling their interest to Cyrus McCormick for about $3,250,000. In November of that year McCormick joined forces with other implement manufacturers in the American Harvester Company, its capital $35,000,000. Early in 1891 the organization broke up, avowedly because of legal technicalities, but it was currently rumored because of internal differences and the open opposition of farmers to an organization considered by them as monopolistic.[55]

San Francisco, and Hamilton, Canada. In 1877 Frank Diesel began the manufacture of cans for fruit, oysters, and meat. *Chicago Tribune*, May 17, 1874; Moses and Kirkland, *op. cit.*, II, 420–21; *Chicago and Its Resources Twenty Years After, 1871–1891*, p. 94.

[53] *Chicago Tribune*, Jan. 1, 1880. For the 1870's see *Lumberman's Gazette*, III (Nov., 1873), 145, 147; *The Western Manufacturer*, VI (Jan. 15, 1879), 909.

[54] Other important manufacturers of agricultural implements were William A. Deering & Company, David Bradley Manufacturing Company, the F. C. Austin Manufacturing Company, the Craver, Steele and Austin Company, the Aermotor Company (maker of windmills). Firm names of many companies engaged in the manufacture of agricultural implements changed throughout the years covered by this volume, just as they did in many other industries. On the whole, the form used was the common one at the time under discussion.

[55] The best source on the McCormick organization to 1885 is Hutchinson's *Cyrus Hall McCormick*, especially Volume II covering the years 1856–1884. Among the twenty members of the American Harvester Company were the Chicago firms McCormick Harvesting Machine

Investment dollars continued to flow into wagon- and carriage-making. Even in the depressed decade of the 'seventies Peter Schuttler had good orders for his freight and plantation wagons, but, as in the case of agricultural implements, wagon production usually reflected the vagaries of crop and other business conditions. To get rid of the deleterious effects of these price determinants by controlling production, the National Wagon Manufacturers' Association was revived in 1886 with the active support of Chicago producers. By 1890 over four and a half million dollars in the gross value of the product attested the prosperity of those providing the buggies, phaetons, sulkies, and other vehicles popular in late nineteenth-century America.[56]

The combination of an abundance of raw material with an insistent demand predetermined the monetary rewards received by those interested in a variety of wood products. An extraordinary growth of manufactories requiring wood for plant buildings and the construction of dwellings for the rapidly increasing population, among other needs, stimulated production. Lumber- and planing-mill products, including sash, doors, and blinds, responded favorably to the generative economic tendencies at play. In their estimated value through manufacture, only four other industries exceeded lumber and timber products by 1890. The turned and carved wood output at the same time also showed evidence of greater popularity.[57]

Men engaged at first in one form of the manufacture and trade in wood frequently became associated with other aspects and prospered through them. Such was the case of Herman Paepcke, who had a planing mill and a box factory through which he laid the basis of a sizable fortune.[58] Boxes and buckets, picture frames, dumb-waiters,

Company, William A. Deering & Company, and Warder, Bushnell and Glessner Company. Cyrus McCormick was made president. *Chicago Tribune*, Dec. 7, 1890, Jan. 10, 1891; *The Economist*, IV (Nov. 22, 1890), 836.

[56] *The Drovers' Journal*, Oct. 22, Dec. 17, 1886; *The Western Manufacturer*, III (July, 1876), 167. The gross value was $4,565,136; the value added by manufacture was $2,785,-517. U. S., *Eleventh Census, 1890*, "Manufacturing Industries," pt. II, 136–37.

[57] In 1870 Chicago had 17 sash, door, and blind factories with a production value of $874,550. In 1890 there were 116 plants, including lumber and planing mills, with products valued at $17,604,494. *Industrial Chicago*, III, *The Manufacturing Interests*, 619–20; U. S., *Eleventh Census, 1890*, "Manufacturing Industries," pt. II, 666; *Northwestern Lumberman*, XXXVII (April 18, 1891), 14.

[58] Paepcke migrated to the United States when twenty-one from his native Germany. At first he lived in Texas. In 1881, at the age of thirty, he came to Chicago. Like other Chicagoans, he invested in southern timberlands. In 1887 the firm was called H. Paepcke

and even baseball bats added to a list of wood products almost too numerous to mention. By the early 'eighties A. G. Spalding & Bros. manufactured more bats than any other concern in the business, reporting in the spring of 1883 that about five hundred thousand would be turned out.[59]

The healthy condition of the woodworking industry was no better illustrated than in the making of furniture, progressing from the crudely constructed pieces of the first factories to the finished products of the 1880's. Indeed, as early as the 'seventies, local boosters proudly proclaimed that there were few points in the country which did not know about Chicago-made furniture, and, by the 'eighties, they advertised the city as the leading producer of parlor furniture in the world. Standing in the first six of the principal manufactures in 1890 both in number of employees and in the estimated value the industry had through manufacture, furniture and chair factories were said to have given Chicago the enviable position of leading producer of the country.[60]

No less a matter of pride was the infant undertaking of musical instrument production, especially since it discounted in the minds of Chicagoans the observation of outsiders that the city's whole energy was directed toward the quest of the Almighty Dollar, a quest hurried, unremitting, and astutely channeled. From the 'eighties on, the manufacture of musical instruments was appreciably stepped up over that of a decade before, placing Chicago by 1890 third among the big four — New York, Philadelphia, Chicago, and Boston. In the mid-'seventies there was no reed-organ factory in the city to satisfy the needs of the musically conscious, but before the 'eighties closed Chicago produced almost four times as many organs according to value as did her nearest competitor, Boston. Equally gratifying was

& Co. In 1893 it became the Paepcke-Leicht Lumber Co. The American Lumberman, *American Lumbermen*, pp. 177–80.

[59] *Zgoda*, Sept. 24, 1890; Stephenson, *Recollections of a Long Life*, p. 166; *The Railway Age*, XV (May 10, 1890), 335; *Industrial Chicago*, III, *The Manufacturing Interests*, 625; *Der Westen*, June 13, 1875; *Northwestern Lumberman*, XXI (March 24, 1883), 6; *Year Book of the Commercial, Banking, and Manufacturing Interests of Chicago, 1885–6*, pp. 309–10.

[60] *The Western Manufacturer*, VI (Jan. 15, 1879), 908; Chicago Board of Trade, *Thirty-first Annual Report, 1888*, pp. xv–xvi; Andreas, *History of Chicago*, III, 733–34; *Chicago Tribune*, Jan. 1, 1890. Cabinetmaking, in which the Germans and Scandinavians especially were occupied, is not included in the census classification of "Furniture, factory product."

the accelerated construction of pianos, which, trumpeted the locally conscious *Tribune,* reached about nine thousand in 1891, an astounding gain over the fifty of the late 'eighties.[61]

In the list of important firms the W. W. Kimball Company, starting as distributor rather than manufacturer, took up the role of the latter in 1881 in organs and four years after in pianos.[62] Other names, well known in a later day, such as the Story & Clark organs, the Chicago Cottage Organ Company, and the Wilcox & White Organ Co., became popular chiefly in Chicago and the near-by territory. The house of Lyon and Healy, important since 1864 as importers, wholesalers, and retailers, began in 1885 the manufacture of musical instruments which, seven years later, was reported as hitting the mark of 100,000.[63]

Far more significant as a contributor to Chicago's economy was the industry of printing and publishing, which, along with the making of musical instruments, exemplified the city's cultural manufactures, giving to her, as the *Western Manufacturer* saw it, " a certain '*éclat*' not enjoyed by places devoted more exclusively to merely mechanical industries." Rising from third place in 1880, printing and publishing was second ten years later as measured in terms of value added by manufacture. At this time the city was outdistanced only by " her ancient rival on Manhattan." Although the disparity was not slight, aspiring and unrealistic Chicagoans boasted that the day was not far distant when the relative positions would be reversed. In 1889 more than nine million dollars were paid out in wages, the second highest amount in the city, and the industry's output, as in most other cases, found the readiest sale in the growing states to the west. This was particularly true of books, which, with newspapers and periodicals, rated the most lucrative of the various individual undertakings.[64]

[61] U. S., *Eleventh Census, 1890,* "Manufacturing Industries," pt. II, 77, 141, 405, 409; *Chicago Tribune,* Jan. 1, 1892.

[62] William Wallace Kimball established his business in Chicago in 1875. In 1864 he had become a prosperous wholesaler. In 1882 his company was incorporated as the W. W. Kimball Company. *Chicago and Its Resources Twenty Years After, 1871–1891,* pp. 125–26.

[63] *Ibid.,* pp. 124–29; Moses and Kirkland, *op. cit.,* II, 447–53; *Year Book of the Commercial, Banking, and Manufacturing Interests of Chicago, 1885–6,* pp. 300–1; *The Knights of Labor,* VI (Aug. 31, 1889), 4; *Der Westen,* July 15, 1879; *Illinois Staats-Zeitung,* Nov. 26, 1879; *Chicago Tribune,* Jan. 1, 1892.

[64] *The Western Manufacturer,* V (Dec. 15, 1878), 886; Chicago Board of Trade, *Thirty-*

Before the Fire not many books had been issued with the imprint of a Chicago house, and the general destruction of October, 1871 delayed any incipient expansion which the early 'seventies might have nurtured. This hiatus, however, was of brief duration, for in 1878 it was estimated that nearly 350,000 Chicago-manufactured books had been sold that year. This gratifying showing was in part the result of the demand for low-cost books to which Donnelley, Loyd & Co. had contributed with their *Lakeside Library,* started in 1875. Made up of noncopyrighted, paper-covered fiction selling for as low as ten cents, the Library soon had wide appeal. The standard works of Scott, Dickens, and Cooper even at this price proved a profitable venture because of economies effected in manufacture. In 1879 the *Lakeside* series of quarto novels was discontinued because of the greater popularity of the *Seaside Library* published by George Munro of New York.

More than the *Lakeside Library,* however, came from the Donnelley presses. In 1877, for example, in order to appeal to the Christmas trade the *Fireside Library* of twenty-four volumes, bound in English muslin, made available the works of Wilkie Collins, Jules Verne, Anthony Trollope, Charles Reade, and other popular authors.[65] In 1883 the firm became R. R. Donnelley & Sons and began focusing its chief attention upon printing rather than book publishing.[66] The demand for inexpensive reading matter stimulated other ventures similar to that of the Donnelley establishment. Cheap cloth-bound books were put out by W. B. Conkey; and Louis Schick in 1884 be-

---

first Annual Report, 1888, p. xvi; *The Chicago Times,* March 12, 1881; *Chicago Tribune,* Jan. 1, 1893; *Industrial Chicago,* III, *The Manufacturing Interests,* 622–24.

[65] Richard R. Donnelley, along with Thomas Hutchinson, Joseph F. Bonfield, and John R. Walsh, organized the Chicago Directory Company in 1879, and from 1880 to 1916 were the publishers of the important Chicago directories with their extensive listings of persons, businesses, organizations, and other items of current interest. From 1879 to 1883 R. R. Donnelley was associate compiler of the directory; in 1887 he became manager of the Chicago Directory Company. The Donnelley firm became R. R. Donnelley & Sons Company in 1890.

[66] Raymond Howard Shove, *Cheap Book Production in the United States, 1870 to 1891* (unpublished M.A. Thesis, University of Illinois, 1936; planograph, 1937), pp. 71–74; *Cambridge History of American Literature* (4 v. 1st ed., William P. Trent *et al.,* eds., New York, 1917–21), IV, 551; Joe L. Norris, *Pioneer Marketing Associations of the American Book Trade 1873–1901* (unpublished Ph.D. Thesis, The University of Chicago, 1938), p. 90; *The American Bookseller,* IX (Jan. 15, 1880), 65; *The Publisher's Weekly,* XV (March 15, 1879), 308.

gan printing fiction in the German language — books in bright-orange paper covers which he sold at twenty cents the copy.[67]

Particularly well known was Belford, Clarke & Co., who reprinted extensively many standard works which they unconventionally allowed to be marketed at less than list prices, not through regular booksellers, but at bookstalls and department stores. They poured out editions of Ruskin, Bulwer-Lytton, George Eliot, Thackeray, and Scott, and, in 1885 alone, 75,000 of their fifteen-volume set of Charles Dickens. In addition to their publications, this venturesome house had on its lists Dante's *Inferno* and *Purgatory* and *Paradise,* and volumes devoted to history, such as Guizot's *A History of France from the Earliest Times to 1848,* profusely illustrated, as well as other serious books of prose and poetry. They carried on a coast-to-coast business, locating agencies in New York and San Francisco, thus emulating the example of eastern publishers with an eye to a good market in Chicago. In addition, they included among their ventures juvenile publications and the monthly *Belford's Magazine,* a journal to popularize serious subjects. It was first issued in June, 1888, but was discontinued in July, 1893, after failing to capture public favor.[68]

The field of cheap book publishing, however, was not the domain solely of those whose primary interest was the satisfaction of the masses for reading matter. Like others, Donohue & Henneberry, well known for the printing of catalogues and similar items, were by the late 1880's issuing twelvemos. About the same time Rand, McNally & Co. started their *Globe Library,* popular authors' works in paper books, which included editions of Bertha M. Clay, H. Rider Haggard, and George Meredith. These books sold at twenty-five cents,

[67] Walter B. Conkey was first listed in 1879 as a bookbinder. In 1891 the firm was known as W. B. Conkey Company and had expanded into manufacturing and publishing books. Schick carried his enterprise to 1888. Shove, *op. cit.,* p. 139; *Industrial Chicago,* III, *The Manufacturing Interests,* 801–2; *The American Bookseller,* XVIII (May 15, 1885), 287.

[68] Belford, Clarke & Co. was established in 1879 having been preceded by Rose-Belford Publishing Co. The firm later appears as Belford-Clarke Company. Alexander Belford and James Clarke had come to Chicago from Canada in 1875. Their price-cutting activities involved them in a series of difficulties and in 1889 they went into receivership, reorganizing shortly thereafter. The Chicago branch was known as the Belford-Clarke Company. It went out of business in 1892. *The Publisher's Weekly,* XXXVI (Sept. 28, 1889), 478, (Oct. 12, 1889), 537, 539–40, (Dec. 14, 1889), 930–31; *The American Bookseller,* XVII (March 16, 1885), 168, XXI (May 2, 1887), 272, XXII (Christmas, 1887), 452–53, XXVI (Oct. 15, 1889), 494; Shove, *op. cit.,* pp. 82–87; Herbert E. Fleming, *Magazines of a Market Metropolis* (Chicago, 1906), pp. 530–31.

principally at newsstands and on railroad trains. To meet the demand for a more substantially made book the *Rialto Series* was put out on better paper, and by 1892 had about fifty titles to the 170 in the *Globe*. Railroad timetables and tickets and shippers' guides became the company's specialty, and reference books, including encyclopedias, directories, guidebooks, maps and atlases, were printed in impressive number.[69]

By the 'seventies subscription books, too, had become an important aspect of both manufacture and selling. Not only did publishers in general frequently engage in this form of merchandising, but houses were organized especially for this purpose. Baird & Dillon, starting in Chicago in 1877, had sales of over $1,000,000 within six years. In 1884 they reported 1,500 canvassers calling upon the American public, from which they realized about $20,000 a week. During the 1880's G. W. Borland & Co. and J. M. Wing & Co. were among those active in this type of book merchandising.[70]

In addition to making books, some manufacturers, indeed most of them, distributed their products by both wholesaling and retailing them. These different functions were performed by Jansen, McClurg & Co., by 1886 A. C. McClurg & Co., whose traveling salesmen made known the firm's name in many an out-of-the-way village. In their retail store on " Booksellers' Row " could be found not only the company's own publications, such as Mrs. Kate Brownlee Sherwood's short-lived *Camp-Fire, Memorial Day, and Other Poems* and Mrs. Helen Ekin Starrett's discussion of *The Future of Educated Women,* but many American books of permanent value in various fields, and rare imports, often expensively bound. This nice perception as to the ephemeral and lasting literature of the day was exhibited in the long rows of shelves frequented by book-loving men and women. Nor did the services of McClurg end here, for they put out the *Dial,*

---

[69] Flinn, *Chicago . . . A Guide, 1891,* pp. 497–98, 503; Shove, *op. cit.,* pp. 141, 144; *The American Bookseller,* XVII (April, 1885), 191, XXII (Aug. 1, 1887), 95. The Rand, McNally & Co. building, planned by Burnham & Root in 1889 and located at Adams and Quincy streets, was the first skeleton structure of rolled-steel beams and columns of bridge steel in Chicago. Fourteen stories high, the building's cost was reported as $450,000. (*The Economist,* I [June 15, 1889], 500; W. A. Starrett, *Skyscrapers and the Men Who Build Them* [New York, 1928], p. 34.) The passage of the International Copyright Act in 1891 restricted publication of these cheap libraries, and spelled, in some cases, the downfall of presses which had relied heavily on them.

[70] Norris, *op. cit.,* p. 103. Frederick B. Baird and Frank Dillon were members of Baird & Dillon.

a superior journal of literary criticism, sometimes sold from the newsstands in drugstores. All this, commented Charles Dudley Warner, reflected a "cultivation, a special love of books themselves," which would be "noticeable in any city." [71]

To this cultivation other publishers and bookstores contributed. Brentano Bros. opened a Chicago bookstore in 1884, and the Western News Company, until 1883 under John R. Walsh, having abandoned its retailing in 1872, broadcast in wholesale lots newspapers, periodicals, and books, often sensational and generally cheap, to news depots and similar agencies. The well-established S. C. Griggs & Co. continued bookmaking and publishing, and nineteen days after the Fire gave to the citizens of the devastated city Elias Colbert's and Everett Chamberlin's *Chicago and the Great Conflagration*.

On the whole, publishers dealt in general rather than specialized books, although the Open Court put out scientific, philosophical, and religious writings, often operating with little or no profit, but kept in business by E. C. Hegeler of LaSalle in the hope he could elevate the American reading public through the publication of philosophical literature.[72] As was the case of other pre-Fire publishers, Chicago-born Fleming H. Revell found his establishment burned in the Fire of October, 1871. Like other men of courage, he, too, rebuilt and by 1880 had produced about one hundred titles, chiefly hymnals, gospel tracts, and Sunday-school literature. By 1890 he was reported the largest publisher of religious books in the United States, including the writings of his brother-in-law Dwight L. Moody.[73]

The zeal for publishing proliferated into scores of booklets, pamphlets, and books for and about labor, particularly from the press of William C. Hollister & Bro., Eight-Hour Printers, popular with la-

[71] *The Western Manufacturer*, III (Jan., 1876), 18, IV (March, 1877), 363, V (Dec., 1878), 886; Warner, "Studies of the Great West," III "Chicago," *Harper's New Monthly Magazine*, LXXVI (May, 1888), 878; Arthur Meier Schlesinger, *The Rise of the City 1878–1898* (Arthur M. Schlesinger and Dixon Ryan Fox, eds., *A History of American Life*, X, New York, 1933), p. 179; *The American Bookseller*, III (June 15, 1877), 374, XVII (May 15, 1885), 288, (July 15, 1885), 48; William M. Payne, "Literary Chicago," *The New England Magazine*, VII (Feb., 1893), 690–93; Fleming, *op. cit.*, pp. 513–14.

[72] Norris, *op. cit.*, pp. 7–8, 93–94; *The American Bookseller*, XV (June 16, 1884), 572; *The Publisher's Weekly*, XXVII (Jan. 3, 1885), 15, XXXV (Feb. 9, 1889), 262, (Feb. 23, 1889), 339; Payne, *loc. cit.*, p. 169; Andreas, *History of Chicago*, III, 684.

[73] Oliver W. Holmes, "Fleming Hewitt Revell," *Dictionary of American Biography*, XV, 512. In 1890 Revell's was incorporated as Fleming H. Revell Co. *The National Cyclopaedia of American Biography*, XXVI (New York, 1937), 442.

bor organizations because of their adherence to the short working day. Schoolbook publishers such as A. Flanagan, A. S. Barnes & Co., and Thomas S. Denison entered the field, and eastern houses, including Harper & Brothers, carried textbooks alongside their other publications on the shelves of their branch establishments in Chicago.[74]

With the consolidation in December, 1892 of R. S. Peale & Co. and the Werner Printing & Lithographing Co. of Akron, Ohio, the absorption of the encyclopedias and subscription books of Belford-Clarke Company and the Webster Dictionary Publishing Co., the *Tribune* exultantly declared that Chicago now had the largest publishing house in America. Indeed, continued the paper, the city, the great provisioner of the world, had now become "the Leipsic of the United States," an analogy more wishful than truthful.[75]

The vast printing industry exacted a heavy toll on the manufacturers of paper. Besides, paper became increasingly popular for a variety of things. In 1871 Pullman's Palace Car Company gave its first order for paper car wheels, and ten years later the Allen Paper Car-Wheel Company had a shop at Pullman, as well as at Hudson, New York. Paper bathtubs, baskets, picture frames, butter plates, and lead pencils likewise appeared.[76]

Contributing, as most of Chicago's industries did, directly to the physical wants of man, the factory production of clothing developed notably during the late nineteenth century. By 1890 ready-to-wear men's garments alone stood fourth among the fifteen major industries of the city in terms of value added by manufacture, an imposing advance from the small beginnings of the 1850's.[77] As in other endeavors, the 'eighties were especially fruitful, although as early as the mid-'seventies the *Tribune* was pointing with pride to the nine-

[74] *The Publisher's Weekly*, XXXVI (July 20, 1879), 44; *The American Bookseller*, III (May 15, 1877), 298. Advertisements appear in Chicago newspapers.

[75] *Chicago Tribune*, Dec. 12, 1892. In December, 1893, Herbert Stone and Ingalls Kimball started publishing in Chicago under the name of Stone & Kimball, the beginning of a distinguished though brief publishing history. *The Publisher's Weekly*, XLIV (Sept. 9, 1893), 311; Sidney Kramer, *A History of Stone & Kimball and Herbert S. Stone & Co. . . .* (Chicago, 1940), p. 197.

[76] R. R. Bowker, "A Sheet of Paper," *Harper's New Monthly Magazine*, LXXV (June, 1887), 127; *The Rights of Labor* (Chicago), VI (July 19, 1890), 12; *The Western Manufacturer*, V (Oct. 15, 1878), 840. A Stationers' Board of Trade was active in 1879. A. C. McClurg was president. *The American Bookseller*, VII (April 1, 1879), 255.

[77] Custom work and the repair of men's clothing, not included in the computation, would have increased the value added by manufacture by $6,658,126 in 1890.

fold growth of the city's industry over 1870 is indicative that the styles were better suited to the western buyer and were also competing successfully with those from the East for the trade of the South and Southwest.

Gradually the quality and styles of Chicago ready-to-wear garments improved enough to attract not only those in the lower income groups, for whom they were first designed, but those who could pay more. Advertisements to entice the latter to become purchasers emphasized the high styling and good fit of ready-to-wear apparel said to be made from as fine and durable fabric as the tailor-made, and at much less cost. Those individuals who could not bring themselves to buy from stocks available from mass production and who could not afford the prices of the best tailors could, at times, purchase from manufacturers suits made to order. To the purchaser would be furnished, if desired, samples of material, self-measurement blanks, and fashion plates for everyday suits costing, in the early 'eighties, only ten dollars, and "Sunday-go-to-meeting suits" priced at fifteen.[78]

Often manufacturers and wholesalers were identical, and sometimes they took on the function of retailers. This triple service was performed, for example, by E. Rothschild & Bros., who, as early as 1883, put out an average of 2,500 to 3,000 suits daily, ranging from low- to high-cost garments. Along with Rothschild's, B. Kuppenheimer & Co., Kuh, Nathan & Fischer, Kahn, Schoenbrun & Co., C. P. Kellogg & Co., and Clement, Bane & Co. became leading manufacturers and sellers of men's and boys' wear.[79] Hart, Schaffner & Marx, the offspring of first a retail and then a wholesale establishment in which Harry and Max Hart were active, was organized in 1887. In the same year Henry C. Lytton founded his clothing store,

[78] *Chicago Tribune,* Jan. 1 issue annually, Sept. 23, 1888; *The Western Manufacturer,* III (Jan. 15, 1876), 2, VI (Jan. 15, 1879), 907, 909; Chicago Board of Trade, *Thirty-first Annual Report, 1888,* pp. xiv–xv.

[79] In 1876 Bernhard Kuppenheimer organized his company from the older firm of Kohn, Clayburgh and Einstein. C. P. Kellogg & Co. succeeded Palmer and Kellogg, established in 1852, and direct descendants of the latter in the 1860's. Charles Kellogg died in 1883 but the firm name continued. Abraham Kuh, Adolph Nathan, and S. M. Fischer organized in 1880. Felix Kahn and Leopold Schoenbrun began in 1882. Henry C. Clement, Oscar F. and Levi B. Bane, and Clement & Sons made up Clement, Bane & Co. from 1878, successor to Clement, Morton & Co. established in 1867 as wholesalers. Many important men in the industry were German Jews.

devoted to retail merchandising only and commonly known as " The Hub."

Some of these firms were lineal descendants of those of an earlier day. Such was Henry W. King & Co., whose factories in New York and Maine supplied the company's retail stores in Chicago, St. Louis, Cincinnati, and Milwaukee. Following the example of others whose business acumen had brought good returns, King increased his initial holdings by sizable investments in rich timberlands and other popular ventures, and took his place alongside other millionaires in Chicago.[80]

As the demand for inexpensive, ready-made clothing increased, a decentralization of the manufacturing plant took place. Practically all Chicago clothiers instead of expanding their airy and commodious inside shops, from which the needs of an earlier day were met, resorted by the late 1870's to the so-called contract or outside shops to satisfy the call for their goods. Many of these places filled only one part of an order, specializing in vests, trousers, coats, or even the making of buttonholes. Here men, women, and children, most of them foreign born, toiled in crowded, unclean quarters in the tenement districts, their unhealthy bodies transmitting the diseases of which they were the victims, their wages often only a few cents a day.[81]

The same conditions of manufacture prevailed in the making of children's jerseys and jackets and boys' knee-pants and coats, merchandise carried often by the clothiers dealing in men's wear. Although far less extensively than factory-made clothing for men, ready-to-wear women's garments appeared more often than formerly in the urban areas, particularly by the late 1880's. By that time the

[80] Andreas, History of Chicago, III, 721–24; The Western Manufacturer, III (Jan., 1876), 15; Abraham Hart, The 50 Years of Hart, Schaffner & Marx (Pamphlet, Courtesy Hart, Schaffner & Marx); Moses and Kirkland, op. cit., I, 297; Victor F. Lawson to Henry Hall, May 8, 1891, Lawson Papers.

[81] Illinois Bureau of Labor Statistics, Seventh Biennial Report, 1892, pp. xvii, 141, 361–402, 419–42; Illinois Factory Inspectors, First Annual Report, 1893, pp. 32–69; U. S. House of Representatives, Report of the Committee on Manufactures on the Sweating System, 52 Cong., 2 sess., H. Rept. 2309 [1893], pp. 74–83, 89, 93; Chicago Tribune, March 4, 1892; The Chicago Times, Aug. 4, 9, 17, 1888; Illinois Staats-Zeitung, April 7, 1892; Chicago Evening Post, April 5, 1892; Wilfred Carsel, A History of the Chicago Ladies' Garment Workers' Union (Chicago, 1940), pp. 4–14. The real conditions of work in the outside shops were unknown to the manufacturers, according to testimony before the Committee of the House of Representatives investigating the sweating system. See Report cited above.

manufacture of women's clothing, not noted ten years previously among the fifteen most important industries of the city, stood fourteenth and had already taken on the aspects of the contract and sweatshop labor, so general in the making of men's apparel not only in Chicago but throughout the country. Leading wholesalers of women's cloaks, including the prominent firms of John V. Farwell & Co. and Marshall Field & Company, used in part the outside shops to fill demands for their goods.[82]

A variety of other manufactured articles appeared. Neckwear for both men and women, underwear, and knit goods added to the imposing total of things made in Chicago. With her leadership in meat packing it was inescapable that the city acquire great importance first as a hide market and then as a leather-manufacturing point. For the packers the sale of skins added to an already rich return on their investment. By the late 'eighties, not only did they ship millions of pounds from the city, particularly to Boston, Massachusetts, Louisville, Kentucky, and Allegheny, Pennsylvania, but they also contributed to thriving Chicago enterprises. By 1887 Chicagoans engaged in the tanning business were reported to be producing about five million dollars' worth of goods a year, their capital amounting to two and a half million. In addition to what was received from the Chicago slaughterhouses, dealers got pelts and skins from other places. From the West came deer and antelope skins, as well as the popular buffalo hides, tanned and made into coats and lap robes. Many of the skins prepared by the tanneries in Chicago and near-by Wisconsin were sold in the East, and some were shipped to Europe, particularly France and Belgium, where they were made into knapsacks.[83]

Saddles and harness, trunks, valises, leather belts, and similar goods increased in quantity as time went on. In addition to currying and tanning, the manufacture of leather articles, including boots and shoes, put the industry ahead of the much heralded iron and steel in 1879. But the most important of these undertakings — the factory

[82] Illinois Factory Inspectors, *First Annual Report, 1893*, pp. 24–31, *Second Annual Report, 1894*, pp. 119–24; *The Baker's Journal*, VIII (Nov. 12, 1892), 4; Florence Kelley to Henry D. Lloyd, June 30, 1892, *Lloyd Papers*.

[83] Wolf & Epstein were leading dealers. Buffalo robes in the 1870's retailed in Chicago for $4.50. *Chicago Tribune*, June 28, 1873, Dec. 31, 1881; Marshall Field, *Papers*, pt. I, 52; *The Drovers' Journal*, June 6, 1883, Jan. 27, 1887.

production of boots and shoes — was, in itself, thirteenth in rank among the fifteen leading industries. Before the 'seventies ended, machinery had superseded hand labor in many of the shops and had so speeded up production that Chicago in 1889 stood fifth among the thirteen leading shoe centers of the country.[84]

As in the clothing industry, the outside shop in which women as well as men found employment often provided the labor for Chicago-made shoes, although some were produced within the assembly factory. Also like ready-to-wear garments, boots and shoes were generally designed for heavy wear. Advertisements emphasized their durability and other "sterling qualities." Not until the late 'seventies did Chicago manufacturers enter the market with women's shoes, and then they were of plain and ordinary design. The suède and kid slippers for evening wear and ladies' patent-leather and colored shoes, which gained favor in the late 1880's over the previously popular black kid, were not the product of Chicago factories. These and men's fine shoes had to be imported from the East and purchased in the retail establishments catering to such a trade.[85] But local boosters, on the whole, were not disturbed about this failure to meet the demands of the home market, for the factories of C. M. Henderson & Co. with their "Red Schoolhouse Shoe" for children and boots and shoes for men and women, the "solid makes" of Selz, Schwab & Co., and, by the early 'nineties, of Florsheim & Co. had captured a considerable market throughout the trade area to which Chicago more and more laid claim.[86]

[84] For the first time the Board of Trade commented in 1888 on the boot and shoe industry. (Chicago Board of Trade, *Thirty-first Annual Report, 1888*, p. xv.) U. S., *Census of Manufactures: 1905 Boots and Shoes, Leather, and Leather Gloves and Mittens*, Bul. 72, p. 19.

[85] *City of Chicago, A Half Century's Progress*, p. 103; *The Sun* [New York], Feb. 12, 1881; Illinois Factory Inspectors, *First Annual Report, 1893*, p. 100, *Second Annual Report, 1894*, p. 125; Illinois Bureau of Labor Statistics, *Seventh Biennial Report, 1892*, pp. 122–30; *Chicago Daily News*, April 17, 1888; *The Knights of Labor*, IV (Dec. 8, 1888), 3; *The Rights of Labor*, VII (Oct. 10, 1891), 5; *Chicago Tribune*, Dec. 26, 1873, Jan. 1, 1881. With petticoats shorter and of lighter weight, women were urged in 1891 to wear leather leggings (price, five dollars). *The Rights of Labor*, VII (Aug. 15, 1891), 9.

[86] Selz, Schwab & Co. was the successor to M. Selz & Co. In 1878 it became Selz, Schwab & Co., with Morris Selz, Charles Schwab, and John Bunn as members. Incorporated in 1890, it had factories in Chicago, Joliet, Genoa, and Elgin. ([The Inter Ocean], *A History of the City of Chicago . . .* [Chicago, 1900], p. 268; *The Rights of Labor*, VI [March 15, 1890], 12; *Chicago Tribune*, Jan. 1, 1887.) Florsheim & Co. appear in 1893 as manufacturers. The firm was composed of Milton S. Florsheim and Siegmund Florsheim (*Lakeside Annual Directory, 1893*, pp. 569, 1835). Andreas, *History of Chicago*, III, 729; *Chicago*

Despite the many substantial gains Chicago made in manufacturing, many of man's daily needs had to be supplied by importations. This was particularly true of the articles sold by the dry goods merchants, who even before the Fire had, on the whole, realized good profits both locally and wherever Chicago promoters had penetrated with their products. By the mid-'seventies, those engaged in the dry goods business were enjoying a growing market, competing successfully with eastern wholesalers not only because of proximity to the customer, but often because of lower prices and easier terms of credit. As early as 1875 an estimated $54,000,000 represented the share of $293,000,000 total sales which dry goods wholesalers pocketed. In 1883 dry goods moved into first place, outranking in dollar volume other wholesale lines, a position consistently held through 1892.[87] Not even the establishment of branch houses by well-known eastern concerns could stem the tide moving against the East in favor of Chicago.[88]

In this aspect of Chicago's economic life the pioneering firms of Field, Leiter & Co., John V. Farwell & Co., Carson, Pirie & Co., and Mandel Brothers at some time participated. The heads of these concerns engaged also in the retail trade, and after 1872 Mandel's carried it on exclusively. Outdistancing all in the breadth of activities and in financial returns was the organization under the guidance of the modest New Englander, Marshall Field. Drawing upon the rich legacy bequeathed him in the business policies established by Potter Palmer, Field, with Levi Z. Leiter, his financially astute partner, built up a business whose wholesale and retail sales of about $13,581,-000 in the year of the Fire rose to approximately $24,703,000 by 1881, when the firm became Marshall Field & Company upon the withdrawal of Leiter. The next ten years were equally satisfying, reaching over thirty-four and a half million in 1891 and adding another million in 'ninety-three. To these totals the wholesale section of

---

Tribune, Jan. 1, 1885; *Year Book of the Commercial, Banking, and Manufacturing Interests of Chicago, 1885–6*, pp. 279–81.

[87] *The Commercial and Financial Chronicle*, XIX (Aug. 29, 1874), 231, XX (May 15, 1875), 483, XXI (Sept. 25, 1875), 308; *The Chicago Times*, May 2, 1883; Moses and Kirkland, *op. cit.*, I, 289. For a survey of the previous years' mercantile and financial activities, see *Chicago Tribune*, Jan. 1, annually.

[88] One of the most important branch houses was that of A. T. Stewart and Company established in 1876 and abandoned in 1882. Arnold Constable & Co. and Calhoun, Robbins & Co. were other New York firms which had branch houses in Chicago by 1892.

DOWNTOWN MADISON STREET IN THE EARLY 'NINETIES

From Frank T. Neely, *Neely's Photographs* . . . (Chicago: F. T. Neely, 18—).

A DRAWING OF THE CHICAGO RIVER IN THE EARLY 'EIGHTIES MADE FROM THE WELLS STREET BRIDGE LOOKING WEST

From *Picturesque Chicago* (Chicago: Chicago Engraving Co., 1884).

the business contributed by far the larger amount, sometimes running in dollar volume more than five times ahead of the retail.[89]

The latter benefited from supplies right at hand and gave Field's an advantage over some of its retail contemporaries. To keep ahead of its rivals the firm introduced new brands of goods to the Chicago market and also made a practice, whenever possible, of becoming the exclusive agent of popular makes. By 1880, for example, Field had become sole distributor of the French-made Alexandre kid gloves, so ardently desired by the best-dressed woman. From resident buyers in France and Germany and the Manchester, England, office established in 1871, Field obtained foreign goods of outstanding quality. As time went on, he made available to Chicago buyers other foreign-made articles, notably those from Italy and the Orient.[90]

At first the wholesale absorbed more of Field's interest than did the retail. But it was the latter which gave glamor to the name of Field, as not only Chicagoans but residents from other parts of this country and abroad visited the store as one of the great institutions of the city. In 1872 the retail was separated from the wholesale with the removal of the latter from the old horsecar barn at State and Twentieth, taken over immediately after the Fire, to Market and Madison, which was to become the city's new wholesale district. Along with the new wholesale store, Field and Leiter had a second retail outlet, to be incorporated with the other retail store, in the autumn of 1873, at State and Washington. From this location a program of expansion began, which, though briefly interrupted by a fire in 1877, culminated in a great block-square store in 1912, six years after Field's death.[91] Here at the retail store the most fastidious could satisfy their needs from a variety of goods organized by kind

[89] Harlow N. Higinbotham became a member of the Field firm in 1879, Harry Gordon Selfridge in 1890, and John Shedd in 1893. All were former employees. *The Chicago Times,* Jan. 27, 28, 1881; *Field Papers,* pt. II, 1, 56–58, 132–34, 194; Robert W. Twyman, *History of Marshall Field and Company 1865–1906* (Ph.D. Thesis, The University of Chicago, 1950), pp. 442–44. Published as *Marshall Field & Co. 1852–1906* (Philadelphia, 1954). Henry J. Willing, a junior partner of Field, Leiter & Co., was important in the wholesale outlet of Marshall Field & Company, retiring in 1883.

[90] *Field Papers,* pt. I, 176, 179, pt. II, 52, 65, 90; Marshall Field, "Our Organization" (*Ms.* Field Archives), p. 3; William O. Stoddard, *Men of Business* (New York, 1905), p. 292.

[91] *Chicago Tribune,* Nov. 3, 1871, March 3, 1872, Sept. 29, Oct. 8, 9, 1873, Nov. 16, 18, 25, 27, 28, 1877, Feb. 27, March 2, 8, 1878, April 25, 26, 28, 1879, Jan. 28, 1881, April 15, 1888; *The Chicago Times,* Oct. 20, 1871, Nov. 15, 1877; Marshall Field, "Complete Inventory Estate of Marshall Field" (Field Estate Office); Twyman, *op. cit.,* pp. 96, 101–3, 113, 121, 144, 148–49, 150, 153, 391, 405.

upon different floors, forecasting the later-day department store, first tried out in the East.

As departments multiplied and the city grew, customers more and more turned to Field's and other stores similarly equipped where numerous purchases could be made quickly and easily. The measure of success which Field enjoyed was reflected in retail sales mounting from $3,109,000 in 1872 to $7,450,000 twenty years later. As with many other Chicago business giants, Marshall Field had risen from lowly beginnings — a clerkship paying $400 a year in 1856 — to the headship of a mercantile establishment with the largest dry goods business in the United States, if not in the world, and possessing, in 1890, a fortune estimated at $25,000,000. Like others, he prospered by investments in banking, real estate, railroads, iron mines, and city traction. Also like other economic leaders, his influence in community affairs was extensive, an influence exercised both directly and indirectly far beyond the confines of mere merchandising.[92]

A few days after Field's moved to Market and Madison, John V. Farwell & Co. had taken up greatly expanded quarters in a new five-story building at Monroe and Franklin streets. From here Farwell's carried on a retail division until March, 1873, but the firm's long-range interest lay in wholesaling, in which Farwell had so long engaged. By 1883 "the Merchant Prince," as he was often called, had put up a new building, fronting Monroe, Market, and Adams streets and reported to have cost $1,000,000, to care for stock estimated as worth five times that amount. Six hundred employees served customers in a trade area where increasingly Field was an active competitor and with whom rivalry was not only keen but at times bitter. In October, 1890 plans to reorganize the Farwell business were drawn up, to be put into effect the following January 1. By this time Farwell's was rated as the third wholesale dry goods house in the country in the size of its business, preceded only by Field's and H. B. Claflin & Co. of New York.[93]

[92] *Field Papers,* pt. I, 126; Marshall Field, "Statement of My Affairs," Memorandum (Field Archives), Jan. 1, 1874; *Chicago Tribune,* Oct. 15, 1873; John Dennis, Jr., "Marshall Field," *Everybody's Magazine,* XIV (March, 1906), 291–302; see Lloyd Wendt and Herman Kogan, *Give the Lady What She Wants* (Chicago, 1952), particularly for kinds of goods sold and policies of selling.

[93] *The Chicago Times,* March 31, 1872, Oct. 9, 1881; *Chicago Tribune,* March 30, 31, April 28, 1872; Abby (Farwell) Ferry, *Reminiscences of John V. Farwell by His Elder Daughter* (2 v. Chicago, 1928), I, 123–24; *The Economist,* IV (Oct. 4, 1890), 537; *The Inter*

Carson, Pirie & Co., retail, became Carson Pirie Scott & Co. in 1891, the name of the wholesale outlet taken in the early 'seventies. In both aspects of trade the firm competed aggressively with others carrying on a similar line of business. Contemporary accounts glowingly described the firm's stocks as " immense," and so successfully exploited that they won wide acclaim, indeed " the most generous recognition of the trade." After the Fire the wholesale was located on East Madison, but in 1874 it was moved to Franklin and Madison in the center of the wholesale district.[94] The year before, Carson, Pirie opened what they chose to call " the West End Dry Goods House " at Peoria and West Madison streets, and advertised " It pays to trade on the West Side." Here, in their retail outlet, the canny Scotchmen who guided the destinies of this well-knit partnership prospered so well that, in 1883, they bought out the popular Charles Gossage & Co., retaining the Gossage name until 1891, when it disappeared in the new organization of Carson Pirie Scott & Co. Three years before this merger took place, the West Side retail store had been moved to Wabash and Adams. With the combination in 1891, business was taken up at State and Washington, where the firm proudly pointed to its four open courts running to the roof, declaring that this upward open space made it the best lighted store in the city.

Sensitive to the trend of Chicago trade, Carson's through its buyers brought its patrons the finest products of foreign countries, particularly dress goods and linens. By the mid-'seventies French hats were imported with their heavy feather trimmings for wear in the winter and fragile flowers for summer. In 1881 the firm expanded its stock to include shoes, and in so doing antedated Field's by eight years and Mandel's by two.[95]

Ocean, Oct. 1, 1890; John Villiers Farwell, Some Recollections of John V. Farwell (Chicago, 1911), pp. 70–71; Andreas, History of Chicago, II, 694.

[94] In 1891 the wholesale was moved to Adams and Franklin streets. For a biographical sketch of Andrew MacLeish and his relations with Samuel Carson, John T. Pirie, George and Robert Scott, see Thomas Wakefield Goodspeed, The University of Chicago Biographical Sketches (Chicago, 1925), II, 55–76; Andrew MacLeish, Life of Andrew MacLeish 1838–1928 (Chicago, 1929), pp. 1–66.

[95] Chicago and Its Resources Twenty Years After, 1871–1891, p. 101; Chicago Tribune, May 6, 1873, Sept. 24, 1874, April 28, 1876, April 8, 1881, Sept. 16, 1883, March 14, 1888, March 30, 1889, June 29, 1891; The Chicago Times, Feb. 27, 1883; The Economist, V (Feb. 21, 1891), 293. Gossage had a shoe department in 1879 and sold kid and velvet slippers as early as 1877. Chicago Tribune, Dec. 7, 1877, March 25, 1879.

The name Mandel became a part of Chicago merchandising history in 1855, when Solomon Mandel and his uncle Simon Kline, both German immigrants, entered into a partnership to conduct a dry goods and notions store. In the next five and six years Solomon's brothers Leon and Emanuel joined the firm as clerks, the one a former cashboy, the other an errand runner for Chicago stores. In another two years Solomon, having saved some money, branched out for himself and took young Emanuel along. The year 1865 was the capstone of these early years of struggle, for it was then that the organization of the house of Mandel into the well-known establishment of Mandel Bros. took place.[96] Burned out, in the Fire of 1871, they started anew the following day, setting up the little they had saved in a small cigar shop at Twenty-second Street and Michigan Avenue. Here they remained for over twenty years, although in the meantime they had made several moves with another stock of goods, the last move into a large building at State and Madison.

The Mandels prospered. Buying agencies in New York and Paris provided them with the latest in materials and styles. Imported French hats, advertised as early as 1874, and a model of the Empress of Brazil hat in 1876, kindled a longing for the exotic in the minds of feminine devotees of unusual headgear. By 1874 the firm offered its goods to mail-order purchasers with the privilege of return. Upon the enlargement of its quarters in 1883 it installed elevators and electric lights and opened up an art department where pottery vases, bisques, and china from abroad, as well as statues of marble, could be found. Like many others in the thriving city who knew success, the Mandels, risen from the humble financial estate of their youth, were, by the late 'eighties, counted among the very wealthy of Chicago.[97]

The expansion of such stores, by multiplying the kinds of things offered for sale and by creating new departments, was neither hasty nor untimely in a period when the structure of business was experiencing change to meet the challenges of the new economic day. The transformation of the old-time staple dry goods establishment into

[96] Sources vary as to the spelling of Kline's name, but Mandels have adopted Kline rather than Klein, probably the original spelling. Solomon Mandel died in 1864. The three brothers, Simon, Leon, and Emanuel took over the stock of Solomon's store.

[97] Thomas Wakefield Goodspeed, *The University of Chicago Biographical Sketches,* II (Chicago, 1925), 155–74; Andreas, *History of Chicago,* III, 718; *Chicago Tribune,* Nov. 23, 1872, Sept. 25, Dec. 3, 1874, April 11, May 9, 1876, Sept. 8, 16, 1883, Oct. 12, 1884, Feb. 2, 1890, July 5, 1891, April 16, 1893; *The Drovers' Journal,* Nov. 26, 1883.

one of numerous lines, however, called forth angry remonstrance from small businessmen against what was described as " a veritable leviathan " endeavoring " to crush the retail business of the middle class." [98] Equally denounced by merchants specializing in single lines were the large variety stores such as the Fair, which realized a considerable Chicago patronage. Founded in 1875 by German-born Ernest J. Lehmann as a notions and jewelry store and housed in a little building on State near Adams with floor dimensions of 2,000 square feet, the Fair by 1891 occupied 286,000 square feet, and carried a varied assortment from children's toys to games for adults, baby carriages, dry goods, furniture, kitchen equipment, fancy groceries, and sewing machines. A store school gave instruction in arithmetic, spelling, and writing two hours daily for the cashgirls, professedly at least fourteen years of age, but believed younger. Thus Lehmann preceded other merchants by several years in providing some education for working girls.[99]

In May, 1887 Henry Siegel, Frank H. Cooper, and Isaac Keim set up a store at the corner of Adams and State and engaged in sales of general merchandise to be conducted on " a strictly cash basis." Like many of their business contemporaries they rose from small beginnings to a position of considerable financial standing. In 1892 they moved to an enlarged building at State and Van Buren where " every manufactured product known to the traffic of the world," it was said, could be found in seventy-three departments, all " under a single roof."

Among the store's unique features was a department of dentistry where patients were assured of " positively no disagreeable after-effects " from " the painless method of extracting teeth," which was used. The establishment of a dental department, a notable departure from the traditional, was paralleled by another innovation — the employment of a physician to oversee the health of the employees and to devote his time solely to this service. The moderate prices charged for its goods commended Siegel, Cooper's to the laboring

[98] *Illinois Staats-Zeitung,* July 30, 31, 1879; Chicago Department of Health, *Report, 1889,* pp. 69, 85.
[99] Emil Dietzch, *Geschichte der Deutsch-Amerikaner von Chicago (von der Gründung der Stadt an bis auf die neueste Zeit)* (Chicago, 1881), p. 332; *Chicago Tribune,* Sept. 1, 7, 1878, Feb. 26, 1879, May 28, 1882, May 18, 1884, March 25, 1888, Feb. 24, 1889; *The Economist,* V (Feb. 21, 1891), 293; *Co-operation,* I (Jan. 26, 1901), 5–6.

population of the city, who were urged by *The Vanguard,* a Chicago journal of Populist leanings, to demonstrate an appreciation of such a price policy by increasing their patronage. To its farm readers *The Vanguard* stressed the almost unmatched advantage of the merchandise offered for the payment required, and advised them to make use of the mail-order department which Siegel inaugurated in 1892.[100]

Antedating Siegel, Cooper & Co.'s entrance into the mail-order business by twenty years was the venture of Montgomery Ward. Onetime employee of Field, Palmer & Leiter, where he had started at a five-dollar weekly wage, Ward conceived of a business which would make available to the farmer and small-town dweller articles familiar to and easily obtainable by the city resident, at a reasonable price kept so through his direct purchase from the manufacturer. In the spring of 1872 Ward and his brother-in-law George R. Thorne opened headquarters in a room twelve by fourteen feet in a building at Clark and Kinzie. The capital invested was $2400.

Pursuing the policy of guaranteeing satisfaction to customers, the company saw its business mount rapidly, despite the open and sometimes vituperative opposition of wholesalers and retail merchants bent on preserving traditional methods of selling, and who held this type of unorthodoxy little short of a betrayal of trust. But Ward's new scheme was destined to succeed, for it had not only the blessings of the Patrons of Husbandry as an official grange supply house, but it brought to the lonely and distant of the rural world the embellishments of the new urban industrialism. By 1886 the *Buyers' Guide* was made up of 304 pages of purchasable articles, tangible evidence of the growth of business since its first issue, fourteen years before, when a one-page circular was enough to list the goods the youthful merchants had for sale.[101]

The success story exemplified in the career of the founders and directors of such stores was duplicated in this exciting era by others, although perhaps in somewhat less spectacular degree. It could

---

[100] *Chicago Tribune,* May 22, 23, 29, 1887, Sept. 24, 1891; *Department Store Journal,* II (June, 1897), 248; *The Vanguard,* I (June 4, 11, 1892), 5.

[101] Rae Elizabeth Rips, *An Introductory Study of the Role of the Mail Order Business in American History, 1872–1914* (unpublished M.A. Thesis, The University of Chicago, 1938), pp. 6–19; *The Drovers' Journal,* Feb. 21, April 2, 1883, March 29, 1886; *Chicago Tribune,* Nov. 8, 10, 1873.

scarcely be otherwise in a place where the growth of the city was in reality " one of the marvels of the world," and to which the peoples from near and far had come, seeking to earn a living and gain the satisfaction of their wants. Not all could or probably desired to patronize the large establishments of Field's, Carson's, and Mandel's. Some preferred the less expensive outlay of C. W. and E. Pardridge, started in 1870, or the Boston Store run by them and Charles Netcher after 1873, whose operations were based entirely on cash purchases. Others, living on the growing West Side with its large foreign population, turned to Schlesinger & Mayer, until that firm's removal to the State Street retail district in 1881.[102]

A variety of establishments, in some cases specializing in only one kind of goods, also enjoyed a lively though smaller trade than did the large downtown stores handling many things. Among these was Chas. A. Stevens & Bros., according to local reports the largest dealers in silk in the world. Organized in 1889 by five brothers, the firm was the successor of one started on a small scale by Charles Stevens who, three years before, had begun importing silks in an office in Central Music Hall and conducting both a wholesale and a retail business.[103]

The making of hats and other headgear, already important before the Great Fire, remained so in the years which followed. D. B. Fisk & Co., the pioneer of the three largest manufacturers and wholesalers of women's headwear, A. S. Gage & Co., and Edson Keith & Co. carrying also caps and gloves were all offshoots of similar enterprises started in the 1850's. Good fortune blessed them; munificent returns from their primary business interests made possible for them also investments in other economic endeavors; and Fisk and Keith at least were commonly mentioned as belonging to the select but increasing number of Chicago millionaires. By the mid-'eighties sev-

102 Schlesinger & Mayer was established in 1872 by Leopold Schlesinger and Daniel Mayer, both German immigrants. The Bee Hive, run by the Morgenthau Brothers (Maximilian and Gustav L.) and the Bauland Brothers (Jacob H. and Joseph H.), started in 1883 and was one of the popular lower-price stores. *Chicago Tribune*, Jan. 1, Oct. 9, 1881, March 4, 1888, Jan. 4, 1891; *The Chicago Times*, Aug. 5, 26, 1888; *The Workingman's Advocate*, July 3, 1875; Flinn, *Chicago . . . A Guide, 1892*, p. 592; Andreas, *History of Chicago*, III, 718–19; Warner, " Studies of the Great West. III. — Chicago," *Harper's New Monthly Magazine*, LXXVI (May, 1888), 870, 878.

103 The members of the Stevens firm were Charles A., Edward D., James W., John W., and Thomas A. *Chicago and Its Resources Twenty Years After, 1871–1891*, p. 102; *The Eight-Hour Herald*, Nov. 25, 1893.

enteen wholesale headwear establishments were in operation which, with 235 retail, not associated with dressmaking shops as some others were, carried on a trade approximating seven million dollars — a small amount compared with the large business of dry goods.[104]

The spectacular rise of those who dealt in dry goods was in a less noticeable degree experienced by those who handled groceries. Up to 1883 the dollar volume of the latter exceeded that of the former in wholesaling, but the decade following saw an over-all decrease, comparatively speaking. Still, the firms of Sprague, Warner & Co.; Reid, Murdoch & Fischer, to become Reid, Murdoch & Co. by 1888; and Franklin MacVeagh & Co. enjoyed a prosperity which fortified them against the vagaries of trading conditions that forced some of their contemporaries out of business.[105] Like the leaders of the dry goods fraternity, the heads of these grocery concerns exhibited so much business acumen that their organizations became a continuing factor in the economic well-being of the city.[106] Sharing the varying fortunes of business were also the dealers in salt, a commodity that already before the Fire had attained an important position in Chicago commerce. In 1885 a new name appeared among their number with the organization of Joy Morton & Company, which under the vigorous direction of Joy and his brother Mark soon made the name "Morton" almost synonymous with salt.

As the city's population grew and her wealth increased, modified habits mirrored the extravagance of luxurious living among the well-to-do in what they ate as well as in what they wore and how they were sheltered. Delicacies unknown in an early day appeared in many of the over four thousand retail stores of the city before the close of the 'eighties. They were, in many cases, made available by

104 *Year Book of the Commercial, Banking, and Manufacturing Interests of Chicago, 1885–6,* pp. 264–71; *Industrial Chicago,* IV, *The Commercial Interests,* 398–404; Chicago Board of Trade, *Thirty-first Annual Report, 1888,* p. xiv; *Chicago Tribune,* Jan. 1, 1872; Currey, *Chicago: Its History and Its Builders,* V, 373–74; Andreas, *History of Chicago,* II, 696, III, 725. Among wholesalers of hats were King Brothers & Co. and after 1885 Bush, Simmons & Co. Martin Ryerson was a partner of A. S. Gage & Co.

105 Albert A. Sprague, Ezra J. Warner, and Otho S. A. Sprague composed Sprague, Warner & Co.; Simon Reid, Frederick Fischer, and Thomas Murdoch, Reid, Murdoch & Fischer; and Franklin and Wayne MacVeagh, Rollin A. Keyes, and Walter T. Chandler, Franklin MacVeagh & Co. Franklin MacVeagh became Secretary of the Treasury in President William Howard Taft's Cabinet.

106 William M. Hoyt Company, important in wholesaling groceries, was established before the Fire but not incorporated until 1882. *Industrial Chicago,* IV, *The Commercial Interests,* 420–22.

the wholesalers to the trade area into which the so-called "drummer" or traveling salesman carried the message of Chicago-made and distributed products.

By the early 'seventies huge chests of tea reached Chicago directly from Japan. So popular did both tea and coffee become that their importers were twenty times more numerous in 1889 than in 1870. The Great Atlantic and Pacific Tea Co., sensing the large market open to those early on the scene, was advertising by November following the Great Fire " the choicest new crop teas in every variety " and " coffee roasted and ground daily," available in their first store in Chicago, whither they had rushed with goods from their New York headquarters.

Fruit in season from Alabama, California, southern Illinois, and Michigan was occasionally added to the grocer's usual supply of foods. It was, however, more often found in the stalls on the sidewalks for several blocks from Wells to State along South Water Street and on West Lake and Kinzie, where there were also crowded the many commission firms which were doing a good business even before the mid-'seventies. As time went on more and more of the retail grocers made fruits available to their customers just as they carried small stocks of bulk candy. They had not yet, however, entered into the sale of high-grade confections by the box, which Charles Frederick Gunther had been making and selling since 1868; his caramels, particularly, having become popular throughout this country and even in Europe.[107]

More than in some other cases, wholesaling and retailing hardware was a post-Fire development. New and different commodities came out of more plentiful supplies of iron, steel, and other metals. Urbanism increasingly set its mark upon the trade. With more buildings heated by furnaces than in an earlier day, and with the increase of commercial laundries, fewer called for stovepipes and the old movable washtub, at one time featured by well-stocked retailers. This changing pattern of wants was, however, less apparent as yet

---

107 *The Commercial and Financial Chronicle,* XIII (Oct. 14, 1871), 505; Moses and Kirkland, *op. cit.,* I, 292–94; Andreas, *History of Chicago,* III, 347–48; *Chicago Tribune,* Nov. 7, Dec. 22, 1871, Dec. 26, 1873, Oct. 18, 1874, and Jan. 1 annually; *The Economist,* III (May 10, 1890), 578, IV (Sept. 20, 1890), 447–48; *Saturday Evening Post,* no. 27 (Dec. 31, 1938), pp. 8–9, 53–55; *The Biographical Dictionary and Portrait Gallery of Representative Men of Chicago . . . ,* p. 313.

in the orders received by the wholesalers from the still ruralized trade area where they sought patronage, and they must, perforce satisfy such desires as well as those of the city. Of the wholesale dealers Hibbard, Spencer, Bartlett & Co. outranked their competitors in all aspects of the business.[108] Chronologically this organization had been preceded by William Blair & Co., said to have been the first concern in the city to deal exclusively in hardware.[109]

Both wholesale and retail establishments tended toward specialization in the kind of goods sold. Some concentrated on shelf hardware, others on tinware and hardware proper, while others carried the very important list of articles designated heavy hardware. As dealer in the last, Seneca D. Kimbark enjoyed not only the prestige of a house long established, but the satisfactions of wealth gained through that business. By 1889, 340 retail dealers outdistanced the seventy-eight firms listed as wholesalers and manufacturers of hardware and cutlery but it was a preponderance chiefly in numbers.[110]

It was, however, to the numerous small neighborhood stores that many Chicagoans turned for the things they must have. These had sprung up as the territory of the city had been extended, and in no way were they comparable to the large and pretentious establishments in the central business section. Nor did they approximate the department stores — small duplicates of those in the downtown business district — found on some of the outlying main streets of the more densely populated divisions of the city. Like the general store of the small communities scattered throughout the country, the little neighborhood shop with its popularly priced merchandise was for the people who lived near by — the working people who must live frugally and buy near their homes.

Such a place was that of William A. Wieboldt, who first located in 1883 at 604 West Indiana Avenue (renamed Grand Avenue in

108 The firm was made up of William G. Hibbard, Franklin F. Spencer, Adolphus C. Bartlett, and Charles H. Conover.

109 Moses and Kirkland, op. cit., I, 300–2; Fred C. Kelly, Seventy Years of Hibbard Hardware (Chicago, 1930. Courtesy of Hibbard, Spencer, Bartlett & Co.), passim; The Economist, II (Sept. 7, 1889), 788–89; Industrial Chicago, IV, The Commercial Interests, 409–10, 445; Chicago and Its Resources Twenty Years After, 1871–1891, pp. 110, 111. In 1888 the Blair company was taken over by Norton, Gilmore, Williams & Co.

110 Year Book of the Commercial, Banking, and Manufacturing Interests of Chicago, 1885–6, pp. 296–97; Chicago and Its Resources Twenty Years After, 1871–1891, p. 110; The American Artisan, Tinner, and House Furnisher, XXI (Oct. 31, 1891), 18; Chicago Department of Health, Report, 1889, p. 68.

1895), where he paid sixty-five dollars a month rental for the building. On the first floor he put his stock of goods, and on the second he had his living quarters. Unlike many of his contemporaries whose names soon disappeared from the painted wooden sign above the front door, Wieboldt, blessed with a resolute boldness and keen discernment, continued to prosper, and during the twentieth century he developed a merchandising empire of considerable size.

Like Wieboldt, another German-born immigrant was also to experience the exhilaration of success and to expand his business so effectively that he, too, was to become one of Chicago's economic giants in the years that lay ahead. In 1883, the year when Wieboldt opened his modest store, Oscar Mayer with his brother Gottfried set up a small retail meat shop in the 1400 block on Sedgwick Street. Shortly, Oscar F. Mayer & Bro. became identified with those engaged in wholesaling, and by 1895 they had undertaken the packing of meats.[111]

The multiplication of facilities of merchandising, like the expansion of manufactories, denoted not only an ability to perceive a lucrative and growing market, but a capacity to satisfy the miscellaneous and new demands of a buying public near at hand. In their multiform aspects they had, in the years following the Great Fire, gone far beyond the elementary needs of early days. This transition from simplicity to sophistication occurred in many enterprises including the furniture store, which was no longer only the cabinetmaker's workshop. Rather, it was like that of J. A. Colby & Sons and the Tobey Furniture Co., who not only designed and made furniture on special commissions, but had extensive showrooms of furniture ready for sale, besides curtains, draperies, and other decorative furnishing for interiors.[112]

Establishments concentrating in the main on selling furniture on hand also assumed a real importance in the over-all trade of the city.

111 [Wieboldt Stores, Inc.], Typescript untitled (courtesy of Wieboldt, Inc.); Chicago Department of Health, *Report, 1889*, pp. 69, 85, 1891; [Oscar Mayer & Co.], *Sixty Years of Service, 1883–1943* (Pamphlet, courtesy of Mr. Oscar Mayer, Jr.).

112 John A. Colby started in 1867 in the furniture business. In 1885 his sons Henry C. and Edward A. went into a partnership with him. (*Biographical Dictionary and Portrait Gallery of Representative Men of Chicago . . .*, p. 150.) The Tobey Furniture Co. was incorporated in 1870, with Charles Tobey, president and F. B. Tobey vice-president. *A Half-Century's Progress of . . . Chicago*, pt. I, 117. The manufacturing of furniture is treated earlier in this chapter.

In this aspect of economic undertaking Spiegel & Co. and John M. Smyth were particularly well known. The former by 1893 had become Spiegel's Home Furnishing Co., its name descriptive of the stock it carried. Smyth, located on the West Side, made available his extensive line of furniture to many who could not pay cash for purchases by instituting installment buying, a method of payment which spread rapidly and was destined to become an important part of business transactions such as he carried on.[113]

A flourishing business was conducted also by an increasing number of druggists who, by 1889, numbered 1,050, twenty-five of whom were women. Descendants of an organization known as far back as 1836, Morrisson, Plummer & Co. participated in wholesaling, selling many drugs prepared in their own laboratory. In retailing, the Sargent Drug Store played a comparable part. Ezekiel H. Sargent, the head of the concern, starting in Chicago in 1852, assumed a leadership reflected in his presidency of the Chicago College of Pharmacy, 1865 to 1872, and of the American Pharmaceutical Association in 1869–70.[114] Catering to those who could indulge a taste for opulent living was the store of C. D. Peacock, with an array of silver appointments, clocks, and personal jewelry; and, after 1888, Spaulding & Co., according to a contemporary enthusiast, the " Tiffany's " of Chicago, with its rare display of gems, ornaments, and jewelry.[115]

Nor was the desire for rare and imported china and exotic glassware unrequited. Besides the domestic crockery and glass, majolica, and other popular dishes sold, both wholesalers and retailers conducted an import business of notable proportions. Pitkin & Brooks were numbered among the former, and Chas. Pick & Co. and the

[113] Andreas, *History of Chicago*, III, 734, 738; Gilbert and Bryson, *Chicago and Its Makers*, p. 664; Flinn, *Chicago . . . A Guide, 1892*, p. 613; *The Workingman's Advocate*, June 13, 1874; Chicago Department of Health, *Report, 1889*, p. 85.

[114] The firm of [Robert] Morrison, [Jonathan W.] Plummer, & Co. [Leonard A. Lange] competed with [Oliver F.] Fuller & [Henry W.] Fuller in the wholesale business. [George] Buck and [James B.] Rayner were important in the retail trade. Andreas, *History of Chicago*, II, 539, III, 546–47; *Year Book of the Commercial, Banking, and Manufacturing Interests of Chicago, 1885–6*, pp. 272–76; Chicago Department of Health, *Report, 1889*, p. 67; *Dziennik Chicagoski*, May 18, 1892.

[115] The pioneering firm of Charles D. Peacock was established in 1837. Giles Bros. & Co. were wholesalers of some importance. The firm of Spaulding & Co. was made up of Henry A. Spaulding, Edward Forman, and Lloyd Milner. *Chicago Tribune*, Nov. 27, 29, 1873, Jan. 1, 1879, Jan. 1, 1880, Jan. 2, 1888, Jan. 1, 1889; *Chicago Commerce, Manufactures, Banking and Transportation Facilities, 1884*, pp. 159–63; *The Economist*, VII (Jan. 2, 1892), 8. For Elgin watches see *Skandinaven*, Jan. 1, 1887.

French & Potter company at some time carried on both wholesaling and retailing.[116]

This diverse and far-flung business community was knitted together by the strong bond of a common interest — the interest in enhancing the prospects of success within the framework of the Chicago economy. Journals devoted to special segments of the business structure accented the principles and problems facing the particular enterprise which they represented. These organs of special pleading varied, of course, in the breadth of their coverage and in the length of time they were active. But all had in common a persisting faith in Chicago as an important center of manufacture and distribution.

Of these, *The Western Manufacturer,* with its news of factories, inventions, and general trade conditions, had widespread appeal. It carried on a vigorous campaign to extend the city's trade area not only within this country but to Latin America, Europe, and the Orient. It editorialized on and publicized aspects of the protective tariff, labor and capital, industrial education, and international goodwill. From 1874 to 1888 *The Western Manufacturer* served not only as disseminator of information about old and new products, but acted as vigilant guardian of the interests it represented.

In 1888, when *The Western Manufacturer* issued its last number, an equally important journal, to be known as *The Economist,* came into existence. Published weekly as a financial and real estate organ, it carried many items relating to manufacturing and merchandising in connection with and related to its expressed purpose. At the same time, periodicals having both local and national circulation such as the *Dry Goods Reporter,* which started in 1871, and the *Grocers' Criterion,* after 1873, furnished information on the persisting and varying factors affecting the trade.[117]

Closely allied in purpose to the many trade journals which were published in Chicago were organizations of men whose investments lay in some special enterprise. Manufacturer, wholesaler, and re-

[116] In 1890 French & Potter entered into retailing, having been recorded as wholesalers under various firm names from 1872 until 1890. Pick had a porcelain works, the United States Porcelain Works at South Bend, Indiana. Andreas, *History of Chicago,* III, 752; *Chicago Commerce, Manufactures, Banking and Transportation Facilities, 1884,* pp. 212–13; *Illinois Staats-Zeitung,* April 9, 1893.

[117] *The Economist* was published from 1888 to May 11, 1946, when its title was changed to *Realty and Building; Dry Goods Reporter,* 1871–1929; *Grocers' Criterion,* 1873–1912. During dates of publication titles at times changed slightly.

tailer, all subscribed to the belief that concerted effort eased the way to eventual success. Pools to control output, to direct distribution, and to fix prices were frequently the order of the day; and the refusal of manufacturers or wholesalers to sell to those outside the acquiescent group proved a convincing weapon whenever applied.[118]

Broader in purpose and in the scope of its activities than most associations was the Commercial Club, organized on December 27, 1877. Its membership, limited to sixty men outstanding in the most important branches of Chicago business life, in a very real sense lived up to the purpose announced in its charter — advancing " by social intercourse and by a friendly interchange of views the prosperity and growth of the city of Chicago." Besides the activities generally sponsored by organizations of this type, the Club worked for social and civic reform, condemning the spoilsman in politics, urging better methods of municipal accounting, greater educational facilities, adequate housing, and extensive physical improvements such as paving streets and building bridges. At its meetings national and international political and economic problems came into its purview, each considered in an atmosphere hospitable to diverse opinions.[119]

Similar in aim was the Mercantile Club, made up of important young businessmen of the city. The Sunset Club, although less exclusive in the selection and size of its membership and not established primarily to enhance the business interests of the city, nevertheless played a significant role in promoting an understanding of the varied questions which perplexed thoughtful men of the day. From March 22, 1889, when it first assembled for " intelligent conversation," until 1901, this group by lectures and discussions was informed of contradictory points of view in a forum notable for the coverage of the issues presented and the tolerance uniformly exhibited.[120]

At the same time other instrumentalities of information and opin-

[118] Examples of such attempts can be found in: *The Drovers' Journal*, April 13, 27, May 10, 1886; Chicago Coal Exchange, *Constitution and By-Laws, 1874*, pp. iv–l; *Chicago Tribune*, Jan. 1, 1885, Jan. 1, 1886, May 1, 1892; *The Western Manufacturer*, V (Dec. 15, 1878), 890; *The Workingman's Advocate*, Aug. 26, 1876; *The Inland Architect and Builder*, III (Feb., 1884), 6.

[119] John Jacob Glessner, *The Commercial Club of Chicago Its Beginning and Something of Its Work* (Chicago, 1910), *passim*.

[120] *Commercial and Architectural Chicago*, p. 71; W. W. Catlin, comp., *Echoes of the Sunset Club* (Chicago, 1891), pp. 3–7; *Chicago Tribune*, March 22, 1889.

ion vigorously prosecuted their programs. An increasing number of conventions and conferences held in Chicago dealt with internal and foreign commerce and allied issues. In 1880, from Chicago, the Industrial League of America inaugurated, in the interest of protectionism, its attack on the National Free Trade League which had originated in this city in 1877; and in 1893 anti-trust agitators met in solemn conclave to plan some way to stem the swelling tide of concentration in business.[121]

These evidences of business self-consciousness and cohesiveness were, of course, recognizable marks of the maturing economy of the city. As for the men who had contributed so generously to this maturity, it now seemed in retrospect as if, once having started, their ultimate success and riches had been not only natural but assured. Enveloped in the optimism of the latter part of the nineteenth century, these giants of enterprise looked to the future with undimmed confidence, believing that each man by serving his own interests would inevitably promote the welfare of all.

[121] *Washburne Papers; The Western Manufacturer,* IV (Oct. 15, 1877), 548–49, V (Nov. 15, 1878), 864, VII (July 15, 1879), 56, (Oct. 15, 1879), 123, VIII (Sept. 15, 1880), 175, 183, IX (Oct. 15, 1881), 191; *The Economist,* II (July 20, 1889), 618; *Chicago Tribune,* April 19, 1889, Jan. 1, 1893; *The Vanguard,* I (May 20, 1893), 5.

CHAPTER VI

THE ECONOMIC EMPIRE OF
CHICAGO: BANKING,
INVESTMENTS, AND FINANCE

THREE DAYS after the Great Fire a group of anxious bankers met at the Wabash Avenue home of Calvin T. Wheeler, vice-president of the Union National Bank, in the hope of finding answers to the questions raised by countless disheartened local depositors, by neighboring small-town bankers, farmers from the near-by countryside, and investors from the eastern seaboard, most of whom saw in the destruction of the city their own ruin. Only two small state banks within the city limits had withstood the ravages of the conflagration; and for the other banks there were heavy losses of personal property and of money running to about a million dollars.[1]

Only the Saturday before (October 7), the twenty leading banks were reported by the *Tribune* to have held an average of cash means (currency, bonds, and New York exchange) equal to 35 per cent of their collective deposits, an estimate later revised to 40 or 50 per cent. Two-thirds of their loans had been made to those engaged in the great strongholds of Chicago's economy — the trade in grain, lum-

---

[1] The Prairie State Loan & Trust Co. at 95 West Randolph Street and the Twenty-second Street State Bank between State and Wabash survived. The Union Stock Yards National Bank was not burned, but was outside the south limits of the city. *Chicago Tribune,* Oct. 12, 15, 1871; F. Cyril James, *The Growth of Chicago Banks* (2 v. New York, 1938), I, 404; Frank Gilbert, "Commercial and Public Institutions," *The Lakeside Monthly,* VII (Jan., 1872), 66.

ber, and provisions, where the loss had been less than in mercantile paper, and even in this a 60 per cent recovery seemed assured.[2]

With a confidence born of a knowledge of long-run financial soundness and a realization of the physical resources from which Chicago derived her economic strength, a committee named by the bankers at the Wheeler home resolved to resume business at once and to make an initial payment of 15 per cent to all patrons.[3] State banks and savings organizations as a gesture of their good faith also offered to see that each depositor having twenty dollars or more to his credit would receive that sum. Before the officers of the national banks could act, however, Hiland R. Hulburd, the federally appointed Comptroller of the Currency, arrived in Chicago and, finding the banks solvent, announced they would open temporary quarters on the seventeenth and would make payment in full.[4]

His words were like magic. Receipts rather than withdrawals became general; fixed capital which had appeared frozen began to flow into channels of exchange; eastern financial interests in many cases did not press for an immediate payment of debts, and loans for reconstruction were easily obtained. Chicago, remarked the *Commercial and Financial Chronicle,* " has become a necessity to the great west. Capital, discovering this fact, is pouring in from all sides seeking profitable investment. Nothing can ever replace, it is true, the large amount of wealth destroyed, but the loss has been distributed, to a great extent, over the whole country, and from present indications the city itself will pass through her hard experience to the attainment of a prosperity as unprecedented as her calamity was

[2] *Chicago Tribune,* Oct. 11–13, 1871. According to the Comptroller of the Currency the national banks had a reserve of 30 per cent of their liabilities. He also reported that the amount of bills receivable held by the national banks was more than $21,000,000, and the indebtedness to correspondents nearly $9,000,000, and to individual depositors about $17,000,-000. U. S., *Annual Report of the Comptroller of the Currency* . . . (Washington, 1872), p. xxiv (hereafter cited as U. S. Comptroller of the Currency, *Report*).

[3] The chairman of the meeting was William F. Coolbaugh, president of the Union National Bank. The committee on resolutions was composed of outstanding men in the field of banking: in addition to Coolbaugh, Chauncey B. Blair, president of Merchants' National; Julian S. Rumsey, president, Corn Exchange National; Solomon A. Smith, president, Merchants' Savings, Loan & Trust Co.; Leverett B. Sidway of State Savings Institution; J. Irving Pearce, president, Third National; Jonathan Young Scammon, president, Mechanics' National; and Lyman J. Gage, cashier, First National Bank.

[4] *Chicago Tribune,* Oct. 12, 13, 15, 1871; Gilbert, *loc. cit.,* p. 66; U. S. Comptroller of the Currency, *Report, 1872,* p. xxiv; William Hudson Harper and Charles H. Ravell, *Fifty Years of Banking in Chicago* (Chicago, 1907), pp. 46–53.

sudden and terrible." [5] Eastern and foreign institutions set up branch establishments eager to take advantage of what very shortly appeared new and profitable opportunities.[6]

The resiliency of the banking structure and the incentive to financial expansion arising out of the needs created by the Fire spurred businessmen not only to restore old enterprises but to adventure into the new and untried. The wave of speculation and business growth of the years just before 1871, which the Fire had so unexpectedly checked, was, by 1873, as the well-known attorney Mark Skinner observed, " prospering every-wise much to everybody's surprise." National and regional well-being paralleled Chicago's and fed it, and it seemed as if the city had crossed the threshold of a new era unrivaled even in the storied years now gone. But disillusionment as to its permanency came September 18, 1873, when the New York banking firm of Jay Cooke & Co., the most powerful in the country, failed. Chicago banks started to call in loans in an attempt to fortify themselves by credit contraction; New York exchange became less and less salable and this, in turn, affected adversely the movement of agricultural products. Before long Chicago, in spite of her brave pronouncements of self-sufficiency, was in the midst of the financial crisis, feeling the reverberations of the money tightness in New York which was, as the prominent physician Charles W. Hempstead put it, " shaking the business centers of the entire states like an earthquake." Chicago bankers with considerably more hindsight than foresight reflected ruefully on the disadvantages of unrestrained purchases of real estate and speculative stocks.[7]

[5] *The Commercial and Financial Chronicle*, XIV (April 20, 1872), 513, XV (Oct. 19, 1872), 514; Rollin George Thomas, *The Development of State Banks in Chicago* (unpublished Ph.D. Thesis, The University of Chicago, 1930), pp. 85–86.

[6] The Bank of Montreal re-established its branch in Chicago, originally opened in 1862 but closed a few years later. Three other Canadian banks, the British North America, the Canadian Bank of Commerce, and the Merchants' Bank of Canada, opened branches. All but the Bank of Montreal, however, had closed their branches or been incorporated in other Chicago banks by the end of 1891. Don Marcus Dailey, *The Development of Banking in Chicago before 1890* (unpublished Ph.D. Thesis, Northwestern University, 1934), p. 319; *Rand, McNally & Co.'s Bankers' Monthly*, III (March, Dec., 1886), 33, 236. The Scandinavian National Bank, first to be chartered after the Fire, was more than half owned by residents of Stockholm, Copenhagen, and other foreign centers. U. S. Comptroller of the Currency, *Report, 1892*, I, 206, 212; *The Bankers' Magazine*, XXX (May, 1876), 904.

[7] *Chicago Tribune*, Oct. 28, 1871, Oct. 9, 1872, Sept. 29, Oct. 4, Nov. 12, 1873; Mark Skinner to Elihu Washburne, May 26, 1873, *Washburne Papers;* C. W. Hempstead to Washburne, Oct. 1, 1873, *ibid.;* James, *op. cit.*, I, 430–34, 436–38.

With the failure of several important New York banks, country correspondents of Chicago institutions, fearful as to what the western city's banks might do, asked for their deposits. On September 21, to guard against disastrous runs, most Chicago savings banks adopted the practice of requiring an advance notice from depositors wishing to withdraw their money. In another three days representatives of member banks in the Chicago Clearing House Association had voted that members could suspend payment of currency on large demands either from country correspondents or across the counter, a drastic measure not approved by all, notably the First National, which, with the Merchants' Savings, Loan & Trust Co., and the Bank of Montreal, continued throughout the crisis to meet all demands.[8] The temporary suspension on September 26 of five of the city's national banks, including the Union National, especially interested in produce loans, whose president, William F. Coolbaugh, feared an unrestricted distribution of the currency, affected at least two hundred country institutions.[9]

This rapid sequence of events was followed by numerous attempts to better the bad condition enveloping the economy of the only recently revived city. Banks reduced loans some 25 per cent, balances and reserves with eastern correspondents were heavily tapped, and credit contraction went far beyond the canons of good banking procedure. But withal, despite intense suffering and despair, Chicago weathered the depression better than did many other places, particularly the cities of the East. Before December things seemed to be better.[10]

The slight improvement which had come in the last weeks of 'seventy-three was not, however, the harbinger of the good times so

[8] The meeting of the Clearing House Association was called for eight o'clock Sept. 24. The vote came after midnight. (*The Chicago Times*, Sept. 25, 1873.) Not all banks belonged to the Clearing House Association. James, *op cit.*, I, 449–50; David Davis to Judge Thomas Drummond, Sept. 29, 1873, *The David Davis Letters, 1872–1884* (Typescript, University of Illinois, Urbana); *Chicago Tribune*, Sept. 28, 1873.

[9] Those banks suspending Sept. 26 were the Cook County, Union, Manufacturers', and Second National banks and the National Bank of Commerce. Chicago had nineteen national banks besides the Union Stock Yards National. (U. S. Comptroller of the Currency, *Report, 1872*, pp. 564–70; *Chicago Tribune*, Sept. 27, 1873.) Other banks followed. *Ibid.*, Sept. 28, 30, Oct. 2, 1873; Francis Murray Huston, *Financing an Empire: History of Banking in Illinois* (Chicago, 1928), I, 230.

[10] *The Chicago Times*, Jan. 1, 1874; *The Commercial and Financial Chronicle*, XVII (Dec. 13, 1873), 793; Dailey, *op. cit.*, p. 457; U. S. Comptroller of the Currency, *Report, 1873*, pp. lxvii, lxxix.

earnestly coveted. An unsettled economy continued for the next several years, leading the *Western Manufacturer* to remark plaintively in the spring of 1877 that for " more than three years . . . we have been passing through the valley, with the waves of adversity rising gradually higher and higher, and ever and anon carrying off some new victim into the slough of bankruptcy." By autumn of that year more than twenty banks had failed, climaxed with the crash of savings banks. In the panic of '73 the latter had been relatively secure because, with the decline in real estate and real estate securities, more money was invested in them. An avid and irresponsible competition for these funds boosted interest rates as high as 6 per cent, beyond the point of a safe profit. Besides, unsound banking practices and fraudulent operation in some instances laid open the savings institutions to attack and ultimate failure.[11]

To unsettle still more the confidence of the public in the soundness of the banking structure and bankers' procedures, a confidence already badly shaken, a run on the important Union National occurred following the suicide of the president, William F. Coolbaugh, on November 14 at the foot of the Douglas Monument.[12] Withdrawals of funds spread to other banks. Charges of embezzlement and violations of the National Bank Act further confirmed the opinion of those hostile to the banking fraternity that its operations were not always in the interest of depositors. No longer were the failures which continued throughout the 'seventies a cause for surprise. " Another consumptive gone," commented the *Times,* and the *Tribune* heatedly ascribed the reported defalcations and frauds as designed primarily to " sustain a little ring of banks and certain real estate operations." [13]

    11 *The Western Manufacturer,* IV (March 8, 1877), 359; *The Workingman's Advocate,* Oct. 13, 1877; *The Chicago Times,* Sept. 3, 27, Nov. 12, 1877; *Chicago Tribune,* Aug. 29, 30, Sept. 19, 20, 25, 27, 29, 1877; *The Bankers' Magazine,* XXIX (July, 1874), 77; *Pomeroy's Democrat,* Sept. 1, 1877; *The Commercial and Financial Chronicle,* XXV (Sept. 8, 1877), 221–22.
    12 Firm action by Calvin T. Wheeler, Coolbaugh's successor, stopped the run on the Union National. Coolbaugh was the outstanding banker of his day in the Middle West, if not in the country. He lost prestige after 1873 and was preyed upon also by the fear of paralysis. James, *op. cit.,* I, 506–8; *Chicago Tribune,* Nov. 15, 1877.
    13 *The Bankers' Magazine,* XXXII (Dec., 1877), 486; James, *op. cit.,* I, 504–6; U. S. Comptroller of the Currency, *Report, 1877,* p. 569, *1892,* I, 216–17, 222–23; *Illinois Staats-Zeitung,* April 28, 1879; *Chicagoer Arbeiter-Zeitung,* June 5, 1879, April 24, 27, 28, 1880; *The Chicago Times,* Nov. 23, 24, Dec. 20, 1877; *Chicago Tribune,* Nov. 22, 24, Dec. 6, 7, 8, 12, 18, 1877, July 4, Nov. 6, 1879.

With the 'eighties came a return of prosperity. Aside from some tightness in funds available for business transactions in 1884, banks, on the whole, did not repeat the same tale of the disasters of the 1870's. Failures were fewer and less spectacular, and instances of injudicious banking practices less numerous.[14] The decade, however, was little more than a hiatus before failures in 1890 mirrored the worsening of industrial activity and increasing unemployment, despite the anticipated glamor and enchantment of the World's Fair soon to be held in the city. The failure of the Chemical National [15] and Columbia National banks in May, 1893, so demoralized depositors that again a run on the savings banks betokened the distrust in which financial institutions were held.[16] To restore the confidence so sorely needed for successful operations the Illinois Trust and Savings Bank remained open all night to prove its solvency, and was sustained in its effort by the announcement of Marshall Field and P. D. Armour that all depositors presenting their passbooks at Field's store and Armour's offices would be paid in full.[17]

With increasing amounts of currency coming into the city from the trade in grain and more and more visitors arriving for the Fair after its opening May 1, the money market turned upward and gold was shipped to New York as proof of the improved financial position. To demonstrate further the omnipresent optimism indigenous in what may best be called " the Chicago spirit," the midwest city declined to follow the lead of the East and use clearinghouse certificates, although by July an epidemic of bank failures in the Mississippi Valley left its mark on Chicago. Between May and July deposits

14 *Rand, McNally & Co.'s Bankers' Monthly*, I (Sept., 1884), 72–73, VI (March, 1889), 48, VIII (Jan., March, Aug., 1891), 15, 80, 257–59; *Chicago Tribune*, Oct. 3–6, Nov. 27, 1888; *The Knights of Labor*, I (Jan. 15, 1887), 12; *The Economist*, III (June 21, 1890), 799, (June 28, 1890), 840, IV (Sept. 27, 1890), 488; U. S. Comptroller of the Currency, *Report, 1892*, I, 73, 210, 216–17, 222–23.

15 The Chemical National Bank held deposits of World's Fair exhibitors. After its failure, wealthy citizens gave guarantees against losses. The group included, among others, Martin A. Ryerson, George M. Pullman, Erskine M. Phelps, William T. Baker, Arthur Dixon, and H. N. Higinbotham. *Chicago Tribune*, May 5, 1893.

16 Both the Columbia and Chemical were considered unwisely managed and had met the disapproval of the Clearing House Association when they applied for a loan. The Columbia disaster involved also the United States Loan and Trust Company as well as country banks. They were controlled by the L. and E. Dwiggins chain, which rested on unorthodox principles of banking. See Huston, *op. cit.*, I, 248–50; Henry S. Henschen, *A History of the State Bank of Chicago from 1879 to 1904* (Chicago, 1905), p. 26; *The Economist*, IX (May 13, 1893), 658, 664, X (July 15, 1893), 46, (Aug. 12, 1893), 158.

17 *Ibid.*, IX (June 10, 1893), 795, 800; James, *op. cit.*, I, 588–89.

in national banks had shrunk over twenty-three million dollars and loans had been considerably curtailed to build up the banks' reserves, the latter measure accelerating other stagnating forces at play in the commercial life of the city.[18] So serious did conditions appear to business leaders that P. D. Armour, Marshall Field, and Ransom R. Cable openly urged the adoption of a more liberal policy for loans and, if necessary, that the clearinghouse issue loan certificates. Although such an issue was shortly permitted, it was not resorted to, probably because of the banking fraternity's hostility, which, instead, offered easement to those temporarily embarrassed by rediscounting their commercial paper or by other similar means.[19]

Such expedients, however, turned out to be only temporary cures in an economy whose basis of prosperity was caught inextricably in the web of national and international trade. And despite the fact that the impact of the financial crises of the post-Fire years may have varied in intensity from east to west, Chicago, " the Great Gateway of the West," as the city delighted to think of herself, was forced, willy-nilly, to become an eventual though reluctant victim. Nor were all the causative factors recognized as having the same relative force as elsewhere. Yet Chicago was no longer free from the repercussions of a national consumer market, of business distress abroad, nor of the impaired confidence of the people of the country in the silver policy of the federal government and the often acridly expressed disapproval of bankers of the national currency.

Before August the entire country was in the throes of a collapsed market. New York banks refused to ship out currency, and in Chicago the eastern city's exchange was disposed of at discounts ranging from fifteen to forty dollars a thousand. And what to many seemed worse, grain and meat dealers found it necessary either to hold back their products or sell them at a loss.[20]

In a context of tense uncertainty as to how widespread and disas-

[18] *Ibid.*, 590–92; *The Commercial and Financial Chronicle,* LVI (June 10, 1893), 946, 959; *The Economist,* IX (June 17, 1893), 834; *Chicago Tribune,* July 18, 19, 24, 1893. For similar conditions throughout the country see U. S. Comptroller of the Currency, *Report, 1893,* I, 5–6.

[19] *Chicago Tribune,* July 28, 29, 1893, Jan. 1, 1894; Huston, *op. cit.,* I, 505; James, *op. cit.,* I, 596–98; James Graham Cannon, *Clearing Houses* (National Monetary Commission, U. S. Senate, 61 Cong., 2 sess., Doc. 491, Washington, 1910), p. 292. Not until 1907 were clearinghouse certificates issued in Chicago. *Ibid.,* p. 121.

[20] *Chicago Tribune,* April 23, Aug. 1, 7, 10, 1893; *The Economist,* X (Aug. 5, 1893), 131, 139, (Aug. 26, 1893), 214.

trous the panic would be, the city's money market was rescued in August through the leadership of Lyman J. Gage, president of the First National Bank, by using foreign balances to buy gold in London, which was then shipped to Chicago.[21] " This striking development," as *The Economist* described it, participated in by other bankers and industrialists, gave the city renewed courage, reanimated the money market, and evidenced a sense of responsibility to banks and business beyond those of the city alone. Demands of country banks abated, hoarded currency returned to the normal channels of circulation and bank deposit. The statesmanship thus exhibited gave Chicago increased prestige throughout the country, and kindled anew the ever persisting but unrealistic hope that the city could at last be emancipated from dependence upon New York and become, in essence, the financial capital of the entire country. Sober observers realized, however, that this could not happen, much as fellow Chicagoans desired it, for, as *The Economist* sententiously observed: " The habit of a nation in carrying on its financial operations at a certain point cannot be broken in a day." [22]

Of the twenty-three national banks doing business in March, 1893, all but the Chemical and Columbia had withstood the strain of what was at times called " the bankers' panic." Three private institutions also closed their doors, including that of Lazarus Silverman, for forty years the guardian of the funds of Hebrew peddlers and small merchants whose confidence in the Silverman bank did not falter even in the time of crisis.[23]

The general unsettlement, which had been occasioned by the various crises through which Chicago passed, naturally raised questions as to the real effectiveness of legal controls already imposed upon

[21] The First National, Illinois Trust and Savings, the Bank of Nova Scotia, Armour and Company, the Illinois Steel Co., and others purchased about eight million dollars' worth of gold in London for shipment to Chicago. In carrying out the operation some bought New York exchange at the great discount then current and ordered London banks to draw against these credits; others with London or Continental balances used them to purchase gold.

[22] James, *op. cit.*, I, 603–6; *The Economist*, X (Aug. 12, 1893), 160, (Aug. 26, 1893), 214, 215; *Chicago Tribune*, Sept. 13, 18, 1893; *The Lumber Trade Journal*, XXIV (Sept. 1, 1893), 4.

[23] Herman Schaffner & Co. and Meadowcroft Brothers were also casualties. U. S. Comptroller of the Currency, *Report, 1893*, I, 304; *The Economist*, X (Aug. 5, 1893), 131; *Chicago Tribune*, Aug. 6, 1893; *The Rand-McNally Bankers' Monthly*, X (Sept., 1893), 357, (Nov., 1893), 447.

banking operations. The national banks were, of course, under the standards prescribed in 1863 and '64, and the Illinois Constitution of 1870 had placed state banks under regulations. But many of the latter had been chartered prior to the enactment of 1870 and were able to avoid some of its provisions. As a result, those under the state's jurisdiction were at times far less stable than their national counterpart and their advertised capital was not always what their officials had claimed.[24] A demand for stricter controls led the legislature, in 1879, to attempt to set up stronger safeguards for those institutions under the state's jurisdiction. Significantly, the regulations provided that officers henceforth accepting deposits with the knowledge that their banks were insolvent were subject to charges of embezzlement, and they were forbidden to borrow money from their savings deposits or trust funds. Furthermore, savings banks and banks receiving savings deposits or trust funds were prohibited from becoming liable as guarantors.[25]

The law, however, did not correct the defects in the operation of banks licensed by the state to do business. It was not until June, 1887 that more effective regulations were placed on the statute books. Then a general banking law provided that banks and banking associations could be established to conduct a discount and deposit business, to buy and sell exchange, to loan money on personal and real security, to accept and execute trusts, and to perform general banking functions. The issue of currency was forbidden and reports of financial standing at quarterly intervals were to be submitted to the state auditor and to be publicized in the local press. Examination by the auditor annually was also prescribed. The act further stipulated that the minimum capital of such institutions should be $25,000 in municipalities of not over 5,000 people, and $50,000 in places not

[24] Under the Constitution of 1870, requirements for state banks included the liability of stockholders to the bank's creditors over and above the stock held and a quarterly statement of the bank's condition. Emil Joseph Verlie, ed., *Illinois Constitutions* (Illinois State Historical Library, *Collections,* XIII. Constitutional Series, I. Springfield, 1919), pp. 157–58; Joseph William Charlton, *The History of Banking in Illinois since 1863* (unpublished Ph.D. Thesis, The University of Chicago, 1938), pp. 57–61. See Pierce, *A History of Chicago,* II, 119–30 for legislation prior to 1870.

[25] Act of June 4, 1879, Illinois, *Laws, 1879,* pp. 113–14. The crash of the State Savings Bank, said to be the largest of its kind west of New York, in Aug., 1877, and the flight of its president pointed up the dangers inherent in lack of control. Charles H. Dennis, *Victor Lawson His Times and His Work* (Chicago, 1935), p. 46.

over 10,000, a wording so peculiar that the Supreme Court of the state later interpreted it as not excluding cities of over 10,000.[26]

Besides this effort to protect the money which people had entrusted to banks and to determine orderly processes of banking, the legislature provided for the supervision of savings societies and institutions. This act, however, the people of Illinois failed to ratify as was mandatory under the Constitution of 1870, and it was therefore declared unconstitutional in 1888 by the Illinois Supreme Court.[27] The first effective statutory regulation of trust companies also was undertaken in 1887. This function of banking, slow to develop in Chicago, was destined to expand in importance in the years to come. By 1893 seven companies, of which the Northern Trust Company, founded in 1889, was a notable example, were conducting business in a climate hospitable to their successful existence.[28]

In spite of setbacks, however, state and national banks grew appreciably in significance as agents of the business community, particularly after the late 'seventies. The former rose from eight, in December, 1872, to twenty-three in October, 1892, and the capital and surplus from an estimated $2,811,000 to $16,780,000. Alongside these evidences of expansion was the total of deposits, which mounted over twenty-two times in the same twenty years to reach $69,162,884. To the state-chartered banks could be added the state savings institutions with their capital and surplus of nearly two million dollars and deposits totaling about twelve million. These savings banks declined considerably, especially after the crash of 1877, and their holdings in official reports are combined with the state-chartered establishments and are therefore indistinguishable.[29]

[26] The act also prohibited a loan to an individual or an association in excess of one-tenth of the paid-in capital. Act of June 16, 1887, Illinois, *Laws, 1887*, pp. 89–95; Charles A. Dupee *et al. v.* Charles P. Swigert, Auditor, 127 Ill. 494–507 (1889).

[27] Act of May 23, 1887, Illinois, *Laws, 1887*, pp. 77–88; William Kelsey Reed *et al. v.* The People *ex rel.* George Hunt, 125 Ill. 592 (1888).

[28] The law stated that trust companies acting as trustees should deposit some $200,000 in bonds or mortgages and should file an annual report with the Auditor of Public Accounts; it further required the auditor to make an annual inspection of the records of such companies. Act of June 15, 1887, Illinois, *Laws, 1887*, pp. 144–48; Thomas, *op. cit.*, pp. 341–45, 349–50; Illinois Auditor of Public Accounts, *Biennial Report, 1894*, pp. 391–94; James, *op. cit.*, II, 1336.

[29] The total deposits in 1872 of state banks was $3,056,627. Fawcette, *loc. cit.*, p. 138; Chicago Board of Trade, *Thirty-fifth Annual Report, 1892*, pp. 122–23.

Even more impressive was the showing made by the national banks in financing Chicago's economic empire. In 1892 they numbered twenty-three; their capital was almost twenty-three million dollars, about eight times more than in 1871, and their surplus had increased nearly five times, to pass ten million in the same period. An equally important yardstick of growth was the multiplication of deposits due other banks, as a result of Chicago's position as a reserve city, by more than seven times, to exceed fifty-two million dollars. In 1892, also, individual deposits of nearly one hundred million testified still further to the prestige the nationals had come to enjoy.[30]

As national and state banks wielded more power, private institutions lost some of the importance which had been theirs in the days prior to the Civil War. They, however, continued to be of consequence in commercial and investment operations, engaging in bond sales and in brokerage activities as well as encouraging savings deposits. Attempts from 1890 to 1892 to license them by the state and require a minimum capitalization met with so much opposition from bankers that such legislation failed to pass. Like the state and national organizations, however, the private institutions made a gratifying showing in deposits, holding by 1882 almost 15 per cent of all deposits in the banks of the city.[31]

As time went on, the influence Chicago exercised in trade over the surrounding territory was extended to the realm of banking and the promotion of other financial enterprises. National banks, in particular, served as the correspondents of banks located in the hinterland. Thither went traveling agents to extol the advantages of their city just as did the so-called drummers to advertise their wares. Between October, 1872 and the same month in 1892 totals recorded in the nationals alone swelled from $45,914,253.06 to $172,612,219.12. Besides tapping the Great Middle Valley, the city served banks in the East and in Canada, and even in the South and Far West. In 1887 Chi-

[30] The Economist, V (Feb. 14, 1891), 245; Rand, McNally & Co.'s Bankers' Monthly, I (Feb. 23, 1884), 16; U. S. Comptroller of the Currency, Report, 1872, pp. 38–39, 1893, I, 304–5; A. D. Welton, The Making of a Modern Bank, An History of the Origin of the Continental and Commercial Banks of Chicago . . . (Chicago, 1923), pp. 14–15.

[31] Pierce, A History of Chicago, II, 133-34; The Economist, V (Feb. 14, 1891), 249, (Feb. 21, 1891), 284–85; Illinois, Senate Journal, 1891, pp. 481, 584, 945, 1893, 386–87, 560, 847, 871, House Journal, 1891, pp. 81, 362, 1142; Fawcette, loc. cit., p. 138; U. S. Comptroller of the Currency, Report, 1882, pp. c, cii, civ, cvi–cvii.

cago was made a central reserve city.[32] Within another four years she
stood next to New York in total clearings, having, in 1891 and 1892,
outdistanced Philadelphia and Boston, and this enviable position
had been attained without including the huge grain transactions
cared for by the Board of Trade Clearing House. The amount also
held by the state banks as correspondents of those in outlying areas,
although much less than that of the nationals, was, however, appreciable, reaching about five and a quarter million by January, 1893.[33]

It is, therefore, not strange that those with money to invest looked
upon shares of bank stock with great favor. This was particularly
true after the mid-'eighties, when, at times, shares were unavailable
at almost any bid. Those fortunate enough to hold such shares found
dividends high — at the First National, for example, never less than
9 per cent for twenty years (1872–1892); and this was for only one
year. Such manifestations of well-being were reason enough, suggested *Rand, McNally & Co.'s Bankers' Monthly,* that shares of
bank stock were an investment " rare to be had," and one which
" must be paid for on its merits." [34]

Whenever the board of directors of the leading banks met, there
assembled the outstanding businessmen of the city, who, at times,
were joined by prominent Easterners.[35] Within the council chamber
of the important state-chartered Merchants' Loan & Trust Co. convened men of the economic stature of Marshall Field, Cyrus H. Mc-
Cormick, George M. Pullman, Albert Keep, and John De Koven.
The board of the Continental National at one time or another was
composed of representatives of the meat-packing industry in P. D.

[32] U. S. Comptroller of the Currency, *Report, 1872,* p. 38, *1892,* I, 375; *The Economist,*
IX (Jan. 7, 1893), 17; Dailey, *op. cit.,* pp. 366–68; *Rand, McNally & Co.'s Bankers' Monthly,*
IV (Nov., 1887), 334.

[33] *Chicago Tribune,* Sept. 24, 1890; *The Chicago Times,* June 2, 1891; U. S. Comp-
troller of the Currency, *Report, 1892,* I, 80–82; *The Economist,* V (May 16, 1891), 841–42,
VIII (Oct. 15, 1892), 540, (Nov. 19, 1892), 713, IX (Jan. 7, 1893), 8, Annual Number
(Jan. 1, 1894), 10. In July, 1892, the amount had been about one million more. *Ibid.,*
VIII (Aug. 6, 1892), 202.

[34] *Rand, McNally & Co.'s Bankers' Monthly,* I (Feb. 23, 1884), 16, VI (June, 1889),
132, IX (Sept., 1892), 202; Morris, *op. cit.,* pp. 196–98. For " bid " and " asked " prices on
shares see *The Economist.*

[35] Among prominent Easterners were H. G. Lane, I. H. Reed, W. F. Dominick, and
David Davis of New York. Bank directors as of Jan., 1892 are given in *Chicago Tribune,* Jan.
13, 1892. A list of all stockholders of Chicago National Banks who reported holdings to the
assessor of South Town in 1893 is in *ibid.,* Nov. 7, 1893.

Armour and Henry Botsford, of the manufacture of metals in Richard T. Crane, of the grain interests in James H. Dole, of the lumber trade in Anthony G. Van Schaick, and of wholesale hardware in William G. Hibbard. This variety in primary business attachments was found in other instances, but always a likeness in economic thinking and motivation served to cement such alliances and to make them indestructible.[36]

So successful did this *entente cordiale* prove to be that it was duplicated in numerous outlying banks which sprang up to meet the needs of new neighborhoods. John W. Doane, the tea importer and president of the Merchants' Loan & Trust Co. in 1890, served at the same time as a director along with Marshall Field, George M. Pullman, and John De Koven in the Pullman Loan and Savings Bank established in 1883. The oldest of the banks not within the central part of the city, the Union Stock Yards National, to become the National Live Stock Bank in 1888, carried on a flourishing business from its beginning in 1869, under Samuel M. Nickerson, president of the First National from 1867 to 1891. The monopoly the Stock Yards Bank enjoyed was allowed to go virtually unchallenged until 1883, when the Drovers National Bank of the Union Stock Yards was established.[37]

Within the community they served, bankers possessed an economic and social prestige equaled by no other group. Although many, like Mr. Dooley, looked upon banking as a " sthrange business," they willingly gave point to his bit of whimsy:

> Ye'er money makes me a prominent citizen. Th' newspapers intherview one on what shud be done with the toilin' masses, . . . I conthruct th' foreign policy in the governmint, [and] I tell ye how ye shud vote.[38]

Of those who wielded this vast influence no one was better known or more highly regarded than Lyman J. Gage, whose rise from the lowly estate of bank clerk at $100 a year in Rome, New York, to the

---

[36] Harper and Ravell, *op. cit.*, pp. 7, 61, 67–72; *Rand, McNally & Co.'s Bankers' Monthly*, I (Feb. 23, 1884), 17; *Armour Magazine and Morris Standard*, XVI (April, 1927), 7; *Chicago Daily News*, Jan. 8, 1890; Illinois Auditor of Public Accounts, *Biennial Report, 1890*, p. 318.

[37] *Ibid.*, pp. 322, 334; E. M. Baty, *The Story of The Outlying Banks of Chicago* (Chicago, 1924), pp. 9–14.

[38] *Chicago Record-Herald*, Jan. 15, 1905.

presidency of the First National Bank of Chicago in 1891, was one of the " success stories " of the day. Gage not only exemplified outstanding qualities of economic leadership, but possessed a sensitive social and civic conscience. He was, in a very real sense, as the organ of the Chicago *Knights of Labor* in its homely play on words put it, " a broad-gauged " man, one capable of leading " in the solution of the great problem [labor problem]." This willing acknowledgment of his understanding of one of the most crucial issues of the day contrasted markedly with the words of obloquy with which labor enveloped many of his business contemporaries. The attributes which thus commended him to this segment of the city's peoples, commended him also to others searching not only for trustworthy stewardship in financial matters but for leadership in civic and political affairs.[39]

Ties of fraternal relationship in the business of banking just as in other economic endeavors were strengthened by association of those of like mind. For this purpose the Bankers' Club was founded in 1883 under Gage's leadership. In November, 1891 an Illinois State Bankers' Association took shape to consider problems of common interest to the banking business and to marshal public opinion against laws considered inimical to the well-being of banking procedures. The Illinois Private Bankers' Association paralleled in aims the State Bankers' group and counted among its supporters important Chicagoans such as Herman Schaffner, Edward S. Dreyer, and Edward Tilden.[40]

To many in the lower income brackets a safer place than banks to keep their savings was the building and loan associations, which, in the years after the Great Fire, grew in number and in the volume of their financial resources. Privileges were accorded only to their members; loans were made for homes on real estate security; and

[39] Reginald C. McGrane, "Lyman J. Gage," *Dictionary of American Biography*, VII, 85–86; [Lyman J. Gage], *Memoirs of Lyman J. Gage* (New York, 1937), *passim;* [Manhattan Publishing Company], *A Biographical History . . . of Prominent Men of the Great West*, pp. 7–9; Gilbert and Bryson, *op. cit.*, p. 760; *The Knights of Labor*, III (May 16, 1888), 5. Under the title " Chicago Merchants and Business Men in Sympathy with Honest Labor," the First National Bank is listed in *ibid.*, IV (July 21, 1888), 5.

[40] Orear, *Commercial and Architectural Chicago*, p. 71; Flinn, *Chicago . . . A Guide, 1891*, p. 210; *Chicago Blue Book, 1891*, p. 340; *Rand, McNally & Co.'s Bankers' Monthly*, II (Oct., 1885), 94; *The Rand-McNally Bankers' Monthly*, IX (Jan., 1892), 11, (March, 1892), 1, (June, 1892), 132, (Dec., 1892), 310; *Chicago Daily News*, Nov. 6, 1891.

payments were required on account of dues, loans, and interest on loans. The names of these " poor men's banks," as they were sometimes called, frequently represented the national background of the people they most often were asked to accommodate.[41] In 1881 a decision of the Illinois Supreme Court opened the way to the incorporation of many new organizations.[42] The number leaped to over two hundred in 1889 and to 320 in 1892.[43]

As these organizations developed, a demand arose for state supervision similar to that of banks. It was not until 1891, however, that proponents of regulation were successful. Then building and loan associations were required to submit to the state auditor annual reports as to their financial condition and to special examination should such be requested by nine shareholders. In 1891 these associations were said to have an estimated $43,500,000 in assets. Yet, in spite of their growth, most Chicagoans did not own their homes. In 1886, for example, out of a population of over seven hundred thousand fewer than eighteen thousand were in possession of their houses or any real estate, leading Ethelbert Stewart of the Illinois Bureau of Labor Statistics to point out that all the real property belonged to less than 2½ per cent of the people.[44]

Over all still hung the spell of the land which had dominated the investment history of the city from the very beginning. From it men

[41] Seymour Dexter, *A Treatise on Co-operative Savings and Loan Associations* (New York, 1889), pp. 58–60; *The Economist*, VI (Sept. 12, 1891), 447; *Chicago Tribune*, March 25, 1883; Illinois Auditor of Public Accounts, *Annual Report, 1892*, p. 15. Examples of national organizations are Svornost, Pravda, and Praha for Bohemians; Concordia and Germania for Germans; the First Swedish for the Swedes; the Polish National Building & Loan Association for Poles.

[42] The case before the court involved the downstate Monticello Mutual Building, Loan and Homestead Association charged by its borrowers with assessing usurious rates. The Association had been incorporated under a law of 1872 which was repealed along with the first general law (1869) in 1874. In 1879 a law similar to the 1872 statute was passed. (Illinois, *Laws, 1879*, pp. 83–87.) The principles of the 1872 law the court held constitutional. William M. Holmes *et al. v.* Aramentia M. Smythe *et al.*, 100 Ill. 413 (1881).

[43] *Chicago Tribune*, March 25, 1883, Jan. 16, 1889; U. S. Commissioner of Labor, *Ninth Annual Report, 1893* (Washington, 1894), pp. 54–65. For further information on these associations, see Citizens' Association of Chicago, *Annual Report, 1888*, p. 38; *The Rand-McNally Bankers' Monthly*, V (Sept., 1888), 295, VI (April, 1889), 74; Henry S. Rosenthal, ed., *Fifty Years of Service, Golden Jubilee, Historical Review of the Building Association League of Illinois* (n.p., 1929), pp. 20, 22.

[44] Illinois, *Senate Journal, 1885*, pp. 325, 559, *House Journal, 1885*, pp. 598, 698; Act of June 19, 1891, Illinois, *Laws, 1891*, pp. 90–92; *The Rand-McNally Bankers' Monthly*, VIII (Sept., 1891), 283; *The Economist*, VI (Sept. 12, 1891), 447; *The Knights of Labor*, XXII (Sept. 4, 1886), 2.

had been rescued from want to consort with the envied possessors of wealth. It was not necessary for the man who had such aspirations to be ingenious. All, or nearly all, that seemed required was an unwavering boldness, a willingness to adventure, to enroll in the ranks of those famed as speculators. The story of men with no tangible assets becoming rich almost overnight was duplicated time and again. It seemed as if for anyone willing to venture

> Awake — asleep — 'tis all the same,
> Or idle or alert.
> In foreign parts he long may roam —
> It grows as if he were at home.
> There's nothing pays like dirt.[45]

If, perchance, the public fancy might have shifted from the real estate market, potential investors were reminded of the alluring prospect in store through the columns of the daily press, the *Real Estate and Building Journal,* and other business organs.[46] So profitable was the vocation of real estate agent that the listings in the city directory showed an appreciable increase as more and more eagerly grasped at the frequently skyrocketing profits.

On February 21, 1883 the unity of purpose of those engaged in the business led to the incorporation of the Chicago Real Estate Board to exchange information of common interest and to engage in activities to protect it. With the adoption of a standard lease by the Board as one of its first orders of business within a month after its incorporation, renters felt that organization had again insured the property owners' advantage over them, and that the result of the lease now imposed upon them was, as the *Tribune* put it, " that the tenant promises to do everything, and that all the landlord agrees to do is to receive the monthly rent in advance."

Within the range of the Board's activities lay the consideration of state laws and city ordinances concerned with matters affecting tax-

---

[45] George Asher Beecher, "Nothing Pays Like Dirt" [Leaflet] (n.p., n.d.), quoting P. T. in *Toronto Grip; Chicago Tribune,* Jan. 1, 1887. Typical of those who gained wealth through real estate holdings was E. H. Hadduck, a hostler in a tavern where his wife was a chambermaid. Entering the hotel business, he put his savings into real estate and in 1874 was worth $1,500,000. Charles Follansbee, a banker in 1874, was reported worth $1,250,000. He and his brother started a bakery in 1836 on a combined capital of $25. See *The Chicago Times,* March 7, 1874, for other examples.

[46] The *Real Estate and Building Journal* ran from 1866 to 1909.

ation, as well as the preservation of abstract books available for public inspection in the county recorder's office. It was also concerned with the prohibition of certain kinds of "nuisance" business (such as livery stables, blacksmith shops, and foundries) without the consent of property owners on both sides of the street for 300 feet in each direction from the proposed building. During the summer of 1889 it worked zealously to insure the holding of the Columbian Exposition in Chicago. Although its membership was not as large as that of some other organizations of special purpose, the Board included many outstanding dealers in real estate such as Wm. D. Kerfoot & Co., E. S. Dreyer & Co., Eugene S. Pike, Dunlap Smith & Co., Bryan Lathrop, Ogden, Sheldon & Co., and H. C. Morey & Co. By autumn, 1892, the Board reached its goal of 150 members and raised its initiation fee to $200, four times higher than in 1884.[47]

The selling of real estate was, of course, marked by the flurries of prosperity and the dullness of depression which affected both Chicago's and the country's economy. Certain local factors, however, at times proved a temporary and unique stimulus. Such a factor was the Great Fire, which, within two years, produced feverish activity only perceptibly slowed up during the last years of the 'seventies. With the 'eighties came a resurgence of good business conditions, particularly emphasized by the expansion of manufactures and other persistently vivifying components of the city's economic structure. To these were added a demand quickened by the extension of the territorial limits of the city and, in February, 1890, by the announcement that the Columbian Exposition would be held in Chicago. In the latter two instances tracts lying to the south of the main business section sold rapidly. Land near Jackson Park, in the locality of the site of the Exposition, increased as much as 1,000 per cent in 1890 alone, with sections partially under water bringing as much as $15,000 an acre over the $600 asked previously.[48]

In 1890 the aggregate realty transfers by quarters was reported to

[47] The Call Board Bulletin, Sept., 1892, pp. 17, 19, 23, 30, 36, 45, 48; Chicago Real Estate Board, Report of Revenue Reform Committees, 1884, pp. 5–6, 19–20; Chicago Tribune, March 18, 1883, Jan. 15, 1885; Industrial Chicago, IV, The Commercial Interests, 24.

[48] Homer Hoyt, One Hundred Years of Land Values in Chicago, pp. 171, 175, and Earl Johnson, The Natural History of the Central Business District, discuss the shifting areas of important investments in Chicago.

total $227,000,000, tapering off in the next two years to $177,000,000 as the inspiriting effects of the Fair abated and reverberations of a tightness in the national money market were first faintly heard and then clearly felt. The validity of transactions of this nature was assured by the various firms recording the ownership of property, including after 1872 Handy, Simmons and Company. This group was succeeded by the Title Guarantee and Trust Company in 1887. The next year the latter, organized in accordance with the provisions of the General Trust Act of 1887, issued the first guarantee title in Illinois which protected the owner against loss if his title as guaranteed was found invalid. In 1885 the Cook County Abstract Company began operations; six years later it changed its name to the Chicago Title and Trust Company.[49]

The popularity of investing in Chicago real estate and in mortgages upon such property extended far beyond those residents of the city who saved or speculated through them. Eastern capitalists at times so ardently sought the midwest city that their own sections looked jealously upon this migration of capital which, critics declared, should have been kept at home and thus have been of benefit to its own neighborhood.[50] Investors from Europe likewise pursued the same enriching returns, their interest whetted by the publication of speeches of such perennial boosters as ex-Governor William Bross, by enticingly phrased advertisements, and by the direct appeal of companies staffed by persuasive salesmen, both American and foreign.[51]

Fortunate indeed had been the man who had foreseen shifts in desirable residence and business locations. Although the stately man-

[49] The total reported by the *Tribune* for 1890 was higher than the totals listed by quarters. The latter were $225,700,000. *Chicago Tribune*, Jan. 1, 1892, Jan. 1, 1893; Illinois, *Laws, 1887*, pp. 144–48; Chicago Title and Trust Company, *Growing with Chicago 1847–1947* (Chicago, 1947. Courtesy of Chicago Title and Trust Company), [pp. 2–6].

[50] Real estate offices by Easterners were established in Chicago to advance their interests. For example, Mrs. Hetty R. H. Green opened one in 1890. *The Economist*, IV (Nov. 22, 1890), 835.

[51] *Chicago Tribune*, Feb. 7, 1873. In 1874, for example, the Scottish-American Mortgage Company, Limited, was organized by Daniel H. Hale and Henry I. Sheldon of Daniel H. Hale & Co. of Chicago and J. Duncan Smith of Edinburgh, to loan money on first mortgages on real estate. Hale, as American agent, also sponsored Scottish emigration under the ægis of the Anglo-American Land Company. David Ward Wood, ed., *Chicago and Its Distinguished Citizens* (Chicago, 1881), pp. 86–87.

sions of many of the leading citizens on Prairie, Calumet, and South Park avenues remained the focus of much of the social life, Michigan Boulevard by 1880 took on new glory; and after the middle of the decade Drexel and Grand avenues and streets near by reflected the continued movement of Chicagoans in a southerly direction. At the same time the North Side had its devotees and at the west Ashland Avenue and Washington Boulevard enjoyed a considerable popularity.[52] The retail business district, which had moved from Lake Street by the late 'sixties and which extended as far south as Monroe, returned here as soon as possible after the Fire, dimming the hopes of property owners in the part of the city where business had been temporarily carried on. The wholesale district around Franklin, Wells, and Monroe, and the selection by bankers, insurance agencies, brokers, and commission dealers in grains and provisions of sites on LaSalle, the " Wall Street " of Chicago, heralded the advance of property values and rents in this neighborhood.

The movement of industries away from the center of the city to Twenty-second Street and Western Avenue and then to outlying sections, such as the Calumet area, became significant also, and drew with it those who worked in the plants, thus peopling new regions and developing a suburban life rarely if ever thought of in pre-Fire days. The price of land in these new settlements, increasingly serviced by spreading lines of transport, soared to astronomical heights. A stretch of land bought by George M. Pullman in 1880 for from $75 to $200 an acre, for instance, jumped to $1,000 and to $3,000 in three years after the establishment there of Pullman's Palace Car Works, and his experience was not unique in the new and flourishing outlands. Much the same was repeated within the central part of the city under its pulsating and high-powered pressures. When, in 1889, Herman H. Kohlsaat, a heavy purchaser of real estate, acquired a plot of land at Dearborn and Madison at $150,000, or $187.50 a square foot, he caused a stir in real estate circles because the price paid was reported the most ever given west of New York. But there was little question as to the soundness of Kohlsaat's judgment. Shortly the land was leased to a syndicate, an auxiliary of the *Inter Ocean,* at $10,000 a year, along with the Frederick Haskell property to the north and west at $30,000. With the purchase of the

[52] See chapters I and II in which residential areas are discussed.

Haskell Building for $100,000, which was then combined with the others into one property for the use of the *Inter Ocean* and others, Dearborn Street became the center of interest in real estate transfers.[53]

Transactions in mortgage bonds claimed the attention of various organizations committed to conducting financial operations. That it was a profitable undertaking was strikingly attested by the favor with which leading bankers looked upon it.[54] No less a seasoned promoter than Henry Greenebaum carried on an active campaign, especially right after the Fire, not only to entice American investors into the Chicago market, but potential purchasers from Europe — particularly those from his native Germany.[55]

With the demand for larger and costlier buildings, paralleling the economic expansion which occurred notably after the 'seventies, went the necessity of finding the means of financing much construction. Alert to these opportunities, bankers proceeded to sell the securities which were to assure the increasingly popular skyscrapers, those " steepling hives," as Julian Ralph called them, located in the central business section and housing many offices, business establishments, and a variety of other undertakings.

It was through the efforts of the First National Bank, for example, that the mortgage bonds were sold, not only for the important Board of Trade Building, opened April 30, 1885, but also for the fourteen-story Great Northern Hotel at the northeast corner of Dearborn and Jackson, built at a cost of a little over a million dollars in 1891. The Young Men's Christian Association structure, at LaSalle Street and Arcade Court, opened when partially finished, on New Year's Day, 1894, was eventually aided by the First National's purchasing the Association's mortgage bonds up to $600,000 and thereby providing the young men of the city, as the *Tribune* put it, in typically Chicago

53 J. W. Sheahan, " Chicago," *Scribner's Monthly*, X (Sept., 1875), 537–39; *The Economist*, C (Oct. 15, 1938), 114. R. C. Smysers, comp., *Invested Wealth of Chicago* . . . (Chicago, 1889), gives examples of increases in land values. For shifts in business and residential areas see chapters I, II, and V; also Hoyt, *op. cit.*, pp. 89–90, 133–35, 137, and Earl Johnson, *op. cit.*, pp. 248–50.

54 The approval of the General Corporation Act in 1872 legalized the possession of real estate needed in the conduct of a corporation's business. This real estate could be pledged as security of a bond issue. Illinois, *Laws, 1871–72*, pp. 296 ff. The law specifically excluded banking and real estate brokerage firms, railroads (except horse and dummy railroads), and any business involved in loaning money.

55 See *Henry Greenebaum Estate Collection*.

superlatives, with "the largest, costliest, most modern, and best appointed association building in this country or the world." [56]

The bonds for the well-known skyscraper, the Tacoma Building, at the corner of LaSalle and Madison streets, were issued through the private banking firm of Arthur O. Slaughter. The brokerage concern of Peabody, Houghteling & Co. also disposed of some of these securities as well as marketing other Chicago issues, many with their large eastern clientele. The disposition of such bonds formed a part of the business conducted by the real estate firms of H. O. Stone & Co. after 1887, and Aldis, Aldis & Northcote after 1890.[57] The investment practices of these companies followed no set pattern, nor did all of them include all kinds of issues in their offerings. Some, such as the Aldis organization to which were entrusted funds from the East and England as well as from Chicago were mainly concerned with city holdings. Others, like the Red Oak Investment Company, with an interest primarily in southeast Nebraska and southwest Iowa, and like D. K. Pearsons & Co. in Illinois, became important in caring for farm mortgages.[58]

By the 'nineties long-term leases had become almost commonplace as more and more high edifices, attractively appointed but not always beautifully designed, appeared. Even those buildings of less recent construction and design than the skyscrapers, when well located, commanded leases for ninety-nine years, and the *Tribune* commented in its New Year's issue of 1893 that such arrangements were being made throughout the city and even in the suburbs. The pros-

[56] Pierce, *As Others See Chicago*, p. 291; Henry Ericsson collaborating with Lewis E. Myers, *Sixty Years a Builder: The Autobiography of Henry Ericsson* (Chicago, 1942), pp. 212–22, 229–33; *The Economist*, V (May 23, 1891), 897, IX (Feb. 4, 1893), 145, XIII (Jan. 26, 1895), 97; *Chicago Daily News*, March 10, 1884; *Chicago Tribune*, Jan. 1, 1894. The securities for the fireproof seventeen-story Schiller Building at 103–109 Randolph Street owned by the German Opera House Company were handled by N. W. Harris & Co. *The Economist*, IX (March 4, 1893), 300–1.

[57] *Ibid.*, II (March 2, 1889), 167, IV (Aug. 9, 1890), 213, IX (April 15, 1893), 508, 511, (May 6, 1893), 619, XXIII (Feb. 10, 1900), 151, 171.

[58] Harry L. Severson, *History of Investment Banking in Chicago* (In progress, Ph.D. Thesis, The University of Chicago, 1939), chapter "1878–1882," pp. 24–25, "1882–1902," p. 28; *The Economist*, II (Jan. 12, 1889), 20, (May 18, 1889), 406; *Chicago Tribune*, June 30, July 14, 1888, July 5, 1890; undated clipping from *Rand, McNally & Co.'s Bankers' Monthly* in *William L. Trenholm Papers* (Mss. Library of Congress). Aldis, Aldis & Northcote later became Aldis & Company. It had its roots as an investment company in the service Owen Aldis, a lawyer specializing in real estate, rendered Peter C. and Shepherd Brooks of Boston as early as 1879. Russell Tyson, *History of Aldis & Company* (Typescript, 1944. Courtesy of Mr. Graham Aldis).

pect of a continued high level, if not an increase in rents, contributed to the popularity of such definite agreements, five-year rentals at a fixed sum often followed by a larger sum for the next five or for the remainder of the period of the lease. With less room available by 1890 to tenants than since the 'eighties, despite an extraordinary amount of construction, business houses established themselves on floors above the first, and merchants desiring new locations and those wishing to start business in Chicago made contracts three to five years ahead. So great was the need for space that even before construction was completed new buildings had been rented.[59]

With the coming of the 1890's the local real estate market became, on the whole, less speculative, assuming to a greater extent the aspect of outlays for investment. Thereupon those with money to put out went into all parts of the country, just as they had been doing for some years, seeking rich returns either from places attempting to restore the glory of the past or from the country now sparsely peopled but hopeful of a rapid increase in population and a future of unending prosperity. The Southern Investment Company, in the early 'nineties, like its predecessors, dealt, for example, in real estate in the South, where the industrial pace for some years had been quickening enough to attract Chicagoans into expenditures for mills and factories and other business undertakings. Advertisements, convincingly phrased, reaped satisfying rewards in the sale of stocks and bonds. Not only did the thickly timbered lands beckon Chicago lumbermen, but cattle ranges in Texas and the Southwest enlisted the support of other investors.[60]

As the number of enterprises calling for funds increased, schemes to promote them sprang up like mushrooms. Colonization projects received the warm endorsement of the ever-alert Chicago agent who, at times, along with the sale of lands to would-be settlers, urged the

[59] *The Economist*, Annual Number, V (Jan. 1, 1891), 11, 13, IX (Feb. 4, 1893), 152, C (Oct. 15, 1938), 115; *Chicago Tribune*, Jan. 1, 1891, Jan. 1, Oct. 12, 1892; Hoyt, *op. cit.*, p. 130.

[60] *The Economist*, III (Feb. 1, 1890), 112, IV (Nov. 8, 1890), 753. N. W. Harris & Co. was active in such promotions, handling, for example, the 10–20 year 6 per cent bonds for enterprises in Jefferson County, Washington, in 1891. (*The Rand-McNally Bankers' Monthly*, VIII [June, 1891], 193.) *The Western Manufacturer*, V (Dec. 14, 1878), 884; *The Drovers' Journal*, Dec. 27, 1882, Feb. 14, April 6, July 25, Dec. 5, 1883, May 16, 18, July 10, Sept. 23, 1885; *Chicago Record-Herald*, June 14, 1906. In preceding chapters will be found examples of specific investments.

building of railroads to connect Chicago with these outposts of civilization.[61] Projects of town development, notably in Galveston, Texas, and West Superior, Wisconsin, were generously supported, and in the Far West designs for irrigation ditches caught wary and unwary alike.[62] Quick-rich mining stocks found a ready market in Chicago as elsewhere in the country, and plausibly presented opportunities to aid in the development of the new mining towns such as Fremont, Colorado, described as "the greatest gold mining camp in the WORLD to-day," captured the fancy and funds of a trusting public. And those who preferred promotions in silver could be accommodated by the Chicago Silver Mining Company and the Chicago Mining and Milling Company, the latter founded by the prominent German, A. C. Hesing, and controlling twenty mines.[63]

The persisting confidence placed in real estate and closely associated offerings as a sound investment did not, however, deter Chicagoans from distributing their funds among a variety of undertakings. The railroads, which played so great a part in making Chicago the capital of the Middle West, shared in this distribution, especially with the coming of economic sophistication in the 'eighties. Even then, many looked upon investments in rail lines as more hazardous than building and real estate issues, though interest rates might be the same. This, however, does not mean that men of wealth did not diversify their holdings and follow the example of their eastern counterparts. Entrepreneurs of the stature of P. D. Armour, Marshall Field, John V. Farwell, Turlington W. Harvey, Jesse Spalding, and

[61] California fruit lands in the San Joaquin Valley, for instance, were sold chiefly to actual settlers. (*The Economist*, III [May 17, 1890], 616.) Daniel H. Hale wished to link Chicago with Texas and even Mexico by a railroad, the Chicago, Texas and Mexican Central. Wood, *op. cit.*, p. 87; Poor, *Manual of the Railroads of the United States for 1882*, p. 823.

[62] Among promoters of irrigation projects were the North Platte Irrigation and Land Company of Arizona, the Arizona Canal Company, the Pecos Irrigation and Investment Company (interested in northwest Texas and southern New Mexico). Irrigation bonds were pushed in 1889 by Charles W. Greene and the firm of Farson, Leach & Co.

[63] *The Economist*, II (May 11, 1889), 376–77, (June 22, 1889), 525, 528, V (March 28, 1891), 513, (April 18, 1891), 652, VII (April 30, 1892), 655; John A. Logan to Mary Logan, May 25, 1875, *John A. Logan Papers* (Mss., Library of Congress); *The* [London] *Times*, March 22, 1873; *The Western Manufacturer*, VIII (Oct. 15, 1880), 207; Advertisement of Chicago-Cripple Creek Gold Mining Company (John Crerar Library, Chicago); *The Drovers' Journal*, Feb. 20, March 2, May 20, 1885; *Chicago Tribune*, May 5, 14, 1889; *Illinois Staats-Zeitung*, Feb. 7, 1879; *The American Elevator and Grain Trade*, VIII (July 15, 1889), 15; *The Mining Review*, XI (Jan. 3, 1884), 7.

Henry H. Porter saw in the promotion of lines of transportation the means of getting to market new physical resources they had acquired and were exploiting, or a way of speeding merchandise to its destination. When they expended large amounts in such issues the market price sometimes shot up, testifying to the magic of the names of those Chicagoans who, within the memory of their contemporaries, had grown rich through foresight and audacity.[64]

Porter, in particular, devoted his attention to the extension of roads throughout the central part of the country, some along new and hitherto unopened paths. He engaged in the reconstruction and consolidation of others, and he bought the stocks of lines which in depression years he could get cheaply, but which under his astute management reached prices that netted him a handsome profit. He was associated in some of these enterprises with leaders in many fields of business, not only in Chicago, but in the East, where some of them were counted among the wizards of Wall Street. He enjoyed similar connections with members of Congress, particularly Roswell B. Flower of New York and Senator Philetus Sawyer of Wisconsin. As a director of the First National Bank of Chicago he had access to those railroad bonds which it held.[65]

Of the various kinds of investment issues available, municipal bonds especially found ready acceptance. Not only were Chicago's numerous projects thus promoted, but those of growing communities particularly in the city's tributary area. Increased offerings from the South and West beckoned investors even before the 1880's, but noticeably from then on. Sometimes bonds were sold to the individual bidder who marketed them at his discretion; sometimes a financial organization bought an issue and disposed of individual bonds as desired; and sometimes a Chicago house acted as the broker for an

[64] *Chicago Daily News*, March 10, 1884; *Chicago Tribune*, Sept. 19, 1873, May 4, 1879, Jan. 1, 1882; *The Economist*, VIII (July 16, 1892), 84, X (Nov. 25, 1893), 557; *The Chicago Times*, Aug. 6, 1881. When Armour put $4,000,000 into the Chicago, Milwaukee and St. Paul Railway in 1885 the stock rose from 65 to nearly 100. *The Drovers' Journal*, Dec. 8, 1885, April 29, 1886.

[65] Porter's extensive holdings are described in H. A. Porter, *A Short Autobiography* (Chicago, 1915), pp. 26, 32–37. Among the roads he controlled were some short lines including the West Wisconsin Railroad, reorganized into the Chicago, St. Paul & Minneapolis Railway Co. " About 1880 " he consolidated several into the Chicago, St. Paul, Minneapolis and Omaha Railway, which, in 1882, was sold to the Chicago and North Western of which he was a director.

eastern customer who took over a complete issue. It was not until 1890, however, that the practice of payments in New York was in part discontinued, and Chicago began to make payment for her own bonds.

At first the size of the issues was frequently small, school bonds having special popularity. The economic luxuriance of the 1880's and an education as to the value of municipals stimulated more issues to provide for public improvements, for there was hardly a time when there was not a wide market for such offerings. The bond departments of the First National Bank and Preston, Kean & Co. were active during the 'seventies. The entrance into the market of N. W. Harris & Co., J. D. Harvey & Co., and Farson, Leach & Co. in the 1880's evidenced the growing attention directed to municipals, just as did the participation of stockbrokers such as Charles Henrotin, A. O. Slaughter, and Edward L. Brewster.[66]

With the extension of streetcar lines as the city grew, traction issues entered prominently into competition with other kinds of offerings. Distributed in much the same way as were municipals, they were channeled not only through Henrotin, Slaughter, Lobdell-Farwell, and others of the broker fraternity, but also through commercial banks including the First National, associated frequently in such undertakings with N. W. Harris in selling syndicates. A similar consanguinity existed between other leading bankers and brokers, and interlocking directorates bore witness to a growing cohesiveness among those to whom were entrusted the increasingly important utility issues.[67]

Of all those interested in extensions of the traction lines, the man who played the most spectacular role was the skillful manipulator Charles Tyson Yerkes, who had started in Chicago as an inconspic-

[66] *Chicago Tribune,* Jan. 21, July 11, 24, 1879, Jan. 14, 20, 1880, Jan. 1, 1883, July 21, Oct. 6, 1888, July 7, 1890; *The Commercial and Financial Chronicle,* XXII (May 13, 1876), 467; *The Chicago Times,* Jan. 20, 1880; *Rand, McNally & Co.'s Bankers' Monthly,* V (Feb., 1886), 64–65; *The Economist,* I (Oct. 20, 1888), 6, II (Jan. 5, 1889), 5, (April 20, 1889), 311, (May 4, 1889), 354, (May 25, 1889), 424, (Oct. 12, 1889), 920, (Dec. 14, 1889), 1169, III (Jan. 4, 1890), 7, (Jan. 25, 1890), 79, VIII (Oct. 15, 1892), 543, (Oct. 29, 1892), 616, X (Nov. 11, 1893), 500, (Dec. 9, 1893), 611, (Dec. 16, 1893), 634, 638.

[67] *Chicago Tribune,* Jan. 1, June 30, 1873, Jan. 3, April 3, 1876, May 8, 1878, May 16, 1879, April 18, 1888; *The Economist,* I (Dec. 22, 1888), 3, VI (Oct. 24, 1891), 697, IX (Feb. 18, 1893), 208–9, 219, X (July 22, 1893), 65, 66, Investors' Supplement, 1897, pp. 13, 58.

uous broker about 1882, after serving seven months of a two-year-and-nine-month prison sentence for "technical embezzlement" in Pennsylvania.[68] Associating himself with Peter A. B. Widener, William Lukens Elkins, and other Philadelphians, he set out to take over the streetcar systems of Chicago.

In March, 1886 Yerkes acquired a majority interest in the old North Chicago City Railway Company, and on May 18 incorporated the North Chicago Street Railroad Company which leased the property of the former permanently in return for the assumption of certain commitments of the lessor and monetary awards to it. An important part of the arrangement was the construction of a line on North Clark Street, starting not far from the north end of the bridge over the Chicago River and running to a point near Diversey Avenue. The contract for the work was let to the United States Construction Company which the Philadelphia interest also controlled, and which was paid in capital stock of the new company, bonds of the old, and in cash, a total of $6,208,908.39. The cost of construction was estimated as a little over three million dollars, netting the construction company approximately as much as the expenditures involved.

A similar deal was made by the Yerkes affiliates with the West Division Railway Company, and on July 19, 1887 the West Chicago Street Railroad Company was organized, with Yerkes as majority stockholder, its capital $10,000,000. The United States Construction Company thereupon was engaged to build cable lines, which the two companies had agreed upon, at a price affording approximately 100 per cent profit. In 1888 further consolidation was effected with the inclusion in the Yerkes orbit of the Chicago Passenger Railway, organized in 1883 as the Chicago Horse and Dummy Railway Company, and identified with the Chicago West Division Railway Company.[69]

---

[68] The date of Yerkes's arrival in Chicago varies in different sources.

[69] "History and Statistics of Chicago Street Railway Corporations," *The Economist*, Supplement, 1896, pp. 10–11, 15; Illinois Bureau of Labor Statistics, *Ninth Biennial Report, 1896*, "Franchises and Taxation," pp. 56–58; *Rand, McNally & Co.'s Bankers' Monthly*, III (April, 1886), 45, IV (Dec., 1887), 370; The Civic Federation of Chicago, *The Street Railways of Chicago* (Report, Milo Roy Maltbie, ed., reprint from *Municipal Affairs*, 1901. Hereafter cited as Civic Federation of Chicago, *The Street Railways of Chicago*), pp. 30, 36, 84–87, 96, 103, 130–31; *Chicago Tribune*, March 25, 27, 1886, July 24, 31, 1887.

The South Side of the city was served by the Chicago City Railway Company, dominated by local financial giants, who enjoyed a six-fold rise in the company's shares of stock from $1,500,000 in 1871 to $9,000,000 in 1893. With the exception of $250,000 in dividends, all shares were issued at par to stockholders, although they could have been sold on the open market at a premium. A 10 per cent dividend in 1882 was followed by one of 12 per cent every year thereafter to the end of the 1890's. The Civic Federation, studying the local traction situation, estimated that including extra dividends in stock, bonds, and cash, and premiums upon stock and bond issues, an average of 44.63 per cent a year was paid for sixteen years from January 1, 1882. These dividends, the Federation pointed out, were possible upon stock put out to an amount $5,000,000 in excess of the actual value of the plant, not including the value of the franchises held.

Despite this startling expansion of the South Side company it had less watered stock than the two other main systems. The Yerkes stocks were speculative favorites. Within five years after its incorporation the stock of the West Chicago company was marketed for as much as $232 for a $100 share, and that of the North Chicago company climbed from its par of $100 to over $200 in the same period. No less an authority than Frank A. Vanderlip, financial editor of the *Tribune* in the early 'nineties, pointed out a few years later that the history of the Yerkes roads and their auxiliaries was " by all odds the most interesting chapter concerning watered stock in Chicago." When Yerkes in 1886 entered the arena in which he was to be without a peer, the existing lines were capitalized at $11,437,000. Within ten years this figure had skyrocketed to $54,705,736.[70]

Besides the three main street-railway companies others partook of the rich rewards of traction issues. By 1893 five other companies were engaged in transporting the city's populace from one point to another. In addition, the construction of elevated systems was started, in the late 1880's, after an uphill fight to get public support. By 1893 the various transportation lines provided Chicago's swelling pop-

[70] Of the $11,437,000 capitalization $5,750,000 was in stocks and $5,687,000 in bonds. A part of the increase in capitalization represented, of course, some technological improvements. Civic Federation of Chicago, *The Street Railways of Chicago*, pp. 26, 27, 73–74; *The Economist*, Supplement, 1896, *loc. cit.*, pp. 7–8, 20; Illinois Bureau of Labor Statistics, *Ninth Biennial Report, 1896*, pp. 56–58.

A STATE STREET CABLE CAR OF THE 'EIGHTIES

THE MAIN TELEPHONE OFFICE OF CHICAGO, 1888, LOCATED
AT FRANKLIN AND WASHINGTON STREETS

ulation with 529 miles of trackage, graphically reflecting the changes which had taken place since 1871 when there were about fifty.[71]

The first " L," as the elevated came to be called, was the Chicago and South Side Rapid Transit Railroad, promoted by Colonel A. F. Walcott of New York. Known commonly as the " Alley L," the line proposed was to extend from the alley just east of State Street from Van Buren to Thirty-ninth. By autumn of 1889 about one mile had been completed by the Rapid Transit and Bridge Construction Company of New Jersey, of which Walcott was vice-president, a company organized to care for the $15,000,000 contract given Walcott. Since the route of the " Alley L " paralleled the principal lines of the Chicago City Railway, an agreement was reached with the construction company on November 26, 1889, by which the former gave about $4,500,000 toward the $7,500,000 capital stock, and, in the February following, it took over controlling interest in the stocks and bonds of the elevated company after delivering the proceeds of a $500,000 bond issue. Lack of harmony between the interested groups resulted in the withdrawal of the construction company in December, 1892. With funds supplied by the Chicago City Railway the elevated was then extended to Sixty-third Street and Jackson Park and finally completed in time for the opening of the Columbian Exposition in May, 1893. Subsequent financial difficulties forced the " L " into further dependence upon the City Railway so that by September, 1893, when the stocks and bonds of the elevated company were distributed pro rata among the stockholders of the surface line as an extra dividend, the two organizations were one, for all practical purposes.[72]

The story of Chicago's second elevated railway, the Lake Street Elevated, is in large part a duplicate of that of the " Alley L." Organized in 1888 with an authorized capital of $3,000,000, it met the op-

---

[71] In 1893 mileage was distributed among the various companies as follows: North Chicago Street Railroad Company, 80.75; West Chicago Street Railroad Company, 176.93; Chicago City Railroad Company, 161; Calumet Electric Street Railway Company, 44.13; Cicero and Proviso Electric Company, 5; Chicago North Shore Street Railway, 8.18; South Chicago City Railway Company, 31.6; Chicago and South Side Rapid Transit Company (elevated), 8.66; West Lake Street Elevated Railroad Company (elevated), 10.5; Chicago General Street Railway Company, 2.25. (Chicago Department of Public Works, *Eighteenth Annual Report, 1893*, p. 195.) See figure 24, Hoyt, *op. cit.*, p. 145 for the lines in 1891.

[72] *The Economist*, Supplement, 1896, *loc. cit.*, pp. 19, 21; Civic Federation of Chicago, *The Street Railways of Chicago*, pp. 80–81; Hoyt, *op. cit.*, p. 146.

position of rival streetcar companies, and after various vicissitudes it received a new charter in August, 1892, in the name of the Lake Street Elevated Railroad Company, under the leadership of ex-Mayor John A. Roche. During the following spring the capitalization was increased from $5,000,000 to $10,000,000, and on November 6, 1893 the new road was opened for operation from Market and Madison streets west to California Avenue. As in the case of the " Alley L," the new line operated at a deficit, and it was only a matter of time before the company fell under the control of interests representing the North and West Chicago street railroads.[73]

Chicago brokers and others concerned with traction issues, however, did not limit their activities to their own city but embarked upon the construction and rebuilding of street-railway systems in various places. For such a purpose Charles B. Holmes, president of the Chicago City Railway Company from 1882 to 1891, organized in 1888 several syndicates which gained control of the lines in St. Louis, Indianapolis, Davenport, Rock Island, Moline, and Los Angeles. The following year William E. Hale, prominent in the hydraulic-elevator business, and Norman B. Ream, associated with the grain trade as a commission merchant and grain-elevator operator, got hold of the run-down car lines of Toledo, Ohio, and reorganized them into one system, the Consolidated Railway Company, under Ream's presidency.

The roster of the enterprising Chicagoans who branched out into such undertakings read indeed like a *Who's Who* of those in the most flourishing businesses of the city, whose wealth had become great enough to permit and even encourage extensive, and what at times seemed uncertain, ventures.[74] Some found it convenient, rather than becoming associated with syndicates such as those organized by

[73] *Chicago Daily News,* July 4, Sept. 19, 1888; *Chicago Tribune,* Oct. 4, 1889, March 8, Aug. 21, 1890; *The Economist,* X (Sept. 2, 1893), 241, Supplement, 1896, *loc. cit.,* p. 24; Illinois Bureau of Labor Statistics, *Ninth Biennial Report, 1896,* p. 65; Chicago Department of Public Works, *Eighteenth Annual Report, 1893,* p. 195. The grants made by the government to the various lines and to utilities in general are discussed in the chapter dealing with the city's government.

[74] Among those associated with Holmes were Marshall Field, Conrad and William Seipp, S. B. Cobb, Cyrus H. McCormick, John J. Mitchell, Samuel W. Allerton, Charles and W. C. Comstock, and Charles L. Hutchinson. *The Economist,* I (Oct. 20, 1888), 5, (Nov. 3, 1888), 10, (Dec. 8, 1888), 6, (Dec. 22, 1888), 3, 4, II (Aug. 10, 1889), 688. For further investments see *ibid.,* V (June 13, 1891), 1043.

Holmes, to conduct their business through N. W. Harris, who headed the most important house carrying such issues.[75]

Although to many the lines of transportation which linked the different parts of the city seemed the most likely to enjoy unbroken prosperity, other utilities gained in favor as their potentialities were recognized. The securities of the gas companies did much to enhance confidence in such issues, more, in fact, according to the *Economist,* than any others ever put out in Chicago. Up to 1882 two companies, " the old gas companies," supplied consumers — the Chicago Gas Light and Coke Company in the North and South divisions and the People's Gas Light and Coke Company in the West.

In the spring of 1882 a third organization known as the Consumers' Gas, Fuel and Light Company was permitted to distribute gas in the city. In November, 1886 it was succeeded by the Consumers' Gas Company under the sponsorship of Charles T. Yerkes, Columbus R. Cummings, Jacob Rehm, and Sidney A. Kent.[76] The year before, the Equitable Gas Light and Fuel Company had been started to serve the South Side by local interests connected with the People's Gas Light and Coke Company.[77] By early 1887 the total securities of these four main companies totaled $14,984,200 in stocks and $10,-432,000 in bonds, the Chicago Gas Light and Coke Company, the largest producer at that time, having no bonds outstanding.

With the establishment of the Equitable and the Consumers' Gas, a struggle among the different companies to win the competitive game brought about a cutting of rates, although not to the point of unprofitableness. Therefore, as in similar business ventures tending to duplicate each other's activities, a move to consolidate resulted in the establishment of a syndicate, sponsored chiefly by Philadelphians, who incorporated the Chicago Gas Trust, April 28, 1887, under

[75] Among the Harris promotions in 1888 and 1889 were the Omaha Horse Railroad and the Des Moines Street Railway. *Chicago Tribune,* Sept. 12, 1888, Oct. 25, 1889. There were, of course, others besides Harris who promoted traction securities.

[76] Pierce, *A History of Chicago,* II, 319–20; Wallace Rice, *75 Years of Gas Service in Chicago* . . . (Chicago, 1925), pp. 30–31; *The Economist,* I (Dec. 15, 1888), 3–4, XI (May 5, 1894), 485; Illinois Bureau of Labor Statistics, *Ninth Biennial Report, 1896,* pp. 276–78; *Chicago Tribune,* June 16, 1886.

[77] In 1862 the Chicago Gas Light and Coke Company and the People's Gas Light and Coke Company had divided the territory and promised not to compete with each other for one hundred years. Some attempts to ignore this covenant, however, led to court action.

the laws of Illinois.[78] Stocks at once moved upward, that of the Chicago Gas Light and Coke Company, for example, jumping from 107 to 170 and more, and as much as 250 was offered for some shares, so optimistic were investors at the turn of events. Although the various companies retained their corporate identity, all gas sold in the city, even that distributed by minor concerns, was now in the hands of one organization.[79]

According to the agreement, the Gas Trust Company was given possession of the capital stock of the four companies; it was to have charge of all dividends, and to elect directors for each company. The distribution of dividends was entrusted to the Fidelity Trust Company of Philadelphia on a *pro rata* basis. In addition, the eastern agency was to care for the dividends of an issue of $25,000,000 shares of stock par value to be marketed on the New York Stock Exchange in place of the original stock of the companies, in itself alleged to be to a considerable extent nothing but water.

Matters now developed so rapidly and boldly that the average Chicagoan had little understanding of either the immediate or long-range meaning of events. The price in the North and South divisions shot up from one dollar to $1.50 per thousand feet of gas, precipitating so many protests from consumers that the Citizens' Association, through its president, Francis B. Peabody, undertook by legal measures instituted in the Circuit Court of Cook County to dispossess the Gas Trust of its powers. Eventually the case reached the Supreme Court of the state, which filed a decision November 26, 1889, that the monopoly being practiced was illegal. Thereupon the price of Chicago Gas certificates fell from approximately 60 to 34; the Fidelity Trust Company returned to the trust the shares of the various companies, and, in turn, the eastern agency got new shares made out in its name. A week after the filing of the Court's decision the Gas

[78] This Philadelphia group, asserted *The Knights of Labor* (Chicago), controls "the gas supply of fully one half the cities of the union, and puts them under contribution to its coffers. The Philadelphia syndicate is a wing of this American Gas association, and the Philadelphia branch proposes to put $10,000,000 into the Chicago monopoly alone." *The Knights of Labor,* I (March 12, 1887), 8, II (Oct. 8, 1887), 1.

[79] At this time in addition to the four main companies in the combination were the Hyde Park Gas Company, chartered in 1871; the Lake Gas Company, chartered in 1881; the Suburban Gas Company, chartered in 1872; and the Illinois Light, Heat and Power Company, chartered in 1885. The first two were connected with Consumers' Gas; the Suburban was with Chicago Gas Light and Coke. Illinois Heat and Power under Billings' backing served all the city. The last did not exist as a separate company for any length of time.

Trust reopened its contract with the Philadelphia organization. In April, 1890 the Chicago Gas Trust Company altered its name and became known as the Chicago Gas Company. On April 9, 1891, under pressure from public opinion and continued legal action, it surrendered its charter. The Fidelity Trust and Safety Deposit Company of Philadelphia was invited to furnish $25,000,000 of its own certificates to the gas company to be apportioned among the stockholders of the different member companies, subject to a commitment to secure the bonds.[80]

The resiliency of the Gas Trust and its abundant faith in its power to enter into satisfactory arrangements with the various agents of local and state government with which it dealt were matched by the advancement of the financial rewards it enjoyed from the conduct of its business.[81] From July 1, 1888 to January 1, 1894 the expenditures of the allied companies, according to reports to the New York Stock Exchange, were only $3,959,579.07, whereas the bonded indebtedness went up to $25,748,000, representing again, in part, what appeared to be the proverbial "water." Net earnings had, in 1890, reached $2,389,709.49, to be even greater the next year when they attained the appreciable amount of $2,729,642.46. By the time the 1890 federal census recorded the relative rank of Chicago's leading manufactures, gas, illuminating and heating, stood first in capital invested with its $40,851,246, and topped even the giant industry of slaughtering and meat packing.[82]

The amicable relations which had existed among the main companies with their rich financial rewards were, however, not to be dissipated by the action of April, 1891. Key figures in the constituent groups continued in many cases to be identical, and often they were important on the council of more than one company.[83] Seven years

[80] The Central Trust Company of New York was affiliated in the distribution of the certificates of the Fidelity Trust and Safety Deposit Company at this stage.

[81] The Chicago Economic Fuel Gas Company, in which Yerkes was heavily interested, was incorporated in 1890 to pipe fuel gas from Indiana. The council forbade alliance with any other company, but control of the Economic shortly was announced to be in the hands of the Chicago Gas Company.

[82] Besides the companies connected with the combination was the Mutual Fuel Gas Company, organized in 1890 and operating at first only in Hyde Park.

[83] Cornelius K. G. Billings, president of the People's Gas Light and Coke Company 1891–1893, was a director of the Hyde Park, Lake, Consumers', and Suburban Gas Companies. In 1893 George O. Knapp served on the board of directors of all four main companies, as did Billings, and Erazm J. Jerzmanowski. The last represented the Chicago Gas

after the Court dissolved the Trust the Illinois Bureau of Labor Statistics reported it as flourishing " in all its strength." Viewing the evidence it had assembled, the Bureau, disquieted by the course of events, apprehensively raised the question whether " this combination is greater than the State of Illinois." [84]

While gas companies had been extending their sphere of activity similar organizations began to make headway in promoting electricity as a source of illumination.[85] The demonstration in the late 'seventies that electricity could be harnessed for the production of light opened the way for the development of a powerful new commercial interest in the ranks of Chicago business. In 1878 the North Side Water-Works was illuminated for a brief time, and by September of the next year a system of arc lights was permanently installed in the Grand Pacific Hotel. Two years later Edison's new incandescent lamps made their first appearance in the city, furnishing light for a mill of the United States Rolling Stock Co.

Illumination by both forms of electricity was an immediate success, and by 1884 eleven firms doing an annual business of over $1,000,000 had established themselves to supply the city's demand for electric lights. The majority of these companies were branches of parent establishments located elsewhere, such as the Brush Electric Company of Cleveland.[86] Four concerns, however, had arisen in the city: the Van Depoele Electric Light Company in 1880, the Western Edison Company in 1882, the Sperry Electric Light, Motor, and Car Brake Company in 1883, and the Blair Electric Company in 1884.

Company in New York. The Central Trust Company of New York held bonds of the Gas Trust as treasury stock in 1893.

[84] Unless noted otherwise, the chief sources for the discussion of the gas industry and trust are Illinois Bureau of Labor Statistics, *Ninth Biennial Report, 1896,* pp. 239–320; Citizens' Association of Chicago, *Annual Report, 1888,* pp. 8–10; *The Economist,* V (April 11, 1891), 599–600, VI (July 11, 1891), 61, XI (April 28, 1894), 454–56, (May 5, 1894), 484–85, (May 12, 1894), 515–16; *Chicago Tribune,* June 16, 1886, March 8, April 5, 30, 1887, Feb. 25, 1892; Adolph Moses to H. D. Lloyd, May 25, 1891, *Lloyd Papers.* See Appendix table.

[85] The usefulness of electricity as a source of industrial power was demonstrated in the 'eighties, but commercial production of electricity for this purpose did not become important until the turn of the century. Chicago Fire Marshal, *Annual Report, 1888,* p. 80, *1890,* p. 101, *1891,* p. 118, *1892,* p. 127; U. S., *Twelfth Census, 1900,* VII, " Manufactures," pt. I, cccxxii, cccxxxiv.

[86] *Chicago Tribune,* April 26, 27, 1878, Sept. 21, 1879, Jan. 15, 1880, Nov. 18, 1881; *Chicago Commerce, Manufactures, Banking and Transportation Facilities, 1884,* pp. 106–7; Andreas, *History of Chicago,* III, 598.

No one of these firms endured as originally constituted beyond the 'eighties, the Van Depoele Company, for example, passing under the far-flung ægis of the Thomson-Houston Electric Company of Boston in 1889 and Western Edison Light Company dissolving in 1887, its franchise for the distribution of power taken over by the Chicago Edison Company.

Of the four local pioneers of the 'eighties, Western Edison Light Company carried on the biggest business, although its capitalization of $500,000 was only half that of the Sperry and Blair organizations. It, however, attracted to its board of directors and counted among its investors men of wide-ranging financial holdings, as well as those concerned primarily in the promotion of Chicago utilities. Between 1883 and 1887, too, many small arc-light companies mushroomed in various parts of the city, indulging in ruinous competition and then succumbing to its penalties.[87]

In 1887 a new era in the history of Chicago's electrical industry opened with the emergence of two corporations, the Chicago Arc Light and Power Company and the Chicago Edison Company, whose profits came from the sale of electricity produced on a large scale in central generating plants. This development marked the first attempt at centralization and mass production in the field of electric power in the city and made possible a rapid expansion in utilizing electricity in the years that followed. The Chicago Arc Light and Power Co. was incorporated in April, 1887 by backers of the Gas Trust, who, seeing the increasing popularity of electricity, decided to participate in, rather than continue opposition to, the new enterprise.[88] At once the new company began to buy up the numerous small arc-light companies then serving the city, and within a month its success was so complete that the *Tribune* waggishly observed: " Beginning this morning the sun and the Gas

[87] *The Electrical World*, IX (April 16, 1887), 196; *Western Electrician*, V (July 13, 1889), 16; W. C. Jenkins, *Chicago's Marvelous Electrical Development* (reprinted from the *National Magazine*, Boston, 1911), p. 8. Among those interested in the Western Edison Light Company were General Anson Stager of the Chicago Telephone Company; Anthony F. Seeberger of the wholesale hardware firm of Seeberger, Breakey & Co.; Edson Keith, important wholesaler of hats and furnishing goods; Frank S. Gorton, president of Chicago Forging Company; John B. Drake, co-proprietor of the Grand Pacific Hotel; Robert Todd Lincoln, lawyer son of President Lincoln; and John W. Doane, tea importer.

[88] Among the prominent men interested were Marshall Field, Charles Norman Fay, Sidney A. Kent, John H. Barker, and Columbus R. Cummings.

Trust Company have a monopoly of all the light with which Chicago is to be blessed."

This monopoly proved short-lived, however, for a rival corporation, the Chicago Edison Company, had already taken form during the same month, drawing for its support the men who had been connected with the old Western Edison. On August 6, 1888 it opened its first central station of incandescent lighting.[89] The Edison organization boasted of supplying the larger " sky-scraping " buildings such as the Tacoma, Crilly, and the Grand Opera House, as well as the current for the *Chicago Tribune* composing-room. Its spectacular rise in capitalization from $500,000 in 1888 to $3,000,000 in 1893 denoted the company's abounding prosperity, while at the same time Chicago Arc Light and Power within five years from its beginning also showed in a similar way an enlargement from the initial $1,000,-000 to $1,829,200. Although the securities of both firms were listed on the Chicago Stock Exchange, the new stocks put out at each increase in capitalization did not reach the Exchange floor, because each issue was first offered to and accepted by stockholders at par. With production increasing nearly tenfold between 1888 and 1893 and annual profits never less than 13 per cent on the capital invested, Chicago Edison's stockholders were seldom tempted to dispose of their holdings, although the Company held dividends to 8 per cent. Even the highest bids frequently failed to draw out stock for sale.

Paying more modest dividends than its rival, ranging as they did from 6 to 8 per cent, Chicago Arc Light and Power's stock changed hands more often than did that of Chicago Edison, but it was seldom a speculative favorite on the Exchange. The securities of both concerns were valued as " sturdy dividend payers," and were held primarily as investments for the income they produced rather than speculation. In the early 'nineties firms not located in Chicago offered their securities in large quantities, but they were not purchased in sizable amounts, for Chicago investors were interested primarily in those available at home.[90] In the autumn of 1892 rumors were cir-

[89] Samuel Insull, *Public Utilities in Modern Life* (Chicago, 1924), p. 369; Jenkins, *op. cit.*, p. 8; *Chicago Tribune*, April 27, May 1, 7, 1887; *The Electrical World*, IX (May 28, 1887), 261; *The Electrical Review*, X (May 28, 1887), 5; *The Western Electrician*, V (Feb. 15, 1890), 78.

[90] Chicago Department of Electricity, *Rules and Ordinances . . . with an Historical*

culated that a merger between Chicago Edison and Chicago Arc Light and Power was imminent, and early in the following year the former, under its new president, Samuel Insull, took over the holdings of its competitor. Stockholders of the latter were reimbursed for their stock at $120 a share with 6 per cent debenture bonds. Chicago Edison now enjoyed a practical monopoly of the electrical field.[91]

Within less than a decade this new force for illumination had seized upon the imagination of the people as it brought speed in transportation with the electrification, first, of the Calumet Electric Street Railway Company, in 1890, and then gradually of other lines, despite the opposition of owners of the cable system.[92] Electricity, too, by the late 'eighties was occasionally driving small machinery, printing presses, and elevators. New household conveniences such as chafing dishes, coffee pots, and grills, demonstrated at the World's Fair, heralded a new day for those exploiting its use.[93]

But such utensils were no more a cause of wonderment than had been the electric clock which was used as the starter of the races at Washington Park in July, 1889, and not as significant a benefaction as the coal punch which Elmer A. Sperry developed in his Chicago plant in 1888.[94] The thirteen columns in the city directory devoted to the electrical industry and its various outlets in 1893, as compared to less than one in 1880, told a compelling tale of the advances al-

---

Appendix (Chicago, 1900), p. 222; *The Economist*, III (May 3, 1890), 535, X (Nov. 4, 1893), 480, *passim, cf.* especially V (March 7, 1891), 372, VI (Aug. 22, 1891), 327, (Oct. 31, 1891), 734, VII (May 14, 1892), 726, VIII (Oct. 22, 1892), 585, IX (April 22, 1893), 556.

[91] *Ibid.*, VIII (Oct. 8, 1892), 503, IX (Jan. 21, 1893), 78, (Feb. 11, 1893), 191, (April 22, 1893), 556. Samuel Insull, born in England in 1859, came to America in 1881 to act as private secretary to Thomas A. Edison and eight years later became second vice-president of the Edison General Electric Company (and later of the General Electric Company). In 1892, when officials of Chicago Edison consulted with him as to whom they should select as the new president of their firm, he offered himself as a candidate and was accepted. *Who Was Who in America*, I (Chicago, 1942), 619; Insull, *Public Utilities in Modern Life*, pp. 368–69.

[92] *Western Electrician*, V (July 13, 1889), 16; Leonard Marion Zingler, *Financial History of the Chicago Street Railways* (unpublished Ph.D. Thesis, University of Illinois, 1931), pp. 7–13; The Civic Federation of Chicago, *The Street Railways of Chicago*, p. 65; *Chicago Tribune*, Feb. 27, 1891, March 1, 1892, April 21, 1893.

[93] Chicago Fire Marshal, *Annual Report, 1888*, p. 80, *1890*, p. 101, *1891*, p. 118, *1892*, p. 127; National Electrical Manufacturers Association, *A Chronological History of Electrical Development* (New York, 1946), p. 68.

[94] *Western Electrician*, V (July 27, 1889), 42; Herbert E. Goodman, "Early Goodman History," *Electrical Mining* insert, XXXVII (Jan., 1940), [p. 1].

ready made but which only hinted at the great possibilities of future development.

The telephone, too, like other utilities, played an increasingly important role in the investment opportunities in the city as it more and more transformed the mode of living of those able to enjoy its advantages. As on the national level, so in Chicago was the rivalry between the promoters of the Alexander Graham Bell instrument and that of Elisha Gray and Thomas A. Edison reflected in a struggle for dominance. The American District Telegraph Company, with General Anson Stager as president and Leroy B. Firman as general manager, in 1877 installed Gray-Edison telephones using Western Union telegraph wires, and on June 18, 1878 opened the first exchange at 118 LaSalle Street. In April of the same year Horace H. Eldred had come to Chicago from Boston as western agent for the Bell Company to solicit local capital, obtain subscribers, and construct and operate an exchange. The Bell Exchange initiated its service at 125 (later 18 North) LaSalle Street, June 28, 1878, the week after the American District Telegraph Company, which had used the Gray-Edison patents, started operations.

With the growing recognition of its usefulness, the early prejudices against the new device gradually disappeared, and on December 21, 1878 the Bell Telephone Company was incorporated under Illinois laws to formalize the organization of the Bell interests in the city. Gardiner G. Hubbard of Boston, who had brought the Bell instruments to Chicago in June, 1877, became president, and Bernard E. Sunny, onetime manager of a subsidiary of the Western Union Telegraph Company, the Atlantic & Pacific Telegraph Company, was made superintendent.[95]

Until 1881 when the two companies combined, competition between them was exceedingly keen, and the subscribers to the two lines suffered an inconvenience which the consolidation eliminated. The new organization, the Chicago Telephone Company, at first under the direction of General Anson Stager, Norman Williams,

[95] Gardiner Greene Hubbard (1822–1897), a well-known Boston lawyer was the first organizer of the telephone industry. Bernard Edward Sunny (1856–1943) was telegraph operator, night manager, and manager of the Chicago office of the Atlantic & Pacific Telegraph Company, 1875–1879, superintendent of the Chicago Telephone Co., 1888–1891, western manager of Thomson-Houston Electric Co., and western manager and vice-president of its successor, the General Electric Co., 1891 to 1908. Sunny's interests later included in addition to his telephone connections various other business undertakings.

and Charles Norman Fay, enlisted the support of no less influential financiers than Henry H. Porter, Robert T. Lincoln, and John Crerar.[96] Exclusive rights in Cook and several contiguous counties to the use of the Bell instrument forecast consistently enlarging returns on the investments made in it, as the population grew and more and more relied on the telephone to assist in the conduct of the day's duties.

The company expanded its facilities from four exchanges in 1881 to twelve in 1893, to serve a mounting number of patrons, who increased from 3,479 to 10,376 in 1893, during a mere decade. Equally significant as a measure of the company's broadening activities was the jump in capitalization from $500,000 in 1881 to a reported $3,796,200 in 1894. Earnings at the same time followed a similar movement. From 1882 to 1889, for example, a regular dividend of $3.00 was declared for each quarter, with extra dividends distributed in the intervening months. In 1882, the first full calendar year of operation, gross earnings reached $414,972 and net $174,387. During that year the infant industry paid its stockholders $148,000 in dividends, conforming to the high return common to many new and hazardous businesses of the day. Although its shares sometimes sold for as much as twice their par value, they were not often available on the market.[97]

Although by 1881 Bell Telephone had been recognized as paramount, various other companies entered the field chiefly to sell shares of stock to the public. In 1883 Elisha Gray attempted to establish in Chicago the Molecular Telephone Company, a subsidiary of the Postal Telegraph Company, and to set up a long-distance connection between Chicago and New York, a good nine years before the Bell system officially opened such long-distance service. Technically the Molecular Telephone did not infringe upon the

[96] Historical Material, Illinois Bell Telephone Company (Courtesy of W. J. Peak, General Information Manager, and Mr. R. L. Mahon, Chicago); Andreas, *History of Chicago*, III, 597; [Illinois Bell Telephone Company], *A Golden Anniversary, 1878–1928* (Chicago, 1928), pp. 6–7, 11; *Chicago Legal News*, XIII (Jan. 22, 1881), 155.

[97] Herbert N. Casson, *The History of the Telephone* (Chicago, 1910), p. 185; Illinois Bureau of Labor Statistics, *Ninth Biennial Report, 1896*, p. 95; Edward W. Bemis, *Report on the Investigation of the Chicago Telephone Company Submitted to the Committee on Gas, Oil, and Electric Light* (Chicago, 1912), pp. 81–83, 94; Letter to author of June 30, 1953, from Ralph L. Mahon, Illinois Bell Telephone Company, citing company records; *The Economist*, I (Oct. 20, 1888) — II (June 29, 1889), *passim* for securities.

Bell instrument, but it could not be perfected mechanically and failed to displace the latter.[98]

Tied in with the history of the telephone in Chicago is the part played by the Western Electric Company, which originated in 1869 in Cleveland, its promoters Enos M. Barton and Elisha Gray and its capital only $2,500. In 1870 the founders moved to Chicago and concerned themselves with telegraph apparatus. Soon they became a source of supply for the Western Union Telegraph Company, and in 1872 the Western Electric Manufacturing Company under General Anson Stager grew out of the small beginnings for which Barton and Gray were responsible. Absorption of other firms, and promotive skills made Western Electric a huge supply center of electrical materials and telephone instruments. With the surrender of its telephone interests by Western Union in 1879 to the Bell Company, Western Electric began to furnish the latter necessary telephone equipment. In 1882 the Bell people set up a new corporation, the Western Electric Company, and, under the agreement made with the Western Union organization, the American Bell Telephone got at cost the telephone patents of the manufacturing company. Western Electric, on the other hand, was compelled to provide whatever telephones and apparatus the Bell Company desired at cost plus 20 per cent. The American Bell Telephone Company and its offspring, the Chicago Telephone Company, were thus in an enviable position to enjoy with little hindrance a highly lucrative business.[99]

Less favored by the average Chicago investor than utility shares were the industrials. The confidence essential to float large issues developed slowly, and it was not until 1887 that the locally conscious *Tribune* could pridefully point out that each year showed " a gain in the proportion of Chicago capital in the business enterprises of

[98] The establishing of telephone communication with the East was a standing challenge and in Sept., 1884 *The Drovers' Journal* noted that James W. McDonough of Chicago had successfully conversed with a party in New York utilizing telegraph wires and an instrument of his own invention. (*The Drovers' Journal*, Sept. 15, 1884.) By the following year the Bell system had established regular service between New York and Philadelphia and by 1889 similar service was set up between New York and Boston. In 1892 the line from the East reached Hammond, Indiana, which was already connected with Chicago. Jonas Warren Stehman, *The Financial History of the American Telephone and Telegraph Company* (New York, 1925), pp. 32–35.

[99] Casson, *op. cit.*, pp. 183, 185; *Chicago Tribune*, April 6, 1883, Feb. 14, 1892; [Chicago Association of Commerce], *Chicago, The Great Central Market* (Chicago, 1923), pp. 86–87; *The Drovers' Journal*, April 6, 1883; Stehman, *op. cit.*, pp. 29–31.

Chicago and the Northwest generally." Even the rapidly growing iron and steel industry got much of its support from the East. Capital from Europe, notably from the British Isles, likewise contributed to the city's industrial enterprises, foreign investors confident that they would realize as good returns as from similar outlays in real estate, railroads, and municipals.[100]

Despite the indifference of many local investors, several Chicago promoters attempted to harness the industrial forces of not only the city but of the country by consolidations and combinations. The trust, as such organizations came to be called, met with approval on the one hand from the influential Chicago *Economist* as the best means to escape the results of competition in the changing economy then taking place. Overproduction it foresaw as inevitable if the old, free form of competition persisted with the corollary aftermath of inevitable ruin for businessmen and workers alike. This point of view gained converts slowly, even *The Economist* holding that stocks of trusts as speculative investments were " unsafe for the ordinary person to trade in."

Opposed to those backing the trust as a legitimate form of business undertaking were leaders of public opinion like Judge Henry G. Miller, who warned of the dangers to the country's traditional pattern they foresaw in such combinations of business. They are, Miller declared, " the most satanical agencies that affect the people of this country," leading labor in self-defense to organize. " When these two classes of combination are at war," he continued, " production ceases and industry is at a standstill. What can be worse for a nation than that ? "[101]

But the climate of opinion was not so inhospitable that the law firm of Judge William H. Moore, his brother James H., and William A. Purcell could not launch successfully from Chicago their daring and extensive corporative enterprises. One of the best known was the reorganization of the Diamond Match Company on February 13, 1889, under the laws of Illinois, succeeding the company es-

[100] *The Economist*, VIII (Oct. 22, 1892), 579–80; *Chicago Tribune*, Jan. 1, 1887, Oct. 15, Dec. 3, 1876, Aug. 12, 1877, Feb. 10, March 15, 1882. For investments in breweries, meat packing, and other industries see the chapters which deal with them.

[101] *The Economist*, II (Feb. 16, 1889), 118, (July 13, 1889), 592, (July 20, 1889), 616, Annual Number, Jan. 1, 1890, 1; *Chicago Tribune*, Jan. 2, 1888; The Sunset Club, *Year-Book, 1892–93*, p. 101; Citizens' Association of Chicago, *Annual Report, 1888*, pp. 11–13.

tablished in 1880 in New Haven, Connecticut, under the leadership of O. C. Barber, and owning factories in various cities. With incorporation in Illinois, the capital stock was increased to 60,000 shares at a par value of $100 over the $2,250,000 original capitalization. Within the circle of its promoters were enough Chicagoans to lead *The Economist* to describe it as " essentially a Chicago corporation," including, as it did, such important figures as George M. Pullman, George Sturges, Otho S. A. Sprague, William Armour, John W. Doane, and Charles Farwell.[102] No less significant in its implication was the gigantic barbed-wire combination effected in January, 1891, under John W. Gates, sometimes dubbed " Bet-a-million Gates," with headquarters in Chicago. The next year, in December, Gates incorporated under Illinois laws several independent companies, including the Baker Wire Company of Chicago, in a still greater combination, the Consolidated Steel and Wire Company.[103]

Although Chicago was the scene of the organization of these and other trusts, the control was frequently located in New York. It was, indeed, much the same as in the case of stocks and bonds where the eastern city overshadowed the western. Still, this did not mean that Chicago agencies did not arise to care for investment needs, and in some instances they carried on a pretty vigorous business. Besides the ever aggressive brokers and other members of the investment fraternity, special exchanges were created and devoted themselves to satisfying potential clients. For such a purpose the Chicago Mining Board opened for business December 16, 1879, and carried on its promotions with its sixteen stockholders serving as directors. Its charge of $500 for listing stocks excluded the few and relatively un-

[102] The Chicago office was in the Pullman Building at Adams and Michigan. John Moody, *Moody's Manual of Industrial and Miscellaneous Securities* (New York, 1900), pp. 602–3; *Biographical and Portrait Gallery . . . of Chicago*, p. 404; Herbert Manchasen, *The Diamond Match Company A Century of Progress and of Growth 1835–1935* (New York, 1935), pp. 14–66; The Inter Ocean, *A History of the City of Chicago . . .*, p. 466; *The Economist*, Investors' Supplement, 1897, p. 26.

[103] Included in the 1892 combination were the St. Louis Wire Mill Company, Braddock Wire Company of Pittsburgh, Lambert and Bishop Wire Fence Company of Joliet, Iowa Barb-Wire Company of Allentown, Pennsylvania, and the Baker Wire Company of Chicago. The Inter Ocean, *op. cit.*, p. 237; *Chicago Tribune*, Jan. 27, 1891, Dec. 3, 1892; American Iron and Steel Association, *Bulletin*, XXVI (Dec. 7, 1892), 357; Lloyd Wendt and Herman Kogan, *Bet a Million! The Story of John W. Gates* (Indianapolis, 1948), pp. 91, 95, 97–98, 101.

important local firms, and the bulk of its business seems to have been done in mining stocks and government bonds.

The Mining Board in 1881 changed its name to the Chicago Stock Board but the management soon fell into disfavor with brokers and, in 1882, the exchange became a mutual association. On May 15, 1882 the Chicago Stock Exchange opened its offices with Charles Henrotin, John J. Mitchell, and J. B. Breese & Co. among the first promoters. Within a year its membership had expanded to 750, and included in addition to its Chicago constituency representatives of exchanges in New York, San Francisco, Boston, and Philadelphia. It was not until the late 'eighties, however, that the volume of business reflected the usefulness its sponsors had so earnestly hoped for. Then local bonds and stocks, especially traction and gas issues, raised the number of transactions it conducted.[104]

104 Wallace Rice, *The Chicago Stock Exchange: A History* (Chicago, 1923), pp. 14–27; *Chicago Tribune,* Oct. 23, 1879, Jan. 1, 1883, Jan. 1, 1887; *The Economist,* I (Dec. 15, 1888), 3–4, II (March 16, 1889), 202, (May 4, 1889), 353; (May 18, 1889), 400, (Nov. 2, 1889), 996, VII (June 4, 1892), 840.

CHAPTER VII

LABOR'S QUEST FOR SECURITY

As CHICAGO EXPANDED her economic empire and took on the sophistication of a maturing economy, increasing opportunities lured laborers from far and near. Work bench and market counter, profession and craft, the house of business and the factory, all gave promise of employment and complete living. But the golden flow which issued from the city's humming activity seeped inequitably into the hands of those who toiled to produce it, and while some accumulated handsome rewards for their efforts, many found that fortune had passed them by. Even in the best of times, those at the bottom of the economic order subsisted on a narrow margin, and when depression struck they sank into want and wretchedness. The workers' lot was hard. Theirs was a life of struggle, a quest for an elusive industrial democracy. When hope was strong, they fought for a fair share of society's gains. When despair supplanted hope, they fought only to live, their insecurity breeding unrest and hatred.

The mounting importance of Chicago from 1870 to 1890 as a center of industry and commerce and the growth of the labor force operated reflexively. The total employed during the two decades rose over four times to reach 458,313. Although diverse nationalities contributed their brain and brawn, their indigenous skills and aptitudes, native workers more and more dominated the scene as the American-born children of immigrants were added to the early and original stock.[1] In every major occupational field they constituted by

---

[1] For a statistical presentation of the number employed in various occupations and the distribution of national groups, see for 1870 Pierce, *A History of Chicago*, II, 150–55, 499–500; for 1880 and 1890 the Appendix tables of this volume. Unless otherwise noted, figures

1880 the largest national group, with the Germans, the chief foreign-born element, having outdistanced immigrants from the British Isles, principally Irish. Again in 1890 this ranking held, but the relative importance of these two foreign groups was diminished by an influx of workers from Sweden, Norway, and other countries.[2]

That the economy had attained maturity was evidenced conclusively by the distribution of workers among the various occupations. Manufacturing and mechanical work employed the greater number, commanding, by 1890, the services of nearly half the labor force.[3] The city's importance as a center of trading transactions was reflected in the large number of persons connected with them — the bankers and brokers, the merchants, hucksters, and peddlers — each in his own way indispensable to the hegemony Chicago came to enjoy. Despite the over-all dominance of Americans, some lines held a special attraction for certain nationals. Thus the Germans and the Irish, famed as dispensers of food and drink, composed about two-thirds of the foreign born classed in 1890 as bartenders, saloon-keepers, and restaurateurs.[4]

Approximately one-tenth of the labor force gained a living in domestic and personal service, a field in which the proportion of native workers decreased slightly between 1880 and 1890, as their places were filled by immigrants from the British Isles, Germany,

---

for 1880 are based on U. S., *Tenth Census, 1880*, [I], "Population," 703–11, 870, and those for 1890, on U. S., *Eleventh Census, 1890*, [I], "Population," pt. II, 628–29, 634–35, 638–39, 648–51, 704–5, 710–11.

[2] In the 1890 census the classification "colored" appears. It includes persons of Negro descent, Chinese, Japanese, and civilized Indian. No similar classification was made in 1880. Such variations are frequently encountered in the enumerations.

[3] In 1880 laborers, comprising about 26 per cent of the total, were the largest category engaged in manufacturing and mechanical occupations. Carpenters, painters, brick and stone masons, plumbers and pipe fitters accounted for about 15 per cent; coopers, sawmill operatives, and cabinet workers and upholsterers about 5 per cent; iron and steel workers about 3 per cent. In 1890 laborers still made up 26 per cent; the four building trades, 18 per cent; the three woodworking trades, 4 per cent; iron and steel workers, 4 per cent. There was one apprentice for each 83 workers in 1880 and one for each 54 in 1890.

[4] In 1890 merchants, dealers, and peddlers made up the largest employment group in trade, or about 38 per cent. Sales people followed or were about 17 per cent, with agents and collectors about 13 per cent, and messengers, packers, and porters about 10 per cent. Revised occupational classifications based on those used in the census of 1930 have been adopted for 1880 and 1890 as they were for 1870 (Pierce, *A History of Chicago*, II, 151). This reclassification leaves some workers listed as "unclassified and unknown." Figures so adjusted have greater comparability from year to year and are more applicable to present-day conditions. All computations unless otherwise noted in the following pages are based on the itemized totals as shown in the Appendix tables.

Sweden, and Norway. Additional thousands of workers went into transportation and communication. The number in these occupations approximately doubled with the passing of each decade, and the increase from 1870 to 1890 exceeded twenty-five thousand. With the expansion of business and the extension of the city's territory, the number in steam railroading increased from 4,857 to 11,694, while employees of the street railways jumped 269 per cent. Alongside these, the gain of nearly ten thousand in drayage and hauling gave further satisfaction to those looking for such obvious signs of progress in a field closely linked with the major enterprises of manufacturing and distribution.

In most professions Americans predominated, representing in 1880 about 68 per cent and in 1890 about 72 per cent of the total. Next in numbers were the Germans, who in 1880 made up about 12 per cent of those in the professions, but whose relative strength declined during that decade to 9 per cent. Greater numbers in the professions sharply delineated the accelerated tempo of a cultural urbanization. In the decade of the 'eighties a gratifying gain particularly in the fields of medicine and the law occurred, but it failed to keep pace with the needs of the extraordinarily growing population. More men trained as architects and civil engineers mirrored a spreading realization of the values of beauty and accuracy of design and construction. An increasing number of musicians and teachers of music bore striking testimony to a gradual softening of the harsh outlines of living in a rapidly changing society. To this refinement more foreign born contributed by 1890 than did Americans, as they shared with others the trained talent of their homelands. Artists and teachers of art, not listed in the federal census of 1880, also attested by their strength of 376 in the next decennial enumeration to the deepening inroads which the arts were making.[5]

Symptomatic of the greater complexity of the occupational pattern was the relatively high increase in clerical employees. Although this branch trailed in 1870, it climbed to fourth place by 1890. Also

[5] Nurses and midwives, not listed in the 1880 census, number 1,333 in 1890; physicians and surgeons, 918 in 1880, 1,794 in 1890; lawyers, 1,035 in 1880, 2,144 in 1890; musicians and teachers of music 817 in 1880, 2,179 in 1890; dentists 171 in 1880, not listed in federal census 1890. According to the city directory of 1893 there were 600 dentists. The city directories listed 23 civil engineers in 1883, in 1893 there were 110; 126 architects in 1883 and 600 in 1893. The lag of the professionally trained in relation to population growth is illustrated by one physician in 1880 to each 548 people and one to each 613 people in 1893.

symptomatic was the change in the number of accountants from only two just before the Fire to twenty-five in the next twenty years. The modernization of business management made necessary the hiring of typists and stenographers, among whom by 1890 were more women than the number of both sexes in clerical work only ten years before. Least numerous of all were those in the public service and in agriculture, the latter reflecting the rise of Chicago as the great center of the Midwest's industrialization, its smoking factories by 1890 overshadowing all else.

Not all enjoyed an equality of opportunity as they went about the city looking for work. It was always hard for the colored, especially the Negro, unless he joined the ranks of those in domestic and personal service, where, in 1890, there were approximately eleven times as many as in other forms of employment.[6] The colored worker had but token representation in the skilled trades and in the professions, aside from a fairly numerous representation in the latter as musicians and teachers of music. Even as common laborers they accounted for less than 2 per cent of all so employed.[7]

Women, too, faced on the one hand by relentless economic pressures and on the other by a willingness, if not desire, to work outside the home, numbered five times more in 1890 than in 1870 as members of the labor force. Within these twenty years their proportion to the total rose about 3 per cent, and of the 88,088 gainfully employed about 41 per cent went into domestic and personal service. They contributed appreciably to the manufacturing and mechanical pursuits, less so to clerical work and to trade and the professions.[8] As

[6] About 57 per cent of the colored employed were in personal and domestic service in 1890. In that year there were 40,296 servants in Chicago, or one for each 27 inhabitants; Philadelphia had one for each 24, New York one for each 19, Boston one for each 18. About 11 per cent of all servants in Chicago, 24 per cent of those in Philadelphia, and 9 per cent each of those in New York and Boston were colored. In Atlanta, where there was one servant for every 14 people, 96 per cent were colored.

[7] According to the federal census of 1890 there were but 16 colored among the city's 7,847 machinists, 3 among 2,959 cabinetmakers, 2 among 3,679 plumbers and pipe fitters, and 37 among over 20,000 carpenters and joiners. As lawyers, they numbered 6; as physicians and surgeons, 11; as engineers and surveyors, 3; as professors and teachers, 18. For listings of the mid-'eighties see I[saac] C. Harris, comp., *The Colored Men's Professional and Business Directory of Chicago*, pp. 12, 22, *passim*.

[8] Of the number of women employed, about 31 per cent went into manufacturing and mechanical occupations, 10 per cent into clerical work, and 6 per cent into trade and the professions. (Based on adjusted census figures.) Data on women in factories and workshops are reported incompletely each year in the Report of the Tenement and Factory Inspectors to the Commissioner of Health, *Report of the Department of Health*, in *Annual Reports of*

factory hands they were attracted predominantly into the clothing industries, particularly men's, and in smaller numbers into printing and publishing, and the manufacture of boots and shoes, and hosiery and knit wear, which, despite hard working conditions, long hours, and low pay, many preferred to employment as domestic servants.[9] Even in the most appallingly unhealthful sweatshops the female labor force by 1892 was approximately three times that of men, their total having reached 13,000 in about 800 shops.[10]

The economic necessity which took women from the home and made wage earners of them was also responsible for the 5,673 boys and girls from ten to fifteen years of age listed in the 1880 federal census as engaged in some occupation. Within the sweatshops they toiled for ten or more hours a day alongside their elders. Most of these child laborers came from immigrant homes. Here, in ramshackle buildings, in basement, loft, or stable — mere firetraps with no fire escapes — little girls averaged fifty cents a week as pay in the coat shops for sewing on buttons or pulling basting threads. As time went on, they might become hand sewers and they then, perhaps, might get two to two and a half dollars a week. They shortly became twisted and bent in body, the stooped positions familiar in their elders to be theirs also in the years to come.

Less numerous than the little girls in the sweatshops were the boys under sixteen, generally employed as messengers or errand runners, their years, too, empty of play and of schooling. Both sexes labored in the furniture factories, in the publishing and printing

---

the Various Departments of the City of Chicago, 1882–1892. These figures cannot be compared with those from the federal census because different bases of tabulation are used.

[9] In the 'seventies the pay for domestics was $2.00 to $4.00 a week plus board and room (Chicago Board of Trade, Eighteenth Annual Report, 1875, p. 227). In the early 'seventies women received about 85 cents a day for sewing (Mrs. George M. Pullman Papers, Nov. 4, 1871, [Mss. courtesy of Mrs. Philip Miller]). Sales girls often made less than $4.00 a week. (Chicago Tribune, Dec. 17, 1871.) Where women worked with men in the same trade or occupation their wages were from 25 to 50 per cent less than the wages of men employed in the same trade or occupation. Chicago Board of Health, Report, 1881, p. 80.

[10] Illinois Bureau of Labor Statistics, Seventh Biennial Report, 1892, pp. 357–443, XIV–XV. In a group of 4,576 women workers surveyed in 1892, who were employed in 90 different establishments in various types of occupations, about one-third of 1 per cent made $20 or more a week, 15 per cent made less than $4.00. The average wage was $6.22. For a survey of the type of occupations women engaged in and wages paid, see the first section of the above report, which had over 300 pages devoted to working women in Chicago. Another large section dealing with sweatshops has a great amount of information regarding women's employment in this type of work.

establishments, and in places where meat packing was carried on. Indeed, the greatest number of children who worked could be found in the numerous manufactories of the city, and the next highest number went into trade and transportation. In the retail dry goods stores thousands of cash boys and girls answered the clerk's call when transactions were completed, and many little boys added to the family income their small pay of a few cents a day earned in the retail grocery stores.[11] Bootblacks and newsboys in increasing numbers appeared on the streets, especially in the advancing 'eighties, while street musicians and flower venders eagerly solicited a few pennies in exchange for what they had to offer.[12]

Probably no aspect of the increasingly complex problem of labor elicited so much comment as did that of the child worker. As time went on, the voices of those recommending the employment of children as the best way to prevent crime and to train them in thrift and industry grew feebler. In turn, the socially minded — publicists, reformers, and educators — all spoke with unequivocal opposition and earnestness as they comprehended the meaning of signs of physical debility and an uneducated citizenry. More and more the responsibility for a continuation of such deplorable conditions was placed upon those employers who engaged in them. "They are," said Henry Demarest Lloyd, "blood-guilty for every wrong they do to their neighbor's child, just as much as if done to their own. And society is guilty to the extent of the sum of individual guilt."[13]

If the struggle of women and children for daily bread was particularly relentless, it was a struggle shared by all workers. Years of depression beggared those who had not been far from want; even skilled craftsmen were willing to work for board alone in order to eat.[14] But the general insecurity of the working class seemed espe-

[11] U. S., *Tenth Census, 1880*, [I], " Population," 870, " Report on the Social Statistics of Cities," pt. II, 511, *Eleventh Census, 1890*, " Population," pt. II, lxxxv; " Factory and Tenement Inspectors' Report," Chicago Board of Health, *Reports, 1884–93, passim;* Illinois, Bureau of Labor Statistics, *Seventh Biennial Report, 1892*, pp. 364–70, 374–75; *Hull-House Maps and Papers*, pp. 37, 38, 51.

[12] *The Knights of Labor*, III (April 25, 1888), 4, V (June 1, 1889), 8, VII (Nov. 7, 1891), 1; *The Chicago Times*, July 10, Aug. 3, 1888; *Chicago Tribune*, Dec. 13, 1880, Aug. 14, 1887; *The Sanitary News*, I (Feb. 1, 1883), 75; *Chicagoer Arbeiter-Zeitung*, June 14, 1888; *L'Italia*, Dec. 17, 1892.

[13] *The Knights of Labor*, II (May 7, 1887), 1. It should be noted that child labor declined during the 1880's but was not eliminated even with the passage of laws.

[14] *The Inter Ocean*, May 11, 1873; *Chicago Tribune*, Sept. 1, 1873; B. W. Raymond

cially evident and terrifying in the days of prosperity when wages lagged behind soaring prices, and the invisible hand of inflation clutched each man's dollar. Between 1879 and 1881 food prices leaped an estimated 50 to 100 per cent, while wages generally remained stationary, and over-all living costs increased another 15 to 40 per cent the next year. Only the grim alternatives " either to work harder and longer, or eat less food and wear less clothing " were open to the average worker. Even in good times, the Illinois Bureau of Labor Statistics concluded, half of the " more intelligent, industrious and prosperous " were unable to stay solvent through their own efforts, and had " to depend upon the labor of women and children to eke out their miserable existence." [15]

Despite such conditions, laborers nevertheless flocked to Chicago to participate in the prosperity which the expanding city seemed to offer. Directly after the Great Fire there was plenty to do. From as far away as the British Isles came " skilled artisans " hoping to share in a daily wage of five to seven dollars which, it was said, they could earn.[16] But the exhilaration over plentiful work was short-lived, for in another year the panic ravaged the country, and throughout Chicago, as elsewhere, spread unemployment and suffering. Appeals for assistance in finding jobs poured into the Woman's Aid Association Employment Bureau. Skilled and unskilled alike were thrown out of work, and where employees were retained, reductions in wages ensued. The growth of industry, which had been stimulated by the city's rebuilding, stopped dead in its tracks. Closing banks

to Louis Reardley, March 6, 1874, *Benjamin W. Raymond Letter Book, 1874* (Ms. Chicago Historical Society), p. 93.

[15] That workmen benefited by fixed wages when prices fell was sometimes claimed. Higher wages than the " inexorable " laws of supply and demand justified, others held, were unattainable. During the long depression of the 'seventies average earnings of unskilled labor fell from $25 a week in 1873 to $9.00 a week in 1879. *Chicago Tribune*, Nov. 14, 1885; *Chicago Morning News*, April 21, 1881; Illinois, *Report of the Special Committee on Labor* . . . (Springfield, 1879), p. 37; Illinois Bureau of Labor Statistics, *Second Biennial Report, 1882*, pp. 288, 351, *Eighth Biennial Report, 1894*, p. 6; *The Economist*, X (Dec. 16, 1893), 633.

[16] Over forty million dollars were reported spent for supplies and for labor by October, 1872. Maximum wages for bricklayers were $4.00 to $4.50 per day. Carpenters got $3.50 a day, said to have been less than the scale in Pittsburgh, Philadelphia, St. Louis, and other cities. Living costs were high, and carpenters struck in Sept., 1872, for $4.00 a day. The following month bricklayers struck for a $4.00 wage and an eight-hour day. *The Chicago Times*, Jan. 19, 1874; *Chicago Tribune*, Oct. 26, 28, 29, 1871, Sept. 17, 24, Oct. 10, 11, 12, 20, 1872; *The* [London] *Times*, March 22, 1872; *Illinois Staats-Zeitung*, Oct. 5, 8, 1872; *The Western Catholic*, Sept. 28, 1872.

swept away the savings of thrifty thousands, and even the rich were touched by the palsying depression.[17]

By 1873 the city government as well found itself in difficulty. A depleted treasury, exhaustion of the bonding power, and the impossibility of obtaining further loans required that expenses be cut to the bone and a " pay as you go " policy instituted. At the same time, the urgency for relief, supported by appeals " calculated to invoke the sympathy of every right minded citizen," Alderman Michael B. Bailey felt, could not be ignored. Unrest became vocal both individually and collectively.[18] On December 21, thousands of workmen at Turner Hall on West Twelfth Street heard speakers declaim in German, Swedish, Polish, French, and English upon their wrongs, and passed resolutions demanding a program of public works, or direct relief if such jobs could not be provided.

The following day a crowd collected at Union and Washington streets and marched on the City Hall to voice their demands, which, said the *Tribune,* fell upon " the American portion of the population like lightning from a clear sky." While ten thousand somber watchers stood in the streets, their spokesman, Francis A. Hoffman, Jr., prominent liberal attorney, addressed the assembled aldermen. Declaring that he was not insensible to the near-bankruptcy of the city's treasury, Hoffman pleaded that a government, which had announced its intention to satisfy bondholders' demand for interest payments, should have " the wisdom and the honor " to care for the breadless and homeless.[19] In desperation the council turned to other agencies whose financial means, it was hoped, could save the unemployed from pauperism by providing labor. On December 26, Hoffman, a special committee from the Common Council, and representatives of the Chicago Relief and Aid Society met to discuss ways

[17] *Chicago Tribune,* Sept. 27, Nov. 26, 28, 1873; *Illinois Staats-Zeitung,* July 21, 1879; Andreas, *History of Chicago,* III, 714. Failures of savings banks in the later years of the depression, due in considerable measure to corruption and mismanagement which depression conditions exposed, afflicted especially the working class. James, *The Growth of Chicago Banks,* I, 501–9.

[18] Chicago, *Council Proceedings, 1873–74,* pp. 3–5, 29, 33.

[19] Alderman Louis Schaffner of the Seventeenth Ward saw a " spirit of Communism " in the Turner Hall meeting, and protested against those who came, " a knife in hand," to demand assistance " as a right, from those who had been more provident than they." The *Tribune* acidly condemned the meeting, declaring that the government did not have a responsibility in the case of unemployment, and suggested that perhaps Hoffman was motivated by personal interests. *Chicago Tribune,* Dec. 19, 22, 23, 24, 1873.

and means of extending help. Asked to distribute among the needy the remainder of the Fire relief funds, estimated at $500,000 to $1,000,000, the Society refused in the face of much criticism and the demonstrations staged against it. It did, however, promise to care for the destitute, and disbursed as much as $4,000 in a single day during the long, cruel winter of suffering. In the first three weeks of December alone the rolls at the County Agent's office rose from 11,726 to 16,040.[20]

Employed working men, witnessing on all sides the unremitting want of their fellows, had at times only the choice between lower wages and striking, against great odds, to preserve their existing pay. The railroads, hard hit by falling receipts, sought to retrench at the expense of workers, dismissing, in the language of the *Times,* the thought as " unworthy of minds managerial " that officials' salaries might be pared as an alternative. In October, 1873 the Lake Shore and Michigan Southern Railway Co. reduced mechanics' wages 10 per cent and shortened hours of work, and on December 1 lowered engineers' pay 7 per cent. At the same time the Michigan Central Railroad slashed road-repair employees from $1.37½ to $1.25 a day. Even where wages were not actually decreased, frequent lay-offs and rumors of pay cuts generated tenseness and worry.[21]

Threats of lower pay scales for engineers in late December occasioned the first united stand on the part of railway men. A joint resolution of members of the Brotherhood of Locomotive Engineers from the Illinois Central, Chicago, Rock Island and Pacific, Chicago & Alton, Michigan Central, Chicago, Milwaukee and St. Paul, and

[20] The Common Council and the Cook County Board of Commissioners took steps to investigate the affairs of the Society. *The Chicago Times,* Dec. 27, 1873, Jan. 6, 7, 1874; *Chicago Tribune,* Dec. 14, 23, 27, 1873; *Hejmdal,* Feb. 27, 1875; Michael J. Schaack, *Anarchy and Anarchists. A History of the Red Terror and the Social Revolution in America and Europe* . . . (Chicago, 1889), p. 45; Chicago Relief and Aid Society, *The Sixteenth Annual Report of the Chicago Relief and Aid Society to the Common Council of the City of Chicago, 1873* (Chicago, 1874), pp. 7–10, *Seventeenth Annual Report, 1874,* p. 8. See also James Brown, *The History of Public Assistance in Chicago 1833 to 1893* (Chicago, 1941), pp. 118–19; John J. Flinn, *History of the Chicago Police* . . . (Chicago, 1887), pp. 148, 156–58.

[21] Trouble began among the city's railway workers in early June when brakemen on the Chicago & Alton struck over a reduction from fifty to forty-five dollars a month. On Oct. 1, when the Chicago and North Western Railway's pay car failed to appear for the second straight month, 250 men in the shops at Halsted Street and Chicago Avenue walked out. This move obtained their back pay, but they were forced to take a pay cut of nearly 7 per cent. *The Chicago Times,* June 3, Oct. 2, 3, 1873, Jan. 2, 1874; *Chicago Evening Journal,* Aug. 12, 1873; *Chicago Tribune,* Oct. 1, 2, 4, 22, 30, Nov. 12, 28, 1873.

the Chicago, Burlington & Quincy declared that they would accept no reduction. When a 10-per-cent cut on subsidiary lines of the Pennsylvania system led to a walkout, and other roads continued to talk of similar action, a general engineers' strike seemed imminent. Confronted with a partial tie-up of freight and continued opposition from the engineers, most roads yielded. No hope of wage increases, however, could be entertained, for in bad times a plentiful supply of strikebreakers strengthened the hand of the employer, and times were bad indeed. Yet the militancy of the engineers helped hold the line against further attempts at reduction.[22]

For the next few years hardship continued, nurturing resentment and despair. Strikes spawned violence. Not a year in the 'seventies was free of labor disturbances.[23] Radical pronouncements, which might have fallen on deaf ears in happier days, gained converts at a time when wage earners with hungry mouths to feed sought vainly for steady jobs. On June 13, 1875 a labor mass meeting in Bohemian Turner Hall accepted without contradiction the prophecy of John Simmens that a " proletarian revolution within a few decades " with all its attendant terrors would come " if the ruling classes threaten to suffocate the labor movement." The following years saw similar fulminations against what these workingmen described as an " arrogant capitalism." John McAuliffe, among the first English-speaking socialists of Chicago and, by the late 'seventies, something of a political figure in third-party activity, joined with Lauritz Thorsmark, William Jeffers, and others in unrestrainedly condemning the " employing class."

It was during these times that men destined to blaze into prominence a decade later first turned to radicalism. August Spies, in some ways the ablest of those who rose to leadership in the Chicago radical movement, heard his first lecture on socialism in 1875. There he found, he declared, " the *passe partout* to the many interrogation

[22] *Ibid.*, Dec. 27, 30, 1873, Jan. 1, 3, 1874; *The Chicago Times*, Dec. 29, 30, 31, 1873, Jan. 1, 3, 9, 1874.

[23] For a tabulation of Chicago strikes, 1873–1879, see Z. E. Jeffreys, *The Attitude of the Chicago Press toward the Local Labor Movement 1873 to 1879* (unpublished M.A. Thesis, The University of Chicago, 1936), pp. 77–84. When August Hielank, a worker involved in a bloody strike of lumber shovers in May, 1876, committed suicide, the *Evening Journal* reported the incident with icy concision. " No cause, except despondency, caused by poverty, is assigned. The Coroner was notified." *Chicago Evening Journal*, May 9, 1876. See also *Chicago Tribune*, June 4, 1875, May 11, 1876; *The Railway Age*, I (June 17, 1876), 6; *Illinois Staats-Zeitung*, Sept. 5, 1876.

marks which had worried" him "for a number of years." The printer Albert Parsons, onetime Confederate soldier and a resident of Chicago since 1871, aroused by the want of workingmen in 'seventy-three, urged alleviation through political action so insistently that he shortly was identified with radicalism by those less outspoken and more conservative. All these, the *Tribune* declared, were but "a parcel of blatant Communist demagogues" acting "in behalf of the Commune." The summer weeks of 1876 were filled with anxiety and trouble. Wages, hours, and the closed shop were now foci of disagreement between those who did the work and those who paid for it. It needed only the distress of these lean years to fertilize the soil with seeds of future strife.[24]

In this atmosphere the "Great Strikes," judged by some an even heavier strain on republican government than the Civil War, took place in 1877. The hoped-for return to good times which had sustained those in need slipped farther away as the winter and spring of 'seventy-seven passed.[25] Additional wage cuts for rail workers were in prospect, though employers acknowledged that many of these men were already underpaid. Lay-offs cut deeply into actual earnings even when the hourly rate of pay seemed adequate. The opinion that roads were wastefully managed combined with bitterness over the arbitrary decreases of pay to fan the flames of employee resentment.[26] On the other hand, management looked upon wage

[24] *Illinois Staats-Zeitung*, June 14, 1875; *Chicago Tribune*, May 10, 1876; Schaack, *op. cit.*, pp. 47–49; George A. Schilling, "History of the Labor Movement in Chicago," in [Lucy E. Parsons], *Life of Albert R. Parsons* . . . [Chicago, 1889], p. XV; Albert R. Parsons, "The Story of His Life," in L. E. Parsons, *op. cit.*, pp. 10–14; Andreas, *History of Chicago*, III, 874; [August Spies,] *August Spies' Auto-Biography* . . . (Chicago, 1887), p. 10. See also A[lbert] R. Parsons, *Anarchism: Its Philosophy and Scientific Basis* . . . (Chicago, 1887), pp. 86–90 on George Engel and Samuel Fielden, then turning to radicalism.

[25] J[oseph] A. Dacus, *Annals of the Great Strikes in the United States* . . . (St. Louis, 1877), p. 15; *The Railway Age*, II (July 26, 1877), 1161.

[26] Average monthly wages at the time of the strike on some important lines with Chicago termini were as follows for engineers and firemen, respectively: Lake Shore & Michigan Southern, $94.64, $47.32; Illinois Central (passenger), $115, $57, (freight), $100, $54; Chicago, Burlington & Quincy, $81, $52; Chicago & Alton, $90, $45. When an operative's locomotive was laid up for repairs, he received no pay for that period. In many cases men worked only four days a week. *Appleton's Annual Cyclopaedia and Register of Important Events* . . . , *1877* (New York, 1878), n.s. II, 425–26; James Ford Rhodes, "The Railroad Riots of 1877," *Scribner's Magazine*, L (July, 1911), 87; Dacus, *op. cit.*, pp. 20–21; *The Railway Age*, II (April 12, 1877), 872, (April 19, 1877), 891, (Aug. 2, 1877), 1187, (Aug. 19, 1877), 1221, (Aug. 23, 1877), 1241, (Aug. 30, 1877), 1267.

reductions and dismissals as its only hope of survival.[27] A 10-percent cut on the Pennsylvania Railroad, June 1, was followed in July by similar reductions on the New York Central and the Baltimore & Ohio. On July 17, the day after the Baltimore & Ohio took this action, freight was not permitted to move from Martinsburg, West Virginia. The strike spread rapidly to other roads. Almost immediately rioting broke out in the East. The issue was now drawn. That employees had a right to demand higher pay the *Tribune* conceded, but that the company had the right to lower a man's pay to a cent a day, if it desired, appeared to the paper the prerogative of the owners of the road.[28]

As the hot July days passed, agitation mounted. Each edition of the Chicago newspapers teemed with accounts of workers' protests, new strikes, and fresh violence, under such flaming headlines as " Civil War," " Horrid Social Convulsion," and " Red War." Bulletins posted in the windows of newspaper offices were eagerly scanned by men and women, distressed and frightened. Chicago, the great railroad center of the nation, might also have bloodshed and death! Reports of militia and federal troops called out, of incendiarism, of lives snuffed out by the bullets of the militia at Baltimore and still more in riots at Pittsburgh, fed the ever-increasing tension.

Meanwhile, workers in Chicago began to hold meetings. On Saturday, July 21, in an open space at Twelfth and Halsted about a thousand men peaceably passed resolutions of sympathy for their brother workmen in the East. The next afternoon seventy-five or eighty men, gathering in the Turner Hall at West Twelfth Street, adjourned to join a larger meeting called by the American section of the Workingmen's party of the United States at Sack's Hall on Twentieth and Brown streets. Before the great crowd John Simmens,

<hr />

[27] *Chicago Tribune*, July 8, 1877; U. S., *Tenth Census, 1880*, [I], " Population," 737; Rhodes, *loc. cit.*, p. 86. *The Railway Age* pointed out that if each of the 68,244 railroad employees in Illinois belonged to a family of three, approximately one-twelfth of the state's population were supported directly by the fifty-two roads doing business in Illinois, not to mention those " indirectly sustained." Railroad pay rolls throughout the country carried 250,000 names. *The Railway Age*, II (July 5, 1877), 1101. See also Illinois Railroad and Warehouse Commission, *Sixth Annual Report, 1876*, p. 10.

[28] John R. Commons and others, *History of Labour in the United States* (4 v. New York, 1935–36), II, 185, 187–88; *Chicago Tribune*, July 20, 21, 1877; Dacus, *op. cit.*, pp. 32–35.

Lauritz Thorsmark, John Schilling, Albert Parsons, and others reviewed the laboring man's plight and flayed the "capitalist press"
and the railroad "kings." "If the proprietor has a right to fix the
wages and say what labor is worth," cried Parsons, "then we are
bound hand and foot, — slaves, — and we should be perfectly happy;
content with a bowl of rice and a rat a week apiece." To this the
crowd shouted a loud "No! No!"

Stepping up the tempo of agitation, the Workingmen's party
distributed circulars for a mass meeting on Monday evening, July 23.
In words charged with fear, resentment, and portent, they played
upon the emotions of those to whom the call was directed. They beheld in the existing vagrancy laws and legal restraints upon unions,
a conspiracy between the government and the "aristocrats," a conspiracy of "the Money Lords of America" to deprive all but prop-
erty-holders of the ballot. The only hope, they cried out, was in unity,
and unity at once. "For the sake of our wives and children, and our
own self-respect, LET US WAIT NO LONGER! ORGANIZE
AT ONCE!!" [29]

With these stirring words ringing in their ears, thousands of men
massed at Market Square near Madison Street in the heart of the
industrial district. Despite the inflammatory summons, the crowd,
composed in large part, according to the *Tribune,* of "respectable
laboring men," was well-behaved, waving aloft banners captioned
in English, French, and German: "Life by labor or death by fight,"
"Why does overproduction cause starvation?" and "United we
stand, divided we fall." The well-known cooper George A. Schilling,
identified with the moderate faction of labor liberals, opened the
meeting by reminding his hearers that they were assembled not to
proclaim "war," but to discuss calmly the issues of the day. Next
came Albert Parsons, who likewise urged obedience to law and
order.[30] Then John McAuliffe, frankly critical of the industrial sys-

[29] *Chicago Tribune,* July 21, 22, 23, 24, 26, 1877; *The Inter Ocean,* July 20, 21, 23, 24,
Aug. 1, 1877; Flinn, *History of the Chicago Police,* pp. 160, 200–1; Dennis, *Victor Lawson,*
pp. 41–44.

[30] Eugene Staley, *History of the Illinois State Federation of Labor* (Chicago, 1930), pp.
29–97; *The Inter Ocean,* Oct. 1, 1888. The *Tribune* considered Parsons's speech to have
bordered "on the inflammatory," though containing admonitions of restraint. (*Chicago
Tribune,* July 24, 1877.) After his Market Square speech, he was browbeaten at police
headquarters and warned that "those Board of Trade men would as leave hang you to a
lamp-post as not." Albert R. Parsons, "The Story of His Life," in L. E. Parsons, *op. cit.,*

tem, accused it of " glutted greed " and of producing low wages and poverty. To ameliorate the distress he proposed a program of public works, and urged that the constabulary alone deal with disorders and not call in the militia, which had, he feared, a prejudice against workingmen and women. Proceeding with still less restraint, he concluded his address by declaring that " if capital fire upon their Fort Sumter . . . his thought, and voice would be raised for bloody war." Despite this strong language, the temper of the crowd remained calm, and the assemblage dispersed in orderly fashion. Reason had not yet given way to passion.[31]

Those officially responsible for the preservation of order made preparations to curb any uprising which might occur. With newspapers blazoning the prospect of " civil war " in Chicago and the terrifying news of events in Pittsburgh and other eastern points, the question of what the days to come would bring was one of portentous gravity. On the afternoon of the twenty-second, Mayor Monroe Heath, some members of the Common Council, and Brigadier General Joseph T. Torrence, commanding officer of the first brigade of the Illinois militia, met in secret session. Major General Arthur C. Ducat, division commander of the militia, ordered all Chicago armories placed under guard, alerted General Torrence's troops, and hastened to the city to offer his services to the Mayor. Meanwhile, deputations of anxious citizens scurried about, pleading for preparedness to the police, the military, and the sheriff's office. Railroad managers considered the advisability of a lockout. Field, Leiter & Company armed the employees of their wholesale store, and double guards were placed about the reaper plant of C. H. & L. J. McCormick. The press cried to the city government that all neces-

---

pp. 10–14; Allan Pinkerton, *Strikers, Communists, Tramps and Detectives* (New York, 1878), pp. 388–89.

[31] *The Inter Ocean*, July 24, 1877; *Chicago Tribune*, July 24, 1877. Accounts of the meeting are colored by bias. Schaack, a police officer and bitterly antagonistic toward the so-called " communists," held the leaders were too cautious to advocate violence at this time. According to Flinn, whose prejudices paralleled those of Schaack, the speeches were the " wildest harangues," and speakers who counseled prudence were " hissed and howled down." Superintendent of Police Michael C. Hickey reported the meeting as orderly and the speeches as unexceptional. (Schaack, *op. cit.*, p. 60; Flinn, *History of the Chicago Police*, pp. 161–63.) The *Tribune* estimated the crowd at from two thousand to six thousand. (*Chicago Tribune*, July 24, 1877.) While the principal speeches were in progress, other speakers addressed smaller groups about the square from makeshift rostrums. Police in plain clothes circulated through the crowd.

sary precautions must be taken and that any outbreak should be vigorously put down.[32]

On the evening of Monday, July 23, switchmen of the Michigan Central struck, and about eight o'clock the next morning, freight workers of the same road, the Baltimore & Ohio, and the Illinois Central walked off their jobs in the yards along the Chicago River waterfront. After some hesitation, a small group of these strikers began to move southward toward the Illinois Central shops and yards at Sixteenth Street; and as word passed along that "the strike had begun," hangers-on joined the growing crowd. At Polk Street the marchers divided, some continuing south to the railroad shops and others turning westward to the freight offices of the Michigan Southern and the Rock Island roads. No violence was attempted, and, except for occasional outbursts from stragglers, the processions were undemonstrative. At the places visited most men left their jobs without demurring when requested by the railway men to join the strike —their action often sanctioned by supervisors who wished to avoid trouble.[33] By afternoon groups had gathered at various points along the west side of the river, composed of a few workmen but predominantly made up of the idle and curious.

The Chicago and North Western, the Chicago, Milwaukee and St. Paul, the Pittsburgh, Fort Wayne & Chicago, and the Chicago & Alton closed their yards voluntarily before any deputations reached them. Rail workers had now almost vanished from the ranks of the surging crowds. Such leadership as there was seemed to have fallen by default to an assortment of street urchins, roughs, and petty thieves, who roamed through the district between Clinton and Halsted streets across the south branch of the river from the center

[32] *The Inter Ocean*, July 23, 24, 1877; *Chicago Tribune*, July 20, 23, 24, 1877; "Biennial Report of the Adjutant-General of Illinois, 1877–78," *Reports to the General Assembly of Illinois . . . , 1879* (4 v. Springfield, 1879), II, 103 (hereafter cited as Illinois, *Reports, 1879*); Flinn, *History of the Chicago Police*, pp. 160–61; Hutchinson, *Cyrus Hall McCormick*, II, 615.

[33] *The Inter Ocean*, July 25, 1877; *Chicago Tribune*, July 25, 1877. Acutely conscious of the latent danger in the situation, railroad employees and managers alike made determined efforts to keep their differences on the plane of genuine negotiation. Conferences between workers and employers were held. The Rock Island made concessions. The railway strikers kept to the fore their position that they were engaged in a legitimate strike, and neither participated in nor countenanced any excesses. After the disorder had ended, the *Railway Age* cleared employees of complicity in criminal action. *The Railway Age*, II (Aug. 2, 1877), 1181. See also Dacus, *op. cit.*, pp. 310–11; Pinkerton, *op. cit.*, pp. 389–90.

of the city, shouting maledictions and indulging in minor depredations. Many factories and business houses locked their doors. Although most passenger runs continued, railroad freight transportation came to a stop. By nightfall the economic life of Chicago was threatened with paralysis. But notwithstanding these ominous developments, the general absence of violence, and particularly the failure of the so-called " communist " leaders to convert the demonstrations into a " rebellion," gave hope to Chicago citizens that they were yet to escape the fate of Pittsburgh.[34]

The morning of the twenty-fifth saw business coming to a standstill. Those places which attempted to resume normal activity were forced to close by mobs who displayed a more vicious temper than on the previous day. Slowly making its way west on Twenty-second Street one group shut down the Pond & Soper lumber mill, distilleries, and other establishments in the district. Going down " the Black Road," as Blue Island Avenue along the south branch of the river was called, the mob headed for the United States Rolling Stock Company and the McCormick works. Their progress continued until they were scattered by the clubs and revolvers of the police. On the North Side, a mob put a stop to business in distilleries, brick kilns, cooperage shops, James S. Kirk & Company's soap works, along with other enterprises. This done, they turned southward, to be shortly dispersed by fifty policemen in a melee without casualties on either side. All through the day gangs of marauding men and boys spread fear and confusion about the city. That evening when rioters began to smash windows and damage locomotives at the Chicago, Burlington & Quincy roundhouse on Union Street the police closed in. Shots were exchanged and several men were injured in the fighting.[35]

[34] *The Chicago Times*, July 25, 1877; *Chicago Tribune*, July 25, 1877. Responsible elements exerted themselves to prevent open violence. The Labor League, representing twenty trade unions, met that evening at Maskell Hall, where speeches stressed the observance of order and abstinence from liquor. The Workingmen's party, though constantly dubbed " communistic " by the press, issued strict orders forbidding violence and instructing members to turn over to the police anyone found drinking. The Mayor closed the saloons, and Superintendent Hickey requested all pawnbrokers to remove firearms from their windows and secrete them in safe places. *The Inter Ocean*, July 25, 1877; Flinn, *History of the Chicago Police*, p. 165.

[35] *Chicago Tribune*, July 26, 1877; *The Inter Ocean*, July 26, 27, 1877. Some obtained liquor from saloonkeepers despite the Mayor's order, and others served themselves by looting. Officers John Bonfield and Joseph Leonard were beaten and robbed of their " clubs and

Men now feared for the safety of the city. The Common Council in a special meeting authorized the Mayor to make any expenditures necessary " to enforce law and protect lives and property," and issued a call for " all good citizens " to enroll as special police. Citizens, gathered in the Moody and Sankey Tabernacle, cheered the Mayor's appeal for five thousand volunteers, and were comforted to hear leading citizens discuss the preservation of order and the restoration of business life. Ex-soldiers and former police offered aid, the Chicago Veterans equipped two companies with breech-loading rifles, and the North Side Germans organized a company known as the Union Veterans. Alderman James Daly was given command of a hastily assembled cavalry squadron of one hundred whose mounts were furnished by business houses. Members of the Board of Trade prepared to arm themselves and assemble at the Board's rooms " subject to the call of the mayor for defense of the city." Even more reassuring to a nervous citizenry was the arrival of two companies of regular army troops " fresh from the Indian campaign on the plains," who, amid enthusiastic cheers, marched down Madison Street, " their clothing covered with dust an inch thick." [36]

Disorder reached its climax on the twenty-sixth. Fresh alarm swept the city as the morning papers told in bold headlines of terrifying happenings the day before. "TERROR'S REIGN. The Streets of Chicago Given Over to Howling Mobs of Thieves and Cut-Throats," headlined the *Chicago Times.* At the section of Halsted Street which ran through the lumberyards and the Chicago, Burlington & Quincy switching yards, repeated clashes between the police and riotous mobs of thousands of men, women, and children took place. Wearied and footsore from the harassments of the previous two days, and angered by the pelting stones and a flood of curses, the police now resorted freely to their clubs and revolvers. Before

shooting-irons " when they attempted to interfere with those who had broken into Gottfried's brewery. Through the night, men and women, intoxicated and unkempt, milled around the vicinity of Lake Street venting shouts and obscenity.

[36] Among the speakers at the Tabernacle were Carter Harrison, then Representative from the Second Congressional District; Robert Collyer, pastor of Unity Church; Henry Greenebaum, president of the German National Bank; attorney Leonard Swett; ex-Mayor Levi D. Boone. Charles B. Farwell, well-known political leader and active in Chicago banking and mercantile circles, served as chairman. Chicago, *Council Proceedings, 1877–78,* p. 113; *Chicago Tribune,* July 26, 1877; *Chicago Post,* July 26, 1877; Flinn, *History of the Chicago Police,* pp. 179–83, 185; Frederick T. Wilson, *Federal Aid in Domestic Disturbances, 1878–1903,* 57 Cong., 2 sess., S. Doc. no. 209 (Washington, 1903), pp. 329–30.

each charge the mob scattered into alleys, doorways, back yards, and open lots, only to form again at some new location and resume its menacing course, while those who had been laggard in their flight lay prostrate, subjects for the attentions of surgeon or undertaker.

The principal encounters occurred at the viaduct, where Halsted crossed the railroad yards near Sixteenth Street, and at the Halsted Street bridge near Archer Avenue. In the face of an overwhelming crowd at the viaduct, one body of police fled as if in a " race for life." At the bridge another detachment, isolated by the mob, appeared in danger of annihilation when reinforcements broke up the seething mob with heavy fire and sent it scurrying to safety. All day such encounters disrupted the peace. Rumor magnified every fray into a bloody slaughter. Throughout the city, people, unnerved by fear and tension, believed that Gatling guns and the spray of canister shot had claimed thousands in dead and wounded, and that Halsted and Sixteenth streets had become rivers of blood.

Though happily far less sanguinary than such reports depicted, the bruising attacks of the police had let sufficient blood and broken enough bones to extinguish the mob spirit. On Saturday, July 28, the *Tribune* described Chicago as " tranquil." But peace had come at a price. At least thirteen men, some of them the innocent victims of wild shots, had been killed, and scores had been injured more or less seriously.[37] In the realm of economic endeavor the strikes and rioting had cost Chicago about $2,300,000 in livestock, grain, and other produce not shipped in, while wholesalers in various lines totaled a loss of $3,000,000. Added to these were the products of manufactories which would probably have reached $1,750,000 in value had the establishments run, and the cost of calling out auxiliary police, special guards, and the militia.

Even more serious was the rift which now separated worker from employer, the consequence of hate and distrust, malefic and imponderable. The employing public quickly closed ranks and with almost complete unanimity joined press and pulpit in unrestrainedly

[37] Flinn, *History of the Chicago Police*, pp. 192, 195, 199; Dacus, *op. cit.*, pp. 331–33, 335–36, 338; *Chicago Evening Post*, July 26, 27, 1877; *Chicago Evening Journal*, July 26, 1877; *The Chicago Times*, July 26, 27, 28, 1877; *Chicago Tribune*, July 28, 29, 1877; Pinkerton, *op. cit.*, p. 404. The exact number of casualties could not be determined. The *Tribune's* list, which it described as " pretty complete," gave more than fifty policemen and forty-seven others injured.

condemning strikes. As strikers became identified in the minds of many with lawbreakers, communists, and anarchists, much of the public support accorded railroad workers early in July disappeared. The excesses of labor's unsought and unwanted allies beclouded public insight into the causes of labor's dissatisfaction, and accelerated a general tightening of lines. Sometimes, too, trade-unionist leaders used the strikes to campaign for union recruits, and still others seized the occasion to preach the gospel of social revolution.[38]

The public mind, so deeply stirred by the events of these July days, more and more, as time went on, solidified in opposition to the strike as a legitimate and safe weapon. Advocates of a strengthened constabulary and a larger regular army, distributed in such a way as to quell strikes and disorders, gained open and enthusiastic support among leading citizens. Marshall Field, for example, urged that a standing army be constantly on the alert to put down such demonstrations. The Board of Trade memorialized Congress to increase the regular army to 100,000, and, in the years immediately following, new armories in Chicago, as in other large cities, were tangible signs of the concern of the people. Individuals and organizations provided funds for military equipment. The "Military Committee" of the Citizens' Association, for example, raised $30,000 by October, 1880 to sustain the local militia. At the same time it untiringly pushed the passage of militia laws which would be satisfactory to those described as "the most conservative minds." With equal vigor it urged the broadening of the tax base for the support of such a force.[39]

These efforts of men who believed that the police power of the state was designed, among other things, to protect property rights were paralleled in the years following the Great Strikes by those of workingmen to get a protection they, too, felt they needed. In the

[38] *Chicago Tribune*, July 26, 28, 1877; *The Chicago Times*, July 26, 1877; "Biennial Report of the Adjutant-General of Illinois, 1877–78," Illinois, *Reports, 1879*, II, 10–11; *The Railway Age*, II (July 26, 1877), 1162, (Aug. 2, 1877), 1181, (Aug. 16, 1877), 1222; *The Inter Ocean*, July 31, 1877; *Chicago Post*, Jan. 5, 1878; Dacus, *op. cit.*, p. 339; Chicago Board of Trade, *Twentieth Annual Report, 1878*, p. 11; *Illinois Staats-Zeitung*, July 25, 1877; *The American Bookseller*, IV (Aug. 15, 1877), 141–42; Henry A. James, *Communism in America* (New York, 1878), p. 29.

[39] *Chicago Tribune*, May 27, June 2, July 28, 29, 30, 1877; *The Chicago Times*, July 26, 1877; Commons, *op. cit.*, II, 191; Andreas, *History of Chicago*, III, 586–89; *The Inter Ocean*, July 30, 1877; Citizens' Association of Chicago, *Annual Report, 1878*, p. 11, *1880*, pp. 6–7, *1881*, pp. 9–10, *1883*, pp. 18–19, *1888*, p. 37; "Biennial Report of the Adjutant-General of Illinois, 1883–84," Illinois, *Reports, 1885*, I, 7.

riotous days of July, 1877 the lives of workers had not been safe nor had their civil rights been respected at all times.[40] Fired upon and beaten by the regular police and subjected to attacks at the hands of undisciplined irregulars even when engaged in lawful acts, working-men believed that they too had the constitutional rights of American citizens. Radical champions of labor's cause capitalized on the fear that molestations might again be experienced. They demanded the creation of a special armed force more sympathetic to the working class than were the regular police and the militia.[41] Turner societies decided to maintain drill corps, originally recreational in purpose, as guards to prevent the disruption of their meetings by disorderly in-terlopers. From the inception of these corps, with the incorporation of the Lehr und Wehr Verein under Illinois law in 1875, extremists had urged that they be expanded into fighting groups who could meet the "servile" militia "man for man." Following the strikes, proponents of arming used the injustices then committed and the strengthening of the National Guard as arguments to bolster a re-newed campaign for a workers' army.

During 1878 and 1879 the status of the drill corps was debated both by those within the labor movement, who differed on the question of whether the corpsmen should be armed, and by the general public, who were not of one mind as to whether the corps was a real threat to the social order. Even some of conservative bent regarded the corps as harmless. But the more timid, still haunted by memories of 1877, foresaw the dark night of a "communist uprising." Exagger-ated reports of membership growth and abusive epithets used by the

[40] The most flagrant of several incidents in which constitutional rights were disregarded was the police invasion of a peaceable assemblage of cabinet workers to discuss wages and hours July 26 at Turner Hall, West Twelfth Street. Without attempting to discover the purpose of the meeting, the police set upon the assemblage with clubs and revolvers, killing one man and injuring others. This was later taken to the courts as a test case, and Judge William K. McAllister rendered a decision in favor of the workers. It scored the action of the police as having been an indefensible "criminal riot." Schilling, *loc. cit.*, pp. XVII–XVIII; *Chicago Tribune*, July 28, 29, 1877, April 25, 26, 29, May 6, 1879; Chicago Super-intendent of Police, *Report, 1877*, pp. 13–14 and *passim;* Flinn, *History of the Chicago Po-lice*, pp. 197–98; *The Chicago Times*, July 27, 1877; *Illinois Staats-Zeitung*, April 25, 1879.

[41] For the participation of the various law-enforcement agents in the strikes of 1877 see Howard Boston Myers, *The Policing of Labor Disputes in Chicago: A Case Study* (unpub-lished Ph.D. Thesis, The University of Chicago, 1929), pp. 119–32; Flinn, *History of the Chicago Police*, pp. 202–4; Wilson, *op. cit.*, p. 331; "Biennial Report of the Adjutant-General of Illinois, 1877–78," Illinois, *Reports, 1879*, II, 3; *Chicago Tribune*, July 29, 30, 1877.

hotheaded against the police convinced an already overwrought public that the Verein and like bodies were unhealthful organisms that should be eradicated from the body politic. Accordingly, a bill severely restricting the activities of these organizations passed the state legislature in 1879, despite the marching of protestants from the Lehr und Wehr Verein, the Irish Labor Guards, the Bohemian Sharpshooters, and the Jaeger Verein, whose fixed bayonets apparently only hastened the unwanted legislation.[42]

The new law forbade any unofficial body to constitute itself a "military company or organization," and permitted drilling or parading with arms only by license of the governor. Yet in spite of the statute, uniformed, armed men sometimes still marched through the streets of Chicago, and loud-voiced leaders continued to exhort them to guard with their lives the red flag of the "proletarians" that proclaimed the "dawn of a new and just era."[43]

Both the moderates and extremists of labor kept up at the same time a steady fire of criticism of the prevailing capitalistic system in which free competition, they held, was "directly opposed to the interests and common welfare of the working class." There was, however, little agreement as to exactly how the old order should be modified or demolished, or how the new should be constructed. Marxist and Lassallean groups, which had existed in the city since the 'fifties and 'sixties, quarreled over the proper roles of trade-unionism and political action in establishing the socialist state, and others, like the Sovereigns of Industry and the Advocates of Justice, extolled their programs of "education" and "co-operative labor" as pathways to a better society.

The well-known difference among left-wing leaders on various

[42] *Chicago Tribune*, April 26, 27, June 15, 1878, April 21, 1879; Illinois, *Report of the Special Committee on Labor*, p. 39; Presser *v.* Illinois, 116 U. S. 252 (1886); Petition to Governor Richard Oglesby for the pardoning of the Anarchists, Chicago, November 8, 1887, *Lloyd Papers;* Commons, *op. cit.,* II, 280–81; Earl R. Beckner, *A History of Labor Legislation in Illinois* (Chicago, 1929), pp. 11–13; Illinois, *Senate Journal,* 1879, p. 1004; *Svenska Tribunen,* Jan. 1, 1879; *Chicago Post,* April 25, May 17, 1878; Schaack, *op. cit.,* p. 64; Spies, *op. cit.,* pp. 11, 24; John Ehlert, "Anarchists in Chicago," *America, A Journal of To-Day,* I (Nov. 22, 1888), 2; Act of May 28, 1879, Illinois, *Laws, 1879,* pp. 203–4.

[43] *Ibid.; Chicago Tribune*, April 21, Sept. 8, Oct. 5, 1879, July 2, 6, 1880; *Illinois Staats-Zeitung,* June 23, 1879; Schilling, loc. cit., p. XIX. The Irish Labor Guards wore green worsted blouses, the Bohemian Sharpshooters gray dress uniforms, the Jaeger Verein gray uniforms trimmed in green. The Lehr und Wehr Verein had blue cotton blouses and carried white canvas haversacks.

questions should have convinced the timid that the *Post* was fully justified in declaring that the city stood in " no immediate peril from a revolt of fanatics against capitalists." [44] So numerous and troublesome, indeed, were the points of disagreement that it sometimes seemed as though the doctrinaires expended as much effort in attempting to clarify their positions as in promoting their program. " Communism," " socialism," and " anarchism " were terms used interchangeably to brand their beliefs, and the question raised by a speaker, " Are you Anarchists . . . or are you Communists, and if so what separates us? " was heard repeatedly in one form or another, but never answered satisfactorily. Paul Grottkau, the German refugee firebrand of the late 'seventies and early 'eighties, sounded a more practical note when he urged that agitation be pressed regardless of the confusions in ideology.[45]

As the depression became more severe in 1877, discontented workingmen turned with increasing sympathy toward governmental measures to solve their problems. The political actionists, whose leadership included Thomas J. Morgan, George Schilling, and, at this time, Albert R. Parsons, gained ascendancy in socialist circles.[46] In order to propagandize their program more widely they established an English-language paper, the *Socialist,* under the editorship of Frank Hirth with Parsons as assistant editor. Some moderate successes were attained in the campaigns of 1877–79, but dissensions

[44] Illinois, *Report of the Special Committee on Labor, 1879,* p. 39; *Chicagoer Arbeiter-Zeitung,* Jan. 24, March 9, 1883; *The Alarm,* I (Oct. 11, 1884), 2, I (Nov. 8, 1884), 14; *Svenska Tribunen,* Jan. 2, Oct. 2, 1886; Commons, *op. cit.,* II, 227–30; *Chicago Tribune,* Feb. 18, 22, 24, 26, 1874; *Industrial Age,* I (March 21, 1874), 4; *Chicago Post,* April 30, 1878. Both the Sovereigns and the Advocates were established in Chicago in Feb., 1874. Leading figures in the latter organization were Mrs. M. D. Wynkoop, the wife of a mechanic, and Jonathan Periam, best remembered as editor of *Prairie Farmer,* 1876–84, 1887–93. For a statement of the principles of the Sovereigns, see Edwin M. Chamberlin, *The Sovereigns of Industry* (Boston, 1875).

[45] *Chicagoer Arbeiter-Zeitung,* Feb. 14, March 20, May 7, 30, 1884; *The Alarm,* I (April 18, 1885), 1; Spies, *op. cit.,* p. 12. Some declared that socialism attracted a more intelligent and better-educated following than did communism. (*Hejmdal,* July 21, 1876.) For a statement of the differences between trade-unionists and political actionists in Chicago, see Schilling, *loc. cit.,* pp. XV–XVI.

[46] Edward B. Mittelman, " Chicago Labor in Politics 1877–96," *The Journal of Political Economy,* XXVIII (May, 1920), 307–17. Morgan emigrated from England to Chicago in 1869, and after 1875 worked as a machinist for the Illinois Central Railroad. Like many others in the Socialistic Labor party, he had been converted to socialism by bitter experiences during the depression of 1873–78. Though Morgan was an outstanding leader in the American labor movement during the late nineteenth century, there is no adequate biography of him.

soon flared into open conflicts. Only an uneasy peace had been temporarily patched up between the trade-unionist and the political-action wings of the socialists, and a growing conviction that labor tickets would be defrauded of any victories at the polls shook the faith of those but half-persuaded of the efficacy of the ballot for redressing labor's wrongs. Even more debilitating was the drift of third-party voters back to their traditional political loyalties with the return of more prosperous times. The *Socialist,* which had first appeared on September 14, 1878, expired a year later, and by the end of 1880 Parsons had parted company with Morgan and Schilling. The socialists made a confused and half-hearted effort in the elections of 1882, but labor's political movement was collapsing, as Schilling said, " in a condition of unrest, uncertainty, and inertia." [47]

Inspired by the international congress of revolutionary anarchists held in London in July, 1881, leaders among the extreme socialists in the United States tried to inaugurate an American counterpart of the movement in Chicago the following October. The " American Congress of the International Workingmen's Association," as the gathering of a dozen-odd delegates was pretentiously called, opened its three-day meeting on October 21 at North Side Turner Hall. Under the chairmanship of August Spies, delegates represented (in some cases by proxy) organizations in various cities throughout the country, as well as groups in Chicago. The fundamentally radical position of the gathering was made clear in resolutions denouncing private property and " wage slavery," praising the armed sections that stood " ready with the gun " to protect workers' rights, and repudiating the " great American superstition " that redress of social wrongs was to be obtained through the ballot. A " Revolutionary Socialist Party " was founded, to be composed of autonomous groups with a liaison center in Chicago.[48]

[47] Parsons took part in the campaign of 1882, though he later wrote that by 1880 he had concluded that workingmen's conditions resulted in " their practical disfranchisement as voters." Schilling, too, was becoming dissatisfied with the political situation. Mittelman, *loc. cit.,* pp. 417, 425–27; *The Alarm,* I (Feb. 21, 1885), 2; Philip Van Patten to George A. Schilling, Jan. 12, 1882, *Labadie Collection* (Photostat, University of Michigan); Scott, *Newspapers and Periodicals of Illinois, 1814–1879,* pp. 143–44; Commons, *op. cit.,* II, 282; *Chicago Tribune,* Sept. 15, 1878, Jan. 19, 1880; Schilling, *loc. cit.,* p. XXI; Spies, *op. cit.,* p. 11.

[48] *Chicago Tribune,* Oct. 22, 23, 24, 1881. The names of participating cities in addition to Chicago, as reported in the *Tribune* for the opening session, were New York, Philadelphia, Louisville, Cedar Rapids, St. Louis, Jersey City Heights, and Milwaukee. According to

The strain of anarchistic thought in the pronouncements of the Congress was to become more and more characteristic of the philosophy of the extreme leftists in Chicago in the early 'eighties, but the projected national revolutionary party proved premature. The movement lay dormant until galvanized by the arrival of Johann Most in the United States, December 18, 1882. Six days later this slight, full-bearded German, who had suffered imprisonment in England for radical articles in his *Freiheit* praising the assassination of the Czar, was in Chicago. Proclaiming himself an anarchist but protesting that his aim was to give society a " healthier tone " and not to overthrow it, Most spoke to large audiences at various Turner halls where not only Spies, but such moderates as George Schilling and Most's Chicago host, the distinguished physician Dr. Ernst Schmidt, took part. Most differed on some points from Spies, Parsons, and other Chicago leaders, but his vitriolic condemnations of the " aristocracy of capital " and of statesmen who " welded iron chains for the workingmen " had an appeal for all in the extreme fringe.[49] The following October a congress of radicals at Pittsburgh strove to consolidate the unification of revolutionary socialists begun the previous year at Chicago. Spies and Parsons were the chief spokesmen of the Middle West at the convention and Most led the East. The ideological differences between middle-western and eastern groups were not so great as to prevent the formation along federative lines of a national organization known as the International Working People's Association, commonly called the " Black International " as distinguished from the " Red International," founded at San Francisco, July 15, 1881. The Association, in the famous " Pittsburgh Manifesto," now

---

Vorbote, Boston, Omaha, Kansas City, and five New Jersey towns (Jersey City, Jersey City Heights, Hoboken, Union Hill, Paterson) sent representatives in addition to those listed by the *Tribune,* with the exception of Cedar Rapids. (*Vorbote,* Oct. 29, 1881.) Some of the delegates upheld the value of engaging in political action for agitational purposes or to illustrate its "utter wrongfulness and inefficiency." At its final meeting the assemblage took the name of " National Socialistic Congress."

[49] A strong advocacy of trade-unionism, which was always characteristic of the Chicago anarcho-extremists, differentiated them not only from those revolutionaries who adhered closely to Lassallean principles, but also from the anarchists intimately associated with Most. While the revolutionary convention of Oct., 1881 in Chicago had taken an equivocal attitude toward the trade-union movement, even unenthusiastic delegates granted that some favor must be shown the unionists in the form of a supporting resolution. *Chicago Tribune,* Oct. 24, 1881, Dec. 24, 25, 27, 28, 1882, Jan. 1, 1883; *New York Tribune,* Dec. 19, 1882; Commons, *op. cit.,* II, 269–75, 277–84, 293, 294.

gave some degree of unity to the American revolutionary movement.[50]

The general public, of course, had little interest in philosophical differences and doctrinal disputes, but it recoiled instinctively from all radical " isms " as dangers to the body politic and the revered manner of living, and it impartially castigated all who opposed its way of life. Those who listened to Most, whom the *Tribune* described as " a justifier of political murder," were roundly denounced as " idlers, cranks, beer-guzzlers, and discontents." No less abhorrent than their incessant disparagement of the economic system was the radicals' attitude toward religious institutions. Chicagoans were horrified to hear August Spies and others of like mind declare in open meetings that the church was the foundation upon which rested " the barbarous system of robbery " called capitalism, and that the oppressed had awakened to " the truth " that the chains of their slavery would not be broken by God or the Saviour but only by themselves. The earth, said another, had been transformed into " a valley of misery " by " three correlative working forces ": class policy, capitalism, and religion. Another declared that religion was always dissipated when men thought independently, for knowledge was the deadly enemy of faith. Along with " politicians, exploiters," and " the capitalistic press " were classed the clergy, who as " assistants of the robber capitalists " were rewarded by tax exemptions and other privileges.[51]

Through newspapers, books, and pamphlets, the radicals made known their principles. Especially effective was the group of German-language papers built up around the weekly *Vorbote,* which

[50] The " Manifesto of the International Working People's Association to the Workingmen of America " was dated Oct. 16, 1883. Despite dissimilarities, both Pittsburgh and San Francisco groups had a strong affinity to the International Working People's Association, founded in 1881 at London. This body, in turn, considered itself the legitimate successor to the famous " First " International which had existed from 1864 to 1876. Some attempt was made to fasten the name " Blues " on the members of the Socialistic Labor party, but apparently the term enjoyed only little currency. Newspapers and speakers of the time were careless in their use of all these appellations, however. Commons, *op. cit.,* II, 204, 222, 291, 294–95, 296, 298–99; Henry David, *The History of the Haymarket Affair* . . . (New York, 1936), pp. 146–49; Richard T. Ely, *Recent American Socialism* (Johns Hopkins University, *Studies in Historical and Political Science,* III, no. 4, Baltimore, 1885), p. 21; Morris Hillquit, *History of Socialism in the United States* (New York, 1903), pp. 237–38; Spies, *op. cit.,* p. 26; A. R. Parsons, " The Story of His Life," *loc. cit.,* p. 19.

[51] *Chicago Tribune,* Dec. 27, 28, 1882; *Chicagoer Arbeiter-Zeitung,* Oct. 20, 1882, Jan. 2, 18, Feb. 6, April 11, 22, 1884.

had been started as an organ of the Workingmen's Party of Illinois early in 1874. During its first years the *Vorbote*'s career was complicated by financial difficulties that made its solvency dependent on a continuous series of benefit balls, picnics, musicales, and other entertainments, and by the fact that the editor, Conrad Conzett, was in some ways unsympathetic toward the principles of the Workingmen's Party of the United States, of which the paper had become an official publication in July, 1876. The conflict of opinion between the leaders of the party and the editorial staff eventually produced such stress that it severed its connection with the party in February, 1878. Thereafter *Vorbote* appeared as " an independent organ for the true interests of the Proletariat."

To ease the financial strain and to provide a publication that would better serve agitational purposes, a tri-weekly, the *Chicagoer Arbeiter-Zeitung,* was begun in 1877. The following year Conzett sold both papers to the Socialistic Publishing Society, an enterprise maintained co-operatively by members of the German section of the Socialist Labor party. Under the new editor, Paul Grottkau, a recent refugee from Germany, the *Arbeiter-Zeitung* became a daily, with a Sunday edition, *Die Fackel*. In 1880, August Spies assumed the managership and editorship of the publications, and despite futile attempts at restraint by the orthodox socialists, *Vorbote,* the *Arbeiter-Zeitung,* and *Die Fackel* in the next years mirrored the progress of their editor toward forthright anarchism. Whatever objections might be raised to his ideology, Spies's editorial ability could hardly be questioned, and the circulation of his journals mounted until their combined total was well over twenty thousand an issue by 1884.[52]

The fatal weakness of all attempts to establish an effective radical movement was the inability to attract a substantial following among non-German, and, in particular, among English-speaking, elements of the working class. This resistance to socialistic appeals was underlined by the quick collapse of the *Socialist,* which had been founded in the hope that Chicago would support an English-language paper

[52] *Vorbote,* Feb. 14, Oct. 10, Dec. 19, 1874, Jan. 9, 1875, Dec. 2, 1876, Aug. 25, 1877, Feb. 16, July 13, 1878; Commons, *op. cit.,* II, 230, 271–73, 280; Spies, *op. cit.,* p. 22. First issues of these papers were: *Vorbote,* Feb. 14, 1874; *Chicagoer Arbeiter-Zeitung,* May 29, 1877; *Die Fackel,* May 11, 1879. In 1877, circulation of *Vorbote* was 3,997; by 1884, it had reached 7,115. In the latter year, the circulation of *Die Fackel* was 10,035, and of the *Arbeiter-Zeitung,* 5,326. Circulation figures are not always accurately given.

of radical bent.[53] After the demise of the short-lived *Socialist* the extremists had no English-language organ until *The Alarm* was established in 1884. With Parsons as editor and prime spirit, *The Alarm* called for the use of force against the established order and quickened fears among the populace of Chicago as probably no other journal did, perhaps because the English-speaking community could read it.[54] In addition to papers printed in the city, others of like opinion published elsewhere were available. *Truth,* an English-language paper of San Francisco, was advertised as a " lance for the fighter in the revolutionary struggle." Johann Most's *Freiheit,* which had been moved from London to New York in 1882, and *Nemesis,* a Baltimore publication, found sympathetic readers in Chicago, as did similar publications of European origin.[55]

Books on revolutionary theory and kindred subjects were also in demand. In 1884 the central organization of the International Working People's Association in Chicago maintained a library valued at over three hundred dollars, of which Michael Schwab, a member of the *Arbeiter-Zeitung* staff, was librarian. Marx's *Communist Manifesto* was advertised as published by the Central Chicago Committee of the Socialist Federation of North America, and reprints of the debate between Most and Grottkau on communism versus anarchism were sold by *Arbeiter-Zeitung* carriers for ten cents a copy. Schwab offered for sale covers for unbound volumes of Lassalle's works, and *Die Fackel* even translated for its readers Allan Pinkerton's history

[53] The failure of the *Socialist* was typical of the fate of such English-language papers. Of eight others established in 1876–77, which supported the Socialistic Labor party, not one survived after 1879. (Hillquit, *op. cit.,* p. 227.) Of other non-German socialist papers in Chicago, only the Scandinavian weekly, *Den Nye Tid,* with a circulation of 2,800 in 1884, appears to have had some following.

[54] *The Alarm,* I (Oct. 4, 1884), 1, 2, (Oct. 11, 1884), 1, 2. *The Alarm* boasted in its first issue (Oct. 4, 1884) of 15,000 copies that, as a spokesman for the International, it would be the only paper in Chicago not published " in the interest of profit mongering, land robbing . . . schemes." Oddly enough, it took no account of the *Arbeiter-Zeitung* and its associated papers, which had anticipated the *Alarm* as radical organs. Besides the journals of various trade unions, there were a number of publications sympathetic to the labor cause, though of moderate tone. Among these may be noted: *The Western Catholic, Svenska Tribunen, The Knights of Labor, The Standard of Labor,* and the *Telegram.*

[55] A. R. Parsons, " The Story of His Life," *loc. cit.,* p. 23; *Chicagoer Arbeiter-Zeitung,* Jan. 2, March 15, April 1, May 2, June 16, 1884. See also David, *op. cit.,* p. 113; Ely, *Recent American Socialism,* pp. 31–34; Hillquit, *op. cit.,* p. 225; Rudolf Rocker, *Johann Most Das Leben Eines Rebellen* (Berlin, 1924), pp. 135–43. *The Alarm* changed from a weekly to a semimonthly, Oct. 31, 1885. Suppressed the day after the Haymarket riot, it resumed publication briefly in 1887–88 with Dyer D. Lum as editor. *The Alarm,* II (Oct. 31, 1885), 1, n.s. I (Nov. 5, 1887), 2; Schaack, *op. cit.,* pp. 156–57.

of the strikes of 1877, *Strikers, Communists, Tramps and Detectives.*[56]

Along with the printed word as a vehicle of propaganda went protest meetings and demonstrations. Community festivals, picnics, and balls brought solidarity and made for a spirit of camaraderie. Lectures and discussions examining the evils charged against the existing society or threshing over the well-worn but ever-absorbing doctrines of anarchism and socialism were on the agenda of nearly every gathering. " Who Are the Criminals?," " The Crisis and the Workers," " The Development of Socialism," " Authority and Autonomy " were, for example, popular lecture and debate topics. Speakers of rare forensic ability foretold the equality of the sexes in " the new, the free society," railed against " exploiters and oppressors," and condemned what they held was the maleficence of organized government. The audiences, composed of various nationalities, heard their native tongues spoken from various platforms, although the German language communicated the thoughts of speakers most frequently.[57]

Though radicalism was promoted aggressively and occasionally effectively, especially in hard times, the number of converts was not large even among those Germans in the trade-union movement.[58] To labor in general, a more likely means of improving its status appeared to be organization, " a formal law of society and one of the

---

[56] *Chicagoer Arbeiter-Zeitung,* Jan. 22, 1880, July 14, 1883, Feb. 23, April 12, June 26, 1884; *Die Fackel,* May 25, 1884. Schwab, a Bavarian bookbinder, came to Chicago in 1879, but did not take up permanent residence in the city until 1882. He was first a reporter and then co-editor of the *Arbeiter-Zeitung.* John D. Lawson, ed., *American State Trials . . .* (17 v. St. Louis, 1914–36), XII, 16, 143.

[57] For examples of multi-ethnic meetings, note the one held at Thirty-first and Halsted streets, June 2, 1878, where three thousand were reported in attendance, and a joint meeting of Czech, German, English, and Scandinavian groups later the same month. *Svornost,* June 3, 28, 1878. See also the *Chicagoer Arbeiter-Zeitung,* Jan. 29, March 15, 1884; *The Christian Union,* XXXIII (May 6, 1886), 5. Notices of various meetings are found chiefly in the German labor press.

[58] No exact figures can be given on I.W.P.A. membership in the city, but *The Alarm,* a friendly source, placed the number of " active " members at over 2,000 in April, 1885, and claimed a " sympathetic " membership of an additional 10,000. (*The Alarm,* I [April 18, 1885], 4.) According to the *Tribune,* Chicago had nineteen groups of the I.W.P.A. in November of that year. National membership was estimated as then about 7,000 organized into some eighty groups. (*Chicago Tribune,* Nov. 30, 1885; Hillquit, *op. cit.,* p. 243.) See the Captain of Police Michael J. Schaack's list in his notoriously exaggerated discussion. (Schaack, *op. cit.,* pp. 691–94.) Henry David, after careful study, concluded that " it is doubtful if there ever were more than 5,000 real members " of the International Working People's Association. David, *op. cit.,* p. 112.

necessities of civilization," as the Illinois Bureau of Labor Statistics put it. In the 1880's a noticeable acceleration of the union movement took place. Even in the lean years of 1884 and '85 following a fleeting flush of prosperity, progress was not halted, and the nationwide upsurge which swept the country in 1886 generated in Chicago an enthusiasm hitherto unseen. By July one hundred trade-union locals were in Cook County, of which Chicago was the industrial center, with a membership of 38,007 or nearly 94 per cent of all enrolled within the state.[59]

The largest trade unions were to be found among the bricklayers and stone masons, brickmakers, butchers, cigarmakers, carpenters and joiners, furniture workers, hod carriers, metal workers, freight handlers, lake seamen, and typographers. But of those with a membership in excess of 1,000 only the brickmakers, cigarmakers, and masons claimed a total organization of the trade. Complete unionization was generally found in the smaller crafts, for here the ties of acquaintanceship were a unifying force.[60] Although some Chicago unions, like the " divisions " and " lodges " of the railroad brotherhoods and locals among the carpenters, bench molders, telegraphers, and cigarmakers, were branches of national organizations and some had international connections, the independent local union without outside affiliation existed in considerable numbers. Some, like the railroad employees, originally created as benevolent societies, were forced by economic conditions into a militancy indistinguishable from that of regular trade unions. The oldest Chicago local of the Brotherhood of Firemen dated from 1881, the Order of Railway Conductors of America from 1883, and the Brotherhood of Railroad Brakemen from 1884. Division No. 10 of the Brotherhood of Loco-

[59] Four of the one hundred Cook County locals were in outlying communities, the remainder in the city proper. The oldest union was Typographical No. 16 (1852), with 1,200 members in 1886. Illinois Bureau of Labor Statistics, *Fourth Biennial Report, 1886*, pp. 172–78, 196, 199, 215, 219, 226–29. For American and foreign born in Illinois trade unions see Appendix table.

[60] *Ibid.*, pp. 166–67, 172–78; *The Bakers' Journal*, VI (Aug. 16, 1890), 1; *Chicago Tribune*, Aug. 18, 19, 21, 1883; Bench and Machinery Molders' Union No. 239, *By-Laws . . .* [1887] (Chicago, 1887), p. 20. The small size of many of the locals claiming complete unionization is illustrated by the coopers, toolmakers, and dressers, each with 100 members; lumber inspectors and measurers, 56; stereotypers, 50. The solidly organized masons' union of 4,000 members was the largest in the city. The metal-working trade may also have been a completely organized field dominated by large unions, but reports from these unions were confusing and contradictory.

motive Engineers had existed in the city since 1863, the year the national organization (then called the Brotherhood of the Footboard) was founded. A majority of those classified in 1886 by the Illinois Bureau of Labor Statistics as belonging to railroad men's organizations held membership not in these four operative brotherhoods, however, but in the unions of freight handlers and switchmen.[61]

The labor-conscious decade of the 'eighties witnessed the evolution of national federation among the various trades, beginning with the Federation of Organized Trades and Labor Unions of the United States and Canada in 1881. From the first, Chicago labor leaders actively participated until the federation, after a brief and unspectacular existence, was absorbed in the American Federation of Labor in 1886.[62]

The remarkable growth of trade-unionism in 1886 was, however, overshadowed by the phenomenal rise in membership and prestige of the Noble Order of the Knights of Labor, which established its first " local assembly " in Chicago August 19, 1877. The order at first gave little promise of its later leadership, for almost as rapidly as new assemblies were formed old members dropped out, leaving the organization weakened and the treasury empty.[63] In 1882 an extended visit to the city by Myles McPadden of Pittsburgh, general organizer of the Knights, to publicize the purposes of the order resulted in the establishment of a new district assembly and several new local assemblies, but the next year's gain in membership was only about five hundred. Even the visit on January 16, two years later, of the Grand Master Workman, Terence V. Powderly, did not spur Chicago workingmen to affiliate with the Knights. Then a series of strikes led by the Knights against the Gould railroad system

[61] Commons, op. cit., II, 309-10; Pierce, A History of Chicago, II, 165-66; Walter F. McCaleb, Brotherhood of Railroad Trainmen . . . (New York, 1936), pp. 51-52; Florence Peterson, Handbook of Labor Unions (Washington, 1944), pp. 195, 197, 307-8, 319; Illinois Bureau of Labor Statistics, Fourth Biennial Report, 1886, pp. 176-77, 219, 376. Of a total of 6,675 men in railroad men's organizations in Illinois, 3,829 were in Cook County.

[62] Federation of Organized Trades and Labor Unions, Report of the First Annual Session . . . 1881, in American Federation of Labor, Proceedings, 1881-88 (Bloomington, Ill., 1906), pp. 6, 7, 12-13, 23-24, First Annual Convention, 1886, Proceedings, pp. 5, 12-13; Commons, op. cit., II, 318-22.

[63] An example of the financial plight of the order came as early as 1878 when Richard Griffiths, a tobacconist and newsdealer, could not attend as delegate the convention at Reading, Pennsylvania, because the Chicago group's treasury was empty and he could not afford to pay his own expenses.

in the spring and summer of 1885 resulted in the most resounding victory yet won by organized labor. What education and appeals to brotherhood had never done, the bringing to heel of Jay Gould accomplished at a stroke. The manifest potency of the order aroused intense enthusiasm, and growth of the organization in Chicago as elsewhere was little short of miraculous. Nine years' effort in the city had placed less than two thousand on the rolls up to July, 1885, but by July of the following year there were 21,753.[64]

Included in the membership were women, who in Chicago had enrolled in September, 1881, as soon as admission was permitted by the order. Their Local Assembly No. 1789 was the second in the country. A recognition by female workers of common problems led in the mid-'eighties, just as it had with men, to the inauguration of other assemblies such as one composed of Bohemian women, of cloakmakers, tailoresses, and shoe workers. Outstanding in the movement was Mrs. George Rodgers, wife of an iron molder prominent in labor circles, who became the first woman master workman of a district assembly in the order's history. Subsequently, at the national convention of 1886 she was named general treasurer, an honor she declined on the ground that she was the mother of twelve children.[65]

The causes which the Knights of Labor actively promoted were those which had the sanction of the trade unions as well. Together they adopted resolutions, among other things, against child labor in factories, immigrant contract labor, and " monopoly," and urged the adoption of the eight-hour day and the establishment of a national labor bureau. Like the unified trades of the 'sixties, the Knights

[64] Illinois Bureau of Labor Statistics, *Fourth Biennial Report, 1886*, pp. 160, 221; *The Knights of Labor*, I (Jan. 29, 1887), 5; *Chicago Tribune*, March 24, 1882, Jan. 17, 1884, Feb. 16, 1887; T[erence] V. Powderly, *Thirty Years of Labor* . . . (Columbus, 1890), p. 239; [Knights of Labor], *Proceedings of the General Assembly of the * * * [sic]* . . . *1878* (n.p., n.d.), p. 26; Commons, *op. cit.*, II, 347–48, 370; *Svenska Tribunen*, April 3, 1886. The decision to abandon secrecy, the policy of the order since its inception in 1869, was reached Sept. 6, 1881. The move was designed, in part, to remove opposition from Catholic sources. Powderly, *op. cit.*, p. 631. See also Harry J. Carman, Henry David, and Paul N. Guthrie, *The Path I Trod* . . . (New York, 1940), pp. 317–82, and *The Knights of Labor*, II (March 5, 1887), 11. A detailed examination of the relations of the Church with the Knights of Labor is Henry J. Browne, *The Catholic Church and the Knights of Labor* (Washington, 1949). For data on native and foreign born in the Knights of Labor see Appendix tables.

[65] U. S. Senate, *History of Women in Trade Unions*, in *Report on Condition of Woman and Child Wage Earners in the United States*, X, 61 Cong., 2 sess., S. Doc. 645 (19 v. Washington, 1911), 115, 127, 129, hereafter cited as *Women in Trade Unions;* Knights of Labor, *Proceedings of Tenth Regular Session, 1886*, pp. 243, 260.

sponsored with considerable zeal agencies for co-operative production and marketing, through which they hoped ultimately "to supersede the wage system." Although directed most often to undertakings which dealt with the necessities of daily living, they covered
a wide range of economic endeavors, extending from food and fuel
co-operatives to those for publishing.[66]

Though subscribing to "the principle of sound business enterprise," co-operatives seldom enjoyed satisfying financial returns and
long-time existence. A conspicuous exception, however, was in the
publication of *The Knights of Labor,* started as a weekly journal in
1886. Endorsed by Chicago assemblies of the Knights of Labor, it
was, however, not an official organ of the national order. The company employed about sixty men, and its capital stock of $50,000 was
held by the Knights. For several weeks in 1887 publication was suspended because of financial difficulties, but by 1890, with name
changed to *The Rights of Labor,* the journal claimed a circulation
of 17,600.[67]

During the early 'eighties the Knights and trade-unionists were
not very far apart in tactics and objectives. Though the Knights'
disapproval of the strike as an economic weapon seemingly separated them from their trade-union colleagues, their actual conduct
made this difference more theoretical than actual. In Chicago, as
nationally, workingmen in the order walked off their jobs in struggles with employers just as did trade-unionists. Furthermore, memberships of the union locals and Knights' assemblies were by no
means exclusive. Seventeen per cent of all Illinois union members
in July, 1886 were also members of the Knights of Labor, and, while
the order envisaged organization of all occupations, many of their

[66] Knights of Labor, *Constitution of the General Assembly, District Assemblies, and
Local Assemblies . . . , 1885* (n.p., n.d.), p. 4; Pierce, *A History of Chicago,* II, 182–83;
Illinois Staats-Zeitung, July 21, 1879; *Der Westen,* Aug. 17, 1879; *Chicago Tribune,*
Oct. 21, 1879, Jan. 26, 1880; *The Industrial News,* Aug. 2, 1888; *American Labor Budget,*
Dec. 4, 1886; Foundrymen's Co-operative Mfg. Company of Chicago, *By-Laws . . .*(Chi-
cago, 1887), pp. 1–2; Knights of Labor Joint-Stock Co-operative Cigar Co., *By-Laws . . . ,
Adopted November 24, 1882 . . .* (Chicago, 1888), pp. 3–5; Knights of Labor Co-operative
Manufacturing Tailoring Co., *By-Laws . . .* (Chicago, 1887), pp. 3–4.
[67] *The Co-operator,* I (March, 1881), 7, 14; *The Knights of Labor,* I (Nov. 13, 1886), 1,
(Dec. 11, 1886), 7, 8, (Jan. 15, 1887), 7, (May 7, 1887), 8; *The Co-Operative News of
America,* I (July, 1887), 3; *The Rights of Labor,* VI (Jan. 4, 1890), 1. For lists of trade-
union and Knights of Labor co-operatives see Illinois Bureau of Labor Statistics, *Fourth
Biennial Report, 1886,* pp. 455–58.

local assemblies were in fact nothing but craft-union locals which had been absorbed.[68]

Although the two movements worked together for the most part to promote common interests, minor friction already foreshadowed the rancorous disputes which later would bring those in the labor movement into open conflict. Differences between political and direct actionists, socialists and "pure" trade-unionists, radicals and moderates, had always been stumbling-blocks to concerted action. A continued drift of radicalism throughout 1884 and 1885 toward an even more advanced position widened the gap between left and right and pointed to a definite parting of the ways. A climax was reached with the disruption of the city's central labor body, the Trade and Labor Assembly, in 1884.[69]

The city's old Trades Assembly had become moribund by 1870, and although a new central body, the Trade and Labor Council, formed in 1877, had briefly displayed considerable vigor in unifying the various trades making up its constituency, deep-seated disagreements led to a split in January, 1880, when the Morgan faction left the council. Four months later, however, the two factions recombined as the Trade and Labor Assembly. But hopes for unity and harmony dimmed as it became evident that centrifugal forces, created by inherent incompatibilities among different factions within the new Assembly, could not be overcome. The protagonist of rebellion against the Assembly's moderate policies was a dissident minority of Cigar Makers' Union No. 14, whose disruptive tactics were rebuked by the Assembly in September, 1883. Later that year the radical cigarmakers withdrew from their old organization and

<hr/>

[68] The Knights excluded those engaged in the liquor trades, lawyers, bankers, professional gamblers, and stockbrokers. All members of the tailors', cigar packers', salt laborers', and seamen's unions in Chicago belonged to the Knights; in twelve other unions, half or more of the members were Knights. Knights of Labor, *Constitution, 1885*, pp. 4, 62–63; Illinois Bureau of Labor Statistics, *Fourth Biennial Report, 1886*, pp. 172–78, 184, 192, 390–94; Powderly, *op. cit.*, p. 254; Commons, *op. cit.*, II, 344–47; *Chicago Tribune*, May 19, 1882; Harry A. Millis and Royal E. Montgomery, *Organized Labor (The Economics of Labor*, III, New York, 1945), pp. 64–65.

[69] *Skandinaven*, June 3, 1884; *Chicago Tribune*, Feb. 24, 1880, July 28, 1884; *Svenska Tribunen*, Sept. 11, 1886. The co-operation between Knights and trade-unionists at the local level in Chicago and elsewhere in the early 'eighties was paralleled by attempts of the national leadership of the two movements to achieve unification. Knights of Labor, *Proceedings of the Seventh Regular Session of the General Assembly . . . 1883* (n.p., n.d.), p. 506; Federation of Organized Trades and Labor Unions, *Report of the Third Annual Session . . . 1883*, pp. 9–10.

formed the Progressive Cigar Makers' Union. The Progressives boldly advocated an anarchistic social order, and urged "open rebellion of the despoiled" as the "only means" by which "emancipation" could be attained. When the Progressive Union issued its call in June, 1884 for the creation of a new central body with a "progressive policy," delegates from four other unions joined it in establishing the Central Labor Union.[70]

Frankly radical, the Central Labor Union gradually attracted the extremist elements of the more conservative but far from homogeneous Assembly. By October, 1885 thirteen unions belonged to the new organization, and by spring of the following year over twenty. Meanwhile, open avowal of anarchism and advocacy of a nihilistic program by those associated with the *Alarm* and the *Arbeiter-Zeitung* were producing a conservative reaction among some who had hitherto been reckoned in the "radical" camp. During 1884 the "more sober element" of the socialists, as the *Tribune* termed them, grew increasingly distrustful of their anarchistic compatriots, and clashes between the factions led at times to physical violence. Control of the influential radical press group was a critical issue that terminated in its complete capture by the extremists. Even the fiery Grottkau was now unacceptable to the Spies faction and left the city. The Morgan-led socialists, who proclaimed their faith in "intelligence" instead of "dynamite," finally reorganized, April 4, 1886, as a separate body which condemned all attempts at forcible revolution and declared socialism to be "emphatically opposed to anarchy."[71]

Compromise between the labor factions had now become impos-

[70] Pierce, *A History of Chicago*, II, 170; *Chicago Tribune*, Jan. 30, May 7, 1880, Oct. 1, Dec. 4, 1883, Feb. 18, 1884; *Chicagoer Arbeiter-Zeitung*, Jan. 3, 4, 1884; Commons, *op. cit.*, II, 387; Norman J. Ware, *The Labor Movement in the United States, 1860–1895* . . . (New York, 1929), p. 313. In the light of later events, it is worth noting that Parsons presided at the meeting of May 6, 1880, at which the Trade and Labor Assembly was formed. (*Chicago Tribune*, May 7, 1880.) The progressive cigarmakers' revolutionary platform was very strongly worded, declaring its first objective to be the "destruction of the existing class rule by all means — i.e., by energetic, relentless, revolutionary, and international action." *Ibid.*, Feb. 18, 1884.

[71] *The Alarm*, II (Oct. 21, 1885), 4; *Chicago Tribune*, March 10, April 21, Sept. 19, 1884, Feb. 2, Oct. 25, 1885, April 5, 12, 26, 1886; *Chicago Daily News*, April 18, 24, 1884; Commons, *op. cit.*, II, 296, 391. The Central Labor Union, too, suffered from factionalism; by no means were all those in its affiliated unions of the same mind as the Spies group. It was even reported that the Progressive Cigar Makers' Union contemplated withdrawing from the new central body it had taken the lead in establishing. *Chicago Tribune*, Oct. 25, 1885.

sible. Through the columns of his *Alarm,* Parsons, a leading figure in the Central Labor Union, fulminated against the Trade and Labor Assembly for condoning a system of " wage slavery " and " slow starvation." " The social war has come," cried the *Alarm,* " and those who are not with us are against us." Most ominous and significant in the ultra-radicalism which now characterized the extreme left was the open and consistent espousal of violence, the " propaganda of the deed," as a revolutionary tactic. Especially praised were the virtues of a " Minerva " sprung from " Jove's head " — dynamite. " What is dynamite? " inquired the *Alarm.* " It is the latest discovery of science by which power is placed in the hands of the weak and defenseless to protect them against the domination of others." " One pound of DYNAMITE is better than a bushel of BALLOTS," blazed the paper, and specific directions for manufacturing and setting bombs were published in its pages. Incendiarism and assassination were recommended. Articles gave advice on street-fighting tactics, and the *Arbeiter-Zeitung* enjoined its readers to prepare for the coming revolution.[72]

[72] August Spies, " August Spies on Anarchy," in A. R. Parsons, *Anarchism: Its Philosophy and Scientific Basis* . . . , p. 55; A. R. Parsons, " The Story of His Life," *loc. cit.,* p. 23; *The Alarm,* I (Nov. 1, 1884), 2, (May 2, 1885), 3, (May 16, 1885), 3, II (Sept. 5, 1885), 1, III (April 24, 1886), 1, 2; Schaack, *op. cit.,* p. 89. " In filling bombs use a little wooden stick, and never be careless," warned the *Alarm.* " Keep the stuff *pure!* Beware of sand. . . . It is necessary that the revolutionist should experiment for himself; especially should he practice the knack of throwing bombs. For further information address A. S., *Alarm,* 107 Fifth Av., Chicago." *The Alarm,* I (June 27, 1885), 1.

CHAPTER VIII

LABOR'S QUEST FOR SECURITY
(CONTINUED)

No LABOR LEADER in the sorrowful 'seventies had seen a way to bridge the yawning doctrinaire gulf between the various factions of the movement. Nor did the brief prosperity of the early 'eighties effect a reconciliation. By 1884, however, substantial wage reductions in many lines had wiped out the gains of the first years of the decade, and lower wages became the lot of blacksmiths, slaughterers, steel foundrymen, cigar packers, and many others.[1] " Wherever you go and wherever you sit," commented the *Illinois Staats-Zeitung*, " you hear people talk about bad times." A simultaneous decline in living costs was not sufficient to allay the uneasiness of the worker who over the months saw his pay grow less and less. Even such wages as he then enjoyed might, he realized, quickly disappear should he lose his job. Over everyone hovered the specter of unemployment. By October, 1884 twenty-five thousand were estimated out of work. As city relief rolls mounted, the County Agent's office, the St. Vincent de Paul Society, and other charitable organizations were hard pressed to meet demands. Applications to the Chicago Relief and Aid Society in the year ending October 31, 1885 were up 61 per cent from the previous year. Many, declared the *Western Catholic,* were

[1] For example, wages of carpenters, joiners, cabinetmakers, teamsters, and painters declined from 12 to 22 per cent. From 1882 to 1886 wages increased in 23, remained unchanged in 19, and declined in 72 trades in the state. Illinois Bureau of Labor Statistics, *Fourth Biennial Report, 1886*, pp. 336–61; *Illinois Staats-Zeitung*, Jan. 30, 1885; *The Drovers' Journal*, Dec. 3, 1884.

in "a state of destitution that is appalling." And accompanying these evidences of distress was the inevitable question as to who was responsible for these frequently recurring crises.[2]

Difficulties were further multiplied when the workingman tried to borrow money to tide his family over the days of unemployment, especially if he had no security, and he seldom had. Unscrupulous pawnbrokers reaped rich returns by limiting loans to no more than 25 to 50 per cent of the value of the collateral, and by charging interest rates that ran as high as 25 per cent a month. Fake " Intelligence Agencies," or employment offices, victimized the idle who in desperation gambled their last dollar on the chance of finding work. So enraged was the *Tribune* at these activities that it had Alfred S. Trude, prominent attorney, prosecute, as an example to others, one such "bloodsucker" before Justice John K. Prindiville, who fined the defendant $100 and costs for swindling a workman. At the same time, landlords, to quote the Citizens' Association Committee on Tenement Houses, 1884, "fleeced" renters for "the wretched tenements" they occupied at a rate of 25 to 40 per cent a year on the value of the property. In the light of such expenses a weekly wage ranging from two to twenty-five dollars seemed to the laborers of the city, when employed, lamentably small.[3]

In addition to rising unemployment, the economy was still further affected by a continuation of strikes to protest pay reductions, although fewer men deserted their jobs than in the opening years of the 'eighties. Early in 1884 laborers at Pullman's Palace Car Company struck when their daily pay scale was reduced from $1.50 to $1.30 and the working hours lengthened from eight to ten. In the various branches of the metal-working trades a series of walkouts over lower pay in 1884 and 1885 was marked by violence at the McCormick works. There, molders who had been cut 15 per cent late in 1884, "on account of hard times," struck the following March, asserting that the company had shown bad faith in not restoring the

[2] *Chicago Tribune*, Jan. 18, 1883; Ethelbert Stewart to Henry D. Lloyd, Oct. 24, 1884, *Lloyd Papers*; *The Western Catholic*, Jan. 24, 1885. The Chicago Relief and Aid Society granted assistance in 3,994 cases in response to 9,511 applications in the fiscal year ending Oct. 31, 1884; for the following year grants numbered 6,915 and applications 15,312. Chicago Relief and Aid Society, *Twenty-seventh Annual Report, 1884*, p. 18, *Twenty-eighth Annual Report, 1885*, p. 17.
[3] *Chicago Tribune*, Jan. 10, March 25, April 1, 1883; Citizens' Association of Chicago, *Report of the Committee on Tenement Houses, 1884*, pp. 9–10.

original pay scale as promised. On April 8 and 9 encounters between strikers and Pinkerton agents, who had been brought into the plant, occurred. Again, as in 1877, an exchange of shots endangered the lives not only of the participants but of women and children onlookers; and one man was seriously wounded.[4]

At the same time, agitation for an eight-hour workday, vigorously prosecuted in the 1860's, was reinvigorated in the 'eighties after an indifferent response from workmen in the depressed years of the 'seventies.[5] In it, labor saw the advantages of spreading work among more who needed it, of increasing opportunities for intellectual advancement, and extending other benefits now denied those who looked upon themselves as " the creators " of the wealth of the country. To this end, a resolution had been passed in 1882 by the Chicago Trade and Labor Assembly and brought before the Federation of Organized Trades and Labor Unions. While the Federation at its conventions in 1882, 1883, and 1884 endorsed the movement, it took no positive steps to implement it.[6]

By 1885 hard times renewed interest in the cause. Delegates at the Federation's fifth annual convention in Washington that year resolved that the Federation, as " a medium . . . to which belongs the leadership in this movement," carry on the fight for the eight-hour

[4] The action of the Pinkerton men the police described as cowardly and unwarranted, and four of these private agents were booked on manslaughter charges. The strike was over by April 12. In this instance the workers gained their demands. *Chicago Tribune*, March 6, April 8, 10, 12, 1885; *Svenska Tribunen*, April 15, 1885. For causes of Chicago strikes see U. S. Commissioner of Labor, *Third Annual Report, 1887* (Washington, 1888), pp. 100–31.

[5] Illinois Bureau of Labor Statistics, *Fourth Biennial Report, 1886*, p. 472; Pierce, *A History of Chicago*, II, 174–79. For sporadic eight-hour agitation during the 1870's, see *The Chicago Times*, May 18, 1874; *The Railway Age*, II (Aug. 9, 1877), 1201, IV (June 26, 1879), 301; *Die Fackel*, May 11, 1879; *Chicagoer Arbeiter-Zeitung*, May 12, June 6, 27, 28, 1879; *Illinois Staats-Zeitung*, May 14, July 5, 10, 23, 1879; *The Western Manufacturer*, VII (May 15, 1879), 3, (July 15, 1879), 56; *Chicago Tribune*, July 1, 5, 16, Aug. 4, Oct. 27, 1879.

[6] Federation of Organized Trades and Labor Unions, *Report of the Second Annual Session, 1882*, pp. 14–15, *Report of the Third Annual Session, 1883*, pp. 14, 16, *Report of the Fourth Annual Session, 1884*, pp. 11, 14, 17. Unlike the Knights of Labor, an eastern organization during its formative years, the Federation of Organized Trades and Labor Unions of the United States and Canada had close ties with the Middle West from its beginning. The call for the convention in Pittsburgh (Nov., 1881) at which the Federation was founded had among its thirteen endorsers George Rodgers, a leader in both the trade-union and Knights of Labor movements in Chicago. Richard Powers of the seamen's union, one of the Chicago delegates, was chosen president of the Legislative Committee at this convention, a position that made him effectively head of the Federation as it was then organized. Federation of Organized Trades and Labor Unions, *Report of the First Annual Session, 1881*, pp. 6, 23–24.

day. Unions were urged to form a united front for the cause. As a coercive measure a call for a general strike, desired by the extremists, was not endorsed by the convention, and any mention of the word " strike " was carefully avoided in the resolution, although no doubt was left that strikes would be resorted to if employers did not comply peaceably with eight-hour demands.[7]

In Chicago an endorsement of the Federation's eight-hour program by the leaders of the radical wing of labor came unexpectedly and ultimately proved painfully embarrassing to the original sponsors. In the minds of Parsons and his fellow workers in the Black International, the eight-hour day as such still had no promise as a way to improve labor's conditions so long as control of these conditions lay in the hands of employers. This attitude was openly expressed by Fielden when he said: " We do not object to it, but we do not believe in it. As to whether a man works eight hours a day or ten hours a day he is still a slave." Yet, in such a unified movement Chicago extremists now envisaged a potential source for the impregnation of the social revolution. Accordingly, the Central Labor Union, meeting on October 11, 1885, urged all members to unite behind the movement. That the anticipated unrest and conflict arising from eight-hour demands might be converted into a more general uprising was implied in resolutions encouraging members to obtain arms in order to be " in a position of meeting our foe with his own argument, force," if resistance were offered by " the governing class," who " prey[ed] upon the bones and marrow of the useful members of society." [8]

Sponsored by the Federation and spectacularly adopted by the Chicago anarchists, the eight-hour movement drew much of its support from the ranks of the Knights of Labor, though the top leaders of the order were unfriendly. Powderly was " certain that eight hours each day is sufficient for men to labor," but, like Parsons and others

[7] Commons, *op. cit.*, II, 376–77; Federation of Organized Trades and Labor Unions, *Report of the Fifth Annual Session, 1885*, pp. 11–14.

[8] *The Alarm*, Sept. 5, Oct. 17, Dec. 12, 1885; Dyer D. Lum, *A Concise History of the Great Trial of the Chicago Anarchists* . . . (Chicago, n.d.), pp. 16–19; Spies, *An Autobiographical Sketch*, pp. 26–27; A. R. Parsons, *Autobiography* (Ms. Chicago Historical Society), pp. 29–30; *Official Court Record of the Haymarket Trial, 1887*, " J," 425 (Ms. Chicago Historical Society), hereafter cited as *Haymarket Trial*. The use of force by the " depressed classes " was always justified by the extremists on the ground that employers protected their interests through the use of militia and private detectives. See, for example, *The Alarm*, June 13, Aug. 8, 1885, April 3, 1886.

in the radical camp, he believed that only a thoroughgoing reform of the economic system could free the worker from his unfortunate position. " The advocates of the eight-hour system must go beyond a reduction of the number of hours a man must work and labor for the establishment of a just and humane system . . . before he will be able to retain the vantage ground gained when the hours of labor are reduced to eight per day." At first the organ of the Chicago Knights of Labor assemblies, *The Knights of Labor,* favored the movement, though it later withdrew its support, holding the time was not propitious. But despite the coolness among the order's officials, the rank and file responded enthusiastically to the program, and the Knights' able staff of paid organizers zealously worked for it.[9]

The date chosen to make known to the country the determination of the nation's labor forces to inaugurate a general eight-hour day was May 1, 1886. Late 1885 and the early months of '86 were given over to solidifying ranks and publicizing aims. In Chicago an Eight-Hour Association, organized November 22, 1885, drew into nominal unity such diverse forces as the Knights of Labor, the Trade and Labor Assembly, the Socialistic Labor party, trade unions, and the anarchistic radicals. Mass meetings and rallies were held, and literature was distributed to arouse the workers' enthusiasm and educate public opinion. On March 15, four thousand union workmen jammed the West Side Turner Hall as thousands more demonstrated outside, unable to gain admittance. On April 10 an estimated seven thousand filled the Battery D Armory to listen to addresses by the public-spirited George C. Lorimer, pastor of Immanuel Baptist Church, and Judge Richard Prendergast of the County Court, while about two thousand more, unable to make their way into the hall, had to be accommodated at an overflow meeting. Alongside these gatherings, demonstrations under the sponsorship of the Central Labor Union went on. Here Spies, Schwab, Parsons, and other International stalwarts lashed out vigorously at those upon whom the labor-

---

[9] Powderly, *op. cit.,* pp. 514–15; *The Knights of Labor,* I (May 15, 1886), 8; Commons, *op. cit.,* II, 378–80; Carman, David, and Guthrie, *op. cit.,* pp. 142–43. Powderly's opposition to the eight-hour movement probably lost some of its effectiveness because it was issued as a secret circular (March 13, 1886), and apparently was unknown to many of the members. Knights of Labor, *Proceedings of the Tenth Regular Session of the General Assembly, 1886,* p. 39.

ing man must depend for employment, and, when the meetings were over, continued their diatribes in the columns of the radical press.[10]

Against this growing unity of sentiment among laborers, common action on their own part seemed necessary to most employers. Organizations already in existence or established for the specific purposes of resistance formed ranks to oppose the eight-hour day.[11] In the movement the majority of employers saw a threat to profits unless they raised prices, and this they knew would be but a temporary solution. And just what would the worker do with his extra time, they inquired, except to spend it in the neighborhood saloon? Then, too, would not shorter hours for the American laborer glut the market with job-hunting immigrants who, declared the *Drovers' Journal* dolefully, had already overrun it enough even under the hardest working conditions. But overshadowing all was a distrust of a unified labor force and apprehension as to what it might do to the normal process of business life. This anxiety, fanned by a press hostile to labor, by denunciations of labor's demands from the pulpit, and by expressions of opposition from a large segment of the public, mounted as May 1 drew near.[12]

On the other side, with leadership divided, the proponents of the eight-hour day were confronted by the dilemma of conflicting counsels, a situation which their employers did not face. Some soberly urged prudence and calm resolution; others a resort to force if need be. In this charged atmosphere the eight-hour movement surged for-

[10] Federation of Organized Trades and Labor Unions, *Report of the Fifth Annual Session, 1885*, p. 11; *Chicago Tribune*, Nov. 24, 1885, Jan. 19, March 16, April 11, 26, 1886; Ware, *op. cit.*, p. 314; *The Inter Ocean*, April 11, 1886; *The Alarm*, April 24, 1886; David, *op. cit.*, p. 184; Schaack, *op. cit.*, p. 105. For examples of other meetings, resolutions, addresses, and like agitational activities in the eight-hour drive, see *Chicago Tribune*, Nov. 12, 17, 1885, Jan. 19, April 2, 1886; *The Alarm*, Jan. 23, 1886; *Baltimore Labor Free Press*, Jan. 30, 1886; *Puget Sound Weekly Co-operator*, V (March 4, 1886), 3; *Svenska Tribunen*, March 27, 1886.

[11] Some employers promised more pay for ten hours of work. Some acceded to demands for an eight-hour day. *Chicago Tribune*, April 2, 17, 23, 28, 1886; *Svenska Tribunen*, March 27, 1886; George A. Schilling to Chas. Gossage Dry-Goods Store, April 17, 1886, *Labadie Collection* (Photostat, University of Michigan). For a list of firms granting the eight-hour day or making other concessions see *The Knights of Labor*, I (May 8, 1886), 6. The eight-hour movement is discussed in Illinois Bureau of Labor Statistics, *Fourth Biennial Report, 1886*, pp. 466–98.

[12] *The Drovers' Journal*, May 10, 1886. These arguments appeared in almost every English newspaper.

ward as a powerful but confused wave of enthusiasm for a redress of grievances. Alarmists beheld the approach of social revolution. What course events might run none could say. In dread and uncertainty men saw the dawn of May 1. Throughout industrial centers of the nation workers had struck or stood prepared to do so. *Bradstreet's* reported over 105,000 ready to leave their jobs if employers should prove recalcitrant, a figure later acknowledged as " below the mark." The spearhead of the attack lay in Chicago, where numerous strikes were already in progress and 62,000 additional workmen were determined to take up the struggle. Every sign pointed to impending tragedy, but the expected malefic incidents did not occur, and night fell after a day of peace. As yet, the " revolution " had not come.

Sunday, May 2, was also quiet. Employers and citizenry in general relaxed a little from the tension which had gripped them for weeks past, mindful that they were guarded by an alert police and militia. Quite likely, the city newspapers reflected, there would be no revolution after all; mutual restraint, the spirit of compromise, and common sense would span the period of crisis until adjustments could be made peaceably. Yet the peace which these two days had given was an uneasy one, filled with smoldering passions ready to burst forth at any moment. Danger was not yet past. On May 3 more strikes occurred. Again men and women marched through the streets and held meetings.[13]

Finally at the McCormick Harvesting Machine Company, where only the year before violence had occurred, the explosive incident came. Here since mid-February employees and owners had been at loggerheads. Though Cyrus H. McCormick, Jr., president of the company, had met most of the workers' demands — increasing wages and rehiring without prejudice men allegedly let out for engaging in union activity — he refused to dismiss five non-union men, asserting his " right to employ or discharge whom and as many " as he pleased. Union labor continued insistent. To cut short the argument, McCormick closed his plant on February 16 for an indefinite period. On the first of March the plant reopened under the protection of 160

[13] *Chicago Herald*, May 4, 1886; *Bradstreet's*, XIII (May 1, 1886), 274–75, (May 8, 1886), 290; David, *op. cit.*, pp. 183–84; *Chicago Tribune*, Jan. 19, Feb. 2, April 11, 13, May 2, 3, 1886; *The Inter Ocean*, May 2, 3, 4, 1886; *Chicago Evening Journal*, May 3, 1886; Flinn, *History of the Chicago Police*, p. 270; *Chicago Daily News*, May 4, 1886; *The Chicago Times*, May 4, 1886.

uniformed police and 75 detectives, and during March and April more "scabs" were imported with a complement of Pinkerton guards. The situation thus created was, to excited laboring men, another link in the chain of bondage from which they saw no easy escape.[14]

On May 3 the Lumber Shovers' Union, on strike for a reduction of hours, held a mass meeting not far from the McCormick works. Thither August Spies made his way to the "Black Road," where the strikers were gathered. He was at first denied a hearing because of his reputation as a radical, but eventually was allowed to speak.[15] While he was exhorting his listeners to persist in their demands, the dismissal bell rang at the McCormick plant. A small number of hangers-on about the fringes of the meeting left in the direction of the harvester works. Sounds of a clash were heard, but Spies urged his listeners to remain where they were, as they had no part in the McCormick quarrel. Soon several patrol wagons and an estimated seventy-five policemen on foot came hastening by Spies's meeting on their way to McCormick's. There guards had called for reinforcements to repel strikers who had assaulted harvester "scab" workmen as they came from their jobs, and who were now venting part of their wrath on the physical property of the factory. His speech concluded, Spies hurried to the scene. Distraught and filled with horror by the sight of what seemed to him a wanton attack of police on unarmed men, women, and children, he returned to the lumbermen's meeting. Excitedly he thundered that they must now act to aid their fellow workers, but he found his dissolving audience completely "unconcerned and indifferent."[16]

[14] *Chicago Tribune*, Feb. 15–17, 28, March 1, 1886; Schaack, *op. cit.*, pp. 113–15. The workers' demand that five non-union men be discharged was not designed to obtain a closed shop, but grew out of bitterness toward one of the foremen, William Ward, whose "tools" the five were declared to be. The men had confidence in McCormick personally, a legacy from happier days under his father, who had died two years before. See Hutchinson, *op. cit.*, II, 694–98.

[15] *Chicago Tribune*, May 2, 1886; *Svenska Tribunen*, May 8, 1886; Spies, *August Spies' Auto-Biography* . . . , pp. 40–41. It was said that some members of the unions had requested Spies to speak. The McCormick Harvesting Machine Company was located on Blue Island Avenue between Oakley and Western avenues. The Lumber Shovers' meeting was held at the corner of Wood Street and Blue Island, where railroad cars standing on a siding served as convenient platforms for the speakers. About a half-mile of open prairie stretched between the site of the meeting and the McCormick factory.

[16] *Haymarket Trial*, "M," 220–32, "N," 23–26; Spies, *August Spies' Auto-Biography* . . . , p. 42; Lum, *op. cit.*, pp. 129–30, 134. One man was killed and several, including

The restraint which Spies had at first imposed upon himself was now gone. Rushing to the *Arbeiter-Zeitung* office, he penned in both English and German the inflammatory appeal known as the Revenge Circular.

REVENGE!

WORKINGMEN, TO ARMS! ! !

Your masters sent out their bloodhounds — the police — ; they killed six of your brothers at McCormicks [*sic*] this afternoon. They killed the poor wretches, because they, like you, had the courage to disobey the supreme will of your bosses. They killed them, because they dared ask for the shortenin [*sic*] of the hours of toil. They killed them to show you, "Free American Citizens", that you must be satisfied and contended [*sic*] with whatever your bosses condescend to allow you, or you will get killed!

You have for years endured the most abject humiliations; you have for years suffered unmeasurable iniquities; you have worked yourself to death; you have endured the pangs of want and hunger; your Children you have sacrificed to the factory-lords — in short: You have been miserable and obedient slave [*sic*] all these years: Why? To satisfy the insatiable greed, to fill the coffers of your lazy, thieving master? When you ask them now to lessen your burden, he sends his bloodhounds out to shoot you, kill you!

If you are men, if you are the sons of your grand sires, who have shed their blood to free you, then you will rise in your might, Hercules, and destroy the hideous monster that seeks to destroy you. To arms we call you, to arms!

YOUR BROTHERS.

That evening half of the nearly twenty-five hundred circulars which had been printed were distributed.[17]

---

five policemen, injured in the fighting at the McCormick plant. The exact number of casualties was never determined. *Haymarket Trial*, "O," 237; *Chicago Tribune*, May 4, 1886; *Chicago Evening Journal*, May 4, 1886.

[17] Spies disclaimed responsibility for the "REVENGE!" streamer. It was added, he maintained, by a compositor who "thought it made a good heading." The language of the German and English versions of the circular differed. Spies, *August Spies' Auto-Biography . . .* , pp. 42–43; "People's Exhibit 6," *Haymarket Trial Exhibits, 1887* (Ms. Chicago Historical Society, hereafter cited as *Trial Exhibits*); *In the Supreme Court of Illinois, Northern Grand Division, March Term, A.D. 1887. August Spies et al., vs. The People of the State of Illinois, Brief on the Facts for Defendants in Error* (Chicago, 1887), pp. 157–62 (hereafter cited as *Brief on the Facts for Defendants*); *Haymarket Trial*, "N," 23–26, 27; *Chicago Daily News*, May 3, 4, 1886.

The following morning, a circular, struck off in German and English, called in ringing tones for a mass meeting that evening at the Haymarket.[18] Thus was laid the groundwork for what is now commonly called " the Haymarket Riot," the tragic climax to the activities of the Chicago anarchists. On this momentous day of May 4, 1886 the headlines in the daily press served only to alarm and to reinvigorate the hysteria which had been built up in the past months. " A Wild Mob's Work. Ten Thousand Men Storm M'Cormick's Harvester Works. Wrought up to a Frenzy by Anarchistic Harangues They Attack the Employes [sic] as They come from Work. Two Hundred Police Charge the Rabble and Use Their Revolvers. Rioters and Policemen Wounded," screamed the *Tribune*. The *Times* headlines began " Riot Reigns," and the *Journal*'s caption read " POLICE UNDER ARMS . . . Bloodshed." [19]

That evening shortly after eight o'clock Spies reached the Haymarket, where already small and apparently lethargic groups, in which some women were intermingled with the men, had begun to assemble. At Spies's request, in order to be clear of the heavy traffic through the Haymarket, they moved about a half-block north on Desplaines Street near the mouth of Crane's Alley, a driveway at the side of Crane Brothers Manufacturing Company's building. Here Spies mounted an empty express wagon and opened the meeting.[20]

[18] " People's Exhibit 5," *Trial Exhibits.*

Attention Workingmen!
GREAT
MASS–MEETING
TO–NIGHT, at 7.30 o'clock
AT THE

HAYMARKET, Randolph St., Bet. Desplaines and Halsted.

Good Speakers will be present to denounce the latest atrocious act of the police, the shooting of our fellow-workmen yesterday afternoon.

Workingmen Arm Yourselves and Appear in Full Force!

THE EXECUTIVE COMMITTEE

Upon the insistence of Spies, who at first was not aware of the wording of the circular, the final line, " Workingmen Arm Yourselves and Appear in Full Force! " was stricken from the copy, although some of the circulars had already been distributed. *Haymarket Trial,* " N," 32, " O," 236.

[19] *Chicago Tribune*, May 4, 1886; *The Chicago Times*, May 4, 1886; *Chicago Evening Journal*, May 4, 1886.

[20] The " Haymarket," or " Haymarket Square," in 1886 was a widening of Randolph Street between Desplaines and Halsted streets; it was crossed near its center by Union Street. In the course of time this section of the city had changed, and the square was no longer the site of an open-air produce market as it had once been. A detailed map of the area may be found in *Brief on the Facts for Defendants*, p. 267. The wagon, which served as an

Courtesy of the Chicago Historical Society

THE BATTLE AFTER THE EXPLOSION OF THE BOMB AT HAYMARKET SQUARE, CHICAGO, MAY 4, 1886

THE DESPLAINES STREET POLICE STATION AFTER THE RIOT AT HAYMARKET SQUARE

His speech of about twenty minutes was followed by one by Albert R. Parsons, who dwelt principally on the worker's small share of the capitalist's income. Even the occasional intemperate remarks with which Parsons embellished an otherwise moderate discourse failed to arouse the largely unsympathetic crowd, and people began to leave. Among those who departed was Mayor Carter H. Harrison, impressed by the harmlessness of the meeting and the apathy of the listeners. The last to speak was the stone teamster Samuel Fielden, whose description of the worker's insecurity failed to hold the crowd, now scattering rapidly before an approaching storm cloud.

Not far from the scene was the Desplaines Street Police Station, where about one hundred and eighty policemen were stationed for any emergency. On his way from the meeting Mayor Harrison reported to the officer in charge at the station, Inspector John Bonfield, that the speakers had about finished and that it did not look as though any interference would be needed.[21] In spite of this, a few minutes later Bonfield and Captain William Ward formed their men in ranks and, taking their places at the head of the column, marched on the meeting. Just as Fielden was concluding his address, Ward lifted his hand and shouted: "I command you in the name of the people of the State of Illinois to immediately and peaceably disperse." To this, Fielden indignantly protested that the assemblage was peaceable, but he ceased speaking and stepped from the wagon. Suddenly a bomb fell, exploding near the head of the police column.[22] Instantly panic, wild and terrifying, swept through the crowd, magnified still more as an exchange of revolver shots between the

informal rostrum at the meeting, stood at the rear of Crane Brothers Manufacturing Company, which faced Jefferson Street, the next street east of Desplaines. Police asserted that the transfer of the meeting from the Haymarket to Desplaines Street was "plotted" to place them disadvantageously in a narrow area when the anarchists should attack. *Haymarket Trial,* "N," 34–35; Flinn, *History of the Chicago Police,* pp. 299–303; Schaack, *op. cit.,* pp. 141–43.

[21] The actions of Mayor Harrison at the Haymarket are a critical point in discussions of the events of that night. Bonfield's decision to descend on the meeting after the Mayor's report that there was no danger has been severely criticized. On the other hand, it has been asserted that the early moderation of the speakers changed after the Mayor departed. Harrison testified at the trial that he thought Spies had recognized him, and that thereafter Spies had spoken more temperately. *Haymarket Trial,* "L," 28–45. See also Spies, *August Spies' Auto-Biography* . . . , pp. 70–71; David, *op. cit.,* pp. 281–85; Schaack, *op. cit.,* p. 144; *Chicago Tribune,* Aug. 3, 1886.

[22] *Haymarket Trial,* "K," 44–45, "I," 21–22, 24, 234, 429, 439, "L," 28–50; Willis John Abbot, *Carter Henry Harrison* . . . (New York, 1895), pp. 141–43; *Chicago Tribune,* May 5, 1886.

police and armed men took its toll in the death of Policeman Matthias J. Degan, one civilian, and the wounding of sixty-six officers and twelve other persons.[23]

Horror and fear now enveloped Chicago. The press shouted for vengeance, and widespread public opinion endorsed this stand. On Sunday, clergymen exhorted their congregations to oppose lenience — though little enough prevailed — and urged the authorities to hang " the murderers." The liberal David Swing, pastor of the independent Central Church, voiced his alarm when he declared: " We need a careful definition of what freedom is. If it means the license to proclaim the gospel of disorder, to preach destruction, and scatter the seeds of anarchy and death, the sooner we exchange the Republic for an ironhanded monarchy the better it will be for all of us." From men of the law came no greater insistence for a delayed judgment. The eminent attorney Charles C. Bonney held that labor was chiefly responsible for its own ills, that anarchism and labor were allies, and that the bomb constituted " a waiver of trial and a plea of guilty." [24] Even labor leaders joined in the cry. *The Knights of Labor* held the anarchists " cowardly murderers, cutthroats, and robbers," deserving " no more consideration than wild beasts," and the city's oldest trade union, Typographical No. 16, stigmatized those directly responsible for the throwing of the bomb as " the greatest enemy the laboring man has." Throughout the country, public opinion almost unanimously called for reprisals on the radical fringe of society. *The New York Times* demanded death for the " cowardly savages," and the *Philadelphia Inquirer* recommended repression by a " mailed hand " to teach " foreign Anarchists " that the United States was no " shelter for cutthroats and thieves." [25]

[23] As in the case of the riot at the McCormick factory on May 3, it was impossible to determine how many civilians were casualties at the Haymarket. Degan died almost instantly, and six other officers died from wounds between May 6 and May 16, 1886; a seventh died June 13, 1888, from a lingering illness attributed to a bullet wound received at the Haymarket. The city paid $9,000 doctors' bills for wounded policemen. *Chicago Tribune,* May 5, 7, 9, 10, 15, 17, 1886; Chicago Superintendent of Police, *Report, 1886,* pp. 61–63, *1888,* p. 74; *Public Opinion,* II (Jan. 22, 1887), 317.

[24] Bonney tempered his condemnation, however, by declaring that " the greed, the selfishness, the neglect and folly of wealth and power " contributed to the " injurious conflict." Charles Carroll Bonney, *The Present Conflict of Labor and Capital* (Chicago, 1886), pp. 16, 24. For examples of press and pulpit reaction, see the *Chicago Tribune,* May 5, 6, 7, 8, 9, 1886, and for a general discussion see David, *op. cit.,* pp. 208–10.

[25] *The Knights of Labor,* I (May 8, 1886), 1; *Chicago Tribune,* May 11, 1886; *The New York Times,* May 6, 1886; *The Philadelphia Inquirer,* May 5, 1886. For numerous examples

Within the troubled city a wave of anti-foreign sentiment engulfed men of toil who had come from abroad, which often failed to distinguish between the few who subscribed to the theory of anarchism and those who, like the native born, now insisted upon a hasty punishment.[26] Insistence upon more extensive police protection and increased vigilance on the part of the government and the citizenry itself brought into existence the First Council of the Conservators' League of America, a secret organization of businessmen to counteract the "recent labor troubles" and to stand on guard for the future.[27] The Chicago Citizens' Association, which had extended its program beyond the original purpose of promoting better fire protection after the fire of 1874, offered to serve the city in any capacity needed. Police and private operatives engaged in feverish activity. People were thrown into jail without warrants, and freedom of speech and assembly seemed in danger of extinction. The color red became a sign of dishonor, and to be known as a socialist was to be classed among the outcasts.[28]

In this atmosphere of fear, prejudice, and determination to wipe anarchism out, the Haymarket case came to trial.[29] A coroner's in-

of the condemnatory editorials in papers outside Chicago, see the *Chicago Tribune*, May 6, 9, 1886.

[26] *Ibid.*, May 9, 13, 17, 18, Sept. 23, Oct. 1, 1886; *Svenska Tribunen*, May 8, 1886; *Chicagoer Freie Presse*, May 8, 1886; *Chicago Herald*, June 24, 1886. Under the weight of disapproval some Germans withdrew from the Verein. Foreign groups felt the weight of adverse public opinion long after the incident of the bombing, since people failed to remember that anarchists were not all of foreign birth. For attempts to restore public confidence in them see, for example, *L'Italia*, Sept. 17, 1887; *Illinois Staats-Zeitung*, May 23, 1888.

[27] Among the promoters of the Conservators' League were Morris Selz, Mark Bangs, Judson M. W. Jones, and Nathaniel S. Bouton. (*Chicago Tribune*, July 1, 1886.) By Aug. 15, contribution to a police relief fund had reached $70,361.43. Among large individual contributors were Potter Palmer, $1,000; William M. Devine and Levi Z. Leiter, $500 each; Cyrus H. McCormick and Frank Parmelee, $250 each. The Chicago Board of Trade gave $13,046, the Lumberman's Exchange $7,780, and the Iroquois Club $1,900. Chicago Superintendent of Police, *Report, 1886*, pp. 64–79; *Chicago Tribune*, May 6, 14, 1886.

[28] The Citizens' Association named a committee to meet daily. It was made up of wealthy and prominent businessmen: Cyrus McCormick, Philip D. Armour, Murry Nelson, Marshall Field, George M. Pullman, Anthony F. Seeberger, William J. Quan, Henry M. King, and Edward G. Mason. *Chicago Tribune*, May 6, July 1, 1886; Citizens' Association, *Annual Report, 1886*, pp. 33–36. For activities of the police and private detectives see *Haymarket Trial*, "I," 453–54, 462–63, "J," 93–97, "K," 515–17; David, *op. cit.*, pp. 221–26; Schaack, *op. cit.*, pp. 156–375; Charles A. Siringo, *A Cowboy Detective* (Chicago, 1912), pp. 21–23; and issues of the Chicago daily papers during the month of May.

[29] Considerable literature has been inspired by the Haymarket riot and trial. By 1897 works had appeared in English, German, Spanish, Portuguese, Dutch, Italian, Czech, and French. (M[ax] Nettlau, *Bibliographie de L'Anarchie* [Bruxelles, 1897], pp. 179–83.) In addition to the study by Henry David and other works cited in this chapter, see George N.

quest held May 5 over the body of Officer Degan found that death had been caused by " a wound produced by a piece of bomb, thrown by an unknown person, aided, and abetted, and encouraged by August Spies, Christ Spies, Michael Schwab, A. R. Parsons, Samuel Fielden, and other unknown persons," and recommended that these be held to the grand jury without bail. The grand jury, sitting under Judge John G. Rogers, met May 17, and ten days later returned indictments against Parsons, Schwab, Fielden, Engel, August Spies, Adolph Fischer, Louis Lingg, Oscar Neebe, Rudolph Schnaubelt, and William Seliger.[30] A true bill was rendered June 4 which charged these defendants with being accessories before the fact to the murder of Degan by a bomb; with murder by pistol shots; with being accessories to one another in the murder of Degan; and with general conspiracy to murder.[31] Feeling that Judge Rogers was prejudiced, the defense attorneys applied for a change of venue. This was granted on June 10 and the case removed to the court of Judge

McLean, *The Rise and Fall of Anarchy in America* . . . (Chicago, 1888); *The Chicago Anarchists and the Haymarket Massacre* . . . (Chicago, 1887); *Anarchy at an End. Lives, Trial, and Conviction of the Eight Chicago Anarchists* . . . (Chicago, 1886); Charles A. Siringo, *Two Evil Isms, Pinkertonism and Anarchism* (Chicago, 1915). A fictionalized account is Frank Harris, *The Bomb* (New York, 1920).

[30] *Chicago Tribune*, May 6, 28, 29, 1886; Sigmund Zeisler, *Reminiscences of the Anarchist Case* (Chicago, 1927), p. 12. The reports of the grand jury stated that evidence showed that the " deliberate conspiracy " to attack the police was not part of the current labor troubles, but that use had been made of the excitement which accompanied the general unrest. While the danger had been " imminent and serious," the report continued, its extent had been " largely magnified " in the public mind. The jury had been reliably assured that the total number of dangerous anarchists in the country probably did not exceed forty or fifty, but that there might be some two or three thousand communists or socialists who were not necessarily dangerous. *Chicago Daily News*, June 5, 1886; *The Inter Ocean*, June 6, 1886.

[31] Fischer, a compositor on the *Arbeiter-Zeitung*, had been associated with Engel in the publication of the unsuccessful *The Anarchist*. Of all the anarchists prominent in the Chicago movement, Lingg, twenty-one-year-old carpenter, alone seems to have been fitted temperamentally for decisive and desperate action. Prior to his arrest, he was unknown to the public. Neebe was a prosperous yeast salesman. Two of those named in the true bill, Schnaubelt and Seliger, never came to trial. The latter, a carpenter, was Lingg's principal assistant in the manufacture of bombs, the site of their operations being Seliger's house, where Lingg was a boarder. Seliger turned state's evidence and was not prosecuted. Schnaubelt, a brother-in-law of Schwab, was arrested early, but was released as an unimportant figure in the anarchist group. Fielden, a teamster, together with Parsons, were the only two of the anarchists who were not German or of German descent. Schnaubelt was later said to have been the actual bomb-thrower, but he was never apprehended. He has remained the " mystery man " of the Haymarket affair. Positive evidence on these matters has never been found. Lawson, *op. cit.*, XII, 4–5, 15–17, 55–57; Schaack, *op. cit.*, pp. 159, 169, 170–72, 256–77; Zeisler, *op. cit.*, pp. 11–13; David, *op. cit.*, pp. 508–14; *The Chicago Sun Book Week*, June 8, 1947.

Joseph E. Gary, but efforts to postpone the trial until fevered passions had somewhat cooled proved unavailing. On the fifteenth of July, the prosecution opened its case, and the great trial, perhaps unsurpassed for dramatic intensity in the whole annals of American jurisprudence, was under way.[32]

A jury whose open-mindedness was suspect heard the testimony, some of which was of dubious accuracy. In presenting its case, the defense sought to prove that the accused, with the exception of Spies and Fielden, were elsewhere when the bomb was thrown, and that the bomb did not come from the hand of either of these two, because they stood near the front rank of the police when the explosion occurred. If these were the facts, pleaded the defense attorneys, how then could any man in the prisoners' dock be found guilty of murdering Officer Degan? The state, it was contended, must prove that the defendants were themselves guilty of throwing the bomb or that their inciting speeches and plotting had led directly to the deed.

The state, on the other hand, tried to link the accused men to the alleged bomb-thrower, Schnaubelt, by the testimony of an itinerant house-painter, Harry Gilmer. Gilmer's testimony that Spies had slipped from the speakers' wagon, met Schnaubelt at the entrance of Crane's Alley, and there lighted the fuse of the bomb which Schnaubelt held ready to throw, was practically destroyed by the defense. The prosecution took the position that, even if Schnaubelt were not the actual culprit, the guilt of the defendants would be proved were they shown to be engaged in a conspiracy against the established order. The fearsome picture of a city menaced by a desperate band of anarchist plotters, thus drawn by the prosecution and then highlighted by voluminous quotations from the *Alarm,* the *Arbeiter-Zeitung,* and the public speeches of the accused, could not be overcome. "Anarchy is on trial," cried Julius S. Grinnell, the state's

[32] *Haymarket Trial,* "I," 4–20; Zeisler, *op. cit.,* p. 15; *Chicago Tribune,* June 11, 1886; Lawson, *op. cit.,* XII, 24. A trial jury was selected after 981 persons were examined. Some of the jurors admitted opinions as to guilt, but on appeal the Illinois Supreme Court ruled that the fitness of only one, Harry Taylor Sanford, was subject to review, and that he had been a competent juror. *Chicago Tribune,* July 16, 1886; *Haymarket Trial,* "A," 137, 141, "B," 20, 112–14, 277–79, 282, "C," 272, 275, "D," 251, 343, 345, 348, "F," 130–31, "G," 252–54, 266, 355, 360, "H," 30, 46, 298, 308; *In the Supreme Court of Illinois, Northern Grand Division, March Term, A.D. 1887. August Spies et al., vs. The People of the State of Illinois, Brief on the Law for Defendants in Error* (Chicago, 1887), pp. 113–39; Illinois Supreme Court, *Advance Sheets of the Illinois Reports* (Norman L. Freeman, comp.), CXXII, no. 1, *Anarchist Case* (Springfield, 1887), pp. 258–64.

attorney, in his summation, and against the charge of anarchy, un-mentioned in the indictment, there seemed no defense.[33]

On August 19, after deliberating three hours, the jury reached a verdict. The following day the court imposed the death penalty on Spies, Schwab, Fielden, Parsons, Fischer, Engel, and Lingg for mur-der, and sentenced Oscar Neebe to fifteen years' imprisonment on the same grounds. A defense motion for a new trial was denied, and on October 9 Judge Gary set the date for execution as December 3, 1886. The verdict was acclaimed in Chicago as just. To attempt to condemn it as solely a judgment on anarchism placed the critic alongside dangerous and disreputable members of society. The rest of the country, too, hailed the verdict as a demonstration of the power of constituted authority over subversive influences. " I cannot see but that it is good law upon which they are convicted; whether the evidence supported the theory or not, I cannot say," wrote Henry C. Adams to Henry D. Lloyd in November. The example set by this conviction of revolutionaries appeared to the nervous a deathblow to the preachments of anarchism.[34]

Leonard Swett, the well-known lawyer who had lived in Chicago since 1865, was now procured through the tireless efforts of a defense committee which worked assiduously to raise funds to assist in the appeal from Judge Gary's decision. Headed by Dr. Ernst Schmidt and composed of men like justice-loving George Schilling, the com-mittee had an air of respectability that won it some countenance even among those unsympathetic to the prisoners. On November 2, Swett applied to Chief Justice John M. Scott of the Illinois Supreme Court for a writ of error on twenty-eight grounds. The writ was granted and issued as a supersedeas to stay execution of the judg-

[33] *Haymarket Trial,* " K," 408–9, 438, " L," 70, 150–56, 195–203, 222–35, 267–73, 280–81, 326–37, 521–23, " M," 39, 95–105, 148, 190–91, 213, 264–66; Lawson, *op. cit.,* XII, 252. Grinnell was assisted in the prosecution by George C. Ingham, Francis W. Walker, and Edmund Furthmann. Defense attorneys were William P. Black, William A. Foster, Sigmund Zeisler, and Moses Salomon. Judge Gary's address to the jury showed clearly that he was of the same mind as the prosecution. (*Haymarket Trial,* " I," 75–86, " O," 5–6, 23.) For a general statement of the case presented by each side, see David, *op. cit.,* pp. 289–305.

[34] *Haymarket Trial,* " O," 48–52, 143–50; Henry C. Adams to Henry Demarest Lloyd, Nov. 18, 1886, *Lloyd Papers.* Each prisoner was given an opportunity to speak. See *The Accused The Accusers. The Famous Speeches of the Eight Chicago Anarchists in Court* (Chicago, n.d.). An extensive survey of the favorable reaction to the verdict expressed by out-of-town newspapers appeared in the *Chicago Tribune,* Aug. 21, 1886. See also the *Illinois Staats-Zeitung,* Aug. 23, 1886.

ment against the condemned men late that month, but not until March 2, 1887 did the court begin its hearings of the case with Zeisler aiding Swett in the presentation of arguments. Over six months later, on September 14, the court announced " that neither in the record and proceedings . . . nor in the rendition of the judgment . . . is there anything erroneous, vicious, or defective." [35]

Again the court's decision commanded general approval, but time had softened much of the original rancor, and independent-minded persons recognized that public hysteria may breed grave injustice. Protests from William Dean Howells, Robert G. Ingersoll, George Francis Train, and William M. Salter showed in what varied circles the manifest unfairness of the trials had aroused sympathy and indignation. [36] Among Chicagoans holding this opinion, Henry D. Lloyd and Lyman J. Gage played a prominent part. The latter urged executive clemency for the condemned men, and, feeling that moral suasion and understanding must supplement law enforcement within the increasingly complex structure of society, he organized a discussion group, the important Economic Club, which brought together men of all shades of belief. Lloyd, deeply touched by the plight of Spies and his fellows, visited them in jail and called in person on Governor Richard J. Oglesby to plead for a commutation of sentence. [37]

Such protests called for real courage. Gage found businessmen who sympathized with his efforts hanging back because they feared the disfavor of Marshall Field and others who strongly opposed leniency.

[35] Zeisler, *op. cit.*, pp. 16–17; *The Knights of Labor*, I (Jan. 29, 1887), 5; *Haymarket Trial*, " O," 155–60, 169–70; *Chicago Legal News*, XIX (Nov. 27, 1886), 89; *Chicago Tribune*, March 3, 19, Sept. 15, 1887. Defense funds came mostly from workers associated with the German socialist organizations. Powderly ordered the Knights to give no aid, but the local journal *The Knights of Labor*, which had strongly condemned the anarchists immediately after the bombing, by Oct., 1886 expressed grave doubts that any good could come from the executions. (*Chicago Tribune*, May 23, June 14, July 5, Dec. 22, 1886, Aug. 8, 1887; *The Knights of Labor*, I [May 22, 1886], 1, [Oct. 16, 1886], 1.) Justice Benjamin D. Magruder delivered the opinion of the court. *Haymarket Trial*, " O," 172–387.

[36] *Chicago Tribune*, Sept. 15, 23, Oct. 6, Nov. 4, 1887, and the *New York Mail and Express* quoted by the *Tribune*, Sept. 16, 1887; *The Knights of Labor*, II (Nov. 5, 1887), 5; Albert Mordell, *Quaker Militant John Greenleaf Whittier* (Boston, 1933), pp. 261–62. Salter's lecture, delivered at the Grand Opera House, Oct. 23, 1887, created a sensation and brought upon him a storm of abuse, both from those who felt he had gone too far and from those who felt he had not gone far enough in his defense of the anarchists.

[37] [Gage], *Memoirs of Lyman J. Gage*, pp. 69–71; Caro Lloyd, *Henry Demarest Lloyd 1847–1903* . . . (2 v. New York, 1912), I, 87, 93–98, II, 330–39; Henry D. Lloyd to Aaron Lloyd, Nov. 18, 1887. *Lloyd Papers*.

In spite of opposition and disapproval, however, support came from many and diverse quarters. Judges of the Circuit Court Murray F. Tuley, Frank Baker, William K. McAllister, and Thomas Moran; attorneys M. M. Trumbull and Benjamin F. Ayer; business leaders Potter Palmer and William R. Manierre; and the Reverend Emil G. Hirsch of the Sinai Temple joined the number begging clemency. Samuel Gompers, steadfastly maintaining that " trade unionists had no reason to sympathize with the cause of the anarchists as such," solemnly contended to the Illinois governor that a country " great and magnanimous enough to grant amnesty to Jeff Davis " could do as much for the anarchists. General Benjamin F. Butler drew a similar analogy to the amnestied Confederate soldiers. From abroad came a petition for mercy to Governor Oglesby, bearing sixteen thousand signatures obtained by English workingmen's clubs, and Annie Besant, Sir Walter Besant, Walter Crane, Stopford Brooke, and William Morris added their voices to those protesting the court's decision.[38]

Many other appeals went to Springfield, but two events made their success unlikely. On November 6 four bombs, allegedly to be used to destroy the jail, were found in Louis Lingg's cell. Furthermore, Lingg, Engel, and Fischer wrote the Governor, protesting their innocence and demanding that they be either freed or hanged. Oglesby, convinced of their guilt, would not grant their request for pardon, but on November 10 he commuted Fielden's and Schwab's sentences to life imprisonment.[39] Meanwhile, the defendants' last hope faded when the United States Supreme Court, after hearing arguments by General Roger A. Pryor, Benjamin Butler, and J. Randolph Tucker, refused to intervene. At the last minute Lingg cheated the hangman

[38] Caro Lloyd, *op. cit.*, I, 87–90, 101; Gage, *op. cit.*, 71; Samuel Gompers, *Seventy Years of Life and Labor* (2 v. New York, 1925), II, 178, 180; *Chicago Tribune*, Sept. 23, Nov. 9, 13, 1887. Many prominent persons, as well as the less-known, joined the movement for clemency. Judge Gary wrote Oglesby petitioning for commutation of sentence for Fielden and Schwab, as an act of mercy. His article " The Chicago Anarchists of 1886; The Crime, the Trial, and the Punishment," *The Century Magazine*, XLV (April, 1893), 803–37, is a detailed defense of the justice of the trial proceedings and the judgment. M[athew] M. Trumbull, *The Trial of the Judgment* . . . (Chicago, 1888), pp. 73–74; *Chicago Tribune*, Nov. 7, 1887.

[39] Much controversy has surrounded the question of how the bombs got into Lingg's cell. Their discovery, in the midst of the concerted drive for clemency, proved harmful to the men's chances. *Ibid.*, Nov. 2, 7, 11, 1887; David, *op. cit.*, pp. 436–39; *The Pictorial West*, Nov., 1887, p. 13.

by exploding a detonating cap in his mouth. On November 11, 1887 the remaining four unfalteringly met their death in the Cook County jail by hanging. On the bulletin board of the Palmer House appeared the laconic notice: " Trap fell. Spies Parson Fischer & Engle expiate their crime & the law vindicated." [40]

No violent reaction followed; the demonstrations for which the police had so carefully prepared did not take place. Chicago was a city of silence. Huge crowds fringed the streets as the funeral processions passed by, and thousands attended the simple services devoid of religious rites at Waldheim Cemetery. " The spell is over," wrote Schilling to Joseph Labadie. " Really the *gloom* of the County Jail for 2 or 3 nights was my blanket[.] I never had such a bitter experience in my life." For others, the remarks of the *Illinois Staats-Zeitung* epitomized their release from anxiety and a return to normal living: " The bloodshed of May 4, 1886, is now atoned. . . . Yesterday's executions marked the beginning of the end of anarchy in America." [41]

But upon the history of Chicago the fate of this handful of sincere but misguided men left an indelible mark. Remembered for having aroused the ugly reaction of intolerance and fear, they remain representative of the injustice which stems from a public opinion stripped of calm judgment. None, perhaps, so well understood the tragedy and the folly of the Haymarket as did the compassionate Schilling. Tireless in behalf of the condemned men as long as there was anything to be done, he never let his sympathies destroy his perspective. " When you terrorize the public mind with violence," said he, " you create the conditions which place the Bonfields and the Garys in the saddle, hailed as the savior [*sic*] of society. Fear is not the mother of progress and liberty, but oft times of reaction and aggression. . . . They [the anarchists] worshiped at the shrine of force; wrote it and

[40] Spies *v*. Illinois, 123 U. S. 131 (1887); *Bulletin of the Haymarket Riot Execution* (*Ms.* Chicago Historical Society. Spelling and punctuation as in the original). The court's decision was handed down Nov. 2, 1887, nine days before the executions. (*Chicago Tribune*, Nov. 3, 1887.) The unflinching bravery of the men won admiration in many quarters. See, for example, *The Knights of Labor*, II (Nov. 12, 1887), 1–2; *Haymarket Trial*, " I," 130; Zeisler, *op. cit.*, pp. 22–23; David, *op. cit.*, pp. 428–30, 446–48.

[41] *Chicago Tribune*, Nov. 14, 1887; *The Inter Ocean*, Nov. 14, 1887; *The Alarm*, I (Nov. 19, 1887), 1; *Illinois Staats-Zeitung*, Nov. 12, 1887; George A. Schilling to Joseph Labadie, Nov. 6, 1887 [*sic*], *Labadie Collection* (*Ms.* University of Michigan). Schilling's letter is obviously misdated.

preached it; until finally they were overpowered by their own Gods and slain in their own temple." [42]

Several groups continued efforts for pardon or clemency for the surviving anarchists. The flush of panic passed; conscience rode hard upon the hearts of many. " Who that saw it can ever forget that Sunday funeral procession . . . the sobering impression of the amnesty of death, the still more sobering question whether we had done right? " reflected Charles Edward Russell. The election of John Peter Altgeld to the governorship in 1892 gave new hope. Scores of Chicago industrialists, financiers, and professional men joined in signing a petition to the new governor bearing 60,000 names.[43]

On June 26, 1893 Altgeld pardoned Schwab, Fielden, and Neebe on the ground that the jury was packed through the efforts of special bailiff Henry L. Ryce, that the jury was prejudiced, that the defendants were not proved guilty of the crimes charged in the indictment, that there was no case at all against Neebe, and that Judge Gary conducted the trial with marked prejudice for the state. Although a brave manifestation of the high moral courage for which Governor Altgeld was famed, it was unfortunate that in coloring his message with personal animosities he missed the opportunity of writing a great state paper. In liberal circles his action aroused great enthusiasm, but in large groups of conservatives the granting of absolute pardons appeared a shocking miscarriage of a governor's power.[44]

Despite the hostility against labor and its demands following the Haymarket tragedy, workingmen did not entirely lose hope, nor did the eight-hour movement suffer the immediate collapse its opponents

[42] George A. Schilling to Lucy Parsons, Dec. 1, 1893, *Labadie Collection.*

[43] Charles Edward Russell, " The Haymarket and Afterwards, Some Personal Recollections," *Appleton's Magazine,* X (Oct., 1907), 411; Waldo R. Browne, *Altgeld of Illinois* . . . (New York, 1924), p. 87. Still active were Schilling, Lloyd, Gage, Salomon, Butler, and others who had sought to aid the anarchists in earlier years. None worked harder for the pardon of Schwab, Fielden, and Neebe than did the banker Edward S. Dreyer, who had served as foreman of the grand jury and in that capacity had been excoriated by Spies as motivated by a desire for personal revenge. Brand Whitlock, *Forty Years of It* (New York, 1914), p. 74; Spies, *August Spies' Auto-Biography* . . . , pp. 68–69.

[44] *Chicago Tribune,* June 27, 1893; Whitlock, *op. cit.,* pp. 71–74; John P. Altgeld, *Reasons for Pardoning Fielden, Neebe and Schwab* (n.p., n.d.); [Albert Shaw], "The Various Bearings of the Matter," *The Review of Reviews,* VIII (Aug., 1893), 135–36; David, *op. cit.,* p. 499; *Abendpost,* June 27, 1893; *The Chicago Times,* June 27, 1893; Theodore Roosevelt, *Campaigns and Controversies* (Hermann Hagedorn, ed., *The Works of Theodore Roosevelt,* XIV. New York, 1926), pp. 259, 273; Samuel P. McConnell, " The Chicago Bomb Case, Personal Recollections of an American Tragedy," *Harper's Magazine,* CLXVIII (May, 1934), 739.

forecast. Even in the fateful May of 1886 some firms conceded the shorter day to their employees, and by mid-June *Bradstreet's* was cautioning those who were belittling the movement that they would do well to look at the facts. Seventy thousand Chicago workers, particularly in the tobacco factories, furniture, tanning, packing, and in the building trades, had obtained concessions in one form or another; and the majority of the gains had come without walkouts or strikes. But they did not always last, and a return to the ten-hour day, as in the packing plants, again demonstrated the greater bargaining power of employers. On nearly every hand the laboring man had to give way, and by the end of 1886 the Illinois Bureau of Labor Statistics found less than ten thousand men in the state who had achieved the eight-hour objective.[45]

To a considerable extent, therefore, the energies of the workingmen were drained into a defensive fight against restrictions which threatened to reduce them to impotence before the more powerful employers. Even the right to strike seemed in serious jeopardy in the atmosphere of near-hysteria that followed the Haymarket affair.[46] In 1887 the state legislature passed the Merritt Conspiracy Bill, a drastically repressive measure so phrased that any person who had conspired to perform an act of force or violence dangerous to human life, person, or property was liable, even if not a party to the accomplishment; and that anyone whose publicly spoken or written word was an incitement to an unlawful act could be punished without proof that the person committing such an act had known about the statement. Furthermore, proof that those on trial had even come together or had made an agreement was unnecessary if their acts knowingly advanced the unlawful result.[47]

[45] *Bradstreet's*, XIII (June 12, 1886), 394; *The Knights of Labor*, I (June 19, 1886), 4; *The Drovers' Journal*, May 31, 1886; Commons, *op. cit.*, II, 385; *The Chicago Times*, May 30, 1886; *Chicago Tribune*, Oct. 8, 9, 17, 18, 19, Nov. 7, 9, 14, 1886; Illinois Bureau of Labor Statistics, *Fourth Biennial Report, 1886*, pp. 479–80, 491–92. For the packers' association and the ten-hour day see Commons, *op. cit.*, II, 418–19. Some unions tried to advance the eight-hour movement by restricting their members to those working an eight-hour day. Painters' Progressive Union of Evanston, *Constitution, By-Laws and Rules of Order* (Chicago, 1889), p. 2; Carpenters' and Joiners' Progressive Association of Evanston, *Constitution, By-Laws, and Rules of Order* (Chicago, 1889), p. 2; Act of June 17, 1891, Illinois, *Laws, 1891*, p. 68.

[46] The "LaSalle Black Law" of 1863, with its threat to strikers, was practically a dead letter by 1880 although still on the statute books. Pierce, *A History of Chicago*, II, 170.

[47] *Chicago Tribune*, May 5, 1887; Act of June 16, 1887, Illinois, *Laws, 1887*, pp. 168–69. The act was repealed in 1891. *Laws, 1891*, p. 100.

The passage of the Conspiracy Bill was by no means the only step the legislature took in its zeal to afford " protection " to the citizens of the state. A measure, making a city or county responsible for three-fourths of the mob destruction of property within its limits, except property in transit, provided police authorities with even more power to suppress mass disorders than they had before. The law-makers also trained their guns on the conspicuously successful labor tactic of boycotting the products of companies not approved by union labor. The Coles Anti-Boycott Law, passed in June, 1887, affixed penalties of not more than two years' imprisonment and a fine of not more than $2,000 or both for anyone conspiring with another to institute a boycott or blacklist, or for an officer of any society who directed its membership to take such action. Although the law for-bade blacklisting as well as boycotting, no successful effort to en-force it against employers was made, and labor organizations tried in vain to have it repealed.

This law was especially offensive to laboring men and women, be-cause they considered the boycott as only the counterpart of the blacklist. "Who is doing the principal boycotting today?" de-manded the *Knights of Labor*. "Why the McCormicks, the Pull-mans, the Champion Reaper Works, the railroads, the manufacturers and merchants are doing it, because they refuse to employ men who assert their manhood, and claim the right to organize for self pro-tection." [48] While the chief restrictions upon organized labor took the form of legislative enactments, the injunction was used in Chi-cago as early as 1886 in at least five instances, [49] anticipating " gov-

[48] *The Knights of Labor*, I (March, 1886), 8; Acts of June 15, 16, 1887, Illinois, *Laws, 1887*, pp. 167–68, 237–38; Staley, *op. cit.*, p. 285; Beckner, *op. cit.*, pp. 34–37. General dis-cussions of boycotting in the period are George A. Schilling, " The Boycott a Social Force," *The Bakers' Journal*, VII (Dec. 21, 1891), 3, and Illinois Bureau of Labor Statistics, *Fourth Biennial Report, 1886*, pp. 446–53. For examples of boycotting see *Chicagoer Arbeiter-Zeitung*, July 2, 1883; *The Knights of Labor*, I (March, 1886), 4, (April 10, 1886), 5; *Chicago Tribune*, Jan. 6, 1887; American Federation of Labor, *Proceedings of the Twelfth Annual Convention . . . 1892* (Bloomington, 1906), p. 43. Armour probably expressed the employers' attitude when he described the boycott as " not American " and not much above " sheep-stealing." *The Drovers' Journal*, Jan. 5, 1887; *The Knights of Labor*, I (Nov. 6, 1886), 1.

[49] An injunction was issued March 26 and made permanent May 20, 1886 against strik-ing employees of the furniture manufacturers Bruschke and Ricke, to prevent them from interfering with the company's business or property, from parading in front of the plant, and from intimidating other employees. On April 21 an injunction of similar scope was issued against striking switchmen of the Lake Shore and Michigan Southern Railway, on May 6 against employees of Calumet Iron and Steel Company, on May 29 against employees

ernment by injunction" which was to become the bane of labor at a later day.[50]

Labor, too, tried to effect a program for its own protection, though generally failing to match the success of capital in legislative and judicial fields. In order to maintain a demand for its services it objected to the competition it had from convict workers and from immigrant labor. The prevailing practice of letting out convict labor on contract to private employers forced down wages in those industries, although not numerous, where their employment was widespread. Under pressure from labor leaders and others of like mind, an amendment to the state constitution was approved in 1885 that forbade the officials of penitentiaries and reformatory institutions to make such arrangements. The amendment turned out to be ineffective since existing agreements could not be abrogated, and the amendment could also be evaded easily by the "piece price" plan which enabled outside parties to furnish the raw material and take the product at a price based on a given rate of pay per day for labor.[51]

Resentment on the part of old-timers against newcomers who sold their services cheaply was another source of friction, despite the large number of immigrant stock in the labor force. Antagonism was especially bitter against the Chinese, although the 1880 federal census recorded only 171 in the city. Still, workingmen protested the veto by President Arthur of the Chinese exclusion bill passed by Congress. *The Knights of Labor* urged Chicagoans not to patronize Chinese laundries, and included in its "Must Go" list of June 27, 1888 the Chinese as second only to "bosses," who were classed along with "millionaire skinflints," "preachers of plutocracy," "prison contract labor," and "starvation wages."[52]

---

of Northwestern Fertilizing Company, on June 28 against striking switchmen of the Michigan Southern on the ground of interfering with interstate commerce.

[50] *Chicago Tribune*, March 26, April 3, 23, May 12, 21, June 29, 1886; *The Chicago Legal News*, XVIII (May 22, 1886), 306, (June 22, 1886), 334; *The Drovers' Journal*, May 31, 1886; Albion G. Taylor, *Labor Problems and Labor Law* (New York, 1938), p. 543; Felix Frankfurter and Nathan Greene, *The Labor Injunction* (New York, 1930), p. 20; *The Chicago Times*, May 7, 8, 30, 1886.

[51] Beckner, *op. cit.*, pp. 136–41; Myra Bradwell, ed., *All the Laws of the State of Illinois, 1885* ([Chicago], 1885), p. 203 (hereafter cited as *All the Laws*); Illinois Bureau of Labor Statistics, *Fourth Biennial Report, 1886*, pp. 92–121. Agitation against the contract-labor system was primarily responsible for the formation of the Illinois State Federation of Labor (originally the Illinois State Labor Convention) in 1884. Staley, *op. cit.*, pp. 31–32, 46.

[52] U. S., *Compendium of the Tenth Census* (June 1, 1880), p. 383; *Chicago Tribune*,

By no means the least of the grievances for which labor sought legislative help was the practice of employers of hiring private detectives as spies and strikebreakers or as guards for strikebreakers. " The English language," said Thomas J. Morgan, " is inadequate to express the hate of the men in regard to them." Although several Chicago firms used men deputized by the state, the prominence of Pinkerton's National Detective Agency, with headquarters in the city, made the term " Pinkerton " generic for all such operatives. So violent was the opposition to them that Robert W. McClaughry, general superintendent of Chicago police, declared that they acted as " an irritant rather than having a quieting effect," and urged that strikes and riots be handled exclusively by the regular police with supplementary help from the militia if necessary.[53] So impassioned were the expressions of labor against these private agents that the state legislature in a loosely drawn militia law in 1887 unsuccessfully attempted to prevent any usurpation of the police power by private operatives. This was followed in 1893 by another enactment forbidding the appointment by constituted authorities of a special deputy sheriff or special policeman not a citizen of the United States and an actual resident of the county during the preceding year. However beneficial the intent of this statute, it proved of little effect in Chicago, where many private agencies, besides approximately one-fourth of the Pinkerton force of 600, were stationed, their presence to many an assurance of protection should disorders rise again.[54]

Undaunted, however, by a generally unsympathetic public and by openly hostile employers, labor leaders continued to urge a protection they held to be rightfully theirs. They especially resented the

April 16, 1882; *Svenska Tribunen*, Aug. 15, 1885; *The Knights of Labor*, I (April 10, 1886), 5, III (June 27, 1888), 5.

[53] U. S. Senate, *Investigation in Relation to the Employment for Private Purposes of Armed Bodies of Men, or Detectives, in Connection with Differences between Workmen and Employers*, 52 Cong., 2 sess., S. Rept. 1280 (Washington, 1893), pp. 35, 106, 108, 111–13, 122, 235, 242, 250 (hereafter cited as *Investigation in Relation to Detectives*); *Chicagoer Arbeiter-Zeitung*, July 20, 1888; *Chicago Tribune*, Feb. 28, 1882, April 22, July 10, Oct. 9, 19, 20, 1886; *The Railroad Gazette*, XX (April 6, 1888), 225; *The Catholic Home*, V (Aug. 18, 1888), [5]. Twenty-one private detective agencies were listed in the Chicago business directory of 1893, but all did not handle labor cases. *Lakeside Directory, 1893*, pp. 1905–10; *Investigation in Relation to Detectives* (cited above), p. ii.

[54] Act of June 16, 1887, Illinois, *Laws, 1887*, pp. 240–41; Act of June 19, 1893, *All the Laws, 1893*, p. 129; Staley, *op. cit.*, p. 166; U. S. House of Representatives, Committee on the Judiciary, *The Employment of Pinkerton Detectives*, 52 Cong., 2 sess., H. Rept. 2447 (Washington, 1893), pp. 193–94, 215; Beckner, *op. cit.*, p. 65.

refusal of many employers to treat with a union in the heat of a strike; and they abhorred the requirement of some companies that men sign " iron-clad " or " yellow dog " contracts in which they foreswore membership in a union. Pressure upon legislators, whom the labor leaders made it clear they could help to elect, was strong enough to get a law in 1893 making it a misdemeanor for any firm to interfere by discharge or the threat of discharge with the right to organize. But labor's success in this regard was short-lived, for the statute was declared unconstitutional in 1900.[55]

Other salutary legislation suffered in the same way. A law of 1891 provided for compulsory weekly payment of employees by corporations in a rather inclusive list of industries, and another forbade any firm engaged in mining or manufacturing to maintain a truck store or to make pay deductions except for money advanced. The desirability of laws to insure prompt and regular pay and to curtail the practice of forced purchases at a company store had been recognized by workers whether in or out of unions.[56] The reverses suffered through action of the state supreme court were, however, in part offset, largely as a result of the high-voltage campaign of the Cigar Makers' Union, by the state providing legal protection against counterfeiting of union labels by employers who neither hired union workmen nor maintained proper working conditions.[57]

If organized labor's quest for betterment appeared motivated primarily by pragmatic considerations, other efforts for the improvement of conditions rose as well out of humanitarian impulses. Antedating by fourteen years a state law dealing with the inspection of factories and workshops was a city ordinance of 1879 designed to maintain standards of cleanliness, health, and safety. Lack of en-

[55] *Chicago Tribune,* May 17, 1881, May 19, June 11, 1882, April 6, Aug. 19, 1883, May 11, 1886, April 2, 1888; Act of June 17, 1893, *All the Laws, 1893,* p. 78; Gillespie *v.* Illinois, 188 Ill. 176 (1900).

[56] Act of April 23, 1891, Illinois, *Laws, 1891,* pp. 213–14; Braceville Coal Company *v.* Illinois, 147 Ill. 66 (1893); Act of May 28, 1891, Illinois, *Laws, 1891,* pp. 212–13; Frorer *et al. v.* Illinois, 141 Ill. 171 (1892).

[57] The use of union labels was widespread enough to cause the *Tribune* to comment Sept. 5, 1892. The law provided for the registration of labels with the secretary of state, for the issuance of injunctions against counterfeiting labels, and for punishment of violations by fines of $100 to $200, or imprisonment from three months to one year, or both. Act of May 8, 1891, Illinois, *Laws, 1891,* pp. 202–3; Beckner, *op. cit.,* p. 19. The Illinois State Federation of Labor vigorously supported the use of labels. Illinois State Federation of Labor, *Proceedings of the Eleventh Annual Convention, 1893* (n.p., n.d.), pp. 8, 41.

forcement led to another municipal ordinance in 1880 having more stringent provisions affecting ventilation, protection against dangerous machinery and vats, weatherproofing, and like matters. As in the ordinance of 1879, inspection was entrusted to the Commissioner of Public Health, but the later enactment specified a monthly visitation and quarterly reports which were to include employment statistics, violations and abatements, and general working conditions.[58]

In 1881 the city, in revising its code of laws, made important additions to the earlier factory legislation. One affected the employment of children, a practice vigorously opposed by labor not only because of the effect it had on the wage scale but because of the dangers inherent in it. Although this ordinance was not the first enactment either in the state or in the city directed to the problem of child labor, it differed from those previously passed in that it prohibited the work of those under fifteen years of age in places where machinery was used, or for more than eight hours a day between seven o'clock in the morning and six in the evening.[59]

Periodic complaints indicated considerable evasion, though the Health Department, entrusted with the enforcement of the ordinance, attempted to fulfill its obligations. Proprietors of downtown stores convinced the inspectors that they should not be liable to prosecution for hour violations as the children they employed, they declared, rested a good part of the time; but factories were ordered to get into line. Most of them did, but the assessment of purely nominal fines for noncompliance showed that the law could be violated with relative impunity.[60]

Continued pressure from labor and by an increasingly greater number of the socially conscious brought about the first general child-labor law in 1891. It prohibited the employment of children

[58] In both ordinances fines ranging from $50 to $200 could be imposed for refusals to permit inspections or for noncompliance with provisions. Chicago, *Council Proceedings, 1879–80*, p. 247, *1880–81*, p. 157; *Chicago Tribune*, Oct. 28, 1879, Sept. 4, 1880.

[59] In 1874 an ordinance prohibited those under eighteen playing musical instruments for money on the streets or in saloons, unless employed in the saloon. (Chicago, *Council Proceedings, 1873–74*, p. 148.) In 1877 a non-enforceable law which forbade the use of children as entertainers for pay or in begging and peddling was passed by the state. Act of May 17, 1877, Illinois, *Laws, 1877*, p. 90.

[60] Chicago, *The Municipal Code . . .* , pp. 329–31, 467; *Chicago Tribune*, Jan. 4, March 16, May 15, 19, 30, 1883, March 17, 1884; *Skandinaven*, March 17, 1883; Chicago Department of Health, *Report, 1883 and 1884*, p. 40. Despite the merchants' claims, the lot of "cash children" in retail stores appears to have been a hard one. *Hull-House Maps and Papers*, p. 56.

under thirteen unless it could be shown to the school authorities that the child's labor was essential to the support of some aged or infirm relative, and that the child had attended school eight weeks in the current term. Because of the exemption clause and the far from strict enforcement, the statute was not as effective as its promoters had hoped. As a result, the Sweatshop Act, or the Factory and Workshop Act, two years later undertook to remedy the defects of previous laws by making illegal the hiring of children under fourteen in places manufacturing, repairing, or sorting goods for sale or wages; nor could those between fourteen and sixteen be thus employed unless they had certificates of birth from parent or guardian. The factory inspectors appointed by the act could require, furthermore, a statement from reputable physicians as to physical fitness.[61]

The Sweatshop Act, which had thus strengthened regulations relating to child labor, applied, however, only to manufacturing establishments, factories, and workshops, and the law of 1891 was still in force for mercantile occupations. Fortunately, the introduction of the pneumatic tube cut down the need of callboys and girls in retail stores. By the time of the passage of the law the Chief Tenement, Factory and Smoke Inspector was able to report: " There is not much so-called child labor in Chicago — less than 1500 cash boys, cash girls and factory helpers, under 15 years, being employed in the whole city." [62]

While the number of gainfully employed children was declining, women more and more entered the ranks of wage earners, many of them in the sweatshops scattered principally in the southwest, north, and northwest parts of the city. Here in what was described by the Bureau of Labor Statistics as " the forgotten regions," where the streets were unpaved, drainage obstructed, and sidewalks decaying planks, women of various nationalities labored in the dimly lighted tenements.

[61] The Christian Union, XXXIV (Oct. 7, 1886), 1; The Knights of Labor, I (Aug. 14, 1886), 1; The Rights of Labor, VI (Feb. 1, 1890), 1; The Dawn, IV (Nov. 9, 1892), 1; Chicago Tribune, Feb. 19, March 6, 1889, Feb. 11, 14, 1893; Act of June 17, 1891, Illinois, Laws, 1891, pp. 87–88; Hull-House Maps and Papers, p. 53; Jane Addams, Twenty Years at Hull-House (New York, 1910), p. 201; Act of June 17, 1893, Illinois, Laws, 1893, pp. 100–2; Illinois State Federation of Labor, op. cit., p. 14; Florence Kelley to Henry D. Lloyd, Oct. 10, 1893, Lloyd Papers.

[62] Hull-House Maps and Papers, p. 56; Chicago Department of Health, Report, 1891, p. 70.

In 1891 the Chicago Trades and Labor Assembly, distressed by the " enormity of these offenses against humanity and morality," set up a committee to investigate sweatshop labor and to arouse the public to take some action against it. As chairman of the committee, Mrs. Thomas J. Morgan, wife of the socialist labor leader, issued a report which served as the background for continued agitation by the trade unions and a slowly awakening public. The Morgan report was followed by an investigation by the Illinois Bureau of Labor Statistics, conducted under the direction of Mrs. Florence Kelley of Hull House. Although the sweatshops were less numerous than supposed, being estimated as no more than eight hundred, the investigators revealed such alarming conditions that a horrified and frightened public demanded action from the General Assembly.

The legislative committee which was, therefore, named to study further conditions in the sweatshops confirmed the sorry plight of the workers revealed in the preceding investigations and recommended remedial legislation. As finally passed, the act established standards of sanitation to protect the health not only of children but of women in manufacturing; it limited the working hours of the latter to eight a day, six days a week; and it provided for the inspection of many sweatshop products in order to prevent the spread of diseases. Unfortunately, the list of articles was not all-inclusive, the enforcement of the eight-hour day could be only partially successful, and the various loopholes of the law doomed it to miss the goal desired. It was, however, a brave beginning in penetrating the opposition of manufacturers steadfastly holding to the laissez-faire philosophy of the day; and in the case of owners of home shops it broke into the incrusted and time-honored doctrine that " every man's house is his castle." The notable work of Mrs. Florence Kelley, as chief factory inspector, and her assistant Mrs. Alzina P. Stevens and ten deputies, five of whom were women, represented the fruits of a humane and intelligent approach toward the solution of the increasingly complex problem posed by the Economic Revolution. That the accomplishment fell short of a desired reform in no sense beclouds the significance of those gains which were made.[63]

---

[63] *The Chicago Times*, July 29, 1888; *The Rights of Labor*, II (Nov. 7, 1891), 1; Illinois Bureau of Labor Statistics, *Seventh Biennial Report, 1892*, pp. 357–443; *Chicago Tribune*, Feb. 11, 14, July 13, 1893; Beckner, *op. cit.*, pp. 188, 254–68; Illinois Factory Inspectors,

Although the recipients of whatever good laws provided, women workers were, in the very nature of the times in which they lived, beset by even greater difficulties than were men. Direct political action was closed to them by the limitation of the suffrage, and the public's opposition to labor organizations among women was far more effective than toward men's. Membership in a union carried the indelible mark of being " unladylike," and the attitude that their jobs were but temporary expedients until marriage weakened women's bargaining power. Even those who had affiliated with the Knights of Labor found the protection they had enjoyed in its heyday nonexistent as the order lost its effectiveness in 1887, and its Chicago membership plummeted as spectacularly as it had risen a year or two before. Along with men, women then turned to the trade union, into which they were received in small numbers, and not always willingly because of their lower wage scale.[64]

By the late 'eighties trade-unionism, vigorously promoted by its adherents as a saner approach to reform than the plans of the earlier " rainbow chasers," had increased its appeal to Chicago workingmen. Many locals were formed, some shortly to take out charters in the American Federation of Labor. By 1890 around sixty-five thousand men were reported unionized, over a third in the Federation. Women, too, turned to this form of organization, and by 1893 had trade locals of cloakmakers, book-bindery girls, shoe workers, and shirtmakers. Despite threats of dismissal and dismissals by employers, and the realization that " scabs " might supersede them, the enthusiasm of union proponents did not subside. " The tendency on the part of working men to associate and form first local and then national organization is too strong to be repressed," commented the *Tribune* in 1890, " and it is as useless to fight it as the tendency of men who are not working men to form associations for their mutual benefit." [65]

But the union movement was seldom rationalized as an inevitable

First Annual Report, 1893, pp. 7, 9–17, Second Annual Report, 1894, pp. 14–27, Third Annual Report, 1895, pp. 94–95, 126–27.

[64] Official Annual Labor Gazette, 1893 (Chicago, n.d.), p. 119; Illinois State Federation of Labor, op. cit., p. 34. The establishment and program of the Illinois Federation of Labor, whose first convention was held in Chicago in 1884, is discussed by Eugene Staley, History of the Illinois State Federation of Labor.

[65] The Rights of Labor, VI (Feb. 28, 1891), 1, VII (April 18, 1891), 1, (Oct. 18, 1891), 1; Chicago Tribune, Aug. 8, 1890.

manifestation of the changing industrial structure. Businessmen, steeped in the philosophy of a day of simple living, insisted, as did the capitalist Z. S. Holbrook, that such cohesiveness did not menace the employer so much as it did the workman, whose " inherent and inalienable right to labor " was thus transgressed. And John V. Farwell saw in unionization, with its implicit assumption of the right to question the labor policies of employers and to strike, an interference with the laws of supply and demand.[66] With each side clinging to a philosophic justification for its stand, industrial conflicts were inevitable. Labor at times aggressively pressed its demands and, when unsuccessful in attaining them, frequently resorted to the strike. Five hundred and twenty-eight strikes were reported in Chicago by the United States Commissioner of Labor from January 1, 1887 to June 30, 1894, costing the 282,611 employees involved nearly nine million dollars in wages and their employers five million more.[67]

As the processes of organization became more refined and strikes were looked upon as at times labor's only weapon, emphasis on " practicality " increased and was lauded by the post-Haymarket unionists as they cast a skeptical eye at the panaceas and somewhat utopian schemes advanced by others.[68] Pursuit of immediate objectives which put more money in the worker's pocket and gave a higher degree of control over jobs seemed a more promising path than a long-run program aimed at the reorganization of society. With benefits extending into insurance, sick and unemployment relief, the union increasingly appealed to the worker by protecting him in his daily employment, providing opportunities for sociability and relaxation, and sustaining him in time of troubles.[69]

[66] Z[ephaniah] S. Holbrook, "The Lessons of the Homestead Troubles," The Sunset Club, Year-Book, 1892–93 (n.p., n.d.), p. 10; John V. Farwell in The Knights of Labor, I (May 29, 1886), 2.

[67] An important railroad strike, for instance, occurred in 1888 on the Chicago, Burlington, & Quincy. It covered states in the Middle West; was a series of strikes involving engineers to switchmen for higher wages and better rules of employment; was marked by violence; and ended in defeat for the unions. Arthur E. Holder, "Railroad Strikes since 1877," American Federationist, XIX (1912), 615–17; The Railroad Gazette, XX (1888), 137–38, 153–54, 456, 478. The exact amount of wages lost between 1887 and 1894 was recorded as $8,846,494; the amount of loss of employers as $14,444,034. U. S. Commissioner of Labor, Tenth Annual Report, 1894, I, 22.

[68] Union rules pointing to improved working conditions sometimes included fixed hours for labor, rate of pay, restrictions on apprenticeship, and measures to insure the closed shop.

[69] Abendpost, March 12, 1890; Chicago Tribune, Aug. 25, 1890; Illinois Staats-Zeitung,

The general prosperity of the years 1887 to 1892 brought relative quiet to the labor front. Those strikes which did occur did not so fearfully convulse society as had " the Great Strikes " in 'seventy-seven and the Haymarket in 'eighty-six. Largely absent were the roaming mobs, the melodramatic headlines of the press, the horror and tensions of those memorable days. But beneath a more or less quiescent surface all the old explosive forces lay, their activity temporarily restrained, their potential undiminished. As the days of the Columbian Exposition of 1893 drew near, men wondered if America were not ending an era, " passing the borderline into a new epoch." To those thus perplexed, questions which seemed unanswerable rose one after another. Just how was it all to happen? How would the transition come? Would the changes be peaceful or violent? To those not incurably optimistic, to those who remembered the militancy of the past, the future appeared fraught with dangers so great that, unless justice and progress were somehow established, " the much predicted cataclysm of fire and blood " seemed inevitable.[70]

" Upon the one side," said George Schilling, " we find the propertied classes. . . . They are in possession of the earth. Upon the other side we find a large army of workmen who have nothing on earth except their labor." The days of simple living lay behind. The complexity of metropolitan life was upon Chicago. The economic structure was now grown to a magnitude almost beyond comprehension; and thoughtful men asked if already it were so big that ordinary controls were no longer effective. Only time was to tell what lay in store in the new epoch for the workingman, the man at the mercy of the labor market, the man who, as Schilling put it, " had to sell his labor or go under." [71]

Sept. 8, 1891; *Official Annual Labor Gazette, 1893*, p. 47; *Chicagoer Arbeiter-Zeitung*, March 23, 1889. An extensive survey of the beneficiary features of Chicago unions in 1886 is found in Illinois Bureau of Labor Statistics, *Fourth Biennial Report, 1886*, pp. 428–33. A more elaborate plan than most is that given in International Typographical Union, Franklin Union No. 4, *Constitution and By-Laws . . . 1893* (Chicago, n.d.), pp. 37–38.

[70] *The Vanguard*, I (June 4, 1892), 5.

[71] George A. Schilling, " The Lessons of the Homestead Troubles," The Sunset Club, *Year-Book, 1892–93*, p. 15.

CHAPTER IX

THE EXPANDING ROLE
OF GOVERNMENT

THE BASIC FRAMEWORK of the city's government had been established in the years which preceded the Great Fire, but the work of adapting it to the new era which followed 1871 lay in the years ahead. Vast changes occasioned by the coming of many people, some untutored in American traditions and language, by the outward thrust of the city's boundaries, by the momentous swell of the economy, indeed by all the forces unleashed by modern urbanization, often complicated the conduct of government by agencies constituted for a rural age. This was particularly true in the case of the county-town organization and the relationship it bore to the city, notably in the authority exercised over the important function of taxation.

A marked extension of municipal activities, necessitated by the need of reconstruction after the Fire, resulted in a strengthening of the power of the mayor — a placing of " the executive at the head instead of the tail of the municipal organism," as the *Chicago Times* put it. Under the leadership of newly elected Mayor Joseph Medill, a temporary measure called " the Mayor's Bill " passed the Illinois legislature March 9, 1872, thus recording a victory over members of the Common Council, the jealous guardians of the powers of the legislature, and those who traditionally feared a strong executive.[1]

---

[1] *The Chicago Times*, Dec. 8, 11, 12, 1871; Act of March 9, 1872, Illinois, *Public Laws, 1871–72*, p. 269, *House Journal, 1871–72*, II, 548, *Senate Journal, 1871–72*, II, 605. For a curtailment of the mayor's powers by state law in 1869 see Pierce, *A History of Chicago*, II, 305.

When the two-year limit was reached on " that pestiferous relic of the Medillian Era," as opponents chose to call the Mayor's Bill, the city reverted to its charter of 1863 and its succeeding amendments. The inadequacy of this instrument provoked a flood of criticism, particularly from the newly formed Citizens' Association, which promoted a petition for a public vote for incorporation under the state's general incorporation act of 1872. Such incorporation would have set up essentially the same machinery as existed before the expiration of the Mayor's Bill.[2] Not until January 4, 1875, however, after the November municipal election had effected changes of personnel, did the council reach a favorable decision on the petition. Meanwhile, in the weeks following its presentation, the Citizens' Association had changed its stand by advocating an entirely new charter with a bicameral legislature and a cabinet for the mayor.[3] Confused by conflicting counsel, the voters cast only a small vote in the special election, April 23, 1875, which by the slight margin of 11,714 to 10,218 accepted re-incorporation under the 1872 provisions.

Thereupon the Citizens' Association charged that the outcome had been obtained through fraud, " the greatest cheap rascality ever seen in a city election." An appeal to the courts followed, resulting in the state Supreme Court sustaining the vote of April 23, 1875.[4]

The council, known henceforth as the City Council, now became the focal point of government under the new charter, with the mayor the council's presiding officer but without legislative functions except

[2] Chicago, Council Proceedings, 1873–74, pp. 76, 455–56; The Chicago Times, Jan. 31, Oct. 23, 1874; Chicago Tribune, Jan. 31, 1873, Nov. 4, 1874; Citizens' Association of Chicago, Addresses and Reports . . . 1874 to 1876, pp. 6, 20. The Act of April 10, 1872 (the general incorporation act) was enacted because the Constitution of 1870 prohibited special legislation for individual cities. Illinois, Public Laws, 1871–72, pp. 218–64. See also Act of April 10, 1875, Laws, 1875, pp. 41–42; Act of May 28, 1879, Act of May 31, 1879, Laws, 1879, pp. 65, 76.

[3] The Citizens' Association at the same time worked assiduously for the passage of a substitute measure expressing its views. On April 8, 1875, the state legislature by large majorities enacted such a law despite vigorous opposition from the Chicago Common Council. Illinois, Public Laws, 1875, pp. 42–62, House Journal, 1875, p. 447, Senate Journal, 1875, p. 472; Chicago, Council Proceedings, 1874–76, pp. 35, 76. For the part played by the People's party supporters of Mayor Colvin, see Chapter X, "The Profile of Politics."

[4] Chicago, Council Proceedings, 1874–76, pp. 153–54; Citizens' Association of Chicago, Addresses and Reports, 1874 to 1876, pp. 21–23; The Chicago Times, May 7, 14, June 8, 15, 1875; Chicago Tribune, April 25, May 4, 1875; E. C. Larned to C. H. and L. J. McCormick, July 23, 1875, Cyrus H. McCormick Papers (Ms. Chicago Historical Society); The City of Chicago v. The People ex rel. Henry W. King et al., 80 Ill. 496 (1875).

when called upon to cast a vote in the case of a tie. A so-called Mayor's Bill, approved April 10, 1875, supplemented the general law of April 8 of that year, and, although it gave the mayor appointive and removal powers, his dismissal of anyone he named could be overridden by a two-thirds vote of the council which, in the first place, had created the office. This also pertained to the use of the veto. But on May 28, 1879 the Mayor's Bill of April 10, 1875 was repealed, and the mayor was then forced to function under the organic law of 1872.[5]

The authority of the council, especially as to regulation and licensing, extended over a vast field involving public safety, health, and morals. The Act of 1872 enumerated more than ninety specific powers, ranging from control of the finances and property of the city to the prevention and regulation of amusements such as rolling hoops, playing ball, and flying kites. While the 1875 charter required popular election of only the aldermen, the city clerk, the attorney, and the treasurer, other officials might be made subject to election by vote of the council rather than by mayoral appointment. The two aldermen, chosen in alternate years from each ward for two years, served without pay until February 7, 1881, after which they received three dollars for each session attended. To Chicagoans concerned with attracting able and honest candidates this remuneration seemed too slight to attract any but men of wealth or those willing to participate in financial irregularities.[6] In 1889, upon the annexation of new territory, the city was redistricted into thirty-four wards.[7]

The courts functioning in Chicago were a part of the county system established by the 1870 state constitution and subsequent acts of the legislature. Cook County became a judicial circuit with its own

[5] Illinois, *Laws, 1875,* p. 41, *1879,* pp. 65, 76. A detailed account of Chicago government can be found in Samuel Edwin Sparling, *Municipal History and Present Organization of the City of Chicago* (University of Wisconsin, *Bulletin,* no. 23. Economics, Political Science, and History series, II, no. 2. Madison, 1908).

[6] Act of April 10, 1872, Chicago, *Municipal Code of Chicago, 1881* (Egbert Jameson and Francis Adams, eds. Chicago, 1881), pp. 13, 18–25, 27–28, 31, *Council Proceedings, 1880–81,* p. 397. The charter of 1875 allowed three dollars a meeting, but until 1881 efforts to give payment were unsuccessful.

[7] In 1876 the number of wards was decreased from twenty to eighteen. In 1887 the state legislature permitted cities of 350,000 or more to have twenty-four, which Chicago then acquired. In 1889 an increase to thirty-five wards was allowed by the legislature when territory was added. Chicago, *Council Proceedings, 1874–76,* pp. 577–78, *1887–88,* pp. 321–23, *1889–90,* pp. 336–37, *Municipal Code,* pp. 13, 15–16, 31; Act of May 20, 1887, Illinois, *Laws, 1887,* p. 105; Act of June 4, 1889, *Laws, 1889,* p. 55.

court, and the jurisdiction of the old Superior Court of the city was shifted to include the whole county.[8] This was true also of the Recorder's Court of Chicago, which became the Criminal Court of Cook County. The various jurisdictions overlapped, and in practice all the tribunals acted as circuit courts. In addition, Cook County had its regular county court to look after matters of probate and the estates of deceased persons, guardians, and apprentices, as well as the collection of taxes and assessments.[9]

Closest to the people were the justices of the peace, appointed upon the recommendation of a majority of the judges of the Circuit, Superior, and County courts for four years by the governor with senate confirmation. Their selection depended upon party politics, their fee system of remuneration became a source of abuse, and their administration occasioned frequent criticism.[10]

These three main divisions thus constituted, as in the past, the foundations upon which rested the structure of government. Especially in choices for the mayoralty and the council did political party popularity play a deciding role, and, throughout, the influence of the latter varied inversely with the powers of the former. To various other agencies, however, were entrusted responsibilities peculiar to their particular establishment, all of which became vastly more important as the city grew larger. A tendency toward change was especially marked in the shift from the board or department form of administration to the more highly centralized control under a single commissioner. Whereas the council exercised the power of confirmation, the commissioner was in reality the appointee of the mayor and responsible to him.

To the police department, long charged with inefficiency and cor-

[8] The judges of the Circuit Court numbered five at first, then eleven in 1887 and fourteen in 1893. Art. VI, sec. 23, Constitution of Illinois, 1870; Act of May 4, 1887, Illinois, *Laws, 1887,* p. 157; Act of June 26, 1893, *Laws, 1893,* p. 94.

[9] Art. VI, secs. 18, 26, Constitution of Illinois, 1870; Harry M. Fisher, "Judicial Structure of Cook County," *Illinois Law Review,* XXXVI (Feb., 1942), 632–33. A special probate court created in 1877 aroused fear that the Cook County Probate Court was superseded. The Supreme Court in 1882 decided that the county court was legal. Act of April 27, 1877, Illinois, *Laws, 1877,* pp. 79–84; E. F. C. Klokke *v.* John H. P. Dodge, 103 Ill. 125 (1882); Joshua C. Knickerbocker *v.* The People *ex. rel.* Otto C. Butz, 102 Ill. 218 (1882).

[10] Art. VI, sec. 28, Constitution of Illinois, 1870; Citizens' Association of Chicago, *Annual Report, 1880,* p. 22, *1891,* p. 18; *Chicago Legal News,* VII (Oct. 17, 1874), 29, XV (June 2, 1883), 755; *Chicago Record,* Jan. 14, 1893. The office of police magistrate was abolished.

ruption, Mayor Medill early directed his attention. Under "the Mayor's Bill" of 1872 he removed two of three commissioners, but with the lapse of the bill in 1874 the city returned to a board of three to which Medill's successor, Harvey D. Colvin, restored the old political elements. On May 31, 1876 the council abolished the board and vested authority in a superintendent directly responsible to the mayor; but, even so, charges of corruption and inefficiency on the part of the force continued unabated.[11] That the force was numerically inadequate to cope with increasingly complex urban conditions may help to explain why arrests lagged behind the number of crimes committed. Nor was the compensation sufficient to attract men of special ability. As late as 1892 patrolmen were getting as little as $720, and the maximum of $1,000 was the same as twenty years earlier.[12]

Quite apart from the rule of "the pistol and the knife" varying at times in the extent to which it terrorized the community, there was seldom absent the need for the law-abiding, as the *Tribune* put it, to "take the matter into their own hands and enforce the laws for themselves." The ratio of arrests to total population was about one to eleven in 1893. Although some parts of the city seemed safer than others, all of Chicago in the eyes of even her most ardent partisans was ever in the shadow of the dominance of the criminal elements. In the slightly more than three square miles lying roughly between Harrison and Sixteenth streets and running west from the lake to Wood Street, an area thickly populated by an estimated 130,000 persons of diverse nationalities, the number of arrests rose to one in four by 1893. Commitments to the House of Correction, moreover, were classified by place of nativity and followed a proportion generally in keeping with the size of the ethnic groups. More sentences, there-

11 Sparling, *op. cit.*, p. 95; *The Chicago Times*, Jan. 8, 1872, July 1, 15, 17, 1875, July 21, 1879; *Chicago Tribune*, Oct. 12, 1872, Oct. 7, Dec. 21, 1875, June 1, 1876; Chicago, *Council Proceedings, 1874–76*, pp. 37, 120–21; Mark Sheridan *et al. v.* H. D. Colvin, *et al.*, 78 Ill. 237 (1875); Citizens' Association of Chicago, *Annual Report, 1887*, pp. 11–12, *1890*, p. 15; *Abendpost*, Feb. 3, Sept. 16, 1890.

12 In 1874 there were three police precincts; in 1892 there was the insufficient number of forty-three. In 1890, when Chicago's 1,680 patrolmen had to cover 181 square miles, there was about one patrolman to approximately every 715 inhabitants. In 1890 New York's 3,100 patrolmen watched over forty square miles, or one patrolman for every 550 persons. Chicago Board of Police, *Annual Report, 1874*, p. 5, *Council Proceedings, 1891–92*, pp. 7–8, General Superintendent of Police, *Report, 1890*, p. 48, *1891*, pp. 50–53, *1892*, pp. 50, 154–55; Act of March 9, 1867, *Laws and Ordinances of the City of Chicago, 1873*, p. 503. New York in 1890 spent at the rate of $2.60 per capita for the system as compared to Chicago's $1.83. New York, *Report of the Police Department . . . 1893*, p. 85.

fore, were passed against the American-born than any other single group, but over half of these were children of immigrants.[13]

The greatest single source of arrests was disorderly conduct, which increased over six times in the fifteen years following 1878, to reach 55,427. This, however, was not the fastest-growing offense. Arrests for assault leaped more than thirty times in the same period, to total 3,874 in 1893. More than threefold increases were noted for inmates of houses of ill fame, for those accused of burglary, gambling, carrying concealed weapons, resisting an officer, and robbery. There were other arrests for threats, for doing business without a license, and for larceny. The only charge that showed a decrease was vagrancy, which dropped from 2,978 in 1878 to 2,154 in 1893.[14]

No violation of the law occasioned greater public concern than gambling. Between owners of such establishments and the forces of government the alliance appeared so solidly cemented that it seemed well-nigh unbreakable. Not far from the City Hall flourished " Al Smith's Lair," a saloon, and gambling houses; and near by were resorts like Harry Varnell's with its ninety-odd employees of faro dealers, croupiers, and others. For about two decades after the mid-'seventies Michael Cassius McDonald, king of gamblers, operated his fabulous " Store " at 176 Clark Street, and aside from a temporary eclipse following the election of Mayor John A. Roche in 1887 he was virtually the dictator of the City Hall.[15] Faro, roulette, craps, in fact all kinds of games of chance, enjoyed general immunity throughout the city. Not even Carter Harrison's attempt at control through supervision prevented the fleecing of the naïve — an attempt criticized by many as failing in its objective and as selling out the city to gamblers.[16]

---

[13] *Chicago Tribune*, Sept. 4, 1881; *Illinois Staats-Zeitung*, Nov. 29, 1892; Chicago General Superintendent of Police, *Report, 1893*, pp. 6, 25; Chicago Board of Education, *Annual Report, 1892*, p. 367; U. S. Commissioner of Labor, " The Slums of Baltimore, Chicago, New York, and Philadelphia," *Seventh Special Report*, p. 16; Chicago Board of Inspectors of the House of Correction, *Fourth Annual Report of the Board of Inspectors . . . and Reports of the City Physician to the Board, 1875*, p. 13, *Tenth Annual Report, 1881*, p. 10, *Twenty-first Annual Report, 1892*, p. 17.

[14] Chicago General Superintendent of Police, *Reports, 1876–1893*.

[15] *The Chicago Times*, Feb. 23, 1874; *Chicago Record-Herald*, Aug. 18, 1907; Herbert Asbury, *Gem of the Prairie, An Informal History of the Chicago Underworld* (New York, 1940), pp. 142–43, 152; John Philip Quinn, *Fools of Fortune or Gambling and Gamblers . . .* (Chicago, 1892), p. 405.

[16] *Chicago Tribune*, Dec. 4, 1879, Sept. 12, 14, 1880; William T. Stead, *If Christ Came to Chicago* (Chicago, 1894), p. 241.

Equally well entrenched were the houses of prostitution, located in a fairly concentrated section south of Harrison and west of State Street. Occasional raids and the imposition of fines proved so slight a deterrent that the *Chicago Times* stigmatized them as demonstrating the " co-partnership of Chicago with harlotry." When a system of licensing was suggested as a possible way of control, reform groups, especially such organizations as the Ladies' Social Evil Association active in the early 'seventies, objected vigorously. An end to this proposal came in 1874 when the state legislature forbade such licensing by cities or regulation of any sort by boards of health, although proponents of similar measures continued to advocate them as the best means of obtaining what moral suasion and public disapproval seemed unable to prevent.[17]

An unofficial policy of confining vice to small areas and maintaining as high a degree of order as possible, however, appeared to be about the best that could be done. During the Harrison administrations policemen were ordered to prevent solicitation on the streets to end prostitution as " an open and public calling." Even the city ordinance of 1892 to suppress the vice activities of amusement places, saloons, massage parlors, and hotels of a questionable character proved a failure. Nothing, not even the public campaign of Mayor Roche to loosen the stranglehold of vice on Chicago, as the *Chicago Daily News* observed, touched " the gilded dens of infamy along the avenue with marble steps and brazen door-plates," or eliminated " the polluting presence of abandoned women who wandered through the streets." [18]

Even when apprehended and placed in the House of Correction, prisoners found the physical conditions painfully inadequate and the atmosphere not conducive to rehabilitation. Hardened criminals were thrown in with those later found innocent and with youthful offenders who composed about one-tenth of those committed, while the overcrowding was made more acute by the incarceration of the

[17] Hoyt, *One Hundred Years of Land Values in Chicago,* p. 103; *The Chicago Times,* Feb. 15, 26, March 12, 22, 23, 25, 26, 1874; Act of March 27, 1874, *Municipal Code of Chicago, 1881,* p. 83; The Sunset Club of Chicago, *The Meetings of 1892–93* . . . , pp. 211–33.

[18] *Chicago Tribune,* July 17, Aug. 6, 1878, Dec. 19, 1880; *The Chicago Times,* July 17, Dec. 19, 1880; Stead, *op. cit.,* pp. 252–53; *Chicago's Dark Places* (Chicago, 1891), p. 120; Chicago, *Council Proceedings, 1892–93,* pp. 134–35; *Chicago Daily News,* May 7, June 1, 1887.

poor, unable to pay fines imposed upon them, and of those later found innocent. Some steps, however, were taken to improve the deplorable conditions. In 1891 a school for juvenile inmates was opened in the House of Correction, and the year before a library had been started. In 1891, too, dormitories replaced women's cells, and first offenders were separated from repeating inmates.[19]

The introduction of telegraph alarms, first experimentally in 1880 and then extended four years later, not only speeded calls for protection but facilitated the hourly reports of patrolmen to headquarters by telephones installed in the alarm boxes.[20] The 'eighties also witnessed a growing concern on the part of the municipality as to its obligation toward public servants, in a form of aid administered through the Police and Firemen's Relief Fund, established by the General Assembly in 1877. In another ten years a municipal pension fund replaced the former relief system, and compensation was provided those disabled in the discharge of duty. Retirement after twenty years of service on half-pay was also granted.[21]

The city which had suffered so severely in 1871 and which continued to have similar experiences found fire fighters as important for its protection as policemen. Until 1875 these were under the supervision of the police department, their performance determined in part by the honesty and perspicacity of its leadership and in part by that of the fire marshal. From 201 men in 1871, organized along military lines, the force was expanded to 1,037 in 1893. At the same time, better equipment was provided in the extension of the fire-alarm telegraph to more than two thousand miles of aerial wires and over one hundred miles of underground lines in its telegraph circuit;

[19] John P. Altgeld, *Our Penal Machinery and Its Victims* (Chicago, 1886), pp. 7, 16, 28, 31, 144; *The Dawn*, V (Feb. 11, 1893), 3; Chicago Board of Inspectors of the House of Correction, *Annual Report, 1875* (Fourth)–*1893* (Twenty-second), *Council Proceedings, 1891–92*, p. 9, *1892–93*, p. 10.

[20] Chicago General Superintendent of Police, *Annual Report, 1881*, pp. 48–54, *1883*, p. 19, *1884*, p. 110; *Chicago Tribune*, Dec. 16, 17, 19, 1880. Individual citizens were given keys to operate the alarms, " making every key-holder to a considerable extent a policeman." Chicago, *Council Proceedings, 1887–88*, p. 8.

[21] The Policemen's Benevolent Association, set up in 1868 and incorporated in 1877, was in part superseded in 1877 by municipal aid. (*Chicago Tribune*, Feb. 19, 1868; Andreas, *History of Chicago*, III, 115.) Act of May 24, 1877, Illinois, *Laws, 1877*, p. 62, Act of April 29, 1887, *Laws, 1887*, pp. 122–26; Chicago City Comptroller, *Report, 1878*, p. 42, General Superintendent of Police, *Annual Report, 1881*, pp. 37–38, Department of Finance, *Report, 1892*, pp. 18–19. For minor amendments to the law see Act of May 10, 1879, Illinois, *Laws, 1879*, pp. 72–74, Act of June 23, 1883, *Laws, 1883*, p. 59.

and in the acquisition of vehicles like the Babcock hook-and-ladder machine and the Silsby rotary fire engine that threw two streams of water simultaneously.[22] As in the case of the police department, the public assumed greater responsibility for its firemen first in the Police and Firemen's Relief Fund in 1877 and then in expanded pension benefits in a separate fund in 1887.[23]

As often happens in the affairs of men, calamity hastened the adoption of protective measures. Following the devastation of October, 1871, " the fire limits " of the city were extended in 1872, and an important general provision of a new municipal building code prescribed that outside walls be of brick, stone, iron or other incombustible material. Then caution gave way to indiscretion, and public opposition led to nullification of the ordinance.[24] How dangerous this action could be was demonstrated in July, 1874, when fire laid waste to about sixty acres lying south and west of Van Buren Street and Michigan Avenue.[25] Threats of withdrawal from Chicago by insurance underwriters forced not only the purchase of more fire-fighting equipment but the extension of the fire limits to coincide with those of the city. The "insurance embargo" was not lifted, however, until the Citizens' Association, formed as a result of the 1874 conflagration, persuaded General William H. Shaler to come from New York to recommend improvements of the fire department and of the general fire affairs of the city.[26] In 1875 the council created

22 The ordinance which established the fire department as a separate entity was passed Aug. 12, 1875. (Chicago, Council Proceedings, 1874-76, pp. 368-69.) General Order, No. 17, Aug. 2, 1873, Fire Marshal's Office, Order Book (Ms. John Crerar Library); Chicago, Council Proceedings, 1872-73, pp. 343, 417, 1874-76, p. 374, 1879-80, pp. 98-100, 262-63, 1901-2, p. 510, Fire Marshal, Annual Report, 1875-1893. See Chicago Tribune 1872-93 for press comments.

23 Andreas, A History of Chicago, III, 125; Act of May 24, 1877, Illinois, Laws, 1877, p. 62, Act of May 13, 1887, Laws, 1887, pp. 117-22; Chicago Fire Marshal, Annual Report, 1878, p. 6; Chicago Department of Finance, Annual Statement, 1892, pp. 19-21. For amendment to 1887 law see Illinois, Laws, 1889, pp. 80-82.

24 The fire limits comprised a tract roughly triangular in shape, with Thirty-ninth Street from the lake to State Street on the south, Fullerton Avenue between the lake and Lincoln Avenue its greatest extent on the north, and Western Avenue between Van Buren and Lake streets its most westerly extension. Chicago, Council Proceedings, 1871-72, pp. 46-47, 49-50, 84-85; The Chicago Times, Jan. 16, 1872; Chicago Tribune, Jan. 15, 1872.

25 Ibid., July 15, 1874; Chicago Fire Marshal, Annual Report, 1874-75, p. 158. In 1885 the burning of lumberyards between Thirty-fifth and Thirty-ninth to the north of the Stockyards and, in 1890, the destruction of Fowler Brothers' Packing House were among the big fires experienced.

26 Chicago Tribune, July 18, 23, Sept. 24, Nov. 7, 14, Dec. 9, 1874; The Chicago Times, July 17, 21, Sept. 22, 25, 26, Dec. 9, 1874; Chicago Fire Marshal, Annual Report, 1874-75,

an executive department to survey and inspect buildings; and in the next two years took other safety precautions, including one which required metallic fire escapes on non-residential buildings four or more stories high.[27]

Principal expender of municipal revenue in the years between the Great Fire and the World's Fair, the Department of Public Works was the administrative division which offered the most tangible evidence of the city's material growth. In 1876 the City Council abolished the three-man board and instituted a department under a single commissioner with authority over the bureaus of water, sewerage, streets, special assessments, engineering, and maps.

The fires of 1871 and '74 spurred apprehensive Chicagoans to seek ways of increasing the supply of water. In little more than a score of years the city's system grew from a single pumping station to six, with a corresponding increase in the number of gallons supplied. At the same time the spectacular expansion of industry, the extension of the city's corporate limits, and the mounting numbers of people forced the government to enlarge facilities still further.[28] With the annexation of towns came systems often inadequate to care for those living near at hand, and these needs had to be considered. Water pumpage grew from approximately 8,000,000,000 gallons in 1870 to over 86,000,000,000 in 1893, and the per-capita consumption more than doubled from 72.8 gallons per day to 146.8.[29]

p. 24, *Council Proceedings, 1873-74,* pp. 314, 316-17, *1874-76,* pp. 3-5; Citizens' Association of Chicago, *Addresses and Reports, 1874 to 1876,* pp. 3, 14-16; *Weekly Journal,* Nov. 11, 1874.

[27] Chicago, *Council Proceedings, 1874-76,* pp. 231-32, 242, 262, *1877-78,* p. 230; *The Chicago Times,* June 16, 22, 1875; *Chicago Tribune,* Nov. 22, 1877.

[28] The single pumping station had a capacity of 38,000,000 gallons daily, drawing water from a single two-mile tunnel of 50,000,000 gallons capacity. The six main stations had a combined capacity of 357,000,000 gallons daily, supplied with water through five lake tunnels with an aggregate daily capacity of 434,000,000 gallons. Chicago Board of Public Works, *Fourteenth Annual Report, 1875,* pp. 4-5, *Eighteenth Annual Report, 1893,* pp. 11-12, 75-86. The chief sources for the discussion of the water and sewerage systems are the Chicago Department of Public Works, *1876 (First Annual Report)-1893 (Eighteenth Annual Report),* and Chicago *Council Proceedings.* Additional references are cited where especially appropriate. The city's corporate limits in 1889 alone increased by 132,519 square miles.

[29] Water revenue per million gallons decreased from $67.86 in 1870 to $34.18 in 1893. In 1879 a reorganized Water Collection Department instituted a system of registry of receipts to check errors and dishonesty which had not been detected. In 1880 house-to-house collectors were dispensed with by allowing a 10-per-cent discount for prompt payment at the Water Office. Sending out water bills was started in 1889, substations for water bills in 1892. In 1894 water bills were made out not only in English but in foreign languages.

But the ever-increasing use of water was no indication of popular satisfaction. City engineers, answering the complaints of consumers, declared the quality by and large uniformly good, even if sometimes " roily " or " turbid " and tasting as if flavored with creosote. Furthermore, officials felt that those who relished " an oyster or clam " should find no fault if they did discover animal and vegetable matter. By the 'eighties, however, conditions had become so vexatious that municipal authorities were no longer refuting criticism when it was observed that the water was " a good deal like Chicago democracy," in need " of reformation." [30] During these years citizens increasingly insisted on finding out the connection between the city's water supply and the disposal of the sewage. The Department of Public Works perforce began to express alarm at the probability that various impurities soon might reach the water supply.

Such fears had a basis in what was actually taking place. In 1871 Chicago had reversed the current of the river, the city's great open sewer, to carry the wastes downstream into the Illinois River by means of " a deep cut " in the Illinois and Michigan Canal. But this engineering feat provided only a temporary remedy to the problem of diverting the sewage from the lake, the source of the city's water supply. In the same year that the canal was enlarged, the privately promoted " Ogden-Wentworth Ditch," from the Des Plaines River to the west fork of the south branch of the Chicago River, was also constructed to improve property owned by William B. Ogden and John Wentworth. This soon counteracted the westward current of the river and in the flood season forced the liquid filth back into the lake. At the same time it carried into the canal debris and silt that clogged the channel. After several years of agitation, an agreement was finally reached between the Ogden interests and the city authorities to build an embankment with head gates at the Des Plaines River end of the ditch. But the dam, completed in 1877, also proved ineffective in preventing an inflow from the Des Plaines River.[31]

Further difficulties arose following the deep cut in the canal in 1871 when the packing houses at Bridgeport were relocated in the stockyards on the south side of the city. The liquid waste discharged

[30] *The Knights of Labor*, II (March 12, 1887), 1; *The Chicago Times*, Nov. 8, 1883.
[31] George P. Brown, *Drainage Channel and Waterway* (Chicago, 1894), pp. 320–27; *Chicago Tribune*, June 14, 1874; *The Chicago Times*, June 25, 1874; Putnam, *The Illinois and Michigan Canal*, p. 143.

into the south fork of the south branch befouled the river and the sluggish canal until, as the *Times* put it, Chicago was "enveloped" by "solid stink." "The river stinks. The air stinks. People's clothing, permeated by the foul atmosphere, stinks. . . . No other word," continued the *Times,* "expresses it so well as stink. A stench means something finite. Stink reaches the infinite and becomes sublime in the magnitude of odiousness." The sewage passing down the canal wafted an intolerable stench to the citizens of Joliet and other canal towns. Chicago-bred germs were reported as "debilitating the systems of 200,000 people" in the Des Plaines and Illinois River valleys.[32]

By March, 1880 the council had heard enough, and on the twenty-ninth appropriated $100,000 for constructing new pumping works to replace the hydraulic works at Bridgeport, which had been dismantled in 1871. In May of the following year the state legislature ordered Chicago to proceed without delay in erecting and maintaining the pumping works, to increase the flow from the Chicago River into the canal sufficiently to dilute and cleanse the waters of the canal. But the works, located at the junction of the canal and the south fork, were not ready for operation until June, 1884. The situation was further aggravated by the fact that reversal of the river in 1871 had not provided for the purifying of the north branch, not auxiliary to the Illinois and Michigan Canal. Nor did the conduit, built on Fullerton Avenue from the lake to the north branch and completed in 1880, care for the increasing discharge from the business establishments along the north branch.[33]

By the mid-'eighties conditions had become intolerable. Unusual rainfall augmented the flow of sewage from the river into the lake, requiring a program of chemical examination to determine the extent of pollution. In 1886, therefore, after years of urging by the Citizens' Association and the press, the City Council created the Drainage and Water Supply Commission to seek an end to this problem so long plaguing the city.[34] When the Drainage Commission under-

---

[32] *The Chicago Times,* June 22, 1880, June 25, 1874; Illinois, *Senate Journal, 1881,* pp. 43, 809–10, *House Journal, 1881,* p. 848.

[33] Senate Joint Resolution adopted May 19, 1881, Illinois, *Laws, 1881,* pp. 159–61; Brown, *op. cit.,* pp. 170–71, 307–19, 328–35.

[34] Citizens' Association of Chicago, *Report of the Committee on the Main Drainage and Water Supply of Chicago, December, 1880,* pp. 15–23, *Annual Report, 1885,* p. 12, *Report*

took its investigations in 1886 the sewerage system of Chicago was thirty years old.[35] The next year the Commission had reached the conclusion that better drainage could be effected through a modification of the Illinois and Michigan Canal system whereby new channels would carry the sewage away from the lake, and eventually to the Mississippi River. The appointment by the legislature in 1887 of a committee of five to study the situation and propose legislation resulted in the recommendation that a sanitary district be created.

On May 29, 1889 a law of a general nature provided for forming a sanitary district whenever two or more incorporated places in a county agreed on a common drainage system by vote of the legal voters, taken on a petition of 5,000 voters, and it vested an elected nine-man board of trustees with the powers to administer such a district. The right, under restrictions, was given to cut a channel through " the Divide " at Summit, Illinois, to join the waters of Lake Michigan with those of the Mississippi.[36] On November 5, 1889 a metropolitan sanitary district was overwhelmingly approved by the electorate; in July, 1892 contracts were awarded; in the following months bonds for $2,000,000 at 5 per cent were sold; and on September 3, 1892 work on the main channel was inaugurated.[37] The new waterway, it was predicted, would do more than help solve Chicago's sanitary problems. It would, so it was said, make Chicago queen city of both the rivers and the lakes, add vastly to the wealth of Illinois, and provide security to the United States in the event of

of the Committee on the Main Drainage and Water Supply of Chicago, September, 1885, pp. 4–18; Chicago Tribune, Oct. 8, 1884, Nov. 6, 1887; Brown, op. cit., pp. 46–62, 345–73.

[35] The sewers of the North and West divisions and suburbs discharged partly into the lake and partly into the north branch; in the South Division those of Hyde Park into the lake, of the town of Lake into the south fork of the river; Pullman's sewage was disposed of on land. Ibid., pp. 49–62, 345–73.

[36] The board could choose minor officers, construct necessary sewers, buy and sell real estate, and under prescribed limits borrow money, issue bonds, and levy and collect taxes and special assessments. Act of May 29, 1889, Illinois, Laws, 1889, pp. 125–27; Brown, op. cit., pp. 376–91. The constitutionality of the law was upheld in Marshall J. Wilson v. Board of Trustees of the Chicago Sanitary District et al., 133 Ill. 433 (1890).

[37] Acting according to the law, Judge Richard Prendergast and circuit court judges R. S. Tuthill and S. P. McConnell fixed the boundaries of the district to coincide with the city limits along North Seventy-first Street; west, beyond the city limits to include Cicero and Summit; south, to the Calumet region; east, to Lake Michigan. The final selection of the route was made June 29, 1892. Chicago Department of Public Works, Fourteenth Annual Report, 1889, map facing p. 79; Brown, op. cit., pp. 392–404; Chicago Tribune, Aug. 16, Nov. 6, 1889; Chicago Sanitary District, Proceedings of the Board of Trustees . . . , 1890 to 1891, pp. 2, 161–66, 208–11, 228–34, 1892, pp. 404–7, 598, 607–8.

war with Great Britain. But not until January 2, 1900, nearly eight years later, did water pass from Lake Michigan into the canal. On January 17 the dam at Lockport was lowered and water from the lake flowed through the canal to the Des Plaines River.[38]

The task imposed on the Bureau of Streets to rescue Chicagoans from deep, clinging dust in dry, warm weather and bottomless pits of sticky mud during rains was as old as the city itself. Of the over 531 miles of streets in 1870, about 61 were improved, most of them being stretches of monotonous ugliness. The wooden blocks that had served as the chief pavement material at the time of the Fire were after that day scorched and badly damaged. Better surfacing, raising the level, and general repair went on during the 1870's, accelerated in the 'eighties under Mayor Harrison, and having a phenomenal extension after the annexations in 1889 of territory with its miles of rutted roads. In five years from 1889 the Department of Public Works surfaced 570 miles; and by the end of 'ninety-three the over 1,007 miles of improved streets reflected the deep-seated desire of Chicagoans to present a city to World's Fair visitors worthy of its much trumpeted glories. Macadam now covered about 31 per cent of the streets that had been improved, but cedar block continued to be used most frequently.[39]

Like the repair and building of streets, sidewalks, too, were extended and improved. Even as late as 1889, of the more than 2,000 miles, over 1,800 were of wood, while only 156 were stone, and less than 27 concrete. By the day of the Fair, over 4,252 miles led in every direction, but wood continued to provide over four-fifths of the materials which eased the way of the man on foot.

Bridges spanning the Chicago River remained, as in the years before the Fire, a frequent object of public concern and eventually of council regulation as to the hours they might be raised to permit passage of the many boats shuttling back and forth.[40] Even more

[38] *Ibid.*, pp. 472–85, 558–59, 619, 698–700, 719–20, *1900*, p. 6240; Elliott Anthony, *Sanitation and Navigation* (Chicago, 1911), pp. 15–17; Brown, *op. cit.*, pp. 424–59; *Chicago Tribune*, July 23, 1893; Putnam, *op. cit.*, p. 145.

[39] Chicago Board of Public Works, *Ninth Annual Report, 1870*, pp. 42–43. The succeeding annual reports provide similar information. See especially *Eighteenth Annual Report, 1893*, for a table showing pavement laid from 1853 through 1893. As late as 1889, of the total 2,048.43 miles, 1,419.46 were unimproved. Chicago, *Mayor's Annual Message and the Fourteenth Annual Report of the Department of Public Works, 1889*, p. 365.

[40] In 1881, for example, bridges could not be raised between six and seven in the morning or between five-thirty and six-thirty in the evening. Chicago, *Municipal Code, 1881,*

serious to traffic was the maze of railroad tracks and poorly protected grade crossings over which Chicagoans must thread their way.
From 1879 on, viaducts were built as a safety measure, but they and
protective gates failed to solve what became a problem of increasing
magnitude. By 1893 the council decided that its only recourse was
to force the elevation of all tracks into the city, a project not to be
completed for years to come.[41]

The motives of practicality back of improved thoroughfares were
accompanied by a civic determination to fashion the molten mass
that was Chicago in 1871 into spots of recreation, into a " city beautiful." The impulse of beautification accelerated in the post-Fire years
the park system which the state legislature had sanctioned in 1869.
Within two decades parks and boulevards of notable extent and improvement environed the fire-razed " Garden City." By the eve of
her transmutation to the fairness of " the White City " in 1892, Chicago had expended, so it was reported, an estimated aggregate of
$24,000,000, and had developed a system of eight large and twenty-
nine small parks and squares, some two thousand acres connected
by broad boulevards of thirty-five miles circling the city.[42]

By the time of the Fire, the administrative framework had been
virtually completed. The Lincoln Park Commissioners, the South
Park Commissioners, and the West Chicago Park Commissioners
were exercising their right to obtain land and arrange for financing
parks in their own divisions. Progress was to be slowed by litigation
over land purchases, condemnation proceedings, and special assess-

---

p. 252. See also *Council Proceedings, 1885–86*, p. 231, *1893–94*, pp. 172–73. In 1893 there
were fifty-one swing and two folding bridges. In 1890 electricity began to replace steam as
motive power. Chicago Department of Public Works, *Fifteenth Annual Report, 1890*, p. xi,
Eighteenth Annual Report, 1893, p. 42.

[41] Citizens' Association of Chicago, *Annual Report, 1887*, p. 20, *1888*, pp. 33–34; *Chicago Tribune*, Sept. 11, 1887, Sept. 25, 1889; *Svenska Tribunen*, Jan. 2, 1890; Chicago,
Council Proceedings, 1887–88, pp. 441–42, *1889–90*, p. 3, *1891–92*, pp. 1689–91, *1892–93*,
pp. 140–44, 188, 223–25, 572–82, 2381–86, *1914–15*, p. 299.

[42] The annual reports of the park commissioner are a main source for the parks located
in the various divisions of the city. For the following discussion see, in particular, Chicago
South Park Commissioners, *Report of the South Park Commissioners to the Board of County
Commissioners of Cook County, from December 1st, 1889, to December 1st, 1890* (Chicago,
1891), pp. 9, 48; West Park Commissioners, *Twenty-first Annual Report . . . for the Year
Ending February 28, 1890*, pp. 40–41; Chicago Lincoln Park Commissioners, *Report . . .
from January 1, 1893, to March 31, 1894*, pp. 7, 11. See for extent, Chicago Department
of Public Works, " Report of the Superintendent of the Map Department," *Fourteenth
Annual Report, 1889*, p. 392, " Appendix," *Fifteenth Annual Report, 1890*, p. 531.

ments as well as by inadequate revenue due to the Fire, to the commercial crisis of 1873, and to slowness in collecting taxes and selling park bonds.[43] Yet the park commissioners, wrestling with problems of revenue, succeeded by the 'eighties in converting nearly two thousand acres of meadow and wasteland into garden and pleasure grounds that elicited from visitors and local citizenry enthusiastic comparison with long-famed parks of Europe.[44]

In 1872 the Lincoln Park Commission gained control of the 171 acres of city property lying within the park. By 1894 private tracts of 59 acres would be acquired at costs ranging from $5,000 an acre to $21,000, and making the total expenditures for land purchase $889,533.12. Lincoln Park by 1885 had become the 250-acre lakeside garden of the North Side, improved at an expenditure exceeding three million dollars over fifteen years. Shifting sand ridges of a former burying ground had been transformed into tree-shaded expanses of lawns and flower gardens. From the modest appropriation in 'seventy-four — $100 for flowers and $500 for a greenhouse — and the appointment of the first gardener were to develop the magnificent gardens and conservatories that won acclaim in 1893 as " an attraction equal to the World's Fair." In 1874, also, a bear cub, which cost the Commissioners ten dollars, homesteaded in the park zoo. By the late 'eighties animals donated by the other commissioners and a collection purchased from the Barnum and Bailey Circus made the Lincoln Park Zoo unique in its exhibits. But leading in attracting some fifty thousand visitors on a fine Sunday morning were the shaded walks and linking drives over which they could stroll, bicycle by 1882, ride in private carriages, or sightsee in hired phaetons and pony carts after 1892.

Signs printed in both English and German, monuments such as that of Johann von Schiller, the famous Augustus Saint-Gaudens's statue of Lincoln, and the imposing statues of René de La Salle,

[43] Act of February 18, 1874, Illinois, *Laws, 1874,* pp. 125–26; Chicago Lincoln Park Commissioners, *Report of the Commissioners* [*1899*] *and a History of Lincoln Park* (Chicago, 1899), pp. 36, 38. For difficulties attending the west parks in particular, see West Chicago Park Commissioners, *Twelfth Annual Report, 1880–81,* p. 55. For relief of west parks see West Chicago Park Commissioners, *Twenty-third Annual Report, 1891–92,* pp. 6–8; Act of June 12, 1891, Illinois, *Laws, 1891,* pp. 173–74, Act of June 17, 1893, *Laws, 1893,* p. 161.

[44] Chicago Department of Public Works, *Fourteenth Annual Report, 1889,* p. 392; Pierce, *As Others See Chicago,* pp. 225, 229, 304–5, 398.

Carolus Linnæus, and General U. S. Grant — all in place by 1891 — gave the park memorials of the ingredients of the city's melting-pot. In this civic playground, Chicagoans, under the supervision of the park police, organized in 1872, enjoyed ice-skating, baseball, tennis, boating, and band concerts, activities which by the mid-'eighties could continue after sunset under the glow of the arc lamps of the park's first electric lighting, installed in 1883. And on the partially improved beach off North Avenue, where a bathing house was erected in 1873, Chicagoans could catch a vision of the planned park beaches that after 1895 would be developed.[45]

But while the visitor to Lincoln Park in the 'eighties might extol it as " an exquisite piece of restful landscape, looked over by a thickening assemblage of stately mansions," it was the boldness of a project of a city encircled by parks that excited the imagination. As planned by Olmsted, Vaux & Co. in 1871, the South Park system covered more than a thousand acres of uncultivated and uninhabited country, six miles from Chicago's business center in the village of Hyde Park. Title to the 1,045 acres for the two south parks with the 600-foot connecting Midway was acquired in 1874, but inflation of property values within the park site was to bring the total outlay for land purchase by 1886 to approximately three and a half million dollars, a considerable increase over the estimated value of $75,000 in 1867.[46]

By mid-'eighties Washington Park was practically complete and improvements were being extended to Jackson Park. Reached over the fashionable thoroughfares of Drexel, Grand, and Garfield boulevards, the south parks functioned as an important factor in the social life of the flourishing South Side community. When the phaeton line acquired by Washington Park in 1876 was extended to Jackson Park in 1888, the visitor to the south parks could make a round trip of nine miles from Oakwood and Drexel boulevards through the

[45] Chicago Lincoln Park Commissioners, *History of Lincoln Park*, pp. 14, 30, 32, 38, 42, 44, 48–54, 71, 72, 77, 82, 85, 108, 110, *Annual Report, 1893–94*, p. 4, *1895–96*, p. 6; *Chicago Tribune*, Feb. 28, Oct. 10, 1886, Oct. 20, 1887, Jan. 22, Aug. 30, 1888, May 5, 1889, Oct. 8, 1891.
[46] Warner, " Studies of the Great West. III. — Chicago," *Harper's New Monthly Magazine*, LXXVI (May, 1888), 873–74; Olmsted, Vaux & Co., *Report [to the Chicago South Park Commissioners] Accompanying Plan for Laying Out the South Park* (Chicago, 1871), pp. 3, 6; Chicago Department of Public Works, " Appendix," *Fifteenth Annual Report, 1890*, p. 531; *Chicago Tribune*, April 4, 1886; Andreas, *History of Cook County*, pp. 557–60.

two parks and the Midway for thirty cents. Within three years after the Fire, weekly concerts conducted by Hans Balatka were drawing large crowds of the musically appreciative to Washington, while Jackson's semicultivated grounds became the recreational spot of no less than 42,260 picnickers in 1882 alone. Popular centers of diversion by 1889, the two south parks were in season the scenes of "foot ball" games on the lawns, curling and ice-skating on the lagoons, tennis on the forty courts in the two parks, baseball games on the seven diamonds of Washington, and exhibitions of equestrian skill on the sixty-foot speeding driveway adjoining. Favorite rendezvous in all seasons for the privileged of Chicago's social set was the Washington Park Racing Club, with facilities alleged to "exceed anything in the country of the kind."[47]

From the thousand acres of the South Park system or from the quarter-thousand of Lincoln Park in the North Division, the park circuit moved by way of the lake shore to the half-thousand acres of the three large west parks — Garfield, Humboldt, and Douglas. Until 1875 meager funds permitted only the development of Central Park, renamed Garfield in 1881. On July 14, 1877 Humboldt was formally dedicated, and Douglas opened the following year. After 1890 improvements progressed rapidly. To the costs of the three large west parks was added the burden of maintaining many small ones, some like Union Square and Campbell Park but a half-acre in extent.[48] Originally supported by city funds, these small parks and squares were gradually transferred to the management of the park boards, the City Council turning over a considerable number to the West Park Board in 1885. These tiny resorts, although less pretentious than the largest, contributed in considerable measure to "the city beautiful" and proved an unalloyed blessing to those who dwelt near them.[49]

[47] M. L. Osborn, *The Development of Recreation in the South Park System of Chicago* (unpublished M.A. Thesis, The University of Chicago, 1928), pp. 23–24, 28; Chicago South Park Commissioners, *Annual Report, 1873–74,* p. 22, *1875–76,* p. 34, *1879–80,* pp. 5, 33, *1881–82,* p. 19, *1883–84,* p. 16, *1885–86,* pp. 11–32, *1888–89,* p. 14; Warner, "Studies of the Great West. III. — Chicago," *loc. cit.,* pp. 873–74; *The Chicago Times,* Oct. 18, 1879.

[48] The largest was the forty-one-acre Lake Front Park, later to be developed as Grant Park.

[49] West Chicago Park Commissioners, *Third Annual Report, 1871–72,* p. 39, *Fifth Annual Report, 1873–74,* pp. 7–8, *Ninth Annual Report, 1877–78,* pp. 5, 7, *Twelfth Annual Report, 1880–81,* pp. 8–10, 12–16, *Twenty-fifth Annual Report, 1893–94,* p. 75; Chicago, *Council Proceedings, 1885–86,* pp. 187–88, 203, 224; Chicago Board of Public Works,

The park boards in 1879 were granted authority to control the streets which connected the various parks, and an ambitious program was projected. By 1893 progress in the realization of one continuous, pleasant driveway from Lincoln to the west parks and thence to Jackson on the southeast was impressive. When, in 1870, the construction of Lake Shore Drive was undertaken by the Lincoln Park Commission, a still numerous bovine contingent, the property of North Chicago residents, found the greensward of the lake front off-bounds pasture. But for cow and prairie the cause was to be lost in a very short time, as road contractors impounded the trespassing cow and pounded out the Drive in a series of widenings and extensions. By the 'nineties the dream of linking a three-mile Lake Shore Drive with a thirty-mile lake-shore road began to stir the imagination of ambitious and farseeing citizens. When the North Shore Improvement Association in 1892 succeeded in persuading the legislature to grant the Lincoln Park Commission authority to condemn lands in order to build the necessary connection for the southern end of Sheridan Road, fulfillment of this master stroke got under way.[50]

In the West Division the connecting link between Douglas and Garfield parks was opened in 1881. That same year surveys were made for a 250-foot roadway on Western Avenue that would join with Garfield and South Park boulevards to connect Douglas with the south parks — a plan half completed by 1893. Joining the west parks with Lincoln and the Lake Shore Drive by a boulevard extending from Western Avenue to Diversey was to remain on paper until 1895 and not to be completed until 1896.[51]

The prospect of a lakeside drive from Jackson Park to the center of the city was also held out, despite the fact that during these years the section of the lake front between the Chicago River and Sixteenth Street was a matter of continuous litigation between the Illinois Central Railroad on the one hand and the state of Illinois and

Fifteenth Annual Report, 1875, p. 21; Chicago Department of Public Works, *Fourteenth Annual Report, 1889*, p. 392.

[50] Act of April 9, 1879, Illinois, *Laws, 1879*, p. 216; Chicago Lincoln Park Commissioners, *A History of Lincoln Park*, pp. 13, 26, 40, 52, 74; *Chicago Tribune*, Feb. 16, 17, 24, March 15, 1889, May 22, July 28, 1891, Jan. 24, 1892.

[51] West Chicago Park Commissioners, *Twelfth Annual Report, 1880–81*, pp. 17, 22, *Thirteenth Annual Report, 1881–82*, p. 9, *Fourteenth Annual Report, 1882–83*, p. 8, *Twenty-fourth Annual Report, 1892–93*, pp. 48–49, *Twenty-eighth Annual Report, 1896–97*, p. 16.

the city of Chicago on the other. The public outcry against what was commonly known as the " Lake Front Steal " was expressed in the procurement of an injunction by property owners against execution of the act. The repeal of the Act of 1869, or the Lake Front Act, on April 15, 1873 made the disposition of the lake front a matter for judicial review. As fought out in the 1870's and '80's, the issue became a struggle between those seeking to reserve the lands west of the tracks for a public park and the railroad and other business interests who favored its exploitation for commercial enterprises.[52]

The Illinois Central, standing by its claims, was to lose the legal contest. The verdict of the United States Circuit Court in 1888, supporting the claim of the state and city, was upheld by the United States Supreme Court in 1892. The full force of the decision would be felt in later years. The United States Supreme Court had acted to save to the state more than a thousand acres of submerged land, an area, in Justice Stephen J. Field's words, " as large as that embraced by all the merchandise docks along the Thames at London, . . . larger than that included in the famous docks and basins at Liverpool, . . . twice that of the port of Marseilles, and nearly . . . equal to the pier area along the water front of the city of New York." With the port of Chicago having arrivals and clearings of vessels, Field continued, " equal to those of New York and Boston combined " and " nearly twenty-five per cent of the lake carrying trade," it was not " conceivable " that the legislature could " divest the state of the control and management of this harbor and vest it in a private corporation." By the same decision, the city was confirmed in its right as riparian owner of the lake front between Randolph Street and Park Row and given title to property valued in 1893 at $80,000,000.[53]

[52] Pierce, A History of Chicago, II, 342; Chicago Tribune, Nov. 27, 1871, April 3, 1874, Oct. 3, 1876, March 6, 1881, April 10, 1883, Jan. 8, 9, July 18, 1884, March 18, 1888, July 4, 21, Aug. 9, 1889; The Chicago Times, Oct. 1, 1882, May 10, 1883, Feb. 4, 1884; L'Italia, July 6, 1889; Illinois Anti-Monopoly League, Report of the Present Status of the Claims of the Illinois Central Railroad to the Lake Front, and Submerged Lands Adjoining, under the " Lake Front Steal " of 1869 [Chicago, 1881], 8 pp.; Act of April 15, 1873, Illinois, Laws, 1873, p. 115.

[53] Decision of the Circuit Court of the Northern District of Illinois was rendered by the Hon. John M. Harlan, Feb. 23, 1888: State of Illinois v. Illinois Central Railroad Company, 33 Federal Reporter 730 (1888); appeal to the United States Supreme Court decided Dec. 5, 1892; Illinois Central Railroad Company v. Illinois, 146 U. S. 387 (1892). See also Mayor Hempstead Washburne, " Mayor's Annual Message to the City Council of the City of Chicago

No agency of the government had greater and more persisting duties than the Board of Health. Scourges of smallpox, cholera, scarlet fever, diphtheria spread sorrow and suffering, particularly during the 'seventies. In July, 1876, under the new city charter of 1875, the City Council — rather than the Superior Court, which had formerly held the power of appointment — reorganized the municipal health service. The board's powers and duties were transferred to a single commissioner named by the mayor with the advice and consent of the council.[54] The expansion of the personnel of the department from thirty-four in 1876 to a staff of ninety-two, distributed in seven bureaus, in 1893, illustrated the enlarging role that was being played. General inspectors who had been assigned one to a ward to look into various aspects of sanitation were gradually replaced by men with specific duties. In 1893 medical, meat and stockyards, burial, milk, tenement and factory inspectors ferreted out perils to health, while a dozen fumigators attempted to stem the spread of contagious diseases.[55]

The greatest single concern of the health authorities was the scavenger service, carried on by the costly method of hiring teams by the day at from $2.25 to $3.50 until 1887, when contracts were made for some of the work. At first the chief problem was the location of a dump, and vacant lots were requisitioned for this purpose. Beginning in 1881, however, great quantities of waste were moved out of the city by rail, and year by year the amounts grew larger and the distance carried became longer. Even so, low places and the streets remained the repositories of garbage, rubbish, and street sweepings. Those cleaning one section inconsiderately removed the refuse to a neighboring area below grade, until, in 1887, Commissioner of Health Oscar C. De Wolf, weary of unheeded reprimands, reminded his fellow citizens that it was full time that Chicago abandon this village custom.

A garbage furnace, built with funds authorized by the City Coun-

for the Fiscal Year Ending December 31, 1892," Chicago, *Municipal Reports, 1892* (Chicago, 1893), p. xxiv; *The Railway Age and Northwestern Railroader*, XVIII (March 10, 1893), 203.

[54] Chicago, *Council Proceedings, 1876–77*, pp. 16, 111; Act of April 10, 1872, Illinois, *Laws, 1871–72*, pp. 228–33.

[55] The reports of the Chicago Board of Health 1871–1874, from 1875–1893 the Department of Health, are the chief source of information on matters relating to health and sanitation. To these, other references are added when particularly pertinent.

cil in July, 1887, proved more of an expense than the authorities had anticipated, and its destruction in 1889 by its own fire was hailed as a blessing. The refusal of the railroads in 1891 to continue to haul refuse even to the edge of the city, and the rejection by property owners of an ordinance of July 15, 1892 for crematories, on the ground that they would depreciate property or become a nuisance, accentuated the difficulties of scavenger services. To these a Bureau of Street and Alley Cleaning in the Department of Public Works fell heir by council ordinance March 13, 1893. The problem, however, was not solved; a shift of responsibility merely had been accomplished.[56]

Offensive odors, at times almost intolerable for those within range of the garbage-strewn alleys, stockyards, rendering plants, oil-burning rolling mills, soap, glue, and fertilizer factories, gave Chicago the reputation of being one of the most smelly places in the country. As late as the 'nineties there still abounded uncleaned, outside privies, " thousands of those dangerous and disgraceful horrors," as the Board of Health put it in its report of 1891. And, besides, the Chicago River, reeking with filth, befouled the atmosphere. Regulations adopted in 1871 forbade the future building of slaughterhouses, rendering establishments, and soap factories within the area bounded by Fullerton Avenue, Thirty-first Street, Western Avenue, and the lake, while rendering in the district was ordered halted during the months of April through September. Municipal control over packing houses was not effective, however, until after June, 1878, when the Illinois Supreme Court upheld an ordinance, backed by the Citizens' Association, licensing slaughtering, packing, and rendering plants, soap factories, and tanneries within the city and a mile beyond.[57]

More successful was the fight against the pall of black smoke belching from buildings and steam-powered vehicles. From its origin in 1874, the Citizens' Association protested this film of dirt and darkness which enshrouded the city. Under this pressure the council adopted an anti-smoke ordinance May 1, 1881, antedating similar

[56] Chicago Department of Public Works, *Eighteenth Annual Report, 1893,* p. 116; Citizens' Association of Chicago, *Annual Report, 1886,* p. 20, *1889,* p. 14, *1892,* pp. 5–6; Chicago, *Council Proceedings, 1888–89,* p. 2, *1892–93,* pp. 7, 497–98, 772, 2594–97, *1893–94,* pp. 34–35, 38; *Chicago Tribune,* Dec. 13, 1871, Aug. 17, 1873, Sept. 27, 1892.

[57] *Ibid.,* Dec. 13, 1871, Aug. 17, 1873, Sept. 27, 1892; Chicago, *Council Proceedings, 1877–78,* p. 155.

measures in both New York and Boston and affording a legitimate reason for Chicago's usual boasting as the first or biggest in nearly everything. Enforcement of the new regulations, which did not apply to private residences, was lodged jointly in the Commissioner of Health and the Superintendent of Police. Although some good resulted, numerous convictions of violations attested to a callous disregard of the law by many. Long, winding trails of thick black smoke continued to envelop and besmutch the city.[58]

Upon the health officials fell also the duty of food inspection, directed principally to the great packing industry, where seizures of condemned meat rose from a low of 85,950 pounds in 1873 to 1,991,-164 pounds twenty years later. With the work of the Department, the large packers, unlike some of the small producers, readily cooperated, conscious that good products would increase sales and spread throughout the world a reputation for reliability.[59]

Besides meats, the Commissioner of Health was responsible for the inspection of foods such as vegetables, eggs, and fruits, as well as for enforcing an 1880 ordinance requiring the labeling of butter substitutes.[60] Adulteration of milk was a never-ending source of trouble, and it was not until November, 1892 that the City Council established a Milk Division within the Department of Health, staffed by a chemist and nine assistants. The ordinance required the licensing of milk dealers and set up a code to eliminate a substandard product.[61]

Under the jurisdiction of health officials after 1880 also fell the inspection of factories and tenements and other places of employment. Six plumbing inspectors in that year undertook to look into the installation of plumbing equipment, and in 1881 state legislators, having in mind improved sanitary conditions, enacted a law to that

[58] See reports of Citizens' Association of Chicago 1880–1882; reports of the Chicago Department of Health 1881–1893; Chicago, *Municipal Code, 1881*, p. 386, *Council Proceedings, 1890–91*, pp. 33–34; Chicago Association of Commerce, *Smoke Abatement and Electrification of Railway Terminals in Chicago* (Chicago, 1915), pp. 82–83; *The Chicago Times*, July 2, 1880; *Chicago Tribune*, Jan. 22, 24, Feb. 11, March 29, July 10, Nov. 12, 1892.

[59] See reports of the Chicago Board of Health 1870–73, and the Chicago Department of Health, especially 1893; *Chicago Tribune*, Oct. 29, Nov. 23, 1879.

[60] See Chapter IV, "Livestock and Meat Packing."

[61] Chicago, *Council Proceedings, 1892–93*, pp. 1527–34; *Chicago Daily News*, Oct. 17, 1892; *Chicago Tribune*, Nov. 22, 1892.

end. Approval of health authorities of plans and specifications of tenement lodging houses and other dwellings also was prescribed in 'eighty-one by the state. But despite gains each year in the improvement of the sanitary character of buildings put up according to the code of the department, the rapid increase in population accentuated the problem of health and sanitation, especially in the poorer sections of the city. Of 31,171 tenements and rented houses inspected in 1887 alone, a reported 85 per cent were found defective in their sanitary facilities.[62]

In 1893, as thousands trooped to Chicago to view the World's Fair, the city boasted that its death rate was " the lowest of any large city in the world," with the possible exception of Berlin. In 1873 mortality among children under five was 59 per cent of all the deaths in the city; in 1893 the figure stood at 45 per cent. Except for unusual epidemic years, deaths from many contagious diseases showed a satisfactory decrease, but an increase of fatalities was noted among sufferers of heart disease and pneumonia.[63]

Municipal participation in the care of dependent persons, except for those in confinement under the jurisdiction of the police, was of minor importance and, on the whole, restricted to indirect activity. Allotments derived from fines from prostitution cases were made each year by the City Council to the House of the Good Shepherd and the Erring Woman's Refuge for Reform, while the Washingtonian Home, an institution for alcoholics, received money from the appropriate source of saloon licenses. Regular relief to the indigent and ill came from private and county rather than city funds, and Chicago authorities could well rejoice that upon them did not fall the burden of the city's poor. By 1890 more than 92 per cent of the county's population lived in Chicago. The welfare work, however, continued to be administered through the county government, al-

[62] Act of May 30, 1881, Illinois, *Laws, 1881*, p. 66; *The Sanitary News*, I (Jan. 1, 1883), 50, (Feb. 1, 1883), 78, III (Nov. 15, 1883), 14; Chicago, *Supplement to the Municipal Code . . . 1887*, pp. 63–64, *Laws and Ordinances . . . 1890*, pp. 657–61. See for 1873 Board of Health agitation for regulation of tenements, Chicago, *Council Proceedings, 1873–74*, pp. 146, 183.

[63] Frederick L. Hoffman, " The General Death-Rate of Large American Cities, 1871–1904," *Publications of the American Statistical Association*, X (March, 1906), 30–32, 34–35, 40–41. Slightly different figures for Chicago appear in Chicago Department of Health, *Chronological Summary of Chicago Mortality 1843–1902* (n.p., n.d.).

though by 1891 county expenditures for institutions, poorhouse, insane asylum, hospital and outdoor relief or dole reached $631,652, almost four times more than in 1871.[64]

At the same time, the government attempted to meet the challenges of the new day which confronted education. In 1872 the administration of the school system was delegated to a Board of Education of fifteen members appointed by the mayor with confirmation by the council, to be increased to twenty-one in 1891.[65] Only 476 teachers were employed in 1871–72 for the 38,035 pupils enrolled; by the year 1891–92 teachers and principals numbered 3,520 to care for the needs of 166,895, a gain in large part due to the territorial annexations of 1889. The salaries paid the instructional staff did not parallel other signs of urban growth, but men in the high school usually received about four times as much pay as did their women counterparts in the grade schools. At times, especially in the depression years of the late 'seventies, all teachers got only scrip, and in 1877 and '78 their pay was suspended. Building also lagged far behind needs, and as late as 1893 enrollment exceeded seats provided for pupils by 14,000.[66]

The cost of supporting the public schools was paid chiefly from local taxes, receipts from the state, and income from school lands. Local taxes might total 5 per cent of all taxable property, of which two-fifths was for educational expenses and the other three-fifths for building costs. Aid to the city from the state came from the common school fund supported by a two-mill levy on the state property tax, the interest on money distributed to the states by Congress in 1837, and part of the money derived from the sales of the public lands.[67]

The school lands included some of the most valuable plots in the central business district, and, while they provided a substantial part

[64] Pierce, A History of Chicago, II, 440–43; Chicago City Comptroller, Annual Statement 1871–1893; James Brown, The History of Public Assistance in Chicago 1833 to 1893 (Chicago, 1941), p. 80; U. S., Eleventh Census, 1890, " Population," pt. I, 103.

[65] Act of April 1, 1872, Illinois, Public Laws, 1871–72, pp. 740–42; Act of May 21, 1889, Laws, 1889, pp. 306–9; Act of June 22, 1891, Laws, 1891, pp. 195–96; Sparling, op. cit., pp. 132–34. The annual reports of the Board of Education are an invaluable source on the public schools.

[66] Besides reports and proceedings of the Board of Education, see The Chicago Times, March 16, 1878; Chicago Tribune, April 19, 1878, Nov. 13, 1880, June 20, 1883, Nov. 27, 1886, Sept. 6, 1888, Sept. 3, 1892.

[67] Act of May 21, 1889, Illinois, Laws, 1889, pp. 316–35.

of the income of the schools, they were at the same time a source of frequent dispute and litigation between the Board of Education and the lessees. Rental of downtown property was made upon the basis of 6 per cent a year of the appraised value of the property; and land in outlying rural areas was let at prices considered suitable for agricultural use.[68] It was common opinion that values set by School Fund land appraisers appointed by the Board of Education were often below their real worth. Reappraisal in 1885 in turn brought protests that valuations were too high from twenty-six lessees who, in 1880, had signed fifty-year leases to School Fund property. Protracted litigation ensued between the Board of Education and twenty-two of the tenants, including the Tribune Company, McVicker's Theatre, Joseph E. Otis, and George L. Otis, with holdings in the vicinity of State and Dearborn on Madison Street.[69]

Typical of the skyrocketing appraisal values of land was the tract at 81 to 87 Madison Street, which soared from the $136,000 figure of 1880 to $240,000 of 1885, or $3,000 per front foot, an increase of 76.4 per cent for the five years. The land leased by the Tribune Company jumped in its appraised value from $129,600 to $300,000, an increase of 131.5 per cent that brought the valuation per front foot on Madison Street to $2,500. The average increase for the twenty-two plaintiffs, said the *Tribune,* was 95.23 per cent.[70]

Deciding in favor of the plaintiffs, Judges Gwynn Garnett and Henry M. Shepard of the Superior Court ruled that improvements made should not have entered into the consideration and that the appraisals should be set aside. In a series of out-of-court agreements then between the Board of Education and the protesting lessees, the period of appraisals was lengthened from five to ten years and leases were extended to 1985. The Board was guaranteed a rental from 1915 based upon a minimum appraisal value of 60 per cent of the valuation established in 1885. Future appraisals were to be made by

[68] One dollar an acre was the rental in the Town of Lake in 1873. Chicago Board of Education, *Proceedings . . . September, 1873, to September, 1874,* p. 5. For various lengths of leases see list of property in Chicago, *Council Proceedings, 1876–77,* pp. 116–17.

[69] Individual cases are listed in *Plaintiff's General Index,* II (Mss. vault of Office of Clerk of Superior Court of Cook County). Bills of complaint were filed June 20, 1885, and the answers of the Board of Education Nov. 18, 1885.

[70] Walsh *v.* The Board of Education of the City of Chicago, case No. 97,615; Tribune Company *v.* The Board of Education of the City of Chicago, case No. 97,614. Superior Court of Cook County (Mss. vault of Office of Clerk of Superior Court of Cook County); *Chicago Tribune,* Nov. 17, 1887.

a board of three, one member each being appointed by the Board of Education, the United States Circuit Court for the Northern District of Illinois, and the Probate Court of Cook County, and future leases should incorporate the valuation provision " exclusive of improvements." [71]

The destruction by the Great Fire of many institutional and individual libraries quickened a demand for a public library in order that Chicago, as the *Tribune* put it, should not "lag behind other enlightened communities." By an act of March 7, 1872, "to establish and maintain a public library and reading room," the state legislature responded to the public wish. A tax of one-fifth of a mill per dollar of assessed value on taxable property was the basis of support. What came to be called "the Chicago Public Library" a municipal ordinance established April 1, 1872, and one week later the first board of directors, appointed by the mayor to serve without pay, was confirmed by the council.[72] While the tax rate was sufficient to provide an estimated $60,000 annually, library officials found themselves in frequent disputes with the authorities as to their right to withhold or divert some of the tax. When frugal councilmen in 1874 allotted only $25,000 to the institution, the *Tribune* indignantly remarked that this display of economy sprang from the fact that " the Library Board had no contracts to let, no jobs to offer, no commissions to pay." [73] Coming to the aid of the library board in 1881, the state legislature raised the tax to one-half mill, and in 1891 increased the levy to two mills for five years to pay for the new building to be erected in Dearborn Park.[74]

[71] In 1895 the Board of Education granted the first of its long-term leases at fixed rentals. Recipients of these leases to run at fixed rates until 1985 included the Tribune Company, the Chicago Daily News Company, and John M. Smyth. Chicago Board of Education, *Proceedings, 1887–88*, pp. 234–36, 247–48, *1894–95*, pp. 389, 479; *Chicago Tribune*, Nov. 17, 1887.

[72] *Chicago Tribune*, Oct. 8, 1871; *The Chicago Times*, Jan. 9, 21, 1872; Gwladys Spencer, *The Chicago Public Library, Origins and Backgrounds* (Chicago, 1943), pp. 250–53, 275–79; Act of March 7, 1872, Illinois, *Laws, 1871–72*, pp. 609–11; Chicago, *Council Proceedings, 1871–72*, pp. 148–49, 153.

[73] *The Chicago Public Library, 1873–1923* . . . [Chicago, 1923], p. 27; Chicago, *Council Proceedings, 1873–74*, p. 296; *Chicago Tribune*, Dec. 15, 1874.

[74] Act of March 24, 1881, Illinois, *Laws, 1881*, pp. 111–12; Act of March 20, 1883, *Laws, 1883*, p. 112; Act of June 19, 1891, *Laws, 1891*, pp. 154–55; Chicago Public Library, *Nineteenth Annual Report of the Board of Directors . . . June, 1891*, p. 15. Dearborn Park was bounded by Michigan Avenue on the east, Randolph on the north, Washington on the south, and Garland Place (later Garland Court) on the west.

No single function of government reflected more clearly the need for expanding controls than did the regulation of services performed by public service corporations. Through the physical conveniences provided, the economic potential of the city was quickened, its social contacts strengthened, and the comforts of living enhanced. In Chicago, as in other cities, were sometimes heard allegations of collusion between the donors of franchise privileges and those who sought them — a hidden alliance hard to prove and serving as a " sleepless influence," as Frederick C. Howe described it.

As Chicago flung her boundaries outward, facilities for transportation became a prerequisite for the continued well-being of the city. After 1870, buttressed by provisions of the new state constitution forbidding the state legislature to grant franchises to street railway companies except by consent of the local authorities, the city was able to claim almost complete power to permit and regulate their construction. It enjoyed, however, only a poorly defined jurisdiction over franchises and the operation of traction companies. To the North Chicago City Railway Company, the Chicago City Railway Company, and the Chicago West Division Railway Company a generous state legislature had extended, in 1865, city-granted franchises from twenty-five to ninety-nine years. In 1874, however, the state legislature, chastened by public opinion, passed "the Horse and Dummy Act," which added to the provision in the Constitution of 1870 the restriction that grants to street railways be for no more than twenty years. A further safeguard appeared in the 1872 general incorporation act, adopted by Chicago in 1875, repeating these protective measures. In 1883 those franchises already in existence were renewed en masse in the midst of controversy regarding the validity of the ninety-nine-year act; after that new franchises were almost always for a twenty-year period.[75]

Five years before, in March, 1878, the council undertook to derive some financial benefit from the use of the streets over and above each company's maintenance of those on which its tracks were laid, a re-

[75] Act of April 10, 1872, Illinois, *Public Laws, 1871–72*, p. 229; Act of March 19, 1874, Illinois, *Revised Statutes, 1874*, p. 571; Act of March 30, 1887, *Laws, 1887*, p. 108; Verlie, ed., *Illinois Constitutions*, p. 157; Pierce, *A History of Chicago*, II, 327–29; Chicago, *Laws and Ordinances, 1890*, pp. 819–20; James R. B. Van Cleave, *List of Franchises . . .* (Chicago, 1896), *passim*; George C. Sikes, "The Street Railway System in Chicago," *Proceedings of the Boston Conference for Good City Government and Eighth Annual Meeting of the National Municipal League, 1902*, pp. 175–78.

quirement in charters and franchises since the beginning. With this
in mind, the city imposed an annual license fee of fifty dollars for
each car operated, a move vigorously opposed by the railway companies. In 1883 "a convention of truce" resulted in redrawing the
franchises with their terminal date 1903 and in the companies agree-
ing to pay a twenty-five-dollar tax for five years from 1878, but fifty
dollars thereafter. An altered method of assessment so aided the railway companies, however, that the government realized little compensation; so little, in fact, that the Illinois Bureau of Labor Statistics sententiously observed: "In 1886 the dogs paid $27,948 for the
few privileges they enjoy, while the street car companies paid
$30,530.85, but soon afterward the dog, having less influence in
legislative halls than certain financiers, had to bear the larger burden." [76]

In 1880 a new kind of compensation to the government had been
added when the franchises then being issued required that streetcar
companies pay toward the construction and maintenance of bridges
they used.[77] Other levies of a similar nature came before the council
but were not made effective. By the 'nineties the question of payment to the city for the use of the streets by companies operating
local transit systems agitated both public and official circles more
than in the years preceding, but the struggle to resolve the problem
awaited a later day.[78]

Side by side with the consideration of traction franchises arose that
for companies dispensing gas and electricity and operating the telephone. Defining and safeguarding the interest of the public were

[76] Chicago, *Council Proceedings, 1877–78*, pp. 473–74, *1883–84*, pp. 76–85, 110–11,
113–17; Illinois Bureau of Labor Statistics, *Ninth Biennial Report, 1896*, p. 69. The right of
the city to exact a fee for use of the street was upheld in John J. Byrne *v.* The Chicago General Railway Company *et al.,* 169 Ill. 75 (1897). Litigation at the end of the pact period
resulted in a decision by the United States Supreme Court declaring the "ninety-nine
year act" illegal. Blair *v.* City of Chicago, 201 U. S. 400 (1906).

[77] The Chicago West Division Railway Company's franchise of Nov. 29, 1880, required
the company to pay one-half of the cost of a new Lake Street bridge and $1,000 annually
to maintain it. Other franchises granted followed similar stipulations. Chicago, *Council
Proceedings, 1880–81,* p. 245, *1886–87,* pp. 230–31, 434–35, 614–15, *1889–90,* pp. 876–78,
1890–91, p. 1749.

[78] For example, in March, 1888, in connection with the franchise of the Chicago and
South Side Rapid Transit Railroad Company (the "Alley L"), a motion to require 2 per
cent of the company's gross receipts for two years and 5 per cent per annum thereafter was
defeated. In 1891 an ordinance granting the West Chicago Street Railroad Company an
extension on West North Avenue required $800 a mile for this part of the line. This clause
was repealed Sept. 28, 1891. For such information see Chicago, *Council Proceedings.*

first worked out in grants to the gas industry, in which the experience of a long and troubled relationship with the Chicago Gas Light
and Coke Company and the People's Gas Light and Coke Company,
chartered by the state in 1849 and 1855 respectively, gave the
municipality a solid basis from which to fashion franchises granted
to the Consumers' Gas, Fuel and Light Company on April 28, 1882
and the Equitable Gas Light and Fuel Company on August 10,
1885. With vivid memories of the monopolistic practices of the older
companies, the city government inserted in the franchises regulations prohibiting agreements that involved price-fixing with other
business organizations or the transfer of franchise rights. In addition,
the city set up certain standards as to the quality of the companies'
product and prescribed municipal inspection to see that they were
enforced. Finally, the city was empowered to require an extension of
service into the new and improved sections of the city.[79]

In contrast to the specific provisions of the gas franchises of the
early 1880's was the blanket permission for the use of the city streets
given the Bell Telephone Company, September 9, 1878. Restricting
the company only in requiring that its lines be set under the supervision of the Department of Public Works and that free telephones
be provided in four municipal offices, the council was to regret its
lack of foresight. When Bell leased the company's rights and its
franchise to the Chicago Telephone Company, August 2, 1881, the
city became embroiled in a bitter struggle to force wires underground, not unlike that with the Mutual Union Telegraph Company
also seeking a franchise in 1881. Eventually in 1885 the municipality
reached a compromise by which the Chicago Telephone Company
promised to place its wires underground, and the city accepted a delay in the accomplishment of the project.[80]

In dealing with the electrical companies, the city benefited from
this experience, for the earliest franchise, granted Henry Corwith
and his associates on July 31, 1882, directed not only that wires be
put underground but that they be properly insulated. This ordinance,
limited to twenty-five years, also included detailed instructions on

[79] Chicago, *Council Proceedings, 1881–82*, pp. 553–54, *1885–86*, pp. 118–20. The right
of the council to regulate the price was recognized in 1865. For a discussion of the two
older companies before 1871 see Pierce, *A History of Chicago*, II, 320–21.

[80] Chicago, *Council Proceedings, 1878–79*, p. 205, *1888–89*, p. 674; *The Chicago Times*,
Jan. 12, 1883; Van Cleave, *List of Franchises . . .* , p. 60.

the use of the city streets; it required construction to start within six months and extend as rapidly as the council saw fit; and it also prescribed the posting of a bond of $50,000 as indemnity to the city for any damage which might arise against it through the company's exercise of its franchise rights. After three years the council saw fit to modify this franchise, now vested in a corporation formed by the Corwith group, known as the Chicago Underground Electric Company.[81] The amendment, passed on December 9, 1885, protected the company by limiting its obligations to extend its service to those areas where such an extension would yield 6 per cent on the investment, but at the same time required it to furnish the city free use of one duct in its conduits and protected property owners by specifying that no wire be laid under a sidewalk without the permission of the owner of the abutting property. When the Western Edison Light Company received its franchise of March 28, 1887, the provisions of the amended franchise of the underground electric group were also applied to it.[82]

By 1888 the relationship of the city government to the public utilities seemed, on the whole, to be well formulated. More franchises were issued in this year than in any previous one, and these ordinances embodied the accumulated experience of a number of years of dealing with the problem of public service companies.[83] The post-1888 agreements included the important stipulation of financial compensation to the city for the privilege of holding a franchise. Besides the early rather minor gratuities a percentage ranging from 3 to 5 per cent of gross earnings was to be paid into the city treasury. By an agreement of July 16, 1891, this tribute was collected not only from new gas, telephone, and electric companies enfranchised after

[81] The Chicago Sectional Electric Underground Company was the successor of the Chicago Underground Electric Company. This name was taken in 1886.

[82] The Chicago Underground Electric Company was a common carrier. The Western Edison Light Company was not. The former was protected by 1888 ordinances providing that private firms using streets where the common carrier had lines must use them or, if laying their own, must open them to public use. Chicago, Council Proceedings, 1886–87, pp. 634–35, 650–51, 1888–89, pp. 245–53.

[83] A franchise was issued the Chicago Telephone Company Oct. 15, 1888 (amended Jan. 4, 1889). For franchises granted short-lived companies, see Chicago, Council Proceedings, 1887–88, pp. 427, 787–89, 1888–89, pp. 245–53, 443–45, 742–43, 1890–91, pp. 1309–12, 1891–92, pp. 436–37, 1893–94, pp. 2–7. During these same years the franchise of the Chicago Sectional Electric Underground Company was exercised by the Chicago Arc Light and Power Company and that of Western Edison by the Chicago Edison Company. The transfer was made in 1887.

1888, but also from all gas firms doing business in the city regardless of the terms of their individual franchises.[84]

The objections raised by various public service companies to governmental impositions quickened agitation by reform groups for municipal ownership. Moreover, clauses were introduced providing that the city might purchase plant or equipment at the end of the franchise term, or even at periodic intervals within the time of the grant. In some cases, too, the city inserted a provision giving it a right to appoint a person to a company's board of directors whose task it would be to represent the interests of the municipality. A more direct approach toward municipal participation was the first city-owned electric-light plant, established in 1888, which furnished illumination on streets and bridges. By 1893 four such plants were in operation and plans were being made for further expansion. These plants generated power only for city use and did not compete with privately owned companies.[85]

The conduct of numerous agencies of government, some as old as Chicago herself, others created by the exigencies of the modern city, was, of course, complicated by the advancing lines of settlement in the outlands and their eventual annexation to the core city. The charter of 1875 permitted part of one corporate body to be transferred to another by mutual consent through general elections in each municipality, but without affecting or impairing any rights or liabilities. Agitation for such extension was especially vigorous in the 1880's. On June 15, 1887 what was popularly called the Chicago Consolidation and Annexation Bill passed the legislature and clarified various questions involved in the annexation of territory, such as the assumption of debts, the retention of prohibition ordinances, and the re-formation of boundaries. Although the ostensible intent was township reorganization, the bill also made automatic the extension of a city's boundaries to include any territory added to a township wholly within a city. Thus by annexing land to the towns of North, West,

---

[84] Chicago, *Council Proceedings, 1890–91*, pp. 1309–12, *1891–92*, pp. 505–7. This agreement of the gas companies was part of the battle with the Gas Trust. For the struggle waged by the Chicago Telephone Company against rate-setting and the 3-per-cent tax on its gross revenue, see Chicago, *Council Proceedings, 1888–89*, pp. 442–45, 674–83, 741–44. For 1890 and later, *Council Proceedings, 1890–91*, pp. 1680–83, *1893–94*, pp. 2–7.

[85] *Electrical Review*, X (June 4, 1887), 10; *Western Electrician*, V (Sept. 14, 1889), 146, (Oct. 5, 1889), 177; Chicago Fire Marshal, *Annual Report, 1887*, pp. 90–91, *1888*, pp. 81–82, *1893*, p. 161.

and South Chicago, incorporation into the city would also be accomplished.

Passage of the law was the signal for annexation-minded residents of outlying areas to seek attachment to the city. Parts of Cicero, Hyde Park, Lake, Lake View, and Jefferson townships petitioned the County Board of Commissioners to place them under the jurisdiction of the towns of North, West, and South Chicago, and the question then went to the voters of the towns.[86]

Stinging defeats met the pro-annexationists in Lake and Lake View, but in other sections success came, only to be blocked by appeals to the courts on grounds of unconstitutionality, illegality of the petition, and similar points. Those who were opposed to relinquishing the separate existence of their communities were especially active in Hyde Park. Here they appealed with great effectiveness to the old-time aversion to higher taxes, increasing costs of such community needs as transportation, the loss of direct control over schools and other institutions. But most persuasive of all was the argument that aldermen would have no ear for the requests of the newcomers.[87]

The injunction which officials of the village of Hyde Park had obtained in Superior Court was lifted on December 3, and on the seventh Hyde Park, like sections of Cicero and Jefferson before it, was " formally wedded," as the *Tribune* put it, to the greater municipality. The dispute between the village of Hyde Park and the city proper, however, continued until the state Supreme Court separated the two on March 16, 1888. At the same time the portions of

[86] On Sept. 27, 1886 property owners of a square-mile section of the town of Jefferson (section 36) lying north of North and west of Western avenues petitioned the City Council. On April 5, 1887 annexation was approved at the polls. The final ordinance of annexation passed the council May 16, 1887, but not until the next year did it become a part of the town of West Chicago. Chicago, *Municipal Code, 1881,* pp. 121–24, *Council Proceedings, 1886–87,* pp. 59, 274, 505–6; Cook County Board of Commissioners, *Official Proceedings, 1886–87,* pp. 374, 436, 448, 474, 478, *1887–88,* pp. 179, 760–61; Act of June 15, 1887, Illinois, *Laws, 1887,* pp. 300–4, *House Journal, 1887,* p. 1173, *Senate Journal, 1887,* pp. 345–768. See also *Chicago Tribune* on appropriate dates.

[87] *Chicago Tribune,* Nov. 7, 8, 10, 17, 22, 1887; *Chicago Daily News,* Nov. 9, 15, 17, 22, 1887; Cook County Board of Commissioners, *Official Proceedings, 1886–87,* pp. 563, 564, 569, 585, 595, 613. The boundaries of the Village and Town of Hyde Park were identical. The merger was attacked on the grounds that the unannexed portion would be left without most of its best property, that property of the village was annexed along with that of the town, that outstanding village bonds were an obligation on the whole village and were not specifically payable from a particular fund, and that an insufficient number of registered legal voters of Hyde Park had signed the petition for annexation. Village of Hyde Park, *Annual Report of the President and Village Officers, 1887–88,* p. 33.

Cicero and Jefferson which had been annexed were also disassociated from Chicago on the ground of the unconstitutionality of the act of June 15, 1887 as applied to the extension of the limits of a city.[88] In April, 1889 the state legislature in the so-called Knight-Bliss Bill opened the way for the towns of Lake and Jefferson, the city of Lake View, the village of Hyde Park, and a small part of Cicero to unite with Chicago. Later court action upheld the returns of the election of June 29, and Chicago's area, by additions made in 1887 and 1889, now embraced 168.671 square miles.[89]

The various extensions of governmental services which took place after the Great Fire proved an unending cause of irritation to Chicago taxpayers as well as a source of anxiety to officials. Demands for ever larger amounts of money, especially in the 'eighties, outran the natural increase of income accruing from the greater size of the city. Comptrollers and other servants of government joined citizens and press in the cry that expenditures must be reduced through rigid economy and the postponement of expensive improvements.[90] The general property tax remained the keystone of the revenue system, and funds from the general levy were appropriated by the council subject to the veto of the mayor on the basis of estimates from the comptroller.[91] Annual expenditures far exceeded what this, the general property tax, provided toward upkeep,[92] and although the cash

[88] *Chicago Tribune*, Dec. 3, 4, 8, 1887, Jan. 9, March 16, 1888, April 21, 25, May 3–7, 11, 12, 15, 17, 24, 30, July 3, 4, 6, Oct. 30, 1889; Cook County Board of Commissioners, *Official Proceedings, 1886–87*, pp. 563–64, 595, 612–13, *1887–88*, pp. 34, 165, 225, 229–30, 235, *1888–89*, pp. 323–25; Chicago, *Council Proceedings, 1889–90*, pp. 86, 99–100, 110, 295; John Dolese *et al. v.* Daniel A. Pierce, 124 Ill. 140 (1888); Act of April 25, 1889, Illinois, *Laws, 1889*, pp. 66–67, *House Journal, 1889*, p. 381, *Senate Journal*, p. 631; John R. Tree, Treasurer, *v.* George R. Davis, Treasurer, 133 Ill. 522 (1889).

[89] The area of the city until the annexations of 1887 was 35.152 square miles. By the end of 1893 it was 185.017 square miles. Chicago Department of Public Works, Bureau of Maps and Plats, *Map of Chicago Showing Growth of the City by Annexations and Accretions* ([Chicago], 1946, 1950).

[90] Unless otherwise noted, statistical data and generalizations are based on the annual statements of the City Comptroller. See also Illinois Bureau of Labor Statistics, *Eighth Biennial Report, 1894*, dealing with taxation in Chicago and Illinois.

[91] In the fiscal year 1872–73 general taxes made up 31.3 per cent of total receipts; in 1881 they were 48.4 per cent; in 1893 they were 34.6 per cent. In the same year these taxes met the cost of government as follows: 31.6 per cent, 45.9 per cent, and 36.7 per cent. In 1876 the beginning of the fiscal year was changed from April 1 to the first Monday in January.

[92] For example, the levy in 1877 was slightly over four million dollars. The city spent $10,316,812.89. In 1893 the appropriation called for $11,810,969.69, but expenditures exceeded thirty-two million dollars. See Appendix table.

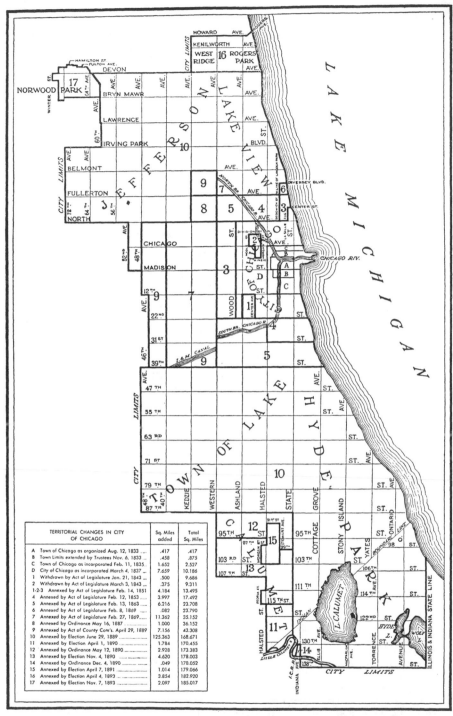

GROWTH OF CHICAGO BY ANNEXATIONS, TO 1893

(From Chicago, Department of Public Works, Bureau of Maps and Plats, *Map of Chicago Showing Growth of the City by Annexations and Accretions.* Chicago, 1946, 1950. Courtesy of Mr. Howard C. Brodman, Superintendent, Bureau of Maps and Plats.)

value of property increased, assessed valuations did not reflect a corresponding advance.[93]

It was in the field of taxation that outmoded instruments appeared in a most unfavorable light. Here the county remained the chief administrative unit, although as early as 1870 the city had over 85 per cent of the population. Upon the County Board of Commissioners devolved the apportionment of taxes among the various towns, which levied and collected them under county supervision. These were tasks the city could have performed far more advantageously. Furthermore, decisions of the town assessors were reviewed by the town board, then reviewed and equalized between towns by the county board of equalization, and between counties by the state board. The state board could raise by as much as 1 per cent but could not lower aggregate assessed valuations. To the county clerk fell the computation of the local tax rate from estimated expenses submitted by governmental bodies, and from the total assessed value published by the state board of equalization. In 1873 the state legislature prescribed that the aggregate amount of taxes levied for any one year should not exceed 3 per cent of the aggregate assessed valuation of all property assessed. Six years later the municipal incorporation act was amended, limiting the rate to 2 per cent.[94]

Still, reason for complaint as to inequities persisted. The frequency with which the state board of equalization reduced the percentage and amount of increase in the valuation of property persisted. Moreover, residents of Cook County felt their burden of state taxes disproportionately high in comparison with other counties, the Citizens' Association pointing out in 1890 that, while the majority of counties frequently were given decreased valuations, Cook County was raised by what was held an exorbitant amount. In turn, those thus accused of profiting at Chicago's expense asserted that by 1894

[93] Valued at $284,197,430 in 1872, the city's property rose in valuation in 1873 to $312,072,995 and then began to decline. The lowest point was reached in 1880, when the assessed value was only $117,133,643. In 1891 it was $256,599,574, slightly higher than 1892 and 1893. In addition to annual statements of comptroller see Illinois, *Report of the Revenue Commission Appointed under the Joint Resolution of the Two Houses of the 34th General Assembly to Propose and Frame a Revenue Code, etc., with Accompanying Address* (Springfield, 1886), pp. iv–v.

[94] Act of March 30, 1872, Illinois, *Laws, 1871–72*, p. 351; Act of April 15, 1873, *Laws, 1873*, p. 53; Act of May 28, 1879, *Laws, 1879*, pp. 66–67. For the situation in the 1850's and '60's see Pierce, *A History of Chicago*, II, 344–51.

it was taking 253,077 acres of farm land to approximate equality in actual value with one acre of Chicago's business district, where values had skyrocketed from twenty dollars a lot in 1830 to $1,250,000 in about sixty-four years.

This difference in the acceleration of values of city and country properties was, to the owner of the latter, merely another example of the advantage enjoyed and exploited by the urban dweller. Tax reform when proposed was, therefore, to suffer the impact of divisive opinions in the halls of the state legislature. In the end it meant that Chicago did not determine this or some other major problems of the city's government. Nor was the antagonism between town and country dulled by Chicago's objection to the state absorbing the tax on the capital stock of corporations and railroads. In the case of the latter, certain properties, including the main track and right of way, rolling stock, stations, and improvements on the right of way, were merged in the cost of the whole road and assessed by the state, while other holdings such as buildings came under the purview of local assessors. The tendency was, therefore, for the numerous lines entering the city to classify as much property as possible in a way to be evaluated by the state; for 1880, for example, these roads, with the exception of the Illinois Central, collectively paid less tax than did one Chicago mercantile firm, including two of its members.

To other protests which poured in a steady stream from critics of the revenue system was added the complaint that payment of the personal property tax was almost non-enforceable, or, if collected, the tax was not representative of all such property held or even a fair estimate of that on which returns were made. Unseen stocks and bonds, warehouse receipts, indeed all kinds of credits and moneys and the trappings of wealth made up what appeared a constantly growing but invisible source of revenue. The tax situation was further complicated by numerous governmental organs legally entitled to levy taxes. Added to the usual state, county, city, and town agencies were special bodies such as the schools, the library, parks, and, after 1889, the Sanitary District — so many, in fact, that to some it appeared as if there were far too much government. Daily bickering among authorities revolved around the chronic grumbling about unfair assessments and the tardy transmission of collections from one agency to another. Receipts in the county treasury trickled slowly into the city's coffers; the various towns within the larger city held on as long as possible to the funds turned over to them in order to realize a profit on returns; and heavier assessments in one division of the city over those in another became a source of ceaseless contention. And throughout, the function of assessment frequently was interlarded with political influences, sometimes sinister, often hidden, powerful, and autocratic, condemned not only by those not able to seek favors but by many of the wealthy who refused to do so.[95]

In order to meet the expenses of governing the city not covered by the inadequate real and personal property tax, the City Council resorted to *ad hoc* assessments that did not fall under the two-per-cent limitation which was exclusive of the payment of interest and principal of the bonded debt. Levies were made for specific improvements such as paving, street lighting, sewerage and drainage, and the charges imposed upon individual property owners who would be benefited. Thus while the property-tax levies increased less than three times between 1872 and 1893, receipts from special assessments mounted nearly fifteen times. Revenues from license fees also provided an increasing amount of support not only because of the greater number of such permissive grants, but because of their higher cost. Between 1881 and 1893 more than a dozen new types of licenses were inaugurated, but here again the city was hampered in attaining a balanced budget by the restraining hand of the state.[96]

Short-term expedients such as interest-bearing scrip, so-called " certificates of indebtedness," were resorted to but declared illegal in 1876;[97] time warrants with interest and principal drawn from specified appropriations were issued until invalidated by the state

[95] For complaints by Chicago on the subject of taxation see annual reports of Citizens' Association of Chicago, especially *1890*, pp. 19–20, 22, *1892*, pp. 21, 31, *1893*, p. 12; *The Chicago Times*, June 20, 1880. Specific valuations of important pieces of Chicago property, contrasts in payments on Chicago property owned by leading citizens, workers, and farmers, comparisons of land values in Cook County with rural counties, can be found in Illinois Bureau of Labor Statistics, *Eighth Biennial Report, 1894*. For the point of view of agricultural sections see *ibid.*, pp. xviii–xx. Chicago City Comptroller, *Annual Statement, 1881*, p. 61.

[96] For enumeration of real estate and personal property tax (1837–93) see Chicago City Comptroller, *Annual Statement, 1893*, pp. 130–31. In 1884, for example, saloon licenses were raised from fifty-two dollars to $500. In 1893, of the total income of $3,734,689.29 from licenses, $3,266,846.70 was derived from saloon fees.

[97] Since no distinction was made by Chicago's charter between short- and long-term loans, the Circuit Court ruled that scrip came within the state limitation of borrowing but 5 per cent of the value of taxable property. *Chicago Tribune*, April 28, 1878.

Supreme Court in 1878; and non-interest warrants for money appropriated but not collected, though considered legal, were used as payment to city employees who, if they accepted them, found they must often cash them at a discount as high as 15 per cent.[98]

State constitutional and legislative restrictions, however, kept municipal indebtedness down to an aggregate not in excess of 5 per cent on the assessed valuation of property subject to taxation, while refunding bonds could be issued only with the consent of the majority of the legal voters of the city. Future generations escaped the burden of additional debts incurred by their predecessors until 1890, when by constitutional amendment a $5,000,000 issue of bonds was authorized for the Columbian Exposition. In spite of this increase, total liabilities of $50,518,906.86 in 1891 for Chicago remained much lower than the indebtedness of other large cities in the country — its bonded debt per capita of $12.30 contrasting with $54.04 for Philadelphia, $96.60 for New York, and $126.03 for Boston. The city's bonds marketed with ease and were readily taken up, particularly by those who lived in the city.[99]

The material nature of the problems with which Chicago government had to deal appeared most vividly in the city's system of revenue. But questions arising out of all aspects of governing the rapidly expanding city persistently challenged the ingenuity and honesty of every public official. In meeting inevitable exigencies, choice of action was restrained not only by the actual frame of government but by state control over many important local affairs. Although the city, with less than 12 per cent of the total population of Illinois in 1870, embraced more than 28 per cent in 1890, its governmental powers did not expand proportionately. Not even the general incorporation act of 1872, designed to eliminate special legislation, emancipated the city from the indifferent, at times hostile, attitude of

[98] Ida Irene Law et al. v. The People ex rel. Louis C. Huck, Collector, etc., 87 Ill. 385 (1877); Henry Fuller v. Monroe Heath et al., 89 Ill. 296 (1878); Chicago Post, April 27, 1878; Chicago Tribune, June 13, 1878.

[99] Art. IX, secs. 12, 13, Constitution of Illinois, 1870; Act of March 26, 1872, Illinois, Public Laws, 1871–72, p. 203; Act of April 14, 1875, Laws, 1875, p. 68; Act of April 27, 1877, Laws, 1877, pp. 158–63; Act of June 4, 1879, Laws, 1879, pp. 229–34; Act of Aug. 5, 1890, Laws, 1890 [Special Session], pp. 6–7. The bonded debt of Chicago in 1891 was $13,530,350. The total debt in 1872 was $14,931,619; in 1893 total liabilities were $56,-604,927.74. For 1891 figures and debts of cities see Chicago Department of Finance, Annual Statement, 1891, pp. 13–16.

rural-minded state legislators; and reapportionment of the General Assembly continued to leave Chicago under-represented.

Within the same geographic area, furthermore, several agencies exercised authority. At times their functions were distinct. At others, they overlapped. This duplication of jurisdiction was found, for example, in the case of the Cook County sheriff and the chief of police of Chicago. The township still operated as a governmental unit, but without a practical excuse for its existence. The town meeting as the legislative organ of the township had been dwarfed to an assembly electing town officers, while the town as such had significance primarily for the part it played in the system of revenue. Efforts to consolidate the towns lying within the city met defeat first at the hands of the Illinois Supreme Court and then by the failure of both the legislature and the electorate to approve legislation or constitutional changes to permit the elimination or consolidation of townships.[100]

This "hydra-headed system of county, city and town governments" covering but one population, as Mayor Washburne put it, with its innumerable clerks, commissioners, and other officials, opened the way for professional politicians to spread their influence, as they capitalized on the voters' unfamiliarity for what and for whom they were voting. To counteract the evils and inequities which seemed to increase rather than diminish with time, Washburne in 1892 urged a new charter for the city, a plea which went unheeded. Years after, succeeding mayors might well have echoed his judgment as he left his post: "Good municipal government is the most urgent necessity of the present day."[101]

[100] In 1881 the legislature failed to pass a consolidation bill. In 1888 and 1892 the people rejected at the polls plans for unification. *Chicago Tribune*, March 17, 1881, Nov. 8, 1888, Nov. 13, 1892; *Illinois Staats-Zeitung*, Feb. 10, 1879.

[101] "Mayor's Annual Message," Chicago, *Municipal Reports, 1892*, pp. xxx–xxxii.

CHAPTER X

THE PROFILE OF POLITICS

BECAUSE CHICAGO had grown so rapidly, political and administrative problems pressed more persistently and sharply for solution than in the average American city. As Chicago drew to herself more and more people, politics cast off the relative simplicity of an earlier day, and became more and more controlled by party machines able to distribute patronage and to obtain large campaign funds. With time laying a healing hand upon voters the old issues of the Civil War gradually subsided, followed on the national level by the question of currency reform and the tariff controversy, which even party labels could not always resolve in the minds of Chicago voters. Economic unrest, too, nourished third-party movements, which plagued the regulars at frequent intervals. At the municipal level the problems of government would have been better solved had the local administration kept independent of state and national politics, but it was generally found advantageous to preserve the same party organization in contests for all officials.

On occasion, however, it was possible to consider local issues on their own merits. In the municipal election of 1871, which, shortly following the Great Fire, came at a time when personal honesty and official reliability were especially needed, party considerations vanished. A non-partisan ticket, the "Union-Fireproof," headed by Republican Joseph Medill, was named by the central committees of the two main parties after agreement on a fair division of the offices. Despite the opposition of professional politicians of unsavory reputation and men the *Tribune* described as "irresponsible soreheads," the Medill ticket swept into office with a flatteringly large vote.

Medill had accepted the nomination as mayor reluctantly because his powers were so restricted that they left him, as he wrote John D. Caton, but "the shadow of authority with all the responsibility that falls on the office." Though "the Mayor's Bill," passed by the state legislature in 1872, granted him additional powers for two years, he was unable to carry out his announced policy of extending the fire limits to the city boundaries because too many people still wished to put up frame buildings. Moreover, he soon became embroiled in the very touchy problem of enforcing the Sunday closing of saloons, an issue which for years had agitated, on the one hand, temperance protagonists and, on the other, voters of foreign extraction.[1] Nearly a year passed, and then, prodded by the Committee of Seventy, composed of prominent citizens to carry out moral reform, the Mayor ordered the Board of Police Commissioners to execute such ordinances. In April and May, 1873, after a further delay due to administrative changes, Elmer Washburn, police superintendent, and two newly appointed commissioners began to clamp down. Thereupon opposition rapidly assumed the form of organized political action.[2]

Meanwhile, the national nominating conventions and the election of 1872 took place, disrupting old party alignments, rekindling personal animosities, and eventually forcing the acceptance of presidential candidates upon unwilling supporters. Opposition to President Grant's renomination shaped up in Chicago, as elsewhere, in the Liberal Republican movement, attracting men of diverse political leanings such as free-trader Horace White of the *Tribune*, the well-

[1] *Chicago Tribune*, Oct. 23, 25, 27, 28, 31, Nov. 1, 1871, Jan. 16, 1872; *Illinois Staats-Zeitung*, Oct. 31, 1871, Feb. 14, 1873; [The Chicago Tribune], "Joseph Medill: The Man," *Joseph Medill, A Brief Biography and an Appreciation* ([Chicago], 1947), p. 19; Joseph Medill to John D. Caton, Dec. 8, 1871, *John D. Caton Papers* (*Mss.* Library of Congress); Chicago, *Council Proceedings, 1870–71*, p. 351, *1871–72*, pp. 2–9; Act of March 9, 1872, Illinois, *Public Laws, 1871–72*, pp. 269–70. For votes cast in elections for president of the United States, governor of Illinois, members of U. S. House of Representatives, and mayor of Chicago, see Appendix tables for years covered by this volume. Annual elections of alderman, elections to minor political offices and those for county and town are detailed only when especially significant.

[2] *The Chicago Times*, Jan. 15, 16, 1872; *Illinois Staats-Zeitung*, Nov. 8, 1871, Dec. 30, 1872, June 30, 1873; *Chicago Tribune*, June 10, Dec. 23, 1871, April 19, Oct. 12, 25, 29, 1872, April 19, 26, May 15, 20, 23, 26, 29, 1873; M. [Michael] L. Ahern, *The Great Revolution, a History of the Rise and Progress of the People's Party in the City of Chicago . . .* (Chicago, 1874), pp. 33–34, 39, 41.

known antebellum Democrat John Wentworth, and onetime Whig David Davis, now Associate Justice of the Supreme Court. Since there were three favorite sons among the Illinois Liberals — Davis, Governor John M. Palmer, and Senator Lyman Trumbull — the contingent to the Cincinnati convention of May 1 was divided in its loyalties and rent by political animosities and personal hatreds. Even Senator John A. Logan, who had announced his sword "unsheathed" against Trumbull, appeared at one time about to join this rebellious group because of a quarrel with Grant. But eventually he remained regular, as did others who could not swallow the nomination of the erratic and picturesque Horace Greeley for the highest office of the land.[3]

The choice of Greeley, so long a foe of the Democratic party and a high-tariff advocate, displeased many anti-Grant men, both Democrats and Republicans; but the Democratic party at length reluctantly endorsed him and the Liberal Republican platform.[4] For the regular Republicans things proved simpler. Even frequently heard charges of corruption against the administration did not prevent Grant's renomination in June. Thereupon Chicago old-line Republicans openly and enthusiastically proceeded to extol the historic role of their party as defender of the Union, their candidate's unique contribution to the war, and the virtues of a protective tariff.[5]

In national, state, county, and Chicago districts Republicans scored a victory, with the campaign pivoting about national issues. By the spring of 'seventy-three, however, purely local matters again claimed

[3] *Chicago Tribune,* April 26, 1872; Koerner, *Memoirs,* II, 549. For correspondence about activities of Illinois leaders in the Liberal Republican movement, see Horace White to Lyman Trumbull, W. Scharit to Trumbull, April 29, 1872, *The Papers of Lyman Trumbull, 1855–1877 (Mss.* Library of Congress); John Wentworth to Jesse W. Fell and Frank D. Orme, care of Judge [David] Davis, May 2, 1872 [telegram], Leonard Swett to "Dear Judge" [Davis], Feb. 25, 1872, Wentworth to Davis, April 25, 1872 [telegram], Wentworth to Fell, April 30, 1872 [telegram], Wentworth to Fell and Orme, May 2, 1872 [telegram], *David Davis Letters, 1858–1894* (Typescript, Illinois Historical Survey, University of Illinois); John A. Logan to Richard Yates [Sr.], Feb. 19, 1870, *Richard Yates Collection, 1870–1900 (Mss.* Illinois State Historical Library); Levi P. Luckey to Elihu Washburne, April 22, 1872, *Washburne Papers;* Wentworth to W. Waller, 1872, *Chicago Vertical File (Ms.* Chicago Historical Society).

[4] The so-called "Bourbon" faction of the Democrats nominated Charles O'Conor of New York for president.

[5] Koerner, *op. cit.,* II, 556–57, 559–60, 574; Horace White, *The Life of Lyman Trumbull* (Boston, 1913), pp. 391–94; Thomas V. Cooper and Hector T. Fenton, *American Politics . . .* (Philadelphia, 1882), Book II, 51–53; Hutchinson, *Cyrus Hall McCormick,* II, 316–19.

the attention of Chicagoans, and opposition to Medill's "Sunday closing" gave birth on May 14 to a new People's party, vigorously proclaiming adherence to personal liberty. Alongside Germans stood their traditional political foes, the Irish; and on August 31 this new alliance obtained the endorsement of the anti-Greeley Anton C. Hesing of the *Illinois Staats-Zeitung* and the Irish boss Daniel O'Hara, important local Liberal Republican. This strange union with its persuasive emphasis on the alleged inequity of "Puritan rule" won over prominent Irishmen like William J. Onahan, Michael Keeley, Alderman John H. McAvoy, and Charles Dennehy, who were willing to pursue their course under the chairmanship of the German-Jewish banker and civic leader Henry Greenebaum, and to work for the election of Harvey D. Colvin for mayor and O'Hara for city treasurer. The usual cry of economy in government, hollow though it may have been, gained recruits among disgruntled taxpayers, while a demand for civil-service reform and for an expansion of educational facilities was designed to lure others less aroused by objections to Sunday closing.[6]

Alarmed by the rising tide of opposition, the "Law and Order" elements recruited a motley group, some favoring the strict enforcement of the Sunday closing law, others avoiding any declaration on the contentious issue. The Committee of Seventy maintained an inflexible no-compromise stand. This attitude, an independent citizens' group held little short of "fanatical"; instead they urged the sale of wine and beer but not distilled liquors on Sunday. On October 8 a fusion ticket entered the field with no platform except one which each candidate might wish to propose. By this time Mayor Medill had gone to Europe, delegating his arduous task to Alderman Lester L. Bond as mayor pro-tem, who now became the candidate of the new Union or Citizens' party against Colvin of the People's.

The lack of a unifying program spelled defeat for the Union ticket. In both city and county the People's party scored a victory with an average majority of approximately ten thousand. Viewing the results of the election, the "Law and Order" leaders sought consolation in the thought that the tie binding Germans and Irish was extremely

---

[6] *The Chicago Times*, May 15, 1873; *Chicago Tribune*, Oct. 25, 1872, May 15, 24, 30, June 26, Sept. 1, Oct. 15, 25, 1873; *Illinois Staats-Zeitung*, Aug. 29, Oct. 10, 1873; Ahern, *op. cit.*, pp. 198–99; *The Advance*, VII (Oct. 16, 1873), 5, (Nov. 13, 1873), 9.

fragile; that, despite failure, they had received the endorsement of all English-language newspapers except the *Times*. But little comfort could be had in the speed with which the new administration on March 16, 1874 repealed the ordinances for Sunday closing.[7]

The marked degree of party irregularity, the crossing of political lines, and the making of new combinations in the elections of 1871, '72, and '73 in Chicago forecast similar deviation in others of the decade. For one reason or another not only men of political stature but also the average voter at times felt dissatisfied with the Republican and Democratic parties. Some, like Lyman Trumbull and Governor Palmer, moved over to the Democrats, while others similarly inclined hesitated to affiliate openly with those held guilty of poor judgment if not disloyalty during the War. Still others like Joseph Medill remained in Republican ranks, at times criticizing officeholders for their policies. With the stabilizing influence of unquestioning party regularity removed, it was not difficult for those who wished to manipulate new combinations to do so, whether the reasons were good or bad.[8]

The formation of successful independent parties, particularly in the early 'seventies, began first and went farthest in the realm of municipal politics. The eventual resumption of traditional party alignments, however, finally occurred. With the disastrous defeat in 1873 of the Citizens' Union, or " Law and Order " party, the bulk of its membership drifted to the Republicans. While the People's party remained substantially intact under Hesing and Mayor Colvin, the necessity of conducting a campaign in 1874 for the state legislature and Congress forced the organization to expand beyond the purely local field. A coalition of Democratic and People's party forces, labeled " the Opposition " by the city's press, proved a successful means of achieving victory that year. It began, however, a transformation which absorbed the local People's party, with most of its members joining the Democratic organization.[9]

[7] *The Chicago Times*, Sept. 2, Oct. 2, 10, 11, 12, 19, 21, 24, 27, 30, 1873; *Chicago Tribune*, July 16, Aug. 19, Sept. 8, 21, Oct. 8, 10, 19, 21, 30, 31, Nov. 1, 2, 3, 1873; *Illinois Staats-Zeitung*, Aug. 29, Oct. 10, 1873; Chicago, *Council Proceedings, 1872–73*, pp. 361, 498–500, *1873–74*, p. 130.

[8] *Chicago Tribune*, July 30, Nov. 2, 1874; *The Chicago Times*, Oct. 22, 27, 1874, Oct. 3, 1875; *Hejmdal*, Oct. 17, 24, 1874; *Illinois Staats-Zeitung*, Oct. 3, 24, 1874.

[9] Joseph Medill to E. B. Washburne, Nov. 1, 1874, *Washburne Papers*. Only in the aldermanic contests did the Republicans achieve real success, filling eleven seats to six for the

The disintegration of the People's party was hastened by a record of corrupt administration in the city and county, by internal dissensions, and by loading its ticket with unqualified candidates — a group of "blacklegs, pimps, grogshop loafers, communist lazzaroni, and other political dead-beats," said the *Times*.[10] The party's ultimate downfall came, however, in connection with a piece of maneuvering which had all the characteristics of high political cunning. Dissatisfaction with the Colvin regime hastened an application for a new city charter under the general act of 1872, which, if granted, would shorten Mayor Colvin's term. In October, 1874 the Citizens' Association obtained the required number of signatures for a petition for a popular referendum, and the Common Council in January, 1875 set April 23 as the time to vote on a new charter. The choice of this date was astute, for the incorporation act provided that a city election should take place, instead of in the autumn, on the third Tuesday in April after the bill was accepted by the people. Since the third Tuesday in April fell on the twentieth, the council's action lengthened the official lives of incumbents from November, 1875 to April, 1876; and because the mayor was to be chosen in an odd year it extended Colvin's term to April, 1877. On the twenty-third the voters in a close election accepted the new charter, though the outcome was inconclusive until the courts decided in its favor.[11]

The high-handed manner in which the People's party and Colvin had engineered the setting of the date, besides the presumption of continued tenure, sparked an incipient flame of indignation which manifested itself in the first municipal election under the new charter, April, 1876. Election of aldermen then was compulsory. The council, foreseeing Colvin's defeat if the move to force a mayoral election was successful, blocked it promptly, and Colvin announced

---

opposition and four independents. *The Chicago Times*, Aug. 28, Nov. 5, 11, 1874; *Chicago Tribune*, July 30, Aug. 18, 27, Oct. 25, 30, Nov. 11, 12, 1874; U. S., *Miscellaneous House Documents*, 44 Cong., 1 sess., III, Doc. 61; *Congressional Record*, 44 Cong., 1 sess., p. 3017.

[10] Citizens' Association of Chicago, *Addresses and Reports, 1874 to 1876*, p. 23; *The Advance*, VIII (Nov. 26, 1874), 234; *Chicago Tribune*, Oct. 6, 8, 18, Nov. 22, 23, 1874; Herbert Asbury, *Gem of the Prairie* (New York, 1940), pp. 144–45; *The Western Catholic*, Feb. 16, 1875; *The Chicago Times*, Sept. 30, 1874, Feb. 6, Sept. 12, 1875.

[11] Act of April 10, 1872, Article I, Section 1; M. Starr and R. H. Curtis, eds., *Annotated Statutes of the State of Illinois in Force January 1, 1885* (Chicago, 1885), I, 452; Citizens' Association of Chicago, *Addresses and Reports, 1874 to 1876*, p. 20; *The Chicago Times*, Oct. 23, Nov. 28, 1874, Jan. 6, Oct. 8, 1875; *Chicago Tribune*, Nov. 4, 1874; Chicago, *Council Proceedings, 1873–74*, p. 450, *1874–76*, p. 35.

his intention to remain in office until April, 1877. Although the courts sustained the council, most of Colvin's supporters were swept out of office in a resounding Republican party victory. Determined to oust the obdurate mayor, Thomas Hoyne, prominent attorney and civic leader, accepted nomination as an independent, and thousands of voters wrote his name in on their ballots.[12]

The final scene of this drama then took place in an atmosphere of animosity, trickery, and stubbornness. The new council, assembling May 8, declared Hoyne mayor of Chicago. Colvin refused to yield. In these circumstances the city had two mayors and two groups of appointive officers. Again the court intervened, and in June in a *quo warranto* hearing declared Hoyne's election illegal, but permitted the council to order a special election. With the success of the recent aldermanic election in mind, the Republicans in convention on July 1 decided to abandon their nonpartisan stand in the choice of Hoyne, a Democrat, and name one of their own party for mayor. As a result, Monroe Heath, a former alderman and a member of the paint firm of Heath and Milligan, was nominated and on July 12 triumphed over Mark Kimball, the regular Democratic nominee, and James McGrath, candidate of the Colvin Democrats, who ran as an independent.[13]

The autumn campaigns of 1876 revealed that Republican landslides in the recent municipal elections were essentially a protest against Colvin and his backers, not a permanent shift to stanch Republicanism. The basic instability in Chicago politics, in fact, remained unchanged. The election on the national level seemed all-engrossing; both old-time parties urged the support of Chicagoans regardless of their differences on the money question and other issues. In the state, however, the Democrats, recognizing the strength

[12] Citizens' Association of Chicago, *Addresses and Reports, 1874 to 1876*, pp. 20–21; *The Western Catholic*, March 23, 1875; *The Chicago Times*, April 3, June 8, Nov. 27, Dec. 25, 1875; *Chicago Tribune*, April 9, 27, May 7, 14, June 8, 1875; Act of April 8, 1875, Illinois, *Laws, 1875*, p. 43, *Journal of the House of Representatives, 1875*, pp. 269, 296, 359, 477, 589–92, 594, 663, *Journal of the Senate, 1875*, pp. 472, 487–90, 577; Chicago, *Council Proceedings, 1874–76*, pp. 153–54, 633, 679–82; Dickey *et al. v.* Reed *et al.*, 78 Ill. 261 (1875); Chicago *v.* The People *ex rel.* King *et al.*, 80 Ill. 496 (1875); *Chicago Post and Mail*, Jan. 3, 26, 1876.

[13] Chicago, *Council Proceedings, 1876–77*, pp. 3, 99–100; The People *ex rel.* Colvin *v.* Hoyne, *quo warranto; The Chicago Times*, June 6, 1876; *Chicago Tribune*, June 6, July 2, 1876. The case was tried in the Circuit Court. Records of this court are not published. Decisions can be found in the newspapers.

of the Greenback or National Independent party, made common cause with it. This bit of "unmitigated stupidity and invincible ignorance," as the *Tribune* derisively described it, paid off, however, in Cook County in the election of Democratic candidates for county commissioner as well as for sheriff.[14]

Although Democratic hopes seemed justifiably high, judged by the Chicago results, Shelby M. Cullom of Springfield, the Republican candidate for governor, was swept into office through downstate votes. When the national returns were in, the Chicago pluralities for two Democratic and one Republican candidate for Congress were overcome by out-of-city voters in the choice of two Republicans and one Democrat. The prolonged uncertainty about the outcome of the presidential race, in which Chicago had gone Democratic, was matched by shortening political tempers in the city. When the decision of the Electoral Commission for Republican Rutherford B. Hayes over Samuel J. Tilden, the Democratic candidate for president, was in, the *Tribune* and others hailed it with relief, not only because the next administration would be Republican, but also because the outcome had not led to civil strife. But " the stolen election of 1876," as it came to be called by the Tilden supporters, supplied the Democratic party in Chicago as elsewhere with campaign ammunition for many a year to come.[15]

Just as revelations of corruption and malfeasance in the national administration had made " Grantism " a term of opprobrium, so did similar revelations at the city and county level alienate men from former party allegiance. However depleted the public coffers, there always seemed to be someone unable to resist the opportunity for illicit gain. Rumors were ever abroad that aldermanic influence could be had for a price, that irregularities attended the award of public utility franchises and fraud the contracts for public works such as street paving and the purchase of supplies for public institutions.[16]

[14] Cooper and Fenton, *op. cit., Book* II, pp. 54–55, 57–59; *Chicago Tribune*, Aug. 6, 11, 13, 14, Sept. 3, 9, 12, 15, Oct. 7, 22, Nov. 8, 1872, July 28, 29, Aug. 5, Oct. 5, 11, 22, 29, 30, 31, Nov. 2, 3, 4, 1876; Bogart and Thompson, *The Industrial State*, pp. 112–13, 116, 119; *Illinois Staats-Zeitung*, July 15, Aug. 7, Sept. 8, 1876; *Hejmdal*, Sept. 22, 1876; *Chicago Post and Mail*, Feb. 4, 1876; Hutchinson, *op. cit.*, II, 336–37.

[15] Bogart and Thompson, *op. cit.*, pp. 113–17, 120–22; Hutchinson, *op. cit.*, II, 340–42, 346–47, 351–53; Koerner, *op. cit.*, II, 619–20; *Chicago Tribune*, Nov. 5, 6, 8, 9, 12, 22, Dec. 14, 1876, Feb. 18, 1877; *The Chicago Times*, Nov. 22, 1876.

[16] The cases of city treasurer David A. Gage (Republican) and city collector George von Hollen (Democrat) showed that irregularities existed not in one party alone. *Chicago*

Graft in the county administration was even more flagrant than in the city government. Disclosures of chicanery in 1874 were followed by others of the county "ring" in 1876 and succeeding years. The rebuilt County Court House, openly called "a thief's monument," along with the failure of purveyors of the County Hospital in 1877 to deliver goods for which payment was made, and the frequent practice of short-weighing goods sold — these and similar evidences made the term "politician" one of reproach.[17] Nor did federally sponsored undertakings such as the construction of the Customs House, completed in 1880, escape the leechlike grasp of the corrupt.[18] In the notorious Whisky Ring of the mid-'seventies Chicago politicians also played a conspicuous part, helping to defraud the government of full payment of the excise tax. Raids by federal agents carried on simultaneously May 10, 1875 in Chicago, Milwaukee, and St. Louis revealed a bold evasion of the law in all these cities. In the Chicago district three distilleries and four rectifying establishments were seized, and the October grand jury returned indictments against distillers, public officials, and others.[19]

What happened in Chicago in the Whisky Ring thus became a matter of national concern. The names and words of men hitherto known chiefly in the city now figured in nationwide press releases. To get immunity or light sentences some of the guilty turned state's evidence. On the heels of his indictment Jacob ("Jake") Rehm, superintendent of police from December, 1873 to October, 1875, and an

Tribune, Aug. 23, 26, 1873, Dec. 1, 27, 1874, March 13, 1876, March 17, 1878, March 25, 26, 1880; *The Chicago Times,* Dec. 5, 1874, July 16, 1875, June 26, Nov. 4, 1877; *Chicago Post,* Jan. 15, 1878; Pierce, *A History of Chicago,* II, 326; *Chicago Daily Law Bulletin,* XX (March 26, 1874), [3]; Chicago Department of Finance, *Twenty-fifth Annual Statement, 1881,* p. 79, *Twenty-sixth Annual Report, 1882,* pp. 28–29; Chicago, *Council Proceedings, 1880–81,* pp. 3, 323–24; City of Chicago *v.* David A. Gage *et al.,* 95 Ill. 593 (1880).

[17] Cook County Board of Commissioners, *Official Proceedings, 1872–73,* pp. 36–37, *1873–74,* pp. 215, 333, *1874–75,* pp. 68–74, 373, 457, *1875–76,* pp. 135, 140, *1876–77,* pp. 42, 46, 49, 58–60; *Report of the Special Committee Appointed March 27, 1882, to Compile All Communications, Reports, and Contracts Pertaining to the Erection of the New Cook County Court House . . .* (Chicago, 1882), pp. 27, 221–22; John O'Neil, *A Compilation of the Cost of Buildings of Cook County . . .* (Chicago, 1884), pp. 125, 331; Citizens' Association of Chicago, *Annual Report, 1881,* p. 20; see also the daily press.

[18] *Chicago Tribune,* Nov. 23, 1878; *The Chicago Times,* Feb. 29, 1876; *Weekly Illinois Staats-Zeitung,* Jan. 29, 1877; *Illinois Staats-Zeitung,* Jan. 27, 1877.

[19] U. S. House of Representatives, *Testimony before the Select Committee Concerning the Whisky Frauds,* 44 Cong., 1 sess., Misc. Doc. IX, no. 186 (Washington, 1876), pp. 437–40. From its establishment in 1862 to June 30, 1887, the First Internal Revenue Collection District of Illinois included Cook County and Chicago. It was enlarged July 1, 1887.

influential German Republican, joined the " first batch " of inform-
ers and received only six months in the county jail and a fine of
$10,000. Anton C. Hesing, another political power and, like Rehm,
accused of being an organizer of the ring, got two years' imprisonment and a fine of $5,000. Gaugers, storekeepers, distillers, and gov-
ernment officials — all were shown to have had a callous disregard of
honesty. And when punishment came, it seemed at times easy to
elude. Within three months, upon payment of his fine, Hesing was
at liberty along with five others. Despite a temporarily aroused public repugnance to this collusion between lawbreakers and a local political machine, this kind of knavery in Chicago, as in the nation,
was not blotted out.[20]

One of the most frequently practiced and flagrant abuses was the
use of repeaters and fraudulently certified voters in elections. Over
all towered the boss and his machine, with his influence reaching
even into the precincts. Within the wards the committeeman and
precinct captain operated, the latter occasionally the neighborhood
saloonkeeper, providing generous " drinks on the house " or gifts of
twenty-five cents and up. But if these gratuities did not avail, strong-
arm squads were able to assist voters in determining how they should
cast their votes.[21]

Tactics other than those clearly unlawful also circumvented the
free expression of the will of the electorate. Behind-the-scene deals,
trading by political bosses, and slates hand-picked by professional
politicians seldom gave the ordinary citizen much voice in the selection of officials. The power of the political boss had already been demonstrated in the years before the Great Fire, and, in the years which
followed, Anton C. Hesing exemplified a matchless opportunism in

[20] Rehm testified that he, as cashier of the ring, had received over $100,000. Henry B.
Miller (" Buffalo Miller "), ex-county treasurer and a member of the firm of Miller and
Reed, was given six months in jail and a $3,000 fine. Some of those indicted fled to Canada;
the trials of others were not pressed. The eminent Chicago attorney Wirt Dexter assisted the
federal government. U. S. House of Representatives, *Testimony . . . Concerning the Whisky
Frauds,* pp. 380–88, 504–40. The men who first turned state's evidence and the places seized
are listed in *ibid.,* pp. 527, 533. See also James H. Hildreth *v.* Monroe Heath *et al.,* 1 Ill.
App. Ct. 82 (1876).

[21] For illustrations see *Chicago Tribune,* Oct. 31, Nov. 1–3, 8, Dec. 6, 13, 1873, April 14,
1875, April 7, 8, 16, 17, 1876, Feb. 1, 1877; Citizens' Association of Chicago, *Addresses
and Reports, 1874–76,* pp. 21–22, 32, 34; The People *ex rel.* Evans *v.* Callaghan, 83 Ill. 128
(1876); William T. Stead, *If Christ Came to Chicago* (London, 1894), p. 35; Lloyd Wendt
and Herman Kogan, *Lords of the Levee* (Indianapolis, 1943), pp. 102–7.

assessing political possibilities and the faculty of converting voters to his point of view. Like other bosses of his era, he shifted from Republican to Democrat, or to a hybrid party when that seemed advantageous. Wherever Hesing went, idolatrous Germans went too, regardless of his changing party labels. Nor was he averse, if the time seemed propitious, to join hands with former bitter opponents, even the Irish, provided such an alliance would back his candidate.[22] Year after year he wove his way along the tortuous paths of Chicago politics, and even his conviction in 1876 for complicity in the Whisky Ring did not break his political power.

The candidate for office, too, must pay his price. From hidden arrangements — those unpublicized agreements which placed him within reach of his nomination — to donations to campaign funds, the candidate from sheriff to Congressman, willy-nilly, was subjected to party assessments. And it was no secret that jobs were the reward of the loyal. Nor were zealous employers, bent on furthering the cause of their party, above resorting at times to printed admonitions to employees that votes for the opposition might prove disastrous for them personally and the country in general.[23]

Redress for such political irregularities was difficult to obtain despite the brave efforts of reform groups such as the Citizens' Association and the Municipal Reform Club. Perjury made indictments hard to get, and the law's delays worked to the disadvantage of a quick justice. A bribery statute of 1874, however, applying to town as well as state officials, prescribed penalties not only on the taker but also on the giver of a bribe, and guaranteed immunity to material witnesses. The County Commissioners, aroused by the frauds in the county, tightened rules in the making of contracts, and the press

---

[22] In 1874 it was reported that Hesing made such an arrangement with the Irish by backing their candidate for sheriff if they would support the candidacy of his son Washington for Congress. The latter withdrew, however, after it was rumored that his father received a "loan" of $40,000 from Jake Rehm and others. *The Chicago Times,* Sept. 13, 1874, Jan. 26, 1876; *The Western Catholic,* Oct. 6, 1877; *Chicago Post and Mail,* March 15, 1876; *Chicago Tribune,* March 15, 1876.

[23] *The Chicago Times,* Sept. 2, 1873, Oct. 22, 29, 1874, Nov. 12, 1875, Nov. 3, 1876; *Chicago Tribune,* Oct. 24, 1873, Oct. 24, 25, 1874, Nov. 5, 1875, March 30, April 6, 1877; *The Western Catholic,* Nov. 1, 1873, Nov. 6, 1875, Oct. 6, 1877; *The Workingman's Advocate,* Dec. 9, 1876. In 1874 it was reported that amounts ranging from $1,000 to $1,500 were extracted from prospective candidates for sheriff and for Congress, from $25 to $50 for aldermen.

waged a ceaseless campaign against a government almost daily accused of " fraud, jobbery, and corruption." [24]

Chicagoans, alarmed by the corruption in the various agencies of government, found some consolation in the victory of Monroe Heath, Republican, in the special election for mayor on July 12, 1876, pledged to an honest administration. The following year, with popularity undimmed, he was returned to office, and that fall the Republicans elected the county treasurer, county clerk, the full judicial ticket, and minor officers.[25] Especially gratifying was the victory of the five candidates for county commissioner, which promised to break the hold of the old " ring." [26] Heath's second term repeated the good government of the first. He brought about a material reduction in taxes and introduced rigorous economies that decreased the amounts of various forms of treasury warrants outstanding. The restoration of quiet with a minimum of bloodshed in the railroad-strike disorders of 1877 further enhanced his popularity. In all his endeavors he was assisted by a council more able than that body often was; and the wholehearted co-operation of the Citizens' Association helped carry him through financial crises.[27]

As the 1870's drew to a close, the majority of Republicans seemed far more attached to their party than in the early years of the decade. Heath could have been renominated for the mayoralty in 1879 had he so desired, but he preferred to retire from public life, just as the colorful and popular Carter Henry Harrison emerged to be five times mayor of Chicago. The latter's first success as Democratic can-

[24] *Chicago Tribune*, March 4, 1876; Illinois, *Revised Statutes . . . 1877*, pp. 353–54; Cook County Board of Commissioners, *Proceedings, 1871–72*, p. 43; Illinois Bureau of Labor Statistics, *First Biennial Report, 1881*, p. 166.

[25] The social and civic leader Perry H. Smith, running as a Democrat, opposed Heath in 1877.

[26] Democrats did fairly well in the aldermanic elections of 1878, but that autumn the Republicans repeated their success of the previous year, taking most of the county offices, and for the first time since 1872 elected all three of their candidates for Congressman from the Chicago districts. *Chicago Tribune*, March 25, 27, April 4, 6, Oct. 24, 26, 27, 28, Nov. 8, 1877; *The Chicago Times*, March 25, 1877, April 3, 4, Nov. 6, 1878; Chicago, *Council Proceedings, 1876–77*, pp. 468–70, *Council Proceedings, 1877–78*, pp. 521–24; Norman Williams to J. D. Caton, Nov. 7, 1877, *Caton Papers*.

[27] Chicago Department of Finance, *Annual Statement, 1877*, p. 173, *1878*, pp. 9–10, 12–13; Chicago, *Council Proceedings, 1877–78*, pp. 3–4, *1878–79*, p. 615; Citizens' Association of Chicago, *Annual Report, 1877*, pp. 10, 13, *1878*, p. 9, *1879*, p. 13; *Chicago Post*, March 14, 16, 18, 1878; *Chicago Tribune*, Feb. 23, 1879.

didate in 1879 did not appear so much a demonstration of growing popularity of the Democrats as the outcome of circumstances, which, in giving birth to third-party movements, had scattered enough votes to provide the Democrats with a minority victory. Harrison went into the 1879 campaign with the added support of the Greenback party, though he failed to acknowledge the formal nomination accorded him on March 8. More substantial assistance came indirectly from the candidacy on the Socialistic Labor ticket of the widely known Dr. Ernst Schmidt, whose popularity among his fellow Germans could not be overcome even by the *Staats-Zeitung*'s insistence that conservative property-owning Germans could not afford to support him.[28]

Throughout the 1870's the interest of workingmen in political action had been growing, nurtured by hard times and continuing unemployment. In the midst of the depression of 'seventy-three, the Workingmen's party of Illinois was founded on January 11, 1874, and the following month it established the weekly *Vorbote* as its German-language party organ. Little success attended the party's venture into the town elections of that year, however, and the organization soon collapsed.[29] Three years later a local Workingmen's party entered the lists, its platform advocating social, political, and economic reforms, with a moderate program of socialization, characterized by the *Tribune* as " a mixture of blatant balderdash and incendiary harrangue [*sic*]." Frank A. Stauber, a retail hardware merchant, was nominated for county treasurer and Albert R. Parsons, the printer, for county clerk. Two other groups, the Workingmen's Industrial party and the National Workingmen's party, also put nominees in the field, their tickets so closely paralleling those of the Democrats and the Republicans, respectively, as to suggest that they were probably decoys designed to pick up a few scattered votes. In

<hr>

[28] *Ibid.*, March 9, 10, 13, 16, 30, 1879; *The Chicago Times*, March 13, 1879; Claudius O. Johnson, *Carter Henry Harrison I, Political Leader* (Chicago, 1928), p. 137; Willis John Abbot, *Carter Henry Harrison, a Memoir* (New York, 1895), pp. 93–94; *Illinois Staats-Zeitung*, March 30, 1879.

[29] *Chicago Tribune*, Jan. 12, March 30, April 8, May 18, 19, 25, June 16, 1874; Fine, *Labor and Farmer Parties in the United States, 1828–1928*, p. 98; *The Chicago Times*, Feb. 9, March 31, April 9, 1874; Schaack, *Anarchy and Anarchists . . .* , p. 48. The party's platform may be found in the *Chicago Tribune*, Jan. 12, 1874. In the autumn of 1874 Francis Hoffman ran as a Workingmen's party candidate in the Third Congressional District but polled only 150 votes out of some 9,000 cast.

spite of these diversionary actions, the regular labor organization made a respectable showing, averaging between six and seven thousand votes for each of its candidates.

Thus encouraged, politically minded laborites entered a full ticket as the Socialistic Labor party in the aldermanic contests of 1878. Stauber won in the Fourteenth Ward, Parsons lost, it was alleged, only by fraud in the Fifteenth, and other candidates polled sizable votes. That fall the party elected a state senator and three representatives to the legislature. Thus it was with some experience that the Socialists engaged in the lively three-way mayoralty race of 1879. The Republican candidate, Albert M. Wright, a commission merchant, had the support of many in the business world. His identification with the temperance movement, however, cost him enough German and other foreign-born votes, on which the party counted, to bring about his defeat.

Harrison was confronted with an equally difficult situation, for he was not only charged with a pro-Southern bias since he was "raised among slaveholders," but he was also accused of an affiliation with Dr. Ernst Schmidt and the advocates of "communism." Even so, the enthusiasm of the Democrats was not dimmed. Parading bands, bonfires, and mass meetings whipped up enthusiasm, effectively contributing to a victory for the Democrats, who seated their first mayor in sixteen years. Into office with Harrison went the party's nominees for treasurer, attorney, and clerk, and enough aldermen to give it a plurality, though not a majority, on the council. The "foreign communists," as the *Tribune* called the Socialistic Laborites, elected three councilmen, and their candidates for major offices received between ten and twelve thousand votes, a doubling of the party's strength since the preceding year.[30]

Though the Democratic judicial ticket was unanimously elected with Socialist support in June, neither Democrats nor Socialists were able to expand these gains, and the co-operation of radicals, Irish, former slaveholders, and "Kentucky squires," as the *Staats-Zeitung*

[30] In the 1878 election Thomas Lynch, a distiller, was a candidate for county treasurer on the tickets of both minor labor parties as well as on that of the Democrats. *Chicago Tribune*, Aug. 21, Oct. 7, 25, 31, Nov. 8, March 11, 17, April 3, 4, 7, 9, Nov. 8, 9, 1878; March 7, 9, 24, 29, April 3, 1879; *Chicago Post*, Feb. 21, April 3, 1878; Carter H. Harrison, II, Typed Statement. Carter H. Harrison, *Papers (Mss. Newberry Library). The Chicago Times*, Feb. 25, 1879; *Der Westen*, March 30, 1879; *Skandinaven*, March 4, 1879; *Illinois Staats-Zeitung*, April 1, 1879; Chicago, *Council Proceedings, 1878–79*, pp. 605–9.

described it, proved short-lived. Thus only briefly checked, the Republicans in the fall of 1880 took all posts in the county election as well as naming ten councilmen to four Democrats, one Socialist, and three Independents. With prosperity now breaking through after long years of economic distress the Socialists started losing ground and, as a party, began to disintegrate. Failure to gain the ends they desired through the ballot played heavily into the hands of those who argued that this method to realize the workers' demands was futile. Particularly bitter was the feeling over a brazen attempt to defraud Stauber of his victory in the Fourteenth Ward. Though the courts declared he had been re-elected, the council did not seat him until March 9, 1881, nearly a year after the election. This tardy triumph of justice did not undo the damage, and without the assistance of its Socialist allies the Chicago Democracy was still too weak to meet on even terms the superior forces of the Republicans.[31]

Both major parties were plagued, moreover, by the controversies attending the money question, which reached the peak of factionalism in 1878. By the time of the 1880 election, however, it had become evident that each wanted to avoid discussion of the issue in so far as possible, in the interest of party harmony. The National Greenback party alone seemed willing to cry out loudly in behalf of inflation, and at their June convention in Chicago they nominated James B. Weaver of Iowa and B. J. Chambers of Texas on a platform reaffirming their demands of unlimited coinage of silver and gold, the substitution of legal-tender currency for notes of national banks, and the abolition of such banks.[32]

To increase the difficulties facing the Republicans, the third-term issue raised by Grant's aspirations separated John A. Logan and his satellites — among whom were Robert Lincoln and Stephen A. Douglas, Jr. — from the equally astute Joseph Medill, Anton C.

[31] *Chicago Tribune,* June 3, 4, Nov. 6, 1879, April 7, July 27, Nov. 4, 5, 1880, March 6, 10, 1881; *The Chicago Times,* June 3, 1879, April 7, 8, May 7, Aug. 1, 1880; *Illinois Staats-Zeitung,* June 4, 1879; Chicago, *Council Proceedings, 1879–80,* pp. 601–4, 610, *1880–81,* pp. 461–62; *Chicagoer Arbeiter-Zeitung,* July 27, Aug. 4, 11, 1880.

[32] The Greenback party attempted to entice labor with planks on mines and workshops, the prohibition of child labor, and the abrogation of the Burlingame treaty. These overtures proved one more disruptive factor in the Chicago labor situation. The English-speaking branch decided to stand by the Greenback nominees, but German and Scandinavian sections objected to co-operation. *Chicago Tribune,* June 26, July 5, 7, 1880; Commons, *History of Labour in the United States,* II, 286–88; Philip Van Patten to George A. Schilling, Sept. 24, 1880, *Labadie Collection* (Photostat, University of Michigan).

Hesing, and Charles B. Farwell. Skillful maneuvering by the Logan forces at the state convention, to which downstate hostility to Chicago contributed, led to the naming of a slate of delegates instead of leaving the choice to the various Congressional districts.[33] But the anti-Grant forces resisted this procedure, selecting from nine districts their own representatives, who were eventually seated by the national credentials committee when the party convention assembled in June in Chicago. Then followed a weary wrangle, which after thirty-five ballots ended in the nomination of a dark horse, James A. Garfield, with Chester A. Arthur as his running-mate.

The Garfield-Arthur team proved too much for the Democratic nominees, Winfield S. Hancock and William H. English. Along with the Republican candidates for president and vice-president, state and county nominees rode to victory. George R. Davis, William Aldrich, and Charles B. Farwell likewise enjoyed sufficient popular support over their Democratic rivals to be carried into Congress from the Chicago districts. During the campaign appeals to nationalistic prejudices again proved effective; the fear of laborers that there would be an influx of Chinese labor and Southern Negroes was preyed upon; and inequities attributed to the economic system sowed the seeds of a cankerous distrust which persisted for years.[34]

Above all others in the local Democracy towered the figure of Carter Harrison. Although overmatched in the general elections of 'eighty, in which he managed the campaign strategy, he demonstrated an astute leadership unexcelled in municipal and county struggles for a long time. Recognizing the magic of symbols on the electorate, he shrewdly capitalized on his black slouch felt hat and

[33] W. C. Goudy to Lambert Tree, May 3, 1880, Lambert Tree Papers (Mss. Newberry Library); The Chicago Times, April 16, 17, May 6, 8, 11, 1880; Chicago Tribune, May 11, 21, 22, 1880; John A. Logan to J. D. Cameron, May 10, 1880 [telegram], Logan to Mary Logan, May 9, 10, 1880 [telegram], John A. Logan Papers (Mss. Library of Congress). Chicago Germans in general and the Scandinavians were not third-termers. The Bohemian Svornost bewailed the " scoundrelism " of both Democrats and Republicans. Chicago Tribune, April 18, 26, 1880; Illinois Staats-Zeitung, May 2, 27, 1880; Skandinaven, May 4, 1880; Svornost, April 2, 1879.

[34] Fremont O. Bennett, comp., Politics and Politicians of Chicago, Cook County, and Illinois (Chicago, 1886), p. 227; Chicago Tribune, May 27, June 5, 9, 11, 25, 26, July 7, Sept. 16, 26, Oct. 6, 10, 26, 27, 28, 31, Nov. 2, 19, 1880; The Chicago Times, May 28, June 3, Sept. 8, Oct. 6, 1880; Philip Kinsley, The Chicago Tribune, Its First Hundred Years (Chicago, 1945), II, 345–46; Cooper and Fenton, op. cit., Book II, 61–63; National Democratic Committee, The Campaign Textbook, Why the People Want a Change . . . (New York, 1880), pp. 3–4.

his white horse. There were no class limitations to his wide popularity. Capitalist and workingman alike succumbed to his charm; the law-abiding and the professional gambler supported him. The fast and deep-running currents of ethnic clannishness he aptly converted to political advantage not only by identifying himself as a lineal descendant of the Irish, Swedes, and the Germans, but also by associating with them. Germans he addressed in the tongue of their homeland. To Italians, as the *News* put it, Harrison was " the 23rd Duke del Piazza " in disguise, and to the Chinese laundryman a descendant of Confucius.[35]

Harrison translated this popularity into votes when he ran again for mayor in 1881 despite a movement to nominate in his stead Levi Z. Leiter, George L. Dunlap, or Cyrus McCormick. Eventually he was opposed by the Republican John M. Clark, leather manufacturer and alderman from the Third Ward, whose candidacy had the blessing of five hundred businessmen of the stature of Joseph T. Ryerson, Marshall Field, Chauncey B. Blair, and Henry W. King. In addition, Clark won the endorsement of " Boss " Hesing, who, as the price of his support, named John Raber, a saloonkeeper, as city treasurer. Disregarding the fact that Harrison himself was a man of wealth, the Democrats untiringly strove to stir up class feeling by describing Clark as " a silk stocking " whose wealth made possible a residence on exclusive Prairie Avenue, and who, they said, was inclined to be anti-Semitic. Unceasing appeals to men's passions issued from the politically shrewd Mike McDonald's " Store." Unblushingly the Clark-Hesing partnership countered with equally degrading tactics. In the end, the tickets put into the field by the two factions of the Socialistic Labor party may have so thinned its ranks that they proved of advantage to Harrison in a more than seven-thousand-vote victory.[36]

[35] Johnson, *op. cit.*, pp. 174–88; Abbot, *Carter Henry Harrison*, pp. 110–13, 240–41; *Chicago Daily News*, March 26, July 19, Aug. 20, 1884, March 2, 12, 1885; *Der Westen*, April 3, 1881; *Chicago Tribune*, April 2, 1881; *The Western Catholic*, April 9, 1881; Mayor's Annual Message, July 13, 1885, in Chicago, *Council Proceedings, 1885–86*, p. 51; Abbot, " The Harrison Dynasty in Chicago," *Munsey's Magazine*, XXIX (Sept., 1903), 809–10.

[36] *Chicago Tribune*, Feb. 24, March 22, April 6, 1881; *The Chicago Times*, March 23, 1881; *Illinois Staats-Zeitung*, March 24, April 6, 1881; *The Western Catholic*, March 26, 1881; Schilling, " History of the Labor Movement in Chicago," in [Lucy R. Parsons], *Life of Albert R. Parsons*, p. xxi; Chicago, *Council Proceedings, 1880–81*, pp. 591–94.

In the months which followed his election Harrison's popularity suffered no decline, and along with him the Democratic party enjoyed success in county offices. All this seemed ominous to Chicago Republicans, not only in the local contests but in the state and national. That party, however, proved successful in 1882 in three seats for Congress in which they supported the independent Democrat John F. Finerty from the Second District, Ransom W. Dunham in the First, and George R. Davis in the Third. For the first time candidates were presented in a fourth district, due to the reapportionment occasioned by the 1880 census, in which Republican George E. Adams defeated in the district Judge Lambert E. Tree, "silk stocking" Democrat who ran ahead in Chicago.

In the selection of state officers the Democrats showed greater proportional strength in Chicago and Cook County than in the state as a whole.[37] It was, therefore, with considerable apprehension that the Republicans viewed the approaching mayoralty contest of 'eighty-three. Allying themselves with reform elements, a committee of twenty-five hoped to stem the tide of Democratic prospects by nominating a leader with wide acquaintance. For this they turned to Levi Z. Leiter, then to Richard T. Crane, to run upon a platform of higher fees for liquor licenses and the elimination from the political scene of so-called disreputable influences.

With the refusal of Leiter and Crane to be candidates, the anti-Harrison forces, handicapped likewise by an apathetic Republican organization, chose Judge Eugene Cary to head the ticket to be known as the Citizens' Union, and solicited votes from the Irish, Germans, and Scandinavians by nominating members of these nationalities. Not even a campaign fund reported as high as $100,000, the appeals to employees by their employers, and the castigation of Harrison by the Protestant clergy could overcome the more numerous supporters of the Democrats, "the great unwashed," as the Baptist organ the *Standard* called them. The Harrison majority was again sizable.[38]

[37] *The Chicago Times*, Nov. 4, 1882; *Chicago Tribune*, Oct. 12, 18, 21, Nov. 11, 18, 1882, Jan. 16–18, 1883; Bennett, *op. cit.*, p. 286; Illinois, *House Journal, 1883*, p. 9, *Senate Journal, 1883*, p. 6; Bogart and Thompson, *op. cit.*, p. 138.

[38] The autumn county elections also went Democratic. *Svornost*, March 26, 1883; *Chicago Tribune*, March 3, 10, 13, 14, 21, 23–26, April 4, 1883; *The Chicago Times*, March

The influence which the Mayor already had over the affairs of the city was strengthened and extended. He was empowered by ordinance to select the standing committees of the council, a function hitherto considered the ultimate prerogative of that body, although choices were often affected by the wishes of the chief executive. By this demonstration of his vigorous leadership Harrison routed the forces led by four especially prominent members of his own party just returned to the council: Edward F. Cullerton of the Sixth Ward; James H. Hildreth of the Seventh, who had been re-elected in 1880 after his indictment in 1876 in the Whisky Ring; John H. Colvin, son of ex-Mayor Harvey D. Colvin, of the Sixteenth Ward; and Frank Lawler of the Eighth. All except Lawler, though they had selections of their own, eventually accepted what appeared to be a situation they could not control, their ultimate authority now restricted by an executive of their own party.[39]

However exciting such local contests were, they did not seem to evoke as intense and prolonged interest as did those fought for national and state offices. In 1884 both major parties held their national conventions in the city, convincing boosters that Chicago was thus recognized as the convention spot of the country. On June 3 the Republicans, assembled in Exposition Hall, chose James G. Blaine of Maine and John A. Logan as standard-bearers. The choice of the latter was especially well received by Chicagoans, who now saw one of their fellow citizens named to the vice-presidency. The following month the Democrats nominated Grover Cleveland of New York and Thomas A. Hendricks of Indiana in the same hall. The opposing platforms, advocating monetary, civil-service, and tariff reform, the exclusion of foreign contract labor, and the reservation of public lands for actual settlers, differed little, and therefore the voter had little assistance in voting on the basis of political principle. Rather,

14, 16, 25, 1883; *Chicagoer Arbeiter-Zeitung*, March 28, 1883; Johnson, *op. cit.*, p. 202; *Northwestern Lumberman*, XXI (March 10, 1883), 3; *The Standard*, XXX (April 12, 1883), 4; Chicago, *Council Proceedings, 1882–83*, pp. 457–60; Abbot, *Carter Henry Harrison*, pp. 124–26.

[39] In 1881, because of disagreement about the list prepared for standing committees, a committee of five aldermen and Mayor Harrison drew it up. Three Republicans (the Republicans held a majority in the council) voted with Democrats and Independents for such a committee. A tie vote of eighteen to eighteen was broken by Harrison, thereby increasing his influence in the council at that time. Chicago, *Council Proceedings, 1881–82*, pp. 8–10, 17–18, *1883–84*, pp. 2, 5, 9; *Chicago Tribune*, May 10, 15, 1881, May 15, 22, 1883; *The Chicago Times*, May 15, 1883.

the campaign degenerated into one of personal issues, a " dirt-evolving campaign," as the *News* put it. Not since 1860 had so much invective been heard in the city; Chicago speakers joined national in charges of dishonesty and immorality; the local press, like the national, found it profitable to satisfy the public thirst for the sordid and sensational as it emphasized, rather than regretted, such tactics of electioneering.

Alongside the major parties appeared minor political organizations — anti-Monopoly, Prohibition, and, most important, the so-called " Mugwumps," independent Republicans supporting Cleveland. Of all the groups the last was, in Chicago, the strongest, claiming no less prominent supporters than Edwin Burritt Smith, Franklin Mac-Veagh, Alexander C. McClurg, Abner M. Wright, Ernst Prussing, and Lyman J. Gage.[40]

By midsummer the major parties had selected their state candidates, the Democrats choosing Carter Harrison and the Republicans Richard J. Oglesby for governor. In the early autumn Congressional and county tickets appeared, including as candidate for Congress from the Fourth District John Peter Altgeld, before many years a name to be known not only in Illinois but throughout the country. Within the Republican party, factionalism played out its sorry game and no full slate could be presented for Congressional and county offices. But even so, the election results in the city showed that the races had been closely run. Blaine received 2,890 more votes than Cleveland, but Harrison had led Oglesby by 4,655, only to be beaten in the state. Congressional honors were evenly divided, and among the losers was Altgeld. The county officers chosen bore, in the main, the label of the party which still found it advantageous at times to wave " the bloody shirt." [41]

[40] *Chicago Daily News*, May 16, June 3–7, July 5, 7, 12, 14, 15, Aug. 16, 28, Sept. 15, 17, 18, 1884; *Chicago Tribune*, May 15, 16, 30, June 4, 7, July 22, 25, Sept. 9, 19, Oct. 6, 19, 23, 1884; Republican National Committee, *Proceedings . . . 1884* (Chicago, [1884]), pp. 91–94; National Democratic Committee, *The Political Reformation of 1884, A Democratic Campaign Book* (New York, 1884), pp. 3–7; Bogart and Thompson, *op. cit.*, p. 149.
[41] *Chicago Daily News*, April 17, July 3, Aug. 19, 21, 25, 26, Sept. 3, 4, 16, 20, 22, Oct. 8, 1884; Andreas, *History of Chicago*, III, 873; Harry Barnard, *Eagle Forgotten* (New York, 1938), p. 66; *The Western Catholic*, July 19, 1884; *Chicago Tribune*, Aug. 24, 29, Sept. 4, 12, 18, 22, 23, Oct. 4, 9, 13, 14, 20, 25, 26, 1884; *Svornost*, Oct. 9, 1884; Chicago Board of Election Commissioners, *First Annual Report . . . 1915* (Chicago, n.d.), p. 15. For election results of county see *Chicago Tribune*, Nov. 23, 1884. For significant contested election for state senator in Sixth District see Illinois, *Senate Journal, 1885*, pp. 41–42, 141–42.

The concern of civic-minded Chicagoans over persisting election frauds led in 1885 to one of the city's periodic reform drives. The November election of 1884 had produced gross irregularities. An investigation by the grand jury revealed that out of Chicago's 171 precincts only seven failed to show violations of the election laws " at every step as the election progressed — fraud at the registration, fraud at the reception and at the counting of the ballots, and fraud at the final canvass of the returns." [42] Here, indeed, was the chance the Republicans had been looking for, which, they thought, might be the key to the door of the City Hall. To the electorate they offered a slate replete with candidates of political strength, men of high standing in the community. For the mayoralty Judge Sidney Smith of the Superior Court was drafted; John F. Finerty, an independent Democrat and editor of the Irish paper the *Citizen,* for treasurer; Hempstead Washburne, son of the politically important Elihu Washburne, for city attorney; and C. Herman Plautz for city clerk in order to attract the large German vote.

The reform spirit likewise seeped into the Democratic ranks as Harrison expressed unwillingness to head the ticket unless the party purged its undesirables. His renomination was, however, taken for granted, and his campaign, supported by only one of the English-language dailies — the *Times* — was waged with heat and vigor. In answer to Republican charges that he represented gang rule, he pointed to his businesslike administration of the city and to the meritorious performance of his department chiefs.[43] His re-election by the slim margin of 375 votes, after a long-drawn-out canvass and a court contest by his defeated opponent, was the narrowest of his career.[44]

[42] Illinois, *Senate Journal, 1885,* p. 138; *Chicago Tribune,* Dec. 12, 17, 1884, Jan. 25, Feb. 6, 17, 18, 22, March 3, 13, July 2, Nov. 20, 1885; Bennett, *op. cit.,* p. 325; D. W. Lusk, *Eighty Years of Illinois* (Springfield, 1889), pp. 480–81, 484; Dennis, *Victor Lawson,* pp. 90–91; Mackin and Another *v.* United States, 117 U. S. 348 (1886). Joseph Mackin, secretary of the Cook County Central Committee and of the Cook County Democratic Club, was sentenced to prison; others escaped through legal technicalities. Mackin *v.* Illinois, 115 Ill. 312 (1885).

[43] One of the able men named by Harrison was Dr. Oscar De Wolf as commissioner of health in 1883. Others were Theodore T. Gurney, as city comptroller first appointed in 1879, and DeWitt C. Cregier, as public works commissioner.

[44] *Chicago Tribune,* March 15, 25, April 5, 8, June 25, 1885, Jan. 26, 1886; *Chicago Daily News,* March 4, 16, 18, 25, 26, April 4, 8, 10, 22, June 11, 1885; Chicago, *Council Proceedings, 1884–85,* pp. 672–75. The charge of the *Inter Ocean* that Harrison was responsible for fraud and violence in the election was withdrawn by that paper when Harrison

During the campaign the objective of reform was fueled by a non-partisan movement for a revision of the election laws, promoted by a joint committee of the Citizens' Association and the Union League, Iroquois, Commercial, Young Men's Republican, and Union Veterans clubs. In June the state legislature, responding to this influence, provided a bipartisan board of election commissioners, appointed by the judge of the county court, which was to form election precincts, reapportion them after each presidential election, and name judges and clerks to serve at registrations and elections. Special precautions sought to prevent the fraudulent counting of votes or tampering with ballot boxes. In November a majority vote in every ward of the city approved the act, and the following January the state Supreme Court declared it constitutional.[45]

Within the scope of the reform movement, as it evolved, was also an assault on the forces dominating the county government. The election in 1886 of five reform members — all Republicans — to the Board of Commissioners brought only slowly the needed regeneration. Outvoted in the general organization, they were unable to change old rules. On the Finance Committee, however, their majority, backed by the county attorney, forced the adoption of resolutions that taxes be raised only for purposes specified in the annual appropriation bills, as state law required; that warrants in any fiscal year could be issued in advance only to a value of 75 per cent of the tax levy for that year; and that old accounts and liabilities exclusive of bonded indebtedness be submitted to the Finance Committee for examination and classification. The intimation that all the floating indebtedness contracted prior to the current fiscal year might be illegal added to the accusations which eventually resulted in 306 indictments, obtained through the efforts of State's Attorney Julius S. Grinnell, not only against men employed in county institutions but also against contractors and even county commissioners.[46]

brought an $800,000 libel suit against the paper. *The Inter Ocean*, April 9, 12, 1885; Abbot, *Carter Henry Harrison*, p. 138.

[45] Act of June 19, 1885, Illinois, *Laws, 1885*, pp. 142–86; Citizens' Association of Chicago, *Annual Report, 1886*, pp. 4–5; The People *ex rel.* Grinnell *v.* Hoffman *et al.*, 116 Ill. 587 (1886).

[46] *Chicago Tribune*, March 10, 16, 20, 26, April 1, 9, 15, 28, May 26, June 19, Aug. 6, 1887; *The Western Catholic*, Aug. 13, 1887; Cook County Board of Commissioners, *Proceedings, 1886–87*, pp. 378, 405, 421, 445, 451, 458–59, 617–18. Unsettled " boodle " claims arose in the following years to plague the county board. Judge Samuel P. McConnell in

These revelations of malfeasance in office proved a lubricant for salutary legislation by the General Assembly which reduced the term of county commissioner from three years to one; provided for the annual election of the entire board; required that two-thirds of the board be from Chicago, the remainder from the rest of the county, and all be county residents during the preceding five years. On June 14, four days after this act was made law, another attempted to regulate the county budget so that " boodlers " could not so brazenly become beneficiaries of their own planning.[47]

The election of November, 1886, which had placed the reform Republicans in a position of power on the county board, was to spell widespread disaster for the Democrats. They lost every county office except three judgeships, were badly beaten in races for the General Assembly, and elected but one Congressman, Frank Lawler, in the Second District. And in this moment of gloom Carter Harrison refused to run for the mayoralty, thus leaving his party without a candidate in 1887. Instead, he advised a fusion with the recently organized United Labor party, sprung out of the vividly stirring memory of the recent Haymarket affair; and to this end he urged the support of Robert Nelson, an iron molder. But the fusion failed to materialize because of " Tommy " Morgan's opposition.[48] Not even the invigorating breath of reform and reorganization sponsored by a " silk stocking " Committee of Eighty, led by the well-known lawyer William C. Goudy, was able to recall for the moment the triumphs of the Democracy. In these circumstances John A. Roche, the Republican, was swept into the city's executive chair. The votes of anti-

1892 ruled the board had no right to make contracts when the county treasury was empty. This decision, it was thought, would end the " boodle " cases. *Chicago Daily News*, June 14, 15, 1892.

[47] Acts of June 10, 14, 1887, Illinois, *Laws, 1887*, pp. 149–55. Among terms of the budget act, approval of the president of the county board was required for any resolution or order making an appropriation; he might veto in whole or in part any measure, and a four-fifths vote was necessary to override the veto; the president was to appoint a superintendent of public service to act as purchasing agent; the county clerk was to be *ex-officio* the comptroller of county finances. Other safeguards were also incorporated.

[48] Abbot, *Carter Henry Harrison*, pp. 145–46; *Chicago Daily News*, March 22, 26, April 1, 4, 1887; *Chicago Tribune*, March 25, 1887; Andreas, *History of Chicago*, III, 492; Green B. Raum, *History of Illinois Republicanism* (Chicago, 1900), pp. 672, 674; Broadside in " Labor 1890–95," *Thomas J. Morgan Collection* (Illinois Historical Survey, University of Illinois); " Minutes of Meeting of Executive Committee of United Labor Party," Sept. 28, 1886, *Thomas J. Morgan Scrapbooks*, IV, 255 (Illinois Historical Survey); Chicago Board of Election Commissioners, *First Annual Report, 1915*, p. 760.

Harrison Democrats and the recency of the Haymarket affair, with its aftermath of fear, militated effectively in favor of the Republicans. For eight years the Democrats had enjoyed dominance in the city. Now, with this dominance no longer theirs in either city or county, they soon were accusing their successful opponent of machine politics as manipulated by Roche and George R. Davis, Republican member of the House of Representatives and now aspiring to the senatorship.[49]

But those who like John A. Logan believed that " the Democracy is now broken up and will never recover again " underestimated the party's resiliency. In a single year the local organization shook off its lethargy, routed confusion and internal dissension, and scored a triumph in November, 1888 unequaled since the memorable election of 1876.[50] For this the nomination of John M. Palmer of Springfield as the Democratic candidate for governor undoubtedly was largely responsible. His opposition to the use of the Pinkertons and other private agents in labor disputes endeared him to workingmen, and his objection to the use of federal troops under General Philip Sheridan at the time of the Chicago Fire established him as a stalwart among Democratic theorists. In the national race, however, the tariff overshadowed all other issues. Illinois Democrats seized upon it with enthusiasm and Chicago Republicans earnestly fought to convert the Northwest to the philosophy of protectionism.[51]

Scarcely had the national platform been adopted before sales of books on the tariff increased, and the subject was frequently discussed by debating societies throughout the city. Congressmen bom-

[49] Chicago Daily News, April 1, 4, 5, 6, Sept. 17, 19–21, 28, Oct. 1, 10–13, 17, 26, 27, 31, Nov. 1, 2, 1887; Chicago Tribune, April 6, Oct. 26, 1887; The Western Catholic, March 5, 1887; Cook County Board of Commissioners, Proceedings, 1886–87, pp. 487–88. Joseph E. Gary was the candidate of both Democratic factions to succeed himself as judge of the Superior Court. The resignation of Julius S. Grinnell as state's attorney to serve on the Circuit Court necessitated another nomination. This was given George H. Kettelle.

[50] J. A. Logan to Mary [Logan], Nov. 3, 1886, Logan Papers; Chicago Daily News, March 14, 15, 24, April 11, 13, 14, 25, May 1, 12, July 16, 21, 1888. Much discussion among Democrats arose over distribution of federal patronage. Chicago Tribune, May 7, 24, 1885; Sept. 22, 1888; H. A. Hurlbut to President Grover Cleveland, July 9, 1886; John C. Cosgrove to Cleveland, July 13, 1886; J. E. Van Pelt to Col. J. B. Lamont, May 19, 1886 [telegram], The Papers of Grover Cleveland (Mss. Library of Congress).

[51] Chicago Daily News, Jan. 28, July 19, Oct. 9, 20, 25, 1888; Palmer, op. cit., pp. 230–34, 258–60; Chicago Tribune, May 3, 4, 24, July 20, Sept. 6, 1888. The free-trade movement in Chicago is discussed in Ralph R. Tingley, American Cobden Clubs (unpublished M.A. Thesis, The University of Chicago, 1947).

barded their constituents with over six million franked copies of tariff speeches, and a million and a half copies of Cleveland's message. Numerous tracts for or against protection were available for all who would read. As early as January, the American Protective Tariff League, organized on a statewide basis in Illinois, established a branch in Chicago with William P. Nixon, general manager of the *Inter Ocean,* as vice-president.

Into the Republican campaign coffers poured the generous donations of industrialists and manufacturers; even workers in protected industries were at times convinced that increased rather than reduced duties would provide them with greater security. Unlike the campaign of 'eighty-four, a widespread discussion of issues prepared voters to cast their ballots. When they were counted after the election was over, they had given victory to the Republicans in Cook County outside Chicago and in the state. In the city proper, however, the Democrats had rolled up majorities for Cleveland, Palmer, and two of their Congressional candidates, and had elected all ten of the county commissioners allotted Chicago. The labor vote, scattered among the various tickets of differing workingmen's groups and the old parties, polled no more than a negligible number for any labor nominee. This led the *Knights of Labor* to observe, what had been the opinion of many labor protagonists, that " the time has not yet arrived when anything can be accomplished by independent political action of the labor party." [52]

The strength of the Democrats in the general election of 1888 filled them with new confidence as to the possibilities in store in the coming municipal campaign. Carter Harrison had returned to the city from abroad in November after his withdrawal the year before from the political ring, and shortly threw his influence to John A. King of the McAvoy Brewing Company instead of to Walter C. Newberry, DeWitt C. Cregier, and Jonas Hutchinson contesting for the Democratic mayoralty post. The nominating convention, " composed of men who by their dress and speech disclosed that they were privates, not captains, in society and politics," and who " represented everything from the church to the saloon," according to the *News,*

[52] *Chicago Daily News,* Jan. 28, July 19, Oct. 9, 20, 25, 1888; Palmer, *op. cit.,* pp. 230–34; *Chicago Tribune,* May 3, 4, 24, July 20, Sept. 6, 1888; *The Knights of Labor,* IV (Nov. 10, 1888), 1.

met on March 17 and, to Harrison's and King's surprise, nominated Cregier in a tumultuous session. The platform, designed to appeal to labor and the radical fringe, contained, said the *News*, "a homeopathic dose of state socialism." It demanded that gas and light, like water, be supplied at cost to the consumer, and that public services in general be performed by the municipality for the benefit of the public.[53]

The situation among Republicans was different. Here all went smoothly. Only one candidate, Roche, appeared, backed by the well-oiled George B. Swift-George R. Davis machine, and Medill of the *Tribune*. Roche's nomination, unpopular in some quarters because of his alleged pro-monopoly attitude particularly toward the West Side elevated railroad, made him a target for those objecting to the transportation monopoly on the West Side held by Charles T. Yerkes and his associates. Furthermore, lax police enforcement of laws against vice and gambling and the toleration of violations of the Sunday closing regulations reminded voters of the criticism directed at the Harrison administrations. The membership of Roche in the secret United Order of Deputies, designed to ostracize Catholics in politics and business, added to the heated charges bandied about by the party out of power. Thus bombarded by the forces of temperance, morality, religion, and economic prejudice, Roche went down to defeat, taking with him other members of his party. To this defeat a ballot, "the Anti-Machine Ticket," carrying both Democrats and Republicans and headed by Cregier contributed.[54]

Almost immediately the air was filled with electioneering for aldermen from the ten wards added by the annexation of territory in 1889, to be chosen at a special election September 10. To the surprise of the *Tribune*, which had expected the suburbs to go solidly Repub-

[53] *Chicago Tribune*, Nov. 16, 1888, Feb. 4, 21, 1889; *The Knights of Labor*, IV (Nov. 17, 1888), 8; *Chicago Daily News*, March 6, 19, 21, 23, 1889; Carter H. Harrison, *Stormy Years*, pp. 35–36; Johnson, *op. cit.*, p. 141.

[54] Roche declared he had not known the purpose of U.O.D. Theodore Brentano, running for attorney, was also accused of membership. Cregier publicized by affidavit that he was not a member. Typescript copies of the constitution and oath of this organization can be found in the *Victor Lawson Papers*, March 28–Aug. 23, 1889 (*Mss.* Newberry Library). *Chicago Daily News*, March 4–6, 11, 13–15, 18, 19, 23, 27–30, Nov. 6, 7, 1889; *Chicago Tribune*, Nov. 16, 1888, March 15, 16, Nov. 6, 1889; Citizens' Association of Chicago, *Annual Report, 1888*, pp. 15–17, 20–21, 42–43; *Chicagoer Arbeiter-Zeitung*, March 28, 1889; Barnard, *op. cit.*, pp. 141–43. Barnard ascribes to Altgeld the idea of "the Anti-Machine Ticket."

lican, that party's successful candidates numbered ten, matched by
ten Democrats, all of whom were chosen to hold office only until
the next regular municipal election, when each ward would again
select one candidate for one year and a second for a two-year term.[55]

This unexpected show of strength was followed by fresh Democratic triumphs in the county elections that fall in a campaign sur-
charged with the anti-Catholicism of the American League, successor to the United Order of Deputies. Through the inflamed speeches
of its members and the bald intemperance of *America,* its journal,
the League propagated its doctrine of nationalism and anti-foreign-
ism, trying to perpetuate and capitalize on the divisive forces of
religious sectarianism and nationality.[56] These successes had filled
brimful the Democrats' cup of optimism. Convinced that one success
foretold another, they looked forward enthusiastically to elections to
come. The 1890 county and state campaigns followed largely successful spring aldermanic and township contests.[57] Although the
county convention was made up of delegates chosen by the primary
election law of 1889 designed to eliminate " the old-style-free-for-all,"
peace did not prevail between the Cregier and Harrison factions.
Once the Democratic slate, however, had been placed in nomination,
it received support of the party.

One of the liveliest issues of the campaign was the question of the
fitness of women to occupy office. Since 1873 they had been eligible
to hold any elective school office, although they did not have suffrage. For the superintendency of the Cook County schools the Democrats nominated Mrs. Marion A. Mulligan, widow of General
James A. Mulligan. Republicans were frankly embarrassed, for if

[55] Chicago, *Council Proceedings, 1889–90,* pp. 110, 307–8, 333–37, 379, 415–16; *Chicago Tribune,* Sept. 11, 1889.

[56] *Ibid.,* Nov. 5, 1889. *America* was sold in 1891 to the *Graphic.* (*America,* VI [Sept. 24,
1891], 754–55.) On June 6, 1889 the state legislature passed a law permitting political
parties to choose delegates to conventions by primary election. It was reported as working
satisfactorily that year, but in future years the harmony it was supposed to effect was not
always apparent. (Bradwell, *All the Laws of the State of Illinois, 1889,* pp. 95–99; *Chicago
Daily News,* Oct. 26, 1889, Oct. 1, 1890; *The Inter Ocean,* Oct. 1, 1890.) The primary law,
it should be noted, provided for the selection of election officers, prescribed their duties, fixed
the manner of establishing election districts, defined who might vote, and laid down penalties for offenses.

[57] The 1890 spring aldermanic and township contests were much more lively than
usual. The spring elections took on interest chiefly when the mayor was among those to be
chosen. *Chicago Tribune,* April 5, 1890; *Chicago Daily News,* March 12, April 2, 1890;
Chicago, *Council Proceedings, 1890–91,* pp. xlv–xlvi.

they criticized her as unfit on account of sex they would be charged
with lack of chivalry toward womankind in general. And that to
some seemed to hold far graver consequences than the charges of
corruption and double-dealing so often heard. Indeed, to be engaged
in " petticoat warfare " proved an unnerving experience. That Harrison had suggested the nomination appears to have been another of
his adroit strokes of political maneuvering, for he must have recognized a force in politics the Republicans had not seen, or, if they had
seen it, they had carefully avoided its pitfalls. As a Roman Catholic
and a candidate lacking experience as an educator, Mrs. Mulligan
was, however, vulnerable on both counts. Some doubt was entertained, too, as to the extent of " chivalry " displayed by the Democrats in naming her, if, as the News reported, she had been asked to
contribute $1,000 to the campaign fund. Not even the fact that she
was the widow of a Civil War general outweighed other considerations, and she went down in defeat before Albert G. Lane, Republican.[58]

That autumn, too, an off-year for state elections, rivalry for the
control of the legislature was particularly keen. A successor to
Charles B. Farwell, Republican, for the United States Senate and a
few candidates for state officers were to be picked. The decision of
labor and farmer groups to work within the old parties laid them
open to an ardent courtship on the part of both. Both Democrats
and Republicans eagerly cultivated a spirit of fraternity with the irregulars despite their espousal of the free and unlimited coinage of
silver, the direct election of United States senators, an income tax,
and, above all, a more favorable attitude toward the problems minor-
ities felt were primarily theirs.

Easily the most controversial and explosive issue of the off-year
state campaign was that of amending the compulsory-school-attend-
ance law. Neither party wanted to touch it. The year before, the
legislature had by law provided that every child between the ages
of seven and fourteen should attend school sixteen weeks a year;
that eight weeks of the time must be put in consecutively in some
public school in his district or in a private school; and that instruc-

58 Chicago Tribune, Oct. 1, 1890; Chicago Daily News, Oct. 1, 28, Nov. 1, 1890; Act
of April 3, 1873, Illinois, Revised Statutes, 1874, p. 982; The Chicago Legal News, XXIII
(Oct. 4, 1890), 40; The Inter Ocean, Oct. 2, 1890; The Rights of Labor, VI (Nov. 1, 1890),
1; Cook County Board of Commissioners, Proceedings, 1890–91, p. ix.

tion using the English language was to be given in reading, writing, arithmetic, United States history, and geography. The provision that English be the medium of teaching roused those groups which wished to perpetuate their native tongues, particularly the Germans, who, whether Lutherans or Catholics, now wished the statute repealed or amended. They attacked it as an interference with personal liberty, the right of parents to control the education of their children. They objected to the English press picturing them as opposed to compulsory education in itself; nor did they — although they denied it — like the part of the law permitting state truant officers to inspect both private and public schools. They earnestly urged voters to elect the German Democratic nominee for state superintendent of schools, Henry Raab, rather than Richard Edwards, the Republican incumbent and father of the enactment.[59]

With the issue forced upon them, Republicans adopted a fence-straddling plank, declaring their faith in compulsory education as necessary for a literate citizenry, and at the same time expressing their desire to see the law so amended that parents would not be subjected to interference. But, willy-nilly, Republican speakers found they must commit themselves in its favor, and campaign literature, adorned with pictures of the " little red schoolhouse," described the disaster to come if the Democrats achieved victory. The Farmers' Alliance and the Farmers' Mutual Benefit Association joined actively in the controversy heavily charged with " foreignism " and all it connoted. With deep-seated convictions as to the dangers they saw in the situation, they adopted the sentiment of English Protestant preachers whose text declared: " Train up a child in the way he should go; and when he is old, he will not depart from it."

While the Democratic party, too, preferred to fight shy of the question, its candidates showed a greater willingness to sign the pledge demanded by the German Lutheran and Evangelical school committees than did their opponents, and party resolutions on the subject by the politically shrewd Judge Richard Prendergast, while paying lip service to popular education, were so phrased as to favor

[59] Act of May 24, 1889, Illinois, *Laws, 1889*, pp. 237–38; *Chicago Daily News*, Sept. 4, Oct. 14, 16, 21, 28, 1890; *Chicago Tribune*, May 3, Oct. 18, 24, 1890; *Abendpost*, April 21, Oct. 24, 30, 1890; *Illinois Staats-Zeitung*, April 22, May 9, Nov. 1, 1890. Aside from the Norwegian Synod, which was in sympathy with the Missouri Synod of Germans, most Scandinavian Lutherans supported the law. *Chicago Daily News*, Oct. 22, 1890.

repeal or wholesale revision of the law. The *News* thought this an excellent and indisputable indication of the Democrats' belief that "a child educated is a democrat lost."

Raab, a key figure in the school-law dispute, carried Cook County and the state. Although the elections on the whole gave a clear-cut victory to neither party, by and large the Democrats strengthened their position. By an alliance of the Democrats with the Farmers' Mutual Benefit Association, gains in the state legislature made possible the selection in March, 1891 of John M. Palmer. He was the first definitely Democratic senator from Illinois to Washington since the Civil War, with the possible exception of the independent David Davis chosen in 1877 by a Democratic-Greenback coalition. Democrats, too, took three of the four places in the Congressional race, thus reversing the proportion in the 1888 election, and for this Republicans held responsible Chicago's disapproval of the much talked-of McKinley tariff bill.[60]

The general outline of political party strategy in the early 1890's did not depart much from that of the years that preceded. Special issues commanding more than the usual degree of the elector's attention, however, had marked the first year of the decade. Most significant in a long-range perspective was the movement for the use of the Australian ballot, which would end the practice of each party printing its own ballot and, moreover, would insure secrecy for the voter. Led by Judge Murray F. Tuley, organized action took shape in January, 1891, in the formation of the Chicago Ballot Reform League. The bill drafted by the League obtained the endorsement of the Democratic Iroquois Club, the Swedish Literary Society, the United Brotherhood of Carpenters and Joiners, and others. In June the bill became law, but too late for the spring election.[61]

Long before the mayoralty contest of 1891 Harrison protagonists were actively nurturing that faction's deeply rooted hostility toward

[60] *Chicago Daily News*, Oct. 9, 11, 14, 16, 18, 20–23, 25, 27, 30, Nov. 6, 19, 1890; *The Inter Ocean*, Nov. 1, 6, 1890; *The Advance*, XXIII (Oct. 23, 1890), 781; Moses and Kirkland, *op. cit.*, I, 245, 251–52; Bogart and Thompson, *op. cit.*, pp. 180–82; Palmer, *op. cit.*, 262–66. See also Barnard, *op. cit.*, pp. 144–45, and Victor F. Lawson to Eugene Field, June 26, 1890, *Lawson Papers*, on the Palmer election. Palmer had been, however, important in the Republican party, serving as governor of Illinois 1868–72.

[61] *Chicago Tribune*, Jan. 3, Feb. 2, 1891; *Chicago Morning Herald*, Jan. 24, 30, 1891; *The Chicago Times*, Jan. 9, 1891; *Chicago Evening Post*, Feb. 6, 1891; *The Inter Ocean*, Feb. 9, 1891; Citizens' Association of Chicago, *Annual Report, 1891*, p. 9; Illinois, *Laws, 1891*, p. 93.

the Cregier administration. It was, furthermore, not hard to capitalize on the mounting criticism of many citizens, regardless of party, who were becoming more and more convinced that the law-abiding never caught up with the law-breaking. Lotteries and gambling, openly conducted policy shops, and well-known resorts of prostitution ran freely, only spasmodically hindered under the pressure of concerted action on the part of the Citizens' Association and others. Then, when evidence was so damaging that the police had no recourse but to act, they did so only in a few instances, imposing upon the guilty punishment so minor that in a short time they carried on as they had formerly. The Cregier machine, moreover, continued to function, and when the Democratic primaries were held in March, Harrison men were denied seats in the convention, which eventually renominated the Mayor. Thereupon the Harrison forces held one of their own, from which the ex-mayor emerged triumphant as the candidate of bolting City Hall Democrats, a large number of Germans, Bohemians, and Poles.[62]

The reform elements, supported by many Republicans, in the meantime moved to enlist Franklin MacVeagh to lead their crusade for cleaner government. Upon his refusal to run, Elmer Washburn, superintendent of police in Medill's administration, took over the drive for the mayoralty, opposed not only by the two Democratic nominees but also by the labor leader Thomas J. Morgan on the Socialist ticket, and Hempstead Washburne, described as " personally unexceptionable " by the Citizens' Association, on the regular Republican slate.

No other contest in the spring election loomed as large in the public eye as that for the mayoralty with its pull, on the one hand, on party loyalties and, on the other, on adherence to good government without regard to political label. From a bitter campaign Hempstead Washburne emerged victor with only a slight lead over Cregier and Harrison, demonstrating to the Citizens' Association the effective participation of the independent voter in electing men to " high offices in defiance of the rough elements " in the city. Again the Citizens' candidate ran far behind all but Morgan. Once more there was

[62] *Chicago Tribune*, June 5, 1890, Feb. 7, March 22, 1891; Citizens' Association of Chicago, *Annual Report, 1889*, pp. 11–12, *1890*, pp. 6–7; Abbot, *Carter Henry Harrison*, p. 191; *The Chicago Times*, March 18, 22, 1891; Harrison, *Stormy Years*, p. 36; Johnson, *op. cit.*, pp. 142–43.

illustrated in Chicago what was becoming increasingly true of reform tickets in city politics in general — the dislodgment of men in
the old-line parties with their facilities for patronage was peculiarly
difficult. Some other means to break through the tangled meshes of
the urban machine had to be found. That day for Chicago was only
a short five years off, when, at long last, the citizens' non-partisan
Municipal League would clear the way for better government.[63]

Although legalizing the use of the Australian ballot had come too
late for the spring election, it was possible to test it in the autumn of
'ninety-one when county officers were chosen. Just as in the recent
mayoralty struggle, intraparty antagonisms were brought into bold
relief as the Harrison-Cregier wings of the Democrats presented
through their own central committees a slate of candidates, later to
be ratified in a joint convention.[64] A similar procedure was followed
also by the Republicans, whose nominations, made by a central committee of seven, were later accepted by a city-wide party convention.[65]

The choice of men to fill vacancies on the Board of Trustees of the
Sanitary District, created in 1889, posed the most difficult question of
all for the voter to answer. Opinion of the public at large as well as
that of the board's membership was divided as to what should be the
size of the Sanitary Canal. Should there be a channel with a flow of
600,000 cubic feet per minute, as set forth in the act of 1889, or a
smaller and less expensive one, half that size? Action in construction

[63] In four of seven town elections Democrats won. The successful city treasurer and city
attorney were also Democrats. In the council the Republicans elected thirteen members, the
Cregier Democrats eighteen, and the Harrison forces three. (Chicago, *Council Proceedings, 1891–
92*, pp. xlvii–xlviii.) *Chicago Tribune*, March 1–13, 15, 16, 18, 20, April 2, 6, 18, 1891;
The Chicago Times, March 10, 13, April 12, 1891; Victor F. Lawson to Frank Drake, Jan.
29, 1892, Lawson to Andrew MacLeish, April 4, 1891, Lawson to T. Benton Leiter, April
9, 1891, *Lawson Papers*; Citizens' Association of Chicago, *Annual Report, 1891*, p. 8.

[64] The Democratic ticket included John S. Cooper as president of the county board;
Jonas Hutchinson as judge for the Circuit Court; Charles F. Babcock as superintendent of
schools. *Chicago Daily News*, Sept. 1, 3, 4, 11, 15, 17, 25, 28, 1891.

[65] Among Republican candidates were John M. Green for president of the county
board, Theodore Brentano for judge of the Superior Court, and Orville T. Bright, superintendent of schools. Ossian Guthrie filed a petition as an independent trustee for the Sanitary
District and demanded a place on the Republican ticket. The Board of Review decided in
his favor since the election law allowed nominations by conventions only when the party
received 2 per cent of the total vote in the preceding election. Because the previous election
had been a nonpartisan judicial election the Republicans lacked a legal basis for the use
of the convention rather than petition. Guthrie's name was on the ballot in a column "Republican by petition." Partial tickets were named by a People's Trade and Labor party and
by the Prohibitionists. *Ibid.*, Sept. 11, 15, 18, 21, 25, 30, Oct. 1, 2, 26, 31, 1891; *Chicago
Tribune*, Oct. 28, Nov. 1, 1891.

had been delayed by the president of the board, Richard Prendergast, abetted by a majority of the trustees in the hope that the legislature would authorize and the voters later accept the smaller canal. In naming Lyman E. Cooley, ex-chief engineer of the Sanitary District and ardent champion of the larger channel, the Democrats thus set the stage for the controversial issue to be aired fully, as they stressed the point of not only more effective sanitation but greater facilities for commerce through this inland waterway, if large enough. Besides, they declared, the advocacy of the Republicans for the smaller outlet was prompted largely by some millionaire land speculators who had in mind the development of the Calumet harbor at government expense and who feared that a ship canal, such as the Democrats proposed, would draw traffic back to Chicago. In the end, majorities were returned for William Boldenweck and Bernard A. Eckhart, Republicans, and Cooley, Democrat, in an election in which three votes could be distributed by the voters among two of the three candidates to be chosen. The county board and officers were now Republican, and for the two judgeships there had been no contest.[66]

But the heat generated in the contest for the officers of the Sanitary District was not the only burning issue of the autumn campaign. In June, 1891 women had been granted suffrage for school officers, after a long, uphill struggle captained by the Illinois Woman Suffrage Association. Shortly before the November election the Board of Election Commissioners ruled that they could not participate in the vote for county superintendent of schools because the constitutionality of the law had been challenged. Not to be denied a civic right for which she had fought, Mary Ahrens attempted to cast a ballot. Not permitted to do so, she thereupon sued the Election Commissioners. The next year the Illinois Supreme Court, acting upon her case, ruled the act unconstitutional insofar as it attempted to give women the ballot in the election of any school official specifically provided for in the state constitution, as was the county superintendent of schools.[67]

[66] Brown, *Drainage Channel and Waterway*, pp. 408–11; *Chicago Daily News*, Oct. 7, 8, 12, 19, 28, 30, 1891; *Chicago Tribune*, Oct. 27, 28, 29, Nov. 1, 1891. According to the law, a voter might vote for the total number of trustees to be elected or might distribute his votes among not less than five-ninths of those to be elected. In 1891 the Board of Review ruled that a voter might have a total of three votes distributed between two candidates.

[67] Act of June 19, 1891, Illinois, *Laws, 1891*, p. 135; Pierce, *A History of Chicago*, II,

Unusual interest for an aldermanic election, when not carried on in connection with choosing the mayor, was aroused in 1892 when rumors freely circulated that votes for a price had been involved in the grant of special privileges to three corporations during the year.[68] One of the ordinances was so objectionable to Mayor Washburne that he vetoed it, only to have it passed by an overwhelming vote over his veto.[69] In March, just before the election, the grand jury indicted seven Democratic aldermen. To the *Times,* since 1891 owned by Carter Harrison, this number seemed small indeed, since so many of both parties had voted in favor of the petitioners. That the widespread publicity and the condemnation of such aldermanic malfeasance affected the election was seen in the re-election of but nine of the thirty-four who retired that year.[70]

On the heels of this excitement came the autumn campaigns, with the county receding in importance to the state and national. Again, as so many times in the past, voters viewed the approach of balloting with an irrepressible partisanship, spellbound by the magic of the fast-flowing oratory of the various candidates and their speakers. For the Democrats, the holding of their convention with all its fanfare in the huge Chicago Wigwam gave additional vigor and animation to already enthusiastic partisans. Chicago Republicans could not receive the nomination of Benjamin Harrison for president for another term with the enthusiasm they wished they could. Some had hoped against hope that a popular uprising might sweep James G.

300, 456–57; *Chicago Daily News,* Nov. 2, 1891; The People *ex rel.* Mary A. Ahrens *v.* William J. English *et al.,* 139 Ill. 622 (1892).

[68] One (June 15, 1891) related to the vacation of streets by the Chicago and Northern Pacific in exchange for the railroad's co-operation in building viaducts. This was repealed and later re-enacted in virtually the same form. The second (July 13, 1891) dealt with the Chicago Economic Fuel Gas Company's request to lay mains in the city streets. The third (Feb. 29, 1892) authorized the Chicago Power-Supply and Smoke Abatement Company to lay mains in the streets to manufacture and distribute compressed air. Chicago, *Council Proceedings, 1891–92,* pp. 274, 337–39, 378–82, 434–37, 554–56, 1863–92.

[69] This was the ordinance of the Chicago Economic Fuel Gas Company, vetoed on the ground that the per cent of gross receipts was insufficient compensation to the city since no minimum sum was guaranteed. Washburne also objected to having the streets torn up during the Columbian Exposition. Chicago, *Council Proceedings, 1891–92,* pp. 434–36.

[70] *The Chicago Times,* March 18, 22, 24, April 6, 1892; *Chicago Daily News,* March 3, 30, Nov. 2, 1892; *Chicago Tribune,* Nov. 1, 1891, March 19, 22, 26, 1892; Carter H. Harrison, *Growing Up with Chicago* (Chicago, 1944), p. 171; *Chicago Morning Herald,* March 22, April 2, 1892; *Dziennik Chicagoski,* March 14, April 1, 1892; *Svenska Tribunen,* April 6, 1892. The cases against the aldermen were *nolle prossed. Chicago Daily News,* June 20, 1892.

Blaine into the nomination.[71] Then, too, there was the McKinley Tariff Act, which had cost a pretty high price in the last Congressional elections. But the therapeutic power of party loyalty lined Chicago up with the Harrison forces. The local Democracy, on the other hand, welcomed the nomination of Cleveland as one to attract votes. His stand on a tariff for revenue only and his endorsement of " hard money " as opposed to the free coinage of silver had strong appeal.[72]

In John Peter Altgeld the Democrats had already selected a first-rate candidate for governor. Associated with the liberal wing of the Democratic party, he now supported the eight-hour day and workers' compensation, although he had not been allied with labor's political endeavors in the 1880's; and he enjoyed the personal loyalty and endorsement of the labor liberal George Schilling. Part of his strength lay also in the backing given him by the Cook County delegation, who chose to ignore attacks on Altgeld, some of which were particularly directed toward his recently published book *Live Questions: Including Our Penal Machinery and Its Victims*. He shrewdly failed to re-announce his onetime sanction of English as the medium of instruction in the schools; instead he turned to a substitute for the Edwards law, one which would provide every child an elementary education without infringing upon his religious liberty.

Against Altgeld the Republicans had renominated Governor Joseph Fifer, " old Private Joe," embarrassed by the Republican resistance in the last legislature to the Democrats' attacks on the controversial education law on the ground that the whole question was not political. Eventually, to hold bolting German Lutherans in line, the Republicans defensively declared themselves for the repeal of the law.[73]

71 The Blaine protagonists included William Lorimer, whose political star was ascending and of whom Chicagoans would hear much in the next quarter-century.

72 *Chicago News Record*, June 2, 4, 1892; *Chicago Tribune*, May 21, June 9, 11, 1892; *The Inter Ocean*, June 22, 23, 1892; *The Chicago Times*, June 22, 23, 1892; *Chicago Morning Herald*, June 16, 1892; Republican National Committee, *The Republican Campaign Text-Book for 1892* (New York, 1892), pp. 8–12; Democratic National Committee, *The Campaign Text-Book of the Democratic Party* (New York, 1892), pp. 5–9. Cleveland's running-mate was Adlai E. Stevenson of Bloomington, Illinois.

73 *Chicago Daily News*, March 4, 11, April 28, 30, May 6, June 14, 1892; *Chicago Tribune*, March 5, April 28, June 14, 1892; Moses and Kirkland, *op. cit.*, I, 252; *Illinois Staats-Zeitung*, May 14, Oct. 5, Nov. 7, 1892; *The Rights of Labor*, VII (June 11, 1892), 1–3, (Nov. 5, 1892), 1; *Dziennik Chicagoski*, April 2, 1892; Bogart and Thompson, *op. cit.*, pp. 33, 153–54. For activities of Populist, Prohibition, and laborite groups, see *Chicago Daily News*, Aug. 30, Oct. 7, 1892; *Chicago Tribune*, Sept. 10, Oct. 18, 1892; *The Rights*

Within the state the campaign revolved chiefly about Altgeld. Altgeld clubs, ephemeral organizations sometimes social in outer form but political in motive, mushroomed under the aegis of the Altgeld Legion, particularly in the workingmen's sections. Especially active in the registration of voters was the Democratic campaign committee under the chairmanship of John P. Hopkins. The Republican counterpart worked also with an unusual burst of energy, until about 95 per cent or slightly over 260,000 Chicagoans eligible to vote were on the lists by the closing day of registration, the heaviest in the history of the city.

For virtually every office, national, state, and local, Chicago and Cook County piled up Democratic majorities. Not since the Civil War had the party had such cause for exultation. Cleveland's majority over Harrison exceeded thirty-five thousand, and Altgeld's over Fifer was nearly as large. Three Congressmen from the Chicago and Cook County area were sent to Washington, and the city's voters gave majorities to two Congressmen-at-large. Similarly, to the General Assembly at Springfield went seven Democratic senators and sixteen representatives against three Republican senators and fourteen representatives of that party.

Retrospectively, beaten Republicans sought the reason. The tariff issue appeared an important factor in their defeat, for men with free-trade leanings were still numerous in Chicago. The tariff and the Homestead steel strike, exploited by the Democrats, further alienated the labor vote. Having once committed himself to a Democratic vote for the national offices, the average voter, moreover, seemed unwilling to scratch his ballot for others. To the state Chicago had contributed the city's first governor. In all, in the twenty wards where naturalized voters outnumbered native, nineteen had gone Democratic and eight of the remaining fourteen where natives predominated fell to the Republicans.[74]

With the approach of the spring of 1893 Hempstead Washburne

of Labor, VII (Sept. 17, 1892), 4, (Sept. 24, 1892), 1, (Oct. 1, 1892), 4, (Oct. 22, 1892), 4.
[74] Chicago Evening Journal, Nov. 9, 10, 1892; Chicago Daily News, Nov. 9, 10, 11, 1892; Chicago Evening Post, Nov. 23, 1892; Chicago Tribune, Nov. 10, 1892; The Chicago Times, Sept. 4, 1892; J. Bernard Hogg, The Homestead Strike of 1892 (unpublished Ph.D. Thesis, The University of Chicago, 1943), pp. 144, 153–56; The Rights of Labor, VII (Nov. 19, 1892), 4, (Nov. 26, 1892), 4; Illinois Staats-Zeitung, Nov. 10, 1892.

was concluding his stewardship as mayor. It was a record of uniformly high achievement to which wisely chosen appointees had made outstanding contributions. Under him the police department was reorganized, mental and physical tests for applicants to the force instituted, and more rigid police discipline executed. In the enforcement of law, the Washburne administration scored triumphs particularly over the long-time politically powerful syndicates of gamblers. For the first time the increasingly powerful gas companies paid the city a part of their gas receipts as compensation for privileges granted, as well as reducing their rates to both municipal and private consumers. Impressive advances in the establishment of better building standards, in the extension of authority relating to the destruction of unsafe structures or those constructed contrary to prescribed regulations, significantly pointed up also the power of officials to carry through major improvements if they so willed.

Such achievements were, of course, not all that a good administration had hoped for. Nor were they accomplished easily. As usual, the city suffered from financial inconveniences due to the debt limitation. Inequality of tax assessments and the lapse in time between levying and collecting taxes further hindered the conduct of governmental undertakings. Again, the slowness with which money passed from the hands of township officials to those of the county treasurer prevented the ready execution of many municipal responsibilities. The tax situation was, furthermore, just as in the years gone by, muddled by attacks on the policy of the county treasurer withholding funds in order to reap the reward of interest upon them. Chicago's antiquated revenue system but added to the increasing complexity implicit in ministering to the needs of the sprawling city. And over all hung the cloud of party partisanship even when unity of purpose should have dictated that there be none. Before the end of his term Washburne indicated his unwillingness to run again.[75]

It had been no secret that Carter Harrison yearned to crown his career by serving as mayor during the approaching Columbian Exposition. To this end the Chicago Carter H. Harrison Club for a

[75] Citizens' Association of Chicago, *Annual Report, 1891,* pp. 9–11, *1892,* pp. 4–5, 16; *Chicago Daily News,* April 29, 1891, Oct. 8, 1892; *Chicago Tribune,* Jan. 10, July 2, 17, 26, 1892; *Chicago Evening Post,* April 29, May 15, 26, 1891; Chicago, *Council Proceedings, 1892–93,* pp. 7–8, 11, 2381–86, 2518–60, *1893–94,* pp. 28–30, 35; *Chicago Herald,* Jan. 11, 1893.

year before the date of election began to broadcast its propaganda. Its colorful publicity so energized and directed sentiment that Harrison emerged from the primaries with a substantial majority. He had, however, been forced to overcome the ambition of his erstwhile supporter Washington Hesing, with his powerful hold on the German-Americans and his influential mouthpiece, the *Illinois Staats-Zeitung.*[76]

The glamor which for years had enveloped Harrison in the eyes of many voters made the selection of an opposing candidate by the Republicans a formidable undertaking. Eventually, Samuel W. Allerton, wealthy packing-house proprietor, was named to make what turned out to be a bitterly fought contest, replete with charges of political alliances between the Democrats and the basest elements of the community. Carter Harrison, however, seasoned by years of this kind of campaigning, drew upon a reservoir of self-confidence, on a congenital independence and mastery over hostile, outside forces, that would have at first dismayed and in the end overwhelmed many others. But this sixty-eight year old veteran, against whom was weighted the hostility of nearly all the English press and many reform leaders of the community, was swept into office by a sizable vote. With him were other Democrats whom he carried into the city offices, but balance in the City Council lay in the ratio of thirty-eight Republicans to thirty Democrats, the former having been successful in twenty wards to the Democrats in eleven and Independent Democrats in three.[77]

Despite the success of the Democrats in both state and city, the party was rent by internal dissensions. This became a matter of public knowledge in the judicial campaign in Cook County in the autumn of 1893. At this time Judge Joseph E. Gary of the Superior Court, the popular Republican judge who had presided in 1887 at the trial of the anarchists, was renominated by his party along with

[76] *The Chicago Times,* April 9, 1891, Oct. 2, 1892; *Chicago Tribune,* July 10, 1891, Feb. 26, 1893; *Abendpost,* March 11, 1892; *Illinois Staats-Zeitung,* Dec. 19, 1892, Feb. 18, 1893.

[77] *The Rights of Labor,* VII (Feb. 4, 1893), 1, (Feb. 18, 1893), 4, VIII (March 25, 1893), 1, (April 1, 1893), 1, 3; *Dziennik Chicagoski,* Feb. 14, 1893; *Chicago Tribune,* Feb. 28, March 1, 2, 4, 5, 8, 10, 11, 16–18, 23–26, 28, April 5, 1893; *The Chicago Times,* Dec. 31, 1893; *Chicago Record,* April 1, 5, 1893; *L'Italia,* April 1, 3, 1893; *Illinois Staats-Zeitung,* March 20, 1893; *Skandinaven,* March 25, 1893; Chicago, *Council Proceedings, 1893–94,* pp. li-lii.

a full judicial and county-board ticket. His name had the endorsement of not only Republicans but prominent Democrats such as Potter Palmer, Marshall Field, Erskine M. Phelps, Andrew Cummings, and William D. and Samuel H. Kerfoot, not to mention the enthusiastic support of the Democratic judges Thomas A. Moran and Murray F. Tuley.

Ranged against Gary were those who approved the pardon Governor Altgeld had granted during the summer to the imprisoned anarchists and who held that their trial had not been fairly conducted. In the vanguard of those who exerted all the influence they could command were labor leaders of the George Schilling and Thomas J. Morgan schools, reformers led by Henry Demarest Lloyd, and the " Harrison City Hall " politicians. But the fearsome shadow of the Haymarket still hung heavily over the city. When the election was over, the Republicans emerged victor with five of their six candidates for the Superior Court, all four of their nominees for the Circuit Court, and their entire county-commissioner ticket, including the president of the county board. The *Tribune* hailed the result as another endorsement before the world of the verdict of 1887 and, with it, the expulsion of Altgeld " into outermost political darkness . . . with his mob of Socialists, Anarchists, single-taxers, and office-holding loots at his heels." [78]

But Carter Harrison did not know that his party's ticket, for which he had so earnestly fought, had thus been repudiated. On the last day of the Columbian Exposition his colorful career was abruptly ended by assassination at the hands of the half-crazed Patrick Eugene Prendergast, who had brooded over the mayor's refusal to appoint him corporation counsel. The city was stunned. Amidst tributes that poured into the city from abroad as well as from all sections of the United States, Harrison's erstwhile political opponents joined his supporters in honoring his memory. Even the *Tribune,* one of his most severe critics, declared that the death by violence of no other Chicagoan would excite more general regret nor elicit the

[78] Barnard, *op. cit.,* p. 258; *Chicago Record,* Oct. 2, 3, 5, 7, 11, 12, 19–21, 23–28, Nov. 4, 7, 8, 1893; *Chicago Tribune,* Sept. 18, Oct. 5, 7, 21, 26–28, 30, Nov. 3, 8, 1893. By the election the village of Norwood Park was annexed to the city and subsequently added to the Twenty-seventh Ward, Chicago, *Council Proceedings, 1893–94,* p. 1244; Gaston, *The History and Government of Chicago,* pp. 10–11.

sympathy of so many of his fellow citizens as had that of Mayor Harrison.[79]

Harrison's death more than a year before his term was to expire obliged the council to call a special election to name a successor, and the date was fixed as December 19. Meanwhile, it devolved upon that body to select one of its own members to serve as mayor pro-tem. The choice fell upon George B. Swift, Republican, who on December 2 was nominated at his party's convention to make the race against the Democrat John P. Hopkins, manager of the Chicago campaign of Cleveland in 1892.

A similarity in policies relating to local government and little difference in the qualifications of the candidates led voters to make their decision chiefly along party lines. The plurality of only 1,290 votes for Hopkins and the usual charges of fraud in the election opened the way for litigation lasting over two years. It was not until March 28, 1896 that the Illinois Supreme Court ruled that no error in the count had been made by County Court Judge Frank Scales. Thus, long after the term in dispute had ended, John P. Hopkins was given the right to occupy the chair of mayor.[80]

The two decades following the Great Fire witnessed Chicago voters placing the responsibility for governing more often upon the Democratic party than upon the Republican. In so doing, the city frequently followed a course independent of that of the state and nation. Although Illinois supported Republican presidential candidates in four out of five elections from 1876 to 1892, Chicago went Democratic in three; at the same time, three of the state's governors were Republican but only one ran ahead of the Democratic candidate in the city. Even more striking was the drift to the Democracy in local elections, for only three Republicans from 1876 to 1893 were victors in the ten mayoralty races. To explain what was a downright

[79] *Chicago Tribune,* Oct. 29, 1893; *Chicago Record,* Oct. 30, 1893; Chicago, *Council Proceedings, 1893–94,* pp. 1123–48; Abbot, *Carter Henry Harrison,* pp. 232–33; Harrison, *Stormy Years,* pp. 46, 128.

[80] Chicago, *Council Proceedings, 1893–94,* pp. 1032–34, 1040; *Chicago Record,* Nov. 1–4, 6, 7, 10, 13–15, 18, Dec. 2, 4, 6, 8, 18, 20, 1893; *Chicago Tribune,* Nov. 5, 6, Dec. 3, 15, 1893, Jan. 21, 31, May 20, June 6, Nov. 11, 1894; *Skandinaven,* Nov. 26, 1893; *Abendpost,* Dec. 4, 1893; *Chicago Evening Journal,* Dec. 22, 1893; *The Inter Ocean,* Jan. 25, Feb. 10, 1895; Samuel W. Allerton *et al. v.* John P. Hopkins, 160 Ill. 448 (1896); *Chicago Times-Herald,* March 30, 1896.

reversal of pre-Fire days was no easy matter for the defeated, unless they agreed that the increasing number of voters of foreign background and workingmen in general gravitated toward the Democrats, and that Carter Harrison was unbeatable.[81]

The primarily local problems which these officials had to face ran the gamut from the old-time demand for economy in government to issues complicated by religious and ethnic differences and the economic and social unrest of depression years. With the mid-'eighties came the increasingly important questions of the control of public utilities and what to do about monopolies. No election was free of charges of fraud and corruption. Critics of political behavior with a depressing persistence bemoaned the state of morality of those engaged in carrying out the duties of their offices. As in other cities of the country, so in Chicago could be found ample justification for Bryce's generalization that the government of cities was "the one conspicuous failure of the United States." Here were sometimes manifested a poverty of leadership and the readiness of elected servants of the people to listen to the siren-like voice of the unscrupulous; here could be found examples of the betrayal of the public trust and the elevation of party above the welfare of the community. Such shortcomings, however, were in some degree offset by occasional bold and honest leadership, by the inevitable expansion of governmental functions which attempted to meet the needs of the growing city and to adjust governmental performance to the demands of the new day. The problems which confronted Chicago were not easy to solve. But the achievement of building a city from the ashes of the Great Fire, to be crowned by the creation of the White City of the Columbian Exposition, could not have been accomplished had not the agents of government contributed to it.[82]

[81] See Appendix table.
[82] Fraud and malfeasance were particularly stressed in the elections 1874–78, 1881, 1883, 1884, 1886, 1887, 1889–93; temperance, Sunday closing, saloon-license fees in 1872–75, 1879, 1881, 1882, 1888, 1889; social and economic reforms in 1877, 1879, 1880, 1888, 1891, 1892; territorial annexations in 1887, 1889, 1892; regulations of public utilities and questions of monopoly control in 1888, 1889, 1893.

CHAPTER XI

THE INCREASE OF KNOWLEDGE

TRADITION AND PRACTICE dictated the continuation and extension of the educational system begun as early as Chicago's incorporation as a town. Within the social structure, resting as it did on a democratic ideology, the public school remained the keystone of the arch to educational and cultural advance. The Fire of 1871 gutted fifteen buildings used for school purposes, five rented, the others owned by the city. It deprived 10,000 children, nearly a third of the total enrollment, of accommodations. Within a relatively short time, however, the number of schoolhouses increased. By 1893 there were 346 buildings to care for the enlarging school population, which exceeded 166,000. In spite of what seemed a considerable expansion in facilities, they failed to keep pace with the rising number of pupils, and in 1888, for example, 10,000 children were reported as able to attend school no more than half a day, particularly in the crowded industrial sections. As the 'eighties advanced, more ethnic elements than in the years past were represented, their cultural backgrounds far different from those of the older stock.[1]

Administratively the basic structure was like that of an earlier day, but the Act of 1872 had centralized authority to a greater degree than formerly in the Board of Education, which functioned generally

[1] Chicago Board of Education, *Eighteenth Annual Report, 1872*, pp. 26, 36–37, 61, 123–26, 141, *Twenty-ninth Annual Report, 1883*, p. 43, *Thirty-ninth Annual Report, 1893*, p. 29; Andreas, *History of Chicago*, III, 144; *Chicago Tribune*, Sept. 6, 1888. The Board of Education reports, 1871–1893, are the chief source on the public schools. Other sources will be cited when used.

382 A HISTORY OF CHICAGO

through committees. Until 1888 women were excluded from the performance of this civic duty, but in that year, despite the plea that only businessmen would serve effectively, Mrs. Ellen M. Mitchell was named because of pressure from the Chicago Woman's Club. Through appointment by the Board a supervisory staff, headed by a superintendent, had general management of school matters and the supervision of the teaching staff, which increased from 476 in 1872 to 3,520 in 1893.[2]

Many of the teachers in the Chicago schools were products of the local school system as normal-school graduates, as cadets aiding teachers in the overcrowded sections, and as apprentices directly from high school after passing required examinations. Lack of adequate supervision in the case of cadets, the passing of qualifying examinations somehow by the poorly qualified, and the temporary interest of many engaged in teaching, meant that the Chicago school system did not offer at all times the best type of instruction despite the high aims of men like superintendents Josiah L. Pickard (1864–1877) and George Howland (1880–1891). Furthermore, salaries were low, particularly for women, who made up the chief force in the lower grades and who, as late as 1893, were receiving compensation ranging from $400 to $775 a year. Pay for women was a little better in the high school, however, for at this level of instruction they got on the average a salary of about $1,245, much lower than the average for male teachers. But there was little hope for better conditions as long as the public erroneously insisted that teachers did not work much after all, having, it was held, short hours and long vacations, and, therefore, that they were receiving more than they deserved.

The school system in 1873 was made up of a high school (the Central High School), a normal school, district schools, grammar schools, and independent primary schools. In the year 1875–76 a change was made from five years each in the primary and grammar grades to four. Then followed the high school — in addition to the old Central, one in each division of the city — offering a two-year curriculum until 1880–81, when a four-year course and a three-year classical preparation were provided. At this time Central High was

[2] Besides Chicago Board of Education reports, see Illinois, *Statutes, 1818–1872*, pp. 421–22; Chicago, *Council Proceedings, 1888–89*, pp. 203–4; *Chicago Tribune*, May 19, 29, June 26, 1888, Sept. 27, 1892.

abandoned and attention focused solely on those high schools located in the three divisions. By 1891 twelve secondary schools accommodated the growing enrollment, which by 1893 approximated six thousand. One of these, the English High and Manual Training School, opened in 1890, catered to the demand of advocates of vocational training for those whose education must end with the high school.[3]

Besides these, there were the special schools — the kindergartens, those devoted to the deaf and mute, evening schools, and, after November, 1889, the school at the Waifs' Mission. It was through private philanthropy that the city was first provided with kindergartens, which by the mid-'eighties numbered twenty-five. Beginning in 1888 the Chicago Froebel Kindergarten Association and the Chicago Kindergarten College received permission to use several rooms in the public schools on the condition that they would arrange for the expense of instruction without charge to pupils or parents. Not until 1892 did the Board of Education assume the responsibility of maintaining this branch of schooling, and then, upon the recommendation of these organizations, it took over the ten kindergartens they had operated.

The city was less tardy in recognizing society's duty to care for the handicapped. In 1874 the Board opened a free public day school for deaf-mute children, where they were taught the sign language and, by 1883 in some cases, articulation and lip reading. An appropriation by the state in 1879 made it possible for the Board to establish such a school in each division of the city and also one for more advanced pupils in a room at the Newsboys' Home, described as the largest of the kind in the United States. The occasional lapses of the state legislature in continuing grants for such purposes, however, placed the burden at times solely upon Chicago for several years following 1886, despite the provision that under state aid all Illinois children were eligible for admission.[4]

³ *The Chicago Times*, Aug. 5, 1875, Jan. 20, 1878, July 1, 1880; *Chicago Tribune*, July 1, 1880, Jan. 15, 1890; Chicago Board of Education reports beginning *Eighteenth* (1872), *Proceedings, July 8, 1891 to June 28, 1892*, p. 390. The average salary of women on high-school faculties was computed from data in *ibid.*, pp. 386–87.

⁴ Illinois, *Laws, 1879*, p. 20; *Chicago Tribune*, April 30, 1887; Chicago Board of Education, *Twenty-first Annual Report, 1875*, p. 20 and following reports, *Proceedings, September, 1887, to September, 1888*, p. 163, *August 21, 1889, to July 9, 1890*, p. 114, *July 6, 1892, to July 5, 1893*, p. 64, 139–40; Andreas, *History of Chicago*, III, 152.

The years following the Great Fire were also marked by a continuation of evening classes, opened in 1863 for the benefit of those employed during regular school hours. By 1873 over 2,600 were reported enrolled, a number which twenty years later increased to 14,530, although attendance was not always constant. Of those who found time to register for courses in reading, writing, and arithmetic, the most popular branches, men in the manufacturing industries were the most numerous; they exceeded those who enrolled in the high school, where they could learn mathematical drawing, mechanical philosophy, drawing of machinery, physics, algebra, geometry, and bookkeeping. In the fall of 1877 stenography, also called phonography, was added to other offerings, attracting within a brief five years no less than 309 students out of a total enrollment of 500 in the Evening High School. English instruction gave to immigrants, who by far outnumbered Americans, a much needed means of communication. In such classes the great majority of students were adults, although the largest single age group among enrollees in the evening schools, as a whole, was somewhat younger — below fifteen years before 1891–92, and from then between fifteen and eighteen.

It was, however, in the daytime hours regularly devoted to instruction that the schools served the greatest number. The 166,895 enrolled in 1892–93 represented a gain of over 278 per cent in twenty years, although in proportion to the general increase in population the number was substantially the same. Costs mounted along with the expansion of the physical plant and a larger teaching staff.[5] At the same time new subjects in the curriculum and attempts to improve instruction mirrored changing concepts of education in its relation to society. Nonetheless, reading, writing, spelling, and arithmetic remained the core in the primary grades, while music, drawing, and the teaching of proper personal habits, such as cleanliness and the right conduct toward public and private property and civil authority, were also emphasized as part of the school program.

A considerable improvement over the purely *memoriter* form of learning was especially noticeable during the 1880's, reading, in particular, by the fourth grade being pointed beyond the mere ability to read to " a nicer discrimination in the use of words." In the gram-

[5] The relation of the government to the schools is treated in Chapter IX, " The Expanding Role of Government."

mar grades the aims of instruction were focused on " the application of the knowledge, the facts acquired, to the business of life "; the abandonment of old-time procedures was recommended — the old formal parsing in rhetoric, for example, being held thoroughly undesirable.[6] Within the high school those subjects designed to open the door to a college education gained popularity by the early 'nineties. For graduation from the general course the Board of Education on August 17, 1892 moved to require a foreign language, algebra, plane geometry, two sciences, a minimum of two years of English, drawing, and music.

The gratifying aspects of the enlargement of educational opportunity were at times marred by unwarranted criticism of the schools and by strife fomented by special interests endeavoring to advance their own ends. With a large foreign population holding political power, Chicago inevitably became the center of groups demanding the teaching of their native tongue. In 1865, through the influence of Lorenz Brentano, then a member of the Board of Education, instruction in German was introduced, and before long it became the target of those who maintained that in such instruction by special teachers the Germanizing of the Chicago schools was under way. With the appointment of Dr. Gustav A. Zimmermann as Special Teacher of German in 1878 the subject was put in the hands of teachers who could handle other courses as well; in 1885 its study could be started as an elective in the third and fourth grades under the assumption that any foreign language could be learned most easily by the young. By the year 1889–90, of the 135,541 students in the public schools, 32,982 were taking the language, over 48 per cent of German parentage.

Other ethnic groups looked with jealous and resentful eye upon the favored position of the Germans. Bohemians, Italians, and even Scandinavians (who loudly protested their unwillingness in any way to neglect the English language in their new homeland) campaigned along with others against the continuation of German as a school subject. Massed antagonism developed to such a degree that in 1887 a proposal to prohibit the teaching of all foreign languages was presented in the state legislature but was not enacted into law,

---

[6] The quotations are from the Chicago Board of Education, *Thirty-fifth Annual Report, 1889*, pp. 43–44.

and German continued on a voluntary basis from the third grade through high school.[7]

The quarrel over the inclusion of German in the public school curriculum, although it attracted the greatest attention, was only one of the subjects which aroused opposition. Those who held that " the three R's " were neglected by the introduction of less practical studies, such as music and drawing at the elementary level, warred also upon the teaching of Greek in the high school. Despite the warning of Superintendent Howland that colleges of good standing required it for entrance, the Board dropped it in 1884. The next year James R. Doolittle, Jr., president of the Board of Education, dared to affirm that as much mental discipline could be had from studies devoted to " the breadth of modern thought, the grasp of modern science, the achievements of modern industry and invention " as from the dead languages and studies of previous eras.

The idea that the emphasis should be placed upon elementary instruction in the essentials for everyday living, even to the point of less support for the high school, reached its peak in 1893. Meetings denouncing and defending the issues at stake multiplied. No less important a citizen than the attorney Alfred S. Trude, a member of the Board and shortly to be its president, assailed with customary vigor the expenditure of money for the so-called fads. Choosing clay modeling as a specific example, he epitomized the sentiment of the " non-faddists " in his inquiry, " What good will a knowledge of mud pies or mud ramparts do a boy if he cannot tell how much nine pounds of liver at 4 cents a pound will cost after he gets through with it all? " The Trude position had the almost unanimous endorsement of the city's leading newspapers except the *Inter Ocean,* which championed a varied curriculum. An alliance of the German forces with labor groups proved effective enough to prevent the elimination of German in the grammar grades and high school, and music and drawing were continued in a modified form.[8]

[7] *Chicago Tribune,* June 19, 1873, June 17, 1883, May 6, 1887, Jan. 24, Sept. 2, 1888, May 16, 1889; *The Chicago Times,* Nov. 11, 1881; *Abendpost,* Oct. 15, 23, 1890, March 9, 1893; *Illinois Staats-Zeitung,* May 5, 1876, Jan. 17, June 13, 1879; *Chicagoer Arbeiter-Zeitung,* Oct. 3, 1879; *The Knights of Labor,* VI (Nov. 2, 1889), 8; *Skandinaven,* March 5, 1893. The percentage of students of German parentage was computed from statistics in Chicago Board of Education, *Thirty-sixth Annual Report, 1890,* p. 99.

[8] *The Chicago Times,* Oct. 19, 29, Nov. 11, 1874, April 8, 1878, March 12, 1893; *Chicago Tribune,* Aug. 1, 3, 29, 1884, Sept. 2, 1888, May 16, 1889, Jan. 21, 22, Feb. 21, 24,

The plea for "useful" rather than so-called "ornamental" subjects took definite shape also in agitation for industrial training in the public schools. Education to equip workers to earn a living had been promoted for some time by individual humanitarians and by organizations such as the Ladies Christian Union. Its purposes, therefore, were a matter of common knowledge when, in his report of 1877–78, the president of the Board of Education urged the development of an industrial spirit and a taste for mechanical pursuits through the use of simple tools by boy pupils and instruction in cooking, sewing, and other branches of domestic economy for girls. By 1881 it was pointed out that the great majority of children stopped school before reaching the fifth grade in order to learn a trade. Some form of industrial education along with the intellectual, it was argued, would thus prolong the time given to education and would tend to dignify labor.

Encouraged by the opening in 1884 of the Chicago Manual Training School under the auspices of the Commercial Club, in which outstanding businessmen like Marshall Field, Edson Keith, and Richard T. Crane had played a substantial role, officials of the schools continued their campaign to persuade taxpayers of the advantages of such training at public expense. In the year 1885–86 an experimental beginning in manual training was made in the first year of high schools. The next year a school dedicated to this type of education was opened in the afternoon for pupils attending regular high-school classes in the morning, and in 1887–88 the course was extended to two years.

By 1890, so successful was the undertaking that authorities ventured to set up a separate high school primarily devoted to the mechanical arts where boys could attend three instead of four years and need not take foreign language. This school also had a commercial course including bookkeeping, shorthand, and typing; but the only special preparation for business that the regular high schools provided was a single-term elective in bookkeeping. Not until January,

1893; The Living Church, XI (Feb. 2, 1889), 696; Chicago Evening Journal, Jan. 12, 1893; Chicago Evening Post, March 14, 1893; Chicago Herald, March 12, Aug. 3, 1893; Chicago Board of Education, Thirtieth Annual Report, 1884, pp. 56, 60–61, Thirty-first Annual Report, 1885, pp. 35–36, Thirty-ninth Annual Report, 1893, p. 21; The Inter Ocean, March 20, 1893; Chas. H. Ham to Henry D. Lloyd, March 15, 1893, Lloyd Papers; Abendpost, Feb. 22, 1893; Illinois Staats-Zeitung, Feb. 21, 26, 1879.

1892 did sewing find a regular place in the curriculum and then only for girls in the second through fifth grades. Cooking was not taught despite increased demands that it be given.[9]

It was during the 'eighties also that the obligation of the school to build healthy bodies was recognized. In 1886 physical culture appeared after a six months' trial in all grammar grades, to be introduced three years later in both primary grades and high school. Upon occasion classed as " a fad," this aspect of educational progress had the active support of the Germans as they joined others in declaring education the guardian of democracy, clean living, and moral uprightness. They were, however, generally opposed to the offering of prayer and the reading of the Scriptures as the opening exercises for the school day, and along with other foreign groups fought for the abolition of this practice. In 1875 the Board of Education acceded to, these demands, but for years powerful dissenters to this action kept up their agitation for the restoration of what was considered an effective weapon against the temptations of life and a fortification against the inroads of communism.[10]

As fears increased, particularly in the 1880's, that the solid pillars of society might crumble under the onslaught of radicalism, efforts to promote an understanding of American institutions and to stimulate patriotism increased. To these efforts aroused citizens lent active support. In 1888, for example, the *Daily News* through its owner and publisher Victor F. Lawson offered the Board of Education the annual income from $10,000 to invest in medals for essays on patriotism written by pupils in the grammar grades and high school. To the end of training in citizenship and an understanding of the meaning of government, less *memoriter* work in history and civics received the endorsement of directors of school instruction; and along with this, it was felt, greater attention should be paid to current events in order to cultivate a better understanding of the present.

[9] *Chicago Tribune*, Oct. 9, 1872, March 26, 27, 1882; *Chicago Daily News*, Feb. 2, 1884; *The Inland Architect and Builder*, III (Feb., 1884), 6; W. C. Larned, *Report of the Committee of the Citizens' Association of Chicago on Education* (Chicago, 1881), pp. 23–24. See Board of Education reports particularly for 1878 and following years. For humanitarian projects in industrial education see Chapter XII, " Religious and Humanitarian Strivings."

[10] *Illinois Staats-Zeitung*, Sept. 30, 1875, Jan. 31, 1876; *Chicagoer Arbeiter-Zeitung*, April 29, 1889; *Abendpost*, July 14, 1890, Jan. 3, 1893; *The Advance*, VIII (Oct. 7, 1875), 975, IX (Nov. 4, 1875), 168–69, XXII (Sept. 13, 1888), 577; *The Western Catholic*, June 26, 1875; *The Standard*, XXXVII (Jan. 23, 1890), 4; Larned, *loc. cit.*, pp. 14–15.

The alliance of the school with politics, as illustrated in appointments to the Board of Education by politically rather than educationally conscious mayors, met outspoken opposition on the part of forces wanting schools free to provide the best instruction available for the youth of the city.[11]

Despite just and unjust criticism of the public school, educational advance was evidenced not only in an expanding curriculum and more agitation for well-prepared teachers, but in more humane methods of dealing with disciplinary problems. After more than a decade of gradual abolition of corporal punishment, the Board of Education ordered its complete discontinuance in 1880. A growing public conscience, furthermore, forced the state in 1883 to enact a law compelling school attendance of children between eight and fourteen for twelve weeks a year. This was followed by another statute in 1889 requiring attendance of those between seven and fourteen for sixteen weeks a year, eight of which had to be consecutive. But an apathetic public, the hostility of some parents, poverty, and inadequate school facilities militated against strict enforcement. With the passage of the Child Labor Law in 1891, theoretically one of the most pressing arguments against compulsory school attendance was eliminated.[12]

Besides publicly supported schools, numerous privately run institutions were scattered throughout the city, reflecting as in the past the religious and ethnic variations characteristic of Chicago peoples. Of these the Roman Catholic had the greatest number of students, by 1893 their total reaching approximately 38,000. Forced to pay taxes for the support of public schools, the backers of parochial institutions continued to press unsuccessfully for a *pro rata* division of such funds, adding to an atmosphere of strife already heavily charged. Private non-sectarian schools such as the Dearborn Seminary for girls and the Harvard School for Boys attracted, as in the

[11] Victor F. Lawson to the Board of Education, Chicago, June 2, 1888, *Lawson Papers;* Dennis, *Victor Lawson,* p. 158; *Chicago Tribune,* Oct. 23, 1881; Swing, *Old Pictures of Life,* II, 64–65. For current events as presented in 1885 see Chicago Board of Education, *Thirty-first Annual Report, 1885,* p. 58. For the need to train for citizenship see, for example, *Thirty-fourth Annual Report, 1888,* pp. 22–23, *Thirty-sixth Annual Report, 1890,* p. 51.

[12] Chicago Board of Education, *Proceedings, September, 1878, to September, 1880,* p. 148; Illinois, *Laws, 1883,* pp. 131–32, *1889,* p. 202. See Chapter VIII, "Labor's Quest for Security," and Chapter X, "The Profile of Politics."

past, a select group of students, as did the Chicago Latin School from 1888.[13]

The capstone of the educational structure was the college or university, through whose doors few passed unless blessed with financial backing. The old University of Chicago, sponsored by the Baptists, badly crippled after the Fire and by administrative dissension, closed in June, 1886.[14] The idea of a university under the auspices of that church, however, was not abandoned. Although other cities indicated that they would be hospitable to such an institution, Chicago was chosen, in large part because of the leadership of Thomas W. Goodspeed. To his and other supporters' agitation the American Baptist Education Society added its endorsement. A gift of $600,000 from John D. Rockefeller, conditioned upon the Society's obtaining pledges of $400,000 more by June 1, 1890, served as an auspicious starting-point. By May 23 this amount was subscribed, and a ten-acre plot valued at $125,000 was provided by Marshall Field for the necessary site.

With the filing of articles of incorporation on September 10, 1890, and the organization of a board of trustees, the new university embarked two years later (October, 1892) upon what was to be a unique undertaking in education, its influence extending far beyond its immediate environment in the heart of the great Middle West.[15] Headed by William Rainey Harper, a former professor of Hebrew at Morgan Park Theological Seminary and later Professor of the

[13] Chicago Board of Education, *Proceedings, July 6, 1892, to July 5, 1893*, pp. 88–100; *The Chicago Times*, Nov. 19, 1876; *Chicago Tribune*, Feb. 7, 10, 1875; *The Western Catholic*, July 10, 1875; Chicago Latin School, *Sigillum, 1938, Fifty Years of Chicago Latin* (Chicago, [1938]), [pp. 6, 14–15]; Harvard School for Boys, *Harvard Review, 1865–1940* (Chicago, [1940]), pp. 14–15; Porter E. Sargent, *A Handbook of the Best Private Schools of the United States and Canada* (Boston, 1915), pp. 72, 152–53. The figure on enrollment in Catholic schools was computed from statistics in *Sadliers' Catholic Directory, 1893* (New York, 1893), pp. 89–94.

[14] Chamberlin, *Chicago and Its Suburbs*, pp. 148–49; Currey, *Chicago: Its History and Its Builders*, II, 13–17; *The Chicago Times*, Jan. 3, 9, 17, 24, July 2, 1874; *The Times* [London], Jan. 9, 1872; *Chicago Tribune*, Oct. 13, 1872, Sept. 7, 1873, Jan. 6, 20, 23, 25, July 3, 1874; Thomas W. Goodspeed, *A History of the University of Chicago* (Chicago, 1916), pp. 16–19.

[15] Thomas W. Goodspeed to John D. Rockefeller, Jan. 7, 1887; William R. Harper to Rockefeller, Jan. 11, 1887; Frederick T. Gates to Henry L. Morehouse, Sept. 14, Oct. 16, 1888; Rockefeller to Gates, May 15, 1889; Gates to Harper, Jan. 15, 1890 (*Mss.* The University of Chicago Archives); The University of Chicago, *Annual Register, July 1, 1892–July 1, 1893*, pp. 3–4; Francis W. Shepardson, "An Historical Sketch," in The University of Chicago, *President's Report, July, 1897–July, 1898*, pp. 1–3. The American Baptist Education Society was organized in May, 1888.

Semitic Languages at Yale, the university benefited by the large donations of Rockefeller, as well as sums from Marshall Field, Martin Ryerson, Sidney A. Kent, Silas B. Cobb, and other public-spirited Chicagoans. Its first faculty, notable for its distinction, focused much of its attention upon graduate instruction, although Harper was also vitally concerned with undergraduate study and other avenues of educational advancement.[16]

To the north of the city Northwestern University more and more extended its influence as it enlarged the number and scope of its offerings, particularly after the 1870's. Under the presidency of Joseph Cummings not only were the liberal arts strengthened but scientific study was accorded more attention than heretofore; professional training in dentistry was inaugurated, and plans for a pharmaceutical education were carefully worked out. In 1886 the school of law, which had been affiliated with the old University of Chicago and since 1873 jointly managed by that university and Northwestern, came under the sole jurisdiction of the Evanston institution. Upon Dr. Cummings's death in 1890, Henry Wade Rogers, the first layman to be so selected, was chosen to pilot the Methodist institution. Working against the opposition of those who wished to preserve the *status quo* of a loosely knit organization of the arts college with the professional schools, Rogers moved not only to a reorganization which brought the associated schools under one head but to a raising of the scholastic standards of the institution.[17]

Also along the lake shore at the north of the city was the Presbyterian-inspired Lake Forest University, chartered by the state legislature in 1857, with an academy for boys and Ferry Hall, a seminary for girls. In 1876 the first college class was held and during the late 'eighties three professional schools became associated with it —

[16] Goodspeed to Harper, Sept. 10, 1890; Harper to Rockefeller, April 5, 1892; Goodspeed to Gates, April 7, Oct. 7, 1892; Gates to Harper, Sept. 3, Dec. 12, 1892; Goodspeed to his sons, June 28, 1891 (*Mss.* The University of Chicago Archives); Shepardson, *loc. cit.,* pp. 3–11, 20, 27; Nott Flint, *The University of Chicago* (Chicago, 1904), pp. 20, 22; Shailer Matthews, " Democracy in Education," *The World To-Day,* VIII (April, 1905), 432–33; *Chicago Daily News,* Nov. 25, 1891; *Chicago Chronicle,* Jan. 1, 1906. A history of the University of Chicago by Richard J. Storr, in progress, will provide detailed information on the founding of the University.

[17] Estelle Frances Ward, *The Story of Northwestern University* (New York, 1924), pp. 167–68, 174–75, 196–99, 309–10, 316–17, 319–20; Moses and Kirkland, *History of Chicago,* II, 113; *Chicago Tribune,* June 20, 1883, Feb. 5, 1887. For the years before 1871 see Pierce, *A History of Chicago,* II, 396–97.

Rush Medical College, the Chicago College of Law, and the Chicago College of Dental Surgery. The Catholics, too, continued educational activities by supporting St. Ignatius College. Here students were taught chiefly the liberal arts, specialization in the professions not yet being provided.[18]

In addition to that available at an institution such as Northwestern, various schools devoted primarily to medicine, law, pharmacy, and dentistry offered professional training. Probably the best known of the four regular, well-established medical schools was Rush Medical College, which had enjoyed a distinguished reputation since 1842. The founding of the College of Physicians and Surgeons in 1881 supplemented the work already being done by Rush, the Chicago Medical College and Medical Department of the Northwestern University, and the Woman's Hospital Medical College. During these post-Fire years the Hahnemann Medical College, dating from 1860, and the Chicago Homeopathic Medical College, formed in 1876, continued to expound the tenets of homeopathic medicine, while the Bennett Medical College gave instruction in the practice of eclectic medicine as it had since 1868.

Those who aspired to the calling of dentistry also found a number of institutions ready to prepare them. In 1881 the Chicago College of Dental Surgery opened its doors, and in 1887 Northwestern University sponsored the establishment of what was to become, in 1891, the Northwestern University Dental School. Active during these years, though somewhat smaller, were the Northwestern College of Dental Surgery, Northwestern Dental College of Chicago, and the American College of Dental Surgery. Pharmacists, too, had their formal training schools, headed by the Chicago College of Pharmacy, founded in 1859 and by 1893 a thriving institution. Similar institutions were the National Institute of Pharmacy, organized in 1885, and the Illinois College of Pharmacy opening in 1886, the latter to become in 1891 the Northwestern University School of Pharmacy.[19]

[18] Moses and Kirkland, *op. cit.*, II, 114–15; Chamberlin, *op. cit.*, pp. 396–97; D. S. Gregory to Elihu Washburne, July 5, 1879, *Washburne Papers;* Caroline Kirkland, *Chicago Yesterdays*, pp. 238–39, 243–44; *Chicago Tribune*, May 31, 1887, May 26, 1889; Flinn, *Chicago . . . A Guide, 1893*, pp. 274, 287. St. Ignatius College was known as Loyola University after 1909.

[19] Moses and Kirkland, *op. cit.*, II, 501–4; Ward, *op. cit.*, pp. 316–21; Andreas, *History of Chicago*, III, 547.

As elsewhere in the United States, the standards prescribed in professional schools for entrance and graduation fell far short of those of a later day.[20] Even the College of Physicians and Surgeons at first required for admission proof only of a fair English or common school education, and for graduation three years of study and attendance on two annual college terms without grading, a graded course being provided only to students electing it. Since the annual term was at first only five months in length, the total time in residence necessary for graduation was a mere ten months. Hospital clinical instruction and work in laboratories were, however, obligatory within this period of the regular college course. In 1889 a full three years' graded course and the extension of the year's college term to six months indicated a growing realization of the need for better-trained physicians. By 1890 Rush had adopted similar requirements, and an eminent physician, Dr. Nathan S. Davis, proudly recorded that all four regular medical schools could be considered " as up to the front line of advancement in both facilities and requirements for medical education."

A Woman's Hospital Medical College, which had opened in 1870, under Dr. Mary H. Thompson and supported by Dr. William H. Byford, turned to the preparation of women, three of whom graduated in 1871 and twenty-four in 1889. By 1891 this Woman's Medical College became an adjunct of Northwestern University and was renamed the Northwestern University Woman's Medical School.[21]

Requirements for other professions were in general less rigid, except in the case of the ministry.[22] For the socially respected position of lawyer even Northwestern required only a common school education, though by 1875–76 almost one-third of the entering students

[20] The *Chicago Tribune,* June 4, 1873, carried a letter to the editor complaining of " mushroom medicos." " Today," said the writer, " they are dry-goods clerks, copyists, and what not. Tomorrow they hang out a shingle and call themselves ' Doctor.' "

[21] *The Chicago Times,* Oct. 8, 1876, Sept. 29, 1880; *Chicago Tribune,* Oct. 5, 1876, Sept. 28, 1891; N. S. Davis and others, " History of the Medical Profession and Medical Institutions of Chicago," *Magazine of Western History,* XI (Jan., 1890), 311–19, (Feb., 1890), 419–24, (April, 1890), 648–50, XII (May, 1890), 35–38, (Sept., 1890), 544–50; Moses and Kirkland, *op. cit.,* II, 25; Chamberlin, *op. cit.,* p. 149; Mary Putnam Jacobi, " Woman in Medicine," in Annie N. Meyer, ed., *Woman's Work in America* (New York, 1891), pp. 174–75; Gilbert and Bryson, *Chicago and Its Makers,* p. 878.

[22] See Chapter XII, " Religious and Humanitarian Strivings," for a discussion of the most important schools of theology.

possessed academic degrees. Although some leading members of the Bar such as Melville W. Fuller and Lambert Tree had the advantage of preparation in an eastern law college, many others, including Julius S. Grinnell, Wirt Dexter, Emery Storrs, James B. Bradwell, and John N. Jewett, received their legal education in some practitioner's office. Between 1874 and 1889 Illinois enacted statutes imposing upon candidates in the fields of law, medicine, dentistry, and pharmacy, examinations or degree requirements for the practice of the profession.[23]

With much of the city's attention focused upon economic endeavors, it was only natural that those sensitive to the desirability of vocational education should advocate manual training. Leading early in the movement for such a school were Augustus Jacobson, lawyer and judge of the Superior Court of Cook County; Charles H. Ham, journalist and appraiser of customs for the port of Chicago; and the Reverend Edward I. Galvin, Unitarian divine and Superintendent of the Atheneum. Backed by the *Tribune* and liberally supported by the Commercial Club, the Chicago Manual Training School opened February 4, 1884. Its start was auspicious, for it had as director Henry H. Belfield, at that time principal of the North Division High School; upon its board of trustees sat men of wealth and influence — Eliphalet W. Blatchford, Richard T. Crane, Marshall Field, Nathaniel K. Fairbank, George M. Pullman, John W. Doane, Edson Keith, John Crerar, and Melville W. Fuller. Shopwork, including woodworking, iron foundry and forge work, consumed one-third of a student's time, while an hour daily was allotted to mechanical drawing. Among the purely academic were scheduled the subjects of algebra, geometry, trigonometry, physics, chemistry, and physiology. At the outset, tuition for the three-year course ranged from $60 for the first year and $80 for the second to $100 for the final term.

Through private benefactions also, technical training was provided at an upper level by Philip D. Armour, who, like many other men of wealth, shared his good fortune with those of less estate. In

[23] Statutory requirements for the various professions were established by the state legislature as follows: Act of March 28, 1874, Illinois, *Laws, 1874,* pp. 169–71 (law); Act of May 29, 1877, *Laws, 1877,* pp. 662–64 (medicine); Act of May 30, 1881, *Laws, 1881,* pp. 727–31 (pharmacy and dentistry); Act of June 16, 1887, *Laws, 1887,* pp. 971–75b (medicine); Act of June 4, 1889, *Laws, 1891,* pp. 944–47 (pharmacy).

1893 Armour Institute, at Thirty-third Street and Armour Avenue, opened its doors to 1,050 students. Within three years enrollment climbed to 1,200, about one-third of whom were women in the scientific department. The Mechanics' Institute continued to carry on its educational program for workers through evening courses in such subjects as mechanical and architectural drawing, arithmetic, and bookkeeping. Besides these there were schools like the Bryant & Stratton Business College and the Catholic De La Salle Institute which equipped those primarily looking toward a career in business.[24]

While technical and business schools in a very real sense mirrored what was considered the most striking characteristic of Chicago, schools for the arts could also be found. The city directory of 1893 listed no less than seventeen in music, which, in addition to private teachers, undertook to train an increasing number of aspirants, just as the school connected with the Art Institute attempted to develop the talent of young artists. Particularly important was the Chicago Musical College, the outgrowth of a school founded by Florenz Ziegfeld in 1867. In 1886 the American Conservatory of Music began its long and distinguished career; by the early 'nineties it was able to boast not only of the competence of its instruction under the guidance of its founder, John J. Hattstaedt, but to point with pride to its large enrollment.[25]

Tangential to the professional training provided by schools were the numerous associations which arose to promote not only good fellowship but to elevate standards of the profession. Such was the Chicago Bar Association, which elected its first officers March 21, 1874 and adopted a constitution which committed it to " the maintenance of the honor and dignity of the profession." In its membership ap-

[24] Andreas, History of Chicago, III, 152–53; Chicago Tribune, March 22, 1882, June 2, 1883, Nov. 22, 1885, May 20, 1889; [Joseph J. Thompson], The Archdiocese of Chicago: Antecedents and Development [Des Plaines, Illinois, 1920], pp. 685, 687; The Inter Ocean, Centennial History of the City of Chicago (Chicago, 1905), p. 59; The Inland Architect and Builder, III (Feb., 1884), 6; Chicago Board of Trade, Thirty-ninth Annual Report, 1896, p. xlvii; The Workingman's Advocate, Nov. 29, 1873, Sept. 18, 1875; The Chicago Times, Sept. 5, 1880. See also Chapter XII, " Religious and Humanitarian Strivings," for other examples of industrial education.

[25] Kenneth Joseph Rehage, Music in Chicago, 1871–1893 (unpublished M.A. Thesis, The University of Chicago, 1935), p. 25–27; Egbert Swayne, " Musical Centers of Chicago," Music, VII (Dec., 1894), 170. For the school in connection with the Art Institute, see Chapter XIII, " Patterns of Urban Living."

peared the names of many outstanding attorneys of the day: William P. Black, Sidney Smith, William H. King, Ezra B. McCagg, Stephen A. Goodwin, and Ira Scott.[26]

Equally important were the various medical societies dedicated to investigating and disseminating scientific knowledge. Leading in exploring new-found aids to health was the Chicago Medical Society, one of the oldest and reportedly one of the largest local medical organizations in the country. In its bimonthly meetings it considered not only past and current research and practice but it actively agitated for better sanitation in the city, for efficient operation of the departments of health, sewerage, and water supply, as well as the keeping of records of vital statistics. The Chicago Society of Physicians and Surgeons numbered in its membership leaders of the profession such as Dr. John Bartlett, Dr. James H. Etheridge, and Dr. James N. Hyde, and was an outstanding forum for the exchange of knowledge about medical discoveries and practice. Committed to elevating professional ethics, it joined in 1874 with the Chicago College of Pharmacy and the Chicago Medical Society in condemning collusion between doctors and druggists in which the latter paid the former for prescriptions sent them.

Besides societies devoted to all aspects of the profession, organizations like the Chicago Gynecological Society, the Chicago Pathological Society, and the Chicago Materia Medical Society (to which women were admitted) attested an awareness on the part of Chicago physicians of research in specific fields not only in this country but in the world at large. Even the layman was kept informed of various advances in science by wide publicity in the daily press. Especially newsworthy were an experiment in blood transfusion with a dog successfully performed in 1874, and the introduction by the Alexian Brothers' Hospital of carbolic acid to sterilize instruments in 1878. Research in microscopy was stimulated by the meetings of the State Microscopical Society of Illinois, which had originated in the Chicago Microscopical Club, formed in 1868. The numerous additions of foreign-born practitioners to the roster of physicians for brief periods, and sometimes for permanent residence, enriched immeasurably the medical history of Chicago, and illustrated in no small

[26] The first officers were William C. Goudy, president; Thomas Hoyne and Lyman Trumbull, vice-presidents; Abram M. Pence, secretary.

way the hospitality accorded by the city to outstanding gains made in science throughout the world.[27]

All these manifestations of interest in the domain of science placed Chicago in line with other leading centers of the country. Contributing no less to the betterment of mankind were the published studies of men like Dr. Henry Gradle, a student of the German scholar Robert Koch, whose *Bacteria and the Germ Theory of Disease* (Chicago, 1883), the first book in the English language on this important subject, placed him in the forefront of his contemporaries. *The History of Medical Education and Institutions in the United States, from the First Settlement of the British Colonies to the Year 1850* (Chicago, 1851) by Dr. Nathan S. Davis remained a matter of pride to his fellow citizens, just as did his numerous articles on medical themes. By 1892 some nineteen medical and dental journals, published in Chicago, kept their readers abreast of current undertakings and advances in their respective fields.[28]

Although nowhere had dentistry attained the status of medical science at its best, there was in Chicago as early as 1864 enough professional spirit to form the Chicago Dental Society. In 1884 another organization, the Odontological Society, was inaugurated, limiting its membership to fifteen, each applicant judged on the basis of a paper on some comparatively unfamiliar topic. The Chicago Dental Club, initiated in 1886, pointed its activities chiefly toward improved professional interests and the discussion of abstruse scientific questions connected with its speciality. The Hayden Society, named in honor of the parent of modern dentistry, Dr. Horace H. Hayden of Baltimore, came into being in 1889, subscribing to the policies and principles adopted by the Odontological Society.[29]

[27] For example, Chicago physicians benefited from translations of German articles made by Dr. Alexander S. von Mansfelde. Dr. Alfred G. Schloesser, onetime assistant physician in the Imperial Hospital of Vienna and later of the Royal Central Institute of Stockholm, was connected with the Swedish Movements Institute. He specialized in spinal deformities. Dr. Antonio Lagorio, of Italian extraction, was the founder of the Pasteur Institute of Rush Medical College in 1890.

[28] The most widely circulated were: the *Western Medical Reporter* (1880–1895), *Medical Era* (1883–1903), *Medical Standard* (1887–1931), *North American Practitioner* (1889–1895), the *Journal of the American Medical Association* (1883–   ), and *Dental Review* (1886–1918).

[29] *The Chicago Times*, March 22, 27, Oct. 27, Nov. 30, 1874; Moses and Kirkland, *op. cit.*, II, 264, 265, 505–6; Schiavo, *The Italians in Chicago*, p. 181; *Chicago Tribune*, Oct. 18, 24, 1873, Feb. 17, Oct. 27, 1874, July 26, 1878, Jan. 20, 1892; *The American Bookseller*, VII (Feb. 15, 1879), 136; Andreas, *History of Chicago*, III, 431.

By no means did the formation of societies by those engaged in the practice of law, medicine, and dentistry circumscribe the spirit of learning, which also penetrated deeply into other fields. With the development of meteorology Chicago began forecasting the city's weather in 1871. During the 1870's, despite the physical task of rebuilding their own city, devotees of archeology became engrossed in discussions concerning the mound builders, especially fascinated when dealing with revelations about near-by Rockford, Davenport in Iowa, and counties in Missouri. As a section of the Chicago Academy of Sciences, the study of archeology was given the benefit of the broadening spirit characteristic of that institution even in its early days of the late 'fifties and early 'sixties. It was much the same with the Chicago Astronomical Society. Although the Fire did not destroy Dearborn Observatory, it left the Society without funds, unable to carry on its research until revived in the spring of 1874. Then, with interest reawakened by a series of four lectures on astronomy by Professor Richard A. Proctor in March and led by J. Young Scammon and others prominent in learned activities, the work of the Society was resumed.[30]

No record of the intellectual aspirations of Chicago would be complete without noting the Philosophical Society of Chicago, organized during September and October, 1873 to bring together men and women for intellectual improvement and to consider problems of human welfare. Committees on social science, natural science, moral science, current history, and speculative philosophy selected the topics for discussion and decided upon the lectures, originally given weekly from October to May. From " The Relation of Socrates to Modern Thought," " The Thinking Faculties," " The Microscope in the Arts," and " The Dispersion of the Roman Empire," to " The Therapeutic Value of Superstition " and " Hypnotism and Thought Transference," the subjects offered a varied intellectual fare, with discussions restricted only by the Society's motto, " What is true ? " [31]

[30] *Chicago Tribune*, April 10, 1873, Jan. 14, March 10, 1874, Feb. 28, 1877, Jan. 10, 1883; *The Chicago Times*, April 17, 1874; Andreas, *History of Chicago*, III, 428; Pierce, *A History of Chicago*, II, 399; " To the Friends and Correspondents of the Chicago Academy of Sciences," *Broadside, Illinois* (Library of Congress); Chicago Astronomical Society, *Collection* (Chicago Historical Society). Numerous other societies carried on specialized studies of merit.

[31] *The Chicago Times*, April 17, 1874, Oct. 1, 1876, Oct. 8, 1880; *Chicago Tribune*, Sept. 3, 1873, Jan. 4, 10, May 31, Oct. 4, 1874, Oct. 1, 15, 1876; Philosophical Society of

Within the Polytechnic Society after 1888, also, restless minds delving into speculative philosophy and social science joined others bent on practical knowledge in art and science. Since 1876, however, those primarily concerned with the social sciences had enjoyed contacts with those of like interest in the Chicago chapter of the American Social Science Association. Besides those societies which had a relatively long existence there arose sporadic, ephemeral associations called into being by issues of the moment that, to the founders, appeared pressing for immediate discussion. Such, for instance, were the various groups organized to explore the theory of evolution, a subject which probably created more widespread argument than others of the time. It was this kind of club which was organized in the winter of 1889–90 by Professor Edson S. Bastin, Herod D. Garrison, Sherburne W. Burnham, Frank A. Johnson, and others, having on its membership roll chiefly men in the professions.[32]

This banding together was mainly among the select few, but the zeal for learning was not confined to them. Among the many not initially endowed with specialized knowledge was an astonishingly large number hungering to know more. For them the public lecture dealing with all manner of subjects satisfied, in some degree, this want. Subjects ranging from the popular travel description to erudite and at times complex scientific discourses offered a wide range of choice. Sometimes, as in the case of Oscar Wilde's lecture in February, 1882, the audience in large part appeared more interested in the speaker than in what he had to say, if press reports can be relied upon.

Particularly did speakers on religious topics find Chicago audiences large and attentive, and the subject of Mormonism invariably meant a good turnout. On January 24, 1882, for instance, no less than twenty-five hundred people heard the locally prominent Thomas Hoyne denounce " the institution of polygamy as the bastard offspring of a vulgar religious impostor," his remarks seconded by no less outstanding political figures than William Bross, Schuyler Col-

Chicago, " Membership Card for . . . 1885–86 " (Chicago Historical Society); G. S. Hubbard Collection in Autograph Letters (Mss. Chicago Historical Society); Philosophical Society of Chicago, " Prospectus for 1877–78," Caton Papers.

[32] The Chicago Times, July 2, 1888; Chicago Post and Mail, Jan. 26, 1876; D. H. Galloway to Dr. Holmes [probably Bayard Holmes], (Ms. Chicago Vertical File 1890, Chicago Historical Society); Journal of Social Science, VIII (1876), 181, 183–87, 189, 190.

fax, and John Wentworth. In turn, those who wished had the opportunity the next month to hear Bishop Joseph Smith, son of the famous founder of the church, defend Mormonism and attempt to distinguish between Mormonism as a religion and polygamy as associated with it. Robert Ingersoll's discourses on Jefferson, Voltaire, Thomas Paine, Franklin, and Emperor Julian, in addition to his attacks on orthodox religion, and Henry Ward Beecher's "Moral Use of Riches," "Moral Uses of Luxury and Beauty," and "Hard Times," and his discussions of the theory of evolution drew large turnouts.

In 1889 the John L. Stoddard series was in its eleventh successful season in Chicago, and lecture-goers had by that time already enjoyed hearing D. R. Locke (Petroleum V. Nasby), Mark Twain, George W. Cable, and Bret Harte, who, along with other writers of the time, was "lionized" in Chicago just as were literary figures elsewhere. Indeed, the list of lecturers who appeared on Chicago platforms was representative of those best known at the time: David Starr Jordan, John Fiske, Henry M. Stanley, Matthew Arnold, Charles Dickens, and George Augustus Sala, to mention only a few. This profusion was increased still more by organizations attempting to raise the level of culture through publicly and privately sponsored lectures. For example, the Dime Lecture Society promoted talks on the early history of the city as well as other subjects, an opportunity seized chiefly by workingmen.[33]

The Atheneum, modeled on Cooper Institute in New York, provided a varied list besides carrying on its formal educational classes. The Chicago Institute's program of literary subjects, for which it charged only a nominal sum, and so-called "literary schools" proffered lectures upon some literary subject or writer for a week or more. In addition to numerous civic and philanthropic clubs which also considered aspects of cultural uplift, those like the Chicago Literary Club, organized by men in 1874, and the Saracen, composed in 1876 of both men and women, attempted to encourage a cultivated

[33] *Chicago Tribune,* Feb. 26, 1873, Dec. 11, 1874, Feb. 8, 1877, Feb. 5, 1878, Feb. 7, 14, March 5, 1882, Feb. 4, 1883, Jan. 20, 23, 1884, Jan. 17, 1885, Dec. 8, 1887, Oct. 13, 1889, Dec. 28, 1890; *The Chicago Times,* Nov. 11, 1873, Feb. 24, March 10, 1874, May 21, 1881, Jan. 24, Feb. 23, 1882; D. H. Galloway to Dr. Holmes (*Ms.* Vertical File, Chicago Historical Society); *The Workingman's Advocate,* April 3, 1875, April 5, 1876; Zebina Eastman, *Collection,* in *Autograph Letters,* XL (*Mss.* Chicago Historical Society).

knowledge befitting the most highly developed civilization of the time.

It was true, unfortunately, that those who came into contact with these definitely formulated programs were relatively few. " Pork, not Plato, has made Chicago," remarked Price Collier even in 1897, " and Chicago people have not arrived at a stage of civilization yet where they can with propriety or advantage change their allegiance." The struggle to master the economic necessities, implicit in building the city, still tended to direct men's thinking into the material, and left the ground largely barren for the development of a local body of authors. But those efforts which were being made to emancipate Chicago from the appellation of " porkopolis " as the most exact description of the city's spirit would, and before long did, bring their rich rewards.[34]

For this day many, even intellectual leaders, were willing to wait, men who looked upon what had already been accomplished as the promise of greater things to come. " Chicago will sooner or later be the literary center of America. How soon or how late I do not know — nobody knows — but the conditions are growing daily more favorable," declared the publisher Francis J. Schulte in 1892. To this optimism Alexander C. McClurg also subscribed, both men being in a position, it was agreed, to gauge accurately the potentialities of local literati. " I do not look to see an impromptu and hasty growth of literary geniuses springing up suddenly around us," McClurg said. " We have been too busy so far to devote much time to the development of what literary possibilities may lie within us. . . . So, as a community, it seems to me we need not worry about our immediate literary product. Let it come, as in due time it will come, without forcing, and as a wholly natural fruit, mellow, ripe, wholesome. . . ."

Nor were these forecasts without some foundation. Books by Chicago authors were already being published in increasing numbers,

[34] *The Workingman's Advocate,* April 3, 1875, April 5, 1876; *Chicago Tribune,* Nov. 15, 1876, April 10, 1883; William Morton Payne, " Literary Chicago," *The New England Magazine,* n.s. VII (Feb., 1893), 683–700; Julian Ralph, *Our Great West* (New York, 1893), pp. 61–63; [Price Collier], *America and the Americans* (8th ed. New York, 1897), p. 263. See also Chapter XIII, " Patterns of Urban Living," for further discussion of intellectual aspirations. The Atheneum evolved from the Chicago Christian Union, organized in 1871 to meet needs created by the Great Fire.

and more readers were providing a market for them. In the fictional realm appeared Charles M. Hertig, John McGovern, Mrs. Celia Parker Woolley, Mrs. Clara Louise Burnham, and Hobart C. Chatfield-Taylor, besides others whose efforts were received with little enthusiasm and soon were forgotten. In 1887 Joseph Kirkland's *Zury: The Meanest Man in Spring County* appeared, to be followed the next year by its sequel, *The McVeys,* vigorously realistic novels of western life, rural rather than urban in spirit. Opie Read, after reaching Chicago in 1887, also contributed to the literature of the great Middle Valley. The novels of Henry B. Fuller, such as *The Chevalier of Pensieri-Vani* (1890) and *The Chatelaine of La Trinité* (1892), clung to old romantic themes and did not partake of the realism of Kirkland's creations, although his outstanding novel, *The Cliff-Dwellers* (1893), was a vivid portrayal of such contemporary Chicago phenomena as the skyscraper and Charles T. Yerkes.

The failure to capture the spirit of the present, the small number of good novels which sketched the local scene, and, on the whole, remoteness from the problems near at hand of those who did write marked Chicago, in the eyes of critics, as still immature in both literary concept and form. In one way or another they could agree with Hamlin Garland (who came to Chicago in 1893) that "the mighty West, with its swarming millions, remains undelineated in the novel, the drama, and the poem." By the 'nineties, however, the competitive struggle of the city had led to the production of some utopian novels describing what the authors felt should be, rather than what really was. Robert H. Cowdrey's *A Tramp in Society* came out in 1891, Henry L. Everett's *The People's Program* appeared in 1892, and *The Beginning: A Romance of Chicago As It Might Be,* written anonymously, was published in 'ninety-three.[35]

As elsewhere, fewer good poets than fictionists appeared, and even those who found a place among their contemporaries failed in general to be known to posterity. This was not true of Harriet Monroe, called the poet laureate of Chicago for her ode celebrating the

[35] *Chicago Tribune,* Dec. 18, 1892; Payne, *loc. cit.,* pp. 696–97; Hugh Dalziel Duncan, *Chicago as a Literary Center* (unpublished Ph.D. Thesis, The University of Chicago, 1948), pp. 55, 74, 113; Lennox Bouton Grey, *Chicago and "The Great American Novel"* (unpublished Ph.D. Thesis, The University of Chicago, 1935), pp. 342–51, 446–51; Moses and Kirkland, *op. cit.,* II, 145, 147; Fred Lewis Pattee, *A History of American Literature since 1870* (New York, 1917), pp. 258–62; Hamlin Garland, *Crumbling Idols* (Chicago, 1894), p. 16.

opening of the Chicago Auditorium in 1889 and for her dedicatory poem for the Columbian Exposition. In 1891 she published *Valeria and Other Poems,* highly praised by the critics. Nor was it true of Eugene Field. To his other writings Field added numerous verses, at times sentimental in tone and contrasting strangely with his prose humor. Even at a later day his touching " Little Boy Blue " and his fanciful lullaby " Wynken, Blynken, and Nod " endeared him to old and young alike.

Of less permanence were the Reverend Frank Gunsaulus's *Phidias and Other Poems* (1891) and the dramatic critic Elwyn A. Barron's *The Viking* (1888), both in blank verse. George Horton sounded a socialistic note in *Songs of the Lowly, and Other Poems* (1892), and Louis J. Block gave expression to a spirit of mysticism in *Dramatic Sketches and Poems* (1891). Still earlier the prominent German political figure Caspar Butz brought out his book of poems *Gedichte eines Deutsch-Amerikaners,* freighted with recollections and praise of his homeland and the stirring events of the American Civil War.[36]

Nor was the city lacking those who qualified as essayists and sketch writers and who, as William Morton Payne, associate editor of the *Dial,* put it, attempted " to bridge the gap between the literature of form and the literature of knowledge." In her works on bird life Mrs. Olive Thorne Miller reflected the prevailing interest in the glories of outdoor life despite the oncoming dominance of the city; in his essays the Reverend James Vila Blake of the Third Unitarian Church strove to capture the style and erudition of an Emerson; while William Mathews, in his studies of philology and literary criticism, rounded out his several books of the 'seventies by his volume on *Oratory and Orators* in 1879.

Books dealing with science, philosophy, and history by Chicagoans appeared in increasing numbers in the bookstores along with those of better-established eastern authors. Within the various fields of science, they ranged, for example, from John W. Foster's *Pre-historic Races of the United States of America* (1873) to Edson S. Bastin's *Elements of Botany* (1887). Particularly well received and more

---

[36] Payne, *loc. cit.,* pp. 694–96; Frank McCall Hursley, *A Survey of Literary Production in Chicago from 1890 to 1900* (unpublished M.A. Thesis, The University of Chicago, 1926), pp. 39–40; *Illinois Staats-Zeitung,* Sept. 30, 1879.

widely read than most essays and the recordings of other learned men were those of a large group of divines, including David Swing and Robert Collyer.

The various fields of learning among the highly literate were broad enough to include several translations of foreign works. Mrs. Kate Newell Doggett rendered into English Charles Blanc's *The Grammar of Painting and Engraving,* George Howland put out translations of Homer, Virgil, and Horace which, without doubt, found fewer readers than did his *Practical Hints for the Teachers of Public Schools,* composed while superintendent of schools in 1889. From 1876 to 1892 John J. Lalor, Alfred B. Mason, and Paul Shorey prepared an English translation of *The Constitutional and Political History of the United States* by the eminent German scholar Hermann Eduard von Holst.[37]

In 1886 Alfred T. Andreas published the third of his detailed three-volume *History of Chicago,* the work of a group of collaborators. Six years later the first of Joseph Kirkland's two-volume *The Story of Chicago* and Judge John Moses's second volume of *Illinois, Historical and Statistical* came from the press.[38] Within the field of biography Lincoln had already become the favorite figure for Chicago chroniclers. Besides numerous short treatments of the life of " the rail splitter " and Isaac N. Arnold's *The Life of Abraham Lincoln,* Chicago admirers of the Civil War president could enjoy Francis F. Browne's *The Every-Day Life of Abraham Lincoln,* written with less political emphasis than some of the others. The eminent librarian William Frederick Poole explored a variety of historical themes in pamphlet form, not to mention his *Anti-Slavery Opinions before the Year 1800,* published in 1873.

Music and education had their exponents as well, in the latter case notably the works of George Howland, Colonel Francis W. Parker, and Charles H. Ham. William S. B. Mathews added to his previous contributions by his *A Popular History of the Art of Music* (1891); and George P. Upton enhanced his reputation through his handbooks in music and *Woman in Music* (1881).[39]

[37] Lalor and Mason were attorneys. Both Shorey and Von Holst joined the first faculty of the new University of Chicago in 1892. Shorey became Professor of Greek, Von Holst Professor and Chairman of the Department of History.

[38] Moses was librarian of the Chicago Historical Society 1887 to 1893.

[39] Payne, *loc. cit.,* pp. 697–99; Moses and Kirkland, *op. cit.,* II, 145; Andreas, *History*

A considerable array of periodicals also poured from the Chicago presses.[40] The outstanding literary magazine of its day was the *Lakeside Monthly*, successor in 1871 to the sectionally minded *Western Monthly*. Following the Fire, it came under the sole direction of the able Francis F. Browne, who raised it from extreme localism to a position comparing favorably in quality and appearance with similar magazines put out in eastern cities. Some fiction lightened its pages, its short stories lending variety and an imaginative touch to the predominantly heavier articles. From the pen of Moses Coit Tyler came literary criticism and from William Mathews philological and miscellaneous essays. Readers could enjoy the poetry of Joaquin Miller, Edgar Fawcett, and Benjamin F. Taylor, and contributions of prominent Chicagoans, including the Reverend Robert Collyer, Mrs. M. L. Rayne, Charles C. Bonney, and George P. Upton. Although the subscription list increased in a flattering manner during the first two years, the Panic of 1873 forced the discontinuance of the magazine the following year. Browne, his health broken, stubbornly resisted all advice to turn over his business to a provisional management, convinced that he could not employ " a man to work his soul for him while he was resting his body."

Also important, especially in the 1880's, was the *Western Magazine* with its eulogistic outpourings of things western. In 1879 it had moved to Chicago from Omaha, its editor the well-known lecturer and journalist Mrs. Helen Ekin Starrett. In 1882 it took over the *Alliance,* an undenominational religious journal started by David Swing and others in 1873, becoming the *Weekly Magazine,* supported by such philanthropically minded businessmen as Marshall Field and George M. Pullman. But, as in many other ventures of this kind, financial reverses forced cessation of publication in a brief two years.

Also distributed from Chicago was the story-paper weekly prepared as " ready prints " for country newspapers. Such was the *Eve-*

---

of Chicago, I, 3; Joseph Kirkland, *The Story of Chicago* (2 v. Chicago, 1892–94); John Moses, *Illinois, Historical and Statistical* (2 v. Chicago, 1889–92). For William Mathews, Poole, W. S. B. Mathews, and Upton see the biographical sketches of these men in the *Dictionary of American Biography*. For a discussion of many titles published in Chicago and books retailed in the bookstores see Chapter V, " Manufacturing and Merchandising."

40 In 1890 periodicals included 193 weeklies, 3 semiweeklies, 5 biweeklies, 20 semimonthlies, and 9 quarterlies, chiefly English but with foreign tongues well represented.

ning Lamp, popular for forty years after its first issue in 1869. Similar to it was the *Chicago Ledger,* founded in 1872 by Samuel H. Williams, which attained a circulation of 10,000 in seven years. Its first-rate stories of the early issues were replaced after a time by sensational material, and eventually in 1891 it became a mail-order paper under the ownership of William D. Boyce.[41] Besides several others of the story-paper type lasting sometimes only a year, as did *The Cottage Monthly* (1873), the *Novelist* ran from 1874 to 1881 and the *Chicago Index* from 1875 to 1891.

Quite unlike these sentimental story-papers was *Carl Pretzel's Magazine Pook,* originated by Charles H. Harris in 1872 and designed to answer the need of a magazine devoted to humor. Written in a pseudo German-English dialect, it had an appreciative audience in a city heavily populated with Germans. Expanded in 1874 into *Carl Pretzel's National Weekly,* it continued its sketches of "Carl Pretzel" until 1893. Besides, it brought its readers news of politics as viewed by John A. Logan and Robert Ingersoll, maintaining at the same time a connection with secret political societies.

Other humor journals in the English idiom appeared, some for only a brief time, some of thoroughly questionable literary quality and, in the light of later years, not at all funny. To critics their jokes were crude and offensively vulgar. Even Mark Twain's humor and the jests of Josh Billings the Congregational *Advance* held to be nothing short of an "indigestible diet." Of higher tone was *The Rambler* (1884–87), imitative of the satirical comments of the New York magazine *Life* and put out first by Reginald de Koven and then Harry B. Smith — men to be better known as collaborators in the field of light opera. In 1887 Opie Read transferred to Chicago from Little Rock his *Arkansaw Traveler* with its humorous sketches and jokes of southern characters couched in the dialect of their region.[42]

Whether the periodicals of the two decades following the Great Fire more nearly than the books produced in Chicago presaged a

---

[41] Moses and Kirkland, *op. cit.,* II, 4; Frank Luther Mott, *A History of American Magazines,* III, *1865–1885* (Cambridge, Mass., 1938), 53–54, 413–16; Fleming, *Magazines of a Market-Metropolis,* pp. 399–404, 407, 501–2, 507–11; F. F. Browne, *Papers (Mss.* and newspaper clippings, Newberry Library).

[42] In 1891 Read abandoned the editorship. *The Arkansaw Traveler,* however, continued under others until 1916.

literary greatness was, of course, subject to disagreement. If any gave this promise it was the *Dial,* founded in 1880 by Francis F. Browne, formerly owner and editor of the *Lakeside Monthly* and at one time literary editor of the *Alliance.* Sustained by Alexander C. McClurg, Browne not only had the encouragement which the former's strong intellectual interests provided, but also the asset of a valuable business connection. He was thus able to publish the outstanding journal of literary criticism of its day. In 1892 he began issuing the magazine himself because he felt a periodical committed to criticism should not have a business connection with a book publisher.

Originally a monthly at $1.00 annually, the *Dial* became a semimonthly at $2.00 a year in 1892. Besides its early practice of reviewing leading books and briefly mentioning others, of announcing plans of publishers, and giving literary news, it added articles on the Columbian Exposition and other contemporary concerns such as the wild enthusiasm for Ibsen which was sweeping the country. It numbered among its authors the ablest writers of the time, including the Chicagoans Melville W. Fuller, Joseph Kirkland, William F. Poole, William Morton Payne, George Upton, and David Swing.[43]

Though of much shorter life than the *Dial,* the *Current,* founded by the journalist Edgar L. Wakeman in 1883, treated its readers to a variety of important features. During the five years of its existence before it became a part of *America,* it had a section on public affairs, poetry by well-known poets like James Whitcomb Riley, and fiction by E. P. Roe and Lucy H. Hooper. Its reputation was such that writers craved the opportunity to be among its contributors because of the prestige that this connection implied.[44]

No other Chicago periodical had the standing of the *Dial,* but it was not the only attempt made in the post-Fire years to produce a journal primarily devoted to literary criticism and comment. In the 'seventies, for example, the *Owl,* under the editorship of Dr. William Frederick Poole, appeared monthly from 1874 to 1876. During 1879

[43] Browne died in 1913 and his son Waldo R. Browne became editor. For a discussion of the *Dial,* see Mott, *History of American Magazines,* III, 539–43; Frederic John Mosher, *Chicago's " Saving Remnant "; Francis Fisher Browne, William Morton Payne, and the Dial (1880–1892)* (unpublished Ph.D. Thesis, University of Illinois, 1950).

[44] For the standing the *Current* enjoyed among writers see Eugene Field, *Culture's Garland, Being Memoranda of the Gradual Rise of Literature, Art, Music and Society in Chicago, and Other Western Ganglia* (Boston, 1887), p. 77.

and '80 the *Literary Review* carried in its pages items about the interests and affairs of the important literary societies of the city.[45] Religious publications, trade journals, and organs of special propaganda groups became legion, reflecting the diverse interests of this growing community with its heterogeneous population.[46]

With even more readers than the magazines had, newspapers assumed an importance second to no other medium of the printed word as they issued from the presses in ever larger numbers. From 1870 to 1892 dailies alone increased nearly three times, totaling twenty-nine by the latter date, their circulation figures showing a correspondingly flattering increase.[47] Both news and editorial columns depicted the broad sweep of Chicago life — urban attitudes and habits intertwined with persisting rural concepts and customs. More provincial in some ways than the press of New York, Chicago newspapers seldom hesitated, however, to claim a greater spirit of enterprise and originality than practiced in New York or in any other place. Leased telegraph wires connected the leading dailies with important centers of interest, and special correspondents at the scene of significant happenings brought readers prompt and first-hand intelligence.

By and large, critics considered editorial pages as having less literary merit than those of the East, particularly New York, despite the presence of some able and original writers. Quality and quantity naturally varied with news conditions, time, and contributors, but

[45] Fleming, *op. cit.,* pp. 503–6, 514–18, 521–23; F. A. Russell, *The Newspaper and Periodical Publishing Industry in Illinois from 1880 to 1915* (unpublished Ph.D. Thesis, University of Illinois, 1916), p. 87; Mott, *History of American Magazines,* III, 54, 233, 266, 270; *The Advance,* VIII (June 3, 1875), 682; Harry B. Smith, *First Nights and First Editions* (Boston, 1931), pp. 98–101; Garland, *op. cit.,* pp. 22, 152; *The American Bookseller,* IX (May 1, 1880), 369; *The Publishers' Weekly,* VI (Nov. 14, 1874), 552.

[46] For religious, business, and other special-group journals see chapters dealing with these aspects of Chicago life. Bibliographical items also refer to many Chicago magazines not discussed in this chapter.

[47] The circulation figures of the three leading English dailies established before the Fire increased from 1870 to 1892 as follows: *Chicago Tribune,* 30,000 to 75,000; *Chicago Evening Journal,* 15,000 to 36,000; *The Chicago Times,* 35,000 to 40,000. The *Illinois Staats-Zeitung* (German) increased from 12,000 to 23,500. Principal English dailies founded after 1871 reported the following circulation in 1892: *The Inter Ocean,* 36,000; *Chicago Daily News* (aggregate of morning and evening editions), 243,619; *Chicago Herald,* 90,000; the *Mail,* 40,000. These figures are those generally given by the papers and not always are they sworn statements. Other estimates appear later in the text. For those given above see *Geo. P. Rowell & Co.'s American Newspaper Directory; N. W. Ayer & Son's American Newspaper Annual.*

in the editorials and special columns undoubtedly appeared much of
the literary work of the city. That such views were considered important and as appealing to readers was demonstrated by the space
devoted to them. According to an 1888 survey by a New York journalist, for example, Chicago had a higher ratio of editorial comment
than any of the leading papers of Boston, New York, Philadelphia,
Cincinnati, and St. Louis. This inquiry into Chicago's greater space
allotment, although not free from the error implicit in such an appraisal, proved to the investigator that the Chicago reading public
had a high degree of interest in such matter. Indeed, the results of
the investigations led him to observe: ". . . if a city can be heard
for its much speaking Chicago should compel attention." [48]

As Chicago read, so read the near-by countryside. Hundreds of
small-town papers received miniature Chicago editions, adding local
items to the general and editorial matter distributed to them. As in
the past, the effect of this dependence was keenly appreciated by the
astute men making up the city's newspaper hierarchy, for not only
was there financial gain but an opportunity to propagate their faith.

Various bureaus insured wider newsgathering than in the past
while they contributed to a monotony of content and presentation.
The City Press Association, concerned chiefly with local news, assumed an active role in the early years of the 'eighties. From the New
York Associated Press the Western Associated Press purchased both
national and international dispatches and, in turn, sent the eastern
association items from the Midwest. In 1882 the western organization
formed a partnership with the eastern, and William Henry Smith,
manager of the former, became general manager. Ten years later
the western group severed its connection with the New York association and became the Associated Press of Illinois under Melville E.
Stone as general manager, shortly to gain leadership in the distribution of national news.[49]

As facilities for gathering and distributing news improved, better

[48] Simeon Gilbert, "The Chicago of the Reader," *The Lakeside Monthly*, X (Oct.,
1873), 312–15; Willis J. Abbot, "Chicago Newspapers and Their Makers," *The Review of
Reviews*, XI (June, 1895), 646–65; Henry R. Elliot, "The Ratio of News," *The Forum*,
V (March, 1888), 99–107; Z. L. White, "Western Journalism," *Harper's New Monthly
Magazine*, LXXVII (Oct., 1888), 687; *Chicago Daily News*, Feb. 28, 1888. The background
of many practices lay in the years before 1871. See Pierce, *A History of Chicago*, II, 412–21.

[49] Gilbert, *loc. cit.*, p. 313; Melville E. Stone, *Fifty Years a Journalist* (Garden City,
1922), pp. 209–16.

reporting developed, with more men of education turning to journalism; at the same time competent critics of the arts and literature contributed regularly to the leading papers of the city. Recognizing the advantages of closer personal relations to raise the standards of the profession, newspapermen formed the Press Club of Chicago on January 11, 1880, by no means the first attempt at professional unity. The Illinois Press Association, organized fifteen years earlier for concerted action in such matters as legislation, the elimination of undesirable and unprofitable business methods, and the development of professional ideals and standards, received the support of numerous Chicagoans. Its eighth convention, in 1872, elected Rodney Welch of the *Prairie Farmer* president, and Mrs. Myra Bradwell, editor of the *Chicago Legal News,* the first woman member of the Association, as one of its three vice-presidents. In 1874 and in 1879 Chicago entertained the annual convention, and again in 1880, '81, and '83, as well as a special session in 1880. In 1885 women members formed the Illinois Woman's Press Association, with Miss Mary Allen West, editor of the *Union Signal,* president. Its membership roll included important Chicago journalists such as Caroline Huling, Frances Willard, and Elizabeth Boynton Harbert.

In the summer of 1889 the Whitechapel Club was established for the cultivation of good fellowship among reporters and others of the newspaper guild. It was during the time when the Cronin murder case was all-absorbing, and its name was taken from the site of London crimes then filling the press. For its first quarters it chose rooms at the rear of a saloon on Calhoun Place, known as " Newspaper Alley," where good liquor could be had and songs sung without restraint. Belonging to it were well-known figures such as Opie Read, Charles Seymour, Frederick Upham Adams, and Wallace Rice, and men then blazing into fame like Finley Peter Dunne, George Ade, and John T. McCutcheon, with the liberal publisher of the *Herald,* James W. Scott, holding honorary membership. Membership, however, was not restricted solely to newspapermen, for Robert Hamill, son of the president of the Board of Trade in 1892 and 1893, Charles Perkins, court clerk, and William E. Mason, Republican Congressman, 1887–91, also attended meetings. The clowning and practical jokes of the Club gave it a unique and not altogether respected place in the annals of the city's club life. Still, the

temper of discussions was serious, often verging on political radicalism inconsistent with what the newspapers published; equally critical were many of the reflections on the new economic order.[50]

Of the eight leading English-language dailies in 1892 only three
had their beginnings in the years before the Great Fire — the *Tribune,* the *Times,* and the *Evening Journal.* Of these three the *Tribune* seldom had reason to worry about circulation or profits. From
1865 to 1874 it was under the editorial direction of the ardent free-
trader Horace White; its important personnel included Alfred
Cowles as secretary and treasurer of the Tribune Company, James
W. Sheahan as assistant editor, and Henry Demarest Lloyd in the
post of literary and later financial editor. In 1872 it turned to Liberal
Republicanism and the candidacy of Horace Greeley.

On November 9, 1874 Joseph Medill gained control of the paper,
announcing that it would be "the organ of no man, however high;
no clique or ring, however influential; or faction, however fanatical
or demonstrative." Convinced that a journal to serve the public good
must express a preference between political parties, he charted its
course into the Republican party, believing that it comprised "a
much larger proportion of the intelligent and educated classes, of
the moral worth and business enterprise, as well as of the patriotic
elements, of the nation."

One of the *Tribune*'s primary purposes was opposition to a high
protective tariff; it advocated a return to specie payment and favored
a bimetallic standard; it disapproved the eight-hour day and other
demands of workingmen, and roundly condemned strikes as a means
of settling labor disputes; throughout, it upheld the rights of the
propertied class which made up a large part of its readers. Until his
death in 1899 Medill dictated the policies of his paper; trenchant
editorials, many of which he wrote, were among the most influential
in the country; in 1874 he chose as managing editor his brother

---

[50] Franc B. Wilkie, *Personal Reminiscences of Thirty-five Years of Journalism* (Chicago,
1891), pp. 306–7; William H. Freeman, comp., *The Press Club of Chicago* (Chicago, 1894),
pp. 9–10; W. D. Eaton, "Clubs That Were and the Club That Is," in *Year Book of the
Press Club of Chicago, 1917,* pp. 7–10; Opie Read, *I Remember* (New York, 1930), pp.
193–94, 232–33; *Illinois Newspaper Directory; History of Illinois Press Association* (Cham-
paign-Urbana, 1930), pp. 9, 23, 25, 42, 44–45, 48, 66–67, 79–82, 121, 129; *Chicago Tribune,*
May 27, 1874; *Railway Age,* II (Feb. 22, 1877), 721; *Chicago Herald,* July 17, 1892; *The
Inter Ocean,* March 6, 1892; Charles H. Dennis, "Whitechapel Nights," *Chicago Daily News,*
July 29, 1936; Elmer Ellis, *Mr. Dooley's America* (New York, 1941), pp. 48–54.

Samuel J. Medill, and, upon the latter's death in 1883, Robert W. Patterson, Jr. He continued on the staff outstanding writers and reporters like Elias Colbert as commercial editor, and George P. Upton as music critic. Writing under the *nom de plume* " Peregrine Pickle," the latter elevated in numberless ways the musical taste of the city.

For its well-packed news columns the *Tribune's* reportorial group searched widely. During the Russo-Turkish War, George Henry Wright went to London in April, 1877 to set up a central bureau from which he delegated correspondents to each army. Other correspondents departed on equally spectacular missions: one to accompany Peary to Greenland in 1891; another, inoculated by haffkine, to Germany to sleep on a cot on which a German had recently died of cholera. The favor accorded the *Tribune* resulted not only from its editorial and news columns but from many other features. Market tables of retail prices for leading articles of food appeared as early as May 13, 1865, but not until November 22, 1879 did the " Gastronomical " column become popular. By February, 1886 " Household Hints " came in the Saturday issue, preceding by eight months " Woman and Her Ways." In 1880 " Farm and Garden " by " Rural Jr.," " Field and Stables " by " Veterinarian " satisfied other interests, while a weather map, introduced November 3, 1879, was editorially declared probably the first adequate one of its kind published by any paper.

By the late 'seventies political cartoons appeared, a crude but effective weapon. With the 'eighties, they figured more often in attempts to influence opinion, although not printed in each issue of the paper. Those of Charles Lederer were particularly praised. One of the earliest, put out on July 21, 1884, represented Cleveland and Hendricks riding on a rickety platform over a swamp toward the Capitol. The 'nineties found etchings brightening a column devoted to humor, the theme focused on incidents of city life; and " Pen Pictures of the Leading Events of Last Week " in the Sunday issues from March, 1892 gave readers a visual résumé of important happenings. By 1893 the *Tribune's* daily circulation was estimated at over 40,000, a figure considered low by Victor Lawson; the Sunday issue was said to reach over 125,000.[51]

51 See issues of *Chicago Tribune*, particularly July 23, Aug. 28, Nov. 9, 1874, April 28, 1877, April 7, 1884, May 24, 1891, Sept. 23, 1892; Kinsley, *The Chicago Tribune, Its*

For years the *Chicago Times* competed with the *Tribune* in news-gathering, its editorials generally reflecting opposite points of view, particularly in politics. Its alliterative and punning headings, especially during the 'seventies, attracted wide and not always complimentary attention, and tended to emphasize the sensationalism to which the paper was addicted. Its most notorious, " Jerked to Jesus," November 27, 1875, which announced the hanging of four murderers, was matched many times by other headlines like " Mortal Monotony " on October 1, 1878, with the subhead " Thirty-five deaths from Yellow Fever in New Orleans on Yesterday," and " Death's Darts " the following day on the same subject. Its " Trooly Rooral," a column detailing suburban matters, and " Fit for the Flames," one devoted to criminal records, were regular features during the mid-'seventies.

If the *Tribune* became the vehicle of Medill's opinions, the *Times* was even more the spokesman of its able, eccentric editor, Wilbur F. Storey. His bold and frequently vitriolic attacks upon persons and conditions he did not like and his tendency to publicize the sensational kept him conspicuously before the public. After the late 'seventies failing health followed by insanity forced him to withdraw from active work. That he was one of the most influential and well known of Chicago newsmen no one doubted. He pioneered in maintaining a cable service and in sending correspondents to Europe, and, like the *Tribune*, had a representative abroad to report the Russo-Turkish War. In January, 1881 Franc B. Wilkie took charge of a London bureau with agents in the principal cities of the Continent, but the bureau's service to *Times* readers was discontinued the following October.

On the Chicago staff appeared names of competent and respected newsmen such as Horatio W. Seymour, Charles Dennett, and Everett Chamberlin; on it also were women in important positions, including the able Margaret Sullivan and Mrs. Julia Holmes Smith. In 1887, three years after Storey's death, the paper fell into the hands of James J. West with Finley Peter Dunne, a member of the editorial and reportorial staffs. But not even the talented Dunne, to be better

---

First Hundred Years, II and III, *passim;* J. Medill to Elihu Washburne, Nov. 1, 1874, *Washburne Papers;* Victor Lawson to Editor of American Newspaper Directory, New York, Aug. 2, 1893, article signed " Columbus," *Lawson Papers.*

known as Mr. Dooley, and his colleagues were able to rescue the *Times* from a rapid deterioration. When Carter Harrison bought the paper in 1891, the circulation had fallen below 18,000; it rose briefly to an average of about 35,000. Its temporary revival rested largely on the paper's claim that it was the only regular Democratic daily in Chicago and as such carried weight in local politics. By 1895, its old glory gone, the *Times* consolidated with the *Herald*.[52]

No newspaper was more ardently a political partisan than the *Inter Ocean,* established by J. Young Scammon in 1872. Standing four-square on the principles of the Republican party, it consistently pursued its motto: " Republican in everything, Independent in nothing." Its first issue appeared March 25, 1872, and after the presidential campaign that year, reorganization in the form of a stock company took place, to be followed in three years by still another. In May, 1872 William Penn Nixon started as business manager, assuming editorial duties in 1875. Upon the *Inter Ocean* he imprinted his personality as effectively as did Medill and Storey on their journals. At no time, however, did Nixon question his party's policies, as Medill did upon occasion. Protectionist to the core in its tariff policy, the paper was also strongly committed to a generous pension system. In local matters it warmly supported public causes and organizations engaged in civic, religious, and philanthropic enterprises. Its refusal to accept advertising from gambling establishments gained warm approval in 1893, especially from religious leaders and other crusaders for law enforcement.

From 1891 to 1894 Herman H. Kohlsaat, prominent baker, restaurateur, and real-estate promoter, brought spectacular business methods into the *Inter Ocean*'s dignified office. Coupons to be clipped and exchanged for some illustrated publication cajoled hesitant subscribers, and the introduction of colored illustrations in the Sunday edition, the first of their kind, gained widespread approval. In 1893 its daily average was over 60,000 and its Sunday sales about 75,000, much of it out of town. By 1894 Nixon again was in control, as a result of differences between him and Kohlsaat.[53]

52 Wilkie, *op. cit.,* pp. 242–67, 286–306; Abbot, *loc. cit.,* pp. 650–52, 664–65; Andreas, *History of Chicago,* III, 696–98; Ellis, *op. cit.,* pp. 32–38; Lawson to Editor of American Newspaper Directory, Aug 2, 1893, *Lawson Papers;* Carter Harrison, *Stormy Years,* pp. 36, 47; the files of *The Chicago Times,* 1871–1893.

53 The Inter Ocean, *A History of the City of Chicago,* pp. 319–20; Abbot, *loc. cit.,* pp.

On Christmas Day, 1875 the *Chicago Daily News* first appeared in an experimental issue announcing that it would be published regularly from the first of the year 1876. Thus what was to be the most important newspaper begun after the Fire started its career. It was to sell as an evening paper for one cent, the " hazardous Odyssey," as Melville E. Stone put it, of William Dougherty and himself, later joined by Percy R. Meggy, an English " remittance man." It was Meggy who provided the capital of about five thousand dollars; Stone and Dougherty, both experienced newsmen, the talent and vision. Idealistically conceived, the paper was to be free of attachment to a political party or any selfish interest; its primary aim was to collect and print the world's news; it proposed to pilot public opinion " aright"; and, as its last function, to furnish entertainment.

But the path led uphill, and the limited financial resources available discouraged all but Stone. By summer both Dougherty and Meggy abandoned the project. In July Stone turned to his former high-school friend Victor Lawson, who was persuaded to take over the proprietorship and act as business manager, leaving the editorship to Stone. Shortly thereafter circulation figures rose, in a year reaching 20,000. Profit rather than loss reflected Lawson's business acumen, the regularity of the patronage of advertisers, and the popularity of the wide news coverage and Stone's sparkling editorials. On March 21, 1881 a morning edition rolled from the presses, to sell for two cents until 1888, when the price was reduced to a penny.

Stories of crime detection became an outstanding feature of the *News*. Through skillful investigations Stone and his staff rounded up wrongdoers before the bar of public opinion and brought about many convictions. During the railroad strikes of 1877 the paper, openly sympathetic with labor, sent reporters to mingle freely with strikers. Hourly editions appeared; on one day circulation reached the amazing total of 77,643.

Whenever the *News* believed the public welfare was endangered, it attacked abuses; when it was unsuccessful in getting the city administration to enforce the laws, it enlisted the aid of public opinion

654–57; White, *loc. cit.*, p. 688; *The Advance*, XXVII (Feb. 16, 1893), 125–26; Andreas, *History of Chicago*, III, 698–700; Frank Luther Mott, *American Journalism* (New York, 1941), pp. 563, 585; Lawson to Editor of American Newspaper Directory, Aug. 2, 1893, *Lawson Papers*. See the files of the *Inter Ocean*, 1872–1893.

and, as in the case of gambling resorts, the co-operation of the sheriff. It led revolts against nominations for political trust bestowed by party bosses; it encouraged a broadening of the curriculum in the schools by awarding medals for essays on patriotism in 1888; it promoted humanitarian enterprises such as a Fresh Air Fund and The Daily News Sanitarium for Sick Babies; and along with other praiseworthy undertakings, it sponsored clubrooms for newsboys.[54]

To the meritorious dissemination of news and the nice perception and independence of its editorials, the *News* added an unusual array of talent in its special features. Without doubt the most notable was the column "Sharps and Flats," written daily by the brilliant and whimsical Eugene Field, who was on the staff from 1883 until 1895. As a humorous columnist, Field had no competitor to challenge his pre-eminence. Clever and irrepressibly biting strictures on attempts of the city's wealthy to appear cultured were interspersed in his columns with serious prose and verse. Calling himself "the bard of pork and lard," he jibed in a generally good-natured fashion at musicians, artists, and their works, at local literati, as well as at society. Many of his columns he reproduced in *Culture's Garland, Being Memoranda of the Gradual Rise of Literature, Art, Music and Society in Chicago and Other Western Ganglia.*

Besides Field, Lawson engaged others of ability to serve in different capacities on the corps of the *News,* its various editions giving evidence of the high standards of his contributors. Among others were Henry Ten Eyck White and Slason Thompson. Amy Leslie (Mrs. Lillie Brown) wrote criticisms of the drama, and in 1889 John T. McCutcheon began his career as artist; his first political cartoon was drawn in the 1890 mayoralty campaign. On May 9, 1892 the morning issue was rechristened the *News Record.*

To other notables Lawson added special correspondents of distinction such as William Dillon and T. P. Gill, prominent in the Irish National party; Grace Greenwood, to contribute news of Paris; Joseph Holton as special London correspondent; and William Ele-

54 Stone, *op. cit.,* pp. 51–109; Dennis, *op. cit.,* pp. 1–20, 41–44, 51, 64, 72, 124, 158–59; Abbot, *loc. cit.,* pp. 657–59; Percy R. Meggy to Henry D. Lloyd, Aug. 23, 1893, *Lloyd Papers;* Victor F. Lawson to the Board of Education, June 2, 1888, to Whitelaw Reid, July 12, 1888, to Charles T. Thompson, May 28, 1892, *Lawson Papers.* See the issues of the *Chicago Daily News,* 1876–1893.

roy Curtis, stationed in Washington. In 1891 Charles H. Dennis was named managing editor of the morning issue. A year earlier George Ade had joined the staff, furnishing articles to the *Record* on the World's Columbian Exposition for which McCutcheon had sketched the scenes. From the pair came the popular feature " Stories of the Streets and of the Town," written by Ade and illustrated by Mc-Cutcheon, which began November 20, 1893.

The success of the Lawson undertakings was depicted in gratifyingly large circulation figures. By 1886, ten years after it started, the *News* sold 160,000 copies daily, said by Lawson to be " the largest daily circulation figure in America," and " probably 40,000 greater than the circulation of all other Chicago daily papers combined." In 1888 Stone unexpectedly retired, despite the prosperity which had crowned his and Lawson's efforts. By August 2, 1893 the *News* was averaging over 200,000 daily, sold to rich and poor alike, thanks to its carrier system to all parts of the city. At the same time, the *Record* boasted 135,019 copies for each day; nearly two-thirds of its circulation was in Chicago, but it was also read throughout Illinois and in Iowa, Indiana, Ohio, Michigan, and Wisconsin.[55]

The large patronage accorded the Lawson publications was not duplicated by others. Some papers trailed considerably. Even the *Chicago Evening Journal,* the oldest of all, was selling only about 20,000 copies in 1893, but these went, in general, to a devoted constituency of conservatively minded folk loyally Republican in politics. The *Chicago Herald,* a morning paper, however, easily doubled the *Journal*'s figures, its advertising department going so far as to claim 80,000. Established in May, 1881, when the *Times* was losing influence, the *Herald* in two years fell into the hands of John R. Walsh, president of the Chicago National Bank and manager of the Western News Company. Through him and his business manager and publisher, James W. Scott, well known and respected in journalistic circles, the paper pursued a so-called independent course, with a leaning toward the Democratic party. Its circulation by the 1890's was divided between Chicago and territory near by. By 1893 its en-

[55] Dennis, *op. cit.,* pp. 64, 83–86, 105, 162, 164; Stone, *op. cit.,* pp. 110–16, 125–40, 179–82; Fred C. Kelly, *George Ade, Warmhearted Satirist* (Indianapolis, 1947), p. 72; Victor F. Lawson, Statement, 1886, Lawson to Editor of American Newspaper Directory, Aug. 2, 1893, *Lawson Papers.*

terprising promoters could declare that its Sunday edition sold 125,-000 copies; and they had introduced funny pictures and circus features into this edition as an innovation.

In 1890 the promoters of the *Herald* embarked on an evening paper, the politically independent *Chicago Evening Post,* in 1893 reported as approaching 30,000 in circulation. Much attention was directed to the theater and to literary subjects, and in its first Sunday edition Finley Peter Dunne's humorous dialect piece "Frank's Visit to Grover" forecast the famous Dooley pieces.[56]

Only the large-scale promoters of newspapers seemed able to stand for long the competitive game in which newspapers engaged. Dwindling financial resources frequently necessitated discontinuing the struggle. Such was the fate, for example, of the *Chicago Post and Mail,* a consolidation in 1874 of the *Post* and *Mail* under the editorship of Oliver A. Willard, the brother of Frances E. Willard. In 1875 Henry D. Lloyd considered buying it because its shaky finances might mean a small purchase price. This, Lloyd thought, would provide him with a vehicle to explain his platform, one through which he could gain converts to his policies: " the pacification of the country, decentralization, free trade, specie payment, administrative reform, anti-Republicanism," and " support for Governor Tilden for the Presidency in 1876." That he failed to realize his wish was evident in the continued control of the paper by the Willard family; Frances E. Willard and Mrs. Oliver A. Willard took over in 1878 after the death of the latter's husband. They aspired to make the *Post* reflect the purifying influence of women in journalism, bringing with them, they declared editorially, " the amenities and elevating influences." Their tenure was of only a few months' duration, for overwhelming financial difficulties led to the sale of the paper to Victor Lawson.[57]

Other papers passed into complete oblivion, their short lives reflecting the insufficient capital back of them or their failure to break through the entrenched positions enjoyed by their prosperous com-

[56] Abbot, *loc. cit.,* pp. 652–53, 660; Dennis, *op. cit.,* pp. 75–79; White, *loc. cit.,* p. 689; Ellis, *op. cit.,* pp. 54, 65–67; Lawson to Editor of American Newspaper Directory, Aug. 2, 1893, *Lawson Papers.*

[57] H. D. Lloyd to "My dear Demarest," April 8, 1875, *Lloyd Papers; Chicago Post,* March 18, 1878; *Chicago Tribune,* April 26, 1878; Frances E. Willard, *Glimpses of Fifty Years* (Chicago, 1889), pp. 503–6. The *Post* ran from 1865 to 1873, the *Evening Mail* from 1870 to 1873.

petitors.[58] This, on the other hand, was not the case of the foreign-language publications, which flourished richly among the nationals to which they were addressed. Of these the German press enjoyed the greatest patronage, as was to be expected in a city with so many German residents.[59]

Among the many agencies extending the boundaries of knowledge, libraries had no peer, with the exception of schools and other institutions of organized learning. The Fire destroyed an unknown number of books and other priceless holdings, including large personal collections, those of the Chicago Library Association, the Chicago Historical Society, the Chicago Academy of Science, the Young Men's Christian Association, as well as the possessions of other private and eleemosynary organizations. The task of restoration began immediately.

At the time of the Fire, Chicago had no free, tax-supported library, although several were semipublic in practice. This was especially true of the Chicago Library Association, considered virtually the public library of the city. The destruction of its possessions deepened the anxiety of its sponsors about an already empty treasury and led its librarian, English-born John Robson, and one of its most loyal members, Thomas D. Lowther, to point out the timeliness of establishing what was in a very real sense a free public library.[60] The suggestion for such an institution was, however, not new. For some time civic-minded Chicagoans had been discussing the need for such a library, one equipped, to quote the *Tribune,* for the " reasonable wishes " of the scholar and where " one who desired a good education could find the means."

[58] Typical of such short-lived papers was the *Chicago Daily Telegraph,* founded in 1878, which was taken over in 1881 by the *Herald.* Mott, *American Journalism,* p. 467; Abbot, *loc. cit.,* p. 662; Andreas, *History of Chicago,* III, 704; Lawson to Editor of American Newspaper Directory, Aug. 2, 1893, *Lawson Papers.*

[59] The principal foreign-language papers were the *Illinois Staats-Zeitung, Abendpost, Chicagoer Freie Presse, Tageblatt,* and *Chicagoer Arbeiter-Zeitung,* all of which were German; *Skandinaven* (Norwegian); *Svornost, Chicagské Listy,* and *Denní Hlasatel,* all three Bohemian; *Dziennik Chicagoski* (Polish); *L'Italia* (Italian); *Svenska Tribunen* and *Svenska Amerikanaren,* both Swedish.

[60] The following are the chief sources on the Chicago Public Library unless noted otherwise: Chicago Public Library Board of Directors, *Annual Report, 1873–93,* bound separately and in *Municipal Reports; The Chicago Public Library, 1873–1923* . . . ; [Thomas D. Lowther, (comp.)], *Memorials of the Old Chicago Library, Formerly Young Men's Association, and of the Advent of the New* (Chicago, 1878); Gwladys Spencer, *The Chicago Public Library, Origins and Backgrounds.*

Following the Fire, Robson returned to England, commissioned by Lowther and others of the Library Association, to obtain, if possible, a new set of the *Patent Office Reports* of Great Britain and to appeal for books for " the old Chicago Library if revived or the new free City Library if established." Meanwhile, A. H. Burgess, a Londoner, proposed to the editor of the *London Daily News* that England present " a new Free Library to Chicago, to remain there as a mark of sympathy now, and a keepsake and a token of true brotherly kindness forever." The suggestion met a warm response, to which the author Thomas Hughes, then a member of Parliament, gave active support. The Anglo-American Association publicized and promoted the scheme, and authors, publishers, societies, and many individuals contributed about seven thousand volumes, a gift Mayor Medill commissioned Robson to receive on behalf of the city.

The generosity of the English hastened legislation authorizing the establishment of free tax-supported libraries in the state. On March 7, 1872, Governor John M. Palmer signed a bill permitting the creation of such an institution in any city, incorporated town, village, or township. On April 3 a Chicago council ordinance established a public library in the city, but not until January 1, 1873, did the new library open its doors, and then in makeshift quarters — an old iron water tank at the rear of a lot at LaSalle and Adams.[61] Other temporary locations followed, but on July 27, 1892 ground was broken for the library's own building in Dearborn Park, into which it moved October 11, 1897.[62]

From the beginning the library was popular, attracting people from all parts of the city. Under the guidance of William Frederick Poole, serving as librarian from January 1, 1874, until January 23, 1887, it expanded its holdings to meet the needs of its growing clientele. By 1893 it possessed a large collection of pamphlets and 189,-

[61] The nine members appointed April 8, 1872 to serve on the board of directors of the Chicago Public Library were the lawyers Thomas Hoyne, Elliott Anthony, Daniel Shorey, Julius Rosenthal (librarian of Chicago Law Institute Library), Samuel Hayes; the journalists James W. Sheahan and Hermann Raster (then of the *Illinois Staats-Zeitung*); Willard Woodward, publisher; and Robert Queal of Robert F. Queal & Co., dealers in lumber.

[62] Chicago, *Council Proceedings, 1890–91*, p. 243; *Chicago Tribune*, Sept. 10, 23, 24, 30, Oct. 7, 8, 1871, Jan. 2, 10, Nov. 2, 1873, June 7, 1874, Feb. 28, 1876, Nov. 22, 1881; Illinois, *Public Laws, 1871–72*, pp. 609–11, *House Journal, 1871*, pp. 282, 667; *The Times* [London], Dec. 8, 1871; Louise G. Pritchard, *A History of the Chicago Public Library* (Urbana, University of Illinois M.S. Thesis, 1928), pp. 30–69.

350 volumes, including many periodicals and other printed documents. As early as 1874 its serial publications in the reading room represented twenty-three nations besides those of Great Britain and the United States. Many volumes contributed by countries of the Continent came in response to requests from their nationals in Chicago, and annual purchases added current publications as well as those printed previously.

Like readers elsewhere in the United States, Chicagoans read more prose fiction and juveniles than other literature, the works of E. P. Roe, Augusta J. Evans, Mary J. Holmes, Oliver Optic, Horatio Alger, and dime novels ranking high on the withdrawal list. Such literary taste, the *American Bookseller* believed justified in a city thoroughly unromantic by nature, where " the pursuit of the almighty dollar " was uppermost. " It needs therefore," observed the writer, " all the romance it can get in the way of parks, pretty girls, and good novels." Though trailing considerably, history and biography stood next, with poetry and drama attracting the smallest number of devotees. With the territorial growth of the city, attempts to supply the wants of readers in outlying sections resulted in the establishment of delivery stations, four as early as 1884 and twenty-nine by 1892. By 1893 and '94 six branch libraries, one the temporary quarters of a library for the blind equipped through the generosity of Byron L. Smith and Mrs. Victor F. Lawson, further increased the library's usefulness to the community. These services were accompanied by others, not the least being closer relations with the schools, both public and private.[63]

Although the public libraries undoubtedly served the greatest number of people, others, privately endowed and supported, also brought to Chicagoans the treasures of the ages. Those connected with professional societies, with institutions of higher learning, with various religious and ethnic groups, as well as with organizations such as the Y.M.C.A., cared for the needs and interests of many. Of those privately sponsored, none was more important to the historically conscious than that of the Chicago Historical Society, which had played a significant part in the city's intellectual life since 1856. In the Fire

[63] *The Publishers' Weekly*, IV (Nov. 15, 1873), 536, VI (Sept. 19, 1874), 313; *The American Bookseller*, III (May 15, 1877), 294; *The Chicago Times*, Sept. 27, 1874; *Chicago Tribune*, April 4, Nov. 10, 1886, Oct. 7, 1888; Katherine L. Sharp, *Illinois Libraries* (University of Illinois, *Studies*, Urbana, 1907), pp. 537-38, 544.

it had lost priceless possessions, including Lincoln's Emancipation Proclamation and collections relating not only to Chicago and Illinois but to all the Northwest. In July, 1874 another conflagration wiped out what had been assembled after the destruction of 1871. But the task of restoration continued, and in a few years the library's holdings represented thousands of volumes, pamphlets, and a valuable collection of manuscripts and portraits. On November 12, 1892 the cornerstone of a fireproof building designed by Henry Ives Cobb was laid; four years later, on December 15, the building was dedicated.

Two other outstanding free reference libraries marked the post-Fire years — because of bequests by Walter L. Newberry and John Crerar. The funds provided by the Newberry will of 1868 were available in 1885 upon Mrs. Newberry's death, and two years later William Frederick Poole of the Chicago Public was named librarian, the first of a distinguished line. Under his able direction, collections, particularly in the humanities and music, immeasurably promoted the advancement and spread of knowledge. The will of Crerar, probated in 1889, gave to the city $2,000,000. This fund the trustees decided to devote largely to the physical, natural, and social sciences, but the library was not opened to readers until 1897.

Thus, with these additions to her other agencies of knowledge, Chicago could well boast of notable achievements in extending the horizon of learning, despite the tremendous task of physical reconstruction the Fire had imposed. It was, indeed, as Theodore Dreiser was to write in *The Titan,* not only a " seething city in the making," but " a very bard of a city, this, singing of high deeds and high hopes, its heavy brogans buried deep in the mire of circumstance." [64]

[64] The Chicago Library Club, *Libraries of the City of Chicago with an Historical Sketch of the Chicago Library Club* (Chicago, 1905), pp. 27–28, 31, 53–56; *The Chicago Times,* Feb. 22, 1874; *Chicago Tribune,* Oct. 17, 1877, Nov. 17, 1886, Dec. 23, 1889, Nov. 19, 1890, April 20, 1892; *Chicago News Record,* June 7, 1892; Chicago South Park Commissioners, *Annual Report, 1906–8,* p. 89.

CHAPTER XII

RELIGIOUS AND HUMANITARIAN
STRIVINGS

It was inevitable that the patterns of religious development and humanitarian aspiration should be modified in the years after the Great Fire — years marked by the strains and stresses of a fast-growing urbanism. On the whole, the changes resembled those of other American cities buffeted by the economic revolution of the late nineteenth century. The massing of many diverse peoples remorselessly battered at the restraints of an older and less complex social order, and the old-time theology had to face the challenge of the scientific thought of the day and attempt as well to answer the higher criticism.

Yet, despite these perils to its authority, the church gained markedly not only in membership but also in the number of congregations. The immediate problem was, therefore, that of physical expansion. Before the 'eighties closed it was a matter of public comment that the building of places of worship lagged noticeably behind Chicago's increase in population, just as in other large centers. By 1889, during a decade of phenomenal growth, the city could count one Protestant edifice to every 315 Protestants, one Roman Catholic church to every 2,202 Roman Catholic communicants, and one synagogue to every 919 of the Jewish faith.[1] Moreover, these

---

[1] Ratios were computed from statistics in U. S., *Eleventh Census, 1890*, "Report on Statistics of Churches," pp. 94–95. Figures for Protestants were calculated by subtracting the sums of Catholic and Jewish edifices and memberships from such totals for the city. By this computation Josiah Strong's statement that there was only one Protestant church to every 3,601 inhabitants in 1890 is incorrect. (*The New Era or The Coming Kingdom*

were more accessible to Chicagoans who could afford to reside at a distance from the hum of the day's work. In 1886, for example, 16,241 persons lived within the city's First Ward, bounded by Harrison Street, the south branch and main stream of the Chicago River, and Lake Michigan. There could be found six churches, including two independent or non-denominational, two Methodist Episcopal, one Friends, and one Swedenborgian temple. In the Third Ward, between Sixteenth and Twenty-sixth streets and from Clark to the lake, the residence of many of Chicago's well-to-do, fourteen churches and two synagogues served the 20,212 inhabitants.[2]

Among the Protestants, the Lutherans outnumbered those of other denominations by the close of the 1880's. The Methodists, however, proudly pointed out that their growth exceeded proportionately the general population increase during the decade. Only the Baptist, of five large Protestant denominations — the Methodist Episcopal, the Presbyterian, the Protestant Episcopal, and the Congregational — had a congregation of a thousand or more members in the early 'seventies. By 1892 all had at least one membership list of over a thousand. Still, according to one authority, only one person in nineteen belonged to the main evangelical groups by the latter part of the 1880's — a ratio which to some critics appeared a reflection on methods of recruiting, to others a foreboding of even greater defections in the years ahead.[3]

By 1890 the Catholic Church, too, with its large immigrant following, reported under its protection 262,047 persons, including the

[New York, 1893], p. 198.) By the evidence available his statement that "in the heart of Chicago there are sixty thousand people without a single church either Protestant or Catholic" also appears an exaggeration. (See Strong's Introduction to Samuel Lane Loomis, *Modern Cities and Their Religious Problems* [New York, 1887], p. 9.)

2 The fourteen churches included three Presbyterian, two Episcopal, and one each, Baptist, Christian, Congregational, Friends, Methodist Episcopal, Reformed Episcopal, Roman Catholic, Unitarian, and Universalist. Ratios of churches to population in the two wards were one to 2,707 in the First, and one to 1,263 in the Third. Population statistics have been taken from Chicago Board of Education, *Thirty-second Annual Report, 1886*, p. 200, and the number of churches from the *Lakeside Annual Directory of the City of Chicago, 1886* (Chicago, 1886), pp. 34–39. City directories, although their listing is not all-inclusive, reveal, on the whole, annual growth and movement of churches. See Appendix table.

3 Loomis, *op. cit.*, p. 89. Membership figures for 1872–1893 can be found in annual reports of the various denominations. See, for example, Methodist Episcopal Church, *Minutes of the Annual Conferences*, and *Fall Conferences;* General Assembly of the Presbyterian Church in the United States of America, *Minutes;* Baptist General Association of Illinois, *Minutes;* Protestant Episcopal Church, Chicago diocese, *Journal of . . . Annual Convention;* *The Congregational Quarterly*, and *The Congregational Year-Book.*

Roman communicants and 2,000 Uniates. This made Chicago the second largest Catholic center in the country. Even more significant was the fact that those referred to as Catholics were more than two and a half times more numerous than all those listed among the seven leading Protestant denominations. The Jews, although they had a far less imposing total than the Catholics, could view with satisfaction the multiplication of their synagogues and small congregations to care for a membership greater than those of either the Episcopal or the German Evangelical churches.

Although Catholics and Lutherans were the chief beneficiaries of the foreign arrivals in the city, the Methodists profited from the addition of Scandinavians and Germans to their membership. These foreign-born congregations usually carried on their services in their native tongues. With the passage of time, however, the Protestant churches absorbed into their membership more and more of those of different lineage, and exemplified within the religious sphere the cosmopolitanism so noticeable in other aspects of the life of the city.[4]

The efforts to save men's souls were aided greatly by denominational missionary undertakings which flourished throughout the city and the near-by suburbs. They superseded to a large extent the activity of individual congregations in initiating and supporting mission ventures in new neighborhoods in the years before the creation of the city missionary societies. By 1878 the Methodists were busily engaged in spreading their special type of sectarianism; by 1882 the Baptists, through the City Mission Society, were proceeding with a vigor equal to that of the Methodists; and the Congregationalists were putting into practice similar methods in their Chicago City Missionary Society.[5] As these denominational offshoots expanded their services to embrace the physical as well as the spiritual wants of men, their numbers grew in proportion to the extent they adopted a program of practical usefulness.[6]

The ardor to Christianize the immediate community was paral-

---

[4] See Appendix table.

[5] *Northwestern Christian Advocate*, XXVI (Jan. 23, 1878), 5, (Oct. 9, 1878), 5; Perry J. Stackhouse, *Chicago and the Baptists, a Century of Progress* (Chicago, 1933), p. 116; *Baptist City Mission Society of Chicago* (Pamphlet, Chicago, n.d.); *The Advance*, XXII (April 19, 1888), 244; J. C. Armstrong, *The Chicago City Missionary Society* (Typescript, Chicago Theological Seminary, [ca. 1914]); Chicago City Missionary Society, *First Annual Report, 1884 — Tenth Annual Report, 1893; Chicago Tribune*, June 17, Aug. 5, 1878.

[6] See later in this chapter.

leled, just as it had been from the early days of the city, by the zeal of home and foreign missionary organizations to gain converts abroad. This effort enjoyed, in particular, the support of women, who often found in such undertakings not only religious but social satisfactions. Through " circles " and " bands," such as the " One Hundredth Band," " Golden Hours," " The Flower Garden," and " Aunt Lizzie's Band of Helpers," salvation, it was hoped, might be made universal.[7] Special periodicals described the scope of the work and encouraged its continuation through the subtle device of fictionalized stories. Often these stories portrayed the gratification gained through financial donations, even if such gifts required great personal sacrifice.[8]

The Sunday schools, both those associated with the missions in the city and those connected with the established churches, continued to propagate the gospel among the young. Along with " the birth and maturity of foreign missions," they were looked upon as perhaps the greatest manifestation of the growth of all instrumentalities for spreading Christianity.[9] Even those churches whose memberships were small, such as the Adventist, Friends, and the German United Evangelical, had at least one school. In 1875, of eighteen Protestant churches reporting the number of schools and attendance, the Methodists led. Then came the Baptists, Lutherans, Presbyterians, and Protestant Episcopalians. But the largest number of schools did not always mean the greatest number of scholars; the Congregational, for instance, with eleven schools exceeded the Protestant Episcopal enrollment in its eighteen. Between 1884 and 1892 membership in these organized bodies increased from 74,975 to 138,183, at times exceeding that of the church itself.[10] A predominance of females over males in attendance, similar to adult participation in religious services, moved one minister to comment on an increasing unwillingness of boys to accept all the things they were frequently

---

[7] *Chicago Tribune*, March 22, 1873, Feb. 1, 1882, Oct. 29, 1887; *The Standard*, XXXVII (March 20, 1890), 4, 5; Chicago Baptist Association, *Proceedings of the Chicago Baptist Association, at Its Forty-seventh Anniversary . . . 1882* (Elgin, 1882), p. 27.

[8] The Baptist monthly *Tidings from the Baptist Home Mission Society* was a journal of this nature. In addition, it printed financial reports and similar material. It was published in Chicago from 1881 until absorbed in 1911 in *Missions*. It cost 25 cents a year.

[9] *The Alliance*, Feb. 19, 1876, p. 75.

[10] See Appendix table.

asked " to receive with implicit faith." [11] To insure effective teaching, journals put out by various denominations carried directions as to the preparation of lessons, the use of a blackboard and chalk, and similar devices to present the Scriptures graphically and interestingly.[12]

Both outside and within the confines of a denomination, the winning of souls to the old orthodoxy continued through camp-meetings and revivals. The pattern remained unchanged from the past — its methods so successful that they were recommended and frequently used by ministers of the evangelical sects. Preachers referred frequently to miracles and reminded the sinful of the wrath of God with its inevitable accompaniment of eternal punishment if they did not repent and affirm their belief in Jesus Christ as a personal Saviour. These fearsome declarations, couched in the language of the market place, workshop, and factory, struck home.[13] Posters, signs, and advertisements in the secular press broadcast the necessity and advantages of salvation. At the Des Plaines camp-meeting grounds, tents, cottages, and restaurants accommodated crowds who listened, in the 1880's particularly, to the ringing tones of the Reverend Thomas Harrison, the " boy evangelist."

No less than twelve regular meetings a day, in addition to informal gatherings under the trees, welcomed the repentant into the fold. Public confession followed the singing of appropriately worded hymns punctuated by booming solicitations from the pious to the wicked to flee the ranks of evildoers. From the 'seventies onward, at their camping grounds at Lake Bluff, north of Chicago along the shores of Lake Michigan, the Methodists found this an effective method of recruitment.[14]

[11] E. C. Hewett, " How Shall We Keep the Boys? ", *The National Sunday School Teacher*, VIII (Oct., 1873), 392–94. A survey of attendance in twenty churches in 1888 showed 3,061 men to 4,018 women. This was explained on the ground that women felt the need for religion more than did men, and that the spiritual seemed more real to them. It was further suggested that pastors did not adapt their sermons sufficiently to men. *The Advance*, XXII (Nov. 29, 1888), 783, (Dec. 6, 1888), 790.

[12] See, for example, the *Baptist Teacher;* Chicago Baptist Association, *Proceedings . . . 1872*, p. 20.

[13] See Rudyard Kipling's account of a sermon in one Chicago church in 1891 which reflected this approach. *American Notes* (Boston, 1899), pp. 97–98.

[14] Pierce, *A History of Chicago*, II, 375–77; *Chicago Tribune*, Aug. 21, 1873, July 1, 1877, Nov. 9, 1880, Aug. 27, 29, Sept. 30, 1881; *The Alliance*, Dec. 16, 1876, p. 17; *The*

A similar procedure obtained in the revival meetings in other seasons of the year. In 1886 the Georgia evangelists Sam Small and Sam Jones, for example, attracted, it was claimed, about 260,000 in their five weeks' stay in Chicago, with the amazing record of only three persons being ejected for bad behavior, and these were little girls wielding spitballs. In 1889 the baseball player William A. Sunday, better known as "Billy," made his first public appearance in Chicago as an evangelist and converted forty-eight youths. But the most important of all the revivalists was Dwight L. Moody, with his famous song-leader, Ira D. Sankey. In 1876, after successfully touring Great Britain and eastern United States, he opened meetings at his tabernacle on Monroe Street. Here in about three months he led 2,500 to take out membership in Protestant churches, a service which made him and his methods acceptable to even the better-educated regular clergy. His Bible Institute, established in 1889, trained women as well as men to spread the gospel without questioning its validity and divine inspiration.[15] In 1890 the evangelist John Alexander Dowie came to Chicago and for three years made his headquarters in Evanston. Carrying on his work under the Divine Healing Association, of which he was president, he held services in tents, halls, and churches throughout the United States and Canada, and on the eve of the World's Fair, he set up Zion's Tabernacle on Sixty-second Street opposite Jackson Park.[16]

Despite the strength thus displayed, orthodox Protestantism in Chicago was confronted with the fierce and divisive force of religious controversy. Proponents of old-time abstractions and dogma saw in the religious debate over biological evolution the demolition of the pillars of their faith; in the textual criticism of the Bible they envisaged the destruction of the spiritual foundation of the ortho-

---

Advance, XX (Jan. 22, 1885), 51–52; *Northwestern Christian Advocate*, XXIX (Aug. 31, 1881), 5; *The Western Catholic*, May 29, 1875; *Skandinaven*, Aug. 14, 1872; *The Chicago Times*, July 30, 1888.

15 *Chicago Tribune*, Oct. 2, 3, 1876, Jan. 17, 1877, Jan. 12, 1885, Feb. 16, 17, 28, March 1, 7, 28, 29, 31, April 5, 6, May 18, 1886, March 5, Dec. 21, 1888, Feb. 18, 1889; *Chicago Evening Journal*, Feb. 18, 1889; *The Alliance*, Sept. 30, 1876, pp. 543, 549; William R. Moody, *The Life of Dwight L. Moody* (New York, 1900), pp. 287–88; E. J. Goodspeed, *A Full History of the Wonderful Career of Moody and Sankey in Great Britain and in America* (Chicago, 1876), p. 315; William G. McLoughlin, Jr., *Billy Sunday Was His Real Name* (Chicago, 1955), pp. 6–8.

16 Rolvix Harlan, *John Alexander Dowie and the Christian Catholic Apostolic Church in Zion* (Evansville, Wis., 1906), p. 34.

doxy to which they subscribed. Alarming, too, was the lively attention which more and more was directed to a consideration of comparative religion. In and around Protestant pulpits the battle raged with fierceness and vigor. From 1872 on, religious periodicals openly attempted to resolve the questions with which religionists were faced. The secular press, too, carried to its readers the significance of discerning the real meaning of the intellectual awakening. " No man with any pretensions to learning," declared the *Tribune* in 1877, " now treats the Development hypothesis in the frivolous manner once so common. . . . Christianity is adapting itself to the Evolution theory much as it did to the Copernican theory." [17] The *Times,* in like vein, saw no challenge to religion in the advancement of science.

> When [said the *Times*] science has taken the field, religion may safely and properly yield it up and pass on toward that realm of mystery where science and religion meet and coalesce in perfect agreement that beyond and above both there exists the same ultimate cause, unconditioned and unknowable. . . . It is perfectly immaterial to any useful religious idea whether human beings were evolved in . . . infinite time from the lowest protoplasmic germ of organic life, or produced instantaneously according to the Mosaic potter's clay theory. Moses and Darwin were alike inquirers after scientific truth, and each proceeded according to the best light of his time. To set up either as an authority, and say that it shall be sinful to inquire further, is not the spirit of religion; it is the function of bigotry. [18]

Foremost in the ranks of liberalism were Dr. David Swing, pastor of the fashionable Fourth Presbyterian Church from 1871 to 1875, and Dr. Hiram W. Thomas, of the Park Avenue Methodist Episcopal Church (1869 to 1872) and of the First Methodist (1872 to 1875). In the pronouncements of these men can be seen the rise of theological liberalism in Chicago; in the opposition to them the persisting play of the forces of traditionalism. Swing, described by an admirer as " the Emerson of our American pulpit " and as " a pulpit essayist rather than a pulpit orator," had from the beginning of his pastorate attracted large audiences, who, not always subscribing to

[17] *Chicago Tribune,* Sept. 9, 1877.
[18] *The Chicago Times,* March 3, 1872.

his views, were nonetheless fascinated by his original interpretations.[19]

It was probably inevitable that charges of heresy be leveled at him by no less a leader of strict construction than Professor Francis L. Patton of the Presbyterian Theological Seminary of the Northwest. Before the Chicago Presbytery on April 13, 1874 he accused Swing of not being "zealous and faithful in maintaining the truths of the Gospel" and of "using equivocal language in respect to fundamental doctrines"; also of rejecting a literal interpretation of the Bible or its plenary inspiration, and of not sincerely receiving and adopting the Confession of Faith of the Presbyterian Church.[20] In public and private discussion the people of the city prepared to defend or condemn, and again the divisive power of opposing ideas permitted little or no neutrality. Those bespeaking toleration for Swing's point of view represented, said the *Times,* "three-fourths of all the brains, courage, and progress of the city of Chicago." They were, of course, in the main a galaxy of the pulpit, representatives of leading Protestant sects, joined by editors of the liberal religious and secular press. In spite of Patton's impassioned appeal Swing was cleared; liberals heralded the verdict of not guilty as a triumph of religion of the spirit over pure dogma. The Congregational *Advance* looked upon the entire controversy as not only a trial of both Swing and Patton but also of Presbyterianism itself, as to whether a man had a right to exercise his own judgment regarding emphasis and methods in matters of creed and dogma.[21]

But Patton was not deterred in pursuing the end he desired. His appeal to the Synod of Illinois North at its October session resulted in the reversal of the decision by the Chicago Presbytery, which directed that the name of David Swing be erased from the roll of the

[19] *The Chicago Pulpit,* I (Jan. 27, 1872), "The Church Reporter"; *Chicago Tribune,* Jan. 4, 1872. Swing had served in the pulpit of Westminster Presbyterian Church from 1866 until it was consolidated with North Presbyterian to form the Fourth in 1871.

[20] *The Chicago Times,* Feb. 24, March 3, April 14, 1874; *Chicago Tribune,* March 1, 5, 6, 8, April 14, 1874; Andreas, *History of Chicago,* II, 802–3; [David S. Johnson, Francis L. Patton, and George C. Noyes, eds.], *The Trial of the Rev. David Swing before the Presbytery of Chicago* (Chicago, 1874), pp. 4–13, 67–133, 173–86; *The World's Edition of the Great Presbyterian Conflict* (Chicago, 1874), pp. 4–5, 92–100.

[21] *Trial of David Swing,* pp. 16–20, 138–47, 204–78; David Swing, *Truths for To-Day* (Chicago, 1874), pp. 313–25; *Chicago Tribune,* May 21, 1874; *The Chicago Times,* May 21, 1874; *The World's Edition of the Great Presbyterian Conflict,* pp. 7, 163–67; *The Advance,* VII (April 30, 1874), 8.

Presbytery of Chicago. Even before this decision Swing, on May 25, announced his resignation from the Presbyterian Church but not from his congregation. In so doing, he based his action on the conviction that Christian brotherhood could be maintained only by love and not by dogma. Nor could he, he declared, continue a relationship so fraught with unhappiness, one which had brought power to another to arraign him as desired " on some dead dogma."

The trial prevented, for a time at least, the broadening of preachments from the Presbyterian pulpit, and liberal theologians as well as laymen were, therefore, forced outside the denomination. Even before the trial was finished a large part of Swing's congregation had signified its intention of retaining him whether within or without the Presbyterian Church. He decided, however, that in the circumstances he should resign also from his pastorate of the Fourth Presbyterian. Inside a week after his resignation, arrangements for establishing a new church society resulted in what came to be called the Central Church of Chicago. On December 5, 1875 services were first held at McVicker's Theatre, and in early March, 1876 steps were taken to organize formally a non-denominational church with Swing as its minister. Over two hundred subscribed to the creed he formulated, declaring themselves desirous of promoting their " own spiritual welfare " and of participating " in the great work of helping others to lead the Christian life, living in a large city, where the moral work to be done " was great.[22] No less important leaders in the community than the eminent Wirt Dexter, solicitor of the Chicago, Burlington & Quincy Railroad, Franklin MacVeagh, wholesale grocer, Leonard Swett, prominent lawyer, and the wealthy Ferdinand W. Peck, energetic promoter of various cultural enterprises, supported the new church.[23]

Soon increasingly large audiences taxed the capacity of McVicker's, and in 1879 the board of trustees leased the newly opened Cen-

[22] *Chicago Tribune,* May 20, 21, 22, 26, June 4, 5, July 6, Oct. 24, 1874, Dec. 6, 1875; *The Chicago Times,* April 24, 29, May 22, 23, Oct. 24, 1874; *Trial of David Swing,* pp. 273, 278, 283; *The Advance,* IX (March 16, 1876), 526; *The Alliance,* March 11, 1876, p. 121.

[23] The above men were on the first board of trustees, besides W. W. Kimball, Orrin W. Potter, Abraham M. Pence, William R. Page, Oliver F. Fuller, and Nathaniel K. Fairbank. Swing's salary was $7,000 at first; in 1878 it was $8,000, and in 1880 it was $10,000. Central Church of Chicago, *Record (Ms.* Chicago Historical Society), pp. 9, 11, 18; *The Advance,* IX (Dec. 9, 1875), 253.

tral Music Hall, where on January 4, 1880 Swing held the first service. Until his death on October 3, 1894 this quiet, unassuming man, who found a refuge in the Congregational Church, became, as Franklin H. Head observed, the guide of those trying to keep touch with the life they were living; for those searching for " a modification of the earlier and sterner tenets of theology," a modification which dwelt more upon " the love and less upon the rigid justice " of God. Through both the spoken and the written word Swing courageously and at times eloquently answered the increased questioning of those longing to reconcile their religious faith and the new urban setting in which they now found themselves.[24]

The case of Dr. Hiram W. Thomas pivoted, as had that of Swing, around his announced deviation from the commonly accepted doctrines of his denomination — the Methodist Episcopal Church. In 1875 he was transferred from Chicago to Aurora for two years by the Rock River Conference, after which he returned to Chicago to serve as pastor of Centenary Methodist Episcopal Church.[25] His substitution of the moral-influence theory for vicarious atonement brought him into conflict with those who held to the old orthodoxy, as did his confession that he did not have settled convictions that after-death punishment was eternal. Nor could he, though believing that those who wrote the Scriptures were inspired, accept the verbal theory of Scripture inspiration. In 1878 the Rock River Conference censured him; two years later it requested his resignation from the Methodist Church.[26]

Thomas, however, refused to resign and insisted upon a formal trial. On October 10, 1881 he was expelled from the ministry and the church, in what his counsel chose to call " a test case," one

[24] *Chicago Tribune*, Dec. 14, 24, 1879; Andreas, *History of Chicago*, III, 652; *The Advance*, VII (Nov. 12, 1874), 187; Franklin H. Head, "Introduction," pp. xv–xviii in David Swing, *Old Pictures of Life*, I (Chicago, 1894). For Swing's sermons and opinions see the Monday issue of *The Inter Ocean* and the *Chicago Tribune*. Writings by Swing are numerous. With Thomas, Helmer, and Horatio Powers, he was editor of the periodical *The Alliance*, which aired their views on religious and moral questions. He also contributed to *The Advance*. Central Music Hall was located on the southeast corner of State and Randolph.

[25] *Chicago Tribune*, Oct. 18, 1875, Oct. 20, 22, 1878; *The Chicago Times*, May 4, 1874; *Northwestern Christian Advocate*, XXIII (Oct. 20, 1875), 4; *Aurora Daily Star*, Feb. 3, 1922, in *Hiram Washington Thomas, 1832–1910, Scrapbook* (Chicago Historical Society).

[26] Rock River Conference, *Minutes of the Annual Conference of the Methodist Episcopal Church . . . 1878*, pp. 12–14, *1880*, pp. 10–18; *Chicago Tribune*, Oct. 11, 12, 16, 18, 19, 1880; *Northwestern Christian Advocate*, XXVIII (Oct. 27, 1880), 1.

which was "looked to by many anxious preachers as settling, not the status of himself, but of the church; . . . and the church, . . . rather than he is condemned." [27] But a way whereby Thomas could carry out his intention to be free, "free to live, and think, and grow with the life of my age," as he put it, had been provided even before the trial was begun. On November 7, 1880 he preached his first sermon in "The People's Church of Chicago," housed in Hooley's Theatre.[28]

All these reconsiderations of the traditional view of the Bible and the origin of man involved, on the one hand, those who held such arguments destructive of all the religious tenets to which men had clung for ages. On the other were ranged those who subscribed to the Swing-Thomas conviction that science need not undermine faith in God. But wherever men stood, their interest in religion had been powerfully stimulated. The ferment of the controversy even seeped into the solid confines of the Roman Catholic Church, through questions raised by the young Father Edward A. Terry of St. Patrick's Church. Addressing the Union Catholic Library Association in May, 1874, he declared it absurd to attempt to circumscribe science through a literal interpretation of the Scriptures. That he had "reconciled Science and Religion in such a way that they can never quarrel again," as the *Tribune* enthusiastically put it, proved, however, far from the truth, for the contemporary controversy but slightly touched the Catholic Church, and Protestant sects continued divided in an unresolved debate.[29]

For some, the best way out was not to attempt any reconciliation between faith and reason. Their conviction that reconciliation was not possible found expression, as early as 1873, in Robert G. Ingersoll's arraignment of religion as intolerant of liberty of thought and as an obstacle to human progress. The trial of Professor Swing gave

[27] *Ibid.,* XXIX (Sept. 14, 1881), 4; *Chicago Tribune,* Sept. 2, 10, Oct. 6, 7, 8, 11, 1881; *The Chicago Times,* Sept. 2, 10, Oct. 6, 8, 11, 1881; Austin Bierbower, "Dr. Thomas and the Methodist Church," in *The People's Pulpit. Complete Sermons of Rev. H. W. Thomas, D.D. Delivered at the People's Church, Chicago, During Church Year Sept. 4, 1887–June 24, 1888* (Chicago, 1888), pp. xliv–xlv.

[28] *Chicago Tribune,* Oct. 11, Nov. 8, 1880; *The Chicago Times,* Oct. 21, 24, 29, 1880; *Northwestern Christian Advocate,* XXVIII (Oct. 27, 1880), 4.

[29] *Chicago Tribune,* May 29, 30, 1874. For the opinion that men of science were not necessarily authorities in religion see *The Standard* [Baptist], XX (Jan. 23, 1873), 2; *The Advance* [Congregational], VII (Oct. 9, 1873), 8–9, VIII (Oct. 1, 1874), 10; *The New World* [Roman Catholic], III (July 13, 1895), 8.

him an opportunity to castigate the Presbytery's endeavor to throttle Swing's speech. In his " Heretics and Heresies of To-Day " Ingersoll made heresy synonymous with progress, later expanding intellectual liberty into " the right to think right and the right to think wrong." As divergent views became more common and more openly expressed, Ingersoll attracted mounting numbers of the curious to his lectures. Throughout the 'seventies and the 'eighties the exposition of his agnosticism, his plea for " the gospel of intelligence," for " the gospel of deed, the gospel of charity, the gospel of self-denial " as a substitute for the doctrine of salvation by faith, challenged all those who saw in religion the hope of the future.[30] Condemnation of " Pope Bob," as the *Times* delighted to call him, ranged from the tolerant tones of Swing and Thomas, who regretted that so powerful an influence dealt with extremes, rather than taking a middle ground, to the unqualified censure of the Reverend William H. Knowlton of St. Andrew's Episcopal Church, who saw him merely as " the blasphemer, the filth dispenser, the willful falsifier of facts." [31]

Holding views similar to those of the spellbinding Ingersoll were less eloquent but equally sincere agnostics such as Circuit Court Judge Henry Booth and General Israel N. Stiles, also a member of the legal profession. Through an open forum the Philosophical Society permitted them to set forth their convictions freely and fully.[32] On October 8, 1880 a group of radical Free-thinkers formed the Chicago Liberal League No. 212, a branch of the National Liberal League, organized in 1876, whose object was to consolidate the liberals to insure the total separation of church and state and the complete secularization of government. Later merged into the American Secular Union, the local chapter broadened the base of its attack on

[30] *Chicago Tribune*, Dec. 22, 1873, May 4, 1874, March 24, April 21, 1879, May 21, 1881, Nov. 26, 1882, May 18, 1885; *The Chicago Times,* May 4, 5, 1874, Sept. 20, 1880; Robert G. Ingersoll, *The Works of Robert G. Ingersoll* (12 v. New York, 1929), I, 188–89, 193, 329–98.

[31] *Chicago Tribune*, Dec. 1, 16, 1878, March 31, April 7, 14, 28, May 19, 1879, Sept. 27, Oct. 4, 1880, Nov. 27, 1882, March 24, 1884; *The Chicago Times,* April 28, 1879; *The Alliance,* Dec. 14, 1878, p. 17; Bert Stewart to Henry D. Lloyd, March 5, 1887, *Lloyd Papers.*

[32] Among the lectures on religious subjects at the meetings of the Philosophical Society in 1873, for example, were " Christianity, the Correlate of Humanity " by the Reverend Minot Judson Savage, "The Origin of Evil: or, Why does not God kill the Devil? " by Gerald Massey, "Inspiration " by Henry Booth. Philosophical Society of Chicago, *Lectures* (*Mss.* Booklet, Chicago Historical Society).

the Christian religion, demanding, among other things, the taxation of church property and the repeal of Sabbath laws.[33]

The establishment of the Society for Ethical Culture of Chicago came in February, 1883, following its organization the previous autumn. On October 1 Professor Felix Adler of New York, the society's founder, spoke on " The True Method of Religious Reform," and set forth his program of ethics without reference to specific theological doctrines. From 1883 to 1892 the Chicago society was under the leadership of the learned William M. Salter, onetime Unitarian minister. Under his guidance pioneering humanitarian projects of wide social significance were undertaken. In 1883 the Society inaugurated district nursing among the sick poor on the North and West sides, an innovation leading to the Visiting Nurses' Association. Five years later it made an equally important contribution to community betterment in the Bureau of Justice, formed to obtain legal aid and protection for the poor, and later merged into the Legal Aid Society.[34]

Both the Society for Ethical Culture and its predecessor the Free Religious Association relied to a considerable extent upon the support of middle-class intellectuals who found Chicago, as Judge Booth put it, a place where freedom in religious belief could survive. Not alone were the native born disbelievers. Along with them went many of alien birth, particularly the better-educated and prosperous Bohemians. The latter, openly describing themselves as Free-thinkers, quoted liberally from the writings of Voltaire, Huxley, Darwin, Thomas Paine, and Ingersoll. Free-thought societies flourished, attracting not only Bohemians but small though vocal groups of Scandinavians and Germans. A Sunday school established in 1888 on the Northwest Side reflected the intention of German workingmen to instill early in life what was considered " a good education in contrast to the so-called Christian education." Particularly conspicuous was the Agnostic Church promoted by the Reverend George Crich-

<hr>

[33] *Chicago Tribune*, Oct. 3, 11, 1875, Oct. 9, 1880, Dec. 25, 1882; *The Chicago Times*, Sept. 19, 1880; *The Western Catholic*, Jan. 24, 1885; *The Knights of Labor*, II (Oct. 22, 1887), 13, III (Feb. 15, 1888), 4; National Liberal League, *Patriotic Address to the People of the United States, adopted at Philadelphia on the Fourth of July, 1876, by the National Liberal League* . . . (Boston, 1876. Newberry Library).

[34] *The Chicago Times*, Oct. 15, 1883; Chicago Ethical Society, *The Chicago Ethical Society. Its History and Its Aims, a Handbook of Information for Inquirers* (Chicago, 1930); American Ethical Union, *The Ethical Societies: A Brief Account of Their Origin, History and Purposes* (New York, 1942), p. 3.

ton Miln in 1882, onetime pastor of Unity (Unitarian) Church. But the radicalism of his ideas failed to attract enough adherents for a continuing forum for their exposition, and shortly Miln abandoned the pulpit altogether.[35]

The impact of these dissident groups was marked. The intellectual crisis thus precipitated was aggravated still more by the higher criticism of the Scriptures. The examination by German scholars of the books of the Bible as historical and literary accounts rather than as the result of divine inspiration deeply shocked the orthodox. In this " rationalistic view of the Scriptures " the *Northwestern Christian Advocate* (Methodist) saw nothing but " absurdity." " It is," commented the journal, " absurd to profess to believe the New Testament, and deny all that is miraculous and supernatural. When all that is miraculous is expunged from the New Testament, but little of the record is left." The appearance of a revised edition of the King James version of the Bible heightened the interest in the new point of view. On May 14, 1881, six days in advance of the publication of the new edition of the New Testament, *The Chicago Times* printed some of the changes it claimed had been made in the revision of both the Old and New Testaments. A printing of the entire revised edition of the New Testament followed on the twenty-second. On the same day the *Tribune* ran a somewhat different version from that of its rival. There followed a bitter controversy about which had printed the authentic edition. Since the Old Testament revision did not appear until 1885 the *Tribune* seemed to have the better of the argument. The vitriolic exchange between the *Times* and the *Tribune,* however, quickened the already deep interest taken by the public in the new version, and sales of the new edition leaped upward.[36]

To add to the divisive forces of the Darwinian theory and the higher criticism, exponents of mysticism warred against traditional practices. Spiritualism gained recruits, claiming no less prominent a

---

[35] *Chicago Tribune,* Jan. 30, 1880, March 13, 14, 19, 27, May 30, Oct. 15, Nov. 24, 1882, Dec. 7, 1885, March 7, 1886; *Svornost,* May 27, Sept. 16, 1884, March 12, 1885; Chicago City Missionary Society, *First Annual Report,* 1884, pp. 6, 10; *The Chicago Times,* Jan. 30, 1875, Oct. 2, 1882; *Illinois Staats-Zeitung,* Jan. 30, 1877; *Chicagoer Arbeiter-Zeitung,* Feb. 16, April 22, 1889.

[36] *The Chicago Times,* May 14, 21, 22, 1881; *Chicago Tribune,* May 22–24, 30, 1881; *Northwestern Christian Advocate,* XXII (July 1, 1874), 6; *The Standard,* XXVIII (May 26, 1881), 4; *The Advance,* XVI (May 26, 1881), 328.

figure than Wilbur F. Storey of *The Chicago Times*. Scant approval was the lot of the spiritualists. Full-length diatribes were directed against them in the form of Sunday sermons, newspaper editorials, and news reports. The reasons for the growth of the cult became the theme of books such as Dr. William A. Hammond's *Spiritualism and Allied Causes of Nervous Derangement,* which held, according to the *Alliance,* that "there is [an] abundant substratum of ignorance and superstition for the mushroom growth of spiritualism." At the same time, the *Alliance* summed up its opinion by declaring: "Spiritualism has revealed many modes of communicating truth, but not any truth." [37]

Others seeking the better life found refuge in Buddhism. In the late 'eighties particularly, those who turned to theosophy were sufficiently influential to attract to Chicago the convention of the American section of the Theosophical Society. Also deviating from those subscribing to the usual pattern of religious expression were the adherents of Mary Baker Eddy, who incorporated June 13, 1886. Their numbers increased rapidly, as they stoically ignored the bitter attacks on their faith that were leveled relentlessly at them. [38]

To these erosions to which historic theology was subjected was added the widespread defection of workingmen from the ranks of Protestantism. In the desperate struggle which was taking place over the distribution of this world's goods, workingmen beheld the clergy, in general, accepting the economic principles of their well-to-do parishioners. They found themselves, moreover, strangers to the rich trappings which wealth now provided in houses of worship. Pew rents too high for them to pay isolated them from those who could afford desirable locations. A sense of loneliness, of degradation, more

---

[37] George C. Lorimer, *Isms Old and New* (2d ed. Chicago, 1881), pp. 211, 212; *Northwestern Christian Advocate,* XXVI (May 15, 1878), 5; *The Knights of Labor,* II (March 12, 1887), 3; *The Standard,* XIX (Dec. 21, 1871), 2; *The Chicago Pulpit,* I (May 11, 1872), "The Church Reporter"; *The Alliance,* Oct. 7, 1876, p. 567, Jan. 12, 1878, pp. 83–84; *The Chicago Times,* March 2, April 1, 1874, Nov. 22, 1875; *Industrial Age,* I (Jan. 31, 1874), 4: *Chicago Tribune,* Aug. 4, 1872, Sept. 17, 18, 1873, Jan. 25, Sept. 19, 1874, Sept. 12, 1881, March 20, June 5, 1882, March 7, 1887, April 2, 1888, March 3, 1890; *Abendpost,* Dec. 14, 1891; Pierce, *A History of Chicago,* II, 411.

[38] *Chicago Tribune,* Sept. 19, 1886, June 15, Dec. 25, 1888, April 29, 30, 1889; *Chicago Daily News,* Feb. 8, March 27, April 23, 1888; *The Standard,* XXXVII (May 1, 1890), 4; Lorimer, *op. cit.,* pp. 156–58; *The Advance,* XXII (May 31, 1888), 337; Church of Christ, Scientist, *Annual of the Church of Christ of Chicago, Illinois* (Chicago, 1887), pp. 6–7. For the establishment of the Society for Natural Healing (Verein für Naturheilkunde) in Jan., 1889, in Chicago, see *Chicagoer Arbeiter-Zeitung,* Feb. 3, 1889.

and more enwrapped them as the 'seventies merged into the 'eighties. " Have the working classes fallen away from the churches or have the churches fallen away from the working classes? " inquired the Reverend Charles F. Goss of the Chicago Avenue Church, as he meditated upon the workingman's indifference and, at times, hostility toward religious institutions. " There is no place," said he, " in the average Chicago church for the poor man . . . surrounded by individuals who not only regard poverty as a disgrace, but by their vulgar display endeavor to perpetually remind the poor man of his poverty." [39]

When workers engaged in a strike to gain what they believed theirs, they heard the clergy voice from the pulpit opinions similar to those held by the men who hired them — that wage reductions stemmed not from the caprice of employers but came as a result of economic laws " as inexorable as the laws of gravitation." In a statement reflecting the general point of view, the Reverend S. J. McPherson of the Second Presbyterian Church declared that labor was merely a commodity, and, therefore, any attempt to evade the laws which controlled it, particularly through collective action, connoted abysmal ignorance. Others, like the Reverend H. M. Paynter of Calvary Tabernacle, condemned the strike as wrong by its very nature, whatever the provocation, and urged that such matters be taken to God for aid and counsel. Throughout, the strike was described not only as an instrument of defiance but as an actual infringement of the law, and as such to be put down and punished.[40]

As strikes spawned violence and laborers united, the clergy, along with other citizens, attacked workingmen in general as socialists and communists who should be hunted down like " mad dogs." To quell radicalism they approved of a strong militia, prompt suppression of independent drill clubs, absolute prohibition of free assem-

[39] The Knights of Labor, I (Nov. 13, 1886), 8, III (Feb. 1, 1888), 4, (Feb. 8, 1888), 4; Chicago Daily News, June 13, 1892.

[40] Chicago Herald, May 10, 1886, Aug. 28, 1893; The Standard, XIX (Jan. 11, 1872), 4; The Advance, VII (Oct. 9, 1873), 5; Northwestern Christian Advocate, XXI (Dec. 31, 1873), 420; Chicago Tribune, Jan. 4, 1874, July 30, 1877, July 6, 1885, July 18, 1892; Public Opinion, I (May 8, 1886), 68; The Knights of Labor, IV (Oct. 20, 1888), 1; Chicagoer Arbeiter-Zeitung, Oct. 15, 1888. For Swing's attitude in the 1870's see The Alliance, May 13, 1876, June 22, 1878; Helen (Swing) Starring, comp., David Swing: A Memorial Volume (Chicago, 1894), p. 392; David Swing, " The Duty of the Pulpit," The Message of David Swing to His Generation, Addresses and Papers (Newell Dwight Hillis, comp., Chicago, 1913), p. 195.

bly where inflammatory speeches might be made, a rigid censorship of the press and of all printed material, and the denial of the vote to communists. On the Sunday following the Haymarket affair, pulpits rang with denunciations of labor. Little, if any, distinction was drawn between violent and law-abiding workingmen.

For much of the ferment, particularly after the late 'seventies, the immigrant received the blame. Preachers piously proclaimed that for the benefit of the country there must be some form of restriction on their entrance to the United States. The alien, too, was held responsible for the growing secularization of the Sabbath, although long working hours for six days a week played their part in a decreasing church attendance. The insistence of Germans on keeping their beer gardens open on Sunday, the customs of the Irish and other foreign born permitting some recreation on Sunday, and the observance of Saturday by the Jews as their day of rest, all appeared to point toward a destruction of the old-time Puritan Sabbath. " The ministers of Jesus Christ who profess to view with such horror the desecration of the Lord's day, can assist in making the [eight-hour] movement a success," commented *The Knights of Labor,* " but to be candid we don't expect much assistance from that source, preachers as a rule are never great leaders in any reform, and the Chicago preachers especially are timid souls without a realizing sense of their responsibility." [41]

Although spokesmen of Protestantism often failed either to understand or to treat sympathetically the growing restiveness of labor in the years following the Great Fire, others faced up to the complex issues posed. In the late 'seventies the Methodist Ministerial Association, in order to get the viewpoint of workingmen, opened their sessions to leading Socialists on May 20, 1878 and invited George Schilling to explain the stand of the moderates. The following summer, Socialist leaders, in turn, inaugurated a series of debates with representatives of the pulpit. But intemperate statements by both sides failed to achieve the reconciliation which might have bridged the gap ever widening between these two vocal segments of society.

No one was more sensitive to the meaning of the alienation of

---

[41] *Chicago Tribune,* July 30, 1877, July 15, 1878; *Chicago Post,* May 13, 20, 1878; *Chicago Herald,* May 10, 1886; *The Knights of Labor,* I (Nov. 6, 1886), 10, IV (Sept. 1, 1888), 1.

workingmen from religious forces than was George C. Lorimer, pastor of the First Baptist Church from 1879 to 1881 and then for ten years of Immanuel Baptist. "Mammonism having no conscience, no truth, it regards those whom it uses for its own advancement as having no soul," he observed on one occasion. "Long hours, short pay for the laborer, short hours and long pay for the capitalist, is its doctrine. It believes in the divine and exclusive right of money. . . . And it stupidly fails to perceive that the science of worldly interests, as now understood, is a monstrous piece of botching, as absurd as it is inhuman, and that as long as it is relied on we need not expect to see any radical abatement of evils which are perpetuating barbarism and breeding dissensions." [42]

With the coming of prosperity in the latter years of the 'eighties, the harsh outlines of the labor protest movement softened. As it did so, Protestant ministers in increasing numbers turned to discussions of the sweating system, of children and women in industry, of the leisure-time activities of men and women who toiled in the factories, and of the hardships of unemployment. They endorsed remedial legislation; they condemned manufacturing and mercantile establishments responsible for long hours, low wages, and poor working conditions. Gradually a more lenient attitude toward the unionization of workers began to break through the almost impregnable hostility of preceding years.[43]

Within the fold of Roman Catholicism, workingmen, often of foreign birth or of alien parentage, felt the warmth of understanding and tolerance. There they predominated in number of communicants, and there they met fellow worshippers on a plane of equality. With the priest looking upon his field of service as primarily among the poor, and the Church's leadership recognizing that the increasingly powerful business corporations were not controlled by Catholics, workingmen by and large found a religious haven in the Catholic faith. Even the Church's hostility toward the secrecy of the Knights of Labor diminished under the influence of Cardinal Gib-

[42] *Chicago Tribune*, May 21, July 4, Nov. 30, 1878; *Chicago Post*, May 20, 1878; Lorimer, *op. cit.*, pp. 306, 310, 315, 321–22; *The Knights of Labor*, II (May 7, 1887), 12.
[43] *The Christian Union*, XXXIII (March 18, 1886), 6, XXXIII (April 8, 1886), 1, 5, XXXIV (Oct. 7, 1886), 1; *The Knights of Labor*, II (May 7, 1887), 6; *The Advance*, XXVII (Feb. 23, 1893), 146, (Dec. 21, 1893), 957; American Federation of Labor, *Proceedings, 1893*, "Report of Proceedings of the Thirteenth Annual Convention," pp. 26, 28.

bons of Baltimore, and his insistence upon a sympathetic approach to the problems of the worker preserved for the Church the loyalty of this vast part of the American population. The *Rerum Novarum* of Pope Leo XIII in 1891, by giving approval to combinations of labor and by endorsing a broad social program, while condemning socialism, placed that church in the vanguard of humanitarians.[44]

The humanitarianism of the Catholics was, therefore, in a very real sense collective, strengthened by official sanction. Not so was that of Protestantism. Here the movement for social welfare received impetus from isolated undertakings, sponsored more often than not by individual churches under the leadership of a liberal theologian. Within the city, missions were expanded beyond the mere design of gaining converts, to the consideration and care of daily human needs. As mission chapels became churches, they frequently extended the number of their services. When the Congregational City Missionary Society, later called the Chicago Congregational Union, was established in 1882, its founders recognized the new conditions which a growing city imposed upon the religious structure. Conscious of the antithetical forces of urban anonymity and multifarious personal contacts attended by a deepening social stratification, the Union's leaders enlarged their ministrations to include kindergartens, an industrial school for girls, mothers' meetings, and rooms for reading and recreation especially for young men. From 1883 to 1890, for instance, the Chicago City Missionary Society had organized twenty-four churches and proudly pointed to their 1,552 members, their twenty-seven Sunday schools with 7,649 in attendance, not to mention the aid given forty-two churches and missions. Teachers were trained to carry on the expanded program of the missions, which, in many instances, was pointed toward inducting the immigrant into the American way of life.

Although the Congregationalists were particularly active from the 1880's on in many of these services, other denominations recognized the duties with which the church was faced. The Episcopalians, for

[44] *The Knights of Labor*, I (Oct. 16, 1886), 6; *The Western Catholic*, June 19, 1875, March 5, 19, 1887; *Chicago Tribune*, March 3, 4, May 1, 1887; John Gilmary Shea, "Labor Discontent," *The American Catholic Quarterly Review*, VII (Oct., 1882), 700–12; Monseigneur Charles de T'Serclaes, *The Life and Labors of Pope Leo XIII* (Maurice Francis Egan, ed., New York, 1903), pp. 224–25. For a discussion of the attitude toward the Knights of Labor see Browne, *The Catholic Church and the Knights of Labor*.

example, in the late 'eighties sponsored a school for deaf mutes and a home for incurables. In addition, they continued their support of St. Luke's Hospital, located at 1426 to 1430 Indiana Avenue, where all but a few rooms were devoted to charity patients, and where a training school for nurses and a diet school were conducted. In 1890 they founded the Church Home for Aged Women, at 4327 Ellis Avenue.[45]

Particularly well known for its early ministrations to the floating population, which frequented the so-called "vicious" section down-town, was the Pacific Garden Mission. Established in 1877 by Colonel George R. Clarke, a veteran of the Union army, this non-sectarian mission on " Bum Boulevard " not only sought converts to religion but conducted a Sunday school and, from 1881, a kindergarten, of which Mrs. Robert D. Fowler was a benefactor.[46]

Also non-sectarian in preaching the gospel, and representative of the philanthropy of Chicago's wealthy men, was the Armour Mission, opened December 5, 1886, at Thirty-third and Butterfield streets. Here were provided educational opportunities — including a kindergarten, library, literary societies, and lectures, a free medical dispensary, a kitchen garden, a sewing or workroom for women, nurseries, and bathrooms. The mission was named for Joseph F. Armour, who at his death had left $100,000 for its endowment, a sum supplemented by his brother Philip D. Armour.[47]

Organizations for youth further broadened the base of Christian

[45] Among others, the Presbyterian Hospital was opened on Wood near Harrison in 1884; the Methodists sponsored the Wesley Hospital at 355 Ohio in 1888; the Baptists established the Chicago Baptist Hospital at Centre and Racine Avenue in 1891; the Swedish Lutheran Church the Augustana Hospital at Lincoln and Cleveland avenues in 1892. John Visher, Hand-Book of Charities (3d ed. Chicago, 1897), pp. 172, 184–86, 189–90, 194, 197, 203–5; The Chicago Times, April 12, 1874, June 3, 1881; The Chicago Pulpit, IV (July 26, 1873), " The Church Reporter "; Chicago City Missionary Society, Seventh Annual Report, 1890, p. 19 (see also fifth and sixth annual reports); Warren E. Thompson, ed., Building a Christian Chicago: A History of the Chicago Congregational Union, 1882–1932 (n.p., n.d.), p. 13; Andreas, History of Chicago, III, 806; The Advance, XXII (April 19, 1888), 244, (July 19, 1888), 460; The Living Church, XII (June 8, 1889), 148, (July 20, 1889), 244; Protestant Episcopal Church, Journal, 1892, p. 14; Chicago Baptist Association, Proceedings, 1892, p. 7; Roswell Park, " The Medical Charities of Cook County, Illinois," in Illinois Board of State Commissioners of Public Charities, Sixth Biennial Report, 1880, p. 319; Pierce, A History of Chicago, II, 451.
[46] The Advance, XXXI (Feb. 6, 1896), 193; Chicago Tribune, Dec. 24, 1882, Dec. 25, 1888; Carl F. H. Henry, The Pacific Garden Mission (4th ed. Grand Rapids, Mich., [1942]).
[47] Chicago Tribune, Dec. 5, 1886; The Christian Union, XXXIV (Dec. 9, 1886), 8, (Dec. 16, 1886), 8.

and humanitarian service. The Chicago Christian Endeavor Union took shape in 1887 and embraced representatives of the Congregational, Reformed Episcopalian, Presbyterian, and the Dwight L. Moody churches. During the 'eighties the Methodists set up the Epworth League, and the Episcopalians turned with similar interest to the Brotherhood of St. Andrew. The annual celebration of Children's Day on the second Sunday in June as early as 1872 presaged a day when child welfare was to become one of the important movements for social betterment. The special attention paid by religious organizations to the problems confronting youth in a growing city was no better illustrated than in the Youth's Training and Employment Association, which, among other things, agitated in 1888 for a grant of funds from the state legislature to be used in the training of young people.[48]

While organizations took shape in growing numbers under religious auspices, those like the Chicago Christian Union and the Young Men's Christian Association extended their original programs. The former, established eight days after the Great Fire, to give aid to young men thrown out of work, enjoyed the support of prominent Chicagoans such as George M. Pullman, W. F. Coolbaugh, George B. Carpenter, A. B. Meeker, C. C. Bonney, William E. Doggett, and David Swing. By 1873 two divisions, reflecting the prosperity and popularity of the Union, maintained a library of about two thousand volumes, two literary societies, and an employment bureau.

There was, however, no more useful organization than the Young Men's Christian Association, which had originated in 1858. By 1873 its membership reached 1,011; its library contained 2,600 volumes; and its *Everybody's Paper,* published in Chicago, attained a satisfying 60,000 copies a month. Not the least of its recreational facilities was the gymnasium, where a variety of equipment attracted 1,600 to its classes in 1886. As outlying parts of the city were peopled,

[48] Samuel Nicholas Reep, *The Organization of the Ecclesiastical Institutions of a Metropolitan Community* (Minneapolis, 1910), pp. 49–57; *The Standard,* XXXVII (June 19, 1890), 1; Protestant Episcopal Church, *Journal, 1888,* p. 46; *The Congregational Year-Book, 1892,* pp. 130–33; *The Advance,* XXII (July 5, 1888), 424, (July 12, 1888), 436; Rock River Conference, *Register of the Thirty-third Annual Session . . . of the Methodist Church . . . 1872,* p. 23; *Northwestern Christian Advocate,* XXVI (June 12, 1878), 4, XXXIX (Jan. 21, 1891), 1; *The Advance,* XXII (April 5, 1888), 209, (July 5, 1888), 424, (July 12, 1888), 436.

branches of the Association were set up to care for neighborhood needs. Here gospel meetings were held, musical and literary entertainments were provided, and, as soon as possible, libraries were made available. The Association's work, broadened to include those from foreign lands, was directed principally to Scandinavian young men from 1872 and to German especially after 1889. In its three divisions devoted to work among railroad employees, the Association by 1882 had set up courses in vocational training, in penmanship, and in arithmetic. Its social rooms were designed to be so attractive to visitors that they would displace the interest many had in beer gardens. Throughout the wide range of its activities, from the religious instruction to the secular programs, the Y.M.C.A. had the support of some of the wealthiest and most prominent men of Chicago, including the John V. Farwells, Cyrus H. McCormick, J. L. Houghteling, Henry J. Willing, T. W. Harvey, and H. E. Sargent.[49]

The Y.M.C.A.'s sister organization, the Young Women's Christian Association, began in 1876, incorporating as the Woman's Christian Association of Chicago on April 12, 1877. In 1886 it became known as the Young Women's Christian Association. On its board of managers were representatives of many of the Protestant denominations of the city. They bound themselves to assist the Association " to seek out women taking up their residence in Chicago, and endeavor to bring them under moral and religious influences, by aiding them in the selection of suitable boarding places and employment, by introducing them to the members and privileges of this Association, securing their attendance at some place of worship on the Sabbath, and by every means in their power surrounding them with Christian associates."

An important service of the women's organization, as of the Y.M.C.A., was its employment bureau. The Young Women's Association also sponsored visitation of the sick, hospital care, and, until 1884, tract distribution in the local jails. In the decade 1884–94 a

[49] Pamphlet, pp. 7–8, 13, in Charles C. Bonney, *Personal Miscellany* (14 v. John Crerar Library), IV (1871–1873); Young Men's Christian Associations of the United States and Dominion of Canada, *Year Book . . . 1891*, pp. 3, 114–15, 141, 152, 156, 160; Young Men's Christian Association, Board of Managers, *Minutes, June, 1858 — December, 1888* (*Mss.* vol. Central Y.M.C.A., Chicago), Meeting of Nov. 1, 1873, p 294; *Chicago Tribune*, March 22, Oct. 18, 1873, Nov. 8, 1878, April 2, 1883, March 8, 14, 1886.

Protective and Provident League for Working Women, a free dispensary, and a Travelers' Aid department were added as important aspects of the Association's work. Only women could become active and associate members of the Y.W. but men could enroll as honorary life members, and the dues assessed from all these became a part of the support fund.[50]

The religious fervor which was in essence the wellspring of the various activities of the Y.M.C.A. and Y.W.C.A. permeated also the drum-beating and cymbal-playing Salvation Army. It was not until January 31, 1885, five years after coming to the United States, that the Army reached Chicago; its first emissaries were Captain and Mrs. William Evans and Captain Edwin Gay. On Sunday afternoon, March 1, the first meeting took place in Bush's Hall, corner of North Clark Street and Chicago Avenue. In this place, equipped with rough wooden benches and a pine-board platform fronted by a kneeling-bench for the penitent, about sixty people listened to the revivalist message of Captain Evans and the warm-throated songs of Mrs. Evans, sung to the accompaniment of a concertina. But there was no "awakening" in any of the listeners; no converts sought the kneeling-bench. By the last of March, however, the Captain and his assistants proudly reported the conversion of fifteen within a week. Shortly thereafter they announced the establishment of district offices at 865 West Madison Street.

Great hardship, derision and disdain not only from the law-breakers and the irreligious, but many times from the law-abiding and religious marked the early months of the Salvation Army in Chicago. But the Army workers were undismayed, and openly proclaimed that they were " willing to be martyrs to the Lord . . . willing to be persecuted in the cause of right." By the latter part of the 'eighties a change in attitude toward the Army became apparent, and, in spite of its noise and unorthodox methods, it received more sympathy than at first. The launching of its general social services did not come until June, 1892, with the opening of a slum post in

50 Woman's Christian Association of Chicago, Illinois, Seventh Annual Report . . . ending November 1, 1883 (Chicago, 1884), pp. 5–7, 10–11, 13–17, 24, Eighth Annual Report, 1884, pp. 18, 21; Young Women's Christian Association of Chicago, Illinois, Tenth Annual Report . . . ending November 1, 1886, pp. 18, 20, Eleventh Annual Report, 1887, pp. 3, 5–8, 18–21, 32, Eighteenth Annual Report, 1894, pp. 27–28, 30–33, 35. In 1887 men enrolled as honorary members included J. V. Farwell, P. D. Armour, William G. Hibbard, H. A. Hurlbut, and H. J. Willing.

the vicinity of Twelfth and Halsted streets, and in Chicago, as elsewhere, these services were designed to regenerate through a humanitarianism coexistent with conversion to the Protestant religion.[51]

The fragmentation in Protestantism as seen in rival denominations
was, of course, not present in Roman Catholicism. All agencies
which spread the faith had their source, their purpose, and their
destiny residing in one body. This unity, marred at times by the dissension between communicants of different national backgrounds
and even of factions within one ethnic group, nevertheless maintained with considerable unanimity the faith to which they subscribed.[52] This solidarity and the large number of Catholics in Chicago indicated the predominance of that church in a variety of ways.
In the realm of humanitarian undertakings this was particularly
apparent. The Catholics had more hospitals to care for the sick than
any Protestant group had. Outstanding among them was the Alexian
Brothers' Hospital, founded in 1866 and restored the year after the
Great Fire. It accepted both charity and pay male patients having
non-contagious diseases, and it conducted a training school for male
nurses. In its dispensary both men and women, chiefly of the Catholic faith, received treatment. Mercy Hospital, incorporated in 1852
and operated by the Sisters of Mercy; St. Joseph's, opened in 1872
and supervised by the Sisters of Charity of St. Joseph; and St. Elizabeth's Hospital, from 1887 under the direction of the Poor Hand-
Maids of Jesus Christ, added to an increasing number of facilities of
this nature.[53]

The Catholics extended their ministrations widely, caring for the
poverty-stricken as well as the sick. Dependent children received

[51] *Chicago Tribune,* Feb. 4, 27, March 2, 3, 4, 8, 9, 10, April 1, 2, 4, 11, May 31, Aug.
27, 28, 1885, Nov. 1, 2, 3, 1886, Jan. 9, May 31, 1887, April 30, 1888, April 24, May 15,
26, 1893; *Chicago Daily News,* Nov. 17, 1890; *War Cry* (New York edition) scattered
issues beginning April, 1885, through year 1893 (Courtesy Mr. Allen Bosch from his *The
Salvation Army in Chicago* [Ph.D. thesis in progress, The University of Chicago]).

[52] For example, the Polish parishes of St. Stanislaus Kostka and the Holy Trinity warred
intermittently between 1874 and 1893 over the matter of separate priests. (*Chicago Tribune,*
Nov. 4, 1878, Jan. 5, 1891; Thompson, *The Archdiocese of Chicago: Antecedents and
Development,* p. 425.) The Germans objected to what they considered a subordination of
German to Irish priests. *The Western Catholic,* Sept. 10, 1887.

[53] *The New World,* V (Oct. 3, 1896), 9; Illinois Board of State Commissioners of
Public Charities, *Sixth Biennial Report, 1880,* pp. 318, 319; *Chicago Tribune,* Aug. 30,
1873; *Appeal in Behalf of the New Saint Elizabeth's Hospital* (Pamphlet, n.d., Chicago
Historical Society); *Illinois Staats-Zeitung,* Oct. 13, 1887; *The Western Catholic,* May 4,
1872; Visher, *op. cit.,* pp. 173, 178.

serious consideration, notably from 1877 in the Chicago Industrial School for Girls and from 1882 in St. Mary's Training School for Boys. Orphans and children whose parents could not provide for them were looked after in institutions such as the Guardian Angel Orphan Asylum, the Holy Family Orphan Asylum for Polish and Bohemian children, St. Joseph's Orphan Asylum, St. Joseph's Providence Orphan Asylum for boys, and St. Vincent's Infant Asylum. A Catholic Day Home, one of the enterprises of the Poor Hand-Maids of Jesus Christ, provided a kindergarten to relieve poor working mothers of the responsibility of their children. The House of Mercy (also known as the House of Providence for Young Women) gave assistance to distressed women of good character, and St. Joseph's Home and St. Francis' House of Providence furnished accommodations to employed women.[54]

Performing many of the services for the Catholics that the Y.M.C.A. did for the Protestants was the Union Catholic Library Association, established in 1868 and reorganized in 1889. Originally, the Association set up a library and reading room and carried on a series of lectures and debates in which the prominent Catholic layman William J. Onahan played a major role. It also held entertainments. Upon reorganization in 1889, the Association changed its name to the Columbus Club, and outlined a program of mutual benefit among Catholic laymen and the advancement of Catholic principles and interests in general. Despite the high hopes of its backers, it lacked support from the Catholic public, and fell victim to the Panic of 1893.[55]

No religious group was more affected by the swift-moving currents of the late nineteenth century than were the Jews. The changes that occurred among them were as profound, if not more so, than those that took place in Protestantism as it responded to the impact of the theory of evolution and the higher criticism. Not only was religious doctrine itself drastically changed, but its form and expression were adapted to the Reform Movement then under way. In this movement, Sinai Temple was especially active, in 1872 present-

[54] *Ibid.*, pp. 173–75, 177–80, 183; Illinois Board of State Commissioners of Public Charities, *Eighth Biennial Report, 1884*, pp. 273–75, 277.

[55] Sister M. Sevina Pahorezki, *The Social and Political Activities of William James Onahan* (Washington, 1942), pp. 42–44; *The Chicago Pulpit*, III (May 24, 1873), "The Church Reporter"; *Chicago Tribune*, Jan. 15, June 13, 1873.

ing lectures on Sunday and deciding to employ a rabbi who could speak English for the benefit of the young people attending services. To this congregation in 1880 came the young, brilliant, dynamic Dr. Emil G. Hirsch, at an early time recognized as one of the leaders giving social emphasis to Judaism. In 1884 all but a few Hebrew prayers were dropped from Sinai's ritual. Dr. Hirsch appeared in broadcloth rather than in the regulation costume of orthodox Jewry as he addressed his fashionable congregation of Jewish bankers, merchants, lawyers, and other professional men, chiefly of German extraction.

The Reform Movement also had the aggressive support of the Reverend Dr. Samuel Sale, successor in 1883 to Dr. Liebman Adler at Kehilath Anshe Maariv, the oldest and probably the largest Jewish society in Chicago. As a member of the committee to draft the set of declarations at the Pittsburgh rabbinical conference in 1885, he openly placed himself in the vanguard of the Reform Movement. This, of course, meant his acquiescence in the adoption of ceremonies harmonizing with modern civilization; the rejection of laws regulating diet, priestly purity, and dress as inappropriate to the times; and the substitution of the concept of the Jews as a religious community for that of the Jews as a nation. On the whole, however, the Reform Movement did not attract the Jews of Russo-Polish, Galician, and Rumanian background, who worshipped according to the traditional ritual, with the men separated from the women, their heads covered with prayer shawls, and standing as they read with the cantor. At most synagogues in the city this kind of service prevailed on Saturday despite the economic hardship imposed upon workers forced thus to lose two days in earning a livelihood.[56]

The humanitarian projects of the Jews were broadly gauged, thoughtfully conceived, and well conducted. The United Hebrew Relief Association had a long record of outstanding relief work, since 1859 directed to a considerable extent toward the relief of the poverty-stricken. Its services were assured only after careful investigation as to the necessity of aid. In October, 1889 the Association passed into the hands of what was known as the United Hebrew

    [56] *The Occident,* May 30, 1884, Nov. 20, 1885, June 18, Sept. 17, 1886, March 23, 1888, Feb. 14, 1890; Sinai Congregation Executive Board, *Minutes,* Sept. 1, 1872, Feb. 19, 1880, Dec. 28, 1885; *The Reform Advocate,* Sept. 4, 26, 1891; *Chicago Tribune,* May 15, 1893. See Chapter II, "The Fabric of Society."

Charities of Chicago, whose well co-ordinated activities reflected good management and effective assistance to the needy. The laying of the cornerstone of Michael Reese Hospital, November 4, 1880, promised the sick of the day outstanding medical attention; its training school for nurses attained high standing, and its dispensary, opened in 1887, was reported one of the best-equipped in the Middle West. An employment bureau, as in the case of other relief agencies, helped prevent the extension of relief rolls after it was instituted January 1, 1884 as a part of the Relief Association work. A Young Men's Hebrew Charity Association assisted in promoting these worth-while undertakings, as did several women's sewing groups and the Young Ladies' Aid Society.

All these activities of Chicago Jewry were interpreted to the gentiles of the community with special effectiveness, particularly by the Reform rabbis, and notably by Dr. Hirsch. His advocacy of social betterment gained the support of non-Jews as well as Jews as he championed mothers' pensions, the placement of orphans in homes rather than the so-called asylums of the day, and psychological studies of those who committed crimes. He urged federated charities in a day when federation was seldom thought of, and he promoted with untiring zeal vocational guidance and training. He softened the harsh outlines of intolerance existing among faiths by encouraging and accepting opportunities to exchange pulpits with his gentile counterparts.[57]

A gradual breakdown of hitherto impenetrable barriers among sects had, however, been going on ever since the Great Fire, when the spirit of compassion which wells out of disasters had led unharmed churches to share their quarters with members of those burned down. Union meetings became common, and nurtured as never before the hope that sectarianism would not continue to set apart members of the Christian community. The plea of church periodicals for a strengthening of this spirit of unity through the abandonment of denominational labels and the reconciliation of creedal differences eventually proved, as one journal put it, " more amiable in intent than successful in fact." Amalgamation of different churches, however, as in the case of the consolidation of the North

---

[57] United Hebrew Relief Association annual reports; *The Reform Advocate*, June 12, Nov. 28, 1891. See *The Universal Jewish Encyclopedia* for biographical essay on Hirsch.

Presbyterian with Swing's Westminster Presbyterian in 1871, took place under the impulse of the broadening humanitarianism of the day. All Souls' Unitarian Church, organized in 1882 under the leadership of the tireless and aggressive Jenkin Lloyd Jones, sought to promote the same general objective. It became an outstanding example of the institutional church consecrated to the practice of democracy and the brotherhood of man. Also laboring to extend the frontiers of the new liberalism was the Reverend Frank W. Gunsaulus, who took over the pastorate of Plymouth Congregational Church in 1887 and, after a prosperous twelve years' ministry there, succeeded to the pulpit of the famous Central Church.[58]

While it seemed impractical to abandon sectarianism as such, it nevertheless was feasible to resort to concerted action to disseminate the social gospel program among the various evangelical denominations and non-sectarian organizations. It was easy through intra-city conferences to advance schemes for social betterment; it was equally easy to exchange views at the various national conventions held more frequently from the 1880's on. Typical and outstanding was the consolidation of activities within the city of the Methodist Institutional churches through the Chicago Home Missionary and Church Extension Society, incorporated in 1885. Indeed, where the city-wide missionary societies had been infiltrated with the philosophy of social service along with spreading the gospel, modest church buildings arose where not only religious services but humanitarian activities were conducted.

The mid-'eighties were, by and large, a flowering of the incentive toward co-operative action. Conferences and conventions in Chicago paid tribute to the city's alertness to the implications of the immediate social obligations of religious agencies. Sometimes non-denominational in membership, they were designed as a free exchange of opinion and experience, untheoretical in character. Such was the gathering which occurred on June 16, 1886, when the Convention of

[58] *The Chicago Pulpit*, I (Jan. 6, 1872), (Feb. 10, 1872), (April 7, 1872), (April 27, 1872), (May 11, 1872), "The Church Reporter"; *Chicago Post and Mail*, Feb. 4, 1876; *The Standard*, XIX (March 28, 1872), 1, XX (Oct. 31, 1872), 1; *The Advance*, VII (Oct. 9, 1873), 1, (Nov. 6, 1873), 8, (March 26, 1874), 1, VIII (Oct. 8, 1874), 1, (Jan. 14, 1875), 366, (Jan. 21, 1875), 383, (Feb. 11, 1875), 430, XXII (Jan. 12, 1888), 24, (March 1, 1888), 137; Aaron Ignatius Abell, *The Urban Impact on American Protestantism 1865–1900* (Cambridge, 1943), pp. 159–60; William Kent, "Jenkin Lloyd Jones," *The American Magazine*, LXX (July, 1910), 320–21, 323; Moses and Kirkland, *op. cit.*, II, 343.

Christian Workers, made up of various groups of missionaries in cities and towns, ministers, and evangelists, assembled. For eight days they pondered the complex problems commonly faced by those working among people not reached by the usual sources. In the end they resolved " to promote union among the various city evangelization agencies " and to " co-operate with the churches without regard to denomination."

Different in purpose and deliberation was the Bible and Prophetic Conference, called by distinguished leaders of various denominations whose delegates indulged in learned and sometimes bitter discussions on the aim of world-wide evangelism as found in the doctrine of the Second Coming. *The Christian Union,* reporting the strained atmosphere of the conference, observed philosophically, however, that " without doubt the result of the meeting will be to quicken Bible study."

The year 1890 saw the culmination of years of effort on the part of a few Protestant divines to bring about a better climate of opinion regarding the Jews. Thanks primarily to the persistence of the Reverend William E. Blackstone, a conference of Jewish rabbis and gentile clergymen was called on November 24 and 25. The name, the Conference on the Past, Present, and Future of Israel, under which the conference assembled, gave the key to its eventual purpose. Resolutions of sympathy with the oppressed Jews of Russia were passed and forwarded to the Czar by the conference; as a result of the meeting, the Reverend Blackstone drew up a memorial, signed by important figures in the country, to the President of the United States, requesting him to promote a congress of European powers which should return Palestine to the Jews.

The spirit of brotherhood which had motivated all such gatherings, whether successful or unsuccessful judged in terms of accomplishments, culminated in the World's Parliament of Religions, the first of its kind, at the Columbian Exposition in 1893. Here the motto, in the words of Malachi, " Have we not all one Father? Hath not one God created us? " epitomized the aim in mind and served as a beacon of tolerance to men of the East and the West.[59]

---

[59] *The Christian Union,* XXXIII (May 6, 1886), 20, XXXIV (July 8, 1886), 20, (Nov. 25, 1886), 8; Abell, *op. cit.,* pp. 95–96, 168; *The Jewish Era,* I (Jan., 1892), 15; Meites, *History of the Jews of Chicago,* pp. 164–67; F. H. Stead, " The Story of the World's Parliament of Religions," *Review of Reviews* [New York], IX (March, 1894), 299–310. The

Whatever the signs of a growing tolerance among the various sects, few, if any, included the Roman Catholics. Within the larger framework of Protestant antagonism there was little new; nor did the Catholic response in any degree differ from what it had been since the earliest days. As in the past, a center of controversy was the public school — the use of taxes for its sole support, and the reading of the Bible. With its large foreign-born membership, the Catholic Church also continued to be the target of those who found all immigrants objectionable. The fear that the solid pillars of government would eventually be undermined by an increasing number of newcomers held in its grip the minds of many. The cohesiveness of the Catholics against assaults that varied from mild criticisms to insidious imputations and open charges of anti-Americanism only cemented, on the other hand, the forces opposed to them.[60]

All these charges were aired in the anti-Catholic columns of religious publications and in such a journal as *America,* put out in Chicago as the expositor of the American Protective Association's opinions. In 1889 a cartoon in *America* epitomized this stand. An Irishman, sitting astride a bag captioned " The Irish Bagging Trust — Public Schools, Public Office, Public Money," brandishes a club at Uncle Sam. Then follow the words of an Irish agitator: " I am going to start an Irish Republic." To this Uncle Sam replies: " I wish you would start something of your own. You will soon push me out of house and home." [61]

A wide range of journals and other publications reflected the shadings of denominational doctrines and mirrored a profound public in-

Parliament of Religions is discussed more fully at a later point. The preceding are by no means inclusive of all the co-operative efforts in which Chicagoans engaged. The Chicago Bible Society, organized as an auxiliary to the American Bible Society, for example, was incorporated in 1889. Chicago Bible Society, *Fifty-first Annual Report . . . 1891* (Chicago, 1891), title page. For its earlier activities see Pierce, *A History of Chicago,* II, 374–75.

[60] *Ibid.,* I, 232, 295–96, II, 379–81; *The Chicago Times,* June 16, 1874, Nov. 26, 1875; *America,* I (Oct. 18, 1888), 2, III (March 13, 1890), 745–46, IV (Sept. 18, 1890), 682; *Chicago Daily News,* Oct. 17, 1892; *Chicago Tribune,* July 28, Oct. 18, 1873, Feb. 10, 1875, Feb. 27, 29, March 1, 1888; *The Inter Ocean,* Nov. 1, 1890; *The Standard,* XIX (March 28, 1872), 4, XXXVII (April 10, 1890), 4; *The Advance,* XXII (Nov. 22, 1888), 749; *Northwestern Christian Advocate,* XXIII (Oct. 13, 1875), 4; *The Living Church,* XI (Jan. 12, 1889), 648–49, XII (Oct. 5, 1889), 424.

[61] *America,* III (Oct. 3, 1889), 3. For a series of sermons on the relation of the Catholic Church to American institutions see *ibid.,* Dec. 19, 1889, p. 362. For comment on the A.P.A. movement see *Illinois Staats-Zeitung,* Oct. 20, 1892; Thomas Jefferson Jenkins, " The A.P.A. Conspirators," *The Catholic World,* LVII (Aug., 1893), 685–93.

terest in religion in its varied aspects. As time went on, periodical literature was extended in many instances to embrace discussions about
conditions created by the rapidly growing city. The Congregational
Advance, the Methodist Episcopal *Northwestern Christian Advocate,* the Baptist *Standard,* the Presbyterian *Interior,* and *The Western Catholic* carried on as in the years before the Great Fire. In 1878
the Unitarians established *Unity. The Universalist* started publication in 1883, succeeding the former *New Covenant;* and *The Free
Methodist,* the only organ of that denomination, moved to Chicago
in 1880. For the Episcopalians *The Living Church,* founded in 1878
as a weekly, soon exceeded in circulation that denomination's weeklies in New York and Philadelphia. *St. Andrew's Cross,* begun in
September, 1886 under the aegis of the Brotherhood of St. Andrew,
promoted zealously the ideals of the social gospel as envisaged by that
Episcopal organization.

Besides the well-established *Western Catholic,* Catholic families
and societies had *The Catholic Home.* Numerous journals put out
by Germans and Irish bespoke the strong influence of these groups
in the Roman Catholic Church. The Second Adventists published
Our Rest and Signs of the Times, and the Reformed Jews *The Occident* and *The Reform Advocate,* the latter edited by Rabbi Hirsch.
In 1873 the *Alliance* was started to express the liberal thought of various well-known divines including Swing, H. W. Thomas, the Episcopalian H. N. Powers, the Congregationalist C. D. Helmer, the
Unitarian Robert Collyer, and the Baptist William Mathews. Following the Reverend J. B. McClure, its first managing editor, were various members of the liberal clergy including David Swing, under
whom the journal became the advocate of the independent church
movement. In 1882 it was merged into the new *Weekly Magazine,*
a literary journal that terminated in bankruptcy two years later. To
this imposing list should be added the *Chicago Pulpit,* which began
in December, 1871, to publish weekly important news and announcements. Its columns made available also the sermons of leading ministers, a service of some of the lay press antedating the Great Fire.[62]

The lively concern over religion so evident in many ways was expressed in the growing number of theological seminaries, some of

[62] The names and runs of most of these journals may be found in Scott, *Newspapers
and Periodicals of Illinois,* and W.P.A., *Bibliography of Foreign Language Newspapers.*

which had been in existence since the 1850's. Garrett Biblical Institute (Methodist) in Evanston, the Chicago Theological Seminary (Congregational), the Presbyterian Theological Seminary of the Northwest, to be known in 1886 as the McCormick Theological Seminary of the Presbyterian Church because of the large gifts of Cyrus McCormick, and the Baptist Union Theological Seminary were among the leading Protestant schools. In 1883 the Western Theological Semin ary of the Episcopal Church was established to train candidates for the ministry; the German Theological Seminary of the Lutheran Church was dedicated in 1885, and the Norwegian Theological Seminary of the Evangelical Lutheran Church in 1891.[63]

Lack of financial resources frequently plagued the administration of these institutions, relying as they did to a considerable extent on the beneficence of well-to-do members of the various churches with which they were linked. In 1877 the Baptists, burdened by debt, transferred their school to Morgan Park on the grant of lands and a building by the Blue Island Land and Building Company. In the early 'eighties the generosity of John D. Rockefeller, in addition to the large gifts of E. Nelson Blake, placed the seminary on a sounder financial basis than it had previously enjoyed. The Western Education Society, which gave financial assistance to students enrolled in the Chicago Theological Seminary and other Congregational establishments, found its treasury so depleted that in 1872 it begged for more support from contributors. " It seems to be increasingly true at this epoch of the Church," commented the secretary of the Society, " that sons of affluence do not enter upon preparation for the gospel ministry. Forty of the fifty members of the Chicago Theological Seminary, last year, were aided by this society. Several young men of decided promise, in different stages of preparation, have been compelled to stop in their course, because the Executive Committee absolutely had no funds to disburse." [64]

[63] Pierce, A History of Chicago, II, 397; The Christian Union, XXXIII (June 3, 1886), 6; Chicago Tribune, April 3, 1891; The Chicago Times, May 16, 1879; Moses and Kirkland, op. cit., II, 119–21; Skandinaven, Oct. 6, 1911; Curry, Chicago: Its History and Its Builders, II, 331–32. Lakeside Directory, 1893, p. 27, lists a Christian Science Theological Seminary.
[64] The Chicago Times, May 14, 1874, Oct. 24, 1880; Thomas Wakefield Goodspeed, A History of the University of Chicago (Chicago, 1916), pp. 23–27; Moses Smith, Secretary of the Western Education Society, Chicago, to " Its Constituency," May 1, 1872 (Mss. Chicago Historical Society); Congregational Quarterly, n.s. IV (Jan., 1872), 163; The Advance, VI (Jan. 16, 1872), 9.

As churches became alert to the implications of urban development and embarked on plans for the betterment of society, theological seminaries gradually undertook to equip students for the new approach. After 1880 sociological instruction, supplemented by lectures on prevailing social conditions heralded the day of the domination of the social gospel in most theological circles. The first department of sociology as such was initiated by the Chicago Theological Seminary in 1890. In 1892 this program was given impetus by the call to Graham Taylor, then at the Hartford Theological Seminary and pastor of the Fourth Congregational Church and Ecclesiastical Society of Hartford, to accept the professorship of Christian Sociology. Here in Chicago he felt he could fulfill his " life purpose " — that is, " to study, teach and exemplify the application of our common Christianity to our common life and its social conditions." In the autumn of 1892 Taylor began his teaching in the midst of an industrial section with its mixed population, where he could be associated closely with the work of Hull House and eventually of similar institutions.[65]

In 1892 the Baptist Theological Seminary was merged with the University of Chicago, where graduate study accented the benefits of outstanding scholarship. Although the Seminary was under the auspices of the Baptist church, it did not exclude students from other denominations. Here, as well as in the Chicago Theological Seminary, the discipline of sociology was emphasized, that department in its first year having first rank in registration.[66]

Closely tied in with the work of the churches was the agitation against the liquor traffic. Intemperance became synonymous with a debasement associated in the minds of many with vice and crime. The spread of drinking among women and children, the growing number of saloons within the city, and the predominance of arrests for disorderly conduct to which drunkenness contributed heavily — all these gave point to the plea that the consumption of intoxicants

---

[65] Graham Taylor to Prof. Pratt, Aug. 11, 1892; to the Rev. G. S. F. Savage, Secretary of the Board of Directors of the Chicago Theological Seminary, Aug. 17, 1892; to the Fourth Congregational Church and Ecclesiastical Society of Hartford (n.d.), *Graham Taylor Papers* (*Mss.* Newberry Library); Graham Taylor, " Sociological Work in Theological Seminaries," in International Congress of Charities, Correction and Philanthropy, Chicago, 1893, Seventh Section, *Sociology in Institutions of Learning* (Baltimore, 1894), pp. 64–79; Taylor, *Pioneering on Social Frontiers* (Chicago, 1931), pp. 4, 403, 430.

[66] The University of Chicago, *The President's Report, July, 1892–July, 1902* (Chicago, 1903), pp. 182–83, 197.

be legislated out of existence. The Sons of Temperance, the Independent Order of Good Templars, the Red Ribbon and Blue Ribbon clubs, the United Order of American Temperance, and many other lodges and societies reflected a contagious zeal for reformation. To them voluntary restraint seemed an important first step, a view sustained by no less a religious leader than David Swing. " It is very certain," said he, " that no laws can be passed and executed until the voluntary measures shall have furnished the land with temperate men enough to make and enforce a law." [67]

Both Protestants and Roman Catholics engaged actively in the crusade, hoping, as *The Western Catholic* put it, to rout forever " that accursed hireling of Satan — King Alcohol." Erin's Hope Temperance and Benevolent Society directed its attention particularly to the inhabitants of heavily settled Irish sections with statistically rewarding results. The pledge of the " League of the Cross," the renunciation of drinking intoxicants in saloons, became a sign of respectability. Temperance lectures, sometimes sponsored by the Roman Catholic Total Abstinence and Benevolent Society, frequently provided arguments convincing enough to effect reform, stressing, as they often did, the costs of excessive drinking in nourishing crime, in increased idleness, and in the great burden placed on society. To consolidate the efforts of various groups, Archbishop Patrick Feehan, who became head of the Chicago archdiocese when it was created in 1880, set about the organization of a central union or clearinghouse in 1882, in order to bring about more extensive and lasting results than in the past. [68]

By 1874 the upsurge of emotion which had swept women throughout the country into the ranks of reformers gripped Chicago. In February they invaded saloons located at Lake and Halsted and at Madison and Clinton streets. Here, following the example set in other places, they knelt in prayer and sang the hymns they believed might save their listeners from a drunkard's grave. But, as the *Times* put

[67] Illinois Board of State Commissioners of Public Charities, *First Biennial Report, 1870,* p. 178; Chicago, *Municipal Reports, 1887,* " Mayor's Message," p. 17; *Chicago Daily News,* Jan. 11, 1884; *Skandinaven,* Feb. 5, 1884; *Chicago Tribune,* March 6, 15, Nov. 4, 1878, July 1, 1883, June 28, 1884; *The Chicago Times,* March 2, 1874; Loomis, *op. cit.,* pp. 102–4. See Chapter IX, " The Expanding Role of Government."

[68] *The Western Catholic,* Feb. 26, 1881, July 19, Aug. 9, 1884; *Chicago Post,* Feb. 2, 1878; *Chicago Tribune,* Aug. 17, 18, Sept. 7, Oct. 10, 1873, Dec. 11, 1882, March 16, 1883; *The Irish World and American Industrial Liberator,* Aug. 23, 1884.

it, the conditions for success in a movement against saloons in Chicago were in no sense favorable. " There is no more use of these women launching themselves in praying bands against saloons," observed the *Times*, " than there would be of attempting to stop by similar means the flow of Niagara river." [69]

The invasion of the saloons was but a first step in the crusade about to take place. On March 16 some two thousand women met in the Clark Street Methodist Church and prayerfully drew up a statement protesting saloons opening on the Sabbath. Relying upon the time-honored appeal through petition, sixty of their numbers visited the Court House and presented to the council their plea backed by 16,000 signatures.

What they achieved fell far short of the mark, for they were unable to prevent the passage of the ordinance permitting the sale of liquor on Sundays. Instead, the council, as a mild gesture of appeasement, ordered all saloons so engaged to close and curtain all doors and windows opening on the street. The climate of opinion in which these women henceforth had to carry on their work of reform became clear as they were showered by onlookers with tobacco juice, their chignons pulled and disarranged, their dresses torn, and their escorts subjected to physical blows. Such treatment kindled all the combative instincts of womankind. Twelve determined temperance enthusiasts then moved upon the state legislature, hoping to induce members to " take the pledge." Political adroitness in the Senate saved its members from so committing themselves; the House, in a more tractable frame of mind, acceded.[70]

By this time it had become obvious that some formal organization was essential to success. In the autumn of 'seventy-four (October 8) Frances E. Willard, onetime Dean of the Woman's College and Professor of Aesthetics in Northwestern University at Evanston, took over the leadership of the local movement. Reared in the tradition of Puritanism, Miss Willard waged her battle tirelessly and with conviction. In November, 1874 she was made corresponding secretary of the national group at its first meeting, held in Cleveland. In 1879 she

[69] *The Chicago Times*, March 1, 18, 1874; *Chicago Post and Mail*, Feb. 18, 1874; Willard, *Glimpses of Fifty Years*, p. 334.

[70] *Chicago Post and Mail*, March 24, 1874; *The Chicago Times*, March 17, 24, 28, 1874; Chicago, *Council Proceedings, 1873–74*, pp. 129–30; *The Illinois State Register*, March 21, 1874; Bogart and Thompson, *The Industrial State*, pp. 49–50.

was called to head the national organization, a position she retained until her death twenty years later.[71]

Under Miss Willard's vigorous direction, agitation for restrictive statutes gained momentum. In 1883 the so-called Harper bill, passed by the state legislature, provided that dramshops be assessed a license fee of $500 annually, unless only malt liquors were dispensed; then $150 would be required. Resentment of local saloonkeepers toward all temperance groups reached fever pitch upon the dates when payment for licenses fell due. For " the tribute " demanded, preachers and reformers were universally condemned. But even as late as the eventful year 1893, the influence of the W.C.T.U. and kindred groups did not close the saloons on Sunday. The teaching of temperance through the subject of physiology in the schools, however, represented a success commensurate with the efforts expended. In 1889 Illinois required that such instruction be given " with special reference to the effects of alcoholic beverages, stimulants and narcotics on the human system."

The W.C.T.U. extended its activities in an ever-widening circle. Gospel temperance meetings undertook conversion; abstention societies, such as the Temperance Reform Club and clubs maintained by the Washingtonian Home, received the support of the Union. The Bethesda Day Nursery, an adjunct of Bethesda Mission, which provided lodging for men and women, was established in 1886 to care for children of working parents.[72] The Woman's Temperance Publishing Association, formed in 1880, and the construction of the Woman's Temple at the corner of LaSalle and Monroe streets, completed in 1893, came about largely through the efforts of Mrs. Matilda B. Carse. In 1883 *Our Union,* the national W.C.T.U. journal, was consolidated with *The Signal,* owned and published in Chicago by the Woman's Temperance Publishing Association. The first issue

---

[71] Willard, *op. cit.,* pp. 337, 339, 342, 343, 348–50; *The Chicago Times,* March 27, 1874; Chicago Woman's Christian Temperance Union, *Report for 1874–75,* in Bonney, *Personal Miscellany,* VI; Mary Earhart, *Frances Willard* (Chicago, 1944), pp. 144–45; *Chicago Post and Mail,* April 17, Nov. 21, 1874; August F. Fehlandt, *A Century of Drink Reform* (New York, 1904), p. 246.

[72] Bogart and Thompson, *op. cit.,* p. 140; Illinois, *Laws, 1883,* pp. 92–93, *1889,* p. 204; *Chicago Post and Mail,* Nov. 27, 1874, April 29, 1876; *Mixed Drinks,* I (Dec. 1, 1889). 1; *The Advance,* XXVII (Jan. 5, 1893), 6; Willard, *op. cit.,* p. 348; Frances E. Willard. " A Day among Chicago Philanthropists," *The Chautauquan,* VII (March, 1887), 349; Noble Canby, " Some Characteristics of Chicago," *ibid.,* XV (Aug., 1892), 613; *Chicago Tribune,* Feb. 15, 1891.

of *The Union Signal* came from the presses January 4, 1883, its editorial policy under the control of the national organization. By 1892 its average circulation was reported as high as 80,000.[73]

Closely allied with the W.C.T.U.'s temperance work were attempts to extend the ballot to women as " Home Protection," in order that they could participate in elections touching upon the licensing of spirituous liquor. Although unsuccessful in this as well as in some other altruistic endeavors, the organization had a measure of satisfaction in the establishment of the office of police matron and of promoting refuges for unfortunate women and children. In its battle against the saloon, however, the Union suffered repeated setbacks, for any move toward prohibition met the united stand of all producers and dealers in liquor, whose pressure-group methods managed to prevent any serious inroads by legislation on the power they possessed.[74] Among the various temperance forces the Woman's Christian Temperance Union carried on the widest range of activities; others, like the Washingtonian Home Association, engaged in the reformation of drunkards. The Washingtonian Home for Men, supported by the association since 1867, had a sister institution in 1882, the Martha Washington Home for women inebriates.[75]

In 1877 alarm over the number of crimes attributable to drinking among juvenile offenders brought into being the Citizens' League, made up of prominent Chicagoans bent on the enforcement of all laws and ordinances concerning the sale of liquor to minors.[76] Its path was thorny, as was the path of all reformers. By 1883, however, three divisions of the league actively sought evidence against lawbreakers and pressed their prosecution. That success at times crowned

[73] Canby, *loc. cit.;* Earhart, *op. cit.,* pp. 345–46; *Chicago Tribune,* Nov. 2, 1890, Jan. 8, Feb. 25, 1893; Willard, *Glimpses of Fifty Years,* p. 353; Fehlandt, *op. cit.,* p. 242; *A Brief History of the Woman's Christian Temperance Union* (3d ed. Evanston, Ill., 1907), p. 116.

[74] Willard, *Glimpses of Fifty Years,* pp. 351–55, 363–64; Illinois, *Journal of the Senate of the Thirty-first General Assembly, 1879,* p. 723, *Journal of the House of Representatives of the Thirty-first General Assembly, 1879,* pp. 445, 575; Elizabeth Cady Stanton, Susan B. Anthony, and Matilda Joslyn Gage, eds., *History of Woman Suffrage* (6 v. Rochester, N.Y., 1881–1922), III, 587–88.

[75] *Chicago Tribune,* Jan. 14, 1873, July 1, 1883, Sept. 19, 1888; *The Chicago Times,* Jan. 20, 1874, Dec. 13, 1878, Dec. 17, 1880, May 14, 1882; Chicago Woman's Christian Temperance Union, *Report for 1874–75,* Bonney Pamphlets, VI.

[76] Among the members of the league were Marshall Field, the Rev. E. P. Goodwin, Potter Palmer, O. S. A. Sprague, Ferd. W. Peck, George M. Pullman, W. J. Onahan, the Rev. David Swing, C. H. McCormick, Franklin MacVeigh, A. C. McClurg, and Martin Ryerson.

their efforts was evidenced by a proportional decrease in the number of minors sent to the workhouse.[77]

Paralleling efforts to curb the use of intoxicating liquors and to aid in the reformation of drunkards were those focused upon the problem of prostitution and the reformation of "fallen women." The two outstanding institutions, the House of the Good Shepherd and the Chicago Erring Woman's Refuge for Reform, continued from an earlier day their humanitarian and religious programs. Industry rather than indolence was encouraged by the establishment of laundries and sewing rooms, but the benefits of recreation were not ignored. The Florence Crittenton Anchorage of the W.C.T.U., founded in 1886 "to care for unfortunate girls who have been led astray and to protect the innocent and friendless from being led into the haunts of sin of a great city," typified the home supported by private contributions. Hull House also provided temporary shelter for these outcasts of society, while the Protective Agency for Women and Children, organized in 1886, endeavored to afford "protection from all offences and crimes against the purity and virtue of women and children." [78]

Despite the valor and determination that characterized attempts to prevent or reform wrongdoing, their success to a considerable degree depended upon the extent of community support which they enjoyed. The path of the reformer was not easy. It was sometimes found, as Mr. Dooley once pertinently pointed out, that " th' frinds iv vice is too sthrong in this wurruld iv sin f'r th' frinds iv varchue. Th' good man, th' crusader, on'y wurruks at th' crusade wanst in five years, an' on'y whin he has time to spare fr'm his other jooties. . . . But th' definse iv vice is a business with th' other la-ad an' he nails away at it, week days an' Sundays, holy days an' fish days, mornin', noon an' night."

[77] *Chicago Tribune*, Feb. 8, March 12, 1878, Jan. 10, 1883, Jan. 9, 1884, Jan. 21, 1885, Jan. 20, 1886; in Bonney, *Personal Miscellany*, VII; *Chicago Legal News*, X (March 16, 1878), 591–92; Citizens' League of Chicago, *Sixth Annual Report, 1884*, pp. 5, 11, *Eleventh Annual Report, 1889*, pp. 6–7, *Fourteenth Annual Meeting, 1892*, pp. 7–9; *The Christian Union*, Feb. 6, 1892, p. 270.

[78] Pierce, *A History of Chicago*, II, 442–43; *Chicago Tribune*, Feb. 8, 1886; Chicago Erring Woman's Refuge for Reform, *Annual Report, 1873–92*; Protective Agency for Women and Children, *Second Annual Report, 1888*, p. 5; Visher, *op. cit.*, pp. 139–40, 174; Aaron M. Powell, *The National Purity Congress, Its Papers, Addresses, Portraits* (New York, 1896), p. 152; Jane Addams, *Forty Years at Hull-House*, pp. 145–46; *Chicago's Dark Places*, pp. 152–53, 157, 160; Willard, " A Day among Chicago Philanthropists," pp. 348–49.

However true this may have been on the whole, it did not put to rout all those bent on the reformation or improvement of society. Under the influence of the social gospel and the currents of humanitarianism which normally flowed in men's hearts, old attempts at amelioration were prolonged or resuscitated; others came into being to meet new and challenging situations. Not always well defined were the incentives of the reformer, the humanitarian intent on improving the status of his fellow men and making them and their kind fit the pattern acceptable to society in general. When explanations of why men and women departed from the path of righteousness and good behavior were sought, agreement seldom was reached except on one point — that economic hardship and poor living conditions many times contributed heavily. The unevenness of economic returns, whatever the reason for it, had for years necessitated assistance to the unfortunate, and, as in the past, governmental agencies shared in providing this aid. Favoritism and costly administration, appointees chosen for political reasons rather than competence, left much to be desired in the extent and character of the relief provided. To private agencies, therefore, fell much of the care of the destitute.[79]

As in the years before the Fire, so in the grievous days which followed it the Chicago Relief and Aid Society carried on its ministrations of mercy to those in distress. It supported lodginghouses where strangers and homeless people could find temporary quarters. Separate soup kitchens and employment bureaus, a wood yard where men could work and earn a meal, assistance to widows and old people in need, and other eleemosynary activities pointed to a usefulness during years marked by devastation through fire, economic distress accentuated by panics, and maladjustments implicit in a planless urban expansion. In 1888 the society merged with the Charity Organization Society, since 1883 a non-sectarian association of city charities designed to cut down on the duplication of services and to distribute through a central clearinghouse relief in a more equitable manner than before such an organization took shape.[80]

Women and children claimed the attention of many who wished to aid those deemed particularly unable to cope with the complexi-

[79] See Chapter IX, "The Expanding Role of Government."

[80] Chicago Relief and Aid Society, *Annual Report,* 1872–93. For the part played in relief work after the Fire of 1871 by the Chicago Relief and Aid Society see Chapter I, "The Great Chicago Fire."

ties of the life they faced. Like the Chicago Relief and Aid Society, the Home for the Friendless carried on the program for which it was established before the Civil War (1858), sustained chiefly by donations from the well-to-do. Jonathan Burr, Henry Hobart Taylor, and Mrs. Mancel Talcott contributed generously to the work of the organization, which provided aid for the indigent. In so doing, the Home's benefactors hopefully declared they might prevent a departure from " the path of rectitude and virtue." To this end two industrial schools were established, one at the Home and the other at the Burr Mission. The *Home Visitor,* edited by Eliza W. Bowman until 1885, was published each month to " counsel the imprudent and erring, help the destitute, and invite the co-operation and sympathy of friends."

Numerous other organizations carried on similar work, focusing, as did the Woman's Aid Association, upon getting employment for women and girls, but never ignoring the help needed by destitute families. The Chicago Exchange, founded in 1878, provided a depot for the reception and sale of marketable articles which women could make at home. For this service the Exchange exacted a 10-per-cent commission and annual consignor's fee of one dollar. By 1893 it recorded that to women who brought goods for sale had been paid the satisfying sum of $22,067.52.[81]

An increasing number of undertakings showed a warmth toward the problem of dependent children equal to that exhibited toward needy women. This concern assured the support of orphanages such as the Chicago Orphan Asylum, known in the city since 1849; the Chicago Nursery and Half-Orphan Asylum, rebuilt after the Great Fire by appropriations made by the Chicago Relief and Aid Society; the Chicago Foundlings' Home to care for infants and obtain permanent homes for them, sponsored by Protestants; not to mention the denominationally supported establishments such as the Uhlich Evangelical Lutheran Asylum and the Church Home for Orphans under Episcopal auspices.[82]

[81] See the annual reports of the Home for the Friendless; *Industrial Age,* I (March 14, 1874), 5; *Chicago Tribune,* Jan. 8, 1873, July 8, 1883; *The Chicago Times,* March 11, 1881, March 11, 1883; Visher, *op. cit.,* pp. 22–23.

[82] Brown, *The History of Public Assistance in Chicago 1833 to 1893,* pp. 162–63; Mrs. Charles G. Wheeler, *Annals of the Chicago Orphan Asylum from 1849 to 1892* (Chicago, 1892), pp. 9, 13–14, 26–28, 43–45, 66–67, 70–71, 74, 77; Visher, *op. cit.,* pp. 33, 39,

These institutions often provided educational opportunities, particularly industrial training that included work in a print shop or in blacksmithing. Such instruction was carried on at the Waifs' Mission and Training School with flattering results. At the Newsboys' Home educational and cultural opportunities and amusements were designed to rear properly those children who already were engaged on the streets in earning their living.[83]

While the spirit of humanitarianism was thus expressing itself by means of organized movements in the churches, lay groups independent of sectarian supervision, ethnic associations, and individual philanthropy were concerned also with the rehabilitation of ex-convicts. The Prisoners' Aid Association of Illinois, organized in Chicago in 1882 and incorporated two years later, provided temporary lodging and assistance in obtaining employment to men just restored to freedom. A Home of Industry, as it was described by its founder, Michael Dunn (for thirty-five years a prisoner), opened in 1885 to bring those released from prison under Christian influences and teach them how to earn an honest living.[84] Another demonstration of a growing sensitiveness to the needs of the unfortunate was the establishment in 1888 of a Bureau of Justice to furnish legal protection for the helpless and to promote better laws and methods of legal procedure. At the same time, the Protective Agency for Women and Children, which provided legal service to those in need and unable to procure it themselves, came into existence.

The progress of reform was further illustrated by the crusade to prevent cruelty to dumb beasts. The Illinois Society for the Prevention of Cruelty to Animals, incorporated in 1869, was instrumental in bringing about the passage of such a law that year. In 1870 the society completed its organization with Edwin Lee Brown, manufacturer of sidewalk and vault lights, as president, and took steps to enforce the law. The society fought an uphill fight to improve the

192; Mamie Ruth Davis, *A History of Policies and Methods of Social Work in the Chicago Orphan Asylum* (unpublished M.A. Thesis, The University of Chicago, 1927), p. 3; *Chicago Tribune*, Jan. 16, 1873, Jan. 7, 31, April 25, 1874, Jan. 3, Aug. 5, 1883; Illinois Board of State Commissioners of Public Charities, *Eighth Biennial Report, 1884*, pp. 272, 274, 276.

[83] Visher, *op. cit.*, pp. 168–69; *Chicago Tribune,* Sept. 4, Oct. 8, 13, 19, 1873, Feb. 22, 1875, Feb. 8, 1883, June 28, 1888, Oct. 18, 1889, Jan. 26, 1890; Joseph Kirkland, "Among the Poor of Chicago," in *The Poor in Great Cities* (New York, 1895), pp. 226–27.

[84] *The Chicago Times*, April 9, 1882; *Chicago Daily News*, March 1, 1884; Illinois Board of State Commissioners of Public Charities, *Eighth Biennial Report, 1884*, p. 275.

treatment of animals, particularly in the stockyards. It labored to prevent the overworking and beating of animals, their confinement more than twenty-eight consecutive hours in railroad cars unless properly watered and fed, and the elimination of steeplechase and hurdle riding at the Washington Park track. It instigated cases in the courts whenever voluntary compliance with the law could not be obtained. Even the docking of a horse's tail engaged the attention of the society because some held that, inasmuch as God had made the horse about right, man could not improve it. Those who approved of "haggling off the tail" countered with the argument that by such an operation the nourishment which went to support it and the force expended by the horse in switching it could be "diverted into his general system."

Despite arguments — some valid and some invalid in the light of a later day — the society accomplished many of the things it had set out to do, for it prevented much of the mistreatment to which animals had been subjected. Its ancillary activities included the erection of water troughs throughout the city and providing an ambulance for disabled horses. Extending its work also to include cases of cruelty to children, the organization changed its name in 1877 to the Illinois Humane Society.[85]

In many of these movements for social betterment, women played an important role. More and more they carried on their work outside the auspices of some religious association, sometimes as individuals, often as members of organized groups. Their fields of activity ranged widely, from the care of the poor to work in institutions for the mentally ill. It became increasingly popular for leaders of society to manifest interest in various humanitarian projects that were under way or, still better, to venture into the new and untried. Young women of prominence such as Fannie Gary, daughter of Judge Gary, gained wide acclaim from working women and their friends for serving as a substitute for a girl in a tailor shop in the summer of 1890, in order

---

[85] *The Christian Union,* XXXIV (Aug. 19, 1886), 6, (Nov. 11, 1886), 6; Visher, *op. cit.,* pp. 15–16, 75, 98–99; Andreas, *History of Chicago,* III, 609–10; Illinois, *Public Laws, 1869,* pp. 114–17; *Chicago Tribune,* Oct. 26, Dec. 8, 1872, May 22, Sept. 5, Dec. 14, 1873, June 27, 1874, Feb. 22, 1877, Oct. 1, 1879, April 27, 1880, Feb. 13, Nov. 27, Dec. 6, 1881, May 6, 1883, May 3, 1885, Dec. 18, 1887, May 6, 1888, Jan. 5, 1892; *Mixed Drinks,* VIII (Feb. 8, 1893), 2. Humanitarian undertakings of various ethnic groups are discussed also in Chapter II, "The Fabric of Society."

that the girl might enjoy a two weeks' vacation. Others followed in like train, abandoning the carefree life to which wealth entitled them, to set up kindergartens, to teach cooking to poor girls, or to engage in many undertakings promoted by members of organizations such as the Daughters of the King.

The first Chicago chapter of the Daughters of the King was established in 1886 on the pattern of the New York society formed that same year. Taking as their inspiration the text " Inasmuch as ye did it unto the least of these ye did it unto me," they supported the aged poor, set up free kindergartens, visited the sick, worked for cleaner streets and other sanitary improvements such as the prohibition of spitting in streetcars. Under the leadership of Ada C. Sweet, the Chicago Woman's Club successfully campaigned to have matrons on duty at night in jails for the benefit of female prisoners. A provision for daytime matrons had already been made in 1882, through the efforts of the W.C.T.U. The Chicago Woman's Club, among its many activities, successfully promoted separate facilities for men and women inmates of police stations, as well as schooling and vocational training for youthful lawbreakers.[86]

Undoubtedly the outstanding humanitarian undertaking of the time was Hull House, established in September, 1889 by Jane Addams, " the civic saviour of Chicago." Here in an old residence on South Halsted Street near the corner of Polk, with shipbuilding yards to its north and the stockyards to its south, Miss Addams and Ellen G. Starr rendered their humanitarian and civic services as need and demand dictated, to the Polish and Russian Jews, Canadian French, Irish, Germans, Italians, Bohemians, and some old-line Americans in the Nineteenth Ward.

The program ranged widely, from bathing babies, solving domestic problems, and caring for the homeless and delinquent, to providing educational facilities for those who wished them. From the beginning, a kindergarten was carried on; savings were placed in the " Penny Provident Fund Savings Bank "; and a wide number of

[86] The Rights of Labor, VI (Aug. 2, 1890), 1; Chicago Tribune, May 3, 1891; Chicago's Dark Places, p. 153; Henriette Greenebaum Frank and Amalie Hofer Jerome, comps., Annals of the Chicago Woman's Club (Chicago, 1916), pp. 38, 42; Dorothy Edwards Powers, The Chicago Woman's Club (unpublished M.A. Thesis, The University of Chicago, 1939), pp. 186–87; Chicago, Council Proceedings, 1882–83, p. 200; Pierce, As Others See Chicago, pp. 312, 318.

benevolent agencies received active support from the staff of Hull House, which included the renowned Julia Lathrop and Florence Kelley.[87]

Similar undertakings reflected the role Hull House played in attempts to solve the problem of mass humanity in the city. In 1891 the Northwestern University Settlement was started by Charles Zueblin and others at 143 West Division " to serve as a neighborhood center for the community." While seeking to improve physical conditions through efforts such as those in behalf of more adequate play areas, it also strove to reduce barriers between diverse immigrant groups by fostering the development of a common American citizenship. In 1893 two young college-bred Jews, Jacob Abt and Jesse Lowenhaupt, took up residence in the heart of the ghetto at 185 Maxwell Street " to afford opportunity for personal fellowship and to be of some social service." Although the original objective was chiefly educational and directed toward young men and boys, the interests of the Maxwell Street Settlement soon expanded to include a variety of activities and participants.[88]

These humanizing forces, to which church and laymen contributed, brought much that was good to the conglomerate mass within the gates of the city, although amelioration was never complete. But the very fact that they envisaged man's better adjustment to the complex social and economic order was, in itself, beneficence, an enlargement of living, at once significant and humane.

[87] For Hull House see in particular Jane Addams, *Twenty Years at Hull-House* (New York, 1910), and her *Forty Years at Hull-House;* Residents of Hull-House, *Hull-House Maps and Papers;* "The Civic Life of Chicago," *Review of Reviews,* VIII (Aug., 1893), 182; Alice Hamilton, *Exploring the Dangerous Trades* (Boston, 1943), pp. 59, 65–66. Miss Addams used a hyphen in speaking of Hull House. All settlement publications still do so. In general usage the name appears without hyphen.

[88] Visher, *op. cit.,* p. 66; *Hull-House Maps and Papers,* pp. 100–1; Robert A. Woods and Albert J. Kennedy, eds., *Handbook of Settlements* (New York, 1911), pp. 66–67, 78; Bregstone, *Chicago and Its Jews,* pp. 48–49; Robert A. Woods and Albert J. Kennedy, *The Settlement Horizon: A National Estimate* (New York, 1922), p. 48.

CHAPTER XIII

PATTERNS OF URBAN LIVING

IN THE TWO DECADES after the Great Fire, Chicago rapidly shed most of the aspects of small-town life that had persisted until then. In many ways, however, the transformed city retained the crudity and bristling energy of a place only recently emerged from the frontier, where the struggle for life was harsh and at times ruthless. Wealth became the main criterion for social standing, and the group qualifying for leadership was constantly augmented as the number of rich men grew. They were the ones who set the pattern which those of lower estate aspired to and imitated whenever they could. Social life in Chicago was indeed, as Charles Dudley Warner observed, " as unformed, unselected, as the city — that is, more fluid and undetermined than in Eastern large cities."

Love of display, of the symbols of wealth, reflected generally the sophistication characteristic of the social elite. As time went on, the novelty of luxuries tended to wear off, and grace and charm rather than an offensive ostentatiousness became the index of good taste. In this evolution, contacts with the many visitors of refinement both from abroad and from the rest the United States played an important part. Even more destructive of the barriers of provincialism was travel in Europe, to which more and more Chicagoans eagerly turned. Rest and pleasure at well-known watering places frequently crowned a tour of historic sites and art galleries. The custom of finishing an education, much of which had been in schools of the East, by a year's travel in Europe became increasingly common for the children of the well-to-do.

Others chose to view the vast stretches of their own country, either attracted by the wonders of Niagara and other well-advertised places of the East, or enticed westward by the marvels of Yellowstone and the Yosemite.[1] The increased leisure which wealth made possible led still others to the summer resorts in the near-by states of Wisconsin, Michigan, and Minnesota, and to the more fashionable places of the East.[2]

In the winter, society reveled in the ball, particularly popular for introducing debutantes to society or for complimenting some distinguished guest. To assure polished behavior at such affairs, young people received instruction at the well-known dancing academies of Augustus E. Bournique and J. Edwin Martine. At the latter's academy the young smart set initiated "the Cinders" (in honor of the Fire), an organization which, in the late 'seventies, evolved into the exclusive Assembly, patterned after its predecessors in Philadelphia and other eastern points.

Of outstanding magnificence were the benefit or charity balls, which netted from the sale of tickets as much as the then considerable sum of ten or twelve thousand dollars, as in the case of St. Luke's Hospital Ball in 1885 and 1886. The next year the Grand Charity Ball inaugurated the practice of dividing the returns among several institutions, but as these events came to be more elaborate the amounts which could be disbursed as charity decreased. This means of bestowing largess was by no means universally commended, for, in the minds of some clergymen and their conservative parishioners, it violated denominational injunctions against such amusements, and evinced questionable moral tendencies. Furthermore, the ostentation, the display of rival social leaders seeking to outdo each other in elegance of dress, and similar betrayals of the primary purpose of the event evoked criticism from those who deplored the widening gulf between rich and poor, so graphically

[1] Warner, "Studies of the Great West. III. — Chicago," *Harper's New Monthly Magazine,* LXXVI (May, 1888), 877; Ralph, *Our Great West,* pp. 33–36. The newspapers, particularly the society columns, are the chief source for social events unless other sources are given.

[2] For example, Levi Leiter, George Sturges, and Samuel Allerton had summer homes at Lake Geneva, Wisconsin. Victor Lawson had a cottage on Green Lake. Oconomowoc, Lakeside, Devil's Lake, Neenah, Waukesha, and Pewaukee were other popular Wisconsin resorts. In the East, Bar Harbor, Newport, Long Branch, and Cape May especially attracted Chicagoans.

illustrated in what appeared to them a desecration of the spirit of charity.[3]

On the calendar of the older members of the social set New Year's Day held special favor. It was at this time that custom dictated calling upon one's friends, and the January 1 issue of the city's newspapers carried lists of the hostesses who held what was designated as " open house," until well into the 'eighties. Then the increasing size of the city and the complexity of urban living tended to curtail the more intimate forms of contact enjoyed in earlier days, and receptions sometimes gave way in popular appeal to smaller gatherings. In the latter, the dinner provided ways to test the hostesses' resourcefulness not only in menus but in the elaborate details which accompanied the food. Here wine often flowed freely; a camaraderie in this form of entertaining assured its long-time popularity. A freedom granted women, seldom found in the older cities of the East, permitted them, upon occasion, to share in the after-dinner entertainment instead of leaving the men guests after the coffee.

Despite the pretentiousness of the homes of the rich, their capacity was not always great enough to care for the more elaborate functions which held so important a place on the list of social gatherings. At such times, the well-known hotels of the city became the center of conviviality. The Tremont House, reopened in 1874 and the favorite rendezvous of theater people, held high place in the affections of Chicagoans throughout its many years. It was, however, exceeded in the extent of its accommodations by the Grand Pacific at Clark and Jackson streets, and the Palmer House on State Street, their size described as no less than " monstrous " by the eminent newspaper publisher Sir John Leng in his visit to Chicago in 1876. In the latter was the much talked-of barber shop floored with silver dollars; the hotel itself, adorned by tessellated marble and gold trimmings, afforded service to its clientele consistent with its lavish furnishings. It catered, as did the Grand Pacific, to visitors of political renown and the great of the theater and opera. With the erection of the Auditorium Hotel, opened in 1890, the acknowledged social hegemony of the Grand Pacific and the Palmer House was seriously challenged.

[3] For critical comments on charity balls see *Svenska Tribunen*, Jan. 21, 1885; Clark, *The Elegant Eighties*, p. 224. Charley Seymour of the *Chicago Herald* pointed out the irony of charity balls as conducted. *Chicago Daily News*, Aug. 18, 1936.

In these hotels could be had the most elaborate cuisine of the day. Menus made up of heavy foods and served in many courses were replete with roast and broiled meats varying from fowl to buffalo, antelope, bear, and mountain sheep, not to mention the " ornamental dishes " from which boned quail in plumage, partridge in nest prairie, and blackbirds could be selected. To these three of the hotel aristocracy should be added the Sherman House (opened in 1873), which made up the so-called " Big Four " of the hotel hierarchy. At the Sherman House gathered prominent stock and agricultural personages and those described as " the sporting fraternity." The Leland and Clifton were also counted among those which contributed to the social and economic development of the city; and until past the mid-'eighties the Matteson was also considered among the best. These were, of course, not all the hotels that made good accommodations a matter of pride to the boosters of the city. As early as 1874 a total of $20,000,000 was reported invested in the more than five thousand rooms available, and to these could be added an indefinite list of boardinghouses.

In the downtown hotels, where the number of stories increased with the costliness of the land upon which they were located, elevator service carried guests to their rooms. The adoption of modern plumbing, the introduction of electricity for lighting before the 'eighties closed, and the replacement of the American by the European plan of service evoked amazed comment as they rapidly became a part of hotel equipment and practice. As the European plan came to prevail in the downtown area, restaurants enjoyed a prosperity hitherto unknown. The Saratoga, the Lakeside Oyster House, and the Stock Exchange Restaurant were accorded a wide patronage, while smaller and less expensive establishments dotted the streets leading to the business center.[4]

As for amusements, there was at hand a wide choice ranging from amateur to professional performances. To the latter, especially in the polite drama, the theater managers James H. McVicker, John Haverly, William J. Davis, and John A. Hamlin paid considerable attention, and left Chicago deeply indebted to them for the high type

[4] Ralph, *op. cit.*, p. 4; *The Grand Pacific Hotel Twenty-ninth Annual Game Dinner, November 22, 1884* (Chicago Historical Society); Sir John Leng, *America in 1876* (Dundee, 1877), p. 76; Clark, *op. cit.*, pp. 4–6. For an uncomplimentary description of the Palmer House see Rudyard Kipling's account quoted in Pierce, *As Others See Chicago*, p. 251.

THE GRAND STAIRCASE OF THE PALMER HOUSE, IN ITS TIME ONE OF THE MOST MAGNIFICENT HOTELS IN THE NATION. OPENED IN 1875

From *Seven Days in Chicago* (Chicago: J. M. Wing & Co., 1877).

"GUNTHER'S," A POPULAR DOWNTOWN SODA FOUNTAIN AND CONFECTIONARY

Photograph taken around 1888.

of production and the outstanding actors they presented. After the late 1870's McVicker's Theatre, the Academy of Music, Haverly's, the Grand Opera House, and the Auditorium Theatre, in particular, offered performances by well-trained traveling troupes supporting stars of renown.[5] At the Adelphi Theatre after 1874, first-class variety shows satisfied lovers of that form of entertainment, and Hooley's Theatre reopened in 1872 for plays and operettas.[6]

Among the stars Chicagoans delighted to welcome were Charlotte Cushman, Edwin Booth, Lawrence Barrett, Thomas W. Keene, and John McCullough. In the late 1880's a younger generation engaged the fancy of theatergoers, who then, and later, found in Edward H. Sothern, Julia Marlowe, Robert Mantell, and Richard Mansfield the promise of genius.[7] Beginning in 1884 the English actor Henry Irving and his leading lady, Ellen Terry, made repeated visits to Chicago, offering finished performances in a Shakespearean repertoire as well as in other plays.

To this rich fare were added appearances by Mme. Helena Modjeska in " Camille " and " Adrienne Lecouvreur," first presented in April and May, 1878. Sarah Bernhardt opened her first Chicago engagement at McVicker's on January 10, 1881, with a repertoire including " Adrienne Lecouvreur," " Frou-Frou," " Le Sphinx," " Camille," and " Phèdre." In the 1880's the lovely Lily Langtry, assisted by Maurice Barrymore; Mrs. James Brown Potter, supported by the matinee idol Kyrle Bellew; and Mary Anderson gave a large measure of personal grace and beauty to performances not always accorded the highest praise. To enumerate all the great who enriched

[5] After the Great Fire, McVicker's Theatre opened in 1872; the Academy of Music, under the management of Charles R. Gardiner, opened in 1873; Haverly's new theater under John Haverly opened in 1881, but Haverly went bankrupt in 1883 and Charles H. McConnell succeeded him as proprietor; the Grand Opera House opened under William J. Davis and John Hamlin in 1880; the Auditorium opened under Milward Adams in Dec., 1889.

[6] See newspapers, particularly the following issues: *Chicago Tribune,* Oct. 9, 13, 1872, Aug. 17, Sept. 1, 1873, Feb. 5, 1878, May 29, Sept. 1, 13, Dec. 20, 1881, Aug. 13, 1882, June 8, 1883; *The Chicago Times,* Feb. 1, 1874, Oct. 3, 13, 1880; *Eastman Collection* in *Autograph Letters,* XL; W. J. Davis, *Scrap Book, 1881–1882* (Chicago Historical Society), p. 9; O. Bersbach, *Scrapbook of Chicago Theatre and Concert Programs* (Chicago Historical Society), II; Flinn, *Chicago . . . A Guide, 1891,* pp. 119–22.

[7] Charlotte Cushman played in " Guy Mannering " (1872), Edwin Booth in " Brutus " (1873), Lawrence Barrett in " Julius Caesar " (1880), Thomas W. Keene in " Richard III " (1880), John McCullough in " Virginius" (1880), Edward H. Sothern in "The Highest Bidder " (1887), Julia Marlowe in " Ingomar " (1888), Richard Mansfield in " Prince Karl " (1886), Robert Mantell in " Tangled Lives " (1887).

the offerings theater producers provided Chicagoans would include substantially every actor of distinction — both Americans and Europeans who came to the United States. From the classics to light comedies and dramas the selection embraced those known in the older cities of the country. Judged by the external evidence of patronage, the appearance of *The Play,* a journal devoted to the theater, and the severe criticism of the drama by writers in the press, Chicago had attained by the late 'eighties a much desired position of culture.[8]

But equally attractive, and perhaps actually more so, were the numerous melodramas with their startling climaxes. Packed houses for four weeks in 1883 saw " The Silver King," and the *Tribune* was of the opinion it could have continued profitably for many more. Bartley Campbell's " The White Slave " and other melodramas left lasting impressions after each performance; and " East Lynne " and " Uncle Tom's Cabin " continued to be played endlessly. Despite the low price of twenty-five cents and the high of fifty cents, Mrs. Stowe's perennial was forced, by the growing competition with newer productions, to resort to special pleading, in 1882, for example, advertising:

NEW AND BEAUTIFUL SCENERY,

THE MAGNOLIA JUBILEE SINGERS,

THE TRICK DONKEY " JERRY,"

AND THE FAMOUS

TRAINED SIBERIAN BLOODHOUNDS

The most savage of their species, which will engage
in the Realistic Picture of the terrible SLAVE
HUNT. During this engagement the people's prices,
25¢, 35¢ and 50¢. No Higher.

Crowded houses saw " Little Lord Fauntleroy," and many parents went home with the fixed determination to model their children

[8] Minnie Maddern appeared for the first time in July, 1882. Chicagoans enjoyed the lighter comedies and drama of Augustin Daly brought from New York in 1882 and later years. Leading roles were played by Ada Rehan, John Drew, Otis Skinner, Agnes Perrins, among others. *Chicago Tribune,* June 11, 13, 25, July 9, 1882, Feb. 25, March 4, June 3, 1883, June 1, 1884, May 31, 1885, May 22, 1887, May 12, 1889. *The Play* ran from 1877 to 1883.

after the curly-haired little gentleman. Daniel Frohman brought the child actress Elsie Leslie to Chicago on March 17, 1890. Like the character actors beloved by the city — Joseph Jefferson in particular — Elsie Leslie held a high place in the affections of those who saw her in " The Prince and the Pauper." [9]

While most of these productions were in English, the large foreign colonies of the city were also entertained by plays, both amateur and professional, in their own language. The most ambitious were German, but Scandinavian and other national groups also offered a variety of programs to their constituencies. Sometimes they were presented in neighborhood theaters, upon occasion as a benefit for some cause or institution; but downtown theaters, notably McVicker's, were used extensively especially by the Germans for their Sunday performances, many of which were the light comedy-farce type such as *"Durchgegangene Weiber"* (" Runaway Wives ").[10]

Vaudeville or variety shows had fascination for lovers of light and cheap entertainment. Tony Pastor's " Go West on the Emigrant Train " and " Fun on the Stage " drew big crowds, and box-office receipts were large whenever the magician Alexander Herrmann, " the greatest of prestidigitators," and his company were advertised. Considered less respectable were the variety acts of cancan dancers such as Mlle. De Lacour's troupe, which appeared in 1875. As vaudeville gained in vogue, the blackface minstrel show gradually lost its favored position, although as late as 1885 Lester & Allen's Minstrels still proved to be an attraction. Along with the vaudeville, the dime museum appealed to many. Here could be viewed a dwarf and his physical opposite the giant, squirming serpents and fluttering, brightly feathered birds, bearded ladies, and the modern centaur.

[9] *Chicago Tribune,* Jan. 1, April 9, 30, 1882, April 22, 24, Aug. 5, Sept. 2, 1883, May 12, 18, July 7, 1889, March 16, 1890.

[10] *Ibid.,* Sept. 18, 1876, Sept. 16, Nov. 10, 1878, Sept. 8, 1879, May 14, Aug. 19, 1883, Sept. 15, 1884, Sept. 21, 1885, Sept. 30, Nov. 11, 1892; *Illinois Staats-Zeitung,* Aug. 28, 1876, May 5, 1877, Jan. 27, 1879; *The Drovers' Journal,* Jan. 6, 1883, July 4, 1886; *Abendpost,* Aug. 5, 8, 9, Sept. 3, 12, 19, Oct. 3, 24, 31, 1890, Aug. 21, 1891; *Chicagoer Arbeiter-Zeitung,* Sept. 3, 1879; *Hejmdal,* Jan. 15, Feb. 25, March 24, April 15, 1876; *Svenska Tribunen,* Oct. 1, 1879, July 28, 1882, April 24, Oct. 29, 1890, Jan. 19, Sept. 6, 1892; *Dziennik Chicagoski,* Jan. 28, Oct. 19, Dec. 30, 1891, Feb. 29, Oct. 12, 19, 1892, Jan. 23, Oct. 30, 1893; *The Occident,* May 27, 1887, Feb. 26, 1892; *The Reform Advocate,* June 24, 1893; *Forward,* April 23, 1922; Geza Kenda, *Magyars in America* (Cleveland, 1927), II, chap. xiv. For an exaggerated and amusing account of a Negro parody of "Othello" see *Chicago Tribune,* Jan. 19, 1889.

Also featured were a Punch and Judy show and horror displays, such as the ropes used in hanging well-known murderers and even wax figures of notorious criminals and their victims.[11]

During the summer months there would be exhibitions of human freaks and unfamiliar animals in the various circuses visiting Chicago. In 1873, following a visit the year before, P. T. Barnum brought his "Equestrian and Hippodromatic Exposition" to the city. Presenting "three silver cornet bands," an expertly trained and well-stocked menagerie, and special attractions such as "Professor Faber's Talking Machine," one hundred life-size oil paintings, midgets, and acrobats, Barnum's circus was equipped to satisfy the varied tastes of the many who visited its tents dotting the lake front. Each successive visit enhanced the popularity of the "Greatest Show on Earth" as it became larger and more spectacular; in 1883 its nineteen performances brought in $125,131.25.

Other circuses also came, always with their fun-making clowns. Adam Forepaugh's was billed as early as June 3, 1872, and in 1884 it introduced for the first time in Chicago, so it was claimed, "the Sacred White Elephant of Siam" — one which required, however, frequent applications of a special preparation to preserve the white paint on his hide. Sells Brothers' Circus and Menagerie, the United States Circus, and many smaller shows filled the roster of this form of entertainment, which had special appeal to the common people of the city and to the residents of the near-by rural hinterland.[12]

Wild West shows by the early 'eighties became as well esteemed, if not more so, than the ever popular circus. In 1883 no less than the bold and adventuresome Buffalo Bill (William F. Cody) and Dr. Carver's Wild West Show entranced an estimated five thousand people in the first performance at the Chicago Driving Park. Return engagements played to crowds whose enthusiasm never wavered as they witnessed "an attack" on a mail coach, a buffalo hunt, and

[11] See especially *ibid.,* Jan. 7, 8, 10, 1875, Sept. 12, Dec. 19, 1880, Feb. 5, June 4, 5, Oct. 22, 1882, Feb. 25, June 3, 5, 1883, June 8, 1884, June 7, Sept. 8, Oct. 4, 1885, Jan. 20, Dec. 20, 1886, Nov. 13, 1892; *The Drovers' Journal,* Nov. 10, 1882; Douglas Gilbert, *American Vaudeville* (New York, 1940), p. 4; Davis, *Scrap Book, 1884,* p. 72, clipping from *The Inter Ocean,* Feb. 24, 1884.

[12] Newspapers, particularly May–September issues, are good sources on the circus just as they are on similar topics. See also Waldo R. Browne, ed., *Barnum's Own Story: The Autobiography of P. T. Barnum* (New York, 1927), p. 417; M. R. Werner, *Barnum* (New York, 1923), p. 354.

other scenes of the dangerous and hair-raising days of the Far West.[13]

Fairs continued their wide appeal, bringing visitors to the city to enjoy along with Chicagoans the many displays available. To a greater extent than in the years before the Fire of 1871 they were directed toward the achievements of trade and industry. The Inter-State Industrial Exposition, opening for the first time on September 25, 1873, was probably the most important and continuous. It was initiated by leading business and professional men with the avowed purpose of making it a permanent establishment.[14] Despite its emphasis on the economic, it did not exclude the cultural contributions of the day, and displays of the fine arts and natural history figured prominently in the Exposition's offerings. The first annual exhibition found the good, poor, and indifferent in art being shown together: paintings by Bierstadt, De Hass, Eastman Johnson, and David Neal next to crayon portraits of dubious merit by the favorite photographer. The eighteen annual exhibitions following showed some, but not an astonishingly great, improvement. The building housing the pretentious exhibits so characteristic of the Exposition was the handiwork of the architect William W. Boyington. Located at Adams and Michigan, it was, in the words of the *Tribune,* a place of " grandeur." In 1892 it was torn down to make way for a permanent structure to care for the Art Institute.[15]

Before the 'sixties closed, Chicago had been the site of the historic State Fair several times. Here the products of agriculture were assembled by the side of the achievements of industry. Here also convened associations such as the Illinois Wool Growers' Association and the National Swine Breeders, not to mention the State Grange. But financial success was never certain, being conspired against by

[13] Buffalo Bill came to Chicago as early as Jan., 1878, playing at Haverly's in western dramas in which were introduced two Sioux Indian chiefs, a rifle team, and other features of the early days of the Far West. See *Chicago Tribune,* Jan. 6, Dec. 22, 1878.

[14] Articles of incorporation for the Inter-State Exposition were signed on July 3, 1872, by Oramel S. Hough, meat packer; Jonathan Young Scammon, banker; Leverett B. Sidway, manufacturer; Josiah W. Preston, merchant; John B. Drake, hotel owner; George S. Bowen, merchant; and J. Irving Pearce, banker.

[15] *The Inter-State Exposition Souvenir . . . 1873, passim; Chicago Tribune,* July 5, 14, 1872, April 25, 29, Aug. 31, Sept. 22, 23, 25, 27, Dec. 24, 1873, Nov. 18, 1877, Nov. 17, 1878, Sept. 14, Nov. 16, 1879, Sept. 6, 1883; Lucy B. Monroe, " Art in Chicago," *The New England Magazine,* n.s. VI (June, 1892), 412; *The Chicago Times,* Sept. 8, 1881; Flinn, *Chicago . . . A Guide, 1893,* p. 408; Andreas, *History of Chicago,* III, 655-57.

bad weather and poor crops, and by a slackening of interest on the part of Chicago residents in matters primarily rural in importance. Then, too, attendance was cut down by the competition of local fairs, including those promoted by the Chicago Fair Association, which, after the first one in 1881, emphasized horse racing as their main attraction, with livestock and agricultural exhibitions only as background.[16]

Among the spectator sports to which the resident of Chicago was attracted, old-time thoroughbred horse racing continued to enjoy large crowds. In 1873 prizes totaling $45,000 brought to the city owners of outstanding racers, and the gratifying attendance of approximately 10,000 on July 5 certified a deep interest on the part of Chicagoans. In 1878 the Chicago Jockey and Trotting Club race drew 35,000 attentive spectators, and, in typical Chicago fashion, the press declared this was the largest crowd ever at such an event in America. In 1880 William Vanderbilt's famous six-year-old filly "Maud S." broke the record of others of her class by trotting the mile in 2:13½.[17]

In 1883 the Washington Park Club purchased eighty acres on the South Side and built a clubhouse near their mile track at Sixty-first Street and South Park Avenue. The new track was opened in the summer of the next year with an eight-day racing meet at which $87,000 in stakes and purses was offered. But the fraud and gambling that often accompanied such events cast horse racing among the sports lacking the support of a respectable public opinion. This became fully apparent by the mid-'eighties, when it was reported that some of the most notorious promoters of gambling in the city — Harry Varnell, the Hankins brothers, and Mike McDonald — were in control of a syndicate which made $800,000 in one season. Public opinion was inflamed still further in 1890 when the news was widely

[16] Illinois Department of Agriculture, *Transactions . . . 1883*, n.s. XIII, 10–12, *1884*, n.s. XIV, 124; *Chicago Tribune*, Aug. 6, Sept. 4, 15, 24, 1881, Sept. 16, 20, 21, 1882, Sept. 5, 22, 26, 1883, Sept. 13, 14, 1884, Sept. 11, 1886, April 12, 14, 16, 1887. For the Fat Stock Show see Chapter IV, "The Economic Empire of Chicago: Livestock and Meat Packing."

[17] *Chicago Tribune*, March 23, June 29, July 6, 13, Oct. 1, 17, 23, 1873, Oct. 9, 11, 1878, July 25, 1880; *The Chicago Times*, April 13, 1873, Sept. 16, 1880. See also Pierce, *A History of Chicago*, II, 467. Races were held in the early 'seventies at Dexter Park, near the Union Stock Yards. The Chicago Jockey and Trotting Club Park, later known as the Chicago Driving Park, was located just east of Crawford Avenue, then the western boundary of the city, between Madison and Harrison.

circulated that one operator selling pools had cleared $190,000 during the previous year.[18]

Of all professionalized sports, baseball by all odds enjoyed the greatest and most enduring popularity. This popularity rested upon more than a decade of enjoyment before the Great Fire, which cut short temporarily the career of the White Stockings. Interest, however, was kept alive by amateur contests, a semi-professional club, and visiting professional teams until 1874, when the White Stockings were reorganized and their grounds at Twenty-third and State streets put in readiness. In 1875 William A. Hulbert, president of the Chicago Base Ball Club, signed Albert G. Spalding of the Boston Champions along with other players of pennant caliber, and the next year Spalding, as player and secretary-manager of the White Stockings, produced a team which took the championship of the National League.

On February 2, 1876, under Hulbert and Spalding, the National League of Professional Base Ball Clubs had been organized by four teams from the West and an equal number from the East. Its formation aided in establishing rules against gambling, adopting regulations to protect both players and management, and instituting business methods. In 1879 Adrian C. Anson, better known as "Cap," assumed the position of manager of the White Stockings, with Spalding retaining his secretaryship until 1882, when he became president. Under Anson, the Chicago Club, beginning in 1880, won the championship of the National League five times in seven successive seasons and took second another year. Financial success also attended the White Stockings when they played in Chicago. Throngs of fans, seldom less than two or three thousand and at times up to eight, crowded into the ballgrounds, from 1878 to 1884 located on the lake front near the foot of Randolph Street and thereafter on property at Congress, Harrison, Throop, and Loomis streets. The year 1885 saw the unprecedented number of 40,000 paid admissions to the four games between Chicago and New York in Chicago. The attendance at games played in the home of the White Stockings, larger than was generally recorded elsewhere, was due, in the opin-

[18] *Chicago Tribune*, July 15, 1883, June 23, 29, 1884, Jan. 24, 1885, July 24, 1887, Feb. 22, Sept. 8, 1888; *The Chicago Times*, Jan. 14, 1883; Asbury, *Gem of the Prairie*, pp. 145–46; Quinn, *Fools of Fortune or Gambling and Gamblers*, p. 405.

ion of the *Tribune,* to the " many baseball-maniacs " in the city who left their occupations and regularly paid their 50 cents.[19]

The financial success enjoyed by the Chicago Club from gate receipts was augmented at times by the sale of players, which in 1886 alone reached $13,000. In addition, profits that year came to more than $15,000, permitting dividends as high as 20 per cent and still leaving in the treasury enough to run the club for a while. Top players by the mid-'seventies were receiving $2,000; they were identified by team uniforms; and they participated in a game in which regulations as to playing and protective equipment reflected the specialized and mature game baseball had become. Even so, this " fashionable and extravagant craze," as *The Rights of Labor* described it, was at times unfortunately beset by widespread intemperance among many players, with scandals of players throwing games for money, and with a continuation of gambling despite the efforts of men like Hulbert, Spalding, and Anson.

In 1888 Spalding arranged a world tour for Anson and the Chicago Club, accompanied by an All-American team under John M. Ward. After playing before the great and famous of ten countries on five continents, the White Stockings returned in April, 1889 to a tumultuous welcome by Chicago fans, despite defeats inflicted at the hands of the All-Americans. In 1890 a revolt on the part of some of the players led to the formation of a new league. Charles A. Comiskey came from St. Louis to manage the affiliated Chicago team, which played its games in a new park at Thirty-fifth and Wentworth.[20] Though lasting only one year, the new organization demoralized Anson's outfit by taking over most of his players, thereby forcing him to rely upon beginners whom the fans at first called Anson's " Colts " and eventually named " Cubs " (1901).

The almost universal fascination of baseball for American lovers of sport led to the organization of leagues besides the National. In

[19] Pierce, *A History of Chicago,* II, 470; Jacob C. Morse, "Chicago in Baseball," *The Baseball Magazine,* II (April, 1909), 1–2; Albert G. Spalding, *America's National Game* (New York, 1911), pp. 199–201, 203, 207–11, 213; Adrian C. Anson, *A Ball Player's Career* (Chicago, 1900), pp. 92–94, 103, 106; Warren Brown, *The Chicago Cubs* (New York, 1946), pp. 7, 10–11; *Chicago Tribune,* Sept. 27, 1876, March 31, 1878, Aug. 28, 1881, April 22, May 6, Sept. 30, 1883, June 25, 1884, Feb. 25, Sept. 30, Oct. 1, 2, 4, 7, 1885, Oct. 10, 1886, April 15, 1891; *The Chicago Times,* Feb. 22, April 19, May 14, 1874, Oct. 1, 1880, Dec. 7, 1882; *Chicago Daily News Almanac, 1890,* p. 166.
[20] Comiskey in 1900 headed the White Sox, organized that year.

1882 the American Association became its competitor, as did the Union Association in 1883 in addition to many minor or "bush" leagues. In 1888 a University Base Ball Association was organized to promote a nine composed of college students who had already participated in the game. Five years later the Chicago Athletic Club assembled a group of college graduates and placed Spalding in charge with the avowed purpose of engaging in contests in the East. Amateurs, too, associated with each other in clubs, eventually coordinating their activities in an Amateur Baseball Association. Fields laid out in the city parks and the use of "sand lots" throughout the city allowed devotees of the game to demonstrate informally their skill among their peers.[21]

Although less popular than baseball, boxing and wrestling were professionalized sports with some following. Those who attended such matches, however, openly flouted public opinion, which generally considered them as inhuman and immoral. Prize fights were forbidden by state law after 1869, and enthusiasts therefore had to travel across the Indiana line or, upon occasion, to be saved from arrest by the friendly "ignorance" of the city police. In 1882 the heavyweight pugilist John L. Sullivan visited Chicago and exhibited his well-known prowess in sparring, wrestling, and club swinging. His appearance was the forerunner of others that winter, with James Elliot fighting under the Marquis of Queensberry rules, and Tom Chandler and John Files contending for the middleweight medal. Matches continued, despite the state law against them. In September, 1892, so avid were fight fans to see the bout between James J. Corbett and Sullivan that many journeyed to New Orleans, and the *Tribune,* in order to satisfy the interest of those who stayed at home, devoted the entire first two pages and one-third of a third page to a description of the fight.

[21] *The Western Catholic,* April 23, 1887; *The Rights of Labor,* VI (March 22, 1890), 5, VII (July 25, 1891), 10; *Chicago Daily News,* Jan. 26, 1888; *The Chicago Times,* Dec. 5, 1880, Dec. 9, 1883; *Chicago Tribune,* Aug. 17, 1884, Dec. 2, 1886, April 25, 1889, Jan. 7, 1890, Jan. 29, 1893; *Spalding, op. cit.,* pp. 240, 242, 251–65, 269–81; Anson, *op. cit.,* pp. 92, 120, 140–294; G. W. Axelson, "*Commy*": *The Life Story of Charles A. Comiskey* (Chicago, 1919), p. 111; *Mixed Drinks,* I (Oct. 1, 1889), 3; Osborn, *The Development of Recreation in the South Park System of Chicago,* p. 30. As early as 1887 two diamonds were laid out in Jackson Park; another was added the following year, and at the same time three were constructed in Washington Park. Chicago South Park Commissioners, *Annual Report, 1886–87,* p. 10, *1887–88,* p. 12.

Even cruder and more brutal, and just as reprehensible in the eyes of the general public as prize fighting, were dog and cock championship contests, a holdover of earlier days. Such exhibitions, too, were against the law, but, as in the case of prize fighting, it was not always necessary for onlookers to go into Indiana in order to witness what appeared to many a relic of barbarism.[22]

The craze of cycling which gripped the country in the late nineteenth century found Chicagoans eagerly following the practices adopted elsewhere. The Chicago Bicycle Club, organized in 1879, was the forerunner of others at first largely informal in procedure. As ardent cyclists, Chicagoans were hosts to the second annual convention of the League of American Wheelmen in 1882, a group which they joined two years later by forming the Illinois State Division of the League. Annual bicycle tournaments became an important part of the sportsman's life by the early 'eighties; six-day races between eleven o'clock in the morning and eleven at night tested both the skill and endurance of individual contestants; the annual Pullman road race, first attempted in 1887, was won by Horace R. Winship; and the professional cyclist Ralph Friedberg brought renown to his home town from as far away as England.

Though organized and professionalized in a degree, bicycling was by and large an informal means of recreation. It was fun among friends and neighbors as they swarmed down boulevards and streets, to the discomfiture of those who wanted to pursue their old-time habit of carriage driving or horseback riding unimpeded by such "outlandish machines," as the *Times* put it. While in 1879 bicycles had been banned from Lincoln Park as a foe "to the peace of mind and safety of body necessary to the pursuit of happiness," the journey made from Chicago to New York in June, 1892 was hailed as proof of the "physical and moral endurance" of American youth. The increased use of the bicycle as a means of transportation to work also

---

[22] Pierce, *A History of Chicago*, II, 468; Illinois, *Public Laws, 1869,* pp. 116–17, 307; *Chicago Tribune,* Oct. 19, 1873, April 9, 12, 1874, Jan. 14, 1875, Oct. 1, 1879, Feb. 16, 1880, Dec. 8, 1881, April 8, Oct. 31, Nov. 21, 25, Dec. 19, 20, 1882, Feb. 12, March 16, May 8, Nov. 17, 1883, Sept. 8, 1892; Citizens' Association of Chicago, *Annual Report, 1886,* pp. 11–12; Alexander Johnston, *Ten — and Out!* (New York, 1927), pp. 94–98. Other prize fights and wrestling matches in Chicago are treated in the *Tribune,* May 21, 22, Dec. 16, 1883, July 27, Aug. 27, 1884, Feb. 3, March 3, 24, Dec. 29, 1885, Jan. 29, March 9, May 20, 23, 1886, Feb. 8, April 12, 1887, Feb. 2, 16, 1888.

shared in the widespread approval it had acquired by the close of the 'eighties.[23]

Following its introduction from England in 1874, lawn tennis was received enthusiastically not only by men but by an increasing number of athletically minded women. Four private clubs by 1884 pitted their prowess against one another at the Kenwood Lawn Tennis Club in the Hyde Park area, and by 'eighty-six Washington and Jackson parks had courts where the public was able to play. Cricket, as in the past, continued to provide pleasure to both spectators and amateur participants through local contests and those promoted by various cricket clubs with other American and with Canadian teams.

Football in the meantime was invading the domain of amateur and professional games, but it gained acceptance far more slowly than baseball, tennis, or cycling. In 1876 the Chicago Foot Ball Club scheduled games to be played in May, and in the 'eighties college alumni more and more took on the teams of their alma mater. At the same time the formation of many clubs attested the popularity of shooting matches. Lacrosse, comparatively unknown to Chicagoans before the early 1880's, was viewed by about three hundred spectators in a contest between the Chicago Lacrosse Club and the Calumet Club on August 12, 1882, the second time the game had been exhibited in Chicago. Archery, like lacrosse, had fewer followers than other means of diversion, and golf by the 'eighties was still regarded as an aristocratic pastime, one in which, commented a correspondent of *The Knights of Labor,* " no man can indulge who has not a servant at command to assist him." Of wider appeal was roller skating, enjoyed by young and old at the many rinks in the city.[24]

Among the wealthy, horseback riding had for years been a favorite

[23] The daily papers, especially the Sunday editions, are filled with news of the cyclists, their clubs, and the use to which the bicycle was put. See also Chicago Lincoln Park Commissioners, *History of Lincoln Park,* pp. 48–50; *The Chicago Times,* July 10, 1881; *Mixed Drinks,* VI (June 22, 1892), 3; Andreas, *History of Chicago,* III, 680–81.

[24] *Chicago Post and Mail,* March 7, 1876; *Chicago Tribune,* May 16, Sept. 7, 1873, May 3, 7, 31, July 15, 31, Aug. 13, 1882, Aug. 20, 1883, May 18, Aug. 28, 31, Oct. 2, 1884, June 6, July 4, 1886, July 7, 10, 1887, Nov. 30, 1888, Nov. 29, 1889, July 16, Nov. 28, 1890, July 14, Aug. 23, 1891, April 11, Dec. 14, 1892; *The Chicago Times,* April 19, 1874, Jan. 23, 1881; *The Knights of Labor,* V (March 2, 1889), 15; Chicago South Park Commissioners, *Annual Report, 1885–86,* p. 11, *1886–87,* p. 10, *1887–88,* p. 12, *1888–89,* p. 14, *1889–90,* p. 20; Osborn, *op. cit.,* p. 30; Moses and Kirkland, *History of Chicago,* II, 513, 516, 520.

means of recreation. Bridle paths running through the Chicago parks became the much frequented course of both men and women. Well-groomed horses, sometimes stabled back of the palatial homes in which their owners resided, were the envy of all who could not possess them. In 1879 a few intrepid spirits formed the Chicago Polo Club and borrowed mounts from a near-by stable to hold a match in Lincoln Park. But lack of skill soon disqualified the performers as entertainers, and polo therefore gained little favor from spectators at this time.

With a lake and artificial bodies of water available, sports such as swimming and boating, were, as occasion permitted, indulged in. Swimming was less common than at a later day, though natatoriums were located in all three divisions of the city. In 1883 one on the South Side held " social swims," which appeared to traditionalists a somewhat irregular practice — an opinion the *Tribune* felt pretty close to unnecessary prudery. Indeed, apologists pointed out, the manager of the natatorium had taken the precaution of holding the swims on but one night each week, and had prescribed that only the male escorts of the women, all of whom must be invited, be allowed to attend. But few in Chicago were privileged to enjoy such facilities, for no public beaches equipped with bathhouses and protected by lifeguards were provided.

On the other hand, boating had been popular for a long time. Besides the informal activity of individuals and the more formalized undertakings of small groups, clubs sponsored special events. Regattas promoted by the Farragut and Chicago Yacht clubs, after the mid-'seventies, created considerable interest among those who could afford to sail for pleasure. Organizations of canoe enthusiasts in the warm months were replaced by those whose programs promoted ice-skating in the cold. Sleighing, reminiscent of Chicago's earliest days when diversions were less numerous than in these post-Fire years, still engaged the fancy of many, just as walking continued to do. It was no small matter of pride to Chicagoans, furthermore, that their city was the home of the champion walker Daniel O'Leary who, in a single match, completed a 500-mile walk in 142 hours and 13 minutes.[25]

[25] Arthur Caton to J. D. Caton, March 12, 1879, *Caton Papers; Chicago Tribune,* May 30, Nov. 21, 1875, Dec. 31, 1876, Oct. 18, 1879, Aug. 3–5, 31, Sept. 11, 1883, July 4, 1884,

Many of these pastimes were, of course, restricted to those who were able to participate in them or could, in some cases, afford to attend as spectators. But a growing attention to physical well-being opened up ways whereby many more than in the past were able to spend their leisure moments pleasurably and profitably. The extension of gymnasium facilities through organizations such as the Y.M.C.A and Y.W.C.A., and the introduction of physical training in 1886 by the public schools contributed greatly to the enlargement of the means for recreation as well as for the improvement of health.

Among indoor games, billiards had an increasing number of addicts, who frequented not only the pretentious Foley Hall and the "elegant" Brunswick Hall but other places scattered throughout the city. This pastime, like cards and similar games of chance, met the persisting fire of those who would outlaw them. Despite vigorously conducted crusades against them, so many people continued to enjoy them that the Reverend Regester W. Bland of the Wabash Avenue Methodist Church, addressing fellow ministers in 1885 on "The Relation of the Church to Popular Amusements," declared that the Great Fire was nothing short of a chastisement for people so fallen from grace.[26]

Within the framework of urban social life rested the club, at times the most exclusive of all the symbols of high society. The Chicago Club, since 1868 under that name, had by 1885 over five hundred members — the "old rich," as Julian Ralph described them. In the clubrooms around the whist tables in the afternoon were congregated men with "gray locks and semi-spherical waistcoats," so affluent that they needed to go to their offices only late in the day to see that "the young members of other clubs" had "not stolen their trade while they were playing cards." Here the great who visited the city were entertained, and here brilliant social events took place.

As the 'seventies advanced, other clubs sprang into being. In 1878

July 5, 1885, Jan. 29, 1888, Jan. 10, 1891; *Pomeroy's Democrat*, Aug. 11, 1877; *Abendpost*, July 27, 1892; *The Vanguard*, I (June 11, 1892), 6; *The Chicago Times*, April 14, 1874, Nov. 17, 21, 1875; Osborn, *op. cit.*, p. 29; Chicago South Park Commissioners, *Annual Report, 1878–79*, p. 7, *1880–81*, p. 17, *1881–82*, p. 18, *1883–84*, p. 12, *1886–87*, p. 14, *1887–88*, p. 10, *1888–89*, p. 8; Chicago Lincoln Park Commissioners, *History of Lincoln Park*, p. 110.
[26] Chicago Board of Education, *Thirty-second Annual Report, 1886*, p. 56, *Thirty-eighth Annual Report, 1892*, p. 235; *Chicago Tribune*, Jan. 26, June 13, Nov. 14–22, 1873, Jan. 18, 1874, March 27, April 7, Oct. 25, 1883, May 13, 1884, Dec. 8, 1885, July 31, 1892.

the Calumet Club, interested, among other things, in the early history of Chicago, was organized. Its Old Settlers' Room and annual old settlers' receptions were features of the city's social life from 1879, as was the reception devoted to displays of art. In 1879, too, the Union League Club, social in outlook but dedicated to the perpetuation of Republican party policies, was organized; its Democratic counterpart was the Iroquois Club, called, at first, the Chicago Democratic Club. Other societies rapidly grew in numbers as Chicago increased in population and wealth; these societies generally had the threefold purpose of caring for the social, intellectual, and economic wants of men in the various divisions of the city.[27]

Fraternal organizations proliferated notably, and the roster of members lengthened each year. As early as 1883 the city directory listed no less than 570 lodges inclusive of those predominantly pointed toward insurance and benevolence. The Freemasons were particularly active, having fourteen Negro lodges among their total of seventy-six. Odd Fellows, the Knights of Pythias, the Knights of Maccabees, the Independent Order of Foresters — indeed, about all that were known in the America of that day were represented on the Chicago scene. Veterans' organizations enjoyed an especially flourishing existence. Among them the Grand Army of the Republic emerged as both the social and the political leader. Temperance lodges, military organizations and informal military companies, and many others with special points of view mirrored the American propensity to affiliate in group action.

It was, in truth, as Alexis de Tocqueville observed as early as the 1830's: "Americans of all ages, all conditions, and all dispositions constantly form associations. They have not only commercial and manufacturing companies, in which all take part, but associations of a thousand other kinds, religious, moral, serious, futile, general or

[27] Ralph, *op. cit.*, p. 17; Andreas, *History of Chicago*, III, 390–94, 401–3, 405–7; *The Christian Union*, XXXIII (June 17, 1886), 6; *Chicago Tribune*, May 21, 23, 1878, Feb. 28, April 15, May 1, 18, 1883; *The Chicago Times*, Jan. 1, 1883. The Hamilton Club, chartered in 1890, sought to promote principles of government advocated by the statesman whose name it took. (Flinn, *Chicago . . . A Guide, 1892*, p. 237.) For the Union Club on the North Side and the Illinois Club on the West Side see Andreas, *History of Chicago*, III, 405–8; *Chicago Tribune*, May 21, 1878. For ethnic clubs see Chapter II, "The Fabric of Society"; for commercial and business groups with social outlook, see Chapter V, "Manufacturing and Merchandising." For the LaSalle Club, a Republican organization, see Charles King, "The City of the World's Fair," *Cosmopolitan*, XII (Nov., 1891), 58.

restricted, enormous or diminutive. . . . If it be proposed to incul-
cate some truth or to foster some feeling by the encouragement of a
great example, they form a society. Wherever at the head of some
new undertaking you see the government in France, or a man of
rank in England, in the United States you will be sure to find an
association."

Accompanying the increased number of men's clubs was the extension of women's societies, expressive of the emancipation of the
sex from some of the restrictions of the past. The first major organization established after those of 1869 was the Fortnightly Club,
initiated by Mrs. Kate Newell Doggett, the wife of William E. Doggett, vice-president of the Merchants' Savings, Loan & Trust Co.
From its founding June 4, 1873, the club was primarily interested in
social intercourse and intellectual developments. Among its limited
membership of 175 were some of the ultra-fashionable society figures
of the city — Mrs. John N. Jewett (wife of a prominent lawyer and
state senator), Mrs. Mason B. Loomis (wife of a lawyer and judge of
the county court), Mrs. Charles Henrotin (wife of the well-known
banker and broker), Mrs. Charles Gilman Smith (wife of a physician and member of the Woman's Medical College faculty), and
Mrs. Potter Palmer (wife of the owner of the famous Palmer House
and known as " the Queen " by her friends). In the years which
followed, it served as the source from which sprang similar groups,
including the Chicago Woman's Club, Friday Club, West End
Woman's Club, and the Young Fortnightly.[28]

The Chicago Woman's Club began February 17, 1876, when
women interested in social problems gathered at the home of Mrs.
Caroline M. Brown. Following the adoption of a constitution a week
later, the club started meeting regularly, first in homes, then, in
April, 1884, in rooms at Michigan Avenue and Van Buren Street.
From 21 members in 1876 the Chicago Women's Club, called so
until October 23, 1895, when it became the Chicago Woman's Club,
experienced a rapid growth, attaining a membership of 566 in 1892.

[28] Chicago Tribune, Jan. 7, 1893; Frank and Jerome, Annals of the Chicago Woman's Club, p. 12; Mrs. J. C. (Jennie June) Croly, History of the Woman's Club Movement in America (New York, 1898), pp. 60–61; Mrs. Charles Henrotin, " Two Women I Have Known," Lydia H. Farmer, ed., What America Owes to Women (Chicago, 1893), pp. 370–72; Moses and Kirkland, op. cit., II, 584; Flinn, Chicago . . . A Guide, 1892, p. 235; Joseph Kirkland, The Story of Chicago, [I], 339.

The entrance in the 1880's of social leaders such as Mrs. Charles Henrotin, Mrs. Potter Palmer, and Mrs. William Chalmers (wife of the machinery manufacturer), illustrated Julian Ralph's observation on the honor Chicago society women accorded cultural aspirations, achievements, and persons of intellect. Not only housewives but professional women, including the able lawyers Mrs. Myra Bradwell, Mrs. Catherine Waugh McCulloch, and Miss Ellen Martin, the well-known physicians Sarah Hackett Stevenson and Julia Holmes Smith, and the pioneering journalists Mrs. Helen E. Starrett, Mary Krout, and Mrs. Caroline S. Twyman participated actively in some one of the organization's six main divisions.

Although the club as such did not conceive of itself as an organ either of politics or of charity, it exerted an indirect but effective influence in both fields. Women important in social welfare work — Jane Addams, Mrs. Matilda B. Carse, Frances E. Willard, Julia Lathrop, Mrs. Celia Parker Woolley, and Mrs. Lucy L. Flower — saw in the club an instrument for bettering the condition of the community. Thus its program ranged widely and its successes were as numerous as the enterprises it promoted. With the coming of the World's Fair, the place of prominence and respect the club had attained was attested by its role of official hostess for the city and its leadership in the Women's Auxiliary Congress and on the Board of Lady Managers.[29]

Other societies more modest in size and in number of activities also reflected the breadth of women's interests beyond the home. For example, the Illinois Woman's Press Association opened its membership to those who published original matter in book form, or who were or had been connected with a reputable journal. Avowedly endeavoring to elevate standards among those who wrote, it had its counterpart in groups devoted to the study of a particular author such as Ibsen, Browning, or Shakespeare.

The Amateur Musical Club, organized about 1877 from informal gatherings of friends at piano sessions, eventually included most of

[29] Frank and Jerome, op. cit., pp. 15–18, 33, 37, 39–41, 43, 53, 71, 102, 114, 129–30, 239; The Chicago Blue Book, 1891, pp. 350–52; Powers, The Chicago Woman's Club, pp. 40, 41, 58–62, 64, 132–33, 159–60, 241, 249–50, 330–32; Croly, op. cit., pp. 62–63; Ralph, op. cit., pp. 42, 45, 52, 55, 58–59; National Council of Women, Transactions . . . February 22 to 25, 1891 (Philadelphia, 1891), pp. 260–62; Josephine Shaw Lowell, "Charity," in Meyer, Woman's Work in America, pp. 342–43.

the musically gifted women of the city. The Chicago Society of Decorative Art, also started in 1877, was primarily concerned with the cultivation of artistic decoration, with training in artistic industries and financial support for those so interested. With others of like mind, the society brought instruction in the practical arts to children living in the poorer sections of the city, and aided persons who planned to teach in the schools of the philanthropic Industrial Art Association.[30] In 1880 those imbued with a zeal for scientific knowledge formed the Woman's Physiological Institute, specializing particularly in anatomy, physiology, hygiene, and child training. From 1882 the Moral Educational Society, with a small membership solely of women but with an advisory board upon which men sat, attempted to disseminate information on marriage and parenthood, the abolition of vice, and the moral training of youth.

As women and children were inducted into industry with the changing economy, individual women and the societies to which they belonged turned their attention to the needs that industrialism created. Thus, Mrs. William Penn Nixon, wife of the business manager of the *Inter Ocean,* assisted in the organization of the Chicago Exchange, in which Mrs. Joseph T. Ryerson, Mrs. Nathaniel K. Fairbank, and Mrs. Jasper D. Ward were also active. The establishment of the Illinois Woman's Alliance in November, 1888 betokened the realization that unified action was important if the condition of working women and children was to be improved. In this co-operative undertaking were joined the Order of the Eastern Star, a Christian Science Association, and suffrage, medical, temperance, ethical, labor, and other groups seeking to obtain, among other things, the enforcement of all laws for the protection of women and children and the enactment of further remedial legislation.[31]

The invasion by women into precincts hitherto sacred to men continued, as in the years before the Fire, to meet opposition and ridicule from many. Particularly laughed at were the " ladies' clubs " and

[30] Moses and Kirkland, *op. cit.,* II, 584–85; Ralph, *op. cit.,* pp. 61–62; Warner, *loc. cit.,* pp. 877–78; Marquis, *Marquis' Hand-Book of Chicago,* p. 231; Frank and Jerome, *op. cit.,* pp. 56–57.

[31] Marquis, *op. cit.,* pp. 140, 158; The Woman's Exchange of Chicago, *Year Book, 1911,* pp. 23–25, *Year Book, 1933,* pp. 23–24; National Council of Women, *Transactions, 1891,* pp. 338–41; Lowell, *loc. cit.,* p. 343. For other humanitarian activities see Chapter XII, " Religious and Humanitarian Strivings "; for interest in politics, Chapter X, " The Profile of Politics."

women bent on the reform of wrongdoing, those who noted inequities in the social structure and moved to remedy them. " Are these money-getting, check book-carrying female stockholders and ballot droppers ' the compliment' [*sic*] to man for whom ' he will supply all material needs ' and whom ' he will protect from harm, toil and hardship '? " inquired *The Rights of Labor*. " Are these the charmers who ' will bring into his life beauty and refinement and the tender joys of home '? Will any man care to marry and to ' love and cherish them '? Will they ' look up to him and love and revere him '? O for heaven's sake — in the slang of the day — give us a rest, Helen! " [32]

But, despite obstacles thrown in their way, indomitable women forged ahead. In medicine, for example, over two hundred were recorded as physicians and surgeons by 1893. Although recognition came slowly, some were accorded places of trust in the profession. Dr. Frances Dickinson, for example, in 1883 became an alternate intern at Cook County Hospital, the first woman to be so honored. In 1876 Dr. Sarah Hackett Stevenson was elected to membership in the American Medical Association, and shortly thereafter local and national organizations took in not only Dr. Dickinson but Dr. Emma R. Gaston and Dr. Julia R. Low.

As in medicine, so in law women gave creditable accounts of themselves. Alta M. Hulett, after storming the citadel of legislative opposition, was instrumental in the passage of a law in 1872 providing that sex should not debar a person from any profession or employment except the military. In June, 1873 she was admitted to the practice of law, and before her death in 1877 she had the distinction of being the first woman admitted to practice in both state and federal courts.[33] Once the door had been forced, other women joined the ranks. Mrs. Myra Bradwell, who applied for admission as early as 1869, was granted it in 1890 and continued her work on the *Chicago Legal News*, a highly respected journal started in 1868. Mrs. Catherine V. Waite distinguished herself in the founding of the *Chicago*

[32] Otto Pelzer, "The Social Problem," *The Rights of Labor*, VI (Nov. 29, 1890), 4; Jacobi, "Woman in Medicine," in Meyer, *op. cit.*, p. 192; Gilbert and Bryson, *Chicago and Its Makers*, p. 880; Andreas, *History of Chicago*, III, 520; Stanton, Anthony, and Gage, *History of Woman Suffrage*, III, 579.

[33] *Lakeside Directory, 1893*, pp. 2097–2106; Ralph, *op. cit.*, p. 53; *Hubbard Collection*, in *Autograph Letters*, XVIII; Illinois, *Public Laws, 1872*, p. 578; Stanton, Anthony, and Gage, *op. cit.*, III, 573; *The Chicago Times*, Nov. 24, 1874; *Chicago Legal News*, IX (March 31, 1877), 229; Ada M. Bittenbender, "Woman in Law," in Meyer, *op. cit.*, p. 232.

Law Times in 1886, a quarterly journal devoted to the legal problems of the community, and Catherine Waugh McCulloch, M. Frederica Perry, and Ellen A. Martin also attained high standing as persons versed in the law.

While women did not appear in the pulpits of the old established religious faiths, many assumed the leadership in promoting the humanitarian enterprises of their various denominations. Upon occasion, however, the smaller sects selected a woman as pastor, the most notable for continued service being Florence Kollock, pastor from 1879 to 1891 of the Englewood Universalist Church.[34]

These increasing signs of the emancipation of women were but one of the many broadening aspects of urbanization. Some were, of course, more lasting and uplifting than others. In the city's transition from the age of beginnings toward that of maturity, the fine arts must be accorded an enduring place. Chicagoans for years had been more equably disposed toward music than toward the other arts. The early revival of amateur choral groups and the presentation of church benefit concerts after the Fire, were, therefore, reckoned natural steps toward the day of a cultivated social order. By 1874 concerts by professional soloists, chiefly from elsewhere, and by local amateurs had ready and uncritical listeners. Societies composed of national groups vied with one another in performing — as did the Germans, for example — musical derivatives of the homeland. As early as 1873 over three hundred music-lovers made up the roll of the Orpheus Gesangverein, and numerous smaller organizations reflected either the community spirit of the locale of their membership or some special or eleemosynary purpose. The twenty-second festival of the national North American Sängerbund in 1881 brought to Chicago groups similar to Chicago's singing societies, and their performances together gave Chicagoans the opportunity of hearing much that was worth while and well done.

Although the Germans were undoubtedly the chief promoters of this kind of endeavor in point of numbers, other national groups carried on similar activities. To these were added still others, irre-

[34] *Chicago Legal News,* XXII (April 5, 1890), 265; Stanton, Anthony, and Gage, *op. cit.,* III, 562, 572, 574, 575; National Woman Suffrage Association, comp., *Report of the International Council of Women* (Washington, 1888), p. 176; Julia Ward Howe, "Women in the Professions," *The Chautauquan,* VII (May, 1887), 462; Bittenbender, *loc. cit.,* pp. 233, 242; National Council of Women, *Transactions, 1891,* p. 104.

spective of the national origin of the membership, who engaged in the performance of some special type of musical expression — glees and madrigals, oratorios, and choral music in general. A church choral union, organized in 1884 by Maro L. Bartlett, set about founding branches throughout the city to teach music-reading scientifically. Four years later a more formally established Church Choral Union proposed also to give instruction in reading music at sight, in order to elevate the standards of congregation singing.[35]

Of the choral organizations the Beethoven (1873–1885), the Mozart (1881–1886), and the Apollo (1872–   ) were outstanding. The last two were male choruses, while the Beethoven was made up of mixed voices. An auxiliary chorus of women was added to the Apollo in 1876, a year after William L. Tomlins became Apollo's leader. In 1877 the ladies' chorus took on the form of an independent organization, more to the liking of its members than the designation of "auxiliary." Concerts, while presenting before Chicagoans the works of Haydn, Handel, Mendelssohn, and other composers of high rank, also became occasions of social acclaim. An attempt in 1889 to bring wage earners a series of oratorio concerts, at the nominal price of five to twenty-five cents, reflected Tomlins's desire to provide good music for all, regardless of financial status.

The importation of soloists from outside the city frequently spelled larger box-office receipts, but, even so, many of the concerts put on by the numerous choral groups of the city failed to make expenses. Then, also, attempts to perform compositions beyond the performing abilities of the group often led to a decrease in the number of participants and the demise of some of the organizations. The Apollo Club was, in this respect, an exception, free from debt and always profiting richly from its growing popularity.[36]

The elevation of musical taste was further achieved through per-

[35] Davis, Scrap Book, I, 1871–1876, 202–49; The Workingman's Advocate, Feb. 8, 1873; Rehage, Music in Chicago, 1871–1893, pp. 2–3, 51–52; Chicago Tribune, Jan. 21, Dec. 8, 1872, March 11, May 25, 1873, April 4, 1874, Oct. 14, 1877, March 31, 1878, May 11, 1879, June 19, 1881, Dec. 26, 1886, Jan. 30, Oct. 16, 1887, Feb. 3, March 21, Sept. 2, Dec. 16, 1888, March 21, 1891, Dec. 18, 1892; Chicago Daily News, June 23, 1881, Oct. 18, 1884. See also Chapter II, "The Fabric of Society."

[36] Chicago Tribune, April 16, Sept. 20, Oct. 5, 26, 1873, March 25, June 24, 1877; Chicago Daily News, Dec. 21, 1881, Dec. 17, 27, 1884, Feb. 18, 1885, March 21, 1889; George P. Upton, Musical Memories (Chicago, 1908), pp. 286–88, 290–91; Kirkland, op. cit., II, 273; W. L. Tomlins, "Wanted — Songs of a Better Life," Music, VIII (June, 1895), 219–20; G. F. Root, Story of a Musical Life (Cincinnati, 1891), pp. 204–5.

formances by visiting artists and opera companies. In 1873 an Italian company under the management of Max Maretzek opened at Mc-Vicker's Theatre. Featuring the voices of Pauline Lucca and the young American soprano Clara Louise Kellogg in a premiere performance in Chicago of Thomas's " Mignon," the first post-Fire opera season was launched in brilliant style. Other companies followed, and in 1874 Christine Nilsson made her first Chicago appearance in Meyerbeer's " Les Huguenots." It was not until November, 1877 that the dominance of Italian opera was challenged by the Pappenheim-Adams German troupe in Wagner and Weber at Hooley's Theatre.

In January, 1879 the arrival of Colonel J. H. Mapleson's Italian Company, with its orchestra of fifty-seven and chorus of forty, evoked a lively interest which was translated into an unusually enthusiastic support. The Hungarian soprano Etelka Gerster was an outstanding success in such favorites as " Lucia di Lammermoor " by Donizetti. But despite the warmth of the reception accorded her, it was not equal to that given Adelina Patti in her several " farewell " performances in Chicago. The year 1884 was made memorable to opera-lovers by the appearance of Patti and Gerster in Colonel Mapleson's troupe, and of Christine Nilsson and Marcella Sembrich with Henry E. Abbey's Grand Italian Opera Company. In 1885 Damrosch's German Opera Company from the Metropolitan Opera House in New York enjoyed a phenomenal success, and in the late 'eighties visiting companies from the Metropolitan, the Milan Grand Italian Opera Company, and the Abbott Grand Opera Company provided rich treats for the music-lovers of the city.

Professional music critics and other would-be critics warred as to the respective merits of the Italian and German productions, and extensive reviews appeared in the columns of the press of the city. As for the audience, the well-known critic Frederick Grant Gleason, writing in the *Inter Ocean,* insisted it attended the opera " a little to hear the music, a trifle more to hear the artists (if their names be sufficiently famous) — but mostly because it is the thing to do," and that it was not the musical notes the majority read, but the society notes about such affairs.

It was, however, the light opera that enjoyed the widest acclaim. The productions of Gilbert and Sullivan won particular favor. " Pinafore," first heard on January 27, 1879, was presented by various groups no less than eighty times within the next four months. This, the *Tribune* declared, was a record unparalleled in the musical history of Chicago. Opera in English became a craze. The Boston Ideal Opera Company, the Hess Acme Opera Company, the McCaull Opera Comique Company, and the DeWolf Hopper Comic Opera Company began in the 1880's to present a variety of enjoyable light operas.[37]

In social gatherings, voices were joined — often more gleefully than musically — in the popular songs of the day which individuals whistled or sang when alone. The sentimentality of Reginald de Koven's " Oh, Promise Me " from the operetta " Robin Hood " appealed to many. Equally favored and often heard were " After the Ball," " The Picture That Is Turned toward the Wall," and " The First Little Kiss He Gave Me," which contrasted in mood with the lighter " Where Did You Get That Hat? " and " Down Went McGinty."

Band concerts paralleled in public favor the light opera and popular songs. Performed in various halls and public parks of the city, these concerts had wide patronage, especially if the baton were wielded by Hans Balatka or Johnny Hand. Of far less appeal were the Chamber Music Concerts, principally a development of the 1880's, criticized for their attempt to please the average listener but not satisfying the musically intelligent.[38]

In the production of the more serious orchestral works in Chicago the name of Theodore Thomas was pre-eminent. To be sure, others of lesser achievement from time to time contributed to elevating the

[37] *L'Italia,* Dec. 10, 1887; *Chicago Tribune,* Feb. 10, May 4, 1873, Jan. 14, 15, 25, 1874, Jan. 12, 23, May 27, 1879, Dec. 12, 1880, April 16, 23, Sept. 24, Nov. 5, 1882, Feb. 11, 18, March 18, April 15, 22, 29, May 20, 27, June 3, 1883, Jan. 20, 27, Feb. 1, 3, 1884, March 1, April 18, Nov. 15, 1885, Jan. 3, Nov. 7, Dec. 5, 1886, Dec. 25, 1887, Nov. 17, 28, 1889, Nov. 30, 1890, Jan. 17, 1892; *The Chicago Times,* Jan. 28, 1879; Upton, *op. cit.,* pp. 38–39, 40, 42–43, 148–49, 251–52; Davis, *Scrap Book, 1884,* clipping from *The Inter Ocean,* Feb. 17, 1884.

[38] John Philip Sousa, *Marching Along: Recollections of Men, Women and Music* (Boston, 1928), p. 133; Smith, *First Nights and First Editions,* pp. 145–48; Sigmund Spaeth, *Read 'Em and Weep: The Songs You Forgot to Remember* (Garden City, N.Y., 1927), p. 191; Isaac Goldberg, *Tin Pan Alley* (New York, 1930), pp. 74, 90–98, 102–5; Schlesinger, *Rise of the City,* pp. 300, 302–4; *Chicago Daily News,* Jan. 11, Nov. 12, 1884; *Chicago Tribune,* May 18, Aug. 5, 10, 30, 1873, Aug. 30, 1884, Aug. 21, 1887, Aug. 16, 1891, July 14, 1892, Aug. 11, 1893; *The Chicago Times,* June 8, 1874, Aug. 3, 14, 16, 1880; *The Drovers' Journal,* May 5, 1883.

musical taste of those before whom they performed. Hans Balatka had gained renown in pre-Fire days through his Philharmonic Society Orchestra, and continued after the Fire to stimulate musical interest through various organizations. Under the direction of Adolph Liesegang a fifty-piece orchestra played Beethoven's Fifth Symphony on January 12, 1877, but internal dissensions, as happened at times in other groups, brought about the society's early decline. The Chicago Orchestra, sprung from the Great Western Light Guard Band and Hand and Freiberg's orchestra in 1877, gave what were reported as superior concerts during the next year under Adolph Rosenbecker. But here failure to get sufficient financial backing proved an insurmountable obstacle to continued existence.

The history of orchestral music of the best tradition in Chicago revolves around the masterful figure of Theodore Thomas, who, as leader of an orchestra, had visited Chicago in 1869. From 1872 to 1877 he returned in a series of concerts featuring the music of Beethoven, Gluck, Wagner, and other classical composers. Even in the bleak year of 1877 his summer concerts were well received. Held in the Exposition Building, transformed at one end into a beer garden replete with overhead lights and potted plants, the concerts gave listeners not only brilliant and light music but symphonic movements not frequently presented in the summer. So pleased was Thomas with his reception that, when invited to come back in 1878, he remarked: " Chicago is the only city on the continent, next to New York, where there is sufficient musical culture to enable me to give a series of fifty successive concerts." [39] To these summer night concerts can be traced what may well be described, as Carter Harrison put it, " the real beginnings of the musical education of Chicago." With four exceptions Thomas returned every summer until 1891, when on October 16 he raised his baton over the newly created permanent Chicago Orchestra and inaugurated a golden age of symphonic music in the city.

In the founding of the orchestra, an Orchestral Association, organized in 1890, played a significant role. Though earlier attempts to

[39] Pierce, *A History of Chicago*, II, 426; *Chicago Tribune,* Oct. 13, 1872, June 22, Oct. 7, 1873, Nov. 9, Dec. 10, 1876, Jan. 18, 21, 26, Aug. 12, 1877; Rose Fay Thomas, *Memoirs of Theodore Thomas* (New York, 1911), pp. 122–23, 124, 130; Theodore Thomas, *A Musical Autobiography* (George P. Upton, ed., 2 v. Chicago, 1905), I, 35–36, 57, 63, 71; Harrison, *Stormy Years*, p. 32.

494   A HISTORY OF CHICAGO

establish such a permanent organization for the city had failed, Chicagoans had evinced a great enough interest in symphonic music to accord enthusiastic receptions to such visiting groups as Leopold Damrosch's orchestra in 1882–83, the Boston Symphony in May, 1887, and Strauss and his Vienna Orchestra in October, 1890, not to mention Thomas's appearances. From the very first, the fifty original members of the Association displayed a high-minded generosity and civic pride in handling the financial problems of the new orchestra. In their number were included men of cultivation and wealth such as Philip D. Armour, Nathaniel K. Fairbank, Charles Norman Fay, Marshall Field, Charles L. Hutchinson, Cyrus H. McCormick, and George M. Pullman, who wisely gave Thomas, as director, the sole power of determining the artistic standards of the group.

Two years before Thomas took up the post of director, the Auditorium, dedicated to art, superseded other smaller and acoustically less satisfactory quarters for concerts and similar events. Under the Chicago Auditorium Association, which issued stock to the amount of $2,000,000 and bonds to $900,000, it was constructed from plans drawn by the architectural firm of Adler & Sullivan. The credit for first promoting the undertaking should go to Ferdinand W. Peck, a prominent Chicago capitalist, who made the structure financially feasible by including space to lease for business offices and a hotel.[40]

In comparison with achievements in music, those in painting were provincial, still embryonic. The beginnings of a local school, moreover, were not even faintly distinguishable, and attention to the exhibition of works from other countries and other times had to bolster the more or less feeble efforts of local talent. In the Chicago Academy of Design, reorganized after the Fire, the city's artistic life converged; and in 1877 a board of trustees constituted of prominent businessmen was added to the artist membership.[41] This board shortly

[40] *Chicago Tribune,* Nov. 25, 1882, May 6, 13, 1883, May 3, 1885, May 7, 1887, Oct. 5, 1890, Oct. 16–18, 1891; Theodore Thomas, *op. cit.,* II, 292; Rose Fay Thomas, *op. cit.,* pp. 355–56, 367; Upton, *op. cit.,* pp. 305–6; Hugh Morrison, *Louis Sullivan* (New York, 1935), pp. 85–86, 101; Andreas, *History of Chicago,* III, 652; Frank Lloyd Wright, *An Autobiography* (New York, 1943), p. 108; Edward C. Moore, *Forty Years of Opera in Chicago* (New York, 1930), pp. 17, 24–26.

[41] The men invited to serve as trustees in the rehabilitation of the Academy were William E. Doggett, Potter Palmer, Franklin MacVeagh, Nathaniel K. Fairbank, Levi Z. Leiter, Samuel M. Nickerson (president of the First National Bank), George C. Walker (treasurer of the Blue Island Land & Building Company), Henry W. King (clothier), Mark

resigned, and established the Chicago Academy of Fine Arts in 1879, which three years later became known as the Art Institute of Chicago.

In every way overshadowing its predecessor, the Art Institute was in a real sense the center of art in the city. In 1882 it moved from rented quarters at State and Monroe to the southwest corner of Michigan and Van Buren. Land additional to this site, which was owned by the Institute, was purchased in 1885, and a new building, designed by John W. Root in Romanesque style, was opened on November 19, 1887. A large and brilliant company assembled to view an extensive exhibit, including the Elbridge G. Hall collection of sculpture, the Elihu B. Washburne collection of portraits and paintings, the Society of Decorative Art exhibition, the Century drawings, and the Gibson and Harper collections of drawings. This museum possessed an attractive location fronting Lake Michigan and easily accessible to interested Chicagoans, but it shortly became too small for the growth of the Institute, and in 1892 it was sold to the Chicago Club. On November 1, 1893 the Institute took over the Renaissance-style structure put up for the World's Congresses of the Columbian Exposition on the east side of Michigan Avenue at Adams Street.[42]

Under the guidance of Charles L. Hutchinson, president from 1882 until his death in 1924, and the generosity of Martin Ryerson and other men of wealth, the Institute not only elevated the artistic taste of Chicago but became one of the greatest of its kind in the world. Visitors were admitted to the galleries free of charge two days each week. At the annual receptions, the holdings of Homer N. Hibbard, William S. Crosby, John T. Lester, Francis B. Stockbridge, Nathaniel S. Jones, Eugene A. Lancaster, Charles A. Gregory, Edson Keith, Charles J. Singer, and others were displayed. In 1890 Rembrandt's " The Accountant," the possession of Philander C. Hanford, whose wealth had been amassed in the oil business, was exhibited to Chica-

Skinner (lawyer), and William B. Howard (contractor). *Chicago Tribune*, Nov. 25, 1872; Andreas, *History of Chicago*, III, 420.

42 The Art Institute of Chicago, *Annual Report of the Trustees, June, 1888*, pp. 8, 11, *1891*, pp. 14–21; Kirkland, *op. cit.*, II, 65–66; Currey, *Chicago: Its History and Its Builders*, II, 264–65, III, 67–68; Chicago, *Municipal Reports, 1890*, " Mayor's Message," p. xxi; W. M. R. French, *The Art Institute of Chicago* (Chicago, 1901), pp. 3–5, 7; The Inter Ocean, *Centennial History of the City of Chicago*, pp. 65–66; *Chicago Tribune*, Nov. 2, 1877, May 23, 1879, Nov. 20, 1887, Dec. 9, 1893; Monroe, *loc. cit.*, pp. 410–12, 416.

goans, who at various other times had been privileged to view works of Millet, Diaz, Meissonier, and Rosa Bonheur in the collections loaned by their fellow citizens. In 1890 came the first showing of old masters purchased by Hutchinson and Ryerson from the Demidoff and May collections, including Rembrandt's "Portrait of a Young Girl," Rubens's "Portrait of the Marquis Spinola," and works by Van Dyck, Frans Hals, Holbein, Van Ostade, Van de Velde, Hobbema, and Jan Steen.[43]

Besides the offerings of the Old World, those of contemporary native talent were also shown, frequently in exhibitions where prizes were awarded. The enlargement of cultural education was accelerated also through lectures by specialists at the Institute, including those by Lorado Taft, later world-renowned in the field of sculpture. The art school, organized in 1879, likewise played a considerable part in providing training for those who wished to learn about drawing, painting, sculpture, newspaper illustrating, decorative designing, and architecture. By 1886 the Institute's school had an enrollment of four hundred, instructed chiefly by those who had studied in Europe or served an apprenticeship in the East. Through the influence of Henry F. Spread of the school's staff, the Chicago Society of Artists was organized in 1888 as a successor to the Chicago Art League, with the aim of advancing art and cultivating social relations among its members. Despite various strains and stresses which had brought about the end of less enduring organizations, the Palette Club, originally called the Bohemian Club, flourished after 1881. Its membership, made up exclusively of women, proudly displayed their works in annual exhibitions at the Art Institute.[44]

The exigencies of earning a livelihood, however, forced not a few

[43] French, op. cit., p. 3; James Spencer Dickinson, "The Art Movement in Chicago," The World To-Day, XIV (April, 1908), 374; Chicago Tribune, May 23, 1873, Jan. 14, 1883, Feb. 15, 1885, March 31, Nov. 8, 1890, Nov. 30, 1941; Hubbard Collection, in Autograph Letters, XVIII; Chicago Academy of Design, Circular, Jan. 8, 1880 (Chicago Historical Society); The Art Institute of Chicago, Annual Report, 1891, pp. 30–35; Andreas, History of Chicago, III, 421–25; Edward A. Duddy, "Charles Lawrence Hutchinson," Dictionary of American Biography, IX, 438. For some holdings of wealthy Chicagoans see Chapter II, "The Fabric of Society."

[44] The Art Institute of Chicago, Annual Report, 1890, pp. 11, 26, 1891, pp. 39–41, 42, 1894, p. 29; Chicago Tribune, June 10, 1886, Dec. 9, 1893; Ralph Clarkson, "Chicago Painters, Past and Present," Art and Archaeology, XII (Sept.–Oct., 1921), 129–43; C. Dean, The World's Fair City and Her Enterprising Sons (Chicago, 1892), pp. 162–63; Monroe, loc. cit., pp. 418–19; Andreas, History of Chicago, III, 419.

Chicago artists to turn to teaching and other pursuits more certainly lucrative than painting and sculpture. Even so, Chicago had men and women of the sturdy stuff who put up with hardship and privation in order to devote themselves to their art. Most of them adhered rather consistently to the ideas which had characterized early American painters. George P. A. Healy, whose portrait-painting in pre-Fire days had enriched the art life of the city, Oliver Dennett Grover, John H. Vanderpoel, Henry Peterson, Alden F. Brooks, Arthur J. Pickering, Daniel F. Bigelow, Lucy Hartrath, Annie C. Shaw, Alice Kellogg, and Henry A. Elkins were among those known to local enthusiasts.

Although men of means gave generously to the support of art and polite society patronized it, no Chicago school arose, even as late as 1893, to challenge the productions of the Old World and the East. It was, as Hamlin Garland pointed out, " a universal belief that no good can come out of Nazareth." Still true, but less so than in 1873, was the observation in the *Lakeside Monthly* of that year that the aristocracy of wealth, the " *nouveaux riches,*" extensively demanded such works of art as were turned out " by the dozen under the auspices of the National Academy for the Development of American Art, and sold to the highest bidder at public auction." But along with other thriving centers, Chicago was developing an appreciation of beauty. And Garland and others had already begun to direct the artist to " unhackneyed themes in sky and plain and in the life of the city itself." [45]

Yet for the many, art, whatever its state of refinement, had slight appeal. Pictures of little merit often gave far greater enjoyment than the works of the masters, and the old-time and frequently shown panoramas still drew large crowds. In 1883 the National Panorama Company, organized by Chicago interests, exhibited the " Battle of Gettysburg," and in one year alone (1885) realized a 24-per-cent dividend on their investment. Other companies experienced similar success as

[45] Archie Thompson, *History of Art in Illinois* (Typescript, W.P.A. [1939?]), p. 3; Clarkson, *loc. cit.*, pp. 129, 134, 136–38, 141; Eugenia Remelin Whitridge, *Art in Chicago: The Structure of the Art World in a Metropolitan Community* (unpublished Ph.D. Thesis, The University of Chicago, 1946), pp. 65–66; Hamlin Garland, " Art Conditions in Chicago," Preface to *United Annual Exhibition of the Palette and Cosmopolitan Art Clubs,* Jan., 1895 [n.p.]; [Anon.], " The Chicago of the Societist," *The Lakeside Monthly,* X (Oct., 1873), 326–32; *Chicago Herald,* April 5, 1891.

they, too, benefited from the interest of the public in battle scenes, particularly those of the Civil War.[46]

Within the city the art of sculpture was also moving forward, although, even more than in painting, local influences were not such as to stimulate greatly the creative powers of many. There were, however, the busts and figures by Leonard W. Volk, which already had won recognition in pre-Fire days; and the work of John Donoghue was considered of high order in the 1880's, including a bronze statue of Sophocles and a design for a frieze to be cut into marble for the Board of Trade Building. The consequences of this dearth of local products were to some extent canceled by the visits of renowned sculptors, such as Harriet Hosmer in 1888, and by collections imported into the city. Statuary and other art works could be seen by an interested public when shown at the Art Institute, at the Exposition Hall, and in the studios of the several art dealers.

As in most other American cities, however, it was the monument that was the conspicuous offering of sculptors, portraying the mood of the moment — the commemoration of the heroes of war, giants in the political arena, or some popular historic event. Some works, it is true, mirrored the desire of a donor to beautify the city; these were most frequently seen in the several fountains dedicated particularly in the 'eighties. A few of the monuments and other sculptured objects had high merit, such as Augustus Saint-Gaudens's masterful statue of Lincoln and the Saint-Gaudens and MacMonnies fountain, both placed in Lincoln Park in 1887 as the gift of Eli Bates. The monument " The Alarm," an Indian group, also in Lincoln Park and the gift of Martin Ryerson in 1884, was a good expression of the skill of John J. Boyle in aboriginal themes. Felix Gorling in 1892 immortalized Alexander von Humboldt in a statue executed for Francis J. Dewes, the brewer. Public subscription made possible in 1891 the U. S. Grant monument by Louis T. Rebisso, considered by critics as decidedly inferior to the Saint-Gaudens Lincoln. The police force in the Haymarket affair of May, 1886 was acclaimed in the work of Johannes Gelert placed in Union Park in 1892. Through the generosity of George M. Pullman, the Fort Dearborn Massacre had its me-

---

[46] As in other topics of this nature, see the newspapers, especially *Chicago Tribune*, Nov. 18, 28, 1883, June 20, Dec. 28, 1884, May 4, Aug. 16, Oct. 4, 1885, Jan. 10, Feb. 24, April 13, 1886, May 1, Sept. 18, 1887, March 4, 1888; *The Chicago Times*, April 3, 1892.

morial in 1893 at the foot of Eighteenth Street, the work of the Dane Carl Rohl-Smith.[47]

If the achievements of Chicagoans in painting and sculpture were marked on the whole by mediocrity and lacked the inspiration of genius, this was not true of the city's architects. In the field of business architecture Chicago made a lasting contribution. The pioneers of what may be called the Chicago school of design — William Le Baron Jenney, Dankmar Adler, John W. Root, Daniel H. Burnham, and Louis H. Sullivan — fitted architectural expression to the needs of a rapidly expanding urban industrialism. They revolutionized the building arts with an impact that was world-wide. Reversing building methods, they changed the function and use of masonry walls. Their work was, as Paul Bourget observed, " the first draught of a new sort of art, — an art of democracy made by the masses and for the masses, an art of science, where the invariability of natural laws gives to the most unbridled daring the calmness of geometrical figures." [48]

The Great Fire, the enormous growth of the city, and the spiraling price of land fostered experiments in the use of iron and steel to sustain walls and floors in buildings resting on the city's claylike soil.[49] Conventional masonry, shown in 1871 not to be fireproof, was put upon a metal framework strongly girded to withstand pulls and pressures. The actual building, with its iron or steel skeleton to which were attached thin outer walls of stone masonry or brick, had partitions of firebrick and plaster resting on iron laths. The first of the skyscrapers was the ten-story Home Insurance Building at the corner of Adams and LaSalle streets, designed by Jenney and completed in 1885. The Rookery, with its " floating foundations " — the work of Burnham & Root — rose twelve stories in 1886; the Rialto at Van Buren and LaSalle streets, and the Phoenix at Jackson and Clark further testified to architectural daring.

The Tacoma Building, planned by Holabird & Roche at Madison

[47] *Chicago Tribune,* Jan. 1, 1882, Dec. 9, 1888, Jan. 3, 1892, June 23, 1893; *The Chicago Times,* Sept. 5, 1878; Revyen, Aug. 25, 1900; Lorado Taft, *The History of American Sculpture* (*The History of American Art,* John C. Van Dyke, ed., New York, 1903), pp. 201–2, 404, 407, 431–32, 523. See also list of monuments, fountains, and memorials published by Commissioners of Chicago Park District (Burnham Park), March 29, 1944.
[48] Starrett, *Skyscrapers and the Men Who Build Them,* p. 35; Pierce, *As Others See Chicago,* p. 384, quoting Paul Bourget, *Outre-Mer Impressions of America.*
[49] The style of residences is treated in Chapter II, " The Fabric of Society."

and LaSalle streets and completed in 1889, was another step forward in the use made of rivets, more easily and quickly applied than nuts and bolts in securing the frame.[50] Other skyscrapers followed, reaching a climax just before the Columbian Exposition in the twenty-one-story Masonic Temple (1892) at Randolph and State streets. Apartment buildings and hotels also benefited by the new form of construction. As more edifices rose " skyward," as the *Tribune* put it, some questioned the effect such high structures would have on health and safety if all buildings located on narrow streets soared ten or more stories above ground. Yet, despite the doubts of skeptics, architects continued to develop and perfect the new methods in response to the ever-increasing demands of the city's expanding business life.[51]

[50] *Industrial Chicago,* I, *The Building Interests,* 170, 188–89; Carl W. Condit, *The Rise of the Skyscraper* (Chicago, 1952), p. 14; Frank Randall, *History of the Development of Building Construction in Chicago* (Urbana, 1949), pp. 12, 15, 105–7, 110, 118, 128, 198; Harriet Monroe, *John Wellborn Root* (Boston, 1896), p. 116; Louis H. Sullivan, *The Autobiography of an Idea* (New York, 1926), p. 310; Tallmadge, *Architecture in Old Chicago,* p. 198; *Chicago Tribune,* Jan. 1, 1892.

[51] *Industrial Chicago,* I, *The Building Interests,* 231, 232, 240, 242–43, 255; *Chicago Tribune,* Jan. 1, 1883; *Chicago Legal News,* VII (Feb. 28, 1885), 396, XXII (April 26, 1890), 537; *Abendpost,* Sept. 3, 1891.

CHAPTER XIV

THE WHITE CITY

LIKE 1871, the year 1893 is epochal in the history of Chicago. Both mark the end of the old and the beginning of the new. During the crowded days of the years between, the city had risen out of the ashes of the Great Fire, and Chicago had become second city of the country, outstripping both Philadelphia and Brooklyn in population. At the same time, comparable gains in economic endeavors fortified the faith of Chicago leaders that the city was destined to be first and biggest in nearly all things. Their unabashed " supervoluminous civicism," as Julian Ralph described their unceasing drive to this end, contributed also to the selection of Chicago as the site of the World's Columbian Exposition.

The proposal to commemorate the four-hundredth anniversary of the landing of Columbus in the Western Hemisphere had been a matter of discussion for some time prior to 1885. In that year Edwin Lee Brown suggested that Chicago would be the ideal place for it.[1] By 1889 New York, Washington, and St. Louis as well as Chicago were presenting to Congress the special advantages which each claimed. By summer of that year Chicago had a committee of three hundred at work, prominent citizens appointed by Mayor Cregier under authorization of the City Council. Incorporating as the World's Exposition of 1892, they issued $5,000,000 worth of stock in shares of $10 each, fully subscribed by April 9, 1890.

It was well that Chicago moved quickly. Eastern representatives,

---

[1] Brown offered to stockholders of the Inter-State Exposition the resolution that a world's fair in 1892 be held in Chicago. *Chicago Tribune*, Nov. 15, 1885.

in particular, saw little merit in the midland metropolis. Time, they held, had been too short to develop local traditions such as the older cities enjoyed; New York, the great metropolis of the country, for example, they declared, was not only surrounded by a more thickly populated region, but had the embellishments of a cultured civilization to a greater extent than this raw new outpost, constantly boasting about its grain, lumber, and meat. But back of her braggart phrases lay the ingredients of Chicago's " I will " spirit, which, before long, demonstrated the reliability of the city's financial pledge of a total working capital of $10,000,000. On April 21, 1890 the Senate, convinced of Chicago's good faith, followed the action of the House of Representatives of February 24 designating Chicago as the site of the Fair. To allow for local celebrations of Columbus Day in 1892, Congress set the opening date for the international exposition as 1893.[2]

Meanwhile the local organizers elected a board of forty-five directors, who chose as president Lyman J. Gage. On June 12, 1890 the stockholders changed the company's name from the World's Exposition of 1892 to the more appropriate World's Columbian Exposition.[3] In addition to the local group, a national commission was appointed to exercise broad supervisory powers and arrange for exhibits, especially from foreign nations. A Board of Lady Managers, an offshoot of the Commission, was named to gather from all parts of the world exhibits of women's work. Conflicting judgments arising among the various bodies slowed up preparations, but with the appointment of George R. Davis of Chicago as Director-General in September, 1890, work moved forward. Finally, a Council of Administration, composed of two directors and two commissioners, reconciled the work of all agencies and insured effective direction of what became an increasingly complex and far-flung undertaking.

[2] Telegram to Lyman J. Gage, March 6, 1890 (Ms. Chicago Historical Society); Chicago, Council Proceedings, 1889–90, pp. 313–14, 360–62, 1247; Chicago Tribune, July 30, Aug. 3, 14, 20, 28, Sept. 6, 9, 18, 20, 25, 1889, Feb. 25, April 22, 26, 1890; U. S., Cong. Record, 51 Cong., 1 sess., XXI, pt. 2, 1664–65, pt. 4, 3615. Unless indicated otherwise, the chief sources on the World's Columbian Exposition are: Chicago World's Columbian Exposition, Report of the President (Chicago, 1898); Rossiter Johnson, ed., A History of the World's Columbian Exposition (4 v. New York, 1897–98); Hubert Howe Bancroft, The Book of the Fair (5 v. Chicago, 1893). The dedication of the buildings took place Oct. 21, 1892.

[3] In April, 1891 William T. Baker succeeded Gage in the presidency of the Board of Directors. Harlow N. Higinbotham succeeded Baker in Aug., 1892.

Before President Harrison would proclaim the opening day of the Fair, it was necessary for Chicago to raise $5,000,000 in addition to the amount already subscribed. The Board of Directors therefore turned to the city government, but the city had already reached the legal limit of indebtedness. Financial aid from this source could come only through action of the state legislature proposing a constitutional amendment for consideration in the November election of 1890. On July 31 a special session authorized this procedure, and in November the voters approved the amendment. On December 4 the City Council provided for the bonds by ordinance. With the selection of the site, President Harrison fixed the opening day of the Exposition as May 1, 1893, and invited nations throughout the world to send representatives and exhibits.[4]

The actual site was not definitely settled until February 11, 1891, after a struggle involving residents and business interests of the North, South, and West sides as well as proponents of a location along the lake front adjacent to the heart of the city. In the midst of this intramural contest the Directors sought the advice of Frederick Law Olmsted, America's most noted landscape artist. Eventually the choice fell upon Jackson Park, still largely undeveloped, a stretch of swamps and wind-swept sandbars with only a scrubby growth of trees to break the dull monotony of the landscape. But it was easily accessible to the center of the city, and at the east glistened the dark-blue waters of Lake Michigan; its spaciousness would permit the conversion of dune and marsh into low and broad terraces crossed by canals, lagoons, and, in the southern portion, a formal basin. The conception of loveliness which became a landmark in artistic accomplishment was that of Olmsted and his partner, Henry Sargent Codman, and the principal architects, sculptors, and painters, under the general supervision of Daniel H. Burnham.[5]

[4] *Chicago Tribune*, April 4, 5, May 1, 24, June 10, 28, July 24, 31, Nov. 25, Dec. 5, 1890; Chicago, *Council Proceedings, 1890–91*, pp. 316–18, 1192–93, 1217–21; Moses and Kirkland, *History of Chicago*, II, 472. In addition to the $10,000,000 thus provided, the Exposition floated $4,444,500 in 6-per-cent debenture bonds and realized $2,446,680.43 from the sale of commemorative fifty-cent pieces placed at its disposal by the national government.

[5] *Chicago Tribune*, Aug. 10, 1889, March 2, May 11, 21, 28, June 8, 11, 24, 26, 29, July 24, 29, 30, Aug. 29, Sept. 5, 10, Nov. 12, 22, 1890; *The Chicago Times*, Jan. 11, 1891; *The Drovers' Journal*, June 21, 26, 30, July 1, 1890; *Abendpost*, July 18, 1890; Monroe, *John Wellborn Root*, pp. 219–28, 234–40; Charles Moore, *Daniel H. Burnham, Architect, Planner of Cities* (2 v. Boston, 1921), pp. 32–43, 45–47; Paul Starrett, *Changing the Skyline: An Autobiography* (New York, 1938), p. 46.

For the design of the halls surrounding the formal basin — known as the Court of Honor — the architects adopted certain general principles. They decided upon the classical style, and, for the sake of harmony of the whole, they agreed upon a uniform height for the cornice; otherwise, artistic genius might enjoy free rein. For structures outside the Court even these restrictions did not hold. A spirit of co-operation among the renowned planners found its physical representation in the magnificent ensemble, so inexpressibly beautiful, as Julian Hawthorne put it, as " not to be translated into parts of speech."

No other single structure won more acclaim than the Palace of Fine Arts, the work of the New York architect Charles B. Atwood, whom Burnham had named Designer-in-Chief to succeed Root upon his untimely death on January 15, 1891. A veritable reincarnation of the genius of ancient Greek art, it rose serenely on the shores of a little lake in the northern part of the park. Augustus Saint-Gaudens pronounced it the greatest achievement since the Parthenon, and to the English journalist George Warrington Steevens it appeared " surely as divinely proportioned an edifice as ever filled and satisfied the eye of man." Its builders, hoping it might last for a long time as well as safely house its priceless collection of graphic and plastic arts, used chiefly brick and steel in construction, although its exterior, like that of other halls, was of staff. Later, for two decades it sheltered the collections of the Field Columbian Museum, and in 1933 it became the home of the Museum of Science and Industry.

Southeast, across the little lake, lay one of the most unusual structures of the Exposition: the Fisheries Building, product of the Chicago architect Henry Ives Cobb. Roofs of glazed Spanish tile sloping sharply to a central ridge accented its long, curtain walls while a turreted circular tower rose from the center of its nave. Most striking of all its features was the sculptural decoration, depicting in the capitals of its numerous columns the sundry creatures of river and sea. Flanking the principal structure and connected with it by curved projecting corridors were two other pavilions housing an aquarium and angling exhibits.

More conventional in design but unique in purpose was the Woman's Building, opposite the Fisheries Building, on the western side of the lagoon. The work of the Boston architect Sophia G. Hayden, the building, in Italian Renaissance style, provided extensive space for the exhibition of women's work, as well as meeting rooms and offices. A popular attraction, too, was the model kitchen with tile floor and gas range, where demonstration lessons were given on how to prepare nourishing foods.

Close by stood the simple and unpretentious Children's Building, for which the Board of Lady Managers, under the chairmanship of Mrs. Potter Palmer, was also responsible. Here thousands of children found wholesome amusement under the supervision of trained attendants while their elders toured the Fair grounds. Its importance extended far beyond this limited function, however, for it demonstrated to those interested in education, methods of instructing deaf mutes, and how to conduct classes in manual training and physical culture.[6]

More spectacular than the Children's Building was the neighboring Horticulture Building, designed by the Chicago firm of Jenney & Mundie in the style of the Venetian Renaissance. Its dominant feature was a depressed but expansive crystal dome, covering the tropical verdure that rose nearly to its summit. Outside the main entrance stood two large sculptural groups by Lorado Taft, depicting symbolically " The Sleep " and " The Awaking of the Flowers." The floral collection within was reportedly the most magnificent ever assembled.

Without doubt the Transportation Building, situated slightly southward, was the most original of the large structures. Departing from the prevailing lines and snowy whiteness that characterized the Exposition, the architects Adler & Sullivan gave the walls a rich polychrome decoration which culminated in a great arched doorway intricately ornamented with arabesques and bas-reliefs, and treated with gold and silver leaf. Through this entrancing portal passed throngs of men and women to see the vehicular and marine transportation exhibits, and the particularly large railroad displays.

[6] Moore, op. cit., I, 41–43, 45–46; Homer Saint-Gaudens, ed., The Reminiscences of Augustus Saint-Gaudens (2 v. New York, 1913), II, 66; Henry Van Brunt, " The Columbian Exposition and American Civilization," The Atlantic Monthly, LXXI (May, 1893), 582–83; Julian Hawthorne, " A Description of the Inexpressible," Lippincott's Monthly Magazine, LI (April, 1893), 496–503; Thomas E. Tallmadge, The Story of Architecture in America (New York, 1927), pp. 207–10; G. W. Steevens, The Land of the Dollar, quoted in Pierce, As Others See Chicago, p. 398; Joseph and Caroline Kirkland, The Story of Chicago, II, 145–46.

Besides these halls devoted to the interests and products of mankind, a considerable array of government buildings, foreign and American, shared the northern section of the park. These varied greatly in size and pretentiousness, in style and quality. Unfortunately, the two structures representing the United States and Illinois evoked the severest criticism, but the state headquarters as a whole marked a great advance over those at the Philadelphia Centennial in 1876.[7]

In the Court of Honor, the brilliant artistic center of the Columbian Exposition, formal classicism reigned unchallenged. Five large exhibition halls framed two sides, individual in design yet blending harmoniously to form a picture of transcendent beauty. From the drafting-board of the Chicago architect Solon S. Beman came the Mines and Mining Building, the first structure given over exclusively to the display of ores and minerals, mining and metallurgical machinery, and petroleum products that ever appeared at an international exposition. The Kansas City firm of Van Brunt and Howe planned the neighboring Electricity Building, dedicated to revealing the mysteries of this new-found power. Completing the line of halls on the north side of the basin was the mammoth Manufactures and Liberal Arts Building, not only the largest of the Fair but reported to be the biggest in the world. The work of George B. Post of New York, it covered an area of more than thirty acres and at its highest point equaled a nineteen-story skyscraper.

On the opposite side of the basin rose Machinery Hall, by Peabody and Stearns of Boston. Its long colonnades took their inspiration from Parisian architectural monuments, while its ornamental towers grew from ideas suggested by Italian and French structures. Within were exhibits of man's inventive skill in mechanics. Although second largest of all the buildings, Machinery Hall proved inadequate to care for all the displays, and authorities were compelled to erect several smaller accommodations. On the south side of the Court also was the Roman-styled Agriculture Building, the creation of McKim, Mead & White of New York. Perhaps no structure of the Fair represented a more perfect wedding of the talents of architect, sculptor, and painter. Poised on its low gilded dome was Saint-

[7] Joseph and Caroline Kirkland, *op. cit.*, II, 109, 112–13; Hawthorne, *loc. cit.*, p. 501; Tallmadge, *op. cit.*, p. 210.

WORLD'S COLUMBIAN EXPOSITION
Looking east toward the Court of Honor.

MICHIGAN AVENUE IN THE EARLY 'NINETIES

From Frank T. Neely, *Neely's Photographs* . . . (Chicago: F. T. Neely, 18—).

Gaudens's statue of Diana, while other sculptures by Philip Martiny and murals by George W. Maynard added to its decoration. The exhibits within included various products of the soil and articles made from them; and an annex housed a collection of agricultural machinery. Near by stood the Live-Stock Pavilion.

The Administration Building alone dignified the western end of the Court of Honor. Conceived by Richard M. Hunt of New York, its octagonal gilded dome soared upward, exceeded in dimension only by St. Peter's at Rome. Below, in the basin, lay the beautiful Columbian Fountain of Frederick MacMonnies; near the opposite end a high pedestal rose from the placid waters to support a colossal statue of "The Republic" by Daniel Chester French. Beyond stretched Atwood's graceful Corinthian Peristyle, to enclose the Court on its lakeward side. Impressive as was each of these architectural and sculptural masterpieces, it was the splendor of no single work but the grandeur of them all that was most compelling.[8]

No less noteworthy were the plans for musical events, the task chiefly of a Bureau of Music headed by Theodore Thomas and William L. Tomlins. They arranged an ambitious six months' program of concerts that would demonstrate to the world the musical progress of the nation in all its phases, and also give Americans an opportunity to hear a wide selection of works by world-renowned composers from abroad. The popular orchestral concerts at noon each day, open to all without charge, enjoyed large and appreciative audiences, but those presenting music in its highest forms, for which a fee was charged, did not prosper. Eventually, Fair administrators, harried by financial worries, canceled all appearances of visiting artists and organizations, and on August 4 Thomas resigned. Popular music took over; band concerts drew enthusiastic crowds and justified John Philip Sousa's advice to offer programs not only for the student and lover of music but for the amusement as well as the education of the common listener.[9]

[8] Joseph and Caroline Kirkland, *op. cit.*, II, 117–19, 122–24, 133–39; Tallmadge, *op. cit.*, p. 209; Henry Van Brunt, "Architecture at the World's Columbian Exposition," *The Century Magazine*, XLIV (May, 1892), 90–92; Saint-Gaudens, *op. cit.*, II, 73–74; William R. Thayer, *The Life and Letters of John Hay* (2 v. Boston, 1915), II, 94–95; Hawthorne, *loc. cit.*, p. 500.

[9] Theodore Thomas, *A Musical Autobiography*, I, 193–200, II, 281–91; Rose Fay Thomas, *Memoirs of Theodore Thomas*, pp. 386–416; "Choral Music at the Fair," Bureau of Music, *Official Circular, reprinted in Music*, III (Nov., 1892), 45–48; Charles Edward

Likewise diverting were the attractions along the Midway Plaisance, which stretched westward from the Fair grounds proper. Here picturesque reproductions of foreign streets and villages, cafés, bazaars, a Turkish mosque, and a zoological show attracted thousands. Particularly popular was the giant Ferris Wheel, 250 feet in diameter, hanging high in the air on supports of steel framework, and carrying thirty-six cars, each of which could accommodate as many as sixty passengers. So successful financially were the concessions that they made possible a 10-per-cent dividend for stockholders of the Fair.[10]

The physical beauty of the Fair's buildings, the educational contribution of its exhibits, indeed the many features which created wonderment, awe, and aspiration were but a part of the Exposition's offerings. A series of congresses drew men of similar interest together, and expanded their range of vision by contacts with those of other lands. It was Charles C. Bonney who conceived the plan of meetings in which the industrial aspect of civilization should not be given chief attention. Under the World's Congress Auxiliary, as it was known, various groups convened in the newly erected Art Institute on the lake front to review achievements and to point a way to further progress. " We know the bringing together of men is more than bringing together of things," observed A. S. Hardy. " In these contacts are formed the circuits which constitute the currents of progress."

The privilege of initiating the undertaking on May 15 was accorded to the women. Devoted to the theme " Woman's Progress," a general congress and thirty-one special sessions detailed their advances in education, industry, literature and art, moral and social reform, philanthropy and charity, civil law and government, and religion. Many other congresses reflected the far-flung interests of those in attendance, from conferences dealing with units of measurement for electrical power to those on banking and finance. The National

Russell, *The American Orchestra and Theodore Thomas* (Garden City, N.Y., 1927), pp. 205–36; *Chicago Tribune,* Nov. 9, 23, 1890, June 30, Oct. 2, 1892, May 14, June 11, 25, July 2, 13, 19, 22, 28, Aug. 15, 22, Sept. 10, Oct. 1, 1893; *The Inter Ocean,* Oct. 29, 1893.

[10] Julian Hawthorne, " Foreign Folk at the Fair," *The Cosmopolitan,* XV (Sept., 1893), 567–76; Francis Hopkinson Smith, " The Picturesque Side," *Scribner's Magazine,* XIV (Nov., 1893), 601–11.

Conference of Charities and Corrections in June heard Governor Altgeld; a series of educational meetings filled two weeks in July, and advocates of arbitration and international peace, as well as those concerned with city government and suffrage reform, met in August.

Especially important were the congresses dedicated to problems of labor and religion. Treating issues that touched the lives of all men, and around which divisive opinions revolved, these assemblies attracted wide attention. The Labor Congress came at a timely moment, for the Panic of 1893 was well under way, and the unemployed were tramping the streets of Chicago as well as elsewhere. By August, Chicago organized labor was demanding a public works program through loans from the federal and state governments, a demand the *Tribune* declared impossible to satisfy, since the city and state had no money to loan anybody.

When the Congress convened on August 28, well-known labor and farm leaders were on hand. With an explosive issue within the city, local labor leaders urged the Congress to hold sessions outside the hall, and the city police granted permission for a mass meeting on the lake front. On August 30 a throng of about 25,000 gathered peaceably and heard Henry George, Samuel Gompers, Thomas Morgan, Clarence Darrow, Bishop Samuel Fallows, and Kate Field. A slight rise in employment provided by the government through work on the Sanitary Canal, streets, and parks eased the situation; the homeless were allowed to sleep in the streets and the parks; and the press studiously directed attention from latent labor discontent to the approaching Parliament of Religions. Not until cold weather settled upon the city and the Fair had closed its gates were the sounds of the shuffling feet of the hungry and homeless on Chicago streets enough to cause public alarm.

The Parliament of Religions, the most numerously attended of all the congresses, opened on September 11. As the Reverend John Henry Barrows, chairman of the planning committee, rose to welcome the thousands in attendance, he addressed a notable assemblage of men of many tongues, of many religions, and of many races. His plea for tolerance and harmony, despite differences in creed, in large part set the tone of the various sessions: " We are not here as Baptists and Buddhists, Catholics and Confucians, Parsees and Presbyterian Protestants, Methodists and Moslems; we are here as members of a Parliament of Religions, over which flies no sectarian flag, which is to be stampeded by no sectarian war-cries, but where for the first time in a large council is lifted up the banner of love, fellowship, brotherhood." [11]

After September 22, consideration of the practical role of religion in the social order took the place of papers on metaphysics and theology. A series of forty-one denominational congresses met to discuss problems of special interest; one of the most notable was the Catholic Congress, where Cardinal Gibbons in a memorable address emphasized the Church's responsibility to educate foreigners and to assume leadership in solving the problems of labor and world peace. On September 27 the Parliament closed, its attendants possessing a sense of unity, a feeling that religion, as Julia Ward Howe put it, " is aspiration, the pursuit of the divine in humanity and of our own individual dignity." It gave to liberal, evangelical, and Catholic Christian alike, as F. H. Stead remarked, " a new Divine impulse." [12]

It was fitting that the Parliament of Religions, with its theme of unity, should come during the last weeks of the Fair. On October 30, Chicago, to quote in part the comment of the *Tribune* two days later, reluctantly bade good-bye " to a little ideal world, a realization of Utopia, in which every night was beautiful and every day a festival, in which for the time all thoughts of the great world of toil, of injustice, of cruelty, and of oppression outside its gates disappeared, and in which this splendid fantasy of the artist and architect seemed

---

[11] The planning committee was composed of the Reverend John Henry Barrows, First Presbyterian Church; the Reverend David Swing, Central Church; the Most Reverend P. A. Feehan, Archbishop of the Roman Catholic Church; and representatives of other Chicago denominations.

[12] A. S. Hardy, " Last Impressions," *The Cosmopolitan*, XVI (Dec., 1893), 199; *Chicago Tribune*, June 8, 18, July 31, Aug. 10, 16, 18, 19, 21, 22, 26–28, 31, Sept. 4, 9, 10, Dec. 18, 1893; Charles C. Bonney, *World's Congress Addresses* (Chicago, 1900); Bonney, " The World's Parliament of Religions," *The World's Parliament of Religions and the Religious Parliament Extension* (Chicago, 1896); Bonney, *Personal Miscellany*, XII; John H. Barrows, ed., *The World's Parliament of Religions* (2 v. Chicago, 1893); George S. Goodspeed, ed., *The World's First Parliament of Religions* (Chicago, 1895); Jenkin L. Jones, ed., *A Chorus of Faith as Heard in the Parliament of Religions* (Chicago, 1893); Walter R. Houghton, ed., *Neely's History of the Parliament of Religions and Religious Congresses at the World's Columbian Exposition* (Chicago, 1893); F. H. Stead, " The Story of the World's Parliament of Religions," *Review of Reviews* [New York], IX (March, 1894), 310; the reports of denominations in attendance.

to foreshadow some far-away time when all the earth should be as pure, as beautiful, and as joyous as the White City itself." This detachment from the harsh realities of daily living was the lot of millions, who, after May 28, could visit the Fair even on Sunday despite the bitter opposition of religious groups.[13] Here they could find recreation, but more important was the quickening of the aesthetic sense through the beauties of grounds and buildings. Under the noonday sun these charmed the sophisticated visitor from the East as well as stirring deeply the souls of "tired and dusty pilgrims of the plains." Then, when daylight faded into darkness, the enchanting city burst again into brilliance, transformed by the magical power of electricity. "The wonder and the beauty of it all," wrote Hamlin Garland of the experience of his aged parents from the Dakota plains, "moved these dwellers of the level lands to tears of joy which was almost as poignant as pain."

Although the glory of the Columbian Exposition was a transient thing, its influence lived on long after fire destroyed the imposing façades of the Court of Honor. It marked, in fact, a new epoch in the aesthetic growth not only of Chicago but of the nation. Most immediate and obvious of its effects was the wave of formal classicism that swept the country in the architecture of public buildings, railroad stations, banks, and churches. Perhaps the *Tribune* never uttered a truer prophecy than its declaration of March 10, 1893 that the White City had "set the standards which will affect the national art for years to come." For this reason especially, the Exposition was a keen disappointment to those Americans and Europeans interested in the development of a novel style of design based upon the techniques of steel-frame construction, rather than in the revival of the models of past ages. Probably far more important, however, than the fashion of ancient Greek and Roman or the later Renaissance style of architecture was the artistic interest the Columbian Exposition aroused. Millions of Americans hitherto preoccupied with the material problems of settling a continent and of expanding the nation's industry and trade had experienced an awakening of the desire for

---

[13] July 23 was the only Sunday after this date when the Fair was closed. The total of paid admissions in the six months it lasted was 21,480,141; gate receipts amounted to $10,336,065.75.

loveliness. The White City had opened their eyes to the possibilities of transforming some of the ugliness and unsightliness of their own abodes, the real cities of the country, into a more lasting beauty.[14]

[14] *Chicago Tribune*, March 10, Nov. 1, 1893; Hjalmar H. Boyesen, " A New World Fable," *The Cosmopolitan*, XVI (Dec., 1893), 178; *The Education of Henry Adams: An Autobiography* (Boston, 1918), pp. 339–40; Moore, *op. cit.*, I, 78–79, 86–90; Hamlin Garland, *A Son of the Middle Border* (New York, 1917), pp. 459–60; Tallmadge, *op. cit.*, pp. 211–12; Fiske Kimball, *American Architecture* (Indianapolis, 1928), pp. 168, 171–83; Sullivan, *The Autobiography of an Idea*, pp. 321–22, 324–25; Wright, *An Autobiography*, pp. 123, 126–27; Sigfried Giedion, *Space, Time and Architecture* . . . (Cambridge, 1946), p. 210; Paul Starrett, *op. cit.*, p. 50; *Chicago Record-Herald*, Dec. 17, 1910.

APPENDIX

NATIVE POPULATION OF CHICAGO[1]

Birthplace	Per Cent of Native Population 1870	1880	1890	Per Cent of Total Population 1870	1880	1890
Old Northwest	65.59	75.35	78.11	33.88	44.67	46.11
Illinois	56.98	66.28	67.23	29.43	39.30	39.68
Ohio	3.32	3.04	3.55	1.72	1.80	2.09
Michigan	1.49	1.71	2.05	.77	1.01	1.21
Indiana	1.36	1.34	2.39	.70	.79	1.41
Wisconsin	2.44	2.98	2.90	1.26	1.77	1.71
Middle Atlantic	19.69	13.89	9.97	10.17	8.24	5.88
New York	15.96	10.74	7.09	8.24	6.37	4.18
Pennsylvania	2.79	2.50	2.36	1.44	1.48	1.39
New Jersey	.88	.61	.46	.45	.36	.27
Delaware	.06	.04	.06	.03	.03	.04
New England	8.91	5.37	3.11	4.60	3.18	1.84
Connecticut	1.34	.82	.46	.69	.49	.27
Massachusetts	3.89	2.35	1.37	2.01	1.39	.81
Vermont	1.44	.86	.51	.75	.51	.30
Maine	1.07	.71	.42	.55	.42	.25
New Hampshire	.87	.45	.25	.45	.27	.15
Rhode Island	.28	.18	.11	.15	.11	.06
South	4.70	3.99	3.99	2.43	2.36	2.36
Virginia [a]	.77	.54	.48	.40	.32	.28
Kentucky	1.08	.88	.92	.56	.52	.54
Missouri	.92	.93	.97	.47	.55	.57
Maryland	.69	.56	.44	.36	.33	.26
Mississippi	.12	.11	.11	.06	.06	.07
Louisiana	.21	.20	.19	.11	.12	.11
North Carolina	.08	.06	.06	.04	.03	.03
Alabama	.14	.10	.09	.07	.06	.06
Tennessee	.31	.25	.32	.16	.15	.19
Georgia	.10	.08	.09	.05	.05	.06
District of Columbia	.19	.14	.14	.10	.08	.08

Birthplace	Per Cent of Native Population 1870	1880	1890	Per Cent of Total Population 1870	1880	1890
South Carolina	.07	.07	.05	.04	.04	.03
Florida	.008	.02	.02	.01	.01	.01
Arkansas	.01	.02	.04	.006		.02
West Virginia [a]		.03	.07		.02	.04
Trans-Mississippi West	1.06	1.41	2.17	.55	.83	1.28
Iowa	.69	.85	1.16	.36	.50	.68
Minnesota	.16	.21	.32	.08	.12	.19
California	.09	.09	.12	.05	.05	.07
Kansas	.05	.10	.22	.02	.06	.13
Texas	.03	.06	.08	.02	.04	.05
Oregon	.003	.004	.01	.001	.002	.005
Nebraska	.01	.05	.10	.007	.03	.06
Nevada	.008	.003	.005	.004	.002	.003
Colorado	.005	.02	.04	.003	.01	.03
Montana	.004	.005	.02	.002	.003	.01
New Mexico	.004	.005	.007	.002	.003	.004
Dakota Territory	.002	.006		.001	.003	
North Dakota			.03			.02
South Dakota			.02			.01
Utah	.002	.007	.01	.001	.004	.005
Idaho	.001	.001	.001	.0007	.0006	.0008
Washington Territory	.0006	.001	.01	.0003	.0008	.006
Indian Territory						
Wyoming		.004	.004		.002	.003
Arizona		.003	.005		.002	.003
Oklahoma		.002	.002		.001	.0008
Not Specified	.05		2.59	.03		1.53
Miscellaneous [b]	.0006	.0007	.05	.0003	.0004	.03

[1] Based on figures in U.S., *Ninth Census, 1870*, I, "Population," 380–85; *Tenth Census, 1880*, "Population," pp. 536–37; *Eleventh Census, 1890*, "Population," pt. I, lxvii, 580–83.

[a] Figures for Virginia and West Virginia are combined in U.S., *Ninth Census, 1870*, I, "Population," 384.

[b] Includes figures for persons born in Alaska, at sea under the United States flag, and of American parents abroad.

FOREIGN-BORN POPULATION OF CHICAGO[1]

Birthplace	Per Cent of Foreign-born Population			Per Cent of Total Population		
	1870	1880	1890	1870	1880	1890
British Isles	37.91	30.45	24.23	18.33	12.40	9.93
Ireland	27.66	21.68	15.54	13.37	8.83	6.37
England	6.94	6.37	6.29	3.35	2.59	2.58
Scotland	2.90	2.03	2.05	1.40	.83	.84
Wales	.39	.35	.36	.19	.14	.15
Not Specified	.02	.02	.004	.01	.01	.002
German States [a]	36.68	37.37	37.07	17.73	15.22	15.19
German Empire		36.71	35.73		14.95	14.64
Prussia	17.25	16.07		8.34	6.54	
Bavaria	2.56	1.28		1.24	.52	
Baden	2.24	1.05		1.09	.43	
Mecklenburg	2.35	.94		1.13	.38	
Hanover	1.71	.94		.83	.38	
Saxony	1.17	.79		.56	.32	
Württemberg	1.47	.69		.71	.28	
Hessen	2.35	.36		1.14	.15	
Hamburg	.22	.20		.11	.08	
Nassau	.14	.05		.07	.02	
Oldenburg	.04	.04		.02	.02	
Brunswick	.06	.02		.03	.01	
Weimar	.03	.006		.01	.002	
Lübeck	.008	.004		.004	.001	
Not Specified	4.58	14.28		2.21	5.81	
Austria	.49	.66	1.34	.24	.27	.55
Bohemia	4.34	5.80	5.57	2.10	2.36	2.28
France	.98	.78	.56	.47	.32	.23
Italy	.38	.66	1.26	.18	.27	.52

Birthplace	Per Cent of Foreign-born Population			Per Cent of Total Population		
	1870	1880	1890	1870	1880	1890
Spain	.02	.03	.03	.01	.01	.01
Switzerland	.85	.71	.50	.41	.29	.21
Holland	1.13	1.00	1.20	.55	.41	.49
Belgium	.27	.24	.18	.13	.10	.07
Poland	.83	2.70	5.34	.40	1.10	2.19
Russia	.08	.45	1.70	.04	.18	.70
Turkey	.002	.007	.005	.001	.003	.002
Hungary	.11	.15	.40	.05	.06	.17
Luxemburg	.02	.17	.02	.01	.07	.01
Greece	.006	.01	.05	.003	.005	.02
Portugal	.004	.02	.008	.002	.01	.003
Malta	.001	.002		.0007	.001	
Gibraltar		.002			.001	
Europe — Not Specified	.0007	.007	.14	.0003	.003	.06
Scandinavia	9.53	12.34	15.97	4.61	5.02	6.54
Norway	4.41	4.78	4.85	2.13	1.94	1.99
Sweden	4.26	6.31	9.55	2.06	2.57	3.91
Denmark [b]	.86	1.25	1.57	.42	.51	.64
British America [c]	6.67	6.79	5.39	3.23	2.77	2.21
Canada [d]	6.18	6.48		2.99	2.64	
West Indies [e]	.03	.10	.04	.02	.04	.02
Latin America [f]	.02	.04	.04	.01	.02	.01
Australia [g]	.02	.05	.05	.01	.02	.02
Asia [h]	.02	.14	.17	.01	.06	.07
Africa	.006	.009	.007	.003	.003	.003
Miscellaneous [i]	.07	.04	.06	.03	.02	.02

[1] Based on figures in U.S., Ninth Census, 1870, I, "Population," 386–91; Tenth Census, 1880, "Population," pp. 538–41; Eleventh Census, 1890, "Population," pt. I, lxvii, 670–73.

[a] Includes states composing German Empire of 1871 and Austria proper.

[b] In computing percentages for 1880, aliens born in Greenland are included in total figure for aliens born in Denmark.

[c] In U.S., Ninth Census, 1870, I, "Population," 387, and Tenth Census, 1880, "Population," p. 538, British America includes New Brunswick, Newfoundland, Nova Scotia, Prince Edward Island, and Canada (see footnote d below); in Eleventh Census, 1890, "Population," pt. I, 670, a combined report is given for Canada and Newfoundland, with no separate figures for New Brunswick, Nova Scotia, and Prince Edward Island.

[d] In U.S., Ninth Census, 1870, I, "Population," 387, and Tenth Census, 1880, "Population," p. 538, Canada does not include New Brunswick and Nova Scotia, original members of Canadian Confederation, 1867; in Tenth Census, 1880, "Population," p. 538, Canada does not include Prince Edward Island, which entered the Dominion in 1873; in Eleventh Census, 1890, "Population," pt. I, 670, no separate report is given for Canada (see footnote c above).

[e] In U.S., Eleventh Census, 1890, "Population," pt. I, 670, report for West Indies includes Cuba.

[f] In computing percentages for 1870, Latin America includes Cuba, Mexico, and South America; for 1880, Central America, Cuba, Mexico, and South America; for 1890, Central America, Cuba, Mexico, and South America.

[g] Included in report for Australasia in U.S., Ninth Census, 1870, I, "Population," 386.

[h] Includes persons born in China, India, Japan, and of Asiatic birth but place of nativity not specified.

[i] Includes persons whose origin was not stated, or born in the Atlantic islands, Pacific islands, Sandwich Islands, or at sea.

OCCUPATION AND NATIVITY OF EMPLOYED PERSONS, 1880, 1890 — BY NUMBERS

Occupations	Year	Total	Native Born: Total	Native Born: White[2]	Native Born: Colored	Foreign Born: Total	Germany	Ireland	Great Britain	British America	English Canada[3]	French Canada	Sweden, Norway	Denmark	Others
Manufacturing & Mechanical	1880	91,857	31,708				24,154	12,585	4,951	3,074			7,561		7,734
	1890	208,194	72,082	70,706	1,376	136,112	46,866	19,532	10,473		4,754	1,027	22,385	2,288	28,787
Trade	1880	36,233	21,225				6,677	2,531	1,850	1,089			821		2,040
	1890	62,995	34,459	33,985	474	28,536	11,508	3,547	2,933		1,679	135	2,565	534	5,635
Domestic & Pers. Service	1880	18,339	8,097				2,781	3,383	718	518			1,988		854
	1890	47,386	19,522	14,550	4,972	27,864	7,615	7,132	1,675		878	72	7,440	603	2,449
Transport. & Communication	1880	17,383	9,033				2,166	2,959	930	754			1,083		458
	1890	34,811	17,663	17,268	395	17,148	5,334	4,516	1,562		1,071	120	2,779	353	1,413
Professional Services	1880	5,101	3,488				599	232	229	161			109		283
	1890	12,340	8,880	8,765	115	3,460	1,089	368	598		396	30	280	60	639
Public Services	1880	1,977	1,027				264	403	94	71			51		67
	1890	6,059	2,906	2,858	48	3,153	720	1,446	296		157	19	284	41	190
Agriculture	1880	1,347	446				448	161	65	13			75		139
	1890	1,340	313	306	7	1,027	505	72	97		6		96	28	223
Clerical Services	1880	1,120	888				57	33	63	35			20		24
	1890	41,015	30,080	29,947	133	10,935	2,772	1,778	2,386		1,294	112	1,380	173	1,040
Itemized Totals	1880	173,357	76,002				37,146	22,287	8,900	5,715			11,708		11,599
	1890	414,140	185,905	178,385	7,520	228,235	76,409	38,391	20,020		10,235	1,515	37,209	4,080	40,376
Unclassified & Unknown	1880	18,403	8,765				3,701	1,631	1,118	607			708		1,783
	1890	44,173	21,028	20,468	560	23,145	9,020	2,945	2,308		1,102	269	2,835	379	4,287
Grand Total	1880	191,760	84,767				40,847	23,918	10,018	6,322			12,506		13,382
	1890	458,313	206,933	198,853	8,080	251,380	85,429	41,336	22,328		11,337	1,784	40,044	4,459	44,563

[1] Based on U.S., Tenth Census, 1880, [I], "Population," 1870, and U.S., Eleventh Census, 1890, [II], "Population," pt. II, 650–51.

[2] The 1880 census was not as categorized as the 1890 census; hence there are certain classifications for which no figures are available for the earlier year.

[3] The 1880 census had the classification "British America." In the 1890 census appeared the two headings "English Canada" and "French Canada."

OCCUPATION AND NATIVITY OF EMPLOYED PERSONS, 1880, 1890 —
BY PERCENTAGES OF TOTAL NUMBER EMPLOYED [1]

Occupations	Year	Total Number Employed	Native			Foreign Born									
			Total	White	Colored	Total	Germany	Ireland	Great Britain	British America	English Canada	French Canada	Sweden Norway	Denmark	Others
Manufacturing & Mechanical	1880	91,857	34.62	[2]			26.30[3]	13.70	5.39	3.35	[4]		8.23		8.42
	1890	208,194	34.62	33.96	.66	65.38	22.51	9.33	5.03		2.20	.49	10.75	1.09	13.83
Trade	1880	36,233	58.58				18.43	6.99	5.11	3.01			2.27		5.63
	1890	62,995	54.70	53.95	.75	45.30	18.27	5.63	4.66		2.67	.21	4.07	.85	8.94
Domestic & Pers. Service	1880	18,339	44.15				15.16	18.45	3.92	2.82			10.84	1.27	4.66
	1890	47,386	41.20	30.71	10.49	58.80	16.07	15.05	3.53		1.85	.15	15.70		5.17
Transport. & Communication	1880	17,383	51.96				12.46	17.02	5.35	4.34			6.23	1.01	2.63
	1890	34,811	50.74	49.60	1.14	49.26	15.32	12.97	4.49		3.08	.34	7.98		4.06
Professional Services	1880	5,101	68.38				11.74	4.55	4.51	3.16			2.14		5.55
	1890	12,340	71.96	71.03	.93	28.04	8.83	2.98	4.85		3.21	.24	2.27	.49	5.18
Public Services	1880	1,977	51.94				13.35	20.38	4.75	3.59			2.58		3.39
	1890	6,059	47.96	47.17	.79	52.04	11.88	23.87	4.89		2.59	.31	4.69	.68	3.14
Agriculture	1880	1,347	33.11				33.26	11.95	4.83	.97			5.57		10.32
	1890	1,340	23.36	22.84	.52	76.64	37.69	5.37	7.24		.45		7.16	2.09	16.64
Clerical Services	1880	1,120	79.29				5.09	2.95	5.62	3.13			1.79		2.14
	1890	41,015	73.34	73.01	.33	26.66	6.76	4.34	5.82		3.15	.27	3.36	.42	2.54
Itemized Totals	1880	173,357													
	1890	414,140													
Unclassified & Unknown	1880	18,403	47.63				20.11	8.86	6.08	3.30			4.34		9.69
	1890	44,173	47.60	46.34	1.26	52.40	20.41	6.67	5.22		2.49	.61	6.42	.86	9.71
Grand Total	1880	191,760	44.20				21.30	12.47	5.22	3.30			6.52		6.98
	1890	458,313	45.15	43.39	1.76	54.85	18.64	9.02	4.87		2.47	.39	8.74	.97	9.75

[1] Derived from figures in U.S., Tenth Census, 1880, [I], "Population," 870, and U.S., Eleventh Census, 1890, [I], "Population," pt. II, 650–51.

[2] The 1880 census was not as categorized as the census for 1890, hence there are certain classifications for which no figures are available for the earlier year.

[3] The percentages for the foreign born represent the per cent of the total in a particular occupation rather than the per cent of the total foreign born in that particular occupation.

[4] The 1880 census had the classification "British America." In the 1890 census appeared the two headings "English Canada" and "French Canada."

TOTAL POPULATION ACCORDING TO AGE AND SEX, 1890[1]

Age	Total			Native White with Native Parents			Native White with Foreign Parents			Foreign White			Colored[a]		
	Total	Male	Female	Total	Male	Female	Total	Male	Female	Total	Male	Female	Total	Male	Female
Under 1	30,104	15,281	14,823	6,722	3,419	3,303	22,956	11,658	11,298	249	114	135	177	90	87
1–4	110,679	55,909	54,770	23,960	12,164	11,796	81,326	40,944	40,382	4,728	2,457	2,271	665	344	321
5–9	116,646	58,397	58,249	24,142	12,171	11,971	76,814	38,346	38,468	14,890	7,489	7,401	800	391	409
10–14	97,824	48,521	49,303	17,043	8,417	8,626	56,173	27,879	28,294	23,822	11,876	11,946	786	349	437
15–19	100,472	48,019	52,453	16,883	8,134	8,749	53,431	25,656	27,775	29,033	13,643	15,390	1,125	586	539
20–24	125,030	61,046	63,984	25,572	13,314	12,258	42,730	20,323	22,407	54,580	26,216	28,364	2,148	1,193	955
25–29	126,741	66,828	59,913	25,669	14,159	11,510	31,722	15,327	16,395	66,888	35,891	30,997	2,462	1,451	1,011
30–34	105,445	59,205	46,240	21,701	12,382	9,319	23,151	11,907	11,244	58,594	33,643	24,951	1,999	1,273	726
35–44	137,197	76,065	61,132	28,405	16,020	12,385	17,246	8,794	8,452	88,720	49,458	39,262	2,826	1,793	1,033
45–54	83,390	45,514	37,876	17,292	9,545	7,747	4,707	2,373	2,334	60,333	33,014	27,319	1,058	582	476
55–64	40,623	20,686	19,937	8,475	4,446	4,029	1,229	619	610	30,521	15,416	15,105	398	205	193
65 & over	22,471	10,567	11,904	5,099	2,345	2,754	548	253	295	16,532	7,806	8,726	292	163	129
Age unknown	3,228	2,364	864	2,243	1,714	529	131	68	63	738	500	238	116	82	34
Total	1,099,850	568,402	531,448	223,206	118,230	104,976	412,164	204,147	208,017	449,628	237,523	212,105	14,852	8,502	6,350

[1] Table taken from U.S., *Eleventh Census, 1890*, "Population," pt. II, 117.
[a] Colored includes persons of Negro descent, Chinese, Japanese, and civilized Indians.

ORIGINAL NATIONALITY OF REGISTERED VOTERS IN CHICAGO[1]

1886

Ward	American	Canadian	German	Irish	English	Scotch	Welsh	Swedish	Norwegian	Danish	Bohemian	Austrian	Polish	Russian	Italian	French	Dutch	Other	Total
1	2,259	74	212	287	83	38	4	12	12	5	3	.....	6	4	4	18	8	15	3,044
2	2,392	64	242	249	85	16	2	13	1	4	2	.....	21	42	50	7	18	29	3,237
3	2,070	59	308	313	100	20	2	25	4	13	2	.....	4	3	7	15	5	21	2,971
4	4,173	141	613	381	183	54	7	66	19	18	6	.....	7	6	4	11	6	54	5,749
5	2,868	168	1,405	2,464	225	80	40	201	46	13	46	.....	12	5	6	41	18	93	7,791
6	1,458	76	1,850	846	93	27	2	74	22	15	703	.....	38	8	2	6	71	193	5,484
7	1,801	115	1,035	1,377	129	40	10	19	17	8	88	.....	9	67	3	11	33	95	4,849
8	2,645	246	555	1,564	196	64	11	23	16	14	283	.....	12	6	10	16	33	53	5,736
9	2,465	220	220	452	135	59	8	18	13	3	.....	.....	5	6	29	14	8	27	3,585
10	959	62	256	339	64	35	14	53	191	31	1	.....	.....	11	10	7	5	27	2,059
11	2,806	135	251	381	180	85	27	45	145	28	29	.....	2	2	7	9	21	40	4,180
12	4,852	205	292	321	344	121	5	17	22	17	6	.....	4	8	14	13	23	49	6,335
13	2,328	37	351	606	190	57	4	43	56	34	1	.....	1	1	6	6	20	24	3,766
14	1,472	60	2,419	658	109	45	8	205	592	170	36	.....	237	12	5	19	31	117	6,191
15	2,156	56	1,992	234	88	25	8	88	28	10	16	.....	6	6	4	16	6	80	4,819
16	1,378	36	1,527	184	44	11	2	117	10	15	5	.....	4	5	.....	13	2	69	3,422
17	1,106	55	308	841	66	24	4	703	60	18	3	.....	8	11	33	21	7	32	3,300
18	3,522	104	660	491	127	51	2	105	22	26	3	.....	3	8	10	11	12	58	5,215
Total	42,710	1,803	14,556	11,988	2,441	852	154	1,827	1,276	442	1,233	.....	379	211	204	254	327	1,076	81,733

[1] Figures for 1886 from *Chicago Tribune*, April 7, 1886; for 1892 from the compilation by Lars P. Nelson published in *The Daily News Almanac and Political Register for 1894* (George E. Plumbe, comp., [Chicago, 1894]), p. 318. Totals given in the original sources have been corrected where necessary. Because of redistricting, the first eighteen wards in 1892 generally are not the same as wards bearing the same number in 1886. The *Tribune* noted with regard to the 1886 figures that "the Scandinavians, Bohemians and Poles probably absented themselves largely from the registry through apathy." *Chicago Tribune*, April 7, 1886.

1892

Ward	American	Canadian	German	Irish	English	Scotch	Welsh	Swedish	Norwegian	Danish	Bohemian	Austrian	Polish	Russian	Italian	French	Dutch	Other	Total
1	4,791	143	477	382	138	61		44	19	20	5	35	44	80	137	29		226	6,631
2	5,147	180	448	450	195	44		77	9	37	3	30	23	34	9	25		55	6,766
3	5,275	169	751	371	164	64		133	25	28	12	59	7	19	25	21		66	7,189
4	5,950	196	716	492	260	90		109	24	100	13	51	12	20	7	26		37	8,103
5	3,079	167	1,859	1,166	186	66		521	38	24	185	162	6	40	18	29		132	8,278
6	2,863	196	2,371	2,298	290	73		205	24	19	46	119	45	39	5	13		62	8,668
7	1,732	68	1,542	623	70	20		35	22	4	325	297	20	1,230	11	9		79	6,097
8	1,661	136	839	816	63	22		26	17	5	1,705	225	39	166	4	8		71	5,803
9	2,178	143	1,639	762	136	29		71	32	14	1,512	103	402	40	1	15		204	7,281
10	3,542	201	2,385	839	201	72		306	41	34	723	345	246	21	6	16		102	9,080
11	5,785	309	413	653	331	137		133	382	87	10	69	7	40	5	15		71	8,457
12	10,511	652	703	862	745	281		88	78	35	15	103	15	34	41	34		84	14,371
13	5,967	307	891	936	417	145		174	195	97	8	33	4	17	21	21		112	9,345
14	2,298	112	3,676	211	97	55		393	745	411	15	214	6	114	11	20		107	8,460
15	2,651	46	3,054	575	290	92		599	624	292	35	101	208	41	12	29		94	8,899
16	1,304	89	2,450	218	65	25		312	859	204	86	180	2,631	79	5	15		54	8,593
17	1,718	282	679	523	85	50		248	818	204	1	83	74	39	208	16		60	4,895
18	5,319	436	674	738	320	133		45	34	38	3	63	23	78	32	28		56	7,866
19	4,232	82	721	1,635	285	99		39	18	14	468	189	38	477	278	35		96	9,060
20	2,310	91	2,111	217	101	27		112	25	16	6	45	4	7	1	10		37	5,112
21	2,360	56	2,445	182	120	27		139	30	21	11	84	3	9	2	22		85	5,638
22	2,805	108	2,577	210	92	22		385	34	32	6	86	5	21	9	20		115	6,482
23	2,275	251	682	1,044	104	48		2,121	69	35	2	35	14	59	16	17		47	6,718
24	6,035	159	853	583	225	58		155	22	38	7	51	6	14	58	14		104	8,430
25	3,421	100	1,291	231	198	54		682	66	63	8	40	3	9	11	10		61	6,303
26	2,666	64	3,370	199	213	49		358	66	40	4	69	4	13	3	5		78	7,247
27	1,422	164	750	79	125	36		167	69	38	29	37	2	9	8	5		30	2,865
28	1,396	238	289	370	142	49		158	127	37	63	9		4	3	14		34	2,849
29	3,294	406	978	2,174	240	58		81	22	36	98	42	40	30	2	31		61	7,415
30	6,811	258	2,170	1,563	410	152		974	71	44	264	111	159	42	9	13		164	13,384
31	4,869	329	708	425	292	87		247	26	36	22	52	8	11	12	23		174	7,250
32	7,076	131	406	504	416	130		145	26	41	6	42	4	9	2	23		49	9,208
33	2,022	346	1,003	608	325	59		725	63	83	13	37	645	25	4	15		52	5,810
34	5,010		994	639	503	141		831	112	96	12	79	18	33	25	23		654	9,516
Total	130,435	6,692	47,005	23,578	7,844	2,555		10,838	4,832	2,333	5,721	3,280	4,865	2,903	1,032	643		3,513	258,069

RECEIPTS OF SELECTED ITEMS

Commodity	Chicago & North Western Railway	Illinois Central Railroad	Chicago, Rock Island & Pacific Railway	Chicago, Burlington & Quincy Railroad	Chicago & Alton Railroad	Michigan Central Railroad
Total grain, bu.	220,985,659	122,402,306	142,903,688	320,491,074	77,237,390	1,577,854
Wheat, bu.	93,231,045	23,838,694	26,335,863	54,169,652	6,949,226	89,432
Corn, bu.	63,970,570	69,432,112	88,927,019	197,659,529	61,742,106	96,626
Oats, bu.	42,660,553	24,017,616	21,411,151	53,464,792	7,029,780	110,821
Rye, bu.	2,324,076	1,793,770	2,527,243	5,361,827	1,202,358	5,685
Barley, bu.	18,799,415	3,320,114	3,702,412	9,835,274	313,920	1,275,290
Flour, bbl.	11,872,502	1,579,802	843,012	2,912,966	903,293	151,793
Millstuffs, lbs.	512,846,330	31,178,600	86,808,460	177,283,463	14,612,300	1,212,000
Malt, bu.	1,157,189	39,663	181,242	19,832	500	28,066
Hops, lbs.	13,605,693	161,563	2,342,721	2,945,810	139,620	3,639,898
Flaxseed, lbs.	182,776,626	185,875,861	42,023,130	103,911,296	27,155,805	313,625
Other grass seed, lbs.	111,961,487	118,737,065	71,023,668	118,218,314	30,682,288	7,685,746
Pork, bbl.	179,895	15,824	22,308	119,154	13,046	1,093
Cured meat, lbs. b	167,347,901	53,551,263	142,237,512	231,676,133	13,406,745	1,240,673
Beef, tierces & bbl.	2,900	707	24,946	88,499	28,364	196
Dressed hogs, no.	531,117	419,048	97,772	197,948	4,570	9,053
Lard, lbs.	47,990,227	51,330,039	67,726,383	128,736,516	26,998,420	388,983
Tallow, lbs.	20,854,716	5,146,833	30,377,213	27,009,864	4,350,860	8,825,000
Cheese, lbs.	131,270,430	2,549,014	2,324,514	20,693,492	3,243,542	1,101,105
Butter, lbs.	136,817,350	63,471,928	30,560,362	67,796,653	4,425,195	1,141,738
Wool, lbs.	119,421,497	4,619,110	109,979,040	163,716,855	15,085,735	203,558
Sheep, no.	674,911	373,665	344,946	844,285	245,216	80,620
Live hogs, no.	8,694,650	8,235,166	8,848,817	15,622,648	3,695,031	482,949
Cattle, no.	1,483,508	1,195,725	1,628,108	3,514,865	1,564,692	44,141
Lumber, feet	133,294,644	27,322,400	10,630,030	22,694,550	9,492,700	257,160,000
Coal, tons c	39,884	320,669	303,836	395,600	3,940,995	710,880
Salt, bbl.	2,392	40,050	555	555	90	2,117,297
Iron ore, tons d	35,221	14	185	1,235	5,727	129
Pig iron, tons	127,092	46,919	6,652	3,601	16,629	71,190
Other iron, lbs.	466,441,589	57,459,489	104,547,225	127,779,120	192,249,600	551,840,610

[1] Compiled from Chicago Board of Trade, *Annual Reports, 1872 to 1882*; figures converted to a uniform measure.

a Chicago trackage taken over by the Chicago, St. Louis & Pittsburgh Railroad, 1883; consolidated into the Pittsburgh, Cincinnati, Chicago & St. Louis Railway, 1890.

b Fresh meat included, 1872–75.

c Coke included, 1872–76.

d Only Lake reported 1877 and 1878.

IN CHICAGO'S COMMERCE, 1872 TO 1882 [1]

Commodity	Lake Shore & Michigan Southern Railway	Pittsburgh, Ft. Wayne & Chicago Railway	Pittsburgh, Cincinnati & St. Louis Railway [a]	Chicago, Milwaukee & St. Paul Railway	Lake	Illinois and Michigan Canal
Total grain, bu.	341,505	294,388	260,293	39,254,683	2,912,671	61,842,342
Wheat, bu.	177,776	8,979	41,771	17,299,115	1,642,435	196,036
Corn, bu.	23,442	30,170	37,524	4,139,325	. . . .	53,866,938
Oats, bu.	14,592	45,026	85,198	8,740,148	4,930	7,343,753
Rye, bu.	10,019	7,277	2,230	1,329,898	3,097	428,620
Barley, bu.	115,676	202,936	93,570	7,746,197	1,262,209	6,995
Flour, bbl.	73,804	40,911	31,041	9,989,646	300,163	421,498
Millstuffs, lbs.	400,420	. . . .	140,000	379,761,998	. . . .	127,914
Malt, bu.	8,007	. . . .	47,665	91,150	. . . .	. . . .
Hops, lbs.	8,478,445	5,182	1,028,850	9,138,848	. . . .	. . . .
Flaxseed, lbs.	44,705	38,770	327,986	102,037,070	283,360	. . . .
Other grass seed, lbs.	7,131,913	14,874,100	8,047,346	58,453,527	3,327,110	10,953,589
Pork, bbl.	3,395	299	22,046	115,973	25,801	. . . .
Cured meat, lbs. [b]	451,309	21,416	555,735	282,332,622	1,516,900	. . . .
Beef, tierces & bbl.	539	. . . .	132	590	. . . .	. . . .
Dressed hogs, no.	2,358	15,101	25,642	180,516	. . . .	. . . .
Lard, lbs.	494,021	848,834	1,566,868	62,283,740	1,323,290	. . . .
Tallow, lbs.	5,357,229	1,708,292	1,052,385	7,176,072	354,550	2,500
Cheese, lbs.	4,550,000	8,161,781	741,630	60,060,862	1,058,510	. . . .
Butter, lbs.	1,261,719	2,681,085	1,456,329	75,676,932	9,838,251	38,040
Wool, lbs.	797,957	308,296	279,362	21,383,055	264,578	2,338
Sheep, no.	115,857	23,293	25,451	522,123	. . . .	. . . .
Live hogs, no.	699,013	376,784	433,351	1,475,273	. . . .	. . . .
Cattle, no.	96,297	26,098	38,406	468,735	. . . .	. . . .
Lumber, feet	118,086,000	204,230,790	90,407,466	48,718,410	11,602,675,150	1,204,212
Coal, tons [c]	889,612	1,397,323	1,548,134	26,743	7,307,755	78,886
Salt, bbl.	391,977	86,582	89,265	7,920	7,780,214	15
Iron ore, tons [d]	342	536	214	26,932	1,127,708	1,556
Pig iron, tons	230,092	91,709	56,325	169,763	386,872	. . . .
Other iron, lbs.	971,294,049	957,377,563	251,519,829	24,132,591	214,956,000	9,716,200

RECEIPTS OF SELECTED ITEMS IN

Commodity	Chicago & North Western Railway	Illinois Central Railroad	Chicago, Rock Island & Pacific Railway	Chicago, Burlington & Quincy Railroad	Chicago & Alton Railroad	Michigan Central Railroad
Total grain, bu.	290,820,514	157,574,460	195,087,467	402,061,435	73,283,508	668,462
Wheat, bu.	35,014,499	13,012,975	19,971,031	51,663,185	15,152,891	191,927
Corn, bu.	111,209,100	72,786,574	86,590,391	225,063,629	38,360,239	93,129
Oats, bu.	90,961,323	63,033,829	77,548,160	104,754,577	18,713,884	75,835
Rye, bu.	5,572,721	3,217,220	5,220,371	9,820,476	912,946	17,837
Barley, bu.	48,062,871	5,523,862	5,757,514	10,759,568	143,548	289,734
Flour, bbl.	13,499,337	509,520	3,826,992	8,438,116	1,616,924	312,562
Millstuffs, lbs.	862,952,879	34,313,685	190,166,814	372,772,656	284,805,605	805,745
Malt, bu.	8,764,786	119,138	183,163	63,529	23,965	14,465
Hops, lbs.	19,219,877	1,066,226	2,631,556	11,338,479	553,900	1,665,242
Flaxseed, bu.	16,232,016	3,041,313	2,308,539	3,765,775	871,485	2,569
Other grass seed, lbs.	118,289,988	47,389,021	65,815,231	95,502,462	9,989,983	9,424,701
Pork, bbl.	109,365	19,462	120,566	69,798	8,788	1,319
Cured meat, lbs.	186,995,815	65,781,629	221,846,451	641,122,543	46,519,159	1,597,717
Beef, lbs.	15,072,878	14,322,830	1,245,776	59,495,807	151,785,387	4,750,916
Dressed hogs, no.	48,473	42,489	11,845	18,407	4,694	3,243
Lard, lbs.	103,115,505	50,275,698	111,036,165	278,681,624	42,435,547	2,045,017
Cheese, lbs.	250,157,405	13,310,988	1,956,753	7,013,227	904,880	1,710,674
Butter, lbs.	309,494,254	136,535,296	130,465,898	109,034,533	3,173,387	2,467,138
Wool, lbs.	85,487,907	7,537,426	36,215,595	86,140,242	35,970,834	1,145,928
Hides, lbs.	154,371,456	58,178,824	133,995,114	166,933,895	55,993,011	47,819,399
Sheep, no.	2,648,397	550,800	966,801	2,140,208	1,490,941	182,202
Live hogs, no.	12,239,247	6,377,409	8,267,613	16,121,361	3,418,184	468,807
Cattle, no.	3,518,295	1,444,563	2,527,045	6,273,971	3,039,710	32,277
Lumber, feet	592,964,000	388,953,000	51,115,000	97,896,000	58,565,000	205,098,000
Coal, tons	69,449	1,165,226	222,443	600,176	7,216,209	1,300,358
Salt, bbl.	8,615	162,291	1,590	11,133	26,270	6,445,177
Iron ore, tons [b]	....	....	....	....	....	....
Pig iron, tons [b]	....	....	....	....	....	....
Other iron, lbs. [b]	....	....	....	....	....	....

[1] Based on Chicago Board of Trade, *Annual Reports, 1882 to 1892;* figures converted to a uniform measure.
[a] See note *a, Receipts, 1872 to 1882.*
[b] Figures by rail not available 1882 to 1892.

CHICAGO'S COMMERCE, 1882 TO 1892 [1]

Commodity	Lake Shore & Michigan Southern Railway	Pittsburgh, Ft. Wayne & Chicago Railway	Pittsburgh, Cincinnati & St. Louis Railway [a]	Chicago, Milwaukee & St. Paul Railway	Lake	Illinois and Michigan Canal
Total grain, bu.	718,610	242,739	2,098,597	197,436,187	833,186	24,296,477
Wheat, bu.	508,105	85,075	433,155	38,830,979	542,739	606,589
Corn, bu.	69,079	50,384	25,723	40,188,684	1,868	17,015,648
Oats, bu.	38,726	99,375	42,007	75,215,691	31,930	6,264,015
Rye, bu.	2,822	400	59,734	4,869,047	9,115	410,225
Barley, bu.	99,878	7,505	1,537,978	38,331,786	247,534	. . . .
Flour, bbl.	408,026	14,201	7,875	15,904,854	235,726	949,184
Millstuffs, lbs.	942,049	24,000	674,670	833,924,726	1,184,916	3,816,305
Malt, bu.	16,317	2,294	3,301	1,301,710	486	. . . .
Hops, lbs.	4,448,746	30,000	521,575	3,084,355	9,750	8,050
Flaxseed, bu.	8,136	9,479	107,991	17,090,968	143,224	. . . .
Other grass seed, lbs.	11,599,713	8,751,901	1,739,377	182,319,514	3,422,706	1,474,754
Pork, bbl.	12,608	776	. . . .	166,531	1,963	. . . .
Cured meat, lbs.	1,580,342	140,522	255,862	629,248,756	200,500	. . . .
Beef, lbs.	105,382	53,138	21,935	120,291,930	6,299	. . . .
Dressed hogs, no.	683	970	1,872	97,176	. . . .	. . . .
Lard, lbs.	3,564,955	915,264	1,217,850	111,986,282	972,640	. . . .
Cheese, lbs.	6,208,683	5,966,351	541,191	179,325,822	15,394,428	. . . .
Butter, lbs.	1,063,022	1,459,458	91,549	313,191,673	2,476,167	145
Wool, lbs.	2,934,821	257,914	296,711	46,468,272	2,452,410	. . . .
Hides, lbs.	14,459,554	4,768,846	5,569,864	81,390,188	12,903,270	. . . .
Sheep, no.	176,699	34,226	49,479	2,302,597	. . . .	. . . .
Live hogs, no.	326,247	159,209	284,606	8,110,050	. . . .	. . . .
Cattle, no.	28,825	19,040	54,339	2,830,993	. . . .	. . . .
Lumber, feet	172,440,000	161,321,000	242,698,000	357,441,000	15,351,058,000	320,000
Coal, tons	2,431,540	930,609	4,361,416	116,747	10,760,601	4,484
Salt, bbl.	555,428	2,333	895	7,016	4,392,482	. . . .
Iron ore, tons	. . . .	. . . .	. . . .	. . . .	2,348,333	. . . .
Pig iron, tons	. . . .	. . . .	. . . .	. . . .	238,168	. . . .
Other iron, lbs.	. . . .	. . . .	. . . .	. . . .	197,916,000	555,862

SHIPMENTS OF SELECTED ITEMS IN

Commodity	Chicago & North Western Railway	Illinois Central Railroad	Chicago, Rock Island & Pacific Railway	Chicago, Burlington & Quincy Railroad	Chicago & Alton Railroad	Michigan Central Railroad
Total grain, bu.	6,239,616	3,902,981	1,948,276	1,456,399	3,389,018	105,898,864
Wheat, bu.	3,421,927	905,093	574,069	644,561	1,421,022	24,040,535
Corn, bu.	638,818	370,747	232,388	140,544	61,354	39,183,566
Oats, bu.	378,226	332,395	112,795	29,675	66,831	37,861,390
Rye, bu.	102,966	535,918	26,826	42,211	19,269	880,835
Barley, bu.	1,697,679	1,758,828	1,002,198	599,408	1,820,542	3,932,538
Flour, bbl.	134,200	311,382	115,838	46,540	116,116	6,400,442
Millstuffs, lbs.	23,535,300	4,339,840	583,260	2,670,670	170,000	357,868,219
Malt, bu.	434,225	1,412,218	660,585	86,377	132,545	594,870
Hops, lbs.	893,153	2,284,852	605,984	904,410	823,410	4,161,385
Flaxseed, lbs.	1,709,818	24,524,436	1,648,100	2,748,203	1,491,249	15,368,139
Other grass seed, lbs.	800,017	16,279,495	2,023,127	5,929,238	5,628,262	78,078,127
Pork, bbl.	23,512	196,702	31,593	4,628	104,011	526,822
Cured meat, lbs.[b]	4,044,965	304,974,547	25,201,783	24,431,468	61,652,430	741,546,826
Beef, tierces & bbl.	6,575	4,238	3,951	5,258	3,471	117,448
Dressed hogs, no.	16,293	9,301	. . . .	. . . .	5	515,000
Lard, lbs.	7,153,652	28,515,094	6,322,706	13,766,187	6,540,755	286,702,753
Tallow, lbs.	408,450	4,683,221	1,117,260	478,680	3,264,260	50,958,246
Cheese, lbs.	349,040	14,080,806	11,539,918	7,861,782	16,551,826	45,673,178
Butter, lbs.	1,209,065	7,251,641	2,348,310	2,287,400	4,268,611	106,584,545
Wool, lbs.	1,055,288	1,429,116	730,859	389,467	1,413,768	245,999,059
Hides, lbs.	34,854,845	6,818,721	288,980	97,175	1,570,305	195,453,773
Sheep, no.	21,119	30,528	45,121	44,660	11,076	304,299
Live hogs, no.	40,451	16,884	4,729	6,224	4,330	5,651,478
Cattle, no.	78,135	130,325	185,579	105,471	131,658	1,629,195
Lumber, feet	619,164,316	832,145,931	574,374,795	2,223,827,507	831,506,007	136,492,690
Coal, tons[c]	2,038,201	193,452	226,104	524,454	214,088	10,695
Salt, bbl.	1,602,888	951,170	1,459,865	2,618,897	489,739	16,907
Iron ore, tons[d]	6,331	8,873	19,138	24	161,468	1,054
Pig iron, tons	145,544	8,681	39,599	51,359	132,842	4,988
Other iron, lbs.	691,808,121	123,537,509	503,522,000	950,394,358	375,099,112	86,507,201

[1] Based on Chicago Board of Trade, *Annual Reports, 1872 to 1882;* figures converted to a uniform measure.
[a] See note a, *Receipts, 1872 to 1882.*
[b] Fresh meat included, 1872–75.
[c] Coke included, 1872–76.
[d] Only Canal reported 1877; none reported 1878.

CHICAGO'S COMMERCE, 1872 TO 1882 [1]

Commodity	Lake Shore & Michigan Southern Railway	Pittsburgh, Ft. Wayne & Chicago Railway	Pittsburgh, Cincinnati & St. Louis Railway [a]	Chicago, Milwaukee & St. Paul Railway	Lake	Illinois and Michigan Canal
Total grain, bu.	95,726,978	53,913,204	22,630,624	1,895,176	587,469,175	4,588,326
Wheat, bu.	18,141,264	13,776,478	7,654,965	1,277,104	130,037,804	3,902,688
Corn, bu.	39,320,947	19,075,702	6,047,075	80,681	399,376,881	512,756
Oats, bu.	34,578,813	14,038,990	4,565,354	120,944	44,479,683	171,660
Rye, bu.	726,478	1,566,543	1,199,530	8,840	6,610,894	1,222
Barley, bu.	2,979,476	5,455,491	3,163,700	407,607	6,963,913	....
Flour, bbl.	5,659,733	6,225,892	2,938,431	15,178	3,259,776	10,794
Millstuffs, lbs.	234,816,681	240,101,500	73,062,470	1,610,395	....	....
Malt, bu.	608,263	388,699	1,054,828	284,558	45,654	....
Hops, lbs.	3,188,741	5,757,420	2,035,810	1,088,860	....	....
Flaxseed, lbs.	81,148,959	15,607,840	40,764,449	2,014,780	341,801,721	....
Other grass seed, lbs.	149,505,861	59,516,020	29,303,333	631,726	77,069,081	72,484
Pork, bbl.	624,093	435,939	143,980	49,671	470,979	....
Cured meat, lbs. [b]	1,235,368,947	1,507,780,286	1,158,837,182	3,928,481	42,760,691	3,135
Beef, tierces & bbl.	274,533	240,798	24,454	9,159	57,182	....
Dressed hogs, no.	328,123	140,330	5,464	1,884	....	....
Lard, lbs.	352,718,354	409,156,400	345,093,007	1,496,711	210,164,084	....
Tallow, lbs.	31,884,031	20,809,700	29,309,722	18,000	3,726,420	....
Cheese, lbs.	24,611,605	38,491,677	3,693,889	796,970	59,440	....
Butter, lbs.	53,110,320	157,965,491	1,476,420	346,040	1,011,865	....
Wool, lbs.	46,212,170	125,146,009	6,216,942	1,757,110	752,801	....
Hides, lbs.	146,282,411	79,257,546	16,138,604	19,871,696	22,305,327	....
Sheep, no.	689,316	566,200	3,240	7,805	....	....
Live hogs, no.	6,880,372	2,851,488	10,869	21,527	....	....
Cattle, no.	2,212,252	2,232,013	29,324	14,975	6,590	....
Lumber, feet	49,231,500	59,614,500	299,725,560	44,674,217	14,026,602	438,843,603
Coal, tons [c]	11,358	17,254	14,897	482,157	9,630	59,614
Salt, bbl.	22,518	23,543	28,815	153,492	75,551	171,856
Iron ore, tons [d]	2,849	685	1,196	350	....	199
Pig iron, tons	20,663	12,352	6,207	42,436	3,604	....
Other iron, lbs.	143,847,696	8,492,000	92,395,472	411,163,473	34,036,000	7,107,678

SHIPMENTS OF SELECTED ITEMS IN

Commodity	Chicago & North Western Railway	Illinois Central Railroad	Chicago, Rock Island & Pacific Railway	Chicago, Burlington & Quincy Railroad	Chicago & Alton Railroad	Michigan Central Railroad
Total grain, bu.	13,027,586	10,471,110	9,519,773	2,450,400	6,516,994	81,260,544
Wheat, bu.	5,798,757	1,718,657	2,698,849	373,401	2,313,867	6,272,385
Corn, bu.	2,857,654	3,331,853	1,007,422	1,381,518	136,484	32,653,973
Oats, bu.	1,170,969	3,246,767	3,626,186	165,702	554,647	36,492,852
Rye, bu.	186,902	648,047	607,087	74,851	24,088	633,276
Barley, bu.	3,013,304	1,525,786	1,580,229	454,928	3,487,908	5,208,058
Flour, bbl.	356,813	245,208	104,762	30,319	218,084	4,530,818
Millstuffs, lbs.	83,919,846	19,505,505	30,000	17,416,650	15,283,988	428,395,915
Malt, bu.	390,729	3,064,666	981,601	526,652	269,858	4,534,209
Hops, lbs.	6,611,584	565,343	159,419	687,735	704,673	6,867,475
Flaxseed, bu.	169,128	2,102,750	29,424	67,341	26,392	1,059,043
Other grass seed, lbs.	12,964,702	19,449,475	6,827,489	4,172,710	2,867,520	53,708,809
Pork, bbl.	51,731	309,598	27,557	14,864	70,416	552,610
Cured meat, lbs.	41,191,979	550,846,166	18,800,948	50,635,415	63,276,487	689,258,102
Beef, lbs.	120,868,510	16,910,412	885,165	467,618	11,238,483	580,092,609
Dressed hogs, no.	4,496	222	1	323	314	540,681
Lard, lbs.	22,295,441	75,720,282	5,891,220	6,631,394	7,724,899	302,716,402
Cheese, lbs.	13,065,741	47,153,918	10,351,869	17,596,449	18,161,795	45,746,370
Butter, lbs.	11,864,993	40,446,533	2,526,480	2,574,318	9,901,954	211,300,636
Wool, lbs.	7,797,388	3,762,700	1,491,917	1,742,075	1,896,308	97,720,289
Hides, lbs.	91,497,012	17,134,775	1,957,880	150,590	4,724,508	173,113,216
Sheep, no.	56,182	63,221	54,687	60,583	59,120	228,878
Live hogs, no.	25,179	94,161	2,227	6,285	1,550	3,649,147
Cattle, no.	90,758	148,263	211,613	127,535	132,477	2,002,821
Lumber, feet	725,826,000	745,904,000	582,894,000	2,398,341,000	962,958,000	71,637,000
Coal, tons	4,104,311	487,281	296,823	1,423,981	400,422	18,173
Salt, bbl.	2,226,871	1,207,288	1,408,551	4,282,691	384,541	35,292
Iron ore, tons [b]	....	....	....	....	....	....
Pig iron, tons [b]	....	....	....	....	....	....
Other iron, lbs.[b]	....	....	....	....	....	....

[1] Based on Chicago Board of Trade, *Annual Reports, 1882 to 1892;* figures converted to a uniform measure.
[a] See note *a, Receipts, 1872 to 1882.*
[b] Figures by rail not available 1882 to 1892.

CHICAGO'S COMMERCE, 1882 TO 1892 [1]

Commodity	Lake Shore & Michigan Southern Railway	Pittsburgh, Ft. Wayne & Chicago Railway	Pittsburgh, Cincinnati & St. Louis Railway [a]	Chicago, Milwaukee & St. Paul Railway	Lake	Illinois and Michigan Canal
Total grain, bu.	106,082,051	64,998,497	52,154,399	7,644,367	668,895,992	6,619,265
Wheat, bu.	7,094,701	3,870,957	4,395,146	3,450,697	121,088,513	6,082,188
Corn, bu.	38,605,865	20,852,129	12,383,040	1,064,087	423,828,640	365,159
Oats, bu.	54,767,642	31,226,683	20,072,341	1,218,754	104,092,153	159,614
Rye, bu.	1,115,102	2,604,320	2,454,416	213,767	14,927,620	12,304
Barley, bu.	4,498,741	6,444,408	12,849,456	1,697,062	4,959,066	....
Flour, bbl.	4,429,389	6,426,774	3,841,532	129,482	12,856,344	25,846
Millstuffs, lbs.	554,056,090	597,311,549	196,367,743	36,611,600	73,498,767	4,000
Malt, bu.	4,887,552	4,648,263	7,882,148	279,459	200,304	....
Hops, lbs.	6,887,695	21,801,742	2,085,763	3,902,422	....	....
Flaxseed, bu.	5,731,293	1,580,494	5,394,708	67,542	19,776,751	....
Other grass seed, lbs.	98,416,031	68,418,834	17,563,662	10,319,416	71,980,710	23,496
Pork, bbl.	444,741	225,473	204,066	33,571	392,760	....
Cured meat, lbs.	706,822,260	1,108,195,296	868,980,879	21,772,129	13,226,899	....
Beef, lbs.	829,466,501	388,479,235	573,929,693	21,281,955	1,182,050	....
Dressed hogs, no.	222,508	36,812	39,164	11,489	....	....
Lard, lbs.	359,797,409	305,464,478	338,238,015	15,049,052	450,408,795	137,079
Cheese, lbs.	17,239,419	45,578,560	34,725,682	7,298,509	2,407,700	....
Butter, lbs.	168,515,523	400,692,697	18,242,567	5,653,830	371,230	....
Wool, lbs.	50,189,450	50,576,775	10,826,502	8,074,208	54,822,059	....
Hides, lbs.	230,469,648	226,183,766	86,307,948	92,452,120	16,914,300	....
Sheep, no.	1,587,118	1,315,719	63,623	197,099	....	....
Live hogs, no.	7,015,541	2,711,172	68,447	84,818	....	....
Cattle, no.	1,867,116	1,568,689	333,357	74,610	....	....
Lumber, feet	128,135,000	132,802,000	336,882,000	404,374,000	12,139,000	241,160,000
Coal, tons	19,682	7,890	37,008	1,575,862	11,093	42,709
Salt, bbl.	6,212	8,509	10,576	676,875	34,725	10,867
Iron ore, tons	....	....	....	....	1,350	....
Pig iron, tons	....	....	....	....	1,152	....
Other iron, lbs.	....	....	....	....	65,420,000	1,232,735

STORAGE CAPACITY FOR CHICAGO GRAIN ELEVATOR WAREHOUSES[1]
1893

Elevator Company	Name of Elevator	Receive from	Capacity, bushels
Armour Elevator Co.	Armour Elevator A	C M & St P	1,250,000
Armour Elevator Co.	Armour Elevator B	C M & St P	1,250,000
Armour Elevator Co.	Armour Elevator B Annex	C M & St P	3,000,000
Chicago & Pacific Elev. Co.	Pacific Elevator B	C M & St P	1,000,000
City of Chi. Grain Elevs., Ltd.	St. Paul Elevator	C M & St P	900,000
City of Chi. Grain Elevs., Ltd.	Fulton Elevator	C M & St P; Canal.	400,000
Armour Elevator Co.	Armour Elevator C	C B & Q	1,500,000
Armour Elevator Co.	Armour Elevator D & Annex.	C B & Q	3,000,000
Armour Elevator Co.	Armour Elevator E	C B & Q	1,250,000
Armour Elevator Co.	Armour Elevator F	C B & Q	800,000
Central Elevator Co.	Central Elevator A	I C	1,000,000
Central Elevator Co.	Cen. Elev. B. & Annex	I C	1,800,000
Chas. Counselman & Co.	Rock Island Elevator A	C R I & P	1,100,000
A. C. Davis & Co.	Rock Island Elevator B	C R I & P	800,000
City of Chi. Grain Elevs., Ltd.	Galena Elevator	C & N W	700,000
City of Chi. Grain Elevs., Ltd.	Air Line Elevator	C & N W	700,000
City of Chi. Grain Elevs., Ltd.	Iowa Elevator	C & N W	1,500,000
Seaverns, George A.	Alton Elevator	C & A	1,350,000
Seaverns, George A.	Alton Elevator B	C & A	500,000
National Elevator & Dock Co.	National Elevator	C & A; Canal	1,000,000
National Elevator & Dock Co.	Chicago & St. Louis Elev.	C & A; Canal	1,000,000
Santa Fe Elev. & Dock Co.	Santa Fe Elevator A	A T & S F	1,500,000
Chicago Elevator Co.	Wabash Elevator	W St L & P	1,500,000
Chicago Elevator Co.	Indiana Elevator	Various Railroads.	1,500,000
Ill. Trust & Savings Bank.	Neeley's Elevator	Railroads & Canal.	700,000
City of Chi. Grain Elevs., Ltd.	City Elevator	Railroad & Canal.	1,000,000
City of Chi. Grain Elevs., Ltd.	Union Elevator	Railroad & Canal.	800,000
Total Capacity			32,800,000

[1] Chicago Board of Trade, *Thirty-sixth Annual Report, 1893*, p. 36.

KEY TO RAILROAD ABBREVIATIONS

A T & S F	Atchison, Topeka and Santa Fe Railroad
B & O	Baltimore & Ohio Railroad
Belt Railway of Chicago	Belt Railway of Chicago
C & Alton	Chicago & Alton Railroad
C & Atlantic	Chicago and Atlantic Railroad
Chi & Cal Terminal	Chicago and Calumet Terminal
C & E I	Chicago and Eastern Illinois Railroad
C & Erie	Chicago and Erie Railroad
C & G T	Chicago and Grand Trunk Railway
C & G W	Chicago and Great Western Railroad
C & I S	Chicago and Illinois Southern Railroad
C & N W	Chicago and North Western Railway
C & N P	Chicago and Northern Pacific Railroad
C & O R	Chicago and Ohio River Railroad
C & S L	Chicago and State Line Railroad
C B & N	Chicago, Burlington and Northern Railroad
C B & Q	Chicago, Burlington & Quincy Railroad
C D & V	Chicago, Danville and Vincennes Railroad
C M & St P	Chicago, Milwaukee and St. Paul Railway
C R I & P	Chicago, Rock Island and Pacific Railway
C St L & P	Chicago, St. Louis and Pittsburgh Railroad
C St P & K C	Chicago, St. Paul and Kansas City Railway
C S F & Calif	Chicago, Santa Fe and California Railway

C U T	Chicago Union Transfer Railway
Cin In St L & C	Cincinnati, Indianapolis, St. Louis and Chicago Railway
Clev Cin Chi & St L	Cleveland, Cincinnati, Chicago and St. Louis Railway
I C	Illinois Central Railroad
L S & M S	Lake Shore and Michigan Southern Railway
L N A & C	Louisville, New Albany and Chicago Railway
M C	Michigan Central Railroad
M P	Missouri Pacific Railway
N Y Chi & St L	New York, Chicago and St. Louis Railroad
N P	Northern Pacific Railroad
P Cin & St L	Pittsburgh, Cincinnati and St. Louis Railway
P Cin Chi & St L	Pittsburgh, Cincinnati, Chicago and St. Louis Railway
P Ft W & C	Pittsburgh, Fort Wayne and Chicago Railway
St L A & T H	St. Louis, Alton and Terre Haute Railroad
St P & D	St. Paul and Duluth Railroad
Union Stock Yards and Transit	Union Stock Yards and Transit Company
W St L & P	Wabash, St. Louis and Pacific Railway
Wis Cen Lines	Wisconsin Central Lines

LEADING CITIES IN MANUFACTURING, 1880, 1890 [1]

Rank	Year	Number of Establishments	Average Number of Employees	Total Wages Paid in Year	Capital	Gross Value of Products	Value Added by Manufacture (Approximate)
1	1880	New York 11,273	New York 223,073	New York $95,832,742	New York $179,605,506	New York $468,443,248	New York $182,175,474
	1890	New York 25,403	New York 354,291	New York $230,102,167	New York $426,118,272	New York $777,222,721	New York $410,799,999
2	1880	Philadelphia 8,481	Philadelphia 174,952	Philadelphia $61,152,952	Philadelphia $178,765,206	Philadelphia $309,424,156	Philadelphia $118,972,780
	1890	Philadelphia 18,166	Philadelphia 260,264	Philadelphia $135,917,021	Philadelphia $375,249,715	Chicago $664,567,923	Philadelphia $265,588,642
3	1880	Brooklyn 5,195	Chicago 79,391	Chicago $34,646,812	Chicago $68,831,885	Chicago $248,995,848	Chicago $69,800,923
	1890	Brooklyn 10,583	Chicago 210,366	Chicago $123,955,001	Chicago $359,739,598	Philadelphia $577,234,446	Chicago $255,074,896

[1] Based on U.S., *Eleventh Census, 1890*, "Manufacturing Industries," pt. II, xxx, 3–5. In number of establishments Chicago ranked sixth in 1880 with 3,518, slightly less than Baltimore's 3,680 or Boston's 3,664. In 1890 Chicago was fourth with 9,977.

CHICAGO'S LEADING MANUFACTURES [1]

1880

	No. of Establishments	Capital	Average No. of Employees	Total Wages Paid during Year	Gross Value of Products	Value of Materials	Value Added by Manufacture (Approximate) [a]
Slaughtering & meat packing............ [b]	70	$8,455,200	7,478	$3,392,748	$85,324,371	$74,546,319	$10,778,052
Men's clothing (incl. shirts & men's furnishing goods) [b]	143	7,182,200	10,321	4,054,889	19,808,971	13,195,716	6,703,255
Printing & publishing [c]...............	151	3,495,550	3,906	2,175,508	6,723,236	2,733,209	3,999,027
Foundry & machine shop products (incl. architectural & ornamental ironwork)...	144	4,519,417	5,032	2,439,655	9,238,529	5,259,519	3,979,010
Furniture (incl. chairs) [d].............	155	2,659,675	4,899	2,149,571	6,511,186	3,135,528	3,375,058
Iron & steel (incl. forgings)...........	15	4,010,800	3,111	1,533,603	10,927,472	8,356,307	2,571,165
Lumber & timber products [e]..........	56	2,209,546	3,728	1,517,916	8,925,481	6,362,337	2,563,144
Malt liquors.......................	18	3,395,500	892	445,891	3,429,375	1,886,165	1,543,210
Leather, curried & tanned.............	28	2,414,000	1,334	871,184	9,302,095	6,751,803	1,507,772
Carriages & wagons (incl. wheelwrighting)	158	1,545,285	1,757	803,666	2,342,493	867,581	1,474,912
Tobacco products...................	291	825,850	1,978	778,633	3,702,772	2,265,103	1,437,669
Distilled liquors [b].................	7	1,175,000	750	330,000	4,387,545	2,961,281	1,426,264
Boots & shoes [b]..................	133	997,475	1,811	770,191	2,479,805	1,355,208	1,124,597
Agricultural implements..............	3	3,110,000	1,021	559,532	2,699,480	1,642,748	1,056,732
Tinware, copperware & sheet-ironware ...	106	657,875	1,181	513,329	2,164,496	1,157,831	1,006,665

[1] Based on U.S., *Tenth Census, 1880,* "Manufactures," pp. 391–93, and U.S., *Eleventh Census, 1890,* "Manufacturing Industries," pt. II, "Statistics of Cities," 130–45.

[a] This figure has been computed by subtracting "value of materials" from "gross value of products." The census did not employ the concept of "value added by manufacture" until 1910. It is, however, the most suitable measure of relative importance of the various industries, since it represents only the new value created by the given industry in the process of manufacturing.

[b] The 1880 census does not distinguish between "factory product" and "custom work & repairing" as it did in 1890.

[c] Includes in 1880 lithographing, stereotyping, and electrotyping; in 1890 lithographing and engraving, steel engraving including plate printing, photo-lithographing and engraving, and stereotyping and electrotyping, as well as book and job printing, music publication, newspapers, and periodicals.

[d] The 1880 census does not distinguish between "factory product" and "cabinetmaking & repairing" as it did in 1890.

[e] Includes planing mill products, including sash, doors and blinds, and wooden packing boxes.

CHICAGO'S LEADING MANUFACTURES (Continued)

1890

	No. of Estab- lishments	Capital	Average No. of Employees	Total Wages Paid during Year	Gross Value of Products	Value of Materials	Value Added by Manufacture (Approximate) [a]
Slaughtering & meat packing (incl. sausage making) [c]	52	$38,915,332	17,487	$10,716,817	$194,337,838	$164,908,701	$29,429,137
Printing & publishing [c]	695	15,254,676	13,805	9,836,265	29,076,992	8,274,034	20,802,958
Foundry & machine-shop products (incl. architectural & ornamental ironwork)	303	25,663,073	15,557	9,441,120	35,245,975	16,220,019	19,025,956
Men's clothing, factory product (incl. buttonholes, shirts & men's furnishing goods)	149	14,732,994	17,993	7,281,437	36,318,610	19,602,630	16,706,680
Lumber & timber products [c]	130	10,406,601	9,377	5,525,976	20,440,324	11,786,526	8,653,798
Furniture, factory product (incl. chairs)	157	8,094,833	8,295	4,766,615	13,582,350	5,599,384	7,982,966
Distilled liquors	3	2,290,000	158	130,447	8,030,863	952,916	7,077,947
Agricultural implements	6	28,468,543	3,945	1,971,309	11,883,976	4,993,877	6,890,099
Malt liquors	34	16,200,563	2,051	1,442,804	10,223,718	3,415,306	6,808,412
Steam railroad cars	7	8,840,330	5,878	3,839,495	14,517,719	8,590,147	5,927,572
Iron & steel (incl. forgings)	20	23,491,264	4,585	3,276,310	25,005,231	19,581,937	5,423,294
Gas, illuminating & heating	4	40,851,246	1,186	772,916	4,319,687	635,586	3,684,101
Boots & shoes, factory product (incl. cut stock & uppers)	57	3,275,319	3,600	1,832,668	8,079,791	4,595,411	3,484,380
Women's clothing, factory product	71	2,793,112	2,673	1,181,478	6,422,431	3,257,712	3,164,719
Bread & other bakery products	335	2,526,078	2,665	1,525,819	6,816,788	3,852,951	2,963,837

MUNICIPAL FINANCES FOR SELECTED YEARS [1]

Year	Popula- tion	Appropria- tions [a]	Per-Capita Appropri- ations [b]	Assessed Valuations	Bonded Debt	Floating Debt in the Form of "Scrip"	Expenditures
1872–3	367,396	$4,793,608.36	$13.05	$283,197,430	$13,544,000	$1,194,553.43	$8,325,875.37
1878	436,731	3,777,757.23	8.65	131,981,436	13,057,000	1,958,931.47	5,967,295.83
1880	503,185 [c]	3,899,126.98	7.75	117,133,643	12,752,000	605,759.48 [d]	9,696,510.61
1884	629,985	4,872,456.60	7.73	137,326,980	12,751,500	. . . .	11,788,728.13
1890	1,099,850 [e]	9,558,334.80	8.69	219,354,368	13,545,400	. . . .	24,491,683.57
1892	1,438,010	12,142,448.75	8.44	243,732,138	18,515,450	. . . .	30,069,963.65

[1] Figures on Municipal Finance from Chicago City Comptroller, *Annual Statement*.

[a] Chicago, *Council Proceedings, 1872–73* to *1893–94, passim*.

[b] Per-capita figures obtained by dividing annual appropriation figures by the population figures.

[c] U.S., *Tenth Census, 1880*, "Population," p. 536.

[d] Chicago, *Council Proceedings, 1880–81*, p. 376.

[e] U.S., *Eleventh Census, 1890*, pt. 1, "Population," lxvii.

PLACE OF BIRTH OF TRADE-UNION MEMBERS IN ILLINOIS, 1886[1]

Organization	Total	American	German	Irish	Scandinavian	English	Poles	Bohemian	Scotch	Italian	Welsh	Miscellaneous and Not Reported
Bricklayers & Stonemasons	4,000[a]	250	1,015	1,270	740	165			155	250	155	
Hod Carriers	3,500	150	1,200	1,000	700	45				105		300
Metal Workers	3,023	275	1,815	21	500	312		100				
Seamen	2,500			278	1,666	278			278			
Furniture Workers	2,429	308	1,458	25	396	22		205	15			
Lumbermen's Laborers	1,921		1,545				336	40				
Carpenters & Joiners	1,868	195	1,259	101	45	109			57			
Cigarmakers	1,674	1,044	489	53	17	25		3			7	95
Typographers	1,597	705	358	225	87	222						43
Butchers	1,200	50	700	300	50	100						

[1] Illinois Bureau of Labor Statistics, *Fourth Biennial Report, 1886* (Springfield, 1886), pp. 224–25. No figures are available on the place of birth of trade-organization members in Cook County, but 88% of state trade-union members were from Cook County. *Ibid.*, p. 221.
[a] Some of these figures are based upon estimates. *Ibid.*, p. 227.

PLACE OF BIRTH OF KNIGHTS-OF-LABOR MEMBERS IN COOK COUNTY, 1886[1]

Organization	Total	American	German	Irish	Scandinavian	English	Poles	Bohemian	Scotch	Italian	Welsh	Miscellaneous and Not Reported
Knights of Labor	18,355	6,228	3,804	2,654	897	1,257	850	1,657	39	42	39	888

[1] Illinois Bureau of Labor Statistics, *op. cit.*, p. 226.

FUNDED DEBT OF THE CITY OF CHICAGO FOR KEY
YEARS INDICATED BY PURPOSE OF ISSUE[1]

Year	Miscellaneous	Bridewell	Tunnels	City Hall	Schools	Sewerage	River Improvement	Water System	Water Bonds of Annexed Areas	Total
1872	$1,267,500	$240,000	$699,000	$327,000	$1,171,500	$2,637,000	$2,621,000	$4,581,000		$13,544,000
1876	1,163,500	240,000	699,000	327,000	1,171,500	2,637,000	2,621,000	4,577,000		13,436,000
1881	1,151,500	239,000	694,000	325,000	1,156,500	2,623,000	2,608,000	3,955,000		12,752,000
1884	1,151,500	239,000	694,000	325,000	1,156,500	2,622,500	2,608,000	3,955,000		12,751,500
1888	1,129,500[a]	150,000	694,000	305,000[a]	1,107,500[a]	2,622,500	2,608,000	3,955,000		12,561,500
1893	6,089,450[b]	150,000	992,000		1,105,500	2,622,500	2,608,000[c]	4,089,500	$779,000	18,426,450

[1] Chicago Department of Finance, *Sixteenth Annual Statement, 1872,* pp. 36–37; *Twentieth Annual Statement, 1876,* pp. 116–17; *Twenty-fifth Annual Statement, 1881,* pp. 150–52; *Twenty-eighth Annual Statement, 1884,* pp. 120–23; *Thirty-second Annual Statement, 1888,* pp. 119–23; *Thirty-seventh Annual Statement, 1893,* pp. 113–15.

[a] Less a total of $10,000 for the three categories in cash on hand for bonds not yet redeemed.

[b] Includes $5,000,000 in World's Fair bonds.

[c] Less $5,000 bonds remaining unsold and $4,500 in cash on hand for bonds not yet redeemed.

CHICAGO VOTE FOR MAYOR [1]

Year	Candidate	Vote	Year	Candidate	Vote
1871	Joseph Medill (Fireproof)	16,125	1883	Carter H. Harrison (Dem.)	41,226
	Charles C. P. Holden (Opp.)	5,988		Eugene Cary (Rep.)	30,963
1873	Lester L. Bond (Union)	18,540	1885	Carter H. Harrison (Dem.)	43,352
	Harvey D. Colvin (People's)	28,791		Sidney Smith (Rep.)	42,997
				William Bush (Prohibition)	221
Apr. 18, 1876	Thomas Hoyne [a]	33,064	1887	John A. Roche (Rep.)	51,249
	Scattering	819		Robert S. Nelson (Un. Lab.)	23,490
				Joseph S. Whitlock (Prohibition)	376
July 12, 1876	Monroe Heath (Rep.)	19,248	1889	Dewitt C. Cregier (Dem.)	57,340
	Mark Kimball (Dem.)	7,509		John A. Roche (Rep.)	45,328
	James McGrath (Ind.)	3,363		Charles Orchardson (Socialist)	304
				Ira J. Mason (Prohibition)	411
1877	Monroe Heath (Rep.)	30,881	1891	Dewitt C. Cregier (Dem.)	46,588
	Perry H. Smith (Dem.)	19,449		Carter H. Harrison (Ind. Dem.)	42,931
	Scattering	10		Hempstead Washburne (Rep.)	46,957
				Elmer Washburn (Citizens)	24,027
				Thomas J. Morgan (Socialist)	2,376
1879	Carter H. Harrison (Dem.)	25,685	1893	Carter H. Harrison (Dem.)	114,237
	Abner M. Wright (Rep.)	20,496		Samuel W. Allerton (Rep.)	93,148
	Ernst Schmidt (Socialistic Lab.)	11,829		Dewitt C. Cregier (Un. Citizen)	3,033
	Scattering	13		Henry Ehrenpreis (Socialistic Lab.)	1,000
1881	Carter H. Harrison (Dem.)	35,668			
	John M. Clark (Rep.)	27,925			
	Timothy O'Meara (Ind.)	764			
	George Schilling (Socialistic Lab.)	240			
	Scattering	51			

[1] Election returns, 1871–85 from Chicago, *Council Proceedings;* for 1887–93, from *Mss.* records of the Chicago Board of Election Commissioners.

[a] Thomas Hoyne, chosen in an irregular election, April 18, 1876, did not serve.

CHICAGO VOTE FOR CONGRESSIONAL REPRESENTATIVES [1]

Dis-trict	Candidate	Vote
	1872	
1	Lucius B. Otis (Lib.)	5,286
	John B. Rice (Rep.) ᵃ	8,785
2	Carter H. Harrison (Lib.)	8,873
	Jasper D. Ward (Rep.) ᵃ	12,182
3	John V. LeMoyne (Lib.)	3,128
	Charles B. Farwell (Rep.) ᵃ	3,970
	1874	
1	Bernard G. Caulfield	
	(Opp.) ᵇ]Dem.] ᵃ	7,246
	Sidney Smith (Rep.)	6,578
2	Carter H. Harrison (Opp.) ᵇ [Dem.] ᵃ	9,186
	Jasper D. Ward (Rep.)	9,181
3	John V. LeMoyne (Opp.) ᵇ [Dem.] ᵃ	4,874
	Charles B. Farwell (Rep.)	4,278
	Francis A. Hoffman (Workingmen's)	150
	1876	
1	William Aldrich (Rep.) ᵃ	10,317
	John R. Hoxie (Dem.)	9,986
	George S. Bowen (Ind.)	163 ᶜ
2	Carter H. Harrison (Dem.) ᵃ	14,732 ᶜ
	George R. Davis (Rep.)	14,090 ᶜ
	S. F. Norton (Greenback)	118 ᶜ
3	Lorenzo Brentano (Rep.) ᵃ	5,217
	John V. LeMoyne (Dem.)	7,324
	1878	
1	William Aldrich (Rep.) ᵃ	7,063
	James R. Doolittle, Jr. (Dem.)	4,217
	William V. Barr (Greenback)	1,402
	John McAuliff (Soc. Lab.)	1,944
2	George R. Davis (Rep.) ᵃ	10,347
	Miles Kehoe (Dem.)	6,111
	James Felch (Greenback)	1,600
	George A. Schilling (Soc. Lab.)	2,473
	J. H. Condon (Dem.)	250
	John Seboski (Ind. Soc.)	74
3	Hiram Barber (Rep.) ᵃ	3,987
	Lambert Tree (Dem.)	3,000
	Alanson B. Cornell (Greenback)	450
	Benjamin Sibley (Soc. Lab.)	2,289

Dis-trict	Candidate	Vote
	1880	
1	William Aldrich (Rep.) ᵃ	14,049
	John Mattocks (Dem.)	12,818
	Richard Powers (Greenback)	514 ᶜ
	J. Altpeter (Soc.)	605
2	George R. Davis (Rep.) ᵃ	20,603
	J. F. Farnsworth (Dem.)	16,014
	O. A. Bishop (Soc. and Greenback)	29
	Charles G. Dixon (Greenback)	461
	Richard Lorenz (Socialist)	514
3	Charles B. Farwell (Rep.) ᵃ	7,934
	Perry H. Smith, Jr. (Dem.)	8,408 ᶜ
	Charles H. Adams (Greenback)	106 ᶜ
	Oscar Neebe (Soc. and Greenback)	141 ᶜ
	Adolph Waldemann (Soc.)	114 ᶜ
	1882	
1	Ransom W. Dunham (Rep.) ᵃ	6,903 ᶜ
	J. W. Doane (Dem.)	6,030
	A. J. Grover (Anti-Monopoly)	644 ᶜ
2	John Finerty (Ind. Dem.) ᵃ	9,360
	Henry F. Sheridan (Dem.)	6,939
	J. M. Altpeter (Anti-Monopoly)	189
	S. Artley (Soc.)	180
3	George R. Davis (Rep.) ᵃ	12,511
	William P. Black (Dem.)	10,274
	Caleb G. Hayman (Prohibition)	748
4	George E. Adams (Rep.) ᵃ	6,435
	Lambert Tree (Dem.)	7,353
	Christian Meier (Anti-Monopoly)	125 ᶜ
	Frank P. Crandon (Prohibition)	663 ᶜ
	1884	
1	Ransom W. Dunham (Rep.) ᵃ	20,245 ᶜ
	William M. Tilden (Dem.)	14,655 ᶜ
	William B. Gates (Prohibition)	288 ᶜ
	John B. Clark (Greenback)	501 ᶜ
2	John F. Finerty (Ind. Rep.)	11,552
	Francis Lawler (Dem.) ᵃ	13,954
	William F. Killett (Prohibition)	23
3	Charles Fitz-Simons (Rep.)	8,928
	James H. Ward (Dem.) ᵃ	15,601

[1] Election returns, names and party labels, 1872–84, from Chicago newspapers; Geo. H. Harlow, comp., *Official Directory Illinois 1877*, p. 71; Geo. H. Harlow, comp., *Illinois Legislative Directory . . . 1881*, pp. 161, 172; Geo. H. Harlow and James H. Paddock, comps., . . . *Legislative Directory* [1879], p. 45; D. W. Lusk, comp., *Thirty-fourth General Assembly, Legislative Directory*, Appendix, p. 17. Election returns for 1886–92, from *Mss.* records of the Chicago Board of Election Commissioners; Geo. E. Plumbe, comp., *The Daily News Almanac . . . for 1891*, p. 214; Chicago newspapers.
ᵃ Won in district. ᵇ Coalition of Democratic party and the local People's party.
ᶜ Cook County figures; Chicago vote not available.

CHICAGO VOTE FOR CONGRESSIONAL REPRESENTATIVES (*Continued*) [1]

District	Candidate	Vote
	1884 (continued)	
3	William E. Mason (Rep.)	10,806
	J. C. Boyd (Greenback)	259
	J. E. Lee (Prohibition)	280
4	George E. Adams (Rep.) [a]	18,333 [c]
	John P. Altgeld (Dem.)	15,291 [c]
	H. W. Austin (Prohibition)	467 [c]
	1886	
1	Ransom W. Dunham (Rep.) [a]	6,371
	Edgar Terhune (Dem.)	3,725
	Harvey Sheldon, Jr. (United Lab.)	1,236
	George E. Christian (Prohibition)	112
2	Charles W. Woodman (Rep.)	3,976
	Francis Lawler (Dem.) [a]	7,369
	Daniel F. Gleason (United Lab.)	7,353
	James W. Lee (Prohibition)	33
3	William E. Mason (Rep.) [a]	13,721
	Benjamin W. Goodhue (United Lab.)	6,352
	J. L. Whitlock (Prohibition)	422
	J. J. Higgins	223
4	George E. Adams (Rep.) [a]	6,045
	Jonathan Taylor (Dem.)	5,233
	Samuel Hawkins (United Lab.)	3,012
	George Gray (Prohibition)	109
	1888	
1	Abner Taylor (Rep.) [a]	11,883
	James F. Todd (Dem.)	8,580
	Harry S. Taylor (Prohibition)	211
	Theophile Laramie (Lab.)	31
2	Daniel F. Gleason (Rep.)	12,969
	Francis Lawler (Dem.) [a]	19,051
	Frank Sibley (Prohibition)	142
3	William E. Mason (Rep.) [a]	23,671
	Milton R. Freshwater (Dem.)	21,295
	Charles G. Davis (Prohibition)	734
	Frank A. Stauber (Lab.)	937
4	George E. Adams (Rep.) [a]	12,041
	Jonathan B. Taylor (Dem.)	12,906
	L. D. Rogers (Prohibition)	605
	H. D. Lloyd (Union Lab.)	35

District	Candidate	Vote
	1890	
1	William G. Ewing (Dem.)	19,327
	Abner Taylor (Rep.) [a]	19,421
	Isaac H. Pedrick (Prohibition)	388
2	Lawrence E. McGann (Dem.) [a]	17,383
	John G. Schaar (Rep.)	10,633
	William Bently (Prohibition)	767
3	Allan C. Durborow (Dem.) [a]	21,069
	William E. Mason (Rep.)	17,933
	J. L. Whitlock (Prohibition)	263
4	Walter C. Newberry (Dem.) [a]	16,540
	George E. Adams (Rep.)	14,526
	Samuel Packard (Prohibition)	266
	1892	
1	Edwin Burritt Smith (Dem.)	34,769
	J. Frank Aldrich (Rep.) [a]	36,340
	Winfield McComas (Prohibition)	1,439
	Alfred Clark (People's)	532
	P. J. Weldon (Reform League)	29
2	Lawrence E. McGann (Dem.) [a]	32,609
	Edward D. Connor (Rep.-People's)	14,168
	Andrew J. Wickland (Prohibition)	483
	James Toll	70
3	Allan C. Durborow (Dem.) [a]	38,652
	Thomas C. MacMillan (Rep.)	27,392
	Joseph E. Young (Prohibition)	786
	Charles W. Russell (People's)	387
	Henry Steinbeck (Reform League)	93
4	Julius Goldzier (Dem.) [a]	29,686
	William Vocke (Rep.)	22,834
	L. D. Rogers (Prohibition)	753
	William E. McNally (People's)	325
	Frank Scanlan (Reform League)	28
At large	John C. Black (Dem.) [a]	135,916
	Andrew J. Hunter (Dem.) [a]	134,868
	George Willits (Rep.)	101,653
	Richard Yates (Rep.)	101,531
	Francis E. Andrews (Prohibition)	3,037
	James Felter (Prohibition)	2,962
	Jesse Harper (People's)	1,498
	Michael McDonough (People's)	1,447

[1] Election returns, names and party labels, *1872–84*, from Chicago newspapers; Geo. H. Harlow, comp., *Official Directory Illinois 1877*, p. 71; Geo. H. Harlow, comp., *Illinois Legislative Directory . . . 1881*, pp. 161, 172; Geo. H. Harlow and James H. Paddock, comps., *. . . Legislative Directory* [1879], p. 45; D. W. Lusk, comp., *Thirty-fourth General Assembly, Legislative Directory*, Appendix, p. 17. Election returns for 1886–92, from *Mss.* records of the Chicago Board of Election Commissioners; Geo. E. Plumbe, comp., *The Daily News Almanac . . . for 1891*, p. 214; Chicago newspapers.

[a] Won in district.   [b] Coalition of Democratic party and the local People's party.

[c] Cook County figures; Chicago vote not available.

CHICAGO VOTE FOR PRESIDENT AND GOVERNOR [1]

Year	FOR PRESIDENT		FOR GOVERNOR	
	Candidate	Vote	Candidate	Vote
1872	Ulysses S. Grant (Republican) [a]	25,498	Richard J. Oglesby (Republican) [a]	23,381
	Horace Greeley (Liberal Republican)	17,355	Gustave Koerner (Liberal Republican)	19,304
1876	Rutherford B. Hayes (Republican) [a]	28,576	Shelby M. Cullom (Republican) [a]	29,462
	Samuel J. Tilden (Democrat)	33,424	Lewis Steward (Democrat)	32,548
	Peter Cooper (Greenback)	251		
1880	James A. Garfield (Republican) [a]	42,906	Shelby M. Cullom (Republican) [a]	42,103
	Winfield S. Hancock (Democrat)	38,302	Lyman Trumbull (Democrat)	38,570
	James B. Weaver (Greenback)	1,054	A. J. Streeter (Greenback)	1,235 [b]
			Uriah Copp (Prohibition)	14 [b]
			S. K. Piatt	173 [b]
			Erick Johnson (Socialist)	780 [b]
1884	James G. Blaine (Republican) [a]	51,420	Richard J. Oglesby (Republican) [a]	47,848
	Grover Cleveland (Democrat)	48,530	Carter H. Harrison (Democrat)	52,503
	Benjamin F. Butler (Greenback–Labor)	542	Jesse Harper (Greenback)	287
	John St. John (Prohibition)	484	James B. Hobbs (Prohibition)	481
1888	Benjamin Harrison (Republican) [a]	60,004	Joseph W. Fifer (Republican) [a]	58,107
	Grover Cleveland (Democrat)	63,619	John M. Palmer (Democrat)	65,912
	Clinton B. Fisk (Prohibition)	1,308	David H. Harts (Prohibition)	1,154
	Alson J. Streeter (Union Labor)	575	Willis W. Jones (Union Labor)	605
	Robert H. Cowdry (United Labor)	136		
1892	Benjamin Harrison (Republican)	100,849	John P. Altgeld (Democrat) [a]	135,861
	Grover Cleveland (Democrat) [a]	136,474	Joseph W. Fifer (Republican)	102,660
	John Bidwell (Prohibition)	3,029	Robert R. Link (Prohibition)	3,013
	James B. Weaver (People's)	1,506	Nathan M. Barnett (People's)	1,259

[1] Election returns, 1872–84, from Chicago newspapers and Illinois, *Journal of the House of Representatives, 1881;* for 1888–92, from *Mss.* records of the Chicago Board of Election Commissioners. Party labels from Geo. H. Harlow, comp., *Illinois Legislative Directory . . . 1881,* p. 172; D. W. Lusk, comp., *Thirty-Fourth General Assembly, Legislative Directory,* Appendix, p. 3; Edward McPherson, *A Hand-Book of Politics for 1888 . . . ,* pp. 183, 186, 188–89, 191; Illinois Secretary of State, comp., *Official Vote of the State of Illinois,* 1888–92; Chicago newspapers.

[a] Won in state.   [b] Cook County figures; Chicago vote not available.

GROWTH IN MEMBERSHIP AND NUMBER OF CHURCHES OF
CHICAGO'S MAJOR RELIGIOUS DENOMINATIONS, 1872–1892 [1]

Denomination	Membership					Number of Churches or Congregations		
	1872	1882	1892	Per-Cent Increase 1872–82	Per-Cent Increase 1882–92	1872	1882	1892
Roman Catholic......	.....	.....	262,047 [f]	......	......	23 [b]	33 [d]	99
Protestant								
Lutheran..........	7,567 [a]	.....	34,999 [f]	......	.....	17	30 [d]	55
Baptist...........	5,406	.....	13,506	......	......	19	..	48
Methodist Episcopal	5,026	8,228	21,767 [h]	63.71	164.55	22	31	109 [h]
Presbyterian.......	3,292	6,816	11,789	107.05	72.96	11	17	46
Congregational.....	2,836	4,562	9,498	60.86	108.20	12	12	44
Protestant Episcopal	2,151	4,003	9,589	86.10	139.55	14	15	38
Reformed Episcopal	.....	1,067 [d]	1,399 [g]	......	31.12	..	7	7 [g]
Jewish..............	.....	.....	9,187 [f]	......	......	10 [b]	13 [c]	30 [e]
All Denominations in Chicago..........	.....	.....	388,145 [f]	.....	......	186	276	538

[1] The statistics in this table have been taken from the official records of the respective denominations, city directories, newspapers, and the United States census of 1890. In several instances lack of information for a particular year has necessitated a substitution as indicated in the notes below. For the purpose of comparison, the following data on the growth of the city in population during the same period are available in school census reports: 367,396 in 1872, 560,693 in 1882, and 1,438,010 in 1892. The per-cent increase in the decade 1872–82 was 52.61, and in the decade 1882–92 it was 156.47.

[a] This figure is for 1870.
[b] This figure is for 1871.
[c] This figure is for 1880.
[d] This figure is for 1881.
[e] This figure is for 1889.
[f] This figure is for 1890.
[g] This figure is for 1891.
[h] This figure is for 1893.

FOREIGN CHURCHES OF LEADING DENOMINATIONS
FOUNDED IN CHICAGO, 1872–1892 [1]

Nationality	Catholic	Lutheran	Methodist [a]	Baptist	Congregational	Presbyterian	Totals
German......	15	20	6	3	3	1	48
Scandinavian .	0	12	17	5	1	0	35
Bohemian.....	6	0	3	0	1	0	10
Polish........	9	0	0	0	0	0	9
French.......	2	0	1	0	0	0	3
Italian.......	2	0	0	0	0	1	3
Lithuanian....	1	0	0	0	0	0	1
Welsh........	0	0	0	0	1	0	1
Total founded 1872–92....	35	32	27	8	6	2	110
Total founded prior to 1872	9 [b]	17	7	4	2	2	41
Total in 1892.	44	49	34	12	8	4	151

[1] The data in this table have been compiled mainly from the official records of the respective denominations and from city directories.

[a] In the case of this denomination the period covered extends to 1893.

[b] One French church established in 1850 that apparently failed to survive the Fire is not included.

CHICAGO'S RANK AMONG MAJOR AMERICAN CITIES IN MEMBERSHIP
OF ITS LEADING RELIGIOUS GROUPS, 1890[1]

Name of Religious Group	Chicago	Rank	New York	Philadelphia	Brooklyn	St. Louis	Boston	Baltimore	Cincinnati	Pittsburgh	Washington, D.C.	Louisville
Roman Catholic	262,047	2	386,200	163,658	201,063	75,908	185,188	77,047	72,368	56,916	36,488	33,740
Lutheran	34,999	1	16,125	11,653	14,732	7,458	1,959	10,902	1,252	4,868	2,997	1,483
Methodist Episcopal	15,859	4	14,998	32,925	18,410	3,871	5,963	22,258	6,262	6,701	9,144	1,613
Regular Baptist (North)	12,605	7	14,207	25,193	13,621	5,654	11,626	18,759	4,063	2,256	21,781	13,753
Presbyterian (Northern)	11,094	4	23,873	35,185	16,447	4,389	1,536	5,241	4,599	7,184	4,882	1,843
Congregational	9,704	3	3,047	890	11,153	2,670	10,076	268	1,047	489	1,399	56
Jewish	9,187	2	35,085	4,216	2,645	3,022	2,300	3,500	3,725	1,250	976	515
Protestant Episcopal	8,937	5	37,597	28,319	17,600	3,536	8,167	12,193	2,253	3,545	7,315	3,651
German Evangelical	8,252	4	200	......	......	13,777	......	3,845	13,093	10,657	......	3,450

[1] Data compiled from U.S., *Eleventh Census, 1890*, "Report on Statistics of Churches in the United States," pp. 94–95, 98–99.

CHICAGO AND COOK COUNTY SUNDAY–SCHOOL STATISTICS, 1875, 1886 [1]

Denomination	Number of Schools		Officers and Teachers		Scholars		Total Membership		Average Attendance	
	1875	1886	1875	1886	1875	1886	1875	1886	1875	1886
Adventist...............	1	...	5	...	53	....	58	....	30	....
Baptist.................	26	27	634	830	6,400	7,240	7,034	8,070	5,056	5,805
Christian...............	2	3	49	64	345	609	394	673	310	371
Congregational.........	11	29	426	1,091	4,505	10,111	4,931	11,202	3,564	7,385
Episcopal (Protestant)....	18	19	350	530	2,956	5,174	3,306	5,704	2,764	4,094
Episcopal (Reformed)....	6	8	140	241	1,340	2,789	1,480	3,030	1,011	2,016
Evangelical Association...	6	6	158	160	1,248	1,533	1,406	1,693	1,077	1,380
Evangelical Reformed....	2	2	37	30	368	300	405	330	310	215
Friends.................	1	1	8	15	76	102	84	117	57	73
German United Evangelical..................	3	5	37	196	595	2,083	632	2,279	535	1,700
Lutheran...............	24	27	495	543	5,813	5,806	6,308	6,349	5,365	4,300
Methodist Episcopal......	32	45	943	1,344	8,543	13,118	9,486	14,462	7,124	9,950
New Jerusalem..........	4	4	31	23	271	172	302	195	181	150
Presbyterian............	22	27	645	934	6,486	9,580	7,131	10,514	4,952	7,276
Union and Independent [a] .	6	20	136	430	2,147	8,557	2,283	8,987	1,538	5,643
Unitarian [b]	4	4	....	72	844	650	844	722	748	500
Universalist.............	4	4	....	80	743	764	743	844	652	600
Total..................	172	240	4,094	6,658	42,733	75,070	46,827	81,728	35,364	58,223

[1] Data compiled from Cook County Sunday-School Association, *Statistical Summary of Sunday-Schools in the City of Chicago and Cook County, Ill., for the Year Ending December 31, 1875,* and *Sunday School Work. A Record of Sunday School News and Progress,* "Sunday Schools in Cook County Reported at the Annual Convention, May 7 & 8, 1886."

[a] Includes Y.M.C.A., News Boys' Home, Depot Mission, and Everybody's.

[b] Figures for 1886 are estimates.

SELECTIVE BIBLIOGRAPHY

The following list does not include all sources used in the preparation of *A History of Chicago*, III. Only selected and representative primary materials appear. Separate items such as letters and periodical articles are omitted. The text is fully documented by references in the accompanying footnotes.

I. UNPUBLISHED

Addams, Jane. *The Papers of Jane Addams, 1840–1940. Mss.* Library of Congress.

Altgeld, John Peter. *John P. Altgeld Collection, 1860–1923. Mss.* and pamphlets. Illinois State Historical Library, Springfield.

Autograph Letters. 97 v. *Mss.* Chicago Historical Society.

Bersbach, O. *Scrapbook of Chicago Theatre and Concert Programs.* 3 v. Chicago Historical Society.

Blatchford, Eliphalet W., comp. *Hog Raising and the Pork Packing Industry in America. Investigations of the Committee Appointed by the President of the United States.* 1883–84. *Mss.* and newspaper clippings. John Crerar Library.

Bonney, Charles C. *Personal Miscellany.* 14 v. John Crerar Library.

Breese, Sidney. *Sidney Breese Collection, 1876–1896. Mss.* Illinois State Historical Library, Springfield.

Browne, F. F. *Papers, 1874–1890. Mss.* Newberry Library.

Burley, Augustus H. *Correspondence Relative to Banks and Banking in Illinois, 1871–1875. Mss.* Chicago Historical Society.

Caton, John D. *John D. Caton Papers. Mss.* Library of Congress.

Central Church of Chicago. *Record, December 4, 1875 — December 23, 1919. Ms.* Chicago Historical Society.

Chicago Academy of Design. *Circular, January 8, 1880.* Chicago Historical Society.

Chicago Astronomical Society. *Collection.* Chicago Historical Society.

Chicago, Burlington & Quincy Railroad Archives. *Contract File, 1866–82; Contracts, 1852–1900; Elevator Papers, 1879–1887; Elevator Statements, 1886–1902; Miscellaneous Papers, 1878–1879; Pools, 1880–89; Traffic Manager's Report, 1876–78. Mss.* Newberry Library. By permission of the Director.

" Chicago Fire, 1871." *Miscellaneous Personal Narratives. Mss.* Chicago Historical Society.

Chicago Fire Marshal's Office. *Order Book. Ms.* John Crerar Library.

Cleveland, Grover. *The Papers of Grover Cleveland. Mss.* Library of Congress.

Cook County, Office of Clerk of Superior Court. *Plaintiff's General Index*, II; Tribune Company *v.* The Board of Education of the City of Chicago, case No. 97,614; Walsh *v.* The Board of Education of the City of Chicago, case No. 97,615. *Mss.* Vault of Office of Clerk of Superior Court of Cook County.

Davis, David. *The David Davis Letters, 1872–1884.* Typescript. University of Illinois.

Davis, Will J. *Collection. Scrap Books. Mss.* and clippings. Chicago Historical Society.

Dennis, Charles H. *Charles H. Dennis Papers, 1868–1942. Mss.* Newberry Library.

Dent, Thomas. *Collection. Mss.* Chicago Historical Society.

Eastman, Zebina. *Collection.* Volume XL of *Autograph Letters. Mss.* Chicago Historical Society.

Field, Marshall. " Complete Inventory Estate of Marshall Field." *Ms.* Field Estate Office, later Field Archives, Chicago.

Field, Marshall. *Marshall Field Letter Books. Mss.* Field Estate Office, Chicago.

Field, Marshall. *Marshall Field Papers. Mss.* Marshall Field and Company Archives, Chicago.

Greenebaum, Henry E. *Henry Greenebaum Estate Collection. Mss.* Chicago Historical Society.

Harrison, Carter. *Carter Harrison Papers, 1860–1953. Mss.* Newberry Library.

[Haymarket]. *Bulletin of the Haymarket Riot Execution; Haymarket Trial Exhibits; Official Court Record of the Haymarket Trial, 1887. Mss.* Chicago Historical Society.

Hubbard, Gurdon Saltonstall. *G. S. Hubbard Collection.* Volume XVIII of *Autograph Letters. Mss.* Chicago Historical Society.

Hutchinson, Charles L. *Papers, 1866–1922. Mss.* Newberry Library.

Kirkland, Joseph. *Papers. Mss.* Newberry Library.

Labadie Collection. Mss. University of Michigan.

Lawson, Victor F. *Papers. Mss.* Newberry Library.

Lloyd, Henry D. *Papers, 1840–1893. Mss.* Wisconsin Historical Society.

Logan, John A. *Papers, 1869–1886. Mss.* Library of Congress.

McCormick, Cyrus H. *Cyrus H. McCormick Papers. Mss.* Chicago Historical Society.

Medill, Joseph. *Medill Papers. Mss.* Courtesy of the late Col. Robert R. McCormick, Chicago.

Morgan, Thomas J. *Collection. Mss.* University of Illinois.

Nelson, L[Lars]. P. *Statistics Showing by Divisions, Wards and Voting Precints [sic] The Original Nationality of the Voters in Chicago.* "Copyright 1887 by L. P. Nelson" *Ms.* with printed title page. Newberry Library.

Parsons, Albert R. *Autobiography. Ms.* Chicago Historical Society.

Philosophical Society of Chicago. *Collection. Mss.* Chicago Historical Society.

Pioneer Aid and Support Association. *Minute Book. Ms.* Pioneer Aid and Support Association.

Pullman, Mrs. George M. *Mrs. George M. Pullman Papers. Mss.* Courtesy of Mrs. Philip Miller, Chicago.

Raymond, Benjamin W. *Benjamin W. Raymond Letter Book, 1874. Ms.* Chicago Historical Society.

Schneider, George. *Collection. Mss.* Chicago Historical Society.

Smith, Moses. *Moses Smith, Secretary of the Western Education Society, Chicago, to "Its Constituency," May 1, 1872. Ms.* Chicago Historical Society.

Spies, August. *An Autobiographical Sketch. Ms.* Chicago Historical Society.

Swift & Company. *Mss.* Swift & Company Library.

Taylor, Graham. *Graham Taylor Papers, [1862–1938]. Mss.* Newberry Library.

Thomas, Hiram Washington. *Hiram Washington Thomas, 1832–1910, Scrapbook.* Chicago Historical Society.

Thomas, John Robert. *The Letters of John R. Thomas, 1879–1890. Mss.* Library of Congress.

Tree, Lambert. *Papers. Mss.* Newberry Library.

Trenholm, William Lee. *Papers of William L. Trenholm. Mss.* Library of Congress.

Trumbull, Lyman. *The Papers of Lyman Trumbull, 1855–1877. Mss.* Library of Congress.

The University of Chicago. *Correspondence on the Founding of The University of Chicago. Mss.* The University of Chicago Archives.

Washburne, Elihu B. *The Papers of Elihu B. Washburne, 1829–1882. Mss.* Library of Congress.

Yates, Richard, [Sr. and Jr.]. *Yates Collection, 1870–1900. Mss.* Illinois State Historical Library.

Young Men's Christian Association. Board of Managers. *Minutes, June, 1858 — December, 1888. Mss.* Central Y.M.C.A., Chicago.

II. BOOKS AND PAMPHLETS

The Accused The Accusers. The Famous Speeches of the Eight Chicago Anarchists in Court . . . Chicago: Socialistic Publishing Society, n.d.

Addams, Jane. *Forty Years at Hull-House.* New York: The Macmillan Company, 1935.

——. *Twenty Years at Hull-House* . . . New York: The Macmillan Company, 1930.

Altgeld, John P. *Live Questions: Including Our Penal Machinery and Its Victims.* Chicago: Donohue & Henneberry, 1890.

——. *Reasons for Pardoning Fielden, Neebe and Schwab.* [Springfield, 1893.]

Ames, Sarah E. *An Open Letter to Judge Joseph E. Gary . . . Why the Undertone?* Chicago: n.p., 1893.

Angle, Paul M., ed. *The Great Chicago Fire Described in Seven Letters by Men and Women Who Experienced Its Horrors* . . . Chicago: The Chicago Historical Society, 1946.

Anthony, Elliott. *Sanitation and Navigation.* Chicago: Chicago Legal News Co., 1891.

Appeal in Behalf of the New Saint Elizabeth's Hospital. Pamphlet. n.d. Chicago Historical Society.

Barrows, John H., ed. *The World's Parliament of Religions.* 2 v. Chicago: The Parliament Publishing Company, 1893.

Bisbee, Lewis H., and Simonds, John C. *The Board of Trade and the Produce Exchange, Their History, Methods and Law* . . . Chicago: Callaghan & Company, 1884.

Blatchford, Mary Emily, and Eliphalet Wickes. *Memories of the Chicago Fire.* [Chicago]: Privately printed, 1921.

Bonney, Charles Carroll. *The Present Conflict of Labor and Capital* . . . Chicago: Chicago Legal News Co., 1886.

——. *World's Congress Addresses.* Chicago: The Open Court Publishing Company, 1900.

Brown, G[George]. P. *Drainage Channel and Waterway* . . . Chicago: R. R. Donnelley & Sons Company, 1894.

Chicago's Dark Places . . . Chicago: The Craig Press and Women's Temperance Publishing Association, 1891.

Colbert, Elias, and Chamberlin, Everett. *Chicago and the Great Conflagration.* Cincinnati: C. F. Vent, 1871.

Ericsson, Henry. *Sixty Years a Builder: The Autobiography of Henry Ericsson* (Lewis E. Myers, collaborator). Chicago: A. Kroch and Son, 1942.

Farwell, John V. *Some Recollections of John V. Farwell.* Chicago: R. R. Donnelley & Sons Company, 1911.

[Ferry, Mrs. Abby (Farwell)]. *Reminiscences of John V. Farwell by His Elder Daughter.* 2 v. Chicago: Ralph Fletcher Seymour, 1928.

Field, Eugene. *Culture's Garland, Being Memoranda of the Gradual Rise of Literature, Art, Music and Society in Chicago, and Other Western Ganglia.* Boston: Ticknor and Company, 1887.

First State Pawners Society under State Supervision: Organized 1899 by the Merchants Club of Chicago. n.p., n.d.

Frank, Henriette Greenebaum, and Jerome, Amalie Hofer, comps. *Annals of the Chicago Woman's Club* . . . Chicago: Chicago Woman's Club, 1916.

Freeman, William H., comp. *The Press Club of Chicago* . . . Chicago: The Press Club of Chicago, 1894.

[Gage, Lyman J.]. *Memoirs of Lyman J. Gage.* New York: House of Field, Inc., 1937.

Garland, Hamlin. *Crumbling Idols.* Chicago: Stone and Kimball, 1894.

Gompers, Samuel. *Seventy Years of Life and Labor. An Autobiography.* New York: E. P. Dutton & Company, 1925.

Gregory, Addie Hibbard. *A Great-Grandmother Remembers.* Chicago: A. Kroch, 1940.

Harrison, Carter H. *Stormy Years: The Autobiography of Carter H. Harrison, Five Times Mayor of Chicago.* Indianapolis: The Bobbs-Merrill Company, 1935.

Holbrook, Z[Zephaniah]. S[Swift]. *The Lessons of the Homestead Troubles* . . . Chicago: Knight, Leonard & Co., Printers, 1892.

Hotchkiss, George W. *History of the Lumber and Forest Industry of the Northwest.* Chicago: George W. Hotchkiss & Co., 1898.

Houghton, Walter R., ed. *Neely's History of the Parliament of Religions and Religious Congresses at the World's Columbian Exposition*. Chicago: Frank Tennyson Neely, 1893.

Hull-House, Residents of. *Hull-House Maps and Papers* . . . New York: Thomas Y. Crowell & Co., 1895.

Hunt, Henry M. *The Crime of the Century; or, the Assassination of Dr. Patrick Henry Cronin* . . . [Chicago: n.p., 1889].

Ingersoll, Robert G. *The Works of Robert G. Ingersoll*. Dresden Memorial Edition. 12 v. New York: The Ingersoll League, 1929.

James, Henry Ammon. *Communism in America*. New York: Henry Holt and Company, 1879.

Jones, Jenkin L., ed. *A Chorus of Faith as Heard in the Parliament of Religions*. Chicago: The Unity Publishing Company, 1893.

Kirkland, Caroline, ed. *Chicago Yesterdays; a Sheaf of Reminiscences*. Chicago: Daughaday and Company, 1919.

Koerner, Gustave. *Memoirs of Gustave Koerner, 1809–1896* (Thomas J. McCormack, ed.). 2 v. Cedar Rapids, Iowa: The Torch Press, 1909.

Loesch, Frank J. *Personal Experiences during the Chicago Fire, 1871*. Chicago: Privately printed, 1925.

Lorimer, George C. *Isms Old and New* . . . 2nd ed. Chicago: S. C. Griggs and Company, 1881.

[Lowther, Thomas D., comp.]. *Memorials of the Old Chicago Library, Formerly Young Men's Association, and of the Advent of the New*. Chicago: John K. Scully, Printer, 1878.

McIlvaine, Mabel, ed. *Reminiscences of Chicago during the Great Fire*. Chicago: R. R. Donnelley & Sons Company, 1915.

[MacLeish, Andrew]. *Life of Andrew MacLeish, 1838–1928*. Chicago: Privately printed, 1929.

National Liberal League. *Patriotic Addresses* . . . Boston: National Liberal League, 1876.

Parsons, Albert R. *Anarchism: Its Philosophy and Scientific Basis as Defined by Some of Its Apostles*. Chicago: Mrs. A. R. Parsons, Publisher, 1887.

[Parsons, Lucy E.]. *Life of Albert R. Parsons* . . . Chicago: Mrs. Lucy E. Parsons, Publisher and Proprietor, 1889.

——. *Souvenir Edition of the Famous Speeches of Our Martyrs, Delivered in Court* . . . 6th ed. Chicago: Lucy E. Parsons, Publisher, [1912].

The People's Pulpit. Complete Sermons of Rev. H. W. Thomas, . . . during Church Year Sept. 4, 1887–June 24, 1888. Chicago: Frank L. Strong, 1888.

BIBLIOGRAPHY 553

Pinkerton, Allan. *Strikers, Communists, Tramps and Detectives.* New York: G. W. Carleton & Co., 1878.

Pinkerton's National Detective Agency and Its Connection with the Labor Troubles at Homestead, Penn., July 6, 1892 . . . [New York, 1892].

Porter, H[Henry]. H. *A Short Autobiography.* Chicago: Privately printed, 1915.

Powderly, Terence V. *The Path I Trod: The Autobiography of Terence V. Powderly* (Harry J. Carman, Henry David, and Paul N. Guthrie, eds., *Columbia Studies in American Culture, no. 6*). New York: Columbia University Press, 1940.

——. *Thirty Years of Labor. 1859 to 1889* . . . Columbus, Ohio: Excelsior Publishing House, 1890.

Presbyterian Church in the U.S.A. Chicago Presbytery. *The Trial of the Rev. David Swing before the Presbytery of Chicago* (David S. Johnson, Francis L. Patton, and George C. Noyes, eds.). Chicago: Jansen, McClurg & Co., 1874.

Quinn, John Philip. *Fools of Fortune, or Gambling and Gamblers* . . . Chicago: The Anti-Gambling Association, 1892.

Read, Opie. *I Remember.* New York: Richard R. Smith, Inc., 1930.

[Reed & Company]. *The Lumber Industry of Chicago.* Reed & Company, Publishers, [1882].

Root, George F. *The Story of a Musical Life.* Cincinnati: The John Church Co., 1891.

Saint-Gaudens, Homer, ed. *The Reminiscences of Augustus Saint-Gaudens.* 2 v. New York: The Century Co., 1913.

Salter, William M. *What Shall Be Done with the Anarchists? A Lecture before the Society for Ethical Culture of Chicago* . . . Chicago: The Open Court Publishing Company, 1887.

Schaack, Michael J. *Anarchy and Anarchists. . . . The Chicago Haymarket Conspiracy* . . . Chicago: F. J. Schulte & Company, 1889.

Sheahan, James W., and Upton, George P. *The Great Conflagration.* Chicago: Union Publishing Co., 1872,

Siringo, Charles A. *A Cowboy Detective* . . . Chicago: W. B. Conkey Company, 1912.

——. *Two Evil Isms, Pinkertonism and Anarchism.* Chicago: C. A. Siringo, 1915.

Spalding, Albert G. *America's National Game* . . . New York: American Sports Publishing Company, 1911.

Spies, August. *August Spies' Auto-Biography* . . . Chicago: Nina van Zandt, [1887].

Starrett, Paul. *Changing the Skyline: An Autobiography*. New York: McGraw-Hill Book Company, Inc., 1938.

Starring, Mrs. Helen (Swing), comp. *David Swing: a Memorial Volume* . . . Chicago: F. T. Neely, 1894.

Stead, William T. *If Christ Came to Chicago! A Plea for the Union of All Who Love in the Service of All Who Suffer*. Chicago: Laird & Lee, Publishers, 1894.

Stephenson, Isaac. *Recollections of a Long Life, 1829–1915*. Chicago: Privately printed, 1915.

Stone, Melville E. *Fifty Years a Journalist*. Garden City, N. Y.: Doubleday, Page & Company, 1922.

Sullivan, Louis H. *The Autobiography of an Idea*. New York: Press of The American Institute of Architects, Inc., 1926.

Swing, David. *The Message of David Swing to His Generation: Addresses and Papers* (Newell Dwight Hillis, comp.). New York: Fleming H. Revell Company, 1913.

——. *The Noble Mission of the Humane Societies* . . . Chicago: Albert W. Landon, Publisher, [1886].

——. *Old Pictures of Life*. 2 v. Chicago: Stone and Kimball, 1894.

——. *Truths for To-Day*. Chicago: Jansen, McClurg and Company, 1874.

Taylor, Graham. *Pioneering on Social Frontiers*. Chicago: The University of Chicago Press, 1931.

Thomas, Rose Fay. *Memoirs of Theodore Thomas*. New York: Moffat, Yard and Company, 1911.

Thomas, Theodore. *A Musical Autobiography*. George P. Upton, ed. 2 v. Chicago: A. C. McClurg & Co., 1905.

Upton, George P. *Musical Memories* . . . Chicago: A. C. McClurg & Co., 1908.

[Van Arsdale & Massie]. *The Inter-State Exposition Souvenir* . . . Chicago: Van Arsdale & Massie, 1873.

Wilkie, Franc B. *Personal Reminiscences of Thirty-five Years of Journalism*. Chicago: F. J. Schulte & Company, Publishers, 1891.

Willard, Frances E. *Glimpses of Fifty Years: The Autobiography of an American Woman*. Chicago: Woman's Temperance Publication Association, 1889.

[Woman's Christian Temperance Union]. *A Brief History of the Woman's Christian Temperance Union*. 3d ed. Evanston, Ill., The Union Signal, 1907.

The World's Edition of the Great Presbyterian Conflict: Patton vs. Swing . . . Chicago: G. Macdonald & Co., 1874.

Zeisler, Sigmund. *Reminiscences of the Anarchist Case* [Chicago]: Chicago Literary Club, 1927.

III. NEWSPAPERS AND PERIODICALS

Abendpost. 1889–93. [Newspaper; German; daily; independent; est. Sept. 2, 1889.]

The Advance. 1871–93. [Congregational; weekly.]

The Alarm. 1884–88. [Chicago, 1884–1888 (Oct., 1884–April, 1886, edited by A. R. Parsons). Published by the International Working People's Association. Publication suspended May, 1886–Oct., 1887.]

The Alliance. 1873–82. [Weekly; non-sectarian; religion, literature, government. Consolidated with *Western Magazine* 1882. Prior to this date it had various titles: *Chicago Alliance, Alliance, Alliance and Radical Review.* The *Western Magazine,* which absorbed the *Alliance,* ceased publication in 1884.]

America. 1888–91.

American Brewers' Review. 1887–93. [Trade; English and German. Took over *Der Braumeister* July 8, 1892. Ran to 1939.]

The American Elevator and Grain Trade. 1882–93. [Trade; monthly. Ceased publication Oct. 15, 1930.]

The American Lumberman. 1873–93. [Weekly; lumber interest. Established in 1873 as *Northwestern Lumberman.* Became *The American Lumberman* in 1898.]

Annalen der Alumni des American Brewing Academy. 1901–2. [Chicago, Ill. Wahl Henius, 1901–2.]

The Banker's Magazine and Statistical Register. 1871–93.

Bankers' Monthly. 1883–93. [Chicago.]

The Banking and Insurance Chronicle of Chicago. 1871–72. [Weekly; insurance and real estate.]

Brauer und Mälzer. 1882–93. [German; monthly; trade; est. 1882.]

Der Braumeister. 1887–92. [German; monthly; trade; est. 1887; expired 1892. Continued as *American Brewers' Review and Beverage Bulletin.* Title changed to *Food Research,* 1918.]

Brewer and Maltster and Beverageur. 1882–93. [Monthly; brewing, malt, hop, barley, beverage, trade. I to IX as *Brauer und Mälzer.*]

Brewers' Journal, 1876–93.

The Bulletin of the American Iron and Steel Association. 1871–93. [Published by American Iron and Steel Association, Philadelphia, 1866–1912.]

The Catholic Home. 1882(?)–1892(?). [Weekly; Catholic.]

The Catholic World. 1871–93.

Chicago Chronicle. 1880–93. [Republican.]

Chicago Daily Law Bulletin. 1876.

Chicago Daily News. Dec. 26, 1875–93. [Independent.]

Chicago Evening Journal. 1871–93. [Republican.]

Chicago Evening Post. 1871–73. [Daily. Republican. Consolidated with the *Mail* to form the *Post and Mail,* 1874–76 (daily and weekly); then as *Chicago Post,* 1876–78. Sold in Aug., 1878 to *Chicago News.*]

Chicagoer Arbeiter-Zeitung. 1876–93. [Three times weekly; working-man's organ.]

Chicagoer Freie Presse. July 2, 1874–Dec., 1874. [Other titles: *Die Freie Presse,* 1871–July 1, 1874. *Chicagoer Neue Freie Presse,* 1874–83. Daily; German; independent.]

Chicago Herald. 1881–93. [Independent.]

The Chicago Legal News. 1871–93.

Chicago Morning Herald. 1881–93. [Republican to 1882; independent with Republican leanings to 1892; Democratic thereafter. Combined with *Times* in 1895.]

The Chicago News Record. 1892–93.

Chicago Post. 1871–73; 1876–78. [Daily and weekly; Republican. Became *Post and Mail* in 1874–76. Again *Chicago Post,* 1876–78. Sold to *News* in 1878.]

The Chicago Post and Mail. 1874–76.

The Chicago Pulpit. 1871–73. [Weekly; undenominational.]

The Chicago Times. 1871–93. [Daily. Democratic. Independent. Title varies.]

Chicago Tribune. 1871–93. [Daily; Republican. Title varies.]

The Christian Union. 1871–93. [Title varies.]

The Commercial and Financial Chronicle. 1870–93.

The Congregational Quarterly. 1871–93.

Der Deutsche Pionier, 1871–87.

The Dial. 1880–93. [Monthly; semimonthly.]

The Drovers' Journal. 1873–93. [Title varies.]

Dziennik Chicagoski. 1890–93. [Polish; daily; Democratic.]

The Economist [Chicago]. 1888–93. [Financial and Real Estate.]

The Eight-Hour Herald. 1892–93. [Semimonthly; labor.]

Electrical Review. 1883–93.

Electrical World. 1883–93. [Title varies; *Electrical World and Electrical Engineer; Electrical World and Engineer.*]

Hejmdal. 1874–78. [Danish Weekly.]

Illinois Staats-Zeitung. 1871–93. [Daily; German; independent. Published Sunday edition of *Der Westen,* 1867–1902.]

The Industrial Age. 1873–77.

The Inland Architect and Builder. 1883–87. [Merged into *American Architect and Architecture.* 1887–93.]

The Inter Ocean. 1872–93. [Daily and weekly; Republican. Title varies.]

The Irish World and American Industrial Liberator. 1871–93.

Iron Age. 1873–93.

L'Italia. 1886–93. [Italian; daily; independent Republican.]

The Jewish Advance. 1878–81. [Weekly; English and German.]

The Jewish Era. A Christian Quarterly in Behalf of Israel. 1892–94.

The Knights of Labor. 1886–89. *The Rights of Labor.* 1889–93.

The Lakeside Monthly. Jan., 1869–Feb., 1874. [From 1869 to 1870 the *Western Monthly.* Not issued from Oct., 1870 to Nov.–Dec., 1871.]

The Living Church. 1878–93. [Weekly; religious; Episcopal.]

Lumberman's Gazette. 1872–87. [Est. 1872. Weekly; commercial.]

The Lumber Trade Journal. 1882–93. [Periodical; monthly & semimonthly; commercial; est. 1882.]

Magazine of Western History. 1884–91. [*National Magazine,* 1891–94.]

Mixed Drinks. The Saloon Keeper's Journal. 1878–94. [Became *Fair Play* 1894–97; *Champion of Fair Play* 1898–1929.]

The News Record. 1881–93. [Called *Chicago Record,* 1892–93.]

Northwestern Christian Advocate. 1871–93. [Weekly; Methodist; est. 1852.]

Northwestern Lumberman. 1873–93. [Weekly (monthly in 1874); devoted to lumber interests.]

The Northwestern Review. 1871–74. [Weekly; monthly in 1870 and 1871; devoted to insurance; in 1872 the *Northwestern Weekly Review.*]

The Occident. 1873–93. [Weekly; Jewish; general news, politics, literature, science, art, interests of Hebrews of the Northwest. Ran to 1895.]

Pomeroy's Democrat. 1876–80. [Newspaper; weekly; Greenback organ; after January 26, 1878, title changed to *Pomeroy's Illustrated Democrat.*]

Public Opinion. 1886–93.

The Publishers' Weekly. 1872–93.

Railroad Gazette. 1871–93. [1870–May, 1908 as *Railroad Gazette.* June, 1908–July, 1909 as *Railroad Age Gazette.* Aug., 1909–June, 1917 as *Railway Age Gazette.* 1918– as *Railway Age.* Transportation; engineering; railroad news. Est. 1870.]

The Railway Age. 1876–93. [Weekly; devoted to construction, equipment, operation, maintenance, public relations of railroads. Est. 1856. Ran until 1908.]

The Railway Age and Northwestern Railroader. 1892–93.

Rand, McNally & Co.'s Bankers' Monthly. 1883–87. [*The Rand-McNally Bankers' Monthly,* 1888–1917. After that it was the *Banker's Monthly.*]

Real Estate and Building Journal. 1871–93. [Est. 1868; weekly; real estate and building.]

The Reform Advocate. 1891–93. [Weekly; Jewish; est. 1891.]

Revyen. 1892–93. [Newspaper; Danish; weekly; independent; est. 1892; exp. 1921.]

The St. Louis Lumberman. 1888–93.

The Sanitary News. 1882–91. [Semi-monthly; sanitary science.]

Siebel's Journal. 1890–93. [Zymotechnic bulletin 1890–1915.]

Skandinaven. 1871–93. [Newspaper; semi-weekly; independent; est. 1866; exp. 1941; Norwegian.]

The Spectator. 1871–80. [Periodical; American review of insurance.]

The Standard. 1871–93. [Est. 1867; Baptist.]

Svenska Tribunen. 1876–93. [Newspaper; Swedish; weekly; Republican; est. 1876; exp. 1906.]

Svornost. 1875–93. [Newspaper; daily; independent; Czech; est. 1875.]

The Timberman. 1885–93. [Absorbed by *Northwestern Lumberman* in 1899.]

The Vanguard. 1892–93. [Chicago.]

Der Westen. 1871–93. [Newspaper; weekly; German; independent; est. 1867; exp. 1902; re-est. 1911; exp. 1914(?).]

The Western Brewer and Journal of the Barley, Hop, and Malt Trade. 1876–93. [Monthly; devoted to brewing, malting, hop, kindred trades. In 1907 the name changed to *Western Brewer.*]

The Western Catholic. 1871–81. [Weekly; Catholic; Democratic.]

Western Electrician. 1887–93. [Weekly; electrical; est. 1887.]

The Western Manufacturer. 1874–82. [Monthly.]

The Workingman's Advocate. 1871–79. [Newspaper; official organ of the labor union 1869. Est. 1864.]

Zgoda. 1882–93. [Weekly; Polish; Republican.]

IV. DIRECTORIES, GUIDEBOOKS, AND MAPS

Bradstreets' Pocket Atlas of the United States. New York: The Bradstreet Company, 1880.

The Chicago Blue Book of Selected Names of Chicago and Suburban

Towns . . . for the Year Ending 1891 . . . Chicago: The Chicago Directory Company, Publishers, 1890.

Cram, George F. *New Railroad and Township Map of the N.W. States* [Chicago]: George F. Cram, 1872.

The Daily News Almanac and Political Register . . . Chicago: The Chicago Daily News Company, 1885–94. [Title varies.]

Dunlap, Thomas, comp. and ed. *Wiley's American Iron Trade Manual of the Leading Iron Industries of the United States* . . . New York: J. Wiley and Son, 1874.

Edwards, Richard. . . . *Annual Directory of the Inhabitants, Institutions, Manufacturing Establishments and Incorporated Companies of the City of Chicago* . . . 13th–16th, 1871–73. Chicago: Richard Edwards, 1870–73.

——, comp. *Merchants' Chicago Census Report Embracing a Complete Directory of the City* . . . . Chicago: Richard Edwards, 1871.

The Elite Directory and Club List of Chicago . . . *1885–6, 1887–8.* Chicago: The Elite Publishing Co. (Limited), 1885, 1887.

Flinn, John J., comp. *Chicago . . . A Guide, 1891–93.* Chicago: printer varies. [1891–93.]

——, ed. *The Hand-Book of Chicago Biography.* Chicago: The Standard Guide Company, 1893.

[Glossop, Frank]. *Glossop's Street Guide, Strangers' Directory and Hotel Manual of Chicago.* Chicago: Frank Glossop, 1888.

Harris, I. C., comp. *The Colored Men's Professional and Business Directory of Chicago* . . . Chicago: I. C. Harris, 1885 and 1886.

Hotchkiss, George W., ed. and comp. *Hotchkiss' Lumberman's Directory of Chicago and the Northwest* . . . Chicago: R. R. Donnelley & Sons, Printers, 1886.

Illinois State Federation of Labor. *Official Annual Labor Gazette, 1893* . . . Chicago: Illinois State Federation of Labor, [1893].

The Lakeside Annual Directory of the City of Chicago . . . (Thomas Hutchinson, comp., 1876–86, and Reuben H. Donnelley, comp., 1887–93). Chicago: printer varies, 1874–93.

[Marquis, Albert Nelson]. *Marquis' Hand-Book of Chicago* . . . Chicago: A. N. Marquis & Co., Publishers, 1885.

Merchants and Manufacturers Illustrated Chicago Guide for 1880. Chicago: Fox, Cole & Co., 1880.

Moran, George E., comp. *Moran's Directory of Chicago and Its Vicinity* . . . Chicago: George E. Moran, 1894.

[Orear, George Washington]. *Commercial and Architectural Chicago* . . . [Chicago]: G. W. Orear, Publisher, 1887.

[Rand, McNally & Co.]. *The Bankers' Directory and List of Bank Attorneys . . . July, 1878, January, 1886, July, 1889.* Chicago: Rand, McNally & Co., 1878, 1886, 1889. [Ed. by C. R. Williams, 1889.]

——. *The Bankers' Directory of the United States and Canada . . . July, 1878, July, 1880.* Chicago: Rand, McNally & Co., 1878, 1880.

——. *Chicago Business Directory . . . 1889–91.* Chicago: Rand, McNally & Co., 1889–91.

——. *Rand, McNally & Co.'s Business Atlas . . .* Chicago: Rand, McNally & Co., 1880.

——. *Rand, McNally & Co.'s Business Atlas and Shippers' Guide, 1885.* Chicago: Rand, McNally and Company, 1885.

——. *Rand, McNally & Co.'s Directory and Shipping Guide of Lumber Mills and Lumber Dealers in the United States and Canada . . .* Chicago: Rand, McNally & Co., Publishers, 1884.

——. *Rand, McNally & Co.'s New Official Railroad Map of the United States and Dominion of Canada.* Chicago: Rand, McNally & Co., 1886.

Sadliers' Catholic Directory . . . 1893 . . . New York: D. & J. Sadlier & Co., 1893.

Sargent, Porter E. *A Handbook of the Best Private Schools of the United States and Canada.* Boston: Porter Sargent, [1915].

Schick, Louis. *Chicago and Its Environs . . .* Chicago: L. Schick, 1891.

[Visher, John]. *Hand-Book of Chicago's Charities.* Chicago: The Illinois Conference of Charities and Corrections, 1892.

V. DOCUMENTS AND REPORTS

A. PRIVATE

American Brewing Academy of Chicago. *Constitution and By-Laws of the Alumni of the American Brewing Academy.* Chicago: n.p., 1901.

——. *Tenth Anniversary Reunion, Alumni and Former Students.* Chicago: Blakely Printing Company, 1901.

American Federation of Labor. *Report of Proceedings of the . . . Annual Convention . . . 1881–93.* Title and publication data vary.

American Iron and Steel Association. *Report of the Secretary . . . 1871–74, 1879–80, 1889.* Title varies. Philadelphia: printer varies, 1872–90.

The Art Institute of Chicago. *Annual Report of the Trustees. 1889–91, 1894.* [Chicago], 1889–94.

The Baptist General Association of Illinois. *Minutes . . . 1875, 1882, 1892.* Publication data vary.

B'nai B'rith, Independent Order of. *Constitution . . . Revised and Amended in the General Convention of the Order Held in the City of Richmond, Va. June 1st to 5th, 1890.* New York: Menorah Publishing Company, 1890.

——. *Report of the Secretary to the Twenty-first Annual Convention of District Grand Lodge No. 6, I.O.B.B.* Chicago: Max Stern & Co., [1889].

Charity Organization Society of Chicago. *Annual Report of the Directors . . . , For the Year Ending October 1st, 1886.* Chicago: Hornstein Bros., Printers, 1886.

Chicago Association of Commerce. *Smoke Abatement and Electrification of Railway Terminals in Chicago.* Chicago: [Rand, McNally & Co.], 1915.

Chicago Baptist Association. *Proceedings . . . at Its . . . Anniversary . . .* 1872, 1882, 1892. Publication data vary.

Chicago Bible Society. *. . . Annual Report . . .* 35th (1875–6), 45th (1885), 50th (1890), 51st (1891). Chicago: publisher varies, 1876–1891.

Chicago Board of Trade. *. . . Annual Report of the Trade and Commerce of Chicago, for the Year Ending December 31 . . .* 13th–36th, 1870–93. Chicago: printer varies, 1871–1894.

Chicago City Missionary Society. *. . . Annual Report . . .* 1st (1884)–14th (1896). Chicago: printer varies, 1884–96.

Chicago Daily Commercial Report. *The Thirtieth Annual of the Chicago Daily Commercial Report.* Chicago: Business Publishing Co., 1889.

Chicago Erring Woman's Refuge for Reform. *Annual Report,* 1873–92.

Chicago Home for the Friendless. *. . . Annual Report . . .* 13th (1871)–35th (1893). Chicago: printer varies, 1872–[94].

Chicago Latin School. *Sigillum, 1938, Fifty Years of Chicago Latin.* Chicago, [1938].

The Chicago Library Club. *Libraries of the City of Chicago with an Historical Sketch of the Chicago Library Club.* Chicago: Library Club, 1905.

Chicago Lumber Institute. *Charter and By-Laws.* Available at Lumber Trade Association of Cook County.

Chicago Mining and Stock Exchange. *Constitution, By-Laws and Rules. . . .* Chicago: John Dale, Printer and Binder, 1878.

Chicago Real Estate Board. *Report of Revenue Reform Committee, 1884.* Chicago, 1884.

Chicago Relief and Aid Society. *. . . Annual Report . . . to the Common Council of the City of Chicago . . .* 15th (1872)–19th (1876), 25th (1881–82)–33rd (1889–90). Chicago: printer varies, 1873–90.

——. *Report . . . of Disbursement of Contributions for the Sufferers by the Chicago Fire.* Cambridge: Riverside Press, 1874.

Chicago Trade and Labor Assembly. *Constitution, By-Laws and Rules of Order . . . Adopted May, 1880, Revised October, 1884, and October, 1886.* Chicago: McAbee and Kendig, 1886.

Chicago World's Columbian Exposition. *Report of the President . . .* Chicago: Rand, McNally & Co., 1898.

Chicago World's Columbian Exposition Bureau of Music. " Choral Music at the Fair," *Official Circular,* reprinted in *Music,* III (Nov., 1892), 45–48.

Church of Christ, Scientist. *Annual of the Church of Christ of Chicago, Illinois.* Chicago, 1887.

Citizens' Association of Chicago. *Address and Reports . . . 1874 to 1876. Annual Report . . . 1877–93.* Chicago: printer varies, 1876–93.

——. *Report of the Committee of the Citizens' Association on the Main Drainage and Water Supply of Chicago, September, 1885.* Chicago: n.p., 1885.

——. *Report of the Committee . . . on Education.* Chicago, 1881.

——. *Report of the Committee on Tenement Houses . . . September, 1884.* Chicago: Geo. K. Hazlitt & Co., 1884.

Citizens' League of Chicago. . . . *Annual Report of the Executive Committee . . .* 6th (1884), 8th (1886), 11th (1889). Chicago: printer varies, 1884–89.

——. *Fourteenth Annual Meeting . . . 1892 . . .* Chicago: James Guilbert, Printer, 1892.

The Civic Federation of Chicago. *The Street Railways of Chicago.* Report, Milo Roy Maltbie, ed., reprint from *Municipal Affairs,* 1901. [New York], 1901.

The Congregational Year Book, 1882, 1892. Boston: Congregational Publishing Society, 1882–92.

Democratic National Committee. *The Campaign Text Book of the Democratic Party for the Presidential Election of 1892.* New York: Democratic National Committee, 1892.

——. *The Campaign Text Book, [1880] Why the People Want a Change . . .* New York: National Democratic Committee. 1880.

——. *Official Proceedings of the National Democratic Convention . . . 1888.* St. Louis: Woodward & Tiernan Printing Co., 1888.

——. *The Political Reformation of 1884, A Democratic Campaign Book.* New York: National Democratic Committee, 1884.

Dominion [of Canada] Board of Trade. *Proceedings . . . Annual Meeting . . . 1871, 1878.* Montreal: The Gazette Printing House, 1871–78.

General Assembly of the Presbyterian Church in the United States of America. *Minutes* . . . 1872, 1882, 1892. Publication data vary.

Harvard School for Boys. *Harvard Review, 1865–1940.* Chicago, [1940].

Howe, S. Ferd. *Year Book of the Commercial, Banking, and Manufacturing Interests of Chicago, with a General Review of Its Business Progress. 1885-6.* Chicago: S. Ferd. Howe, 1886.

Illinois Anti-Monopoly League. *Report of the Present Status of the Claims of the Illinois Central Railroad to the Lake Front, and Submerged Lands Adjoining, under the "Lake Front Steal" of 1869.* [Chicago: n.p. 1881].

The Illinois Conference of Charities and Corrections. *Hand-Book of Chicago's Charities.* Chicago: Edwin M. Colvin, 1892.

Illinois State Federation of Labor. [*Proceedings of the Eleventh Annual Convention, 1893*]. Publication data vary.

The Knights of Labor. *Constitution of the General Assembly, District Assemblies, and Local Assemblies of the Order of the Knights of Labor of America.* n.p., n.d.

——. . . . *Proceedings* . . . 1878–86. Publication data vary.

——. *Report of the General Secretary* [John W. Hayes, 1888]. n.p., n.d.

Methodist Episcopal Church. *Minutes of the Annual Conferences* . . . 1872, 1882, 1893. New York: printer varies, n.d.

National Association of Iron Manufacturers. *Statistical Report . . . for 1872.* Philadelphia: J. A. Wagonseller, 1873.

National Board of Trade. *Proceedings of the . . . Annual Meeting . . .* 4th–10th (1871–79), 15th (1885), 18th (1888). Boston and Chicago: printer varies, 1872–88.

National Council of Women of the United States. *Transactions of the National Council . . . Assembled in Washington, D.C., February 22 to 25, 1891.* Philadelphia: J. B. Lippincott Company, 1891.

National Woman Suffrage Association, comp. *Report of the International Council of Women.* Washington: Rufus H. Darby, Printer, 1888.

Protective Agency for Women and Children, Chicago. *Annual Report.* 1st, 2nd, 6th. Chicago: printer varies, 1887–[92].

Protestant Episcopal Church. Diocese of Chicago (before 1883, Diocese of Illinois). *Journal of the . . . Annual Convention . . .* 35th (1872), 45th (1882), 51st (1888), 55th (1892). Chicago: printer varies, 1872–92.

Pullman's Palace Car Company. *Annual Statement, 1889, 1890, 1891.* Courtesy of Pullman, Incorporated, Chicago.

Republican National Committee. *Proceedings of the Eighth Republican National Convention . . . 1884.* Chicago: Republican National Committee, [1884].

——. *Proceedings of the Ninth Republican National Convention . . . 1888 . . .* Chicago: Republican National Committee, 1888.

——. *The Republican Campaign Text-Book for 1892.* New York: Republican National Committee, 1892.

Rock River Annual Conference of the Methodist Episcopal Church. *Minutes of the . . . Session . . .* 39th (1878), 41st (1880), 42nd (1881). Rockford, Illinois: Abraham E. Smith, Printer and Binder, 1878–81.

——. *Register of the Thirty-third Session . . . 1872.* Freeport, [Illinois]: The Journal Steam Printing House, 1872.

Sinai Congregation. *Minutes.* Special Meetings and Executive Board. Chicago: n.p.

The Sunset Club, Chicago. *Year Book, 1892–93.* Chicago: Privately published.

United Hebrew Charities of Chicago. . . . *Annual Report . . .* 1st (1888–89)–4th(1891–92). Chicago: printer varies, 1889–92.

United Hebrew Relief Association of Chicago. . . . *Annual Report . . .* 18th (1876–77), 21st (1879–80)–29th (1887–88). Chicago: printer varies, 1877–88.

The University of Chicago. *Annual Register, July 1, 1892 — July 1, 1893.* Chicago: The University Press of Chicago, 1893.

——. *The President's Report, July, 1892–July, 1902.* Chicago: The University of Chicago Press, 1903.

——. *The President's Report, July, 1897–July, 1898.* Chicago: The University of Chicago Press, 1903.

Woman's Christian Association, of Chicago, Illinois. . . . *Annual Report . . . for the Year Ending November 1 . . .* 7th (1883), 8th (1884), 10th (1886). Chicago: Jameson & Morse, Printers, 1884–87.

Woman's Exchange of Chicago. *Year Book.* 1911, 1933. [Chicago]: n.p., 1911–33.

Young Men's Christian Associations of the United States and the Dominion of Canada. *Year Book . . .* 1882–83, 1891. New York, 1882–91.

Young Women's Christian Association, of Chicago, Illinois. . . . *Annual Report . . . for the Year Ending November 1 . . .* 11th (1887), 18th (1894). Chicago: printer varies, 1888–95.

B. OFFICIAL

United States

Bureau of Animal Industry. *Reports . . .* 1884–93. Washington: Government Printing Office, 1885–93.

Bureau of the Census. *Census of Manufactures: 1905, Boots and Shoes,*

Leather, and Leather Gloves and Mittens. Bul. 72. Washington: Government Printing Office, 1907.

——. *Compendium of the Ninth Census, 1870 to Eleventh, 1890.* Washington: Government Printing Office, 1872–92.

——. *Ninth Census . . . 1870 to Thirteenth . . . 1910.* Washington: Government Printing Office, 1872–1913.

Bureau of Corporations. *The Lumber Industry.* 2 v. Washington: Government Printing Office, 1913–14.

——. *Report . . . on the Beef Industry, 1905.* Washington: Government Printing Office, 1905.

——. Commissioner of Education. *Report for the Year 1876.* Washington: Government Printing Office, 1878.

Bureau of Education. *Public Libraries in the United States of America Their History, Condition and Management.* Special Report. pt. I. Washington: Government Printing Office, 1876.

Bureau of Foreign and Domestic Commerce. " Commercial Organizations of the United States." *Miscellaneous Series,* No. 28. Washington: Government Printing Office, 1915.

Bureau of Foreign Commerce. *Emigration and Immigration: Reports of the Consular Officers of the United States.* Washington: Government Printing Office, 1887.

Bureau of Statistics. *Annual Report . . . on Commerce and Navigation, 1872–92.* Washington: Government Printing Office, 1873–93.

——. *First Annual Report of the Internal Commerce of the United States,* by Joseph Nimmo, Jr., being Part Second of the *Annual Report of the Chief of the Bureau of Statistics on the Commerce and Navigation of the United States, for the Year Ending June 30, 1876.* Washington: Government Printing Office, 1877.

——. " The Grain Trade of the United States," *Monthly Summary of Commerce and Finance of the United States, 1899–1900,* no. 7. Washington: Government Printing Office, 1900.

——. *Report in Regard to the Range and Ranch Cattle Business of the United States.* Washington: Government Printing Office, 1885.

——. *Report on the Internal Commerce of the United States,* by Joseph Nimmo, Jr. . . . *1884.* Washington: Government Printing Office, 1884.

——. *Report on the Internal Commerce of the United States . . . 1891,* pt. 2 of *Commerce and Navigation . . .* Washington: Government Printing Office, 1892.

——. *Special Report on Immigration; Accompanying Information for Immigrants . . .* Washington: Government Printing Office, 1872.

Commissioner of Internal Revenue. *Report* . . . 1870–95. Washington: Government Printing Office, 1890–93.

Commissioner of Labor. *Annual Report,* 1st (1885), 3d (1887), 9th (1893), 10th (1894). Washington: Government Printing Office, 1888, 1894, 1896.

——. "The Italians in Chicago," *Ninth Special Report* . . . Washington: Government Printing Office, 1897.

——. "The Slums of Baltimore, Chicago, New York, and Philadelphia," *Seventh Special Report* . . . Washington: Government Printing Office, 1894.

Commissioner of Patents. *Annual Report,* 1882–84. Washington: Government Printing Office, 1883–85.

Comptroller of the Currency. *Annual Report,* 1871–93. Washington: Government Printing Office, 1871–93.

Congressional Globe, 1871–73.

Congressional Record, 1873–93.

Department of Agriculture. *Annual Report,* 1870–93, 1917. Washington: Government Printing Office, 1871–94, 1918.

Department of the Interior. *Statistics of the Iron and Steel Production of the United States.* James M. Swank, comp. Washington: Government Printing Office, 1881.

Department of State. *Consular Reports, 1885–94.* Washington: Government Printing Office, 1885–94.

——. *Malt and Beer in Spanish America* . . . *Special Consular Reports,* I, 325–90. Washington: Government Printing Office, 1890.

——. *Papers Relating to the Foreign Relations of the United States* . . . *1890.* Washington: Government Printing Office, 1891.

Federal Housing Administration. *The Structure and Growth of Residential Neighborhoods in American Cities.* Washington: Government Printing Office, 1939.

Federal Trade Commission. *Food Investigation. Report* . . . *on the Meat-Packing Industry, 1919.* 6 pts. Washington: Government Printing Office, 1918–20.

——. *Food Investigation. Report* . . . *on Private Car Lines, 1919.* Washington: Government Printing Office, 1920.

——. *Report* . . . *on the Grain Trade.* 5 v. Washington: Government Printing Office, 1920–23.

General Land Office. *Annual Report of the Commissioner* . . . 1871–93. Washington: Government Printing Office, 1872–93.

House of Representatives. *Contested Elections, LeMoyne vs. Farwell, Platt vs. Goode.* 44 Cong., 1 sess., H. Doc. 61. Washington: Government Printing Office, 1876.

——. *The Employment of Pinkerton Detectives.* 52 Cong., 2 sess., H. Rept. 2447. Washington: Government Printing Office, 1893.

——. *Papers Relating to the Foreign Relations of the United States, Transmitted to Congress, with the Annual Message of the President . . .* 1881–91. Washington: Government Printing Office, 1882–93.

——. *Report of the Committee on Manufactures on the Sweating System.* 52 Cong., 2 sess., H. Rept. 2309. Washington: Government Printing Office, 1893.

——. *Report of the Committee on Manufactures, Trusts.* 50 Cong., 2 sess., H. Rept. 4165. 4 v. Washington: Government Printing Office, 1889.

——. *Report of the Committee to Examine Conditions of Hog Raising and Packing Industries of the United States.* 48 Cong., 1 sess., H. Ex. Doc. 106. Washington: Government Printing Office, 1884.

——. *Reports of Diplomatic and Consular Officers concerning Emigration from Europe to the United States . . .* 50 Cong., 2 sess., H. Rept. 3792. Washington: Government Printing Office, 1889.

——. *Testimony before the Select Committee concerning the Whisky Frauds.* 44 Cong., 1 sess., H. Misc. Doc. 186. Washington: Government Printing Office, 1876.

——. *Trusts* [Whisky]. 50 Cong., 2 sess., H. Rept. 4165. Washington: Government Printing Office, 1889.

——. *Whisky Trust Investigation.* 52 Cong., 2 sess., H. Rept. 2601. Washington: Government Printing Office, 1893.

Immigration Commission, 1891–92. *Report on European Immigration to the United States . . .* by Herman J. Schulteis. Washington: Government Printing Office, 1893.

——. *Reports of the Immigration Commission,* 1907–10. 41 v. Washington: Government Printing Office, 1911.

Industrial Commission. *Preliminary Report on Trusts and Industrial Combinations . . .* 56 Cong., 1 sess., H. Doc. 476, pt. 1, 2 v. Washington: Government Printing Office, 1900.

Interstate Commerce Commission. *Annual Report,* 1887–93. Washington: Government Printing Office, 1887–93.

——. *In the Matter of Private Cars.* Washington: Government Printing Office, 1918.

——. *Report and Decisions . . . April 5th 1887 to April 5th 1888.* I. New York: L. K. Strausse, 1888.

National Conservation Commission. *Report*. 60 Cong., 2 sess., S. Doc. 676. 3 v. Washington: Government Printing Office, 1909.

National Monetary Commission. *Clearing Houses,* by James Graham Cannon. 61 Cong., 2 sess., S. Doc. 491. Washington: Government Printing Office, 1910.

Senate. *Economics of Iron and Steel Transportation*. 79 Cong., 1 sess., S. Doc. 80. Washington: Government Printing Office, 1945.

——. *Federal Aid in Domestic Disturbances, 1878–1893,* by Frederick T. Wilson. 57 Cong., 2 sess., S. Doc. 209. Washington: Government Printing Office, 1903.

——. *History of Women in Trade Unions* in *Report on Condition of Woman and Child Wage-Earners in the United States*. 61 Cong., 2 sess., S. Doc. 645, X. 19 v. Washington: Government Printing Office, 1911.

——. *Investigation in Relation to the Employment for Private Purposes of Armed Bodies of Men, or Detectives, in Connection with Differences between Workmen and Employers*. 52 Cong., 2 sess., S. Rept. 1280. Washington: Government Printing Office, 1893.

——. *Report of the Committee on Commerce, February 20, 1873*. 42 Cong., 3 sess., S. Rept. 462. Washington: Government Printing Office, 1872 [*sic*].

——. *Report of the Committee on Foreign Relations on Swine Products of the United States*. 48 Cong., 1 sess., S. Rept. 345. Washington: Government Printing Office, 1884.

——. *Report of the Committee on Immigration*. 52 Cong., 2 sess., S. Rept. 1333. Washington: Government Printing Office, 1893.

——. *Report of the Committee upon Relations between Capital and Labor*. Washington: Government Printing Office, 1885.

——. *Report of the Select Committee on the Transportation and Sale of Meat Products*. 51 Cong., 1 sess., S. Rept. 829. Washington: Government Printing Office, 1890. [Includes *Testimony, 1889*.]

——. *Report of the Select Committee on Transportation-Routes to the Seaboard* . . . 43 Cong., 1 sess., S. Rept. 307, pt. 2. 2 v. Washington: Government Printing Office, 1874.

——. Committee on Labor and Education. *Testimony of Albert Fink. New York, September 17, 1883*. [n.p., 1883].

Statutes at Large . . . 1863–91. XIII–XXVI. Washington: Government Printing Office, 1866–91.

Treasury Department. *Report on the Internal Commerce of the United States* . . . 1879–91. Washington: Government Printing Office, 1879–92.

Treaties and Conventions Concluded between the United States of America and Other Powers since July 4, 1776. Washington: Government Printing Office, 1889.

War Department Corps of Engineers, U.S. Army and United States Shipping Board. *Transportation on the Great Lakes.* Washington: Government Printing Office, 1926.

Illinois

1. DOCUMENTS OF GENERAL ASSEMBLY AND SENATE

House of Representatives. *Report of Special Committee on Labor* . . . Springfield: Weber, Magie & Co., 1879.

Illinois Legislative Manual for 30th General Assembly. 1877 and 1878. Springfield, Ill.: M. G. Tousley & Co., Publishers, 1877.

Journal of the House of Representatives of the . . . General Assembly . . . 1871–93. Springfield: printer varies, 1871–93.

Journal of the Senate of the . . . General Assembly . . . 1871–93. Springfield: printer varies, 1871–93.

Reports Made to the General Assembly . . . 1871–93. Title varies. Springfield: printer varies, 1871–94.

2. DOCUMENTS RELATING TO THE STATE CONSTITUTION

Debates and Proceedings of the Constitutional Convention . . . , Convened . . . December 13, 1869. 2 v. Springfield: E. L. Merritt & Brother, 1870.

Journal of the Constitutional Convention of the State of Illinois Convened at Springfield, December 13, 1869. Springfield: State Journal Printing Office, 1870.

Verlie, Emil Joseph, ed. *Illinois Constitutions* (Illinois State Historical Library, *Collections,* XIII. Constitutional Series, I). Springfield: Illinois State Historical Library, 1919.

3. LAWS

All the Laws of the State of Illinois Passed by the . . . General Assembly . . . 1885–97. [Chicago]: Chicago Legal News Company, 1885–97.

Annotated Statutes of the State of Illinois in Force January 1, 1885 . . . (Merritt Starr and Russell H. Curtis, eds.). 2 v. Chicago: Callaghan and Company, 1885.

A Compilation of the Laws of Illinois, Relating to Township Organization. (Elijah M. Haines, ed. 23d ed.). Chicago: The Legal Adviser Publishing Company, [1901].

Laws of the State of Illinois, Passed by the . . General Assembly . . . 1849, 1859, 1871–1905. Title varies. Springfield: printer varies, 1849–1905.

Private Laws of the State of Illinois, Passed by the . . . General Assembly . . . 1851–69. Springfield: printer varies, 1851–69.

Public Laws of the State of Illinois, Passed by the . . . General Assembly . . . 1863–73. Springfield: printer varies, 1863–73.

The Revised Statutes of the State of Illinois . . . (Harvey B. Hurd, comp. and ed.). 1874, 1877, 1880, 1893. Place and publisher vary, 1874–93.

The Statutes of Illinois: An Analytical Digest of All the General Laws of the State in Force at the Present Time . . . 1818 to 1872, II, Acts of 1871 and 1872 (Eugene L. Gross and William L. Gross, eds.). Springfield: E. L. & W. L. Gross, 1872.

4. REPORTS OF OFFICIALS, BOARDS, COMMISSIONS, AND DEPARTMENTS

Attorney General. *Biennial Report . . .* 1874–95. Springfield: printer varies, [1874?]–95.

Auditor of Public Accounts. *Annual Insurance Report.* 4th (1872)–8th (1876). Springfield: printer varies, 1872–76.

——. *Annual Report . . . of Building and Loan Associations of the State of Illinois.* 1892–96. Springfield: printer varies, 1893–96.

——. *Biennial Report . . .* 1890–96. Springfield: printer varies, 1890–97.

Board of Livestock Commissioners. *Annual Report.* 1888–90. Springfield: printer varies, 1889–90.

Board of State Commissioners of Public Charities. *Biennial Report.* 1st (1870)–12th (1892). Springfield: printer varies, 1871–93.

——. *Special Report of an Investigation of the Management of the Cook County Hospital for the Insane.* Springfield: H. W. Rokker, 1886.

Bureau of Labor Statistics. *Biennial Report.* 1st (1881)–9th (1896), 12th (1902). Springfield: printer varies, 1881–1904.

Department of Agriculture. *Transactions . . .* o.s. XVI–XXXVI, n.s. VIII–XXVIII, 1878–98. Springfield: printer varies, 1880–99.

Factory Inspectors. *Annual Report.* 1st (1893)–3rd (1895). Springfield: printer varies, 1894–96.

Railroad and Warehouse Commission. *Annual Report.* 1st (1871)–25th (1895). Springfield: printer varies, 1872–96.

Revenue Commission. *Report of the Revenue Commission Appointed . . . to Propose and Frame a Revenue Code . . .* Springfield: H. W. Rokker, 1886.

Secretary of State. *Biennial Report . . .* 1874–94. Springfield: printer varies, 1875–95.

——. *Election Returns 1873 to 1882. Ms.,* Illinois State Archives, Springfield, Illinois. [This handwritten ledger book has no title page. Above information is taken from its cover, which lists the author as " Illinois, Secretary's Office."]

——. *Election Returns County Officers.* 1882 [to 1905] *Ms.* Illinois State Archives, Springfield, Illinois. [This handwritten ledger book has no title page. On the cover appears " Illinois, Secretary's Office, *Election Returns County Officers 1882,*" but actually the book contains figures from 1882 to 1905, inclusive.]

Secretary of State, comp. *Official Vote of the State of Illinois Cast at the General Election Held November 6, 1888* . . . Springfield, Illinois: H. W. Rokker, Printer and Binder, 1889.

Cook County

Annual Reports of the Cook County Agent, Warden Insane Asylum and Poor House, Medical Sup't [sic] Cook County Insane Asylum, Warden Cook County Hospital, Cook County Physician, and Coroner . . . 1874-[77]. Chicago: printer varies.

Board of Commissioners. *Annual Statement of the Board of Commissioners of Cook County, 1879-80.* Chicago: J. M. W. Jones Stationery and Printing Co., 1880.

——. *A Compilation of the Cost of the Public Buildings of Cook County from March 8, 1866, to Dec. 3, 1883.* John O'Neill, comp. Chicago: The J. M. W. Jones Stationery and Printing Company, 1884.

——. *Official Proceedings,* 1871-93. Chicago: printer varies.

——. *Report of Special Committee Appointed March 27, 1882, to Compile All Communications, Resolutions, Reports and Contracts Pertaining to the Erection of the New Cook County Court House. Being from June 17, 1872, to July 17, 1882.* Chicago: The J. M. W. Jones Stationery and Printing Company, 1882.

——. *Special Report to County Commissioners Giving a Comparative Statement of Cook County Expenses, and Other Matters, from 1871-2 to 1881-2.* Presented to County Board by Henry C. Senne, Chairman of the Committee on Finance. Chicago: The J. M. W. Jones Stationery and Printing Company, 1882.

Coroner. *Report.* 1874/75-1876/77. Chicago: printer varies.

Department of Public Charities. *Annual Report of the Superintendent and Medical Director of Public Charities* . . . 1872. Chicago.

——. *Report of the Superintendent and Medical Director of Public Charities.* Quarterly. March-June, 1872.

Department of Public Instruction. *Statistical Report of the County Super-*

intendent of Schools . . . 1871/72, 1874/75, 1879/80–1880/81, 1882/84–
1890/92.

Cook County Hospital. *Reports.* 1890. Chicago.

——. *Rules and Regulations for the Government* . . . 1874, 1877, 1881.

——. *Annual Reports of the Warden of the Cook County Hospital for the
Years ending August 31, 1885 and '86.* Chicago: J. M. W. Jones Stationery and Printing Co., 1887.

Cook County Hospital for the Insane. *Report of the Superintendent* . . .
for the Year 1890. Chicago: J. M. W. Jones Stationery and Printing
Company, 1891.

Cook County Normal School. *Catalogue and Circular* . . . 1871/72, 1875/
76, 1878.

——. *Course of Study* . . . Chicago: J. M. W. Jones Stationery and Printing Co., 1893.

Recorder. *Official List. Abstracts of Title to Cook County Real Estate*
. . . May, 1877.

Chicago

Except where noted otherwise, the following cover the years 1871–93.
Published in Chicago. Printer varies.

Board of Education. *Annual Report.*

——. *Proceedings.*

Board of Election Commissioners. *Elections, Nov., 1886. April, June, Nov.,
1887. Jan., April, June, 1888. Mss.* Chicago Board of Election Commissioners.

——. *Elections, April, June, Sept., Nov., Dec., 1889. April, Nov., 1890. Mss.*
Chicago Board of Election Commissioners.

——. *Elections, April, June, Nov., 1891. April, Nov., 1892. Mss.* Chicago
Board of Election Commissioners.

——. *Elections, April, Nov., 1893. Mss.* Chicago Board of Election Commissioners.

——. *First Annual Report, 1915.*

Board of Health. *Report, 1871–75.* Department of Health. *Report, 1876–93.*

Board of Inspectors, House of Correction. *Report, 1875–93.*

Board of Police. *Report, 1871–75.* Superintendent of Police. *Report, 1876–94.*

Board of Public Works. *Report, 1870–75.* Department of Public Works.
Report, 1876–94.

Board of Trustees of the Sanitary District. *Proceedings, 1890–92, 1900.*

City Comptroller. *Annual Statement, 1873–75.* Department of Finance. *Annual Statement, 1876–93.*

Common Council. *Proceedings, 1870–76.* City Council. *Proceedings, 1876–94.*

Special Committee of City Council. *Report of Special Committee of the City Council of Chicago on the Street Railway Franchises and Operations of the Chicago City Railway Company, The North Chicago City Railway Company, The North Chicago Street Railroad Company, The Chicago West Division Railway Company, The Chicago Passenger Railway Company, The West Chicago Street Railroad Company, The West and South Towns Street Railway Company, The Chicago General Railway Company to January 1, 1898.* Chicago: John F. Higgins, 1898.

——. Special Report. *Report on the Investigation of the Chicago Telephone Company, 1912.*

Department of Electricity. *Rules and Ordinances . . . with an Historical Appendix, 1900.*

Fire Department. *Report of the Fire Marshal.*

Laws and Ordinances Governing the City of Chicago . . . 1873 (Murray F. Tuley, comp.), 1890 (Henry Binmore, ed.), Supplement, 1894 (Binmore, ed.); *The Municipal Code of Chicago . . .* Egbert Jamieson and Francis Adams, eds., 1881, *Supplement to the Municipal Code of Chicago . . .* Clarence A. Knight, comp., [1887].

Municipal Reports [binder's title], also cited as *Annual Reports of the Various Departments . . .* , 1883–93, including Mayor's Annual Message, Annual Statement of the Finances, Annual Report of the Department of Public Works, Report of the General Superintendent of Police, Report of the Fire Marshal, Annual Report of the Board of Directors of the Chicago Public Library, Annual Report of the Board of Education, Report of the Department of Health, Annual Report of the Board of Inspectors of the House of Correction.

Park Commissioners:

(a) Lincoln Park Commissioners, *Report, 1894, Report and a History of Lincoln Park,* I. J. Bryan, comp., 1899.

(b) South Park Commissioners, *Annual Report, 1872–93.*

(c) West Park Commissioners, *Annual Report, 1871–93, 1896–97.*

Public Library. *The Chicago Public Library, 1873–1923 . . .* [1923].

Public Library. Board of Directors. *Annual Report, 1873–93.*

Van Cleave, James R. B. *List of Franchises Granted by the City Council of . . . Chicago, from March 4, 1837, to April 10, 1896.* 1896.

Legal Cases

Mary A. Ahrens *v.* William J. English *et al.,* 139 Ill. 622 (1892).

Samuel W. Allerton *et al. v.* John P. Hopkins, 160 Ill. 448 (1896).

In re Barber, 39 Federal Reporter 641 (1889).

Blair *v.* City of Chicago, 201 U. S. 400 (1906).

The Braceville Coal Company *v.* The People of the State of Illinois, 147 Ill. 66 (1893).

John J. Byrne *v.* The Chicago General Railway Company *et al.,* 169 Ill. 75 (1897).

California Cooperative Canneries, Appellant *v.* United States of America, Swift & Company, Armour & Company *et al.,* appellees. Court of Appeals of the District of Columbia, Jan. term, 1924, no. 4071. " Answer of Morris and Company," pp. 77–78, Packer Consent Decree, 1920, I.

The Chicago and Alton Railroad Company *v.* The People *ex rel.* Gustavus Koerner *et al.* Comrs. 67 Ill. 11 (1873).

City of Chicago *v.* David A. Gage *et al.,* 95 Ill. 593 (1880).

The City of Chicago *v.* The People *ex rel.* Henry W. King *et al.,* 80 Ill. 496 (1875).

Dickey *et al. v.* Reed *et al.,* 78 Ill. 261 (1875).

The Distilling and Cattle Feeding Company *v.* The People *ex rel.* M. T. Maloney, Attorney General, 156 Ill. 448 (1895).

John Dolese *et al. v.* Daniel A. Pierce, 124 Ill. 140 (1888).

Charles A. Dupee *et al. v.* Charles P. Swigert, Auditor, 127 Ill. 494 (1889).

Frank Frorer *et al. v.* The People, for use of the school fund, 141 Ill. 171 (1892).

Henry Fuller *v.* Monroe Heath *et al.,* 89 Ill. 296 (1878).

Charles Gillespie *v.* The People of the State of Illinois, 188 Ill. 176 (1900).

James H. Hildreth *v.* Monroe Heath *et al.,* 1 Ill. App. Ct. 82 (1876).

William M. Holmes *et al. v.* Aramentia M. Smythe *et al.,* 100 Ill. 413 (1881).

State of Illinois *v.* Illinois Central Railroad Company, 33 Federal Reporter 730 (1888).

Illinois Central Railroad Company *v.* Illinois, 146 U. S. 387 (1892).

E. F. C. Klokke *v.* John H. P. Dodge, 103 Ill. 125 (1882).

Joshua C. Knickerbocker *v.* The People *ex rel.* Otto C. Butz, 102 Ill. 218 (1882).

Ida Irene Law *et al. v.* The People *ex rel.* Louis C. Huck, Collector, etc., 87 Ill. 385 (1877).

Mackin *v.* Illinois, 115 Ill. 312 (1885).

Mackin and Another *v.* United States, 117 U. S. 348 (1886).

David McIntosh *et al. v.* The People *ex rel.* McCrea, 93 Ill. 540 (1879).

Minnesota *v.* Barber, 136 U. S. 313 (1890).

Munn *v.* Illinois, 94 U. S. 113 (1876).

The New York and Chicago Grain and Stock Exchange *v.* The Board of Trade of the City of Chicago, *et al.,* 127 Ill. 153 (1889).

Packing Company Cases, 105 U. S. 566 (1881).

The People *ex rel.* Evans *v.* Callaghan, 83 Ill. 128 (1876).

The People *ex rel.* Grinnell *v.* Hoffman *et al.,* 116 Ill. 587 (1886).

The People *ex rel.* Francis B. Peabody *v.* The Chicago Gas Trust Company, 130 Ill. 268 (1889).

The People *ex rel.* Franz Schack *v.* Hardin B. Brayton, 94 Ill. 341 (1880).

The People *ex rel.* W. H. Stickney *v.* John M. Palmer, Governor of the State, 64 Ill. 41 (1872).

Presser *v.* Illinois, 116 U. S. 252 (1886).

William Kelsey Reed *et al. v.* The People *ex rel.* George Hunt, Attorney General, 125 Ill. 592 (1888).

Mark Sheridan *et al. v.* H. D. Colvin *et al.,* 78 Ill. 237 (1875).

William Soby *v.* The People of the State of Illinois, 134 Ill. 66 (1890).

Spies *v.* Illinois, 123 U. S. 131 (1887).

August Spies *et al. v.* The People of the State of Illinois, 122 Ill. 1 (1887).

Swift *v.* Sutphin, 39 Federal Reporter, 630 (1889).

John R. Tree, Treasurer, *v.* George R. Davis, Treasurer, 133 Ill. 522 (1889).

Tribune Company *v.* The Board of Education of the City of Chicago, case No. 97, 614. Superior Court of Cook County. *Mss.* vault of Office of Clerk of Superior Court of Cook County.

Walsh *v.* The Board of Education of the City of Chicago, case No. 97, 615. Superior Court of Cook County. *Mss.* vault of Office of Clerk of Superior Court of Cook County.

Marshall J. Wilson *v.* Board of Trustees of the Sanitary District of Chicago *et al.,* 133 Ill. 443 (1890).

VOLUME III

INDEX

mann Medical College, 392; Northwestern University Medical Department, 392; Northwestern University Woman's Medical School, 393; Rush Medical College, 47, 392; Woman's Hospital Medical College, 393; professional journals, 397 (note 28); professional societies: Chicago Gynecological Society, 396; Chicago Materia Medical Society, 396; Chicago Medical Society, 396; Chicago Pathological Society, 396

Medill, Joseph, 19, 60, 300, 304, 340–1, 343–4, 354, 365, 370, 411–12, 420

Medill, Samuel J., 412

Meeker, A. B., 443

Meggy, Percy R., 415

Mercantile Club, 190

Merchants' Loan & Trust Co., 203

Merchants' National Bank, 193 (note 3)

Merchants' Savings, Loan & Trust Co., 193 (note 3), 195, 485

Mercy Hospital, 446

Merritt Conspiracy Bill, 290

Metals, non-ferrous, 162–3

Methodist Episcopal Church, 424, 425, 427, 432–3, 450, 453

Methodist Institutional Churches, 450

Methodist Ministerial Association, 439

Metropolitan National Bank, 99 (note 101)

Mexican Lumber Company, 104 (note 119)

Michael Reese Hospital, 42, 449

Michigan Central Railroad, 51, 67, 95, 110–11, 111, 111 (note 6), 242, 248, 522, 524, 526, 528

Militia, use of in labor troubles, 247, 272 (note 8), 292; see also Strikes

Miller, Henry B. ["Buffalo" Miller], 349 (note 20)

Miller, Judge Henry G., 231

Miller and Reed, 349 (note 20)

Millinery, 183–4

Miln, The Rev. George Crichton, 433–4

Milner, Lloyd, 188 (note 115)

Milwaukee, 66, 147, 149, 150

Milwaukee and Chicago Breweries, Limited, 150, 151

Mining securities, 214

Minstrel shows, 473

Mitchell, Mrs. Ellen M., 382

Mitchell, John J., 220 (note 74), 233

Mixed Drinks. The Saloon Keeper's Journal, 149, 153, 154 (note 27)

Molecular Telephone Company, 229

Monopoly, 225–7, 329, 365; see also Business combinations

Monroe, Harriet, 402–3

Monroe, William H., 129 (note 57)

Montauk Block, 102

Monticello Mutual Building, Loan and Homestead Association, 206 (note 42)

Montreal, Bank of, 14, 14 (note 30), 194 (note 6), 195

Monuments and statues, 29, 34, 37, 37 (note 52), 196, 315, 498, 504

Moody, Dwight L., 170, 428

Moody Bible Institute, 428

Moore, James H., 231

Moore, Orrin E., 7 (notes 11, 12)

Moore, William H., 231

Moral Educational Society, 487

Moran, Judge Thomas, 286, 378

Morey, H. C., & Co., 208

Morgan, Thomas J., 255, 255 (note 46), 256, 266, 267, 292, 362, 370, 378, 509

Morgan, Mrs. Thomas J., 296

Morgan Park, settlement in, 51–2; location of Baptist Theological Seminary, 454

Morris, Nelson, 111–13, 116 (note 20), 119–20, 127, 129–30, 129 (note 57), 132, 134, 138–9, 142, 147

Morrisson, Plummer & Co., 188

Mortality, rate of, 55, 323; see also Health, Sanitation

Mortgage bonds, 211–13

Morton, Joy, 184

Morton, Joy, & Company, 184

Morton, Mark, 184

Motts, J. L., Iron Works, 161 (note 48)

Mozart Society, 490

Mulligan, Mrs. Marion A., candidate for political office, 366–7

Munger, Allison A., 75 (note 27)

Munger, Wesley, 75 (note 27)

Munger, Wheeler & Company, 74, 74 (note 23)

Municipal bonds, 215–16